DEVELOPMENT WITH A HUMAN FACE

Development with a Human Face
Experiences in Social Achievement and Economic Growth

Edited by

SANTOSH MEHROTRA and RICHARD JOLLY

CLARENDON PRESS · OXFORD

1997

Oxford University Press, Great Clarendon Street, Oxford OX2 6DP

Oxford   New York

Athens   Auckland   Bangkok   Bogota   Bombay
Buenos Aires   Calcutta   Cape Town   Dar es Salaam
Delhi   Florence   Hong Kong   Istanbul   Karachi
Kuala Lumpur   Madras   Madrid   Melbourne
Mexico City   Nairobi   Paris   Singapore
Taipei   Tokyo   Toronto   Warsaw

and associated companies in
Berlin   Ibadan

Oxford is a trade mark of Oxford University Press

Published in the United States by
Oxford University Press Inc., New York

The material in this book has been commissioned by the United Nations Children's Fund (UNICEF), but the contents are the
responsibility of the authors and do not necessarily reflect the policies or the views of UNICEF

The designations employed in this publication and the presentation of the material do not imply the expression of any
opinion whatsoever on the part of UNICEF concerning the legal status of any country or territory, or of its authorities, or the
delimitations of its frontiers

The text has not been edited to official publication standards and UNICEF accepts no responsibility for errors

British Library Cataloguing in Publication Data
Data available

Library of Congress Cataloging in Publication Data

Development with a human face : experience in social achievement and
economic growth / edited by Santosh Mehrotra and Richard Jolly.
p.   cm.
Includes bibliographical references and index.
ISBN 0–19–829076–4
1. Economic development—Case studies.   2. Developing countries—
Economic conditions—Case studies.   I. Mehrotra, Santosh K.
II. Jollu, Richard.
HD82.D43   1997
338.9—dc21   97-26762
CIP

1 3 5 7 9 10 8 6 4 2

Typeset by Best-set Typesetter Ltd., Hong Kong
Printed in Great Britain by
Biddles Ltd, Guildford and King's Lynn.

Contents

Preface   vii

Contributors   ix

Foreword   xv

I OVERVIEW

1. Profiles in Success: Reasons for Hope and Priorities for Action   3
   RICHARD JOLLY

2. Social Development in High-Achieving Countries: Common
   Elements and Diversities   21
   SANTOSH MEHROTRA

3. Health and Education Policies in High-Achieving Countries:
   Some Lessons   63
   SANTOSH MEHROTRA

II CASE-STUDIES

4. Botswana: Social Development in a Resource-rich Economy   113
   TYRRELL DUNCAN, KEITH JEFFERIS, and PATRICK MOLUTSI

5. Mauritius: The Roots of Success 1960–1993   149
   EDWARD and BRIDGET DOMMEN

6. Rapid Social Transformation despite Economic Adjustment and
   Slow Growth: The Experience of Zimbabwe   179
   RENE LOEWENSON and MUNHAMO CHISVO

7. The Route to Social Development in Kerala: Social Intermediation
   and Public Action   204
   T. N. KRISHNAN

8. Social Policies in a Slowly Growing Economy: Sri Lanka   235
   PATRICIA ALAILAMA and NIMAL SANDERATNE

9. Social Policies in a Growing Economy: The Role of the State in
   the Republic of Korea   264
   SANTOSH MEHROTRA, IN-HWA PARK, and HWA-JONG BAEK

10. Malaysia: Social Development, Poverty Reduction, and Economic Transformation   297
LEONG CHOON HENG and TAN SIEW HOEY

11. Barbados: Social Development in a Small Island State   323
MYRTLE D. BISHOP, ROSALYN CORBIN, and NEVILLE C. DUNCAN

12. Costa Rica: Social Development and Heterodox Adjustment   355
LEONARDO GARNIER, REBECA GRYNSPAN, ROBERTO HIDALGO, GUILLERMO MONGE, and JUAN DIEGO TREJOS

13. Human Development in Cuba: Growing Risk of Reversal   384
SANTOSH MEHROTRA

III CONCLUSION

14. Paths to Social Development: Lessons from Case-Studies   421
LINCOLN CHEN and MEGHNAD DESAI

15. The Links between Economic Growth, Poverty Reduction, and Social Development: Theory and Policy   435
LANCE TAYLOR, SANTOSH MEHROTRA, and ENRIQUE DELAMONICA

Index   469

Preface

Fifteen years ago it would have been difficult to name more than a few developing countries which managed to make substantial gains in human development. Today this position is dramatically different. In addition to the 10 countries reviewed in this study, there are at least 10 to 15 others demonstrating wide-ranging development success. These 20–25 countries, covering a substantial proportion of the population of the developing world, have shown that broad human development is possible, with or without rapid economic growth.

This success introduces a strong element of hope into the development debate even though qualified in some cases by limited reduction in income poverty. It is this perspective of hope, together with the specific lessons on how these countries were able to achieve rapid advances in health and education, which is analysed in these studies. The studies provide a multi-disciplinary analysis of the experiences of a group of countries, generally recognized as high-achievers in terms of human development.

To produce the studies, UNICEF commissioned two or three national scholars in each of the countries concerned to examine how and why their countries were able to achieve high levels of health and education relatively early in their development process. In most cases, the teams incorporated an economist and health or education expert. The authors examine, on the basis of primary and secondary sources, and interviews with policy-makers, past and present, the historical experiences and policy interventions which made this possible.

A meeting with the authors was held in November 1994 in New York to discuss the initial findings. Some of these results were presented in a short booklet (*Profiles in Success: People's Progress in Africa, Asia and Latin America*, New York, 1995) and issued at the World Summit for Social Development in Copenhagen in March 1995.

We would like to acknowledge with gratitude the support of Professor Lincoln Chen and Professor Lord Meghnad Desai who acted as peer reviewers for the country case studies. Thanks are due to Jan Vandemoortele for his support throughout the project. We also acknowledge with deep gratitude Enrique Delamonica, without whose assistance, always dependable and untiring, the manuscript would have taken much longer to prepare. For detailed comments on all or parts of the manuscript we would like to thank Krishna Bose, Fay Chung, Enrique Delamonica, Ian Hopwood, Stephen Jarrett, Sushma Kapoor, Alberto Minujin, Richard Morgan, Ashok Nigam, Mary Pigozzi, Aung Tun Thet, and Jan Vandemoortele.

We would also like to acknowledge the input and support of UNICEF representatives and staff in country offices where the country studies were undertaken: Marjorie Newman-Williams and Fabio Sabatini (Barbados), Sheila Tacon and

Krishna Belbase (Botswana), Rhea Saab (Costa Rica), Luis Zuñiga (Cuba), Jon Rohde and Shiva Kumar (India), Tony Hewett (Malaysia), Brita Ostberg and David Baker (Sri Lanka), Sally Fegan-Wyles and Lauchlan Munro (Zimbabwe). Special thanks must also go to Luis Zuñiga for extensive assistance, both in the form of materials as well as detailed comments on the Cuba chapter, which would not have been possible without him. Wanda Quiñones was extremely patient with the typing of numerous drafts, and bore it all with a smile. It should be made clear that the analysis and interpretation of country experiences are those of the chapter authors and editors of the volume and do not necessarily reflect any official position of UNICEF.

We hope this publication will be both interesting and motivating, helping to promote understanding of what has been successfully achieved in these countries and encouraging people in other countries to learn from these examples and to pioneer their own advances.

Santosh Mehrotra
Richard Jolly
January 1997

Contributors

Patricia Alailama   Dr Patricia Alailama is currently the Additional Director General (Social Sector Planning) in the National Planning Department of the Ministry of Finance and Planning, Government of Sri Lanka. She has undertaken extensive work in the field of social policy, gender relations and poverty for several international organizations.

Hwa-Jong Baek   Hwa-Jong Baek is an economist and econometrician. Since 1994 he has been a Research Fellow at the Health Policy Research Division of the Korea Institute for Health and Social Affairs.

Myrtle D. Bishop   Myrtle D. Bishop, an economist, is currently a Commercial Counsellor in the Embassy of Barbados in the USA. She has previously been employed as a private consultant, Chief Economist at the Barbados Industrial Development Corporation and Chief of the Industry, Trade and Tourism section in the CARICOM Secretariat. She has undertaken extensive research activities on the industrialization process in Barbados, women in development, gender issues, social policy and social change, and economic integration.

Lincoln C. Chen   Lincoln C. Chen holds an MD and is Taro Takemi Professor of International Health at the Harvard University School of Public Health. At the School, he serves as Chairman of the Department of Population and International Health. He also serves as Director of the Harvard University Center for Population and Development Studies, a Faculty Fellow at the Harvard Institute for International Development, a Faculty Associate at the Harvard Center for International Affairs, and a member of the faculty of the Harvard Medical School. Over the period 1970–80, he worked in Bangladesh with the Ford Foundation and the International Centre for Diarrhoeal Disease Research, Bangladesh. Before joining the Harvard faculty, Dr Chen was the Ford Foundation representative for India, Nepal and Sri Lanka.

Munhamo Chisvo   Munhamo Chisvo, an economist, is an independant consultant in Harare, Zimbabwe.

Rosalyn Corbin   Rosalyn Corbin, a Barbadian, holds a Master's degree in Education, and has done extensive work with several national, regional and international agencies in the areas of women and development, gender and development, literacy and adult education.

Enrique Delamonica   Enrique Delamonica has taught economics at the University of Buenos Aires, the Institute for Economic and Social Development, Buenos Aires, and the New School for Social Research, New York. His areas of interest are macroeconomics, financing of social policies, and poverty reduction policies. Currently he is a consultant with UNICEF.

Meghnad Desai   Meghnad Desai, Professor of Economics at the London School of Economics and Political Science, is currently the Director of the Centre for the Study of Global Governance, LSE. Born in 1940, he was educated at the University of Bombay and secured his Ph.D. from the University of Pennsylvania, USA. From 1984 to 1991 he was co-editor of the Journal of Applied Econometrics. He was made a peer in April 1991.

Bridget and Edward Dommen   Bridget and Edward Dommen lived in Mauritius in the 1960s at the time of Independence. Bridget Dommen was responsible for launching the family planning programme in the Ministry of Health. Edward Dommen had come to take charge of the newly-established Economic Planning Unit, and moved later to the University of Mauritius as its first professor. At present, Bridget Dommen is an economist in the Ministry of Health of Geneva, Switzerland, and Edward Dommen works with UNCTAD and is currently Visiting Professor in the School of Social and International Studies, University of Sunderland.

Neville C. Duncan   Neville C. Duncan is the Director of the Institute of Social and Economic Research, University of the West Indies, Mona Campus, Jamaica. His most recent books are *Mechanisms of Improvement in the Anglophone Caribbean: The Role of Bretton Woods Institutions and the Recommendations of the Caribbean NGOs* (1995); *Global Developments: Caribbean Impacts and Organised Labour* (1995), and *Caribbean Integration: The OECS Experience Revisited* (1995).

Tyrrell Duncan   Tyrrell Duncan has been engaged in research in a wide range of fields including social development policy, poverty alleviation, transport, communications and infrastructure development, and industrial strategy. His current work is mostly in Southern Africa, and South and East Asia. He has worked extensively for UNICEF and UNDP in formulating social development policies in Botswana, Zambia, and Zimbabwe.

Leonardo Garnier   Leonardo Garnier took his Masters and Ph.D. in Economics at the New School for Social Research, New York. During 1991 and 1992 he was the Director of the Secretariat of the Costa Rican Commission of the Reform of the State. He is a professor of Economics at the Universidad Nacional, and has also worked as a researcher and consultant for different agencies of the United Nations as well as for the Inter-American Development Bank. Currently, he is the Minister of Planning and Economic Policy of the Costa Rican Government, where he also worked as a Viceminister (1988–90).

Rebeca Grynspan Rebeca Grynspan is an economist. She has taught at the Universidad de Costa Rica and been a researcher at the Institute of Economic Research of that university and at the Association 'Alternativas de Desarrollo'. She worked as a Viceminister of Public Finance (1986–88). Her latest publication, 'Mujeres de maiz' (1995), in collaboration with M. Chiriboga and L. Perez, is about female agriculturists in Central America. Currently, she is the Second Vice-President of the Republic of Costa Rica and the Co-ordinator of the Social Area of the Government.

Leong Choon Heng Currently a Senior Analyst with the Institute of Strategic and International Studies, Malaysia, he has worked on issues related to social and economic development. After taking a Ph.D. from Harvard University, he lectured in sociology at the National University of Singapore and has worked as a consultant to state governments in Malaysia on industry-specific studies. He has recently been involved in the study of the human resource requirements for the New Industrial Master Plan (1996–2005) of Malaysia.

Roberto Hidalgo Roberto Hidalgo, an economist, is a researcher in San José, Costa Rica. A political scientist and sociologist, he was a researcher at the Universidad de Costa Rica from 1986 to 1992. Currently, he is the Political Adviser to the President of Costa Rica.

Tan Siew Hoey Currently a free-lance consultant with the International Food Policy Research Institute (IFPRI) in Washington, DC, she has served as a consultant to the Malaysian Institute of Economic Research on Malaysia's New Industrial Master Plan (1996–2005). Prior to this, she has worked at the Institute for Strategic and International Studies (ISIS), Malaysia for nine years as Senior Fellow and served as economist for seven years at the Agriculture Bank of Malaysia before joining ISIS.

Keith Jefferis Keith Jefferis is currently Deputy Director in the Research Department of the Bank of Botswana. He previously spent seven years teaching in the Department of Economics of the University of Botswana. His main research interests include the financial and industrial aspects of economic development in Africa, as well as social development, Quality of Life indicators, and poverty alleviation. He has published widely in international academic journals, and consulted extensively for international organizations.

Richard Jolly Richard Jolly's career as a development economist has combined planning and operational involvement with research and teaching in a wide range of countries and situations. Richard Jolly is currently Special Adviser to the Administrator of the United Nations Development Programme (UNDP), and the architect of the Human Development Report. Before this, he was, for 14 years, Deputy Executive Director in UNICEF, with responsibilities for UNICEF's programmes in over 130 countries, including UNICEF's strategy for support to countries in implementing the goals agreed at the 1990 World Summit for Children. He has also been directly involved in efforts to ensure more attention to the needs of children and women in the making of economic adjustment policies, along the lines set out in the book he co-edited *Adjustment with a Human Face*. Before joining UNICEF, Dr Jolly was for nine years Director of the Institute of Development Studies at the University of Sussex.

T. N. Krishnan   T. N. Krishnan, former Director of the Centre for Development Studies, Trivandrum, Kerala, was one of the few Indian economists who had worked extensively on health issues. After taking his Ph.D. from MIT, he taught in several universities in South India. In the sixties and then late seventies he worked for the UN Population Fund, where he was responsible for the *State of the World's Population* report. When he passed away suddenly in late 1996, he was directing (for UNDP) a major research project on human development in India.

Rene Loewenson   Dr Rene Loewenson, a Zimbabwean epidemiologist, has worked as Senior Lecturer in the University of Zimbabwe medical school, as Head of the Health Department of the Zimbabwe Congress of Trade Unions, and as Co-ordinator of an African Regional programme on Health Safety and Environment under the Organisation of African Trade Union Unity. She has since 1980 been involved in research and programmes on child health, children's rights, nutrition, primary health care, child labour and child sexual abuse, and has provided technical support to government and non-government organizations in Zimbabwe on these issues. Her book *Modern Plantation Agriculture: Corporate Wealth and Labour Squalor* was published in 1992 and she has also contributed to various books on health and social development in Zimbabwe.

Santosh Mehrotra   Santosh Mehrotra studied at Jawaharlal Nehru University, New Delhi, at the New School for Social Research, New York (MA Econ.), and at the University of Cambridge (Ph.D. Econ.) in 1985. He worked on international economic policy issues at a government think-tank in New Delhi, taught Economics at the Nehru University while consulting for UNCTAD and ILO, before moving to UNICEF, New York in October 1991. There he works on the links between macroeconomic policy and health and education, and on the economics of basic education. His other books include: *African Economic Development: An Agenda for the*

Future (1987 co-edited), and *India and the Soviet Union: Trade and Technology Transfer* (Cambridge University Press, 1990). He is currently directing a major project on public expenditure in developing countries on basic social services.

Patrick Molutsi   Patrick Molutsi is currently Dean of the Faculty of Social Science, and Senior Lecturer in Sociology, at the University of Botswana. His research interests include rural development, poverty alleviation, and democracy and the political process in African countries. He is a founding member of the Democracy Research Project at the University of Botswana, and has consulted extensively for local and international organizations in the field of social development policy.

Guillermo Monge   Guillermo Monge is an economist based in San José, Costa Rica. A civil engineer and economist, he was a researcher at the Institute of Economic Research of the Universidad de Costa Rica from 1986 to 1991. He currently works as Adviser to the President of Costa Rica.

In-Hwa Park   In-Hwa Park received a Ph.D. in Public Health. Between 1979 and 1995 he was a Research Fellow at the Health Policy Research Division of the Korea Institute for Health and Social Affairs. Since 1995 he has been a Research Fellow at the Division for Health and Welfare of the Legislative Research Service, the Republic of Korea.

Nimal Sanderatne   Nimal Sanderatne is Chairman of the National Development Bank and President of the Sri Lanka Association of Economists. Formerly he was Adviser, Research and Training, Director of Economic Research and Director of Statistics at the Central Bank of Sri Lanka, Senior Research Fellow of the Institute of Policy Studies and Chairman, Bank of Ceylon. He has published on a wide range of issues relating to economic and social development and agrarian change. His recent publications include *Malaysia and Sri Lanka, Poverty Equity and Growth* (with Henry J. Bruton, *et al.*).

Lance Taylor   Lance Taylor is Arnhold Professor of International Cooperation and Development at the New School for Social Research, New York, where he has taught since 1993. Before that he was Professor of Economics at the Massachusetts Institute of Technology and Harvard University. His research concentrates on macroeconomic and distributional problems in developing and post-socialist economies. Recent publications include *The Market Meets its Match: Restructuring the Economies of Eastern Europe* (1994) and *The Rocky Road to Reform* (1993).

Juan Diego Trejos   Juan Diego Trejos, an economist, has been consultant to the IADB, World Bank, UNDP, ECLA and UNICEF. Currently he is Researcher at the Institute of Economic Research of the Universidad de Costa Rica and Advisor of the Second Vice-President of the Republic of Costa Rica, in the fields of poverty alleviation and social policy reform.

Foreword

The United Nations Children's Fund is pleased to present ten striking examples of how governmental policies and commitment can increase longevity and knowledge, enhance human development, and give hope and opportunity to all people, especially children. Within the latter half of this century most developing countries have made health and educational advances which took nearly two centuries to accomplish in the currently industrialized countries. This book is about countries which managed to exceed the scope and pace of social achievement of most other developing countries. It is an attempt to learn the lessons of this success.

These countries offer hope to the rest of the developing world. Hope in these cases comes from the confidence of parents in impoverished communities that their children will have a real chance to survive, be reasonably nourished, go to school, and grow up to be productive participants in society. Governments in these societies chose to empower the most vulnerable of their citizens—women and children—so that, with some support, they could enjoy longevity, knowledge, and well-being. 'Chose' is a key word, for although several of those studied have dynamic economies, some grew very slowly and are still characterized as low-income economies. They demonstrate that it is possible to achieve high levels of social development even without thriving economies if the right priorities are set and the political will is strong. This is an even more dramatic accomplishment, since most of them were able to make progress or hold on to their gains during the 'lost decade' of the 1980s.

While all of them managed to eliminate the social dimensions of poverty, many of them had somewhat limited success at eradicating income-poverty while increasing longevity and knowledge, though some were more successful than others. The reduction of income-poverty is the challenge of the next decade in some of these countries, as well as in the rest of the developing world.

Stephen Lewis
Deputy Executive Director
UNICEF

Part I

Overview

1

Profiles in Success: Reasons for Hope and Priorities for Action

RICHARD JOLLY

Pessimism and Optimism about Development

In many of the industrial countries today, there exists a widespread attitude of pessimism about development. The mood is both excessive and unfortunate. It is excessive because it is at variance with the facts. And it is unfortunate because it saps popular interest in development and political commitment for its support, just as the evidence is accumulating of widespread and long-run success.

In fact, the record of development over the last two or three decades shows widespread human and social progress. Notwithstanding the tragedies and setbacks in situations of conflict, in the least developed countries and more recently in the countries of transition from socialist to market economies, the human indicators of development have with few exceptions advanced impressively in all parts of the world, developed and developing.

UNICEF recently summarized the broad trends as follows:

In little more than one generation, average real incomes (in the developing world) have more than doubled; child death rates have been more than halved; malnutrition rates have been reduced by about 30 per cent; life expectancy has increased by about a third; the proportion of children enrolled in primary school has risen from less than half to more than three-quarters; and the percentage of rural families with access to safe water has risen from less than 10 per cent to more than 60 per cent. In the meantime, the proportion of couples using modern contraceptives has risen from almost nothing to more than 50 per cent. (UNICEF, 1993)

Since that was written, there has been further advance and new evidence to back up the claims. And one could refer also to progress in other areas such as gender, environment, and population. For instance, the proportion of girls enrolled in secondary and higher education has risen enormously in most countries over the last fifty years. Increasing numbers of countries now have environmental plans, and increasingly various forms of action are underway, often in response to an ever more aware general public. And in the area of population, average family size in the developing world has now fallen by more than half the distance between what it was thirty years ago and what is required to provide the conditions for stable population growth. These impressive achievements in the record of development deserve a 'paean of praise'[1] rather than a sour dismissal as failure or futility.

Fortunately, in parallel with the mood of development pessimism in the West, are signs of optimism, confidence, and strengthened leadership in the East. This is hardly surprising. Asia is the region of the world which over the last two or three decades has demonstrated that rapid economic growth and rapid human development are both possible. Four developing countries—China, Thailand, Republic of Korea, and Singapore, together totalling about one-quarter of world population— have achieved rates of economic growth and human development well beyond anything ever experienced even a decade or two ago. Asian performance also far exceeds anything expected in the 1950s and 1960s when the international effort for development was just getting underway.

Other countries—Indonesia and Malaysia, more recently India—have achieved somewhat lower rates of economic growth but still rapid by historical standards. Growth in these countries has also been accompanied by rapid improvements in the indicators of human development and by dramatic reductions in poverty. The number of the poor in India, for example, is estimated to have fallen from 290m. in 1972–3 to 240m. in 1987–8 and the proportion from over half to well under a third (from 52 per cent to 30 per cent).[2]

Not surprisingly, this experience of successful development has created in Asia a strong and positive mood of development confidence. The governments of these countries have not been hesitant to adopt long-term perspectives, with a sense of vision and with plans and pragmatic policies directed in support of them. These lessons are increasingly being explored with interest and inspiration both within Asia, as well as in other parts of the world.

Thus development pessimism is far from world-wide. It is concentrated overwhelmingly in the industrial countries of the West, though shared (with more reason) by many in Africa and the countries of the former Soviet Union.

Since some of the readers of this study may be from industrial countries or donor agencies, it may be useful to speculate on why the mood of development pessimism in industrial countries has grown so strong. One can identify at least five possible reasons:

- Preoccupation in the media with countries in conflict, encouraging a perception that this is typical of the developing world and that many or even most developing countries are in this condition.

- A focus on examples of extreme poverty in fundraising for development, without indicating whether the numbers in poverty is growing or declining.

- A focus on failures of development in political and policy debate, in part because these are the problems for policy-makers to tackle and in part because these are often the focus of criticism from opposition parties.

- Increasing emphasis on poverty reduction as the goal and test of development, combined with insufficient statistical evidence to judge reliably whether poverty is declining or growing and caution over using evidence of economic growth to judge whether poverty has decreased.

- The rise in poverty in a number of industrial countries since the 1980s, particularly the substantial rise in the USA and Britain, which readily encourages the view that 'the poor will be always with us' and, if with us, then surely also in poorer developing countries.

All of the above reasons are understandable, some like the increasing emphasis on poverty reduction are desirable. But combined together, they vastly overemphasize the view that progress in tackling poverty has been weak or non-existent. With the additional fact that statistics in the areas of poverty and social need are usually much more limited than in the areas of economic production, trade, and finance, sceptics can readily argue that the evidence of human development is greatly exaggerated.

In the developing countries, different reasons explain why the extent of progress is often understated, especially in international discussion and debate:

1. For some 100 developing countries, including most of Sub-Saharan Africa and most of the least developed countries, development experience since about 1980 has often been of decline in incomes and living standards rather than of advance. In many cases, the declines have been deeper and usually more sustained than anything experienced by people in the industrial countries during the Great Depression of the 1930s.

2. The wide and sometimes still widening gaps between developed and developing countries in many measures of economic and social progress. Though some of the gaps in the main human indicators have narrowed over the last two or three decades, especially between the industrial and better-off developing countries, the gaps between the poorer developing countries and the industrial countries have still been widening by most measures. In 1960, the economic gap between the richest 20 per cent of the world's population and the poorest 20 per cent was 30 to 1. By the early 1990s, this gap had grown to over 60 to 1. Meanwhile the share of the poorest 20 per cent of the world's population in global income had fallen from 2.3 to 1.4 per cent, while the share of the richest 20 per cent had risen from 70 to 85 per cent. Such experience fuels a reluctance to put too much emphasis internationally on the extent of the progress made as opposed to the distance yet to travel.

3. Colonialism and imperialism, though felt to be part of distant history by many in the industrial countries, are still widely felt within developing countries to be the basis of the continuing inequalities between developing and industrial countries within the world today. This justifies and sustains the repeated emphasis on inequalities within the international economic and political system, and supports some of the political solidarity among the developing countries.

4. For virtually all developing countries, 'development' remains one of their main national objectives. However basic this objective, in the sense that development is never really 'achieved', it none the less serves to define a widely felt ambition, even if it is one which ultimately may prove to be more a political ambition of being classed as one of the powerful, industrial countries than an economic and social objective.

For these reasons too, there is less emphasis than might be on development progress and more on development failures and weaknesses, again feeding the sense that little progress has been made.

In summary, what should the dispassionate observer conclude about the global development scene in the mid 1990s?

In terms of human development, advances clearly outweigh setbacks. There is reason neither for despair nor for complacency. None the less, there are major areas of failure and great distress.

Countries in civil conflict and war present some of the worst human distress and present to the world a major challenge. But as a commentary on the whole long-run effort of development, their failures must be kept in perspective. The countries in severe conflict and collapse involve, in total, at most 100m. people, under 2 per cent of total world population.

The major failures of economic growth and development also need to be kept in perspective. Sub-Saharan Africa is the region of greatest economic difficulty. Its population numbers about 560m. The countries in transition number under 400m. Taken together with the populations of the poorest and least developed countries elsewhere, their total population is about one billion, well under 20 per cent of the global population.

Contrast these with the regions of considerable development advance—the quarter of the world's population experiencing dramatic success as mentioned earlier and perhaps another quarter—in India, Bangladesh, and other countries of Asia, and some in Latin America and the Middle East—where signs of development success are considerable. Many of the countries in these regions are well into a phase of economic recovery and all show clear advance by tests of human development: reduced mortality rates, improved health and education, and increasing incomes and living standards for a sizeable proportion of their populations.

None of these countries is without development problems and few would argue that they have arrived at the development destination, even if that could simply be defined. But most are clearly on the development journey and making progress, measurable in the lives of most of their populations.

To be pessimistic about development in the 1990s is thus to lack historical perspective. 'On a world scale', a recent ILO research paper has stated, 'the risk, intensity and severity of poverty have fallen more sharply in the past fifty years than in the preceding thousand years. So has the risk that poverty will force its victims into illiteracy, illness or death' (Lipton, 1996).

Moods of development pessimism have been seen before. Over sixty years ago, John Maynard Keynes wrote of Britain that

We are suffering now from a bad attack of economic pessimism. It is common to hear people say that the epoch of enormous economic progress which characterized the nineteenth century is over; that the rapid improvement in the standard of life is now going to slow down—at any rate in Britain; that a decline in prosperity is more likely than an improvement in the decade which lies ahead of us.

Keynes continued, 'I believe that this is a wildly mistaken interpretation of what is happening to us. We are suffering, not from the rheumatics of old age, but from the growing-pains of over rapid changes, from the painfulness of readjustment between one economic period and another. The increase in technical efficiency has been taking place faster than we can deal with the problem of labour absorption' (Keynes, 1930).

With hindsight, it is clear that Keynes was right, both for Britain in the 1930s and for other industrial countries. We need to adopt today a similar long-term perspective of confidence and vision, especially with respect to the development prospects and possibilities of developing countries.

Lessons of Success

The purpose of this book is to probe the reasons for these successes in development—and to draw conclusions as to how they can be repeated and sustained. But let it be clear. It is not part of the purpose of this study to suggest that all is satisfactory, that the world can rest on its laurels, that no further effort is required. Far from it. The focus on success is simply and directly to emphasize that successes have been part of the record of the last fifty years—and, with purposeful effort, could be a greater and a more general part of future development—and a part which benefits all the world's people, and more fairly than in the last fifty.

A good part of past success has been the result of human development advancing hand in hand with economic growth. The studies explore this relationship, and ask how it can be strengthened.

But for important periods, especially since about 1980, the advance in human development has occurred *in spite of failures* of economic growth. About 100 countries experienced a 'lost decade' in terms of economic growth over much or more of the period since the late 1970s or early 1980s.[3] Notwithstanding, human advance continued in many cases, sometimes at accelerated rates, even in a number of the cases of very severe economic decline. The studies also explore this unexpected relationship. It is mostly a phenomenon of the 1980s and 1990s and one which so far has been too little studied.

The ten case-studies in this volume combine lessons of both types of advance—with economic growth and without. Six of the studies are of countries with more or less steady growth, mostly quite rapid growth per capita. Four of the studies focus on countries with less growth and interrupted growth, often periods of some years of considerable economic decline. Fig. 1.1 provides the thirty-year perspective for most of the countries in the case-studies. In spite of the great contrasts in the growth patterns, the steady advances in human development can be seen in every case.

The fact that many of the key human indicators continued to advance even with the marked economic declines of the 1980s, is a striking indication that the links between human advance and growth of GNP are not as close as often imagined. Though there are broad correlations, there are important differences in the human performance of different countries which cannot be explained by differences in income or economic growth.[4] All this demonstrates that with clear effort and focused action, human advance is possible even in the absence of economic growth, at least for a period.

The same contrasts between growth and human development are visible in the record of almost all developing countries since 1960. Fig. 1.2 shows the four main patterns of growth over this period. Out of 166 countries for which we have data, some fifty fall into pattern 1—broadly steady or accelerating economic growth, judged by growth of income per capita. Just under fifty fall into pattern 2—a long period of more or less steady growth over the 1960s and 1970s, followed by a major decline starting about 1980 and continuing more or less until the mid-1990s. Pattern 3 includes some forty countries—showing the steady growth followed by major decline of pattern 2 but with a subsequent recovery to a period of resumed growth in the late 1980s or early 1990s. Pattern 4 covers some ten countries—with growth, decline, and resumed growth as in pattern 3 but then faltering again, with a further downturn in the last few years.

It is perhaps surprising that all but ten countries fall into one or other of only four main patterns. But more surprising is that in almost every case, the indicators of human development continued to advance, as also shown in Fig. 1.1. Of course, the advances are not always at the same speed—and it can be argued, may some-times have been at a lower rate than might have been had steady economic growth continued. But none the less the contrasts between growth and human advance are striking.

For some two-thirds of developing countries over the 1980s there was even an acceleration in the rate at which child mortality was reduced. For nearly seventy countries, child mortality was reduced at a faster rate in the 1980s than in the 1960s or 1970s. Moreover, the regions with acceleration in the rate of reduction of child mortality were the regions of economic decline—while countries with slow rates of improvement in child mortality were those of accelerating economic growth.

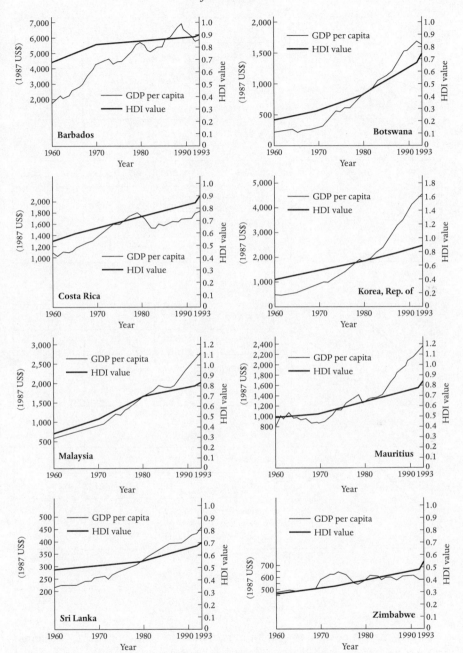

Fig. 1.1 Economic growth and human development

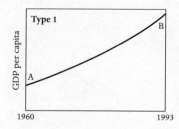

51 countries	AB	BC	CD	DE	Total
Growth % p.a.	3.4				3.4
Cumulative growth	138.5				138.5
Duration (years)	26				26

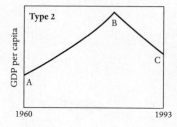

48 countries	AB	BC	CD	DE	Total
Growth % p.a.	3.9	−4.0			1.1
Cumulative growth	91.6	−31.0			32.2
Duration (years)	17	9			26

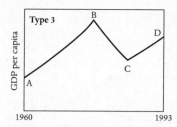

45 countries	AB	BC	CD	DE	Total
Growth % p.a.	4.5	−5.3	3.6		1.7
Cumulative growth	85.2	−32.0	28.1		61.3
Duration (years)	14	7	7		28

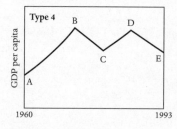

10 countries	AB	BC	CD	DE	Total
Growth % p.a.	4.9	−3.2	3.1	−3.0	1.0
Cumulative growth	69.2	−18.0	20.1	−19.2	34.7
Duration (years)	11	6	6	7	30

Fig. 1.2 Main patterns of economic growth, 1960–1993

Clearly, there is no need to wait for improvements in the economy to accelerate action to reduce child mortality. And the same can also be said of the expansion of basic education, access to clean water and sanitation, and improvements in nutrition. Of course, there is need for prioritization of effort and resources, sustained in the longer run—which seems to require economic growth identified as a long-run condition. A given level of social expenditure (and the concomitant provision of services) can be maintained with a constant per capita income; growth is not a necessary condition for maintaining the corresponding level of social outcomes. While improvement in social indicators *may* require economic growth, well-being may be improved by reallocating resources (public and private) to social sectors, even in the absence of growth. Thus, economic growth is required only for an ever-increasing provision of services with improvement in quality.[5]

Adjustment with a Human Face

How does this finding match the arguments for 'adjustment with a human face', with which UNICEF (and I myself) was much associated in the 1980s. In brief, the evidence of continuing human advance is much more positive than seemed likely in the early 1980s when the call for adjustment with a human face was first put forward. At that time, evidence from individual countries and from data-sets covering many developing countries in Africa and Latin America both suggested a widespread slow-down in the rate of advance and, for some countries in the early 1980s, decline and set-back.[6] The more substantive record which now exists confirms some of these early indications—for instance, in the fact that primary-school enrolment ratios fell over the 1980s in some twenty countries in Sub-Saharan Africa. But in most other cases, the worst does not appear to have happened, judged by child mortality, life expectancy, nutrition, and access to water and sanitation. What explains this?

There are, it seems, four main explanations. First, some remedial action was taken. Beginning in the second half of the 1980s, the World Bank and the International Monetary Fund (IMF) recognized the need for giving more attention to education, health, and human concerns in the making and implementing of adjustment policies. As they have acknowledged, this made these institutions more sensitive to these concerns and more willing to respond positively to countries wanting to incorporate such elements into their economic adjustment programmes. Social conditionality was often introduced into adjustment programmes, social action funds were developed, and efforts were made, at least to prevent new groups falling into poverty.

Second, even before the Bretton Woods institutions changed their tune and their policies, other international institutions, non-government organizations, and certain donors were active in encouraging such actions and providing support for them. Indeed, the very severity of adjustments and the fears of widespread human calamity often encouraged unusually energetic efforts along these lines. Increasingly the World Bank sought ways to work with these groups and has acknowledged their contribution to broadening concerns with adjustment.[7]

Three, many of the remedial actions taken involved a focus on low-cost, high impact interventions, with a special effort to 'go to scale', by extending their coverage to as many of the population as could be reached. This meant that over the 1980s some crucial programmes and interventions—like immunization, oral rehydration therapy, promotion of breast-feeding, attention to young child nutrition, reproductive health and family planning, low-cost water tubewells and boreholes, etc.—were not merely maintained in the midst of adjustment but greatly expanded. Their impact on mortality and life expectancy almost certainly was considerable. Even if limited, they represented selective upward support and improvements against the more general downward economic pressures and setbacks of the lost decade.

A final reason why social indicators could continue to grow through the 1980s despite economic decline was that adjustment policies initially seemed to affect social input indicators more than output or outcome indicators.[8] The main social input indicator that was affected by adjustment policies *per se* was public expenditure on health and education. Significant advances had been made in the preceding two decades especially in creating a social infrastructure—health clinics, schools, rural roads, and so on—and a strong upward tendency in social outcome indicators had come to exist at the end of the 1970s. These tendencies seemed to be a bit more resilient in the 1980s. The upward trend could not be reversed merely by reducing public expenditures, which affected the availability of drugs at clinics, of materials in schools, and the salaries of health personnel and teachers—because private expenditure would compensate for the decline in public expenditure, with the result perhaps of increasing the incidence and the depth of poverty (but on the latter there is little or no information).[9]

None of this means that the constraints and cut-backs of adjustment had no impact. The full story could only be judged by a careful analysis of the 'counterfactual'—of what would have happened if adjustment policies had more effectively combined human concerns from the very beginning, with all other things being in some sense the same. Even attempted analyses of such counterfactuals have become matters of considerable controversy. Parties sympathetic to orthodoxy on adjustment have tended to define their counterfactual as what would have happened *in the absence of any adjustment*. UNICEF always acknowledged the need for some adjustment but defined its counterfactual as what would have happened *given a different sort of adjustment*—one which made protection of basic human concerns and vulnerable groups a central objective and one which was more growth-oriented.

UNICEF also argued for a more pragmatic approach, with more attention to meso- and micro-policy and to actions which would accelerate economic growth. UNICEF identified the need for actions to strengthen small-scale farmers and industrial producers, including women and workers in the informal sector, together with more attention to issues of tax and pricing to encourage this. A more pragmatic approach was also needed in matters of subsidy, with the emphasis on making subsidies efficient and effective judged by the basic objectives of human development and economic growth, as opposed to the doctrinaire attempt to remove all subsidies.

Unfortunately, this part of the call for adjustment with a human face received much less attention. Concern for the poorest and the vulnerable became an 'add on' to an otherwise largely unchanged approach to adjustment. The core of macro-economic policies recommended by the IFIs was little changed. And, perhaps most serious of all, the issues of structural change, required for the reduction of poverty and inequality and for achieving more rapid economic growth, remained on the back burner for most of the decade. Development policies throughout the 1980s were dominated by the concern for macroeconomic stability, with compensatory policies to address the 'new poor', while at the same time the incidence of poverty worsened in both Africa and Latin America over the 1980s.

The consequences were reinforced by the repercussions of globalization. Adjustment policy encouraged countries to open their economies. In cases where an economy was strong, this could bring new opportunities and benefits. But in cases where the economy was weak, rapid opening of the economy meant that it could be swamped by forces of competition beyond its ability to deal with successfully. Production suffered, imports rose, the currency devalued, savings and capital sought refuge abroad. It was not a recipe for increasing growth.

One argument against taking poverty more seriously in the midst of adjustment was the sheer scale of the problem. In countries where the poor formed half or more of the total population, was it not obvious that the priority had to be 'getting the economy right' and only later, when resources were more plentiful, to turn to the question of poverty reduction? UNICEF's answer to this was 'development with a human face'. It was not possible in the short run to tackle all aspects of poverty. But it was possible to focus on some of the most important needs of *all* the poor—and to make progress even at times of the most severe economic constraints. Indeed, not to do so would often be a neglect of the most important priorities of human investment. To give substance to this strategy of development with a human face would require setting clear goals for the medium to longer term and to pursue them steadily with low-cost approaches. This UNICEF did in ways summarized in the next section.

Notwithstanding these important advances, it would be a great mistake to read the positive dimensions of the human record as complacency over the economic setbacks of the 1980s. The lost decade had—and sometimes continues to have—a most terrible impact on the lives and living standards of a billion to a billion and a half people. Incomes fell precipitously for most of these people, with an impact on themselves and their families probably more severe and in most cases more sustained and often deeper than anything experienced in the Great Depression in the industrial countries in the 1930s (countries whose populations even at that time were better off than most of the poor in the developing countries today). And many of the actions required for long-term solutions were neglected.

The fact that advance in life expectancy and education has often continued is a point of importance which moderates somewhat the setbacks. But this silver lining to the dark economic clouds of the 1980s is not a reason for arguing that the lost decade did not represent a human cost of enormous proportions and a tragedy of human suffering. And for many countries the costs still continue, even in the second half of the 1990s.

We must also take account of some other important qualifications to the record of human development. The social indicators used to judge human progress are not always as reliable as one would like, especially in the least developed countries. In spite of these weaknesses, for most countries, the *broad* trends showing *quantitative* advance in human development are not in doubt. The more serious problem is *qualitative*. Most countries lack reasonable indicators of quality in the key areas of education, health, or water.

There is, however, much casual evidence to suggest that qualitative declines frequently occurred. This is hardly surprising, since the quality of services is often highly dependent on resource availability. Schools without books and health clinics without basic medicines, teachers and health workers only occasionally receiving their salaries became common accounts. Almost certainly, therefore, the quality of schooling and health services deteriorated on a wide scale. Readers need only think of their own experience—or their concerns for their children's—in education or health, to realize how important a matter this is. The absence of a minimum of quality at basic levels of education and health can make a mockery of the effort.[10]

Two Types of Lesson

Two different types of lesson need to be distinguished from the successful experiences of recent decades: lessons for more comprehensive development, especially with respect to human development, economic growth, and poverty reduction, and lessons for focused programme action, within a sector or subsector.

Although comprehensive development is the long-run goal, the potential and possibilities of more focused programme advance should not be neglected.[11] Although this may seem obvious, it is often disputed. Much debate and many words have been spent in development arguing that only a comprehensive approach is worthy of being tried. This case neglects three important truths, well borne out from experience in many of the more successful developing countries.

First, experience of accelerated sectoral or focused programme action in many countries shows that substantial progress is possible, and has produced important gains, without having to wait for the longer and more difficult process of achieving broad-based development. Second, investment in basic education and basic health has increasingly been shown to be of critical importance for laying a foundation for broader, more comprehensive development later. Third, the estimated 'partial' rates of return on such actions are often high, and higher than those on the totality of investments in broad-based development. Why wait to achieve this benefit?

This said, the case is for accelerated action in key sectors, not for the long-run neglect of more comprehensive development. Again there are three reasons. In the long run, the goal must be human development and poverty reduction, both of which involve a more holistic approach, not a narrow focus. Second, as more focused action succeeds, the emerging items on the agenda will inevitably require broadening the approach to cover wider range of goals and actions.

Third, recent evidence suggests that though it is possible for a decade or so to accelerate some of the key indicators of human advance, especially in education and health, unless economic growth and more balanced development is then achieved, it becomes difficult to sustain early progress in human development. At that point, either economic growth also begins to accelerate and begins to provide the support required for the expanded social sectors, or the rapid earlier advance in human development begins to slow and, sometimes, even to peter out.[12]

The Human Development Report (1996) explored such experience in detail. It showed that balanced growth was always needed in the long run, not lopsided growth.[13] However, in the early stages of development, there is a strong case for accelerated action focused on education and health, to lay the foundations for later acceleration in growth, and also more balanced growth. This is of course one of the major lessons of Asian experience in the post-Second World War period—and of the earlier experience of the faster-growing industrial countries like Japan and Sweden.[14]

Goals for the Future

How can these success stories be used for further and more widespread human advance in the years ahead?

Each country needs to focus more sharply on the goals of human development—and give clearer priority to their achievement. In the case of the poorest and least developed countries, international support will be needed, not just more aid, but aid and debt relief purposely devoted to support of long-run goals for social transformation.

Basic goals for long-run human advance have already emerged and achieved a consensus of basic support in the series of global conferences held over the 1990s: the World Summit for Children (1990), the Conference on Environment and Development—the Earth Summit (Rio, 1992), the Conference on Human Rights (Vienna, 1994), the International Conference on Population and Development (Cairo, 1994), the World Summit for Social Development (Copenhagen, 1995), the Fourth World Conference on Women (Beijing, 1995), and the Global Conference on Human Settlements (Istanbul, 1996).

The declarations and plans of action with which most of these global meetings ended, comprised several points of basic approach, greatly adding to the realism of the commitments made:

- Action must be country focused and nationally led.
- Each country must produce its own goals and plans of action.
- Effective action must involve a wide range of non-government groups and organizations. Follow-up cannot be seen as simply a government initiated effort, let alone as merely the implementation of a national plan.
- The international community and aid donors in particular have an important supportive role, especially in the poorer and least developed countries.
- Action needs to be publicly monitored, as a measure of accountability, to ensure course corrections as progress proceeds and to mobilize and maintain public interest and support.

These points are important to emphasize. One of the common points of criticism about global conferences is that they fail to be specific about follow-up action. This is less true than is often suggested. Experience shows that in most cases the declarations and plans of action provide a sufficient frame for national action and an effective and enabling frame for international support.

Moreover, the majority of developing countries have already taken some actions to carry forward the commitments made at these conferences. A series of international reports have been prepared to show the actions underway.

The 1990 World Summit for Children was the first to be held and is thus the one for which most specific progress can be reported. One hundred countries prepared national plans of action, of which fifty were decentralized to state, regional, or city level. A whole diversity of actions was set in motion, directed to the achievement of the goals for the year 2000 and in many cases also to 'stepping-stone' goals for 1995.

The latest report suggests 'an encouraging trend towards the achievement of the majority of the [17] goals for children in most countries. There is of course, considerable variation across countries and regions' (UNICEF, 1996). The better-off countries have already achieved many or most of the goals, or soon will. This includes goals for the reduction of infant and child mortality, for the expansion of primary education, for increased access to water and sanitation, for further expansion of immunization, as well as major actions towards the eradication of polio, iodine deficiency, and vitamin A deficiency, as well as ratification of the Convention on the Rights of the Child. Although in many countries, especially in Africa and the least developed countries, progress is not rapid enough to achieve the goals by the year 2000, more than half the developing countries are on track to achieve more than half of the goals by this date. There are few countries which have not made some quantitative advance.

Equally impressive, hard results in terms of reductions in mortality and prevalence of disease have become increasingly evident by the mid-1990s. Polio has been certified as eradicated in all countries of the Americas and in total, some 100 countries for which data are available report no case for the last three years, with another thirteen reporting no case for the last year. The 2.7m. deaths expected to occur each year from measles and the 1.2m. deaths from neonatal tetanus have now fallen, respectively by about 85 and 61 per cent between 1990 and 1995. The incidence of goitre and iodine-deficiency disorder has dropped dramatically world-wide and in the majority of the former most afflicted countries. Guinea-worm disease is now no longer found in Asia or the Middle East and, with the incidence having declined by an estimated 97 per cent, is on the verge of elimination.

It is easy for the eye to glide over such figures, forgetting the human suffering and economic setbacks which such diseases once represented and how recently their incidence was so widespread. Iodine deficiency was in 1990 the largest single cause of mental deficiency world-wide, with 1.6bn. people at risk, some 750m. with symptoms, and some 43m. people affected by brain damage and with lowered IQ as a result of inadequate iodine intake during infancy and early childhood. Yet by 1995, almost all countries with an iodine-deficiency problem were iodizing salt in an effort to reach the end-decade goal and around 1.5bn. more people were consuming iodized salt than in 1990. Data on the human impact is not yet available but an estimated 12m. infants each year are now protected who would otherwise have been susceptible to mental retardation.

But progress is not just in these sectoral areas, but in many respects more widespread, and sustained. Each of the countries studied in this book has demonstrated:

- clear human development over at least two and usually three decades, measured in terms of progress in mortality reduction, in health and education and reduction in gender disparities in social indicators.

- a sustained process of human development, usually in the sense of maintaining a broad process of advance but in every case avoiding any long-term downturn.

- economic advance, though usually at rates and with a pattern which varies considerably between countries. (Our sample ranges from the exceptionally economically successful like Botswana and the Republic of Korea to those like Sri Lanka which over the last three decades has achieved only slow and variable economic performance. Indeed, over the period covered, most of the countries show a variable pattern of economic growth and activity, though most of them demonstrate a much steadier pattern of human development.)

- a continuing dynamic which promises further development in both opens the possibility of reducing poverty as well.[15]

The country case-studies in this volume thus provide a range of experience which, with appropriate adaptation, is applicable to a wide variety of other developing countries.

Our challenge, in this present phase and at the end of the twentieth century, is not to give up on the struggle for development but to complete the task. No one can deny that the world amply possesses the resources to eradicate the worst aspects of world poverty. And as this study shows, an increasing number of countries have demonstrated that it is possible to make rapid progress to this end. The challenge now is to draw on this experience in order that other countries may be set on a path of human advance, poverty reduction, and a pattern of development which enables all their people to achieve control and choice over their lives.

The structure of the rest of the book is as follows. Chapter 2 presents a broad overview of the major social achievements of the selected countries, while avoiding any contextual or country-specific discussion. The common elements of their social development, as well as their differences, are analysed in order to answer why they were able to make such dramatic improvements in health and education status, despite their varying experiences in respect of economic growth. Chapter 3 introduces the main policy initiatives implemented in the case-studies, focusing on how those health and educational improvements were achieved. Also, it summarizes the main policy lessons in each sector while it highlights the complementarity of the sectoral interventions.

Part II contains the case-studies. They have been organized by region and represent a rich description of the major economic and social trends in each country. In each case, the initial conditions and context in which specific policies were implemented is presented. Each country's accomplishments in the social sectors, and their limitations, are examined in greater detail. It is in this part that the reader will find the contextual factors—which are specific to each country—underlying their social achievements.

Finally, the two closing chapters in Part III correspond to two different, if partly overlapping, conclusions. Chapter 14 pulls together the main implications for social policies from the case-studies. Chapter 15 builds on the conclusions of Chapters 2, 3, 14, and the case-studies in regard to social development and explores the linkages among social development, economic growth, and poverty reduction.

Notes

1. The phrase comes from Surendra Patel (1992).
2. The figures quoted are official government estimates (Government of India, 1993). The expert group made their own estimates suggesting that the total number had fallen from 322 to 313m. from 1972–3 to 1987–8 and the percentage of poor had fallen from 55 to 39.
3. For fuller details, see UNDP (1996).
4. Again, the Human Development Report (1996), contains further analysis on this point, though appendix 4 in this report somewhat misses the point, I suspect. By relating the

improvements in life expectancy from 1970 to 1992 to the growth rate of GNP 1960 to 1970 and relating life expectancy in 1992 and child mortality in 1993 to GDP per capita in 1980, the analysis misses out most of the periods of sharp decline. It will be surprising if the relationship as specified and lagged stands up to subsequent testing, when life expectancy and child mortality data are available for the next decade.

5. For further elaboration, see Ch. 15.

6. Some of this evidence was summarized in Cornia (1987).

7. See e.g. the generous tribute to UNICEF: 'when structural adjustment issues came to the fore [in the 1980s], little attention was paid to the effects on the poor. . . . Many observers called attention to the situation, but it was UNICEF that first brought the issue into the centre of the debate on the design and effects of adjustment' (World Bank, 1990: 103).

8. There are two significant exceptions to this statement. First, primary enrolment ratios—an output indicator—definitely declined in many African countries, with the result that the overall Sub-Saharan primary enrolment ratio fell 12 percentage points between 1980 and 1990 (from 81 to 69) (see Mehrotra and Vandemoortele, 1997). Second, the incidence of malnutrition increased in many countries (see Cornia, Jolly, and Stewart, 1987).

9. In the transitional economies of East Europe and the CIS, the decline in output after 1989 was much greater than that experienced in Africa and Latin America in the 1980s. As a result both social input, output and outcome indicators worsened significantly in a short period of time. Most African and Latin American countries were spared comparable declines e.g. in mortality rates.

10. For a discussion of the relationship between slow economic growth and the quality of services, see Ch. 2, and case-studies on Kerala, Sri Lanka, and Zimbabwe.

11. What is implied here is similar to Hirschman's strategy of 'unbalanced growth' (1958). The need to keep in mind the long-run goal of comprehensive development should prevent countries from, again following Hirschman (1995), 'getting stuck', i.e. being unable to move forward once an intermediate objective has been reached.

12. For fuller details, see the analysis in Ch. 3 of UNDP (1996).

13. Lopsided growth was defined there as either rapid economic growth but slow human development, or rapid human development but slow or negative economic growth.

14. Descriptions are given in UNDP (1996: 53–4).

15. This issue is further explored in Ch. 15.

References

Cornia, Giovanni Andrea (1987), 'Economic Decline and Human Welfare in the First Half of the 1980s', in G. A. Cornia, R. Jolly, and F. Stewart (eds.), *Adjustment with a Human Face*, Oxford: Oxford University Press.

Government of India (1993), *Report of the Expert Group on Estimation of the Proportion and Number of Poor*, Planning Commission.

Hirschman, A. O. (1958), *The Strategy of Economic Development*, New Haven: Yale University Press.

—— (1995), *A Propensity to Self-subversion*, Cambridge, Mass.: Harvard University Press.

Keynes, J. M. (1930), 'Economic Possibilities for our Grandchildren', repr. in *The Collected Writings of John Maynard Keynes*, ix: *Essays in Persuasion*, London: Macmillan, 1972.

Lipton, Michael (1996), *Success in Anti-Poverty*, ILO Issues in Development Discussion Paper no. 8, Development and Technical Co-operation Department, ILO, Geneva.

Mehrotra, S., and Vandemoortele, J. (1997), *Cost and Financing of Primary Education: Options for Reform in Sub-Saharan Africa*, UNICEF Staff Working Paper, EPP/UNICEF, New York.

Patel, Surendra (1992), 'In tribute to the Golden Age of the South's Development', *World Development*, 20/5: 767–77.

UNDP (1996), *Human Development Report 1996*, New York: Oxford University Press.

UNICEF (1993), *Progress of Nations 1993*, New York: UNICEF.

—— (1996), 'World Summit for Children Follow-up', Mid-decade Review 1996 (Report of the Secretary General on Progress at Mid-decade 1996), New York: UNICEF.

World Bank (1990), *World Development Report 1990*, New York: Oxford University Press.

2

Social Development in High-Achieving Countries: Common Elements and Diversities

SANTOSH MEHROTRA

The Conceptual Framework of the Book

The ultimate objective of state action in all countries should be the enhancement of human capabilities. This is so for all countries, but more so for developing countries. Capability consists of the basic capacity to avoid ignorance, undernutrition, disease, and early mortality and lead a fuller, longer life, and be able to participate in decision-making in the community (Sen, 1985; Dreze and Sen, 1989). The capability to avoid undernourishment may depend not only on a person's intake of food, but also on the person's access to health care, medical facilities, basic education, drinking-water, and sanitary facilities. The notion of capabilities goes beyond a person's command over income, and in that sense comes much closer to the concept of human development that has recently influenced development thinking (UNDP, 1990).[1]

Leading this literature, the *Human Development Report* has attempted to quantify some of the elements which constitute human development in a well-known index. The human development index combines, with equal weight, longevity, knowledge, and income (as measured by life expectancy, a combination of adult literacy and mean years of schooling, and income measured by average purchasing power, respectively). These are the means to achieving the end of human development or the enhancement of human capabilities. Although the human development index is defined in this manner, it is important to stress that the notion of human development or capability also incorporates the concepts of civil and political liberties and the freedom of individuals to participate in community or state decisions which affect their lives.

Every region in the developing world has some examples of high-achieving countries which have experienced major improvements in life expectancy, literacy, and mean years of schooling over the last few decades. Longevity and knowledge, key elements of human development, have been called social development in the rest of the book. The main objective of the book is to understand why and how these countries achieved these outcomes. The countries in this book are drawn from almost every developing region: the Republic of Korea (hereafter Korea) and Malaysia from East Asia; Sri Lanka and the State of Kerala, India from South Asia; Botswana, Mauritius, and Zimbabwe from Sub-Saharan Africa; and Barbados, Costa Rica, and Cuba from Latin America and the Caribbean.

Although the case-studies in the book are mainly about social development, or about the health and educational development of these societies, every society examined in this book also began with a high incidence of poverty. Hence the studies also look at the relationship between the process of economic or income growth in the society, and the process of social development. However, they deal with the participatory aspects of human development in only a limited way. Although most of these countries are either democracies or have moved in that direction the discussion of civil or political liberties or of the growth or decline of participatory democracy in these countries is limited—otherwise the project would become extremely unwieldy.

In some countries included in this volume, social development has been accompanied by rapid economic growth, while in others it has occurred in spite of modest economic growth. In some (e.g. Korea) market structures dominated economic transactions, while others (e.g. Cuba) stood at the other end of the spectrum in this respect, though most were somewhere in between. This chapter attempts to distil some of the common elements of why and how advances in longevity and knowledge occurred in these successful cases of social development in the past three to four decades, despite the diversity in their economic structure and performance, and in their success at poverty-reduction.

The objective of both economic growth at the macro-level as well as health and education advance should be the development of human capabilities. To pose the question in terms of the primacy of social development or economic growth, or to ask whether the causality runs from social development to economic growth or vice versa, is at best to pose the wrong question and at worst to be misleading, because they both influence and enhance each other.

Evidence from many countries demonstrates that social development is a major contributor to economic growth. The direct effects of educational investment are well known. For instance, better-educated workers earn higher incomes and education raises the output of farmers (Psacharapoulos, 1985). The indirect effects take longer. Investments in health and education have brought down infant-mortality rates. In this context, the education of women has higher social returns than that of men: educated women have healthier children; infant mortality is lower the greater the number of years of mother's schooling; educated women have fewer children; and so on (Colclough, 1982; Psacharapoulos and Woodhall, 1985; Schultz, 1988; Tilak, 1989; Birdsall, 1993). In turn these have an effect on economic development. Similarly empirical evidence has been collected on the impact of health and nutrition on labour productivity, on schooling productivity, of female nutrition on fertility, and of infant mortality on fertility (Behrman and Deolalikar, 1988). But given that human capital is only one of the constraints on economic growth—the others being physical capital and in the case of developing countries, foreign exchange—the accumulation of human capital may not necessarily lead to economic growth, as the evidence from these country studies demonstrates (and as is discussed in Chapter 15).

While human capital is a major contributor to economic growth the latter might promote human development. Cross-country evidence (Anand and Ravallion, 1993) suggests that for basic health, growth matters to the extent that it delivers lower income-poverty and better public services. In fact, the commonly observed positive correlation across countries between life expectancy and affluence disappears once one controls for incidence of poverty and public spending in health.[2] We discuss the relationship between economic growth and social development in the ten cases later in this chapter. We also explore the synergies between income growth and social development and feedback effects further in the final chapter of the book.

While the impact on economic growth at the macro-level of social development is only a minor theme in this book, the real focus is on synergies in interventions in nutrition, health, education, fertility, and income. UNICEF has long recognized these synergies in its own work for child survival and development. The conceptual framework of UNICEF's health and nutrition strategies for country programming implies relationships between particular kinds of interventions. In the 1980s the GOBI-FFF programme strategy was based on these interventions: G = Growth monitoring of children; O = Oral rehydration therapy; B = Breast-feeding; I = Immunization; F = Female education; F = Family spacing; and F = Food supplements (Cash *et al.* 1987). Interventions in health, nutrition, fertility, education, and income complement each other, and thus the economic return to any one from investments in any other (Birdsall, 1993). It was with this understanding that the World Summit for Children formulated a list of goals in these areas in 1990, which 150 governments in the world committed themselves to achieve by the year 2000. With the objective of achieving these goals in health, nutrition, water and sanitation, and education, they prepared National Programmes of Action for women and children.

Underlying UNICEF's global programming and global goals there is a conceptual framework, which recognizes the relationship between the delivery of primary and basic curative care services, the command over food, and the existence of good child-care practices in the household (UNICEF, 1990). This conceptual framework states that low mortality, especially of children, is the outcome of not merely access to health services, but adequate food and child-care practices, and in the absence of even one of these preconditions, mortality can be higher than would otherwise be the case. For instance, control of diarrhoea and measles is very important not only for health outcomes but in reducing malnutrition (by improving the capacity to absorb and retain caloric intake). This means that improved water and sanitation also contributes substantially to achieving the health and nutritional goals. Exclusive breast-feeding is the only human action that fulfils the conditions of 'food', 'health', and 'care' simultaneously. In the conceptual analysis, education is identified as crucial in increasing the capacity of the household to use available human, economic, and organizational resources for satisfying the 'food', 'health', and 'care' conditions.

The synergistic effect of these interventions will also hasten the demographic transition in the developing countries, thus reducing the need over time to allocate more and more resources to health and education merely to provide access to these services for the entire population. It should be made clear, however, that the motivation for the goals was not entirely economic, but rather based on a strong commitment to basic rights of children—rather in the frame of the Convention on the Rights of the Child, now the most ratified of all UN human rights conventions.

In their different ways, the countries discussed here have already shown the direction in this respect. What is striking about the selected countries is that social development occurred despite low-income levels and at early stages of their development process. These countries demonstrate that it is possible for even low-income countries to achieve levels of health status and education for their population comparable to that of industrialized countries.[3] Many of these high achievers in social indicators (including Korea and Mauritius) were seen as 'basket cases' in the early stages of their development, although they may now be middle-income countries.

The choice of countries

Tables 2.1–2.3 and Figs. 2.1 and 2.2 present data on these high-achieving countries for crucial indicators in health and education. It is important here not to compare countries across regions, e.g. Zimbabwe with Cuba, but only with countries in their region. These countries may or may not be high achievers in an absolute sense, but they certainly are relative to other countries in their region.[4] Most indicators for most sectors are superior in the selected countries for the early 1990s when compared to the regional average. Clearly there are other countries for which some indicators are higher than the regional average, but we found that for the chosen countries the indicators were consistently higher than the regional average for most sectors.[5] We also relied on qualitative information and previous research to arrive at this choice of countries. For major selected health indicators, these countries have better indicators than all countries in the region, i.e. for outcome indicators like life expectancy at birth, infant-mortality rate (IMR) and maternal-mortality rate (see Table 2.1), and under-5-mortality rate (U5MR) (see Fig. 2.1). The same holds true for adult literacy rates in 1970 and 1990 (see Table 2.2) and gross enrolment rates in primary schools in 1960 and 1993 (see Fig. 2.2).

TABLE 2.1. Selected high achievers by geographic region: health outcome indicators

	Infant mortality rate		Maternal mortality rate	Life expectancy at birth (years)
			1990–92	1993
	1960	1993		
East Asia and Pacific	132	42	159	68
Korea, Rep. of	88	8	26	71
Malaysia	73	13	59	71
South Asia	146	87	492	59
Kerala[a]	120	17	87	70
Sri Lanka	90	15	80	72
Sub-Saharan Africa	152	109	616	51
Botswana	117	43	250	61
Mauritius	62	19	99	70
Zimbabwe	109	58	—	56
Latin America and Caribbean	105	38	189	68
Barbados	74	9	70	76
Costa Rica	80	14	36	76
Cuba	39	9	39	76

Sources: UNICEF, *State of the World's Children, 1995*; [a] Chapter 7

TABLE 2.2. Selected high achievers by geographic region: adult literacy, 1970–1990

	1970		1990	
	male	female	male	female
East Asia and Pacific	76	56	88	71
Korea, Rep. of	94	81	99	93
Malaysia	71	48	86	70
South Asia	44	19	59	32
Kerala[a]	55	39	95	87
Sri Lanka	85	69	93	83
Sub-Saharan Africa	34	17	61	40
Botswana	37	44	84	65
Mauritius	77	59	85	75
Zimbabwe	63	47	74	60
Latin America and Caribbean	76	69	86	83
Barbados	—	—	—	—
Costa Rica	88	87	93	93
Cuba	86	87	95	93

Note: Comparable regional averages are not available prior to 1970, hence the use of 1970 as the starting date

Sources: UNICEF, *State of the World's Children, 1995*; [a] Chapter 7

TABLE 2.3. Selected social indicators, then and now (% change)

	Education				Health	
	Adult literacy rate, 1970–90		Primary school enrolment ratio, 1960–90		U5MR 1960–90	IMR 1960–90
	male	female	male	female		
East Asia and Pacific	13	20	7	41	−72	−68
Korea, Rep. of	5	16	−2	−16	−93	−91
Malaysia	21	46	−14	18	−82	−81
South Asia	34	68	26	87	−46	−39
Kerala	73	123	—	—	—	—
Sri Lanka	9	22	9	11	−85	−83
Sub-Saharan Africa	79	141	65	150	−29	−27
Botswana	127	48	182	161	−66	−62
Mauritius	—	—	6	16	−71	−68
Zimbabwe	18	28	44	79	−53	−45
Latin America and Caribbean	15	20	40	44	−68	−63
Barbados	0	0	10	11	−88	−87
Costa Rica	6	7	9	10	−86	−83
Cuba	11	7	9	10	−86	−83

Note: A minus sign for primary enrolment denotes that GER and NER were converging

Sources: UNICEF, *State of the World's Children Report, 1995*; Chapters 4–13

A comparison of a 'then and now' nature (Table 2.3) shows that the rate of change in these countries compared with the regional average shows a mixed pattern. It was higher especially for U5MR and IMR among the health indicators, but much less so for the education indicators (the adult literacy rate and primary-school enrolment ratio for males and for females). However, it should be noted that most of the selected countries had a more significant head start in education, in that their indicators are at a higher level at the beginning of the selected period, and hence have a shorter distance to travel. Thus, their rate of change is not as large as the regional average, and in many cases may actually be lower.

We compared the rate of change of outcome and output indicators among the ten countries in our sample and the rest of the developing countries (including the ex-USSR and eastern European countries), i.e. a total of 124 countries. The percentage change in U5MR and primary gross enrolment ratio (GER) for both males and females between 1960 and 1990 was used; in addition, the percentage change in literacy rates for females and males between 1970 and 1990 was used. This comparison of the percentage change in the ten selected countries with all other countries revealed that the rate of improvement in our sample was higher for all variables

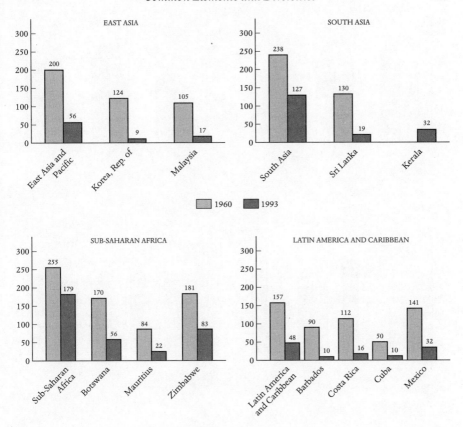

Fig. 2.1 Under-five mortality in high-achieving countries

Source: State of the World's Children, 1995

(except primary enrolment for males), and this difference was statistically significant.

While social development is the common element among the selected countries, the experience with economic growth has been quite varied. In some countries, real per capita income multiplied considerably between 1960 and 1992: in Korea, Malaysia, Botswana, and Mauritius. In other countries, per capita incomes grew two to three times: in Sri Lanka, Zimbabwe, and Costa Rica (see Table 2.4). Given that these per capita incomes are in purchasing-power parity terms, they give a realistic idea of the increases in incomes. In Kerala State income grew more slowly than in India on average, where in real terms it doubled over the period.

There is considerable diversity between the countries in the rate of growth of per capita income experienced during the turbulent decade of the 1980s. In Zim-

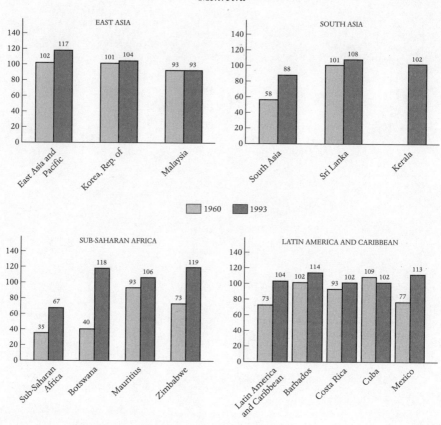

Fig. 2.2 Gross enrolment rates in primary schools

Source: State of the World's Children, 1995

babwe per capita incomes actually fell slightly over the period. However, the East Asian high achievers as well as Botswana and Mauritius weathered the 1980s extremely well (see Table 2.4).

The diversity between countries is evident in regard to economic structure as well. In 1965, while all the economies were, in terms of the structure of their employment, predominantly agricultural (see Table 2.5), Botswana and Zimbabwe were almost entirely so. While Korea and Malaysia considerably diversified the structure of their production by the early 1990s and transformed the structure of their employment, in the other economies there were only moderate changes in this regard.

While all the countries started out with low per capita incomes, today many belong to the middle-income category, while a few (Sri Lanka, Cuba, Kerala,

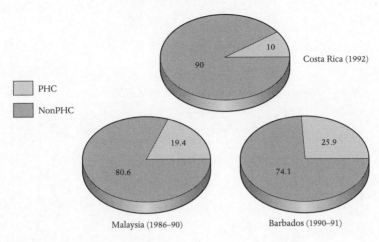

Fig. 2.3 Distribution of health expenditure

Source: Chapters 10–12

and Zimbabwe) still belong to the low-income category. However, all have made remarkable progress in terms of longevity and knowledge available to their people—key aspects of human development.

Common Elements among the High Achievers

There are a number of common elements in the stories of successful social development in the countries included here: (i) a policy of state-supported basic social services for its population, instead of a reliance upon a trickle-down of the benefits of growth (or, as Sen calls it, simply a policy of 'unaimed opulence'); (ii) investment in the health and education of its population, before economic take-off; (iii) resource allocation to the health and education of the population *usually* well above the average for developing countries; (iv) an investment in basic education and attainment of educational status which preceded the improvement in the health status, ensuring high effective demand and utilization of health services; (v) certain cross-sectoral interventions which favoured the status of women; (vi) attempts at ensuring a nutritional floor for the population; and (vii) a number of specific kinds of health and education interventions (the last two discussed in Chapter 3) which ensured high effectiveness of inputs as well as demand for these services.

It should be clarified here that this chapter does not attempt to summarize the contextual factors underlying social achievement in these countries. Factors of a historical or political economy nature specific to the country are best discussed in the case-study.

TABLE 2.4. Output growth and sectoral composition

	Real GDP per capita ($)		GNP per capita Avg. growth rate (%)		Structure of output											
					Agriculture				Industry				Services			
	1960	1992	1965–80	1980–92	1960	1970	1980	1993	1960	1970	1980	1993	1960	1970	1980	1993
East Asia and Pacific																
Korea, Rep. of	690	9,250	7.3	8.5	37	25	16	7	20	37	41	32	43	41	43	50
Malaysia	1,783	7,790	4.7	3.2	37	29	24	—	18	25	37	—	45	46	39	—
South Asia																
Kerala	555[a]	1,107[a]	—	0.3[a]	—	—	—	—	—	—	—	—	—	—	—	—
Sri Lanka	1,389	2,850	2.8	2.6	32	28	28	25	20	22	30	30	48	45	42	50
Sub-Saharan Africa																
Botswana	474	5,120	9.9	6.1	—	33	—	6	—	28	—	47	—	39	—	47
Mauritius	2,113	11,700	3.7	5.6	—	16	—	10	—	22	—	33	—	62	—	57
Zimbabwe	937	1,970	1.7	–0.9	18	15	12	15	35	36	39	36	47	49	49	48
Latin America and Caribbean																
Barbados	—	9,667	—	—	—	—	—	—	—	—	—	—	—	—	—	—
Costa Rica	2,160	5,480	3.3	0.8	26	23	17	15	20	24	29	26	54	53	54	59
Cuba	—	—	—	—	18	15	12	15	55	53	45	—	27	32	44	—

[a] Kerala's real GDP per capita (PPP) is estimated as 90% of that of India's. Growth rate is for the 1980–90 period. Cuban figures are for 1962, 1970, and 1978

Sources: World Bank, *World Development Report, 1982* (for 1960 and 1980 figures) and *1995* (for 1970 and 1993 figures); UNDP, *Human Development Report, 1995*; UNICEF, *State of the World's Children Report, 1995*; Mesa-Lago (1981); IMF, *International Financial Statistics Yearbook*, various issues

TABLE 2.5. Structure of employment

	Agriculture						Industry						Services					
	1965	1970	1975	1980	1985	1992	1965	1970	1975	1980	1985	1992	1965	1970	1975	1980	1985	1992
East Asia and Pacific																		
Korea, Rep. of	55	49	43	36	—	17	15	20	23	27	—	35	30	31	34	37	—	48
Malaysia	59	54	48	42	—	31	13	14	17	19	—	23	28	32	35	39	—	46
South Asia																		
Kerala	—	—	—	—	—	—	—	—	—	—	—	—	—	—	—	—	—	—
Sri Lanka	56	55	54	53	49	—	14	14	14	14	18	—	30	31	32	33	33	—
Sub-Saharan Africa																		
Botswana	89	86	78	70	—	—	4	5	8	13	—	—	7	9	14	17	—	—
Mauritius	37	34	31	28	—	25	25	25	25	24	—	—	38	41	44	48	—	—
Zimbabwe	79	77	75	73	—	17	8	9	10	10	—	—	13	14	15	17	—	—
Latin America and Caribbean																		
Barbados	22	18	14	10	—	—	27	26	23	21	—	11	51	56	63	69	—	—
Costa Rica	47	43	37	31	—	25	19	20	22	23	—	27	34	37	41	46	—	48
Cuba	33	30	27	24	—	17	19	20	22	23	—	27	48	50	51	53	—	56

Source: World Bank, *Social Indicators of Development, 1994*

Public action in all cases

The large improvements in social indicators which characterize all these countries were not the result of trickle-down of growth or complete reliance on market forces. Public action for social development was a common element in all these countries, regardless of whether they experienced rapid economic growth over the last few decades or not. This is significant because there are a number of middle-income countries, especially in Latin America, with per capita incomes comparable to the fast-growing economies of Korea and Malaysia, but which have social indicators much below those found in the latter (or even Thailand or Indonesia, which have a much lower per capita income). For example, Brazil, with many times the income per head of China and Sri Lanka, still has a lower life expectancy than the latter countries. Thus, improvements in the quality of life cannot simply be seen as the simple outcome of increases in income, and in reality it is the public intermediation which is the determining factor.

Among the low-income economies, poor social indicators are the norm rather than the exception. Therefore, the examples of Sri Lanka, Zimbabwe, and Cuba stand out as even more significant. In fact, among the States of India, Kerala has had one of the lowest rates of economic growth, and very little industrialization has occurred since independence. Even agricultural production has tended to decline within the last decade. Nevertheless, committed leadership has ensured that access to basic health care and primary education is available to all.

The two rapidly growing economies of Sub-Saharan Africa (Botswana, Mauritius) among the selected countries have also been characterized by public policies favouring social development. Between 1960 and 1993 Botswana managed to increase life expectancy for its population from 48 years to 67 years and Mauritius from 60 to about 70 years. There is striking contrast here with the most populous country in Africa, Nigeria, whose economy had grown at 9.7 per cent per annum over 1965–73, and thereafter experienced the windfall gains of the oil price increases. In spite of the windfall gains, Nigeria managed to reduce its U5MR by less than 10 per cent (from 212 to 188) over three decades, and the life expectancy of its population increased from about 42 to 51 years. That lack of resources is not the most important constraint to improvements in social indicators is demonstrated not merely by such examples, but even more so by the examples of the relatively slow-growing economies in our sample (Cuba, Kerala, Sri Lanka, Zimbabwe) which show what could have been achieved, given the necessary public policies.

Cuba is a country now thought to have a per capita income comparable to that of its poorest neighbours, but the broad measures of its health remain impressive in spite of the current economic difficulties: IMR, estimated to have fallen to 9.4 deaths for every 1,000 live births in 1994, was only a shade higher than that of the USA; life expectancy at birth, 75.5 years in 1992, nearly equalled that of Luxembourg. These examples demonstrate what is possible even at rather low levels of income, and slow income growth.

The role of ideology and politics cannot be ignored as driving forces behind public action in the selected countries. Thus, in Cuba it was communism; in Kerala it was the competitive politics between the Communist Party and the populist Congress Party; in Sri Lanka, it was a combination of socialist ideology, competitive democracy, and Buddhism; in Zimbabwe, it was the natural consequence of the liberation struggle against white rule. In Costa Rica it was essentially a social-democratic consensus (in a democracy which has lasted almost 150 years, with elections every four years, in strong contrast with the rest of Latin America). Similarly, in the island States of Barbados and Mauritius, it was competitive politics which drove the State's commitment to health and education. In Malaysia social development was the outcome of the State's attempt to correct the social and economic disadvantage of the Malay population based on ethnicity. In Korea, early social development was driven by a military State (supported by the USA) facing a communist 'threat' from the north; once set in motion the process was sustained by a State committed to economic growth.

Public support for improvements in the quality of life was a significant factor in improvements in social indicators even in the now-industrialized countries. For example, England and Wales began this century with a life expectancy no higher than that of developing countries today. In each decade up to 1960, life expectancy tended to grow by about 1 to 4 years, except in the two decades of the two world wars when it grew by more. Those were also the decades of the large increases in public support which included public employment, food rationing, and health care (including the National Health Service in the 1940s) (Dreze and Sen, 1989).

By and large it was the government's commitment to public action which made health and education development possible. Thus, there is limited evidence of NGO involvement in the delivery of programmes in these countries (except in Mauritius and Cuba), either in health or education. The studies do not show much evidence of direct community involvement in the programmes (except Zimbabwe's primary schooling) in the majority of countries. It should be noted, however, that the enhanced role of NGOs and other institutions of civil society in development is a relatively recent phenomenon. Many of the selected countries, on the other hand, made their health and education breakthroughs in an earlier period when the role of the State in development was, and was recognized to be, much more powerful than is the case in the 1990s.

Educational achievement preceded high health status

The selected countries had a head start over the other countries in their regions in regard to the health indicators. However, the rate of improvement of the outcome indicators (U5MR and IMR) were also better in our selected countries than in the region as a whole. A comparison of Tables 3.1 and 3.8 will establish that high education indicators preceded the health breakthrough. These gave the selected countries a tremendous advantage over the others, since high education levels are highly correlated with positive health improvements. While the reasons for the head start in education are discussed in the case-studies, suffice here to say that primary-school enrolment was high. In 1960 the primary GER for girls (normally lower than for boys in most developing countries) was less than 50 only in Botswana and Kerala.

In fact, from the case-studies, an implicit model of social development seems to be emerging: the head start these countries had in education suggests a sequence of investment in education preceding that in the health infrastructure. All our countries started with an advantage in regard to, in particular, female education (see Table 2.2); the female–male differential in educational levels at the beginning of the period was lower, and that differential was closed over the period of analysis, much more so than in the rest of the countries of the region. When the investments in health infrastructure came, high educational levels ensured a high demand and effective utilization of health services.

The classic example of the synergy between educational and health interventions comes from Korea. Before 1976 Korea had no publicly supported health system worth the name, and no form of broad-based medical assistance or medical insurance scheme. Health care was predominantly in the hands of private professionals, especially pharmacists. But its literacy rate was already 90 per cent in 1970. The role of literacy in sustaining high levels of private demand for health care (certainly in Korea's case) is worth noting. When the investment in public health came after 1976, IMR, which was still 53 in 1970 and 41 in 1975 dropped to 17 within a matter of five years (1980). Similarly, in Sri Lanka, literacy levels were already 60 per cent before independence in 1948, higher than they are in India and Pakistan today. Not surprisingly when health services expanded immediately after independence, Sri Lanka experienced a very rapid increase in life expectancy in the first decade after independence.

In Table 2.6 we present the extent of correlation between health outcomes (U5MR and life expectancy) and a number of inputs, related to health, nutrition, water and sanitation and education, for a sample of 124 countries.

Among the input indicators which had the six highest correlation, five were education indicators and one was from nutrition. In fact, 1990 secondary-education levels were more strongly correlated with a lower U5MR and high life expectancy than was primary education. In addition, female education was more strongly correlated than male education. Moreover, 1970 primary and secondary GERs, both total and those for females, were highly correlated with both U5MR and life expectancy. In the pre-eminent importance of the education indicators as determinants of health outcomes we have reinforcement of the implicit model that emerges from the qualitative analysis of the evolution of social policy.

It should be emphasized that these are simple correlations between each individual input indicator and the health outcome, and do not tell us much about the mutually reinforcing effect that, say, education may have on nutritional outcomes and therefore on health outcomes. We began this chapter by saying that health,

TABLE 2.6. Correlation between mortality and various input indicators (144 countries)

Variable	U5MR, 1992 Correlation	Rank	Life expectation at birth, 1990 Correlation	Rank	Total fertility rate Correlation	Rank
1990 GER, secondary ed., females	-0.84	1	0.89	1	-0.83	2
1990 GER, secondary ed., males	-0.80	2	0.86	2	-0.80	4
1990 GER, primary ed., females	-0.79	3	0.78	5	-0.69	5
1970 GER primary ed., females	-0.79	4	0.83	3	-0.85	1
1970 GER primary ed., males	-0.78	5	0.81	4	-0.82	3
Daily per capita calories supply	-0.72	6	0.74	6	-0.69	6
1990 GER, primary ed., males	-0.67	7	0.63	8	-0.54	8
Percentage of population with access to health services, rural	-0.63	8	0.58	9	-0.50	9
Percentage of population with access to safe water, urban	-0.54	9	0.58	10	-0.38	11
Percentage fully immunized, DPT	-0.50	10	0.65	7	-0.57	7
Percentage of population with access to safe water, rural	-0.50	11	0.50	11	-0.42	10
Percentage of population with access to adequate sanitation, rural	-0.49	12	0.48	13	-0.36	13
Percentage of population with access to adequate sanitation, urban	-0.47	13	0.46	14	-0.31	14
Percentage of births attended by professionals	-0.43	14	0.48	12	-0.37	12
Percentage of population with access to health services, urban	-0.28	15	0.30	15	-0.30	15
ORT use rate	-0.22	16	0.23	16	-0.11	16
Population per nurse	0.49	17	-0.60	17	0.53	17
Population per physician	0.84	18	-0.79	18	0.61	18

Sources: UNICEF (1993); World Bank, *Social Development Indicators, 1993*

education, and nutrition interventions have a mutually reinforcing effect on the quality of life—something that a correlation cannot pick up.

The above should also not be taken to mean that health interventions *per se*, and their particular nature in our ten countries, were unimportant—quite the contrary. Within the health system, the imbalance between rural and urban areas in terms of facilities and that between primary and curative care providers was eliminated. Besides, within PHC, the emphasis was on mother and child health (MCH). A food-consumption floor helped to reduce mortality rates (see Chapter 3 for further discussion of these issues). It is significant that interventions within the health sector focused on system-building of the preventive rather than curative services. This involved the provision of comprehensive primary health care, as opposed to a selective approach to primary health (an issue discussed further in Chapter 3).[6]

Women's education and women's agency

As the conceptual framework mentioned earlier made clear, health outcomes for children are not only the result of adequate food consumption and the availability of health services, but proper child-caring practices. In this respect the position of women in the household and in society acquires major significance. Relative to other countries in their region, these countries are also characterized by much greater access to education by women at the beginning of our period of analysis. In the selected countries, 1960 female enrolment ratios at primary level were above the regional average (except in Malaysia). In 1970, female adult literacy rates were also higher than the regional average for all countries, except Malaysia (see Table 2.2); and this country more than made good the lag by 1990, ending the period with better than the regional average for both primary enrolment and adult female literacy. By 1970, primary enrolment ratios were similar for males and females in all the selected countries (see Table 2.7), and substantial parity existed between males and females in secondary-school enrolment. In other words, any disparity in educational levels of men and women was completely eliminated by 1970—in striking contrast to the large disparities that continue to exist to date in the vast majority of countries in Asia and Africa.

While education is an important determinant of women's position in society, there are other factors which are at play as well—some historical and some more recent, the latter particularly mediated by the State. Sen has written about the notion of women's 'agency', and its relationship to women's well-being (Sen, 1995). The notion refers to the freedom women have to engage in work outside the home, to earn an independent income, to have ownership rights, and, of course, to receive education. Wherever these freedoms and rights prevail, the well-being of women is positively affected. Culturally, where there are no taboos attached to girls taking up roles outside the house, the task of setting up an effective health service becomes easier. In Sri Lanka and Kerala, where rural women have become educated, and where parents permit them to engage in work outside the home, it is easier to hire

TABLE 2.7. Women's agency: education (women as a % of men)

	Adult literacy		Enrolment ratio						% of cohort persisting to grade 4	
			Primary		Secondary		Tertiary			
	1970[a]	1992[a]	1970	1990	1970	1990	1970	1990	1970[c]	1988[c]
East Asia and Pacific	74	81	87	96	76	79	53	73	—	82
Korea, Rep. of	86	94	98	100	73	97	38	53	101	100
Malaysia	68	81	89	100	69	106	49	99	—	101
South Asia	43	54	60	75	43	60	30	48	90	—
Kerala	71	92	—	97[b]	—	97[b]	—	—	—	—
Sri Lanka	81	89	92	100	105	108	99	108	—	100
Sub-Saharan Africa	50	66	72	85	60	72	34	46	—	100
Botswana	119	77	112	105	97	111	29	74	95	104
Mauritius	77	88	98	103	79	104	32	75	100	100
Zimbabwe	75	81	85	101	66	95	54	52	100	100
Latin America and Caribbean	91	97	101	98	91	98	96	70	103	—
Barbados	99	98	100	100	109	92	71	149	—	—
Costa Rica	99	100	99	101	102	99	84	85	102	99
Cuba	101	98	101	100	102	110	67	128	—	—

Note: Column 4 data does not correspond exactly to the data in Ch. 3 because figures for all levels were taken from UNDP (1995) to ensure comparability

Sources: UNDP, *Human Development Report, 1995*, pp. 57–68; [a] from UNICEF, *State of the World's Children, 1995*; [b] 1993 data; [c] from World Bank, *World Development Report, 1995*

them as nurses or train them as midwives. Since they work in their own areas in their own language, they are accepted more easily by the community in house-to-house visits. Caldwell found that in a neighbouring State in India, Karnataka, female health workers often came from Kerala and remained strangers to the local population; in fact, nurses in the rest of India also come from Kerala, while in many places the shortage of local recruits meant the absence of female health workers (Caldwell, 1986).

Similarly, the positive feedback from the presence of female teachers on female primary enrolment has been noticed (see Chapter 3). The proportion of female teachers in school is very high in the high-achieving countries. On the other hand, in most South Asian, Middle Eastern, and Sub-Saharan societies, there is a considerable male–female differential even in primary-school enrolment, which in fact tends to worsen at the secondary level. Not surprisingly, many of the education systems of these societies are characterized by a low proportion of female teachers in schools (Dreze and Sen, 1995; Chapter 3).

Work outside the home is reflected in data on the economic activity rate of women in these countries. In most of these societies the economic activity rate (defined as those who supply labour for the production of economic goods and services as defined by the UN System of National Accounts, whether for the market, for barter, or for own-consumption) of women (over 15) has been rising between 1970 and 1994. Since female economic rate includes agricultural activity, column 1 in Table 2.8 does not give us an accurate picture of the situation. In fact, the regional average in East Asia and Africa (and even Latin America) for female economic activity rate tends to be higher than in our sample countries since agricultural work has traditionally been part of female economic activity. Hence, we also present data on the non-agricultural employment of women. In the selected countries, women as a percentage of men in the workforce is high in non-agricultural sectors of employment. In fact, non-agricultural employment is a better indicator than agricultural employment of the propensities to work outside the home and of an independent source of income. Agricultural-sector employment will not give women a source of independent income unless undertaken as wage labour, which is more likely to be undertaken within landless families by the male. On account of the high educational levels achieved by women in the selected countries, women are nearly as well represented as men in the professional categories of employment. This is not to suggest that parity has been reached with men even in these societies, but considerable advances have been made.

In many societies, the modern State has helped to strengthen the position of the woman in society. Nowhere is this more obvious than in Cuba. Many sections of the Cuban constitution explicitly refer to gender equality, and its penal code treats the infringement of the right to equal treatment as a criminal offence (see Cuba case-study for further discussion). In Zimbabwe, women had participated in the liberation struggle, and worked as community health workers pre-1980. From that it

TABLE 2.8. Women's agency: employment

	Female economic activity rate (%) 1994	Women as a % of men				
		Non-agriculture paid employment[a] 1990	Professional and technical 1990	Clerical and sales 1990	Administrative and managerial 1990	Services 1990
East Asia and Pacific	69	—	82	65	13	108
Korea, Rep. of	41	66	74	79	4	156
Malaysia	45	56	—	—	—	—
South Asia	29	—	—	—	—	—
Kerala	—	—	—	—	—	—
Sri Lanka	29	64	98	28	7	61
Sub-Saharan Africa	52	—	—	—	—	—
Botswana	41	50	159	151	56	238
Mauritius	29	59	71	44	17	70
Zimbabwe	43	18	67	52	18	42
Latin America and Caribbean	30	—	—	—	—	—
Barbados	61	84	110	184	48	132
Costa Rica	24	55	81	68	30	146
Cuba	38	72	—	—	—	—

[a] Data from ILO, *Yearbook of Labour Statistics*. For Cuba it corresponds to 1988

Professional and technical includes, e.g. scientists, lawyers, teachers and artists

Clerical and sales includes, e.g. working proprietors (wholesale and retail), cashiers, transport, and mail workers

Administrative and managerial includes legislative officials, government administrators, and managers

Services includes, e.g. managers (catering and lodging), cooks, waiters, building caretakers, maids, and hairdressers

Source: UNDP (1995: 57–9)

was a minor transition for them to be employed as village health workers by the ministry of health. The Zimbabwean State has also taken a number of legislative measures to strengthen the position of women—and is rather unusual on the African continent in this respect. Changes in legislation have conferred majority status on women and given inheritance and maintenance rights; women no longer need their husband's consent to buy immovable property; and the law now allows the equitable distribution of family property between spouses upon divorce. In Botswana there has been no large legislative or societal change in the position of women, but in terms of education Botswanan women too have made considerable strides. Girls now constitute the majority of primary-school children, and even at secondary level their enrolment is higher than that of boys—unlike Zimbabwe. The result is that in professional as well as clerical categories of workers the number of women exceeds that of men (see Table 2.8), as it does in Barbados. In Mauritius it was mainly boys who went to school in the 1950s at all levels. At the primary level the gap had almost closed by 1960, while at the secondary level, the enrolment ratio of girls caught up with that of boys only by the end of the 1980s. As a result (and helped by the smaller size of the family) the participation of Mauritian women in the labour force increased considerably.

In all cases this has contributed to their autonomy in society and an enhancement of their role in decision-making in the household with regard to the health of their children and their own health.

In particular, the education of women will also strengthen women's earning capacity, their caretaking capacity, and their control over household resources. Women's resource control and caretaking capacity comprise one of the conditions for adequate nutrition, along with household food security, access to health services, and a healthy environment. We indicated earlier (in relation to GOBI-FFF) that 'care' is the pivotal link between the other conditions, especially household food security and disease control. In practice, the main responsibility for child care lies with the mother, who often also has a major role as an income-earner. This integral precondition for adequate nutrition may not be as well recognized by policy-makers as household food security and infectious-disease control. Maternal literacy and schooling is known to be associated with a more efficient management of limited household resources, greater utilization of available health services, better health-care practices, lower fertility, and more child-centred caring behaviour (Gillespie and Mason, 1981). Moreover, it raises the awareness of the means to overcome problems and generates effective political demand. In general, therefore, women's education has an enormous effect on nutrition and health, in the long run probably one of the most important.

Resources for social development

Another common element in the high-achieving countries is the higher allocation of budgetary resources to health and education, and in particular, to basic social services. We find that in a sample of 123 developing countries the average health expenditure to GDP for low health achievers (as defined by below-average U5MR) was 1.05 per cent, while that for the high achievers (above average U5MR) was 1.37.[7]

In the selected high achievers governments spent in the range of 5–8 per cent of GDP on health and education together over the fifteen-year period 1978–93 (see Tables 2.9 and 2.10). Rarely did any of these countries spend more than 8 per cent of GDP. (It should be noted that expenditures on food subsidies are not covered by this figure, since it relates exclusively to health and education expenditure.) The Human Development Report 1991 concluded that the human expenditure ratio (or government expenditure on basic social services—primary health, basic education—rather than all health and all education) may need to be around 5 per cent of GDP if a country wishes to do well in human development. It appears that the selected high achievers may be spending somewhat less, given that no more than half of government expenditure on health and education is likely to be going to basic social services in our sample (though it is possible that in earlier decades—for which internationally comparable data are not available—these countries may have been spending more).

Two of the selected countries spend much less than 5 per cent of GDP on health and education—Sri Lanka and Korea. Actually, Sri Lankan spending was very much within the range of the rest of the countries in the sample until the late 1970s, when economic difficulties forced it to curtail social expenditure. As regards Korea, the study points out, the republic has not been a welfare-oriented State, and has kept state expenditure on health and education low relative to the region, and private expenditure on health and education has been quite high. Korea made a substantial investment in education in the early years of its development, but state investment in health services increased only after 1976 (note Korea's particularly low health expenditure to GDP ratio in Table 2.9). Nevertheless, what is important is that Korean government per capita expenditure on human priorities is the same as that of Malaysia, even though Malaysia's human expenditure ratio is twice that of Korea, because the latter's GNP per capita is twice that of Malaysia (UNDP, 1991).

Most of the selected countries spent between 20 and 30 per cent of government expenditure on education and health (over 1978–93) (see Tables 2.11–2.12). There is one country which spends well above this range: Costa Rica's expenditure on health and education has accounted for around 42–50 per cent of all government expenditure—well above the normal even for our high-achieving countries. The latter indicates the very high priority given by Costa Rica to health, but it may also indicate some inefficiencies in government expenditure on health (see Chapter 3 for further discussion).

The *Human Development Report 1991* had recommended that in order to achieve a human expenditure ratio of around 5 per cent, a preferred option is to keep the public expenditure ratio moderate (around 25 per cent), allocate much of this to the social sectors (more than 40 per cent), and focus on the social priority areas of basic

TABLE 2.9. Government health expenditure as a percentage of GDP, 1978–1993

	1978	1979	1980	1981	1982	1983	1984	1985	1986	1987	1988	1989	1990	1991	1992	1993
East Asia and Pacific (mean)	1.5	1.4	1.5	1.6	1.8	1.9	1.9	1.8	1.8	1.7	1.5	1.4	1.5	1.5	1.2	0.8
East Asia and Pacific (median)	1.0	0.9	0.8	1.0	1.2	1.1	1.6	1.5	1.2	1.2	1.2	1.0	1.0	0.8	0.2	0.8
Korea	0.3	0.2	0.2	0.2	0.3	0.3	0.2	0.2	0.2	0.4	0.3	0.3	0.3	0.3	0.2	0.2
Malaysia	1.6	1.4	1.5	1.7	—	—	1.3	1.5	1.7	1.4	1.3	1.4	1.5	1.6	1.6	1.5
South Asia (mean)	0.4	0.6	0.4	0.5	0.7	0.8	0.8	0.5	0.7	0.5	0.9	0.9	0.9	0.8	0.2	0.1
South Asia (median)	0.3	0.3	0.3	0.3	0.6	0.5	0.7	0.3	0.3	0.5	0.3	0.7	0.3	0.3	0.2	0.1
Kerala[a]	—	—	1.5	—	—	—	—	1.6	—	—	—	—	2.0	—	—	—
Sri Lanka[b]	—	—	1.2	—	—	—	—	1.0	—	—	—	—	1.6	—	—	—
Sub-Saharan Africa (mean)	1.4	1.3	1.3	1.4	1.6	1.6	1.3	1.3	1.5	1.5	1.4	1.5	1.9	1.5	1.3	1.9
Sub-Saharan Africa (median)	0.9	0.9	0.8	0.7	0.6	0.8	0.7	0.5	1.6	1.7	1.5	1.4	1.6	1.7	1.5	1.9
Botswana	1.8	1.3	1.7	2.0	1.7	1.7	1.5	1.4	2.0	2.5	1.6	1.5	1.8	1.7	—	—
Mauritius	2.5	2.5	2.2	2.2	2.2	2.3	2.2	2.1	1.9	1.8	1.9	2.3	2.2	2.1	2.1	2.2
Zimbabwe	2.0	1.9	1.9	2.1	2.3	2.0	2.5	2.4	—	—	—	—	2.5	—	—	—
Latin America and Caribbean (mean)	1.7	1.7	1.8	1.7	1.7	1.7	1.8	1.9	1.5	1.7	1.6	1.7	2.0	1.9	2.0	—
Latin America and Caribbean (median)	0.9	0.9	1.1	0.9	1.0	1.0	1.0	1.1	0.9	0.8	0.4	0.4	1.4	1.8	1.6	—
Barbados	3.5	2.8	3.4	3.5	3.2	3.1	3.5	3.7	3.4	3.9	3.7	4.0	—	—	—	—
Costa Rica[a]	—	—	7.2	6.2	6	5.3	5.6	5	5.1	5.5	6.1	7.1	6.7	7.9	—	—
Cuba[a]	—	2.4	—	—	—	—	—	—	—	—	—	—	4.7	—	—	—

[a] as a percentage of State Domestic Product for Kerala, Gross Social Product for Cuba, and GNP for Costa Rica; [b] corresponds to the five-year average up to the date shown

Sources: IMF, Government Finance Statistics, various issues; Chapters 4–13 Mesa Lago (1996); ECLAC (1995)

TABLE 2.10. Government education expenditure as a percentage of GDP, 1978–1993

	1978	1980	1981	1982	1983	1984	1985	1986	1987	1988	1989	1990	1991	1992	1993
East Asia and Pacific (mean)	4.0	3.6	3.4	4.3	4.5	4.3	4.1	4.3	4.2	4.5	3.5	4.0	3.9	4.1	3.3
East Asia and Pacific (median)	2.6	2.8	2.3	3.9	4.1	4.4	4.3	3.1	3.7	4.0	2.9	3.1	3.4	3.1	2.7
Korea, Rep. of	2.6	2.8	2.7	3.6	2.8	3.0	3.1	2.8	2.8	3.4	3.0	2.9	3.0	3.1	2.8
Malaysia	5.5	5.1	5.5	6.5	6.7	5.6	5.3	5.5	5.9	5.6	5.2	5.5	6.1	5.7	4.9
South Asia (mean)	3.5	2.6	3.0	2.6	3.6	3.2	3.1	3.9	3.1	3.4	2.5	3.4	2.7	4.0	2.6
South Asia (median)	3.7	2.6	3.0	2.7	3.3	2.2	2.9	4.3	3.1	2.6	1.4	4.1	1.4	4.1	1.4
Kerala[a]	—	5.0					7.0					6.0			
Sri Lanka[b]		2.3					1.9					2.6			
Sub-Saharan Africa (mean)	4.2	3.8	3.2	4.3	4.1	4.0	4.2	3.9	4.2	4.3	3.7	4.4	3.9	4.3	3.4
Sub-Saharan Africa (median)	2.8	3.8	3.0	2.7	1.6	2.1	2.8	3.5	1.9	3.1	2.9	3.6	2.4	3.5	2.7
Botswana	7.4		—	6.0	6.2	5.0	5.3	5.8	6.0	5.8	6.8	6.3	7.1	7.2	6.1
Mauritius	2.0	2.0	2.1	4.5	2.2	2.6	2.8	2.1	1.9	3.2	5.1	2.5	4.9	2.2	5.4
Zimbabwe				7.9			8.1			7.1	5.4		5.9		4.0
Latin America and Caribbean (mean)	2.6	—	3.2	3.3	3.3	3.6	3.5	2.9	3.1	3.2	3.5	3.4	3.9	2.9	3.6
Latin America and Caribbean (median)	1.8	—	3.2	2.3	2.6	2.8	2.8	2.0	2.0	2.5	2.1	1.8	2.5	0.5	2.2
Barbados				5.7	5.3	6.0	6.0	5.5	5.8	5.4	5.9	6.2	6.3		5.9
Costa Rica				4.2	4.3	4.1	4.2	2.5	4.1	4.6	6.2	2.3	5.0	2.9	6.2
Cuba[a]	7.5											6.8			—

[a] as a percentage of State Domestic Product for Kerala, and Gross Social Product, in 1979, for Cuba; [b] corresponds to five-year average before the date shown

Sources: IMF, Government Finance Statistics, various issues; Chapters 4–13; Mesa-Lago (1996)

TABLE 2.11. Share of health expenditure of total government expenditure (selected high achievers), 1978–1993

	1978	1979	1980	1981	1982	1983	1984	1985	1986	1987	1988	1989	1990	1991	1992	1993
East Asia and Pacific (mean)	6.6	6.4	6.1	6.8	7.6	7.7	7.7	7.6	6.8	6.5	6.4	6.5	6.5	6.3	6.3	6.2
East Asia and Pacific (median)	6.4	6.4	5.1	6.1	6.8	6.8	7.3	6.9	6.2	5.5	5.6	5.0	6.0	6.2	6.7	1.9
Korea, Rep. of	1.7	1.1	1.3	1.4	1.5	1.7	1.5	1.5	1.6	2.5	2.2	2.1	2.0	2.2	1.1	1.0
Malaysia	6.4	6.5	5.1	4.4	—	—	4.8	5.9	5.8	5.5	5.6	5.8	6.0	6.2	6.7	6.5
South Asia (mean)	3.3	3.7	3.1	3.2	3.7	3.9	3.7	3.5	3.2	4.0	3.8	3.9	4.6	3.4	2.6	2.5
South Asia (median)	1.9	3.4	2.5	3.0	4.0	4.3	4.2	3.0	2.9	0.9	3.4	4.8	5.1	3.1	0.2	0.2
Kerala[a]	—	—	9.7	—	—	—	—	8.2	—	—	—	—	9.9	—	—	—
Sri Lanka	4.2	5.2	4.9	3.9	3.4	5.5	4.0	3.9	3.9	5.4	5.7	6.0	5.4	4.8	5.7	5.2
Sub-Saharan Africa (mean)	5.9	5.8	5.7	6.0	5.9	6.1	5.8	5.7	5.9	6.3	6.4	6.1	7.3	7.3	6.2	6.0
Sub-Saharan Africa (median)	5.1	5.2	5.2	4.1	3.7	4.3	3.8	3.0	6.5	6.3	5.7	5.4	7.7	7.1	6.9	6.2
Botswana	6.0	4.7	5.4	5.9	4.9	5.6	4.8	5.0	5.9	7.4	5.4	4.8	5.1	4.7	—	—
Mauritius	8.2	8.0	7.5	7.0	7.1	9.2	9.7	9.0	9.3	8.8	9.1	11.2	10.3	10.8	10.1	11.8
Zimbabwe	5.7	5.9	5.4	7.1	6.4	6.1	6.2	—	—	—	—	—	5.3	—	—	—
Latin America and Caribbean (mean)	7.9	7.7	8.4	7.6	7.4	7.5	8.0	7.7	7.1	7.9	8.0	7.8	8.7	9.4	9.9	10.6
Latin America and Caribbean (median)	5.8	6.5	5.7	5.8	5.2	5.9	6.6	6.6	6.0	3.7	2.3	3.0	7.9	7.7	7.9	10.2
Barbados	—	—	—	—	—	—	—	—	—	—	—	—	—	—	—	—
Costa Rica	5.2	3.3	6.9	5.9	9.2	3.7	7.5	3.0	2.2	2.6	2.3	4.3	3.9	—	—	—
Cuba	—	—	16.2	—	—	—	—	13.0	—	—	—	—	13.8	—	—	—

[a] Refers to state government revenue

Sources: IMF, Government Finance Statistics, various issues; Chapters 4–13

TABLE 2.12. Share of education expenditures of total government expenditure (selected high achievers), 1978–1993

	1978	1979	1980	1981	1982	1983	1984	1985	1986	1987	1988	1989	1990	1991	1992	1993
East Asia and Pacific (mean)	16.4	16.6	15.9	17.5	18.6	19.7	18.7	19.7	19.0	18.3	19.8	19.6	19.7	18.9	18.3	19.2
East Asia and Pacific (median)	15.2	15.8	13.5	16.1	18.0	18.2	19.1	19.4	18.0	16.2	19.7	19.3	20.5	17.4	17.0	18.5
Korea, Rep. of	16.4	17.2	17.9	18.9	21.1	21.2	19.9	19.4	19.0	19.2	19.9	19.3	20.5	17.0	17.2	17.9
Malaysia	21.4	21.9	18.4	15.9	18.0	18.1	19.1	22.7	23.1	22.8	23.3	22.5	22.4	21.6	22.2	23.0
South Asia (mean)	6.6	6.7	6.2	6.6	7.4	7.8	7.8	8.0	7.1	8.3	8.1	9.4	8.2	6.8	4.7	4.6
South Asia (median)	2.4	6.8	4.7	8.2	8.7	7.8	9.5	8.2	7.6	2.6	8.5	10.5	10.5	2.2	2.1	2.2
Kerala[a]	—	—	32.0	—	—	—	—	28.0	—	—	—	—	26.0	—	—	28.1
Sri Lanka	6.9	7.3	6.8	8.2	8.7	7.8	7.2	8.2	8.8	7.8	8.5	10.5	10.5	8.4	10.9	10.4
Sub-Saharan Africa (mean)	15.3	16.5	17.7	17.0	16.9	16.8	16.7	15.9	16.2	17.4	18.5	17.6	19.4	19.6	15.3	12.9
Sub-Saharan Africa (median)	13.3	12.5	12.8	11.2	11.9	12.4	11.7	9.0	14.7	16.7	17.5	15.1	17.7	20.1	22.8	20.4
Botswana	20.5	22.1	22.2	21.2	17.6	19.4	17.5	17.7	18.4	18.1	20.0	20.3	20.5	21.0	—	—
Mauritius	17.7	17.7	17.6	15.8	14.7	12.9	12.3	11.1	10.9	9.5	10.2	12.3	10.7	10.2	10.5	10.7
Zimbabwe	11.9	12.7	15.5	20.0	21.9	21.5	20.4	—	—	—	—	—	18.0	—	—	—
Latin America and Caribbean (mean)	17.1	17.0	17.2	16.5	15.2	15.5	15.4	15.5	15.6	15.0	15.2	15.5	15.0	13.7	13.3	16.2
Latin America and Caribbean (median)	13.5	12.7	12.4	11.7	10.8	13.0	13.4	14.5	13.4	10.7	8.2	8.7	16.2	14.7	16.8	16.9
Barbados	—	—	23.5	—	—	—	—	23.8	—	—	—	—	23.1	—	—	—
Costa Rica	34.5	33.5	34.0	34.1	33.0	25.7	24.4	25.7	21.1	24.8	19.1	17.0	21.0	—	—	—
Cuba	—	—	—	—	—	—	—	—	—	—	—	—	—	—	—	—

[a] as a percentage of total state revenue

Source: IMF, Government Finance Statistics, various issues

social services (giving them more than 50 per cent). Our high-achieving countries do not seem to have been spending as much as 40 per cent of government expenditure on social services (just as they appear to have spent less than 5 per cent of GDP on basic social services). Costa Rica is the only country with an unusually large allocation to health and education (42–52 per cent), but it is also unusual in not having an army.

How did the high achievers' health and education expenditure to GDP ratio compare with the regional average over 1978–93? Education expenditures for each of our countries were higher for the high achievers relative to the region, without exception. For health, too, the expenditures were higher than the regional average, except in the cases of Korea.

Sri Lanka has allocated a consistently lower proportion of government expenditure to education than the South Asian average. This is perhaps explained by the fact that, unlike all its neighbours, by 1960 it had already achieved near-universal primary education with a primary GER for girls of 95 (and 107 for boys). As its population growth rate has also sharply dropped to 1.5 per cent, the school-age population is tending to stabilize.[8] It has, however, consistently spent more than the South Asian average on health, which is perhaps less a reflection on Sri Lanka than on its neighbours, where mortality rates are among the highest in the world and life expectancies among the lowest. In any case, it is interesting that comparing across regions, the share of government expenditure allocated to health is the lowest in South Asia.

Table 2.13 shows that as a share of government education expenditure, all the selected countries spent more on primary education than on the other two levels, but so did the other countries in every region. What is more interesting is that by 1990 none of the selected countries (except Zimbabwe) was allocating a larger share to primary education than the rest of the countries in their region. The investment in primary education had been made early in the development process, and the share of higher education kept low. The weight of secondary level increased in the 1980s. Only Malaysia continued to allocate as much to primary as to secondary education through the 1980s. For the rest, it appears that African countries (Botswana and Mauritius) and Latin American/Caribbean countries (Barbados, Costa Rica, Cuba) were already shifting the focus of government expenditure to secondary education, having achieved their goals for primary education. Zimbabwe, too, after making a massive thrust in primary education, was beginning to shift focus somewhat to secondary education.

For countries for which information is available on the allocation of health expenditure to PHC and non-PHC activities (see Figure 2.3), it appears that Malaysia allocated one-fifth and Barbados a quarter of its health expenditure to primary health activities, while Costa Rica's allocation was quite limited. What is clear, however, is that the primary health activities are the low-cost activities—and ones that do not necessarily absorb a very large part of public expenditure. It is the

TABLE 2.13. Selected high achievers by geographic region: current government expenditures on education by level

	Pre-primary and primary		Secondary		Higher	
	1980	1990	1980	1990	1980	1990
East Asia and Pacific[a]	43.2	51.2	29.1	29.4	19.1	16.9
Korea, Rep. of	49.9	44.4	33.2	34.1	8.7	7.4
Malaysia	35.0	37.9	34.0	37.7	12.4	14.9
South Asia[a]	54.6	51.8	28.1	26.6	19.8	18.8
Kerala	—	42.0	—	—	—	—
Sri Lanka	92.4[b]	84.3[b]	—	—	7.6	13.4
Sub-Saharan Africa[a]	43.7	46.4	30.2	29.6	20.3	18.0
Botswana	52.1	31.1	29.2	48.8	13.2	12.2
Mauritius	44.1	41.2	36.5	39.6	7.7	7.2
Zimbabwe	66.5	54.1	21.4	30.6	7.5	10.3
Latin America[a]	43.1	45.8	23.6	25.1	16.2	14.9
Barbados	32.0	37.5	32.0	37.6	18.1	19.2
Costa Rica	28.0	31.0	21.5	17.1	26.1	35.8
Cuba	29.4	25.7	40.8	39.0	6.9	14.4

[a] Unweighted average; [b] Also includes secondary level

Source: UNESCO, *World Education Report, 1993*

clinical activities which are relatively more expensive (Joseph, 1985). Nevertheless, there is need for a much better information base in regard to public expenditure on basic health services and the distribution of public health expenditure by level— without which it is difficult to estimate the scope for budget restructuring to meet basic needs in developing countries. The number of countries for which such information is available is very limited, though now growing (Mehrotra and Thet, 1996; UNDP, 1991 and 1996).[9]

While the various ratios discussed above give an indication of the salience attached to the population's health and education by governments, what matters at the receiving end is the actual absolute size of the expenditure in per capita terms. Relative to other countries in their region, our high achievers are spending much more per capita than other countries. This is particularly so in education, and to a lesser extent in health as well. Thus in 1992 the median expenditure in education was $49 in East Asia, but $174 in Korea and $123 in Malaysia. The Sub-Saharan median was $11 in 1992, but even a low-income country like Zimbabwe spent $26, while Botswana spent fifteen times and Mauritius twelve times as much. Even though Costa Rica is not one of the countries with the highest per capita income in Latin America, it spent nearly three times as much per capita than the regional median ($43).[10]

For the period for which we have information (1978–93), defence expenditure (see Table 2.14) was not particularly significant in most of the high-achieving countries, except in Korea and in Zimbabwe. In the case of the Republic of Korea the potentially negative effects of the relatively high defence expenditure appears to have been offset by high economic growth rates. In Zimbabwe's case, high defence expenditure was necessitated by its geographical location as a frontline State against the apartheid regime in South Africa, which destabilized the subregion through the 1980s. The tension resulting from unproductive defence expenditure and the commitment to provide social services to the poorest through the 1980s finally resulted in a decline in the capacity to sustain social services in the context of structural adjustment. Like Zimbabwe, Botswana too bore part of the brunt of the destabilization of the subregion by South Africa, and had a relatively high defence expenditure to GDP ratio, though the burden was greater on the Zimbabwean economy. In Sri Lanka, the burden of defence expenditure more than doubled from the mid-1980s onward on account of the civil war conditions prevailing in the north and north-east of the country. However, in the remaining countries, defence was hardly any burden at all. Thus, Mauritius and Costa Rica do not have armies, while in Kerala there is almost no burden of defence expenditure in any case, given that defence expenditure is undertaken by the central government of India rather than by State governments.

In all the cases, the role of foreign resources was significant, though it took extremely varying forms. Foreign aid, properly defined, was critical to the development of human capital in both Korea and Cuba. Similarly, both Botswana and Zimbabwe received sizeable official development assistance, as did Costa Rica, though to a lesser extent. Sri Lanka and Kerala received hardly any external assistance for health and education from donor governments, but the availability of foreign exchange in the form of worker remittances played an important part in fostering a

TABLE 2.14. Expenditure on defence as a percentage of total GDP

	1978	1980	1982	1984	1986	1988	1990	1992
Korea, Rep. of	6.0	5.9	5.8	4.9	4.7	4.1	3.9	3.9
Malaysia	3.7	4.2	—	—	—	2.5	2.6	—
Kerala	—	—	—	—	—	—	—	—
Sri Lanka	0.7	0.7	0.5	0.8	2.4	2.1	2.1	—
Botswana	2.9	3.3	2.2	2.1	2.7	3.6	4.7	—
Mauritius	0.2	0.2	0.3	0.3	0.2	0.2	0.3	0.4
Zimbabwe	6.6	8.7	6.3	6.5	6.8	—	—	—
Barbados	0.2	1.1	0.8	1.0	0.6	0.6	—	—
Costa Rica	0.7	0.6	0.5	0.7	0.6	0.5	—	—
Cuba	—	—	—	—	—	—	—	—

Source: IMF, *Government Finance Statistics*, various issues

private sector in health. The remaining three countries—Barbados, Malaysia, and Mauritius—were the beneficiaries of 'rent' derived partly from the exports of tropical commodities or simply their location (and the concomitant tourist revenues). The point here is not that the availability of foreign exchange was particularly significant for health and education investment specifically (though for Botswana, Cuba, Korea, and Zimbabwe it was), but rather that it weakened the binding constraint lack of foreign exchange is for development of physical capital in most developing countries.

What was the reaction of the States of the high-achieving countries to the economic crisis of the early 1980s, the global economic recession, and the structural adjustments that most of them had to undergo? Did education and health expenditures decline in response to the adjustment process? In regard to both health and education, government expenditure as a proportion of GDP held up in all high achievers through the 1980s. In Sub-Saharan Africa as a whole, health and education expenditure definitely declined in per capita terms and as a ratio of GDP in the vast majority of countries over 1980–93 during adjustment (World Bank, 1994; Jayarajah *et al.* 1996), but it held up in Botswana, Mauritius, and Zimbabwe. In Latin America also health and education expenditure's share in GDP and in per capita terms was lower during adjustment compared to before adjustment, but in the high achievers it held up.[11] What is clear is that the higher-than-average (relative to other countries in their region) macro-economic priority given to health and education expenditures by most of the high achievers was sustained throughout the crisis years of the 1980s (see Tables 2.9–2.12).

An additional striking point is that the studies demonstrate that in most of the countries which have undertaken stabilization/adjustment since 1980, the adjustment process has been a relatively unorthodox one. This is particularly true of Korea, Malaysia, Mauritius, and Costa Rica. In its own way, the transition that Cuba has been attempting to undergo since the early 1990s also contrasts strongly with the experience of the east European economies as well as the countries of the former Soviet Union, where the social costs of the transition to a market economy have been very severe. On the other hand, in Zimbabwe, where the adjustment process in the 1990s has been much more orthodox, in keeping with the 'Washington consensus', the social costs have seen a reversal in the 1990s of some of the social achievements of the 1980s.

Diversity among the Success Stories

While there were common elements in the successes of our high achievers, there is also evidence of considerable diversity among them, not only in the means and methods adopted to achieve the health transition and educational expansion, but in the actual outcome. The main difference in regard to the means and methods lies in the extent of state involvement in social development (to be discussed in Chapter 3). The main divergence in terms of outcome is in regard to the relationship between economic growth and trends in social indicators, the extent of change in the incidence of poverty, and finally the degree to which a demographic transition has set in our high achievers (which is discussed in Chapter 3).

Economic growth and the rate of change of social indicators

We found difference between the countries in terms of the speed with which social indicators changed. We wanted to test the hypothesis that there would be a difference in the rate of improvement in social indicators between the countries with rapid GDP growth and the slow-growing ones. It is likely that while the slow-growing economies made large initial jumps in social indicators as a result of investments in human capital, the growth in those indicators reached a plateau, since the capacity of the economy to finance sustained improvements in health and education inputs was constrained by the lower long-run growth trend of the economy. The studies on the low-income examples in this book—Sri Lanka, Kerala, Cuba, and Zimbabwe—all argue that slow economic growth has ultimately proved to be a constraint. While coverage of services has increased and both output and outcome indicators have improved enormously, the quality of health services as much as the quality of education has remained severely constrained.

To test the hypothesis that slower-growing countries experienced a lower rate of improvement in social indicators as compared to the faster-growing countries, we compared those countries (in a sample of 122 countries) where per capita GDP grew above the average over 1965 to 1980 against those which grew below the average. For all countries the average per capita growth rate of GDP was 2.35 per annum. Of the ten countries (excluding Kerala), the following were in the set of countries growing above this rate: Korea, Malaysia, Sri Lanka, Botswana, Mauritius, and Costa Rica. The comparison was carried out for U5MR (in health) and literacy rates for males and females, and primary-school enrolment ratios for males and females (in education). It was found that the rate of change in U5MR, literacy rates for females, and primary-school enrolment for males showed a statistically significant difference (while literacy rates for males and primary-school enrolment for females did not) between those countries which had a per capita GDP growth rate which was below average and those where it was above average. It is not entirely surprising that there did not exist a significant difference for all the indicators, since the causal relationship between the growth of per capita income and improvements in social indicators is quite complex. Nevertheless, it does tend to confirm what the studies are suggesting anyhow, i.e. that further social development will be affected in various ways by the pace of economic growth, or its lack thereof.

A similar comparison for the period 1980 to 1992 was also carried out. What is critically significant for this period is that the average per capita growth rate of GDP fell to 0.3 per cent—a dramatically lower growth rate for all countries, during the 'lost decade'. Of the ten selected countries, the following grew at a rate above average: Korea, Malaysia, Sri Lanka, Botswana, Mauritius, and Costa Rica. In this case no variable (other than literacy rates for males) showed a statistically significant difference between the two groups of countries, which is hardly surprising given that the growth rate for all economies had fallen so sharply that on the average per capita income had stagnated.

The studies for all the low-income countries in this book draw a strong relationship between the lack of economic growth and stagnation, if not in the quantitative indicators, certainly in the quality of services. Thus, relative economic stagnation—in Sri Lanka, Kerala, Zimbabwe, and, more recently, Cuba (in Cuba mainly caused by external factors)—has created major problems for the social sectors. In Sri Lanka, the food subsidy and free health and education services were made possible by heavy taxation of export plantation crops—tea, rubber, and coconut. When international commodity prices dipped in the late 1950s, and 1960s, and the balance of payments deteriorated, it became increasingly difficult to sustain those expenditures. Nevertheless, on account of the political difficulty of cutting social expenditures and the food subsidy, the government continued to heavily tax the plantation sector, and jeopardized the plantation industry. Quite clearly, the economy needs to generate a surplus for social investment (as the plantation sector did), but excessive surplus extraction may lead to lower economic growth ultimately causing a curtailment of social expenditures.

Kerala offers similar lessons—though for rather different reasons. Kerala ranks ninth among the States of India in terms of per capita income and has had one of the lowest levels of industrialization. In addition, many features of Kerala's labour and land markets are very different from the rest of India. Kerala has experienced extensive reforms in landownership and tenancy and has a more equal landownership pattern than other parts of India. Trade unionism is common not only among industrial and public-sector employees, as in other parts of India, but, unlike the rest of India, even among agricultural workers; it has even spread to the informal labour sector—all aided by the high levels of literacy. One outcome of unionization is that Kerala has the third highest wage rate for agricultural workers in the country (after the bread-basket States of Punjab and Haryana), and Kerala is the only State where real wages have nearly doubled between 1960 and 1990. The result has been that the little industry that existed has tended to shift to neighbouring states, and agricultural output has been declining because it is cheaper for the State to import its food from the rest of India. The economy has been practically stagnant since 1975. Remittances from Keralan migrant workers from the Middle East have also contributed to increasing private expenditure on health. As a result, the demand for quality health care, especially private health services, has expanded. At the same time, the scope for sustaining public expenditure on health care has been limited by slow growth.

Similarly, Zimbabwe's per capita GNP growth was slightly negative (−0.2 per cent) over the 1980s. Hence the concern in the 1990s has shifted from distributional and equity issues which dominated Zimbabwe in the 1980s to aggregate growth and balance-of-payments concerns. The adoption of a structural-adjustment programme has also limited social expenditures, and the study points to a rise in IMR and MMR as real health expenditures shrank and fees were introduced at health services.

While these examples suggest that the sustainability of health and education indicators can be threatened by economic stagnation, what about the relationship in the other direction, i.e. from social development to economic growth? Although we return to this issue in Chapter 15, here one can put forward two fairly strong propositions (on the basis of the case-studies as well as the experience of other developing countries): first, it is noticeable that most of the selected countries with high social indicators (six out of ten over 1965–80, and over 1980–92) grew faster than the developing countries' average in terms of per capita GDP, as we discussed earlier. While we would suggest that social development is a necessary condition of rapid economic growth, it is not a sufficient condition—as the slow growth in Kerala and Zimbabwe would demonstrate.

Second, the growth experience of developing countries in general over nearly the last quarter century demonstrates that for sustained high growth the initial level of social indicators will need to be relatively high (comparable to those in our selected high-achieving countries). Thus comparing the fastest-growing countries over 1965–80 with the fastest-growing ones over 1980–92, it is striking that countries with relatively lower social indicators (Brazil, Ecuador) drop out of the list in the later period, suggesting that the *sustainability* of the growth performance may be importantly dependent upon the level of social development achieved by the majority of the population. A narrowly based economic growth will be exhausted sooner, as the Brazilian miracle of 1974–80 was, or as was the Ecuadorian or Gabonian one based on oil production/exports. On the other hand, a broadly based growth pattern, as demonstrated by Korea, Malaysia, or Mauritius, will be much more sustainable (Malaysia grew at 4.7 and 3.2 per cent respectively).

All the high-growth countries during 1965–80 had initial social indicators significantly better than the regional average: Botswana, Singapore, Korea, Hong Kong. In those which did not, the growth came as a result of special conditions or was not sustained: Oman had windfall oil-price gains, as did Gabon; in Lesotho and Brazil the growth was not sustained, and they disappear from the high-growth economies between 1980 and 1992. During the 1980–92 period, all the high-growth economies had health and education indicators significantly better than their regional neighbours.

Poverty alleviation

While social indicators improved enormously during the thirty-year period under consideration in the selected countries, it is also important to establish what happened to the incidence of poverty. We have information for incidence of poverty for two points of time for six of the countries (see Table 2.15). In Malaysia and Korea, overall poverty incidence declined to negligible levels. In Mauritius and Cuba, too, poverty appears to have declined.

But in the remaining countries, in spite of the high level of social indicators, poverty proved to be more stubborn. In Sri Lanka, several studies estimating the incidence of poverty all produce similar figures: about 20 to 25 per cent of the population lived in poverty, and the figure does not change very much over the decade 1973 to 1982 (Bruton, 1992).[11] The headcount ratio for a low poverty line was 27 per cent in 1985–6 (41 per cent using the higher poverty line), which declined to 22 per cent in 1990–1 (35 per cent using the higher poverty line). Similarly in Kerala, while the incidence of poverty has declined from nearly 59 per cent in 1973–4 to 32 per cent in 1987–8, it still remains high.

Although information is less adequate about poverty incidence in Zimbabwe the studies point out that the unchanged distribution of wealth suggests that the incidence of poverty has not declined. In Botswana too, while poverty has declined, it remains high. Thus, the very poor (who could not cover the food component of the poverty line) accounted for 41 per cent of all individuals in 1985–6, in 1993–4 they were still 30 per cent of the population. Estimates of poverty which use a different definition suggest that even in 1975 the incidence of poverty was about 54 per cent.

TABLE 2.15. Incidence of poverty: percentage of population below poverty line

	Total		Urban		Rural	
	First year	Last year	First year	Last year	First year	Last year
Korea, Rep. of (1965–84)	41	4	55	5	36	4
Malaysia (1970–90)	49[a]	12[a]	21[a]	5[a]	59	22
Kerala (1973/4–1987/8)	60	32	—	—	—	—
Sri Lanka (1985/6–1990/1)	27	22	16	18	31	24
Botswana (1985/6–1993/4)	59	47	30	29	68	55
Mauritius (1975–91)	40	11	—	—	—	—
Zimbabwe (1990/1)	—	25	—	10	—	31
Barbados (1980–9)	—	—	5	2	11	21
Costa Rica (1970–92)[a]	24	25	15	25	30	25
Cuba (1965–88)	—	—	—	—	36	11

[a] % of households

Sources: UNICEF, *State of the World's Children Report, 1995*; Chapters 4, 7, 9, and 10; ECLAC, Social Panorama (for Costa Rica); IFAD, The State of Rural Poverty (for Costa Rica, Cuba, Korea, Malaysia, and Sri Lanka); Morley, *Poverty and Inequality in Latin America* (for Barbados); World Bank, *Country Economic Memoranda* (for Mauritius and Zimbabwe); World Bank, *Poverty Assessment Reports* (for Malaysia and Sri Lanka)

TABLE 2.16. Income distribution

to lower 20%	Year	Share of income (consumption) by quintile (%)					Share of	Ratio highest 20 highest 10%
		1st	2nd	3rd	4th	5th		
Korea	1988	7.4	12.3	16.3	21.8	42.2	27.6	5.8
Malaysia	1989	4.6	8.3	13.0	20.4	53.7	37.9	11.8
Kerala		—	—	—	—	—	—	—
Sri Lanka	1990	8.9	13.1	16.9	21.7	39.3	25.2	4.5
Botswana	1985	3.6	6.9	11.4	19.2	58.9	42.9	16.4
Mauritius[a]	1980	4.0	7.5	11.0	17.0	60.0	—	15.0
Zimbabwe	1990	4.0	6.3	10.0	17.4	62.3	46.9	15.7
Barbados[a]	1975	7.0	12.0	—	37[b]	44.0	—	6.3
Costa Rica	1989	4.0	9.1	14.3	21.9	50.8	34.1	12.7
Cuba		—	—	—	—	—	—	—

[a] from IFAD, *The State of World Rural Poverty, 1992;* [b] third and fourth quintiles combined

Source: World Bank, *World Development Report, 1995*

There is evidence in the case of the Latin American countries (Costa Rica and Barbados) that the incidence of overall poverty may have worsened, as it did in most of Latin America through the 1980s, but here again there is a difference between rural and urban poverty. In Costa Rica, the proportion of households below the poverty line was stagnant in the 1970s, but increased sharply in the urban areas in the 1980s, while it fell somewhat in rural areas. However, the distribution of land remains highly unequal even by Latin American standards, and in 1988 44 per cent of the rural population was landless (IFAD, 1992). While Costa Rican data are based on nationally determined poverty lines, in the case of Barbados an international poverty line of $1 per day was used to arrive at the conclusion that the incidence of poverty in urban areas was negligible (4.9 per cent in 1980), and fell to 2.3 per cent in 1989. In rural areas, however, the incidence of poverty doubled between 1980 and 1989 from 10.5 per cent to 21.1 per cent.

There is thus a striking contrast between the East Asian high achievers on the one hand and the Latin American (and African and South Asian) ones on the other in regard to the reduction of poverty, in spite of the remarkable similarity in regard to improvements in social indicators. In many crucial respects, major pre-existing differences between the high-performing economies in East Asia and those in Latin America, which determine the degree of poverty, were magnified through the 1980s. First, while the East Asian economies managed to maintain rapid economic growth rates, the Latin ones were finally overtaken by the 'fiscal crisis of the state' (Bresser Pereira, 1993). The fiscal crisis and the liberalization of financial markets contributed to a debt crisis, which was followed by bouts of stabilization and neoliberal structural adjustment, and a worsening of poverty. Thus, tax ratios to GDP, which were already lower in the latter compared to the East Asian countries, have tended to fall in the 1980s in Latin America (though not in Costa Rica and Mexico). Second, gross domestic savings relative to GDP, which were already higher in East Asia in 1970, increased further by the early 1990s. In Latin America, while they have grown, especially in the early 1990s in the wake of the economic recovery, they are still much lower than in East Asia. Third, social expenditures in the high-achieving countries of East Asia have tended to be stable through the 1980s, and have increased in some cases, while they were slashed in the Latin American countries (at least in certain years even in Costa Rica). Fourth, inflation rates in East Asia over 1980–93 were 6.3 per cent in the Republic of Korea, 2.2 per cent in Malaysia, 4.3 per cent in Thailand, and 8.5 per cent in Indonesia, compared to Latin American averages measured in thousands of percentage points. Finally, nothing has changed as regards the distribution of land in either East Asia or Latin America: the degree of landlessness characterizing the latter has remained the same (Mehrotra and Pizarro, 1995).

Thus not only did many of the high achievers found poverty a difficult issue, income distribution information presented in Table 2.16 for the selected countries (except for Kerala and Cuba, for which no information is available), mostly for the 1980s, suggests that for most of the countries (except Korea and Sri Lanka) the distribution of income is also rather unequal. In fact, for most of the countries, the top two quintiles of the population accounted for around three-fourths of the income (or consumption) in the economy. The highest 20 per cent of the population accounted for over half of the country's income in most countries. Taken together with the discussion of poverty (which admittedly is measured differently in each country), the relatively unequal income distribution in mainly the Sub-Saharan and Latin American selected countries seems to suggest that while social development was treated as a priority in most, the distribution of wealth and income proved a much more complex issue.

The factors underlying the greater resistance of poverty vary. In the South Asian cases, slow economic growth has remained a barrier. Kerala experienced a landownership reform much more effective than that in the rest of India (Jose, 1985). Communist party governments in Kerala alternated with the Congress party in state elections, and the effect of competitive electoral politics was to bolster the social agenda. However, on account of slow economic growth in the State, incomes have not risen much, and the incidence of poverty has not declined very dramatically since the formation of the State in 1956. Sri Lanka had a land-ownership pattern much more equitable than that which prevails in most parts of the Indian subcontinent, and at least until the 1970s economic policies were also relatively egalitarian—but became much less so in the 1980s. Again, relatively slow growth in income prevented a sharp decline in the incidence of poverty.

An unequal distribution of assets in the African cases has prevented a reduction in the incidence of poverty. Zimbabwe had been through a revolutionary liberation war against racist white rule, and the liberation fervour carried over into social policies. However, in regard to landownership, the government's hands were tied for a decade by the terms of the agreement between the white regime and the winners of the liberation war. Besides, most of industry obviously remained in the hands of white owners after independence, and the income distribution is simply a reflection of the unequal distribution of assets in the economy. Again, in Botswana the ownership of land and cattle (an important source of wealth in this country) is highly unequal, as the case-study points out, and it is hardly surprising that the income distribution is as unequal as it is. Nevertheless, the Botswanian government has succeeded in using its diamond rents to invest in the health and education of the population.

Thus, while high levels of social indicators are common to all the selected countries, this does not necessarily translate into a uniformly high level of human development. Only a few of them (Korea, Malaysia, Mauritius) come out well in terms of all three kinds of desirable outcomes—economic growth, poverty reduction, and social development. Others fail, to a lesser or greater degree, on one or even two other counts (i.e. growth or poverty reduction). The linkages between the processes underlying these desirable outcomes are analysed in the final chapter in order to demonstrate the possible synergies on the one hand within the social sectors, and on the other between interventions in the health and education sectors and those state actions which impact on the level and dispersion of household incomes.

Conclusions

One unmistakable lesson from the success stories is that in those countries which grew rapidly, human development came before and simultaneous with rapid economic growth, generating a virtuous cycle of growth and social development. Equally important, that it is possible for poor countries at an early stage of development to invest in the health and education of their population. In fact, even the poorest countries (which also grew relatively slowly)—Sri Lanka, Zimbabwe, Cuba, and the State of Kerala—could afford to make that investment. That demonstrates that the poorest countries may not have to wait until they become rich to make that investment[12]—which also implies that social development may be a necessary but not a sufficient condition of economic growth.[13]

Whether it is a rich country or a poor one, a slow or rapidly growing one, the lead has to be taken by the State, especially in regard to the provision of basic education and primary health services. Public action for human development was a common factor underlying the success in every country.

It is equally clear that unless countries maintain economic growth, their capacity to sustain quality improvements in health services and the educational system remain sharply limited. Those countries which were unable to grow rapidly may not experience a deterioration in their stock outcome indicators, but they are not able to introduce improvements in quality of health and education services.

What is perhaps also very important is that although social indicators may improve as a result of investments in health and education, special attention must be paid to those in conditions of absolute poverty. We found that in some of our countries poverty worsened, especially during the 1980s. Without public action directed at the poorest and the most vulnerable, there is no guarantee that with economic growth and improvements in social indicators, poverty will automatically decline. Structural adjustment in the 1980s may have limited the capacity of the States for direct action for poverty alleviation.

Most of these countries grew rapidly while they simultaneously managed to improve their social indicators. Those which did not grow so rapidly did not manage to reduce the incidence of poverty as rapidly as those which did. However, even though not growing rapidly, the social investment in the slow-growers ensured a safety net for the vast majority of the population. The synergy between interventions in education, health, nutrition, water, and sanitation mitigated the worst manifestations of poverty. In other words, even though incomes may not have grown, social investments ensured that destitution was not widespread. Most in all countries were assured access to health and education. And if human capabilities were not enhanced in all respects, in some significant respects they were enhanced very substantially.

The specific ways in which the various ingredients of human development evolved in these high-achieving countries have been discussed in this chapter. The specific sectoral policy lessons emerging from the health advances and educational achievements are discussed in Chapter 3.

We are not attempting to offer a blueprint for other developing countries to follow, either in this overview or in the country cases. The country experiences examined in this book offer the strongest possible affirmation that whether countries are able to grow rapidly or not, whether they are able to eliminate poverty or not, it is definitely within the realm of possibility of all developing countries to achieve major gains in key aspects of human development for the vast majority of their people.

Notes

1. The only difference between the notion of human capability and human development is that the former refers to the capacities of the individual, while the latter applies as much to the society as a collectivity.

2. Anand and Ravallion (1993) attribute roughly two-thirds of the elasticity of life expectancy with respect to average income to the positive effect of income on public health expenditure; the rest is attributed to the decline in income poverty that typically accompanies higher-average incomes.

3. What enabled some of the selected countries to grow much more rapidly than others is a subject beyond the scope of this book.

4. While some of the countries (Barbados, Mauritius) may be rather small, the population size of the selected countries exhibits considerable range and is comparable to the population of other countries in their region. Korea has 45m. people and Malaysia 20m.; Kerala (30m.), and Sri Lanka (18m.) have populations comparable to those in the States of India and Pakistan; Zimbabwe's population is larger and Botswana's smaller than that of the average African country; Costa Rica has a population similar to those found in Central America; Barbados is not very different from other Caribbean island States, and Cuba's population is that of a median country in Latin America. Besides, large populations are not typical for developing countries: there are no more than fifteen developing countries with populations larger than 50m.

5. The oil-rich countries have also been able, within the last twenty years or so, to use their windfall gains from rising oil prices to provide widespread access to health and education services for their population, and have improved the social indicators enormously. Thus, between 1960 and 1991, the under-five-mortality rate fell in Saudi Arabia from 292 to 43, in the UAE from 239 to 29, in Oman from 278 to 42, and in Iran from 233 to 62 (UNICEF, 1993). We have deliberately excluded these countries from the high achievers precisely on account of the windfall nature of the rents accruing to these countries in the 1970s in the wake of the quadrupling of oil prices in 1973 and then their doubling in 1979.

6. In 1985, a major conference on 'Good Health at Low Cost' (Halstead *et al.*, 1985) was organized by the Rockefeller Foundation to discuss the lessons emerging from such cases as China, Costa Rica, Kerala, and Sri Lanka. A major conclusion emerging from that conference was the need for comprehensive PHC, which led to a debate within the UN agencies as well, as it was perceived that GOBI-FFF was a selective approach to PHC.

7. A chi-square analysis of a 2×2 table with above and below average spending and above and below USMR was carried out to test for independence of expenditures and outcomes. The null hypothesis (i.e. independence) was rejected at 1%, as most countries fill either in the low–low or high–high quadrants.

8. One implication, however, of the relatively low expenditure is that the country has been unable to improve the quality of services. See later discussion in text.

9. To fill this gap in information and analysis, UNICEF currently has a research project on how much governments spend on basic social services, the scope for restructuring public expenditure inter-sectorally and intra-sectorally (within health and education) in favour of basic services, and the scope for improving efficiency and effectiveness in health and education expenditures.

10. Since exchange rates influence the dollar value of these per capita expenditures, one should be careful in interpreting these numbers, especially for purposes of cross-country comparisons. They are presented here for illustrative purposes.

11. Private consumption per capita in real terms increased by a factor of 3.2 (using the CPI as deflator) between 1953 and 1985 (World Bank, 1995), and while poverty incidence would have declined it remained quite high in 1985.

12. That is because interventions for health delivery in rural areas or cost-effective provision of primary education (instead of higher education at higher cost per pupil) is not extremely resource-intensive.

13. The implication is that social development is a necessary condition for long-term sustained high-growth rates. That does not mean, for example, that the oil-rich countries of the Middle East cannot achieve rapid economic growth for a while without the necessary initial conditions of high social indicators. They have been able to do so because of windfall gains from oil-price increases in 1973 and 1979. Since then, they also managed to provide free education and health services for the majority of the population. However, their economic growth rates collapsed in the 1980s when oil prices plummeted.

References

Anand, Sudhia, and Ravallion, Martin (1993), 'Human Development in Poor Countries: On the Role of Private Incomes and Public Sources', *Journal of Economic Perspectives*, 7/1.

Behrman, J. R., and Deolalikar, A. (1988), 'Health and Nutrition', in H. Chenery and T. N. Srinivasan (1988).

Birdsall, Nancy (1993), 'Social Development in Economic Development', *World Bank WPS/123*, Washington, DC.

Bresser Pereira, L. C. (1993), 'Economic Reforms and Economic Growth: Efficiency and Politics in Latin America', in Bresser Pereira *et al.* 1993.

—— Maravall, J. M., and Przeworski, J. (1993), *Economic Reforms in New Democracies: A Social-Democratic Approach*, Cambridge: Cambridge University Press.

Bruton, Henry J., with Abeyesekera, G., Sanderatine, N., and Yusof, Z. A. (1992), *The Political Economy of Poverty, Equity, and Growth*, Oxford: Oxford University Press.

Caldwell, John C. (1986), 'Routes to Low Mortality in Poor Countries', *Population and Development Review*, 12/2.

Cash, Richard, Keuach, Gerald T., and Lamstein, Joel (1987), *Child Health and Survival. The UNICEF GOBI-FFF Program*, London: Croom Helm.

Chenery, H., and Srinivasan, T. N. (eds.) (1988), *Handbook of Development Economics*, 1, Amsterdam: North-Holland.

Colclough, Christopher (1982), 'The Impact of Primary Schooling on Economic Development: A Review of Evidence', *World Development*, 10/3.

Dreze, Jean, and Sen, Amartya (1989), *Hunger and Public Action*, Oxford: Clarendon Press.

—— —— (1995), *India: Economic Development and Social Opportunity*, Delhi: Oxford University Press.

ECLAC (Economic Commission for Latin America and the Caribbean) (1994), *Social Panorama of Latin America 1994*, Santiago.

—— (1995), *El gasto social en America Latina: un análisis cuantitativo y cualitativo*, Cuadernos de la CEPAL series, no. 73, Santiago.

Gillespie, Stuart, and Mason, John (1981), *Nutrition—Relevant Actions: Some Experiences from the Eighties and Lessons for the Nineties*, Geneva: UN ACC/SCN.

Halstead, Scott B., Walsh, Julia A., and Warren, Kenneth (eds.) (1985), *Good Health at Low Cost*, Conference Report, Rockefeller Foundation, New York.

IFAD (1992), *The State of World Rural Poverty*, Geneva.

Jayarajah, Carl, Branson, William, and Sen, Binayak (1996), *Social Dimensions of Adjustment. World Bank Experience, 1980–93*, World Bank Operations Evaluations Study, Washington, DC.

Jose, A. V. (1985), 'Poverty and Inequality: The Case of Kerala', in A. R. Khan and Eddy Lee (eds.), *Poverty in Rural Asia*, New Delhi: ILO-ARTEP.

Joseph, Stephen (1985), 'The Case for Clinical Services', in Scott B. Halstead, Julia A. Walsh, and Kenneth S. Warren (eds.), *Good Health at Low Cost*, New York: Rockefeller Foundation.

Mata, L., and Rosero, L. (1988), *National Health and Social Development in Costa Rica: A Case Study of Inter-sectoral Action*, Technical Paper 13, Washington, DC: Pan American Health Organization.

Mehrotra, S., Nigam, A., and Thet, A. T. (1996), 'Public and Private Costs of Primary Education: Evidence from Selected African and Asian Countries', UNICEF Staff Working Paper 15, New York.

—— and Pizarro, Cristostomo (1996), 'Social Policies in Chile, Costa Rica and Mexico', in UNICEF, *Social Development in the Nineties: The Case of Chile, Costa Rica and Mexico*, Bogotá: Planeta.

—— and Thet, A. T. (1996), 'Public Expenditure on Basic Social Services: The Scope for Budget Restructuring in Selected Asian and African Economies', UNICEF Staff Working Paper 14.

Mesa-Lago, C. (1981), *The Economy of Socialist Cuba*, Albuquerque.

—— (1996), 'The Social Safety Net in the Two Cuban Transitions', in *Transition in Cuba*: Florida International University, Cuban Research Institute.

Psacharapoulos, G. (1985), 'Returns to Education: A Further International Update and Implications', *Journal of Human Resources*, 20/4.

—— and Woodhall, M., *Education for Development. An Analysis of Investment Choices*, Oxford: Oxford University Press.

Schultz, T. Paul (1988), 'Education Investments and Returns', in H. Chenery and T. N. Srinivasan (1988).

Seers, Dudley (1964), *Cuba: The Economic and Social Revolution*, Chapel Hill, NC: University of North Carolina Press.

Sen, Amartya (1985), *Commodities and Capabilities*, Amsterdam, North-Holland.

—— (1995), 'Agency and Well-Being: The Development Agenda', in Noeleen Heyzer with Sushma Kapoor and Joanne Sandler, *A Commitment to the World's Women: Perspectives on Development for Beijing and Beyond*, New York: UNIFEM.

Tilak, J. B. G. (1989), 'Education and its Relation to Economic Growth, Poverty and Income Distribution: Past Evidence and Further Analysis', *World Bank Discussion Papers*, 46, Washington, DC.

UNDP (1990), *Human Development Report 1990*, New York.

—— (1991), *Human Development Report, 1991*, New York.

—— (1995), *Human Development Report 1995*, New York.

—— (1996), *Human Development Report 1996*, New York.

UNICEF (1990), *Strategy for Improved Nutrition of Children and Women in Developing Countries*, E/ICEF/1990/L.6, New York.

—— (1993), *State of the World's Children*, Oxford: Oxford University Press.

World Bank (1994), *Adjustment in Africa: Reforms, Results, and the Road Ahead*, Oxford: Oxford University Press.

—— (1995), *Sri Lanka Poverty Assessment*, Washington, DC.

Annex 1
Country Groupings

Sub-Saharan Africa	Angola	Eritrea	Malawi	Sierra Leone
	Benin	Ethiopia	Mali	Somalia
	Botswana	Gabon	Mauritania	South Africa
	Burkina Faso	Ghana	Mauritius	Tanzania, U. Rep.
	Burundi	Guinea	Mozambique	Togo
	Cameroon	Guinea-Bissau	Namibia	Uganda
	Central African Rep.	Kenya	Niger	Zaire
	Chad	Lesotho	Nigeria	Zambia
	Congo	Liberia	Rwanda	Zimbabwe
	Côte d'Ivoire	Madagascar	Senegal	
South Asia	Afghanistan	Bhutan	Nepal	Sri Lanka
	Bangladesh	India (State of Kerala)	Pakistan	
East Asia and Pacific	Cambodia	Korea, Dem. Peo. Rep.	Mongolia	Singapore
	China	Korea, Rep. Of	Myanmar	Thailand
	Hong Kong	Lao Peo. Dem. Rep.	Papua New Guinea	Viet Nam
	Indonesia	Malaysia	Philippines	
Latin America	Argentina	Costa Rica	Haiti	Paraguay
	Barbados	Cuba	Honduras	Peru
	Bolivia	Dominican Rep.	Jamaica	Trinidad and Tobago
	Brazil	Ecuador	Mexico	
	Chile	El Salvador	Nicaragua	Uruguay
	Colombia	Guatemala	Panama	Venezuela

3

Health and Education Policies in High-Achieving Countries: Some Lessons

SANTOSH MEHROTRA

In the preceding chapter, we analysed the common elements which help to explain the remarkable achievements of the selected countries in social development, while recognizing the considerable diversities between them. These common elements were: public provision of basic social services for all; investment in health and education early in the development process; public health and education expenditures well above their regional average; and elimination of male–female differentials in social indicators and enabling conditions which favoured the 'agency' role of women. In addition, among these common elements are specific kinds of intervention in the health and education sectors. This chapter looks more closely at these specific health and education interventions and policies with a view to deriving some lessons of policy significance from the experience of these countries. The discussion avoids contextual factors which explain improvements in the social indicators since that can be found in the case-studies in Part II, and tends to focus on the policy related variables. The first section is devoted to health policies and includes discussion of nutritional and water and sanitation interventions. The second section discusses education policies. The chapter closes with some policy lessons which seem to emerge from the case-studies.

We noted in Chapter 2 that the high initial level of the education indicators—the reasons for which are discussed in the case-studies—gave the selected countries a tremendous advantage over the others, since high education levels are highly correlated with health improvements. The experience of the selected countries indicates that the effectiveness of health investments at the primary level is greatly enhanced by building on the foundations of a strong educational base.[1] Inputs of all social services—education, family planning, health, nutrition and water and sanitation—impact on outputs such as knowledge, family size, health status, nutrition status and healthful living conditions. However, education is one social service input which very strongly affects all these outputs, more than the other inputs do. In other words, we would like to emphasize the paramount importance of the high educational level in these societies before the major health interventions began. Second, we should emphasize the synergistic impact on health outcomes of both educational and health interventions. Or as Caldwell (1986) notes in an analysis of data from two Nigerian villages, the equivalent gain in the expectation of life at birth was 20 per cent when the sole intervention was easy access to adequate health facilities for illiterate mothers, 33 per cent when it was education (as measured by mother's schooling) without health facilities, but 87 per cent when it was both, i.e. neither merely additive, nor multiplicative, but greater than either.

Health Policy

Almost half the existing disease burden in the world is from communicable or infectious diseases, poor nutrition, and maternal and peri-natal causes. Under-5s are particularly vulnerable to them and suffer from high mortality risk. Thus in 1891 in England and Wales (when its age-distribution was still bell-shaped) children under 5 constituted only about 12 per cent of the population, but they accounted for over 35 per cent of total deaths. In 1955 in Latin America and the Caribbean under-5s were below 18 per cent of the population, but accounted for over 45 per cent of total deaths. Demographers point out that a health transition or change in disease pattern occurs in two steps. First, a demographic transition, when mortality from communicable disease falls, and, partly as a result, fertility falls as well. As fertility declines, and non-communicable diseases become more important as a cause of death (i.e. an epidemiological or health transition), the population grows older. More infants and under-5s survive, and the age-structure of the population changes from being bell-shaped to rectangular.

If this health and demographic transition is to be hastened, the health system in developing countries has to be structured in response to the pattern of disease. Although developing countries have invested heavily in health, in most countries the facilities and equipment as well as human resources are skewed in favour of the top of the health system pyramid—the specialized, urban-based referral hospitals, as opposed to health centres and district hospitals to serve the preventive health and basic curative care needs of the population. The latter would address most cost-effectively the disease pattern in developing countries. Almost half of the preventable deaths of under-5s in poor countries are the result of diarrhoeal and respiratory illness, exacerbated by malnutrition—all of which are most cost-effectively dealt with through preventive measures at lower level facilities. But in some countries a single teaching hospital—at the top of the pyramid—can take 20 per cent or more of the government's health budget. This leads to both inefficiency and inequity.

The studies were required to address some of these important issues relating to health inputs and outputs that underlie the health problems in most developing countries. First, in regard to investment in health infrastructure and equipment, how did policy ensure that urban bias in distribution of facilities, which existed at the beginning of the period, was removed? Second, how was the imbalance in human resources which existed at the time of independence between rural and urban health services and between primary and tertiary care addressed? Third, what kind of mother and child programmes were organized within a system of primary health care? And finally, how significant were intervention in (a) water and sanitation, and (b) nutrition seen to be in the improvements in health outcomes? In the following pages these issues are discussed by region.

What is significant about most of the selected countries is that they adopted the principles of Primary Health Care underlined in the declaration of Alma Ata in 1978 long before they had been generally accepted by the world community.[2] One principle underlying the declaration is that it is necessary to overtake the lag between the discovery of modern medical knowledge and its use in the setting of the community.

Before the 1930s the contribution of medical technology was limited.[3] Since the introduction of anti-bacterial drugs and new vaccines in the 1930s, many potent interventions have been available against infectious diseases. But the effect of medical innovations on health have depended upon other variables, among them incomes of the poor, improved schooling, and the effect on health systems of public policies. Thus a second principle is that a vertical medical system is not really effective unless it is integrated with other activities in the society in joint attack on the problems of development. Health is not simply a 'sector', a responsibility of the health ministry alone; it must be an explicit goal to be achieved through all sectors with mass participation of the citizens—through education, better nutrition, and national and local community leadership. A third principle is that successful health organization implies reliance on cost-effective strategies for serving the entire population rather than only the well-off. The vast majority of developing countries have examples of major hospitals whose operational costs resulted in the curtailment of health clinics and preventive services. The fact is that while the majority of countries have, since the Alma Ata declaration, paid lip-service to promoting primary health care (e.g. millions of village health workers have been trained but left to their own devices), the majority of health resources are still not applied to achieving it. On the other hand, most of the selected countries applied the principles long before these principles were enshrined in the Alma Ata declaration. The recent declines in mortality in the post-colonial world have been much greater than the earlier declines in the non-industrialized countries, but the selected countries managed to achieve even quicker declines precisely by applying these principles in practice.

The African cases

For Zimbabwe the breakthrough in health status (here defined as the largest percentage decrease in IMR in recent decades) was achieved in the 1980s immediately after independence (see Table 3.1). In 1980 Zimbabwe inherited a health system

TABLE 3.1. Health breakthrough periods for high achievers

Country	Dates	IMR % reduction
Korea, Rep. of	1970–80	68
	esp. 1975–80	58
Malaysia	1960–70	40
	1975–85	50
Kerala	1975–85	40
Sri Lanka	1940–50	40
Botswana	1980–90	37
Mauritius	1945/9–50/4	40
Zimbabwe	1980–90	30
Barbados	1950–60	50
	1970–80	50
Costa Rica	1970–80	68
	1940–50	30
Cuba	1970–80	40[a]
	1975–85	50

[a] refers to U5MR

Sources: UNICEF data files; Chapters 4–13

deeply divided along racial lines with sharp differences in social indicators between the black and white populations. However, at independence the system was reorganized into a four-tier system, with rural health centres, district hospitals, provincial hospitals, and five central hospitals in two major cities.

Access to these health services was free of charge from September 1980 to those earning less than $Z150 per month, a level which ensured the majority of the population was covered (Sanders, 1993).[4] The country doubled the number of its rural health centres, from 500 to more than 1,000, during 1980–90. The goal here was to make essential clinical services available within a distance of 8 km. from home for the entire population. All developing countries, but especially low-income ones, face a problem in keeping health personnel in rural areas. In the mid-1980s housing for rural physicians and nurses was added to the health programme. The result was that vacancy rates for personnel in areas with new housing fell sharply, as against 20 to 30 per cent in other areas.

A dramatic difference between pre-1980 and post-1980 health services was the interface between the community and health services. The community health worker of the liberation struggle was transformed into the village health worker, and by 1984 over 7,000 VHWs were playing a central role in the promotion of primary health care. The number of nurses also increased dramatically between 1981 and 1989 (over 40 per cent increase in nurses per 1,000 population). But the number of doctors in the public sector barely increased at all: from 1,159 in 1981 to 1,290 in 1989, primarily on account of the loss to the private sector, to better paying NGOs, and to other countries—indicating how much more significant is the increase in the ratio of primary-care providers compared to physicians. Thus, Zimbabwe not only emphasized the creation of facilities in the rural areas, but the imbalance in human resources between primary providers and tertiary levels was also eliminated.[5]

Zimbabwe's success in this respect highlights the problem in the majority of developing countries in South Asia and Latin America.[6] During the 1960s and 1970s many countries promoted, mainly through subsidies to education, a major increase in physician training. Soon these countries were having problems absorbing increasing numbers of doctors. There is no optimal level of physicians per capita or optimal nurse-to-physician ratio, but a rule of thumb is that nurses should exceed physicians by at least two to one.[7] But in 1990 the ratio was well under two to one in India, Latin America, and the Middle-Eastern crescent (World Bank, 1993). As far as the public-health delivery system is concerned, the problem in the latter countries is not the oversupply of doctors as the undersupply of nurses. In other words, these countries are very far from resolving the fundamental imbalance in respect of human resources afflicting their health systems.

The expansion of the primary health-care infrastructure in the selected countries was reflected in the revolutionary improvement in mother and child health services. Every year about 600,000 women in developing countries die from complications associated with childbearing (UNICEF, 1996b). Without obstetric care, women who have a birth before age 18 are three times as likely to die in childbirth as those who have a birth between ages 20 and 29—demonstrating how important obstetric care is to avoid maternal mortality. The proportion of births attended by trained health personnel is very high in all the selected countries (Table 3.2). As the Zimbabwe study points out, by 1988 92 per cent of urban women and 64 per cent of communal area women delivered at a health facility and nearly 80 per cent of women surveyed in 1991 delivered in a health facility. The maternal mortality rate (MMR) had dropped from 150/100,000 in 1980 to 87 by 1987.[8]

For the vast majority of developing countries, immunization coverage began to increase from below one-third of all one-year-olds only from the mid-1980s, after the WHO–UNICEF campaign to achieve universal immunization of children by 1990 was launched. However, as Table 3.3 shows, in the selected countries the immunization coverage was at least 40 per cent already in 1980, and by the mid-1980s covered at least two-thirds of all infants born in any given year. The expanded programme of immunization in Zimbabwe was launched in 1981 (long before it was launched as an international campaign in 1985 by WHO and UNICEF). By comparison, even in 1996 there are eighteen developing countries with an immunization coverage of under 50 per cent, 14 of which are in Africa (UNICEF, 1996c).[9]

TABLE 3.2. Selected high achievers by geographic region: health input indicators

	% of pop. with access to health services, 1985–93		% of births attended by trained health personnel 1983–93
	urban	rural	
East Asia and Pacific	98	—	81
Korea, Rep. of	100	100	89
Malaysia	—	—	87
South Asia	77[a]	—	29
Kerala	100	90	98
Sri Lanka	93	—	94
Sub-Saharan Africa	79	50	38
Botswana	100	85	78
Mauritius	100	100	85
Zimbabwe	96	80	80
Latin American and Caribbean	81	51	82
Barbados	100[a]	—	—
Costa Rica	100	63	93
Cuba	99	96	90

[a] Refers to total population

Note: 1. Access to health services is defined as being able to reach a local health service centre by local transport within an hour. 2. Kerala data refers to India: access is better in Kerala than in India on the whole

Sources: UNICEF, *State of the World's Children Report, 1994* and *1996*, Chapters 4–13

In Mauritius immunization coverage for under-1-year-olds was already 80 per cent in 1974. Botswana too launched its primary health-care strategy in 1973 and by 1980 immunization coverage was already 60 per cent, a coverage level which most countries in East and West Africa did not achieve even at the end of the international campaign in 1990.

The South Asian cases

In the State of Kerala (India) and Sri Lanka similar policies have resulted in some dramatic results, when compared with the rest of the subcontinent. Sri Lanka had inherited a health status—and equally importantly, educational status—much better than the Indian average at independence, just as the southern part of Kerala did. The Sri Lankan breakthrough in health, occurred during the period 1945 to 1955: over that period IMR dropped from 131 to 75, and 12 years were added to life expectancy at birth in a period of seven years. The only parallel to this 12-year gain in life expectancy was a similar increase in Japan over the same period, or a gain of

TABLE 3.3. Immunization rate (% of all 1-year-olds and pregnant women)

| | DPT (% of 1-year-olds) | | | | | | | | | Tetanus (% of pregnant women) |
	1980	1982	1984	1986	1988	1990	1992	1994	1992–4
Korea, Rep. of	70	61	76	76	58	74	—	74	—
Malaysia	58	60	54	59	73	89	—	90	86
Kerala	—	—	—	—	—	—	—	99	93
Sri Lanka	46	56	66	75	83	90	59	88	79
Botswana	64	63	79	65	50	—	59	78	97
Mauritius	87	94	83	86	90	—	88	89	78
Zimbabwe	39	—	—	75	—	—	73	80	50
Barbados	60	62	83	84	76	91	—	90	100
Costa Rica	86	81	71	94	87	95	—	88	90
Cuba	67	99	86	99	94	92	—	100	61

Sources: WHO, Expanded Programme on Immunization Information System; UNICEF data file; UNICEF (1995)

12.7 years over nine years from 1953 to 1962 in China (Caldwell, 1986). The key factor which accounted for the decline in the mortality rates, as the case-study points out, was the comprehensive and widespread maternal and child health services at primary level linked to the intermediate institutional level (in Sri Lanka's three-tier health-care system), the training of the midwife, and the relatively manageable area and number of persons under the midwife's care. The midwife has an intimate knowledge of her area and the families she serves, and through a systematic scheme of home visits, she provides the necessary domicillary contact and care to mothers and children. The midwife is trained for eighteen months, longer than is the case in India or Bangladesh—a training which comprises one year in a school of nursing and six months of work experience in a health unit working within the community. She is responsible for the immunization of the children and mothers, and through her home visits is able to undertake early registration of all pregnant mothers and infants, thereby ensuring a systematic follow-up.

Another very significant difference between Sri Lanka and the rest of South Asia is that, until at least the late 1970s, newly graduated doctors, whose training is subsidized throughout South Asia, were required in Sri Lanka to serve government hospitals for a period of at least five years. There is no similar requirement in India, Pakistan, or Bangladesh, and physicians trained at public expense have migrated in the thousands from these countries to provide, by the 1970s, a very substantial part of the staff of the National Health Service in the UK and of health care in the USA.[10]

The death rate in Kerala is half that of rural India, and the IMR (17 per 1,000 live births) is only one-sixth that of rural India. As the case-study points out, this health breakthrough in Kerala was the result of the fact that during the ten years following the formation of the State in 1956, the same health facilities that had been available at independence in 1947 to the southern part of the state (Travancore-Cochin) were extended by the state government[11] to the northern part (Malabar). Kerala has the most extensive medical infrastructure among the States of India—about four times as many hospitals and nearly twice the numbers of hospital beds per 100,000 people as the Indian average (Chatterji, 1993). The level of expenditure per capita in the health sector was higher in Kerala than in all other Indian States between 1974 and 1982, and only somewhat lower than the highest spending States over 1982–9 (Tulasidhar, 1996). The expenditure was also more equitably distributed than in other States. An educated population, politically conscious, and highly unionized (even among agricultural workers)—conditions very different from the rest of India—also ensure that the demand for health services is high and that the public health service delivers what it is supposed to deliver.

In addition, there are two further factors which stand out about the Kerala case. First, Kerala has a long history in Ayurveda, the traditional Indian system of medicine, which has played a role comparable to the one played by the indigenous system in the health transition in China. On account of the marked differences in the cost of treatment between Ayurvedic (and homoeopathic) treatment on the one hand, and allopathic treatment on the other, the former are extremely popular. The public health system of Kerala includes Ayurvedic and homoeopathic hospitals and clinics. In 1987–8, 29.3m. were treated by the allopathic public health system, 16.7m. by the Ayurvedic system, and 9.5m. by the homoeopathic system.

The second striking aspect of the Kerala health transition is the large size of the private health sector. The number of beds in the private allopathic sector is one-third larger than the public system, and the number of private practitioners is 80 per cent higher. The number of Ayurvedic and homoeopathic dispensaries and physicians is four to eight times larger in the private sector. What is important, however, is that the rapid increase in private health care has occurred since 1976 (especially since migrant income from the Middle East increased), by which time the IMR was down to 55 (though it further declined to 17 by 1991). The development of private health care since the mid-1970s is evidence of the general growth in consumption expenditure, including demand for health services, and the incapacity of the public system to expand on account of fiscal constraints.

While Kerala may be different from the other countries in this sample in the prominent role of the traditional system and the private sector, these two features are common in Kerala and in the rest of India. So where is the crux of the problem with the health system in the rest of India? It may be useful, therefore, to dwell briefly on the problem with the rest of Indian States (especially the northern states of Bihar, Madhya Pradesh, Rajasthan, and Uttar Pradesh). An Indian government committee in 1946 had enunciated many of the same principles as the Alma Ata Declaration, and by the early 1980s India's multi-tiered health system was one of the best developed in the developing world. But it emphasized curative, high-technology medicine and urban hospitals, and pursued 'élitist' health manpower policies.[12] In the 1980s the health infrastructure expanded hugely in the rural areas, where three-quarters of the country's population lives. In 1980 there were 5,484 primary health centres (PHCs) and 47,112 sub-health centres in India. By 1991 they had grown to 22,065 and 130,983 respectively. Till 1980 the apex was the district hospital; but over the 1980s a new facility was introduced between the PHC and the hospital, a community health centre (1,932 existed by 1991). This numerical expansion occurred at the expense of quality.

In particular, weaknesses in the quantity and quality of staff are widespread. Doctors remain in short supply especially at the new PHCs, despite India's annual production of 12,000 medical graduates, mostly at public expense. Ensuring adequate staff and their actual presence at health centres is a prerequisite of improving quality of care in the rural health system; in Kerala a literate, politically conscious population ensures that government health personnel are actually present at their posts. The Eighth Plan notes that the greatest shortage in India is of paramedical staff and doctors at PHCs (Government of India, 1992). As a result, the PHC system provides less than 8 per cent of the medical care sought by rural households, and public hospitals a further 18 per cent. The remainder seek out various private practitioners (in the allopathic, homoeopathic, or traditional systems). Only 8 to 10 per cent of births are attended by trained government personnel. Household health surveys reveal that the reasons for not utilizing free government services are the time and cost of travelling to a PHC, the long waiting hours at public-health facilities, and rude treatment by government workers. Utilization of health services in Kerala, on the other hand, is very high.

In 1977 the government of India introduced a scheme of community health workers (CHWs), and within five years 400,000 CHWs were trained—one for every village, constituting the largest health cadre in the world outside China. But hired as volunteers with a small stipend and trained for three months, they focused on undertaking family-planning motivation and sanitation tasks.[13] Worse still, mostly men were hired, so they could not become primary-care workers focusing on women and children, given gender relations in Indian society. In Kerala, on the other hand, the paramedics normally tend to be women, and there is almost no emphasis on family planning in the PHC's activities—yet the contraceptive prevalence rate is one of the highest in the country.

The East Asian cases

The selected East Asian countries also offer useful lessons from their respective health transitions. At independence in 1957, Malaysia inherited a health system with facilities and personnel very unevenly distributed across the country. Seventy per cent of health services were concentrated in urban and semi-urban areas. The rural population had to go to clinics in small towns and hospitals in the larger towns to seek treatment. The government responded by setting up a three-tier system of rural health services. The main breakthrough period was the first fifteen years after independence when IMR fell from 73 to about 44 (1956–70) and life expectancy increased from 58.8 to 68.2 for females and from 55.8 to 63.5 years for males. The study points out that the curative component in the health centre provided the enticement to get the villagers into the habit of seeking medical help from professionals, to bring them to the health centre.[14] While the main government failure in most developing countries in regard to clinical services is to try and provide everything to everybody with no distinction between more or less essential care and more or less needy patients, most of the selected countries seem to make that distinction. Thus Malaysia has followed a pro-poor policy since the 1970s, with the lowest-income groups receiving a larger share of public subsidies on health than the middle-class and above (World Bank, 1993).

What is significant is that the government made a special effort to correct the imbalance between rural and urban areas not only in terms of facilities but also in terms of human resources. After the early 1970s in Malaysia, a law required all medical-degree holders to undergo three years of compulsory service with the government health service. This allowed the government to post doctors to the rural areas earlier avoided by the doctors. Nurses sent to the rural areas would receive one year of rural health training, in addition to their normal training, and also one year of midwifery.

The Latin American cases

The Latin American studies provide an interesting comparison in the routes to low mortality. Costa Rica, a middle-income country, had experienced a gradual increase in life expectancy from 41 to 66 years between 1927 and 1970. Between 1940 and the end of the 1960s, deficiency diseases or malnutrition were seen to be the primary determinant of poor health in Costa Rica (Mohs, 1993). As a result an important part of the strategy was nutritional improvement through public food distribution. In the 1950s, social insurance of the kind that has since been prevalent in the rest of Latin America began, with a major employer's contribution for those in government or private business employment. In all such schemes medical costs are covered and medical services are provided; in Costa Rica this coverage climbed from one-eighth of the population in 1956 to one-half in 1971. Those not covered until the early 1970s included the rural self-employed and those in the urban informal sector.

In 1974 the social security programme was enlarged to include the remaining population through the rural health programme. A major principle was the switch to primary health care with emphasis on coverage of the entire population using appropriate health technologies.[15] The PHC programme (or Rural Health Programme) included development of a sanitary infrastructure (water supply and latrines); organization of the community; periodic house visits to immunize against measles, poliomyelitis, diptheria, pertussis, and tetanus; deworming of the population; referral of medical problems to higher levels of care as needed; and nutrition and health education, including prenatal care and family planning.

Another striking aspect of the Costa Rican success story in health is the inter-sectoral action for health in the evolution of planning and the execution of health programmes, even before this modern concept was endorsed at Alma Ata. The 1970s were particularly characterized by an increase in inter-sectoral health efforts. Thus, programmes to improve water supplies and excreta disposal in the 1960s were intensified in the 1970s. During that decade there was also a significant improvement in incidence and duration of breast-feeding. Thus, more than 90 per cent of women now initiate lactation. The oral rehydration programme was implemented at the national level (Mata and Rosero, 1988). In addition, growth monitoring of children was introduced. The tool employed to monitor health was the child's growth curve, even before the GOBI proposition of UNICEF was applied globally.

In the 1970s the number of admissions to the university medical school was doubled and the curriculum reduced from seven to six years. The school of nursing doubled its intake, and that for nurses' aides tripled its enrolment.

It is hardly surprising then that the 1970s was a breakthrough period in the health status of the Costa Rican people. IMR, which in 1965–9 was 75 per 1,000, averaged 64 over 1970–4 and fell to 22 over 1975–9. Life expectancy, which was 66 years at the beginning of the decade, rose to 73 years within the span of the decade.

Despite economic shocks and cuts in public expenditure in the 1980s due to structural adjustment, Costa Rica's health spending favours the poor. In 1988 about 30 per cent of government health spending went to the poorest 20 per cent, and just over 10 per cent to the richest 20 per cent (World Bank, 1993). The entire population is covered in principle by the social security health system, although only 63 per cent of the working population contributes. Meanwhile, the well-off get most of their outpatient care in the private sector.

While the Republic of Korea (hereafter Korea) may be at one extreme of public–private mix in terms of health-service delivery, Cuba is at the other. After the revolution in 1960, there took place a gradual nationalization of the different private health institutions. The first migratory wave in 1959 and the early 1960s left the country with only half of its doctors (about 3,000). In early 1960, the Rural Medical Service Law was passed, requiring that recent graduates of medical schools had to do one year of social service. Later on the length of social service was doubled. Charges for medical services (as for many other services) were abolished. Health posts, integral polyclinics, and rural hospitals expanded rapidly, which provided health services at the primary level. One of the most powerful reasons for the drop in the IMR was the increase in hospital births made possible by the maternity homes which were established during the second half of the 1960s. The immunization programme, carried out with the support of the health and education sectors, was founded as early as 1960. The result of all these measures was that in the second decade after the revolution U5MR fell 40 per cent from an already low 42 in 1970, and life expectancy increased from 65 in 1970 to 71 in 1980.

In terms of health-related interventions then, what have we learned from the experience of our success stories? A combination of supply and demand factors was responsible for such positive outcomes. Successful health transition depends on making simple, cost-effective technologies available to the population; it depends on providing access to health services—through geographic proximity and low cost—for the people, especially rural, who did not have access to it. In particular, the provision of specific maternal and child health services is critical. It depends on births being supervised preferably at a health facility; household visits, especially if they are timed before and after birth immunization; and on ensuring the presence of health workers, including one physician, in the health centre. Many of the latter interventions are dependent upon ensuring an appropriate ratio of nurses and midwives to physicians. All these are perhaps the same reason—access to a well-functioning health system. For those of these health inputs which can be quantified, Tables 3.2 and 3.3 show that the selected countries have performed better in regard to all of these inputs than the regional average. But supply-related factors alone are not important. The efficiency or responsiveness of the service would depend upon either the patient's insistence (e.g. as in Kerala, where an educated population ensured high utilization) or upon being self- or leadership-induced (e.g. Cuba, Costa Rica, or Malaysia). High initial levels of education ensured high utilization of health facilities.

The organization and financing of health services

Public-supported action was a common element in the success of the health and educational achievements of these countries. However, this should not be taken to mean that there were not major differences between these countries in the private–public mix of service delivery for both health and education. In fact around the world, clinical services are financed in four ways. Two are private—direct payment and voluntary insurance; and two are public—compulsory (social) insurance, which is managed or regulated by government, and financing from general government revenues. Moreover, there are three ways of delivering clinical services: private for-profit, private not-for-profit, and public. All national health systems use at least two of the twelve possible combinations of systems of financing and delivery—which is true of our ten cases as well. Government revenues finance public provision for the poor of public health and clinical services in all the selected countries. At the publicly provided services there was little or no evidence of out-of-pocket expenditure by the poor (except in Zimbabwe after adjustment measures which were introduced in 1990).

Insurance systems were used as an additional means of financing in several of the selected countries—mainly for clinical services. In countries with social insurance (e.g. Korea, Costa Rica, and most of Latin America) mandatory contributions from employees and employers, and some government funds, finance insurance for part of the population (while health care for the poor is financed from general revenues). In most of Latin America middle-income families receive better care in facilities run by the social security agency than the low-income groups receive in the hospitals of the ministry of health. Only Costa Rica has undertaken to place all health facilities under one administration and opened them to all (World Bank, 1993). The Korean social insurance system (introduced in 1976) is a nationwide network of 'sickness funds' and covers all; the government subsidizes the coverage of the old and poor. The providers, however, are all mostly private and paid on a fee-for-service basis. While the government subsidy to the Korean social insurance system is progressive, in Zimbabwe's case, where the government subsidizes voluntary insurance for the well-off, it is regressive.

All over South Asia the State played a key role but private provision of health services is widely practised. In fact, the private sector has been an important player in the health transition in the state of Kerala (according to the case-study). In Zimbabwe and Botswana, however, the role of private suppliers in the health transition was almost non-existent.

In terms of the debates that dominate the health sector today, the selected countries provided universally available (as opposed to targeted) services to all, paid out of government revenues. In many countries the relatively well-off opted out by taking private health insurance, or where private insurance services were not available (e.g. Kerala, Sri Lanka) by making direct payment to private providers.[16] But for the vast majority of the population a universally available and affordable system, financed out of government revenues, functional at the lowest level, made effective by allocating resources at the lower end of the health system pyramid—these were the keys to health status.

In addition to examining health inputs our studies also addressed the following issues. First, how significant were nutritional inputs in explaining health outcomes? Second, what was the role of water and sanitation interventions? Part of the reason why these questions are important is because in the mid-1980s and early 1990s a debate grew between those advocating a 'selective' approach to PHC—the provision of a few key interventions (such as immunization, oral rehydration, basic drugs, growth-monitoring), and those who advocate a 'comprehensive' and co-ordinated approach to health which encompasses all development actors, including locally based health services, water, education, appropriate agricultural technology, and so on.[17] The evidence from the selected countries was that they adopted what would in today's jargon be called 'comprehensive' (though Korea's approach was, as we saw, quite different).

The role of nutritional interventions[18]

Nutritional status is an important component of well-being and health and a main determinant of infant, young-child mortality, and of adult productivity. The key stages of life in this context are pregnancy, infancy, and young childhood; they influence the whole life. The main determinants of protein-energy status are food intake (Table 3.4); access to health services (Table 3.2); safe water and sanitary excreta disposal, which are important measures for prevention of infection (Table 3.5); and care, particularly care of the infant and young child by the mother (which can be represented by women's literacy as a proxy for access to information). A low level of these determinants is usually associated with poverty; however, their effects can be mitigated by policy and services, as illustrated by the cases of Kerala, Sri Lanka, and Zimbabwe.

Among the determinants of nutritional status, it is noticeable that most of our group of countries have a calorie supply at 120 per cent of requirements or above,

TABLE 3.4. Selected high achievers by geographic region: nutritional indicators

	% of infants with low birth weight 1990	Daily per capita calorie supply as a % of requirements 1988–90	% of under-5s suffering from moderate and severe underweight 1980–93
East Asia and Pacific	11	112	27
Korea, Rep. of	9	120	—
Malaysia	10	120	—
South Asia	34	99	64
Kerala	—	—	35
Sri Lanka	25	101	38
Sub-Saharan Africa	16	93	31
Botswana	8	97	15
Mauritius	9	128	23.9
Zimbabwe	14	94	11.5
Latin America and Caribbean	11	114	11
Barbados	—	—	—
Costa Rica	6	121	6
Cuba	8	135	—

Sources: UNICEF, *State of the World's Children, 1995*; UNICEF India Office (1995); Gunasekera (1996)

which is a rough rule of thumb to offset for inequality of distribution among households. Second, most provide geographical access to health services for a substantial part of their population.[19] They reached high immunization coverage early on; immunization against measles reduces mortality from poor nutrition; and tetanus immunization also reduces child mortality (Table 3.3). Usually maternal and child health services include surveillance of young-child growth (weight and growth cards). Third, women's literacy is better for all of them. Fourth, a majority of countries have safe water for most of their population. There is a similar situation in regard to sanitary means of excreta disposal, except in rural areas of Zimbabwe, Sri Lanka, and Kerala. Diarrhoeas, largely caused by infection from water and the environment, are a major cause of malnutrition; the typical growth curve dips below that usually found in industrialized countries at 4-to-6 months of age when the baby begins to crawl on the ground and to take foods complementary to breast milk (which makes access to safe water crucial). Fifth, in addition to their above average expenditure on health and education, several case-study countries survey their nutritional state and take account of it in their health services, e.g. Costa Rica and Cuba.

The three countries with fewer resources—Sri Lanka, Kerala, and Zimbabwe—are particularly interesting because they have maintained levels of nutrition and infant and child mortality better than other low-resource countries. For these countries (and Botswana) the daily calorie supply is not much different from the requirement.[20] What is significant, however, is that a system of food subsidies has been sustained in these countries over several decades. This intervention is an important part of the explanation of the long-run improvement in nutritional and health outcomes. Of course, these food-related measures, however, were accompanied by basic health services and other enabling conditions (e.g. as discussed in Chapter 2, the status of women). Kerala and Sri Lanka had a high level of literacy, and in Zimbabwe and Botswana it increased rapidly over the period. In addition, Sri Lanka had a food and nutrition policy division in the ministry of planning, and Zimbabwe a nutrition unit in the ministry of health. All these factors compensated for the fact that the daily caloric supply was relatively low and that the coverage of safe water and sanitation was substantially less than in the better-off countries, particularly in Zimbabwe, which began to address this problem only after independence in 1980. Kerala gave less attention to these preventive services (water and sanitation) than to health.

Nevertheless, these other interventions should not detract from the fact that all the poorer countries adopted food-distribution programmes of one kind or another. Thus, in Kerala, a comprehensive free meal system was begun in primary schools (attended by all Keralan children) during the breakthrough period, in 1961, and three-fourths of the children took these meals. The meals were refused only by high-caste families fearing pollution, or by the better-off. In addition, food supplements are distributed through the health centres to pregnant and nursing mothers and to pre-school children, and there are special programmes for tribal and slum children. It is likely that these school feeding programmes are more effective in bringing and keeping children in school (on which see next section) than in necessarily raising nutrition levels.[21] More importantly, India's comprehensive system of subsidized food outlets, the fair price shops, expanded in the early 1960s. Although agricultural output in Kerala has declined since the mid-1970s, rice and wheat is available through the public distribution system even in rural areas, unlike in the rest of India, where coverage of the public distribution system has been restricted to urban areas. Not surprisingly, by 1975–9 Kerala had the lowest level of severe malnutrition among Indian States.

Sri Lanka introduced a food-rationing system during the Second World War which guaranteed a minimum level of nutrition for the poor, and established a structure for subsidizing food thereafter. The network of co-operatives established throughout the country continued to implement the food subsidy programme and make available essential food items such as rice, wheat flour, lentils, dried fish, and powdered milk. The subsidized food ration was not only universally applicable but it did in fact reach all people.[22] The rice subsidy was finally removed in 1979, but was substituted with a food stamp scheme, which gradually came to cover 40 per cent of the population. Subsidized food has been supplemented by free school meals.

In Kerala and Sri Lanka the incidence of malnutrition for under-5s may have been lower than in South Asia (see Table 3.4), but it is certainly much higher by any absolute standards. Thus Kerala and Sri Lanka present a parodox in health: while mortality and fertility are low, malnutrition is rather high. As we said earlier, Kerala's families do not meet their caloric requirements—60 per cent of households fell short of recommended caloric intake (Chatterji, 1993). The explanation for higher child survival rates lies perhaps in the health service access and a better intra-household distribution of calories. The latter may itself be a function of the mother's superior education in Kerala and Sri Lanka (compared to the rest of South Asia), which in turn gives her greater control over intra-household allocation of resources.[23]

In Zimbabwe after 1980, the new government responded to the nutritional damage of war and neglect of the rural communal farming areas by first focusing on peasant food production in communal areas, and also feeding of children in war-affected areas. The child supplementary feeding programme was initiated by the government and NGOs in 1980. A daily, energy-rich supplementary meal was supplied to predominantly undernourished young children in communal areas. The programme, which operated from 1980 to 1986, was reinforced by a pro-gramme of nutrition surveillance through the use of a growth chart (established by the nutrition unit in the ministry of health). Between 1980 and 1983–4, the level of malnutrition seems to have fallen sharply. Thus, in spite of a daily calorie supply per capita in the late 1980s below the requirement, the incidence of malnutrition in Zimbabwe still appears to be well below the regional average. Quite clearly this analysis suggests that targeted interventions to provide a nutritional floor can do much to offset the effects of inequitable income distribution, and thus improve health outcomes.[24]

What is very striking is that the incidence of under-5 malnutrition is much lower in Sub-Saharan Africa than in South Asia, and it is lower in Zimbabwe and Botswana than in Kerala and Sri Lanka. What accounts for this phenomenon? One reason is that one-third of babies in South Asia are born with low birth weight (i.e. below 2,500 grams), while that share is much lower in Sub-Saharan Africa—the same holds for the high-achieving countries in our sample (see Table 3.4).[25] A second reason may be more complex: good nutrition is determined by frequency and duration of disease, which inhibits appetite. Frequency of disease depends on several factors, but especially on the absence of safe water and sanitation. Although higher proportion of families have access to safe water and sanitary means of excreta disposal in Sub-Saharan Africa than in South Asia, in the South Asian high-achievers these indicators are worse than in the African ones (see Table 3.5). Hygiene tends to worsen in overcrowded conditions, and the South Asian region (and the high-achieving areas within it) have a much higher density of population than their African counterparts (Ramalingaswami *et al.*, 1996).[26]

A third reason may be differences in breast-feeding and in the timing of the introduction of other foods, occurring within the first year of birth. WHO and UNICEF recommend exclusive breast-feeding of the baby for the first six months, but breast-feeding in South Asia may be inadequate, because there is a significant difference in the well-being of women in the two regions. African women have better health, better nutrition, and better care—all reflected in a ratio of female life expectancy to male life expectancy in South Asia that is significantly below the world-wide norms. The other difference is in the timing of the introduction of complementary foods. In Sub-Saharan Africa the proportion of children aged 6 to 9 months receiving complementary foods is almost two-thirds. In Bangladesh, India, and Pakistan it is one-third. Even in Kerala the proportion of infants receiving foods in addition to breast-milk at the age of 6 to 9 months is only 69 per cent, the highest for any Indian State; in Rajasthan in the north, it is 9 per cent (UNICEF, 1995). In other words, because of inadequate breast-feeding, children in India need other foods earlier but receive it later.

A general food subsidy, as provided in Kerala and Sri Lanka, is generally quite costly, and does not appear to have succeeded in impacting malnutrition strongly. This is hardly surprising, given that the process of malnutrition sets in during the first weeks after birth. Hence nutritionists today argue strongly for targeted subsidies which are aimed mainly at households facing food insecurity (Gillespie and Mason, 1991) and at the very young child (6 months to 3 years).[27] What is clear is that in low-income countries with a high incidence of poverty the provision of a nutritional floor in the form of a general subsidy may be one among a variety of factors which account for a better nutritional outcome. In Kerala the incidence of severe malnutrition is lower than in the rest of India, and in Sri Lanka and Zimbabwe malnutrition is lower than their respective regional averages. This is likely to be an outcome of the combined, cumulative effect of food subsidies, health services, and higher levels of education.

In middle-income countries, direct nutritional intervention may be less cost-effective than the expansion of the PHC programme or improvement in its quality. In Costa Rica nutritional interventions began in 1950, when the urban-centred social security programme (with a health component) was introduced. Nutrition levels improved following the provision of nutrition centres for mothers and pre-school children as well as school hot-meal dining-rooms; the State also subsidized certain foods, regulated basic food prices, and financed the fortification of foods (vitamin A in sugar, iodine in salt, and vitamins in wheat flour). Increasing numbers of these centres were built after 1975. However, a PAHO study in Costa Rica has concluded that when malnutrition is confined only to infants and young children, such as in Central America, the primary causal role is infection and social pathology rather than inadequate food supply (Mata and Rosero, 1988). The PAHO study questions the whole concept of supplementary feeding in a country like Costa Rica because there is no evidence of food shortage even at times of crisis. Thus, during the economic crisis of 1979–83, when the decreased budget resulted in cut-backs in the scope of the food programme, there was continued steady reduction in severe malnutrition. In fact, the cost per child of the feeding programme is much higher than that of the rural health programme, which needs to be extended and improved, given that rural access to health services is not yet complete. Besides, a World Bank study of feeding programmes in nineteen Latin American countries came to the conclusion that the cost of the programmes was not justified by its nutritional impact (World Bank, 1991). It appears then that in Costa Rica, feeding programmes are designed less with nutritional levels in view, but promote the inclusion of specific vulnerable groups in universal programmes. The child-care programme, for instance, is aimed at providing comprehensive care of children under 6 years and their mothers, and besides food it offers pre-school education and medical care. The school-lunch programme aims to trigger a nutritional impact on learning, and to encourage poor families to keep sending their children to school— an objective we support later in this chapter.

Water and sanitation

We noted in the preceding chapter that the correlation coefficient for access to safe water and sanitation with U5MR and life expectancy was not particularly high (around 0.5 for both rural and urban areas). In the case-studies it was found that, for instance, Malaysia had achieved a life expectancy of 66.7 for males and 71.6 for females by 1980, and an IMR of about 28, while access to safe water in rural areas was still around 43 per cent (total 59 per cent). Similarly, in Kerala, the study points out, the coverage of protected public water supply or the availability of improved sanitary facilities is not significantly better than in other Indian States—but while the Indian IMR is 93, that in Kerala is 17.[28] For Costa Rica as well, when the decrease in IMR during 1970–80 is correlated with changes in socio-economic and water-supply variables, the conclusion is that water supply and sanitation did not play an important role in reducing IMR prior to or since 1970 (Feachem, 1985).

Nevertheless, the interpretation here should be that water and sanitation interventions play a minor role if the reference period is relatively limited, but are significant over a longer time-frame. In fact, it could be argued that the dramatic health improvements in the short term come from specific interventions aimed at children and their mothers, while health improvements for adult males and the aged require a longer time. Second, the great majority of the literature on the health impacts of water supply and sanitation concerns their impacts on morbidity from infectious disease and especially from diarrhoea (and on nutrition by disease depressing appetite and inhibiting nutrient absorption), rather than on mortality. In other words, falling mortality may have been reached in many high achievers in spite of low levels of access to safe water and sanitation.[29]

TABLE 3.5. Selected high achievers by geographic region: water and sanitation coverage

	% of pop. with access to safe water, 1988–93		% of pop. with access to adequate sanitation, 1988–93	
	urban	rural	urban	rural
East Asia and Pacific	91	57	63	13
Korea, Rep. of	100	76	100	100
Malaysia	96	66	—	—
South Asia	84	74	61	14
Kerala	85	71	—	—
Sri Lanka	80	55	68	45
Sub-Saharan Africa	73	35	58	28
Botswana	100	77	91	41
Mauritius	98	96	99	99
Zimbabwe	95	80	95	22
Latin America and Caribbean	90	55	79	33
Barbados	99[a]	—	100[a]	—
Costa Rica	100	86	100	94
Cuba	100	91	100	68

[a] Refers to total population

Source: UNICEF, *State of the World's Children, 1995*

Demographic transition in the selected countries

In the majority of cases the health transition has been accompanied by a demographic transition. In fact, the case-studies strongly suggest that it was non-family-planning interventions—mortality decline and rising education, with rising marriage age and women's economic participation—that has resulted in the decline of fertility. Only in Korea is there evidence of a strong family-planning programme.

But falling infant and child mortality has not necessarily meant all of them have also initiated their demographic transition. Population growth rates in Malaysia, Botswana, Zimbabwe, and Costa Rica have not declined when the average for 1965–80 is compared with that for 1980–92 (see Table 3.6). If anything, in Malaysia and Zimbabwe population growth rates have actually grown, from 2.5 per cent per annum (1965–80) to 2.6 per cent (1980–92) in the former, and from 3.1 to 3.3 per cent in the latter. In Botswana, the population growth rate has declined slightly from 3.3 to 3.1 per cent over the period, and in fact remains above the regional Sub-Saharan average. Thus, neither of the two Sub-Saharan countries in the sample have been able to buck the continent-wide trend so far of over 3 per cent per annum population growth rates. What is heartening, however, is that both have a contra-ceptive prevalence rate (CPR) much higher than the regional average of 12 per cent. In addition, they also have a much lower total fertility rate (TFR) (Botswana 5.0 and Zimbabwe 5.3) compared to the regional average of 6.4 children per woman. These facts suggest that the breakthrough in child mortality and female education has occurred too recently to manifest itself in reduced population growth. Lower TFR and higher than average CPR both suggest that the effects of falling mortality and increased education will begin to filter through to the population growth rate. It must be recognized that the breakthrough in child mortality and female education has occurred in both countries only within the last decade.

Malaysia is an Islamic society, and like many other Islamic countries, has not nec-essarily adopted family planning with any vigour.[30] Malaysia in fact adopted pro-natalist policies on account of the relatively small total population size. Clearly, improved health and education will not automatically result in a demographic tran-sition, without consciously adopted family-planning practices. The country has not only higher than average population growth rates, but also a TFR well above the average for the region, and a CPR of only 51 per cent in a region where three-quarters of the couples practise family planning. For this oil-rich State, where per capita incomes have continued to grow in the past thirty years, family planning may not have been seen as a particular priority by the government. Here Indonesia's suc-cessful family-planning programme in the same region offers an interesting con-

TABLE 3.6. Selected high achievers by geographic region: demographic indicators

	Population (million) 1993	Population annual growth rate (%)		Total fertility rate 1993	Contraceptive use (%) 1980–93
		1965–80	1980–93		
East Asia and Pacific	1754	2.2	1.7	2.5	74
Korea, Rep. of	44.5	1.9	1.2	1.8	79
Malaysia	19.2	2.5	2.6	3.6	48
South Asia	1208	2.3	2.2	4.2	39
Kerala	29.1	—	—	1.7	80
Sri Lanka	17.9	1.9	1.5	2.5	62
Sub-Saharan Africa	547	2.8	3	6.4	12
Botswana	1.4	3.3	3.1	5	33
Mauritius	1.1	1.7	1.1	2	75
Zimbabwe	10.9	3.1	3.3	5.3	43
Latin America and Caribbean	459	2.5	2.1	3	59
Barbados	—	—	—	1.8	—
Costa Rica	3.3	2.9	2.8	3.1	75
Cuba	10.9	1.5	0.9	1.9	70

Sources: UNICEF, *State of the World's Children, 1995*; UNICEF, India Office (1995)

trast, but then Indonesia has a larger absolute population, with a strong imperative to adopt family-planning measures.

In the remaining seven countries in the sample, however, the health transition has already begun to translate into demographic transition. The transition is, naturally, at different stages in the selected countries. Only in Korea, Kerala, Mauritius, Barbados, and Cuba has the total fertility rate dropped below the replacement level of just over two children per woman. Although it has been declining in Costa Rica, Malaysia, Botswana, Zimbabwe, and Sri Lanka, it is still not below the replacement level. Among the latter, only in Costa Rica is contraceptive use at a level comparable to that found in industrialized countries (see Table 3.6), though in Sri Lanka it is quite high as well.

There has raged a debate in the population literature as to whether the supply of family-planning services is a more important determinant of fertility decline or fertility desires (which in turn depends on health/education status of the couple). The main arguments of the advocates of family planning programmes in respect of their impact on fertility are: (i) there is considerable unwanted (and mistimed) fertility in most societies; and (ii) well-designed family planning programmes can reduce unwanted child-bearing (Bongaarts, 1994). However, Pritchett (1994a) argues that to achieve low fertility, 'it is fertility desires and *not* contraceptive access that matter'. He argues that changes in socio-economic conditions are very important causes of fertility declines, and the effect of family planning programmes on fertility is quantitatively small. Given that the world spends nearly $5 billion annually on the supply of family-planning services, this is a critical question. The proponents of family planning have argued that currently 120 million women in developing countries have unmet needs of family-planning services. In other words, inadequate family-planning services account for the unmet need for contraceptives, and hence, higher births. On the other hand, the advocates of demand-side factors in determining use of family-planning services argue, partly on the basis of a twelve-country study across developing countries, that lack of access accounts for only 4 per cent of the cases of unmet needs, and cost for 3 per cent, while other factors are far more important in explaining lack of use of family-planning services—husband disapproval (9 per cent), health concerns (20 per cent), and lack of knowledge (25 per cent).

It appears that both schools of thought may have some strength in their arguments. The supply-side school argues for improving the effectiveness of family-planning programmes and investing more in them, since their analysis of distribution of programme efforts in developing countries suggests that 74 per cent of countries have weak programmes or none at all. However, an analysis of programme coverage based on percentage of the developing world's total population shows that 70 per cent of that population is covered by strong/moderately good programmes, while only 30 per cent is covered by weak programmes or none at all. In other words, the future scope for reducing the developing world's population growth rate by focusing on the supply of family-planning services is limited, except in countries where the programme is weak (Bongaarts, 1995).[31] Past programmes have indeed substantially reduced the TFR (by about 1 birth per woman on average) and population growth, but future programmes will only have a modest impact on TFR. Non-family-planning issues will have to be addressed directly and up front now in order to reduce TFR, a conclusion which was reinforced by the International Conference on Population and Development (in Cairo in 1994). Our case-studies certainly suggest that none (except Korea) had very active family-planning programmes early in their development, and it was non-family-planning interventions (leading to the reduction in infant mortality) that resulted in the decline of fertility. This is a conclusion on which there is now an emerging consensus (Sen *et al.*, 1994).

It should be noted, however, that there is evidence from history that gender inequality may persist inspite of the occurrence of a demographic transition. Thus the transition in Western Europe occurred despite ineffective contraception methods, high maternal mortality, continuing domestic drudgery for women, and their limited access to income. More recently in India and China as fertility has fallen, the ratio of females to males has fallen as well (suggesting female infanticide and neglect of female children) (Population Council, 1995). Similarly, recent demographic and economic change in the former Soviet Union and Eastern Europe has not reduced gender inequalities, and domestic burdens of women may have increased. However, apart from having intrinsic value, we would argue on the basis of our case-studies, much as others have argued (Population Council 1995; Sen, 1995), that improvements in women's status and gender equity have created and will create the enabling conditions for fertility decline and better reproductive health.

The Achievement of Universal Primary Education

We noticed earlier that the selected countries started with better education indicators than the regional average. For the purposes of this chapter, by education indicators we mean those which relate primarily to primary and secondary education. This is so for two main reasons. First, it is well known that the social rate of return is highest for primary, followed by secondary education, and the social rate of return for higher education is the lowest (World Bank, 1995). Second, it is also well known that primary and secondary education have high health benefits for society, as we have argued in Chapter 2. Therefore, the rest of this discussion will focus on primary and secondary education.

The quantitative, qualitative, and policy aspects of the achievement of universal primary education in the selected countries are examined in this section. On the quantitative side, we were interested in understanding how gross/net enrolment rates of 100 or near 100 per cent were achieved when the vast majority of developing countries over the same period have made only moderate progress. Another critical aspect of the effectiveness of the education system that is examined is the primary completion rate. Without completing at least four years of education, it is unlikely that children can remain literate, and will indeed lose the skills acquired very quickly. Also, it is well known that drop-outs at the primary or early secondary stage normally join the millions of child labourers, so common in South Asia, Africa, and Latin America, where child labour is growing in many countries (at least in absolute terms) (Grootaert and Kanbur, 1994; Siddiqui and Patrinos, 1995). A final issue in quantitative expansion of education that is examined is the gender-equity issue. For the vast majority of developing countries, there are very substantial gender differences in every educational indicator, with ramifications not only for the health of all and the productivity of women (and thus their capacity to earn higher incomes), but also with major implications for hastening the demographic transition.

We found that in 1960, the gross enrolment rate for males at the primary level was already very high (over or close to 100) in all countries except Botswana.[32] For girls it was somewhat lower than for boys, but still remarkably high compared to the respective regional averages (Table 3.7).

TABLE 3.7. Selected high achievers by geographic region: education indicators

| | Primary school enrolment ratio | | | | Secondary school enrolment ratio | |
| | 1960 (gross) | | 1986–92 (gross) | | 1986–92 (gross) | |
	male	female	male	female	male	female
East Asia and Pacific	120	85	121	113	54	46
Korea, Rep. of	108	94	103	106	90	91
Malaysia	108	79	93	93	57	59
South Asia	77	39	101	75	47	28
Kerala	—	—	103	—	108	106
Sri Lanka	107	95	110	106	71	77
Sub-Saharan Africa	47	24	74	60	22	14
Botswana	38	43	116	121	50	57
Mauritius	96	90	104	108	52	56
Zimbabwe	82	65	120	118	54	42
Latin America and Caribbean	75	71	105	103	45	49
Barbados	—	—	114	113	90	83
Costa Rica	94	92	103	102	42	45
Cuba	109	110	103	102	81	94

Source: UNICEF, *State of the World's Children, 1995*

For instance, the Republic of Korea made very early investment in education in general and primary education in particular; most of the primary school-age children entered school during the 1950s. In Malaysia, the breakthrough came in the first decade after independence in 1956 (Table 3.8). In Kerala, the breakthrough came within the first decade after the formation of the State in 1956; in Sri Lanka it came within a decade of independence in 1947 by building on achievements in the last decade preceding independence. In Sub-Saharan Africa, the earliest successes came in Mauritius, followed by Botswana (independence 1966), and then by Zimbabwe during the 1980s. In the Caribbean, Barbados had achieved an NER of 88 by 1938, i.e. before independence in 1966. In Costa Rica, the big push for primary enrolment came during the 1950s, and in Cuba the first few years after the revolution were crucial.

In spite of the early achievement of universal primary education, gross enrolment ratio at the secondary level is less than 75 in all countries except Barbados, Cuba, Sri Lanka, and the Republic of Korea. Nevertheless, it is much higher than the respective regional average in all countries. The net enrolment ratio (Table 3.9) measures whether children in the relevant age-group at the primary level are in school, and by that standard already in 1980 the countries were doing extremely well. However, at the secondary level, much remains to be achieved.

The internal efficiency of the system is given by the repetition rate and the percentage of children starting school who complete primary school. It is clear from Table 3.10 that (for countries for which we have information) repetition rates were already very low in 1980. Also, it is clear that almost all children remained in school

---

TABLE 3.8. Enrolment breakthrough periods for high achievers

Country	Date	Reached
Korea, Rep. of	1960–70	GER = 100
Malaysia	1947–60	GER (m) = 103
		GER (f) = 79
Kerala	1956–60	GER = 98
Sri Lanka	1947–60	GER = 95
Botswana	1970–80	NER = 91
Mauritius	Before 1950 (m)	GER = 105
	1950–60 (f)	GER = 95
Zimbabwe	1980–85	GER = 124
Barbados	Before 1938	NER = 88
	1970–80	NER = 97
Costa Rica	Before 1960	GER = 93
Cuba	1958–60	GER = 110

Sources: UNICEF, *State of the World's Children, 1995*; Chapters 4–13

TABLE 3.9. Net enrolment ratios[a]

	Primary				Secondary			
	1980		1991–2		1980		1989–92	
	male	female	male	female	male	female	male	female
Korea, Rep. of	100	100	100	100	72	65	87	89
Malaysia	—	—	93	93	—	—	—	—
Kerala	—	—	—	—	—	—	—	—
Sri Lanka	—	—	100	100	—	—	71	78
Botswana	70	83	94	96	14	18	40	47
Mauritius	84	84	87	90	—	—	—	—
Zimbabwe	—	—	84	84	—	—	—	—
Barbados	96	97	88	92	87	86	87	74
Costa Rica	89	90	87	88	36	43	35	38
Cuba[a]	95	95	97	98	63	71	62	72

[a] Secondary figures are for 1985 and 1991 for Cuba, and gross ratios for Sri Lanka

Sources: UNESCO, *Statistical Yearbook, 1994*; UNESCO (*1995*)

till grade 4. Even more impressive, nearly all completed the final grade of primary school in the selected countries—which also gives some indication of the quality of primary schooling.

What policy measures made these achievements possible?

Ensuring equity and cost-effectiveness in public education expenditure

We know from the previous chapter that the allocations to education in the selected countries were among the highest in their region. Table 3.11 shows that public expenditure on primary education as a share of GNP per capita was generally higher in these countries in 1980 than the regional average (except in Sri Lanka). Ten years later this priority to public spending on primary education, relative to the region, remained in all cases, but in the African countries this priority was shifting to secondary education.

The allocation of the education expenditure to primary, secondary, and tertiary levels of education was very equitable in the selected countries by the standards of most developing countries. Thus, per pupil expenditure at secondary level, as a multiple of per pupil expenditure in primary schools, was in no case (except Botswana) greater than 2.[33] Even more remarkable, the tertiary-level pupils were not particularly pampered, as is normal in most developing countries. Thus, in India and China the ratio of expenditure per pupil at the tertiary level, relative to the primary level, was 38.5 and 40.3 respectively in the mid-1980s (Tan and Mingat, 1992). In Africa,

TABLE 3.10. Internal efficiency of primary education

	Duration (in years)		Repeaters (%)		Percentage of 1989 entrants reaching					
	Compulsory	First level	1980	1990	Grade 4			Final grade		
					Total	Male	Female	Total	Male	Female
Korea, Rep. of	6	6			100	100	100	99	99	100
Malaysia	9	6			98	98	98	96	95	96
Kerala										
Sri Lanka	10	5	10	8	99	100	97	97	98	95
Botswana		7	3	5	90	88	93	90	71	88
Mauritius		6		5	99	100	99	97	97	97
Zimbabwe	8	7			94	96	93	94	96	93
Barbados	11	6			93	81	86	75	76	71
Costa Rica	9	6	8	11	89			79		
Cuba	6	6	6	3	92			89		

Source: UNESCO, World Education Report, 1993

TABLE 3.11. Primary education expenditure per pupil as % of per capita GNP, 1980 and 1990 (public current expenditure, including pre-primary)

	1980	1990
East Asia	0.05	0.08
Korea, Rep. of	0.11	0.12
Malaysia	0.11	0.15
South Asia	0.15	0.10
Kerala	—	—
Sri Lanka	0.09	0.06
Sub-Saharan Africa	0.13	0.14
Botswana	0.15	0.09
Mauritius	0.14	0.10
Zimbabwe	0.25	0.21
Latin America and Caribbean	0.08	0.11
Barbados	0.12	0.21
Costa Rica	0.12	0.09
Cuba	0.12	0.16

Note: Sri Lanka also includes secondary education

Source: UNESCO, *World Education Report, 1993*

the comparable ratios were 66 in Burkina, 22 in Mali, 108 in Malawi, 157 in Uganda, and 255 in Tanzania. These figures reflect the extremely poor funding of primary education in these countries. In the high-achieving countries, on the other hand, that ratio exceeded 10 only in Botswana (18.4) and Mauritius (27.4) (see Table 3.12), demonstrating that unlike India, China, and most African countries, tertiary-level education was not heavily subsidized at the expense of primary schooling.

There are two consequences of this equity and the consequently high levels of funding of primary schooling. First, unlike in the majority of developing countries where most public current expenditure on primary education (over 95 per cent in most cases) is devoted to teacher salaries, there is reasonable allocation for learning materials, supervision, and teacher upgradation. Although internationally available data are not sufficiently disaggregated nor go back far enough to enable us to establish this, there is enough evidence in the case-studies to show that the quality of education did not decline sharply as the system expanded (though in the poorer countries quality has not improved as much as in the rest, as discussed in Chapter 2).

A second consequence is that when governments underspend on primary education, there is a heavy incidence of costs on parents (Bray, 1988)—but there is little evidence of the latter in our selected countries. The parents' expenditure in poor countries does not make up for the low public expenditure, as low enrolment and

TABLE 3.12. Public education expenditure per pupil by level, 1980 and 1992

	Ratio of secondary to primary expenditure		Ratio of higher to primary expenditure	
	1980	1992	1980	1992
Korea, Rep. of	0.88	0.93	1.52	0.39
Malaysia	1.80	1.88	12.35	10.43
Kerala	—	—	—	—
Sri Lanka	1.50	—	13.70	—
Botswana	4.59	5.82	40.40	18.45
Mauritius	1.30	1.65	21.66	27.40
Zimbabwe	5.32	1.80	16.70	8.19
Barbados	1.08	1.11	4.37	1.98
Costa Rica	1.97	1.90	5.85	6.35
Cuba	1.77	2.04	2.26	3.12

Source: UNESCO, *Statistical Yearbook, 1994*; Tan and Mingat (1992)

completion rates show. When private costs of primary schooling are low, as in low-income countries like Myanmar and Vietnam, demand for primary schooling tends to be high. But where household costs are so high as to serve as a disincentive to enrolment, female children are more affected than male children (Mehrotra *et al.*, 1996).

The evidence from the selected countries also suggests that it is critical that unit costs per pupil are kept low if the system is to expand without a precipitous loss in quality. This is because education is, in most developing countries, the single largest category in the budget, and in most countries the primary system accounts for half of that expenditure. In other words, unless costs are kept low it rapidly becomes nearly impossible for the public exchequer to bear the burden of expanding coverage while at the same time maintaining quality. The experience of many of the selected countries seems to confirm this hypothesis.

In this quantitative expansion, we are interested not only in the supply-side issues, but also in finding out how important the following factors were in increasing demand for education. First, how was the cost to parents kept low, in order to ensure that all disincentives to sending children to school were, if not eliminated, at least mitigated? Second, how important were school feeding programmes in ensuring a low drop-out rate? Third, was the mother tongue used as the medium of instruction or not? Table 3.13 attempts to summarize the relevant information, as it emerges from the case-studies.

TABLE 3.13. Some factors determining demand for primary schooling

	Cost of primary education	School feeding programme	Mother-tongue instruction
Korea, Rep. of			yes
Malaysia	free		mostly Malay[a]
Kerala	free	yes	yes
Sri Lanka	free	yes	yes
Botswana	free		yes
Mauritius	free		yes
Zimbabwe	free	yes	yes
Barbados	free	yes	yes
Costa Rica	free	yes	yes
Cuba	free	yes	yes

[a] Ethnic minorities—Chinese and Tamil—have own language schools as well

Source: Chapters 4–13

The African cases

As in the case of its health achievements, Zimbabwe is a success story *par excellence* in the field of universal primary education on a continent where the vast majority of countries are very far from achieving it. Zimbabwe tripled its gross enrolment ratio (GER) at primary level from around 42 to more than 120 within ten years of achieving independence in 1980—over precisely the period when the average primary GER for Sub-Saharan declined, the only developing region where this happened. With Botswana and Mauritius Zimbabwe is one of the few Sub-Saharan countries where the net enrolment ratio is about 100 per cent. How was this achieved? No explanation of Zimbabwean success in social development would be complete without an appreciation of the role of the liberation struggle against white rule (including the role played by women in that struggle) lasting ten years. The new State desired to achieve for the black people most of the basic needs that the white population in the country took for granted. To fulfil rising expectations, the State adopted a number of innovations that made these educational achievements possible.

After introducing racial integration in all schools, it harnessed popular enthusiasm for the school-expansion programme. Most communities were not serviced by schools, and since resources were limited as reconstruction began, all capital investment became the responsibility of the local communities, especially of parents (Colclough, 1993). The government provided only a modest subsidy, technical support, and quality supervision. Parents provided the bricks and the labour for constructing schools. However, the government covered the main recurrent expenditures, which included teachers' salaries and the cost of educational materials. Additional recurrent costs were met by parents who funded more facilities, teachers, and materials than could be met by government funds. Since self-financing by parents can skew the availability of facilities and their quality, the government adopted a programme, supported by international donors, of construction in disadvantaged areas which serve the poorer communities. Many other African countries (e.g. Kenya and Tanzania) have adopted community-based expansion programmes, which are quite significant in the countries' education systems. But a major difference, for instance, between the Kenyan *harambee* programme and the Zimbabwean case is that the former hardly receives any assistance from the State, while the latter programme is an integral part of the Zimbabwean education system and is financed partially by the government.

Policy-makers mapped the existing school facilities and compared them to the distribution of Zimbabwe's population. Thus it was planned that each primary school would serve a 5-km radius, and five to eight primary schools would feed into each secondary school (Chung, 1993).

The result was that enrolment at both primary and secondary levels doubled over the two years 1979–81, and universal primary education was achieved very quickly. Tuition fees were abolished at the primary level, though tuition fees were retained at secondary level. Primary schooling is free in the sense that those who are unable to pay the fees are not expelled from school, as happens in secondary schools. In fact, the case-study suggests that one-third of children graduating from primary school do not enter secondary school on account of the fees at that level. To ensure maximum utilization of existing equipment and facilities, schools ran two sessions per day with two sets of teachers. Drop-out rates were kept low by ensuring automatic promotion throughout primary and the first four years of secondary schooling. Not surprisingly, the survival rate to grade 4 was higher than any other Sub-Saharan country. Another means of achieving reduction in unit costs of schooling was the standardization of class-sizes throughout the system by increasing class-size in many privileged schools.

Teacher supply was increased by two methods: first, as enrolments built up, untrained teachers were employed particularly at primary level; by 1990 almost half of the primary-school teachers then employed had no formal teacher training. Second, an accelerated teacher-training programme, the Zimbabwe Integrated National Teacher Education Course (ZINTEC), was introduced. This course lasted four years, but only the first and last terms of this period were spent in college, with the remainder being spent teaching in the schools. ZINTEC has been highly successful in terms of both quality and cost-effectiveness—the cost of training a teacher under the ZINTEC programme is less than half the cost of conventional training (Chung, 1993). These cost-saving measures were critical in keeping real unit costs down at the primary level over the 1980s even though the salaries of African teachers rose as discrimination between black and white salaries ended.

As regards materials, the government decided in 1983 to publish essential primary- and secondary-school texts at low cost by using inexpensive newsprint and covers as well as inexpensive typesetting and printing.

The policy of developing educational facilities at lower cost and close to the children's homes has contributed substantially to enabling girls to attend primary and secondary schools. Besides, although boarding-schools are preferred in many African countries to day-schools at the secondary level (less so in francophone than anglophone countries), there has been a policy decision in Zimbabwe to provide day-schools instead of boarding-schools. This has cut costs dramatically, since in Zimbabwe the capital costs of a boarding-school are seven times that of a similar size day-school, and recurrent costs four times higher (Chung, 1993). In fact, real unit costs at the secondary level fell consistently between 1979–80 and 1988–9 as a result (Colclough, 1993).

The experience of Botswana and Mauritius also emphasizes the importance of cutting the direct costs of schooling for parents—which is often a function of the size of the government's own allocation to education. We know from the experience of Uganda and Burkina Faso, that the cost of sending a child to school could be at least 20 per cent of per capita income—a major disincentive to sending a child to school (Mehrotra *et al.*, 1996). With considerable donor support the Botswana government (not the communities) initiated a major primary-school construction programme. Enrolment received a major boost from the decision to cut fees by half in 1973, and to eliminate them in 1980. Transition rates to secondary school were only 41 per cent in 1980. Secondary-school fees were abolished in 1988, and as the supply of secondary schools expanded, by 1991 the transition rate had increased to 65 per cent. Needless to say, the superior resource base of the Botswanan economy permits the abolition of school fees altogether, which the Zimbabwean economy does not. Similarly, Mauritius was able to introduce free primary education in the 1950s (free textbooks at primary level only since 1988); secondary education became free in 1976, and tertiary education in 1988. Quite clearly, not all countries would be able to follow the example of Botswana and Mauritius by making both primary and secondary education free, but one of the largest challenges for education policy in most Sub-Saharan countries is to cut the direct costs of education to parents (Lockheed and Verspoor, 1991; Mehrotra and Vandemoortele, 1996).

The South Asian cases

The largest number of children in the world who are out of school are concentrated in three countries on the Indian subcontinent—India, Bangladesh, and Pakistan. On the same continent, the State of Kerala has achieved near total literacy. Similarly, Sri Lanka has made very substantial strides toward universal primary education and also achieved a total literacy rate of 89 per cent (1990). Sri Lanka had a higher literacy rate (60 per cent) at the time of independence in 1948 than the literacy rate of neighbouring countries today (India 52 per cent in 1991 and Pakistan 39 per cent in 1990). This was made possible because the colonial government, enriched by tea and rubber revenues, decided, in contrast to most colonial governments, to invest in primary education. This process was helped by the spread of missionary schools (as in Kerala) and Buddhist temple education, apart from the granting of self-government in 1931. The most important reasons for the high literacy rate since independence, according to the case-study, are the scheme of free education, the relative proximity of schools to the home (no child needs to travel more than 4 km.), the adoption of the mother tongue as the medium of instruction, the provision of a midday meal for children in schools, and free textbooks.

The male–female literacy gap was reduced not by taking any special measures, but by providing equal opportunities for free schooling, and by expanding the number of schools to provide easy access to girls and boys. Before independence, female literacy doubled from 21 per cent in 1920 to 44 per cent in 1945, and these increases were sustained by policies after independence. A major factor accounting for the sustained increases since independence was the allocation of educational expenditure amounting to over 4 per cent of GNP by the 1960s—partially made possible by the fact that there was practically no army (and hence little unproductive expenditure). This enabled the physical expansion of the school network, of which 95 per cent were coeducational schools by 1971. Free education for primary, secondary, and university education was introduced in 1945.

The system as a whole has to serve all children effectively. A separate system for girls at an early age did not exist, nor would it be desirable. But in many societies the cultural factors and special needs of girls have to be addressed. Recent evidence has shown, for instance, that a lack of toilets and water supply deters girls from attending, as do the distance to school which impinges on parents' sense of security about the modesty of girls.

In addition to free primary education and locational access, what appears to have helped girls' enrolment is the high proportion of female teachers. It is noticeable in Table 3.14 that the share of female teachers in total teaching staff is higher in the selected countries than the regional average. In India, in particular, it has been noticed that in the northern States, where female primary enrolments are quite low and certainly much lower than in Kerala State, the proportion of female teachers is known to be very low (e.g. 20 per cent in Uttar Pradesh) (Dreze and Sen, 1995).

In Kerala (as in Malaysia) there was a combination of public and private investment in education, and financial incentives were given to the private sector to establish and run educational institutions. A high demand was assured by making schooling progressively free up to and including high school. Even in private schools nearly half the children receive free primary schooling (i.e. tuition-fee free) in Kerala (Tilak, 1995). Children in need were also provided with midday meals.

TABLE 3.14. Women teaching staff (as a % of total)

	Primary education		Secondary education	
	1980	1992	1980	1992
Asia	39	45	28	36
Korea, Rep. of	37	53	26	36
Malaysia	44	58	45	54
Kerala	—	—	—	—
Sri Lanka	—	80	—	59
Sub-Saharan Africa	34	40	33	38
Botswana	72	77	37	40
Mauritius	43	45	39	41
Zimbabwe[a]	43	41	—	—
Latin America	76	77	47	49
Barbados	—	72	—	55
Costa Rica	—	80	—	—
Cuba	—	66	46	49

[a] Zimbabwe data are for 1985 and 1992

Source: UNESCO, *Statistical Yearbook, 1994*

Kerala has now achieved mean years of schooling equivalent to that of East Asia as a result of a very low drop-out rate; the drop-out rate remains a serious problem in the rest of India. It appears that Kerala's success has resulted from a policy of promotion which limits the failures in each class to 10 per cent or less. The case-study points out that while this policy raises some questions about the quality of schooling (reflected in the low graduation rates in the high school exams), the larger social impact of the high level of schooling is undeniable.

What is equally striking about the Kerala case is that the extremely low drop-out rate in the State correlates highly with a very low incidence of child labour (Government of India, 1995). The eleven Indian States that have the highest drop-out rates for classes 1–8, ranging between 36 and 79 per cent, also have the highest incidence of child labour in the country (Bihar, West Bengal, Andhra Pradesh, Rajasthan, Karnataka, Orissa, Gujarat, Maharashtra, Madhya Pradesh, Uttar Pradesh, and Tamil Nadu. Clearly, ensuring that children not only join school but remain there has implications going well beyond the school system.

How important is legislation in favour of compulsory education? This issue arises because it has been argued (Weiner, 1991) that no country in the industrialized world was able to eliminate child labour without enforcing compulsory education legislation, and that it is easier to enforce and monitor attendance of children in school than monitor through labour inspectors factories where children may be working. However, the States in India where enrolment rates are highest (Kerala, Himachal, Pradesh, and Manipur) are also the States where there is no compulsory education legislation; in fact, in States where the legislation does exist (Bihar, Uttar Pradesh, Rajasthan are among the fifteen such States) the enrolment ratio is relatively low (Tilak, 1995). In Sri Lanka too there was no such legislation, and although the Education Ordinance 1939 provided for enabling legislation to enforce compulsory school attendance, such regulations were never implemented. Education had already been accepted as a valued attribute, and there was a great demand for education. However, the case-study suggests, more recently, with an increase in the incidence of child employment and child prostitution, the need for such legislation is emerging. In Malaysia too primary schooling was not made compulsory in the early years.

Legislation by itself clearly cannot make much difference unless the conditions are created for its implementation and measures are taken for doing so. If compulsory education legislation specifies the obligations of various parties, especially of the State and it is used to rally support of all sections of society, the compulsory education law can be a boost to universal primary education.

Particularly interesting in Kerala were the means adopted to ensure total adult literacy. In the late 1980s, a total literacy campaign was launched with the co-operation of the government, all political parties, many NGOs, and interested individuals. It involved the free services of about 400,000 volunteers to teach the illiterates. Later, the National Literacy Mission, set up by the central government of India, and many States in the country which had begun a total literacy campaign adopted the Kerala approach. A similar campaign approach was adopted in Cuba to reach illiterate peasants in the countryside, soon after the revolution. In fact, Kerala and Cuba are two outstanding examples of adult literacy programmes, an area in which failed programmes tend to dominate. Given that there are nearly a billion illiterate adults in the world (or nearly one-fifth of humanity), compared to about 130 million children worldwide who are out-of-school, the Kerala and Cuba examples offer a lesson for similar programmes in the developing world.[34]

The East Asian cases

In all the selected countries, the mother tongue was adopted as the medium of instruction. In Sri Lanka, the adoption of the mother tongue had two effects: equalizing education throughout the country (in other words, removing the class bias inherent in an education system inherited from colonial times based on the English medium); and enabling the vast majority of children to enter the school system. However, in societies where there is more than one language, the mother-tongue issue becomes much more complicated. In Malaysia there were four kinds of schools: English-medium, Tamil-medium, Chinese-medium, and Malay-medium. With the promulgation of Malay as the national language, all schools were required to teach Malay. By inning in 1970 the English-medium schools were converted to the Malay-medium one grade at a time. Thus, the main road which non-Malays had been taking to higher socio-economic status, the English-medium schools, was closed (Snodgrass, 1980). Above all, all schools were required to teach a standard curriculum, regardless of the language in which instruction was imparted. In other words, parents were free to choose the medium of instruction for their children at the primary level, and the government provided assistance to non-Malay schools which taught the standard curriculum.

What about the external efficiency of the system? In both Kerala and Sri Lanka, while the literacy rate has been high for a long period, the rate of growth of the economy has been too slow to absorb the large numbers of secondary-school graduates. The result has been that both these regions have experienced a massive flow of workers to the Middle East, which have provided valuable foreign exchange remittances. However, in East Asia, the results of the massive expansion of first primary and then secondary education were internalized domestically, and as the economy expanded, there was little or no absorption problem. On the contrary, a well-educated and healthy work-force became a key to the expansion of the economy. How was this achieved?

Since the Korean case is particularly instructive, we dwell more on that country, particularly in the 1950s and 1960s. Most importantly, the growth of enrolment was not accompanied by fiscal pressures experienced in other countries (Mason *et al.*, 1980). A major reason for the internal efficiency was the low costs per pupil, which was in turn the outcome of very high pupil–teacher ratios at the primary level. As in Zimbabwe and Malaysia, there was substantial double- and triple-shift teaching, and thus a high utilization rate of existing facilities—this tended to fall as the number of classrooms increased. Costs per pupil were also kept low by reducing drop-out rates. This was done (as in Zimbabwe and Malaysia) by offering automatic promotion from grade to grade. Therefore, the transition rate from primary to secondary level was very high. Moreover, the cost per pupil was kept low by keeping teacher salaries low. Given that throughout the developing world teacher salaries account for around 90 per cent of educational expenditures, especially at the primary level, this fact deserves special mention.[35]

Another major factor that kept government costs for education low is the manner in which different levels of education were financed. Almost all primary-school children (99.5 per cent in 1965 and 98.8 per cent in 1975) were in publicly funded schools. But at the secondary level, private financing of schooling was and still is much more important, while all primary education is financed publicly. Thus, while government expenditure on education as a percentage of GDP is much lower for Korea compared to the other selected countries, almost three-quarters of government expenditure on education in the earlier decades went to primary education. Even in 1990 half of public education expenditure was still going to primary schooling.

A third, and possibly less important factor, except in the early years, which explains Korea's expansion of educational enrolment was foreign aid, especially from the USA. A final reason for the educational achievement in Korea (as in other East Asian economies) was that they moved to a demographic transition before other regions, which reduced the growth rate of the number of children of school-going age.

The Latin American cases

The Latin American cases also provide some interesting insights into the processes and methods by which primary schooling was universalized and near-total adult literacy achieved. Cuba's adult literacy campaign was a massive success (and to some extent similar to Kerala's total literacy campaign). The country inherited one million total illiterates and over a million semi-illiterates at the time of the revolution. Beginning in 1961, Cuba captured the world's attention by conducting a literacy campaign in which the government mobilized over 100,000 secondary-school students and other volunteers to teach adults from all over the country to read and write. Women in particular have played a significant role since then: the women's federation has been involved in improving the education of rural women and in helping to raise the education of all workers to the 6th-grade level.

In both cases (as in other cases) where literacy campaigns have led to near-universal literacy, primary education has already expanded considerably with almost universal enrolment and the literacy rate was also in the 60–80 per cent range. On account of the sheer demographic pressure, little dent on illiteracy can be made when large numbers of children are spewed out by the primary school system as illiterates, or large numbers are not even in primary school (as in large parts of Sub-Saharan Africa and South Asia). It is therefore necessary to be realistic regarding where and in what conditions sustainable and functional literacy can be achieved. It is never achievable without universal primary education. At the same time, given the large evidence that the children of educated mothers are more likely to enter, and then remain in school, and the other large externalities of educating adults, the importance of realistic and sustainable literacy campaigns cannot be overemphasized.[36]

Some policy implications emerge from the contrast between the Latin American high achievers and those from East Asia. The East Asian countries had already made a substantial investment in education in the 1950s. By 1960, gross enrolment ratios at the primary level for both males and females were higher on average in East Asia than in Latin America. Even more important was the difference in a key indicator of quality of primary education—proportion of primary-school children reaching final grade. Drop-out rates in Latin America are commonly known to be very high compared to other developing countries, especially other countries at the same level of per capita income. Thus, even among the high achievers in Latin America the proportion of children completing primary schooling is smaller than among high achievers in East Asia. Through the 1980s the East Asians were able to sustain their social expenditures, and maintain and improve quality in schools. On the other hand, for all Latin American countries—including such high achievers as Chile, Costa Rica, and Mexico—the 1980s were a period of intense economic adjustment during which they found it difficult to maintain social expenditures, unemployment and poverty tended to increase, and per capita incomes were stagnant. Thus, the gap in the stock of human capital between the two sets of countries is likely to have widened over the 'lost decade' of the 1980s (Mehrotra and Pizarro, 1996).

Some Lessons

Health development and mortality decline

The preceding analysis suggests that the following were the health- and non-health-related interventions that were responsible for mortality decline and health status improvement in the selected countries.

• The high initial level of education indicators in the selected countries and the early investment in primary education gave them a tremendous advantage given that high levels of education in the population are known to strongly impact on family size, health status, nutrition status, and healthy living conditions (through its impact on environmental sanitation).

• Most of the selected countries focused on primary health care in the organization of their health system and attenuated the urban bias in health services that existed hitherto. All the selected countries succeeded in providing access to health services—in both a physical and cost sense—in both rural and urban areas to a very substantial portion of the population. Access to health services was nearly 100 per cent in urban areas for almost all the selected countries by the late 1980s, and in the range of 80 to 100 per cent in rural areas (except Costa Rica), which was not the case for other countries in their region.

• While these countries emphasized system-building and a comprehensive approach to primary health care, they achieved major reductions in mortality of mothers and children by focusing their PHC activities on mother and child health. This was done by ensuring deliveries supported by good health-referral systems. This was followed by household visits by the first-level health worker. Immunization coverage was found to be particularly high in all our countries. It should be noted that immunization tends to be an indicator of a relatively effective formal health system that can reach a high percentage of the population. Many of the selected countries were easy to cover because of the small size of the population and no major problems of access. In the majority of countries in our sample, immunization coverage had reached a very high level long before the UNICEF–WHO campaign for universal immunization was launched. Growth monitoring of children was found to be an important tool for early detection of nutritionally vulnerable children (in Zimbabwe and Costa Rica).

• Primary health-care is supposed to be delivered by first-level health workers (who may or may not be community-based health workers) acting as a team. In different societies in the world they have included people with limited education who have been given elementary training in health care, 'barefoot doctors', medical assistants, practical and professionally trained nurses, trained birth atten-dants and midwives, as well as traditional practitioners. Some variant of this approach was adopted in many of these countries. Zimbabwe specifically trained a large number of community health workers. Sri Lanka too relied heavily on the primary health midwife (PHM). In many societies, it is advantageous if these health workers come from the community in which they live and are chosen by it, so that they have local support. We found this to be the case in Kerala and in Sri Lanka.

• When more complicated care is needed, the first-level health worker should be able to turn for help to more highly trained staff. A serious problem that most developing countries have faced in the past is that physicians and other health pro-fessionals trained at public expense have not been willing to work in rural hospitals or health centres. Malaysia ensured that all doctors trained at public expense were required to serve the public health system for at least three years. This allowed the government to post doctors to the rural areas. Sri Lanka too required doctors to work with the government health service.

• The Alma Ata Declaration (1978) had not recognized a strong role for the private sector in primary health care. However, it appears that the private sector has played a not insignificant role in the provision of health care in Kerala and to a lesser extent in Sri Lanka. However, this role has been largely supportive and com-plementary, rather than substitutive. The State's role has been dominant in expand-ing health services to the rural areas in most cases. While the issue of financing has been dealt with more fully in the previous chapter, we found little evidence of user charges at the primary level of health services in the selected countries.

• Traditional medical practitioners are found in most societies, and can be effec-tively used to supplement the work of the modern health system. In at least two of the studies (Kerala and Sri Lanka), we found that the traditional practitioners were a very significant part of the health delivery system. In Kerala, homoeopathy was found to be playing a very important role, though largely of a curative nature. Sim-ilarly, herb doctors filled a much needed gap in the health sector in Korea for several decades. (Likewise, traditional medicine played a very significant role in the health transition of a large country like China.) In fact, the number of traditional healers in Asia and Africa is many times larger than the number of medical physicians (9 to 1 in Sri Lanka, 17 to 1 in Indonesia, 25 to 1 in Ghana, 28 to 1 in Nigeria) and they offer an opportunity to governments to improve essential health services.

• The provision of a nutritional floor in low-income countries in the selected countries was found to be an effective mechanism of reducing malnutrition. In three of them (Cuba, Sri Lanka, and Kerala) a system of food subsidies has been maintained from the 1960s to date. Fair price shops have existed in other States of India as well since the 1960s, but the point here is that in Kerala they are found in the rural areas, while they are effectively non-existent in the rest of rural India. However, provision of the nutritional floor was one among a number of factors which accounted for the low level of malnutrition in these countries, the others being better disease control through health services and women's control over resources (that in turn was determined by other variables).

• Water and sanitation interventions play a minor role in mortality (as opposed to morbidity reduction) if the reference period is relatively limited, but are significant over a longer time-frame. The quickest results seem to be achieved by the direct provision of mother-and-child-oriented health services to the population, complemented with measures aimed at improved personal hygiene.

• Relative to other countries in their region, these countries were characterized by a much higher level of education indicators for women at the beginning of the period of analysis. In addition, in the late 1980s these countries also had substantial parity between males and females in secondary-school enrolment, quite apart from having nearly 100 per cent gross enrolment ratios for females at the primary level. Most importantly, it ensures the effective demand for health services and their utilization.

• Although all of them have managed to reduce IMRs below 20 (except Botswana and Zimbabwe), those that have not raised CPRs over 50 per cent (Malaysia, Botswana, Zimbabwe) still seem to have total fertility rates over 3. Hastening the demographic transition will require more than ensuring a health transition in some of these countries. However, in most of the selected countries the demand for family-planning services followed the health/education breakthroughs. In fact, it should be noted that all industrialized countries were down to a very low TFR before modern contraception was even around.

Education policies

What needs to be stressed is that in the universalization of primary education it is the combination of a number of policies and interventions, many of which are illustrated in the selected countries, that make the difference, rather than individual policies.

• In all the selected countries, primary education has been the responsibility of the State, while there are considerable differences between our high achievers when it comes to secondary education. The private sector's role in primary education is rather limited in all our high achievers. In almost all cases the physical infrastructure (school buildings and facilities) was created by the State. However, in Zimbabwe it was the community which undertook the responsibility for building the schools, supported by the State.

• On the supply side, a critical factor underlying the achievement of universal primary education in nearly all the selected countries is the high allocation of the government budget to primary education (an issue also addressed in Chapter 2). Intrasectoral allocation of resources within education was highly equitable compared to most developing countries. The adequacy and equity of the allocation was a prerequisite for the proper use of funds within primary education—with provision for an effective packaging of essential inputs.

• In most countries several devices were adopted to ensure that primary education expenditures were used cost-effectively.

• In several of the selected countries, automatic promotion was adopted as policy (Kerala, Malaysia, Korea, and Zimbabwe), which ensured that drop-out rates remained low. Automatic promotion, however, is not a matter of an administrative procedure; the educational rationale behind it is that the school and the teacher are responsible for ensuring that the child has a meaningful learning experience and actually learns. Another mechanism used (in Korea, Malaysia, and Zimbabwe) to reduce costs was to utilize existing facilities more fully by having double shifts in schools. Korea managed to keep per pupil costs low by maintaining a very high pupil–teacher ratio and by containing teacher salaries within reasonable bounds. The studies suggest that unit cost containment is a key to maintaining high expenditures on education and sustaining coverage and quality.

• On the demand side, the reduction of costs to parents of sending children to school seems to have been a primary reason for the rapid expansion of primary enrolment in most of the selected countries. In all countries, primary education is entirely free of direct tuition fees, and has been so for decades. In Zimbabwe, while the parents contribute to the parent–teacher association, the building fund, and extracurricular activities, there are no tuition fees. No child is expelled at the primary level for non-payment. On the demand side, this has been the key to the quantitative expansion in enrolment in these countries.

• Another demand side explanatory factor has been the use of the mother tongue for instruction at the primary level in all cases. Thus, unlike the vast majority of West African countries where primary schooling is still carried out in the language of the former metropolitan country (France) and the primary gross enrolment ratios are among the lowest in the world, all the selected countries adopted the mother tongue.[37]

• Another common factor on the demand side were school feeding programmes, which were common to all the selected low-income countries—Cuba, Kerala, Sri Lanka, and Zimbabwe (though in the last case it was ended in 1986). Other countries, including middle-income ones like Costa Rica, also had a school feeding programme, but its nutritional value is not seen to be high. The school feeding programme is a motivational issue, and through nutritional impact on learning, was seen to be an important factor underlying the very low drop-out rate in these countries. This is being increasingly used in India as an incentive, given that while gross enrolment rate is reasonably high, the survival rate to grade 4 (according to official figures which may not be entirely reliable) was only 61 per cent in 1988, showing how high the wastage rate is in the country with the largest number of illiterates in the world. Nevertheless, what is important is that without improved school quality, school feeding programmes will not ensure improved learning outcomes.

• These demand-side factors are of considerable importance in the context of the widespread existence of child labour in South Asia, Africa, and Latin America. By reducing the direct and opportunity costs of schooling not only can drop-out rates be reduced, but the compulsion for parents to send children to work (rather than to school) can be mitigated. However, in addition to demand for schooling, supply-side or school-related factors, especially the quality and relevance of primary schooling, are equally important in order to reduce drop-outs.

• Compulsory primary education legislation was not seen in the case-studies as being essential to achieving universal primary education. A legal framework that specifies the obligation of State and other parties backed by a commitment to implement the legislation would be helpful, but only when enrolment rates are already quite high.

• None of the countries seem to have reported any special policies to ensure growth in female enrolment. The efforts made to reach all children, including girls, certainly played a role. The expansion of physical facilities and physical proximity to the schools laid the basis for the participation of girls. A critical factor underlying high school girls' enrolment was the high proportion of female teachers in schools.

• While all countries managed to universalize primary education, two of them adopted very effective means of providing adult literacy as well. Given the evidence that the children of parents with education are more likely to remain in school, the effectiveness of Cuba's and Kerala's literacy campaign, is noteworthy. Both adopted the same means; volunteers from secondary schools were drafted to run well-organized literacy campaigns. However, the literacy gains were sustained in Cuba following the campaign, as a result of follow-up activities, which has not been the case in Kerala.

These policy interventions in health and education are discussed further in the case-studies in Part II. In addition, the contextual reasons for social achievement—the why and how of social development—are examined in the country studies.

Notes

1. In an examination of the relationship of child health and other factors in four countries (Costa Rica, Côte d'Ivoire, Egypt, and Japan) over 1960–87, Lau *et al.* (1993) suggest that part of the gain in child health depends upon the initial levels of schooling (in 1960) of the population and of income per capita. Because schooling and income per capita lead to health benefits that persist over time, they argue that health in a population may be improved simply by maintaining initial levels of schooling and income.

2. This is not to suggest that systemic approaches did not differ between countries. Thus, while Cuba focused on equality in health access, reliance on paramedics was low. The principles of primary health were certainly not very actively promoted in the Republic of Korea in the first three decades after independence from Japan.

3. The exception was smallpox vaccination, which was widely used in Europe from the late eighteenth century on, and diphtheria anti-toxin (discovered 1894).

4. However, since the responsibility of proving eligibility for free health care rests with users, many of whom have difficulty in providing the requisite evidence, many are excluded. Also, to place the $Z150 eligibility in perspective, it is useful to know that the minimum industrial wage of $Z243.50 set in 1980, exceeds this limit (Sanders, 1993).

5. This is not to suggest that challenges to equity in health care do not remain in Zimbabwe. See Loewenson *et al.* (1991), and also World Bank (1993) for regressivity of public subsidies to private insurance for the well-off.

6. Given its resource constraints, the relatively high ratio of nurses to physicians (5 to 1) in Sub-Saharan Africa is a good sign. However, Africa has the fewest physicians and nurses of any region, which is an impediment to the delivery of public health interventions and essential clinical services because some of existing personnel are providing tertiary-level care, mostly in urban areas.

7. The World Bank recommended a package of health services for developing countries, including public health and minimum essential clinical interventions, which require about 0.1 physician per 1,000 population and between two and four graduate nurses per physician (World Bank, 1993).

8. There is considerable debate as to whether trained birth attendants (TBAs) are very effective on their own in reducing infant or maternal mortality. The relevant point in the case of the selected countries is that they had a well-integrated and functional health delivery *system*, with the appropriate referral system to back up the lower-level health personnel.

9. It is now widely recognized in the 1990s that in developing countries an EPI package that also incorporated vaccines against hepatitis B and yellow fever together with supplements of micro-nutrients Vitamin A and iodine (the 'EPI Plus') would have the highest cost-effectiveness of any health measure available today (WHO and UNICEF, 1996).

10. In the late 1970s when the availability of foreign exchange contributed to an exodus of doctors from Sri Lanka, the government decided to permit doctors employed by the state to

engage in private practice to counteract the brain drain. Often in South Asia doctors working in government hospitals are not permitted to engage in private practice in off-duty hours, but are given a non-practising allowance. The permission to engage in private practice has the potential of raising physicians' incomes beyond their salaries plus non-practising allowances.

11. Health and education are both in the provincial domain according to the Indian constitution.

12. This discussion draws heavily from Chatterji (1993) and the Government of India (1992).

13. In fact, the primary health system in India has generally been excessively focused on achieving family-planning targets, to the detriment of preventive or promotive services. Only in mid-1996 was the target-based incentive system for lower level health personnel abrogated.

14. Earlier research suggested that universal demand for clinical services may serve as a motivator and incentive for people to utilize and accept preventive and public health services. In the 1950s, Sri Lanka had responded to demands for clinical services by decentralization and stress on rural services. Kerala too put a strong emphasis on easy access to clinical services, with resultant high utilization and immunization rates.

15. Table 3.2 states that the percentage of population with access to health services in rural areas is 60 per cent. This requires clarification. The Rural Health Programme covers only 60 per cent of the population (Mata and Rosero, 1988). Currently, the government is engaged in creating basic teams of integral health care, composed of a doctor, a nurse, and one or two primary health-care technicians covering 3,000 to 5,000 inhabitants, which will cover the entire population by the end of the present government's term.

16. Thus in many of the selected countries private health expenditures as a per cent of GDP are quite high: Korea 3.9% (public spending is 2.7%), Malaysia 1.7% (1.3%), Sri Lanka 1.9% (1.8%), and Zimbabwe 3% (3.2%) (World Bank, 1993).

17. There is general consensus now that the debate was somewhat sterile. Both groups accepted the centrality of health services in the determination of health, in line with the Alma Ata Declaration (Klouda, 1993), and the ultimate vision of both approaches is the same—a comprehensive health system (Hill *et al.*, 1993). Only the timing is at issue. Given that resources are scarce, equity demands that all people should have access to at least the selective services which reduce suffering, morbidity, and death.

18. The discussion in this section focuses on protein-energy malnutrition, as opposed to micro-nutrient deficiencies (iron, Vitamin A, iodine). Hence the interventions needed to address the latter—micro-nutrient supplementation and micro-nutrient fortification of food—are not discussed. However, most of the other interventions—food supplementation, food price subsidies, disease control (especially control of intestinal parasites), nutrition education—needed to address protein–energy malnutrition, are discussed.

19. Access to health services is defined as living within an hour by local transport of a local health service centre.

20. Micro-nutrient deficiences are not reflected in the use of calorie supply as an indicator of the food component of nutritional status, and they are only beginning to be addressed in many of the selected countries. Several have an iron-deficiency problem (an important factor in maternal mortality as well as many other problems), many have areas of iodine deficiency, and some have areas of vitamin A deficiency; some of the countries have multiple micro-nutrient deficiencies. Addressing these deficiencies offers one cost-effective way of improving nutrition.

21. UNICEF has usually argued that school feeding programmes are not an efficient means of raising nutrition levels. This is because serious malnutrition begins early, in the pre-school years—and the target years for interventions should be these early years (see UNICEF, 1990).

22. The proportion of rationed rice to total rice consumption exceeded 70% at one time but declined to about 50% after 1966. As a proportion of total calories, rationed rice represented about 20% in 1970. The lower-income groups benefited much more from this programme than those better off (Martorell and Sharma, 1985).

23. This may be part of the explanation for the higher survival chances of girls in Kerala than in the rest of India, and the more favourable female to male ratio in the population found in Kerala compared to the rest of the country.

24. Other studies (of Cuba, Sri Lanka, Kerala, China, and Costa Rica) also show a clear associa-tion between changes in energy (calories) per capita availability and changes in infant mortal-ity. Short, acute fluctuations in the food supply in these countries were associated with an almost immediate inverse response in infant mortality (Martorell and Sharma, 1985).

25. Low birth weight implies that the infant was malnourished in the womb, which reflects the condition of women during pregnancy and their young lives. For an explanation of these differences see Ramalingaswami *et al.* (1996).

26. Ramalingaswami *et al.* (1996) offer additional reasons for this differential in incidence of malnutrition.

27. The Tamil Nadu Integrated Nutrition Project in India is directed precisely at the young child, which explains its high success rate in reducing malnutrition (Balachander, 1993).

28. Panikar noted that water-supply coverage is low in Kerala by Indian standards, with 37% of villages (compared to 18% for India) and 71% of the rural population unserved in 1981. Cited in Feachem (1985).

29. Positive health outcomes may also emerge on account of other compensating factors. Thus, access to safe water and sanitation refers only to hardware, and not necessarily to water/san-itation-related behaviour or personal hygiene. Improved personal hygiene can have an effect on diarrhoea incidence rates without any improvements in hardware. For example, hand-washing and the use of soap can reduce the incidence of diarrhoea, and education is likely to foster such behaviour. Education may also contribute to decreased morbidity if it leads to adults rendering water safe by boiling it. (However, our studies did not examine these aspects). Besides, the benefits of the provision of safe water and sanitation go beyond their impact on morbidity. The provision of the hardware of safe water supply close to home can improve girls' educational opportunities and otherwise significantly free the time of women and children. It also saves energy, the equivalent of as many as 500 calories or one meal per day.

30. It is not possible to make a case that in all Islamic societies family-planning programmes have proved unsuccessful, as major increases in contraceptive prevalence rates in Bangladesh and Indonesia demonstrate.

31. In our view the demand-based argument is much stronger than the opposite view. Thus, as Pritchett (1994b) points out, most of the populous countries (China, India, Bangladesh, Indonesia) already have strong programmes. The regression analysis (in which fertility is the dependent variable and derived fertility and family planning effort are the explanatory vari-ables) suggests that a 50-point (on a scale of 0 to 100) increase in family planning effort would reduce fertility by just one birth. First, a 50-point increase means a change from a effectively non-existent programme like that of Chad (20), Mauritania (21), or Bhutan (22) to one like

that of Bangladesh (72). Second, only one country (Botswana) actually improved family-planning effort by 50 points over seven years from 1982 to 1989. Third, the practical maximum for family planning effort is around 80 per cent of the theoretical maximum effort (e.g. where Korea, Sri Lanka, Indonesia are clustered)—even China achieves only 87 per cent of the maximum. And only twenty-eight countries of 98 countries score below 30 in family-planning effort. Therefore achieving a reduction of even one birth by a 50-point increase in family-planning effort looks very difficult.

32. GER is the total number of children enrolled in a schooling level—whether or not they belong in the relevant age-group for that level—expressed as a percentage of the total number of children in the relevant age-group for that level. The net enrolment ratio is the total number of children enrolled in a schooling level who belong in the relevant age-group, expressed as a percentage of the total number in that age-group.

33. The higher per pupil expenditure in Botswana can be explained by the need for boarding secondary schools, which are more expensive than day-schools. A low density of population, with small cohorts of children in a given geographic location, makes boarding necessary.

34. Recent evidence from Kerala is that since there has been limited follow-up activity. After the campaign many adult neo-literates have fallen again into illiteracy after a few years. On the other hand, in Cuba neo-literates joined schools in the countryside following the literacy campaign, and were thus able to consolidate their skills.

35. Mehrotra and Vandemoortele (1996) argue strongly for many similar reforms in Sub-Saharan countries.

36. Yet it is remarkable that the World Bank (1995)— in its recent policy review on education— completely ignores the issue.

37. In West African Francophone countries, the language of instruction is one among other factors which explains the low level of enrolment, the others being distance to school, the lack of facilities, poor quality of education, and the presence of nomads.

References

Balachander, J. (1993), 'Tamil Nadu's Successful Nutrition Effort', in Rohde *et al.* (1993).

Bongaarts, John (1994), 'The Impact of Population Policies: Comment', *Population and Development Review*, 20/3.

—— (1995), 'The Role of Family Planning Programs in Contemporary Fertility Transitions', Working Paper 71, New York: Population Council.

Bray, Mark, with Lillis, K. (1988), *Community Financing of Education: Issues and Policy Implications in Less Developed Countries*, Oxford: Pergamon Press.

Caldwell, John C. (1986), 'Routes to Low Mortality in Poor Countries', *Population and Development Review*, 12/2.

Chatterji, Meera (1993), 'Health for Too Many: India's Experiments with Truth', in Rohde *et al.* (1993).

Chung, Fay (1993), 'Educational Expansion, Cost-Considerations and Curriculum Development in Zimbabwe', in Jill K. Conway and Susan C. Bourque (eds.), *The Politics of Women: Education Perspectives from Asia, Africa and Latin America*, University of Michigan Press, 1993.

Colclough, C., with Levin, Keith M. (1993), *Educating All the Children. Strategies for Primary Schooling in the South*, Oxford: Clarendon Press.

Dreze, J., and Sen, A. (1995), *India: Economic Development and Social Opportunity*, Delhi: Oxford University Press.

Feachem, R.G. (1985), 'The Role of Water Supply and Sanitation in Reducing Mortality in China, Costa Rica, Kerala State (India) and Sri Lanka', in Halstead *et al.* (1985).

Gillespie, Stuart, and Mason, John (1991), *Nutrition-Relevant Actions: Some Experiences from the Eighties and Lessons for the Nineties*, ACC/SCN State-of-the-Art Series, Nutrition Policy Discussion Paper 10, Geneva.

Government of India (1992), *The Eighth Five-Year Plan* (1992/3–96/7), Planning Commission, New Delhi.

—— (1995), *Children and Work*, Workshop of District Collectors in Child Labour, Ministry of Labour, New Delhi.

Grootaert, Christian, and Kanbur, Ravi (1994), *Child Labour: A Review*, background paper for the 1995 World Development Report, Washington, DC, mimeo.

Gunasekera, H. R. (1996), *Nutrition Status of Children in Sri Lanka*, DHS Further Analysis Series no. 1, Dept. of Census and Statistics, Ministry of Finance and Planning, Colombo.

Halstead, S. B., Walsh, J. A., and Warren, K. S. (1985), *Good Health at Low Cost*, Conference Report, New York: Rockefeller Foundation.

Hill, Terrel, Kim-Farley, Robert, and Rohde, Jon (1993), 'Expanded Programme on Immunisation: A Goal Achieved towards Health for All', in Rohde *et al.* (1993).

Klouda, Anthony (1993), 'Prevention is *still* more costly than cure', in Rohde *et al.* (1993).

Law, L., Yazbeck, A., Hill, K., Jamison D. T., and Tan, J-P. (1993), 'Sources of Child Health Gains since the 1960s: An International Comparison', background paper for World Bank (1993).

Lockheed, M., Verspoor, A. M., and associates (1991), *Improving Primary Education in Developing Countries*, Oxford: Oxford University Press.

Loewenson, R., Sanders, D., and Davies, R. (1991), 'Challenges to Equity in Health and Health Care: A Zimbabwean CaseStudy', *Soc. Sci. Med.*, 32, 10.

Martorell, R., and Sharma, R. (1985), 'Trends in Nutrition, Food Supply and Infant Mortality Rates', in Halstead *et al.* (1985).

Mason, Edward S., Kim, Maha Je, Perkins, Dwight H., Kim, K. S., and Cole, David C. (1980), *The Economic and Social Modernization of the Republic of Korea*, Cambridge, Mass.: Harvard University Press.

Mata, L., and Rosero, L. (1988), *National Health and Social Development in Costa Rica: A Case Study of Inter-sectoral Action*, Technical Paper 13, Washington, DC: Pan-American Health Organization.

Mehrotra, Santosh (forthcoming), 'Improving Cost-effectiveness and Mobilizing Resources for Primary Education in Sub-Saharan Africa', *Prospects*.

—— and Pizarro, Crisostomo (1996), 'Social Policies in Chile, Costa Rica and Mexico: An Inter-Regional Perspective', in UNICEF (1966).

—— Nigam, A., and Thet, A. T. (1996), 'Public and Private Costs of Primary Education: Evidence from Selected African and Asian Countries' *UNICEF Staff Working Paper 15*, New York.

Mohs, Edgar (1993), 'Changing Health Paradigms in Costa Rica', in Rohde *et al.* (1993).

Population Council, *The Unfinished Transition*, New York: Issues Paper.

Pritchett, Lant (1994), 'Desired Fertility and the Impact of Population Policies', *Population and Development Review*, 20/1.

—— (1994b), 'The Impact of Population Policies: Reply', *Population and Development Review*, 20/3.

Ramalingaswami, V., Jonsson, U., and Rohde, Jon (1996), 'The Asian Enigma', in *The Progress of Nations*, New York: UNICEF.

Rohde, Jon, Chatterji, Meera, and Morley, David (eds.) (1993), *Reaching Health for All*, Delhi: Oxford University Press.

Sanders, David (1993), 'The Potential and Limits of Health Sector Reforms in Zimbabwe', in Rohde *et al.* (1993).

Sen, Amartya (1995), 'Agency and Well-Being: The Development Agenda', in Noeleen Heyzer with Sushma Kapoor and J. Sandler, *A Commitment to the World's Women—Perspectives for Development for Beijing and Beyond*, New York: UNIFEM.

Sen, Gita, Germain, A., and Chen, Lincoln (1994), *Population Policies Reconsidered: Health Empowerment and Rights*, Cambridge, Mass.: Harvard University Press.

Snodgrass, Donald R. (1980), *Inequality and Economic Development in Malaysia*, Oxford University Press, Kuala Lumpur.

Siddiqui, F., and Patrinos, H. A. (1995), 'Child Labour Issues, Causes and Intervention', Human Resources Development and Operations Policy, *Working Paper 56*, Washington, DC: World Bank.

Tan, Jee-Peng, and Mingat, Alain (1992), *Education in Asia. A Comparative Study of Cost and Financing*, Washington, DC: World Bank.

Tilak, Jandhyala B. C. (1995), 'How Free is "Free" Primary Education in India?' *NIEPA Occasional Paper* 21, New Delhi.

Tulasidhar, V. B. (1996), *Government Health Expenditure in India*, International Health Policy Programme Working Paper, Washington, DC.

UNESCO (1995), *Educating People: Improving Chances, Expanding Choices*, Paris.

—— (various years), *Statistical Year Book*, Paris.

UNICEF (1990), *Strategy for Improved Nutrition of Children and Women in Developing Countries*, Policy Review Paper E/ICEF/1990/1.6, New York.

—— (1995), *The Progress of Indian States*, New Delhi: India Office.

—— (1996a), *Social Development in the Nineties: The Case of Chile, Costa Rica and Mexico*, Bogota: Planeta.

—— (1996b), *Progress of Nations 1996*, New York.

—— (1996c), *Mid-Decade Review 1996*, World Summit for Children Follow-up, New York.

Weiner, Myron (1991), *The State and the Child in India*, New Delhi: Oxford University Press.

WHO and UNICEF (1996), *State of the World's Vaccines and Immunization*, Geneva.

World Bank (1991), *Feeding Latin America's Children. An Analytical Survey of Food Programmes*, Washington, DC.

—— (1993), *World Development Report 1993*, Washington, DC.

—— (1995), *Priorities and Strategies for Education: A World Bank Review*, Washington, DC.

Part II

Case-Studies

4

Botswana: Social Development in a Resource-rich Economy

TYRRELL DUNCAN, KEITH JEFFERIS,
AND PATRICK MOLUTSI

Overall Trends in Social Development

Introduction

Botswana is a landlocked country traversing the Tropic of Capricorn. The country is largely arid or semi-arid and is prone to droughts that are often prolonged. With a land area of 582,000 sq. km. (roughly the same size as France) and a population of 1.3m. in 1991, it is one of the world's most sparsely populated countries. More than two-thirds of the country is covered with the thick sand layers of the Kgalagadi (Kalahari) Desert; only 5 per cent of the land area is arable. Most of the population lives in the eastern part of the country, along the line of the north–south railway, where rainfall and soil conditions are moderately better.

When Botswana gained independence in 1966—after eighty years as a British protectorate—it was one of the poorest and least developed countries in the world, still depending on Britain to meet half of its recurrent budget. It had no capital city and only a few miles of tarred roads; most of the population depended on subsistence farming and most were illiterate—there were only a handful of university and high-school graduates and only eighty students in the final year of secondary school (Harvey and Lewis, 1990). Soon after independence, large, exploitable deposits of diamonds were discovered and Botswana entered a period of more than two decades of rapid and sustained economic growth that has continued to the present day. From the early 1970s on, Botswana's development was supported by considerable foreign aid.

The impact of diamonds on the economy was enormous, and over the twenty-five years from 1965 to 1990 Botswana was the fastest-growing country in the world,[1] with GDP increasing at an average annual rate of 13 per cent, and GNP per capita at 8.5 per cent. As a result, average real incomes were nearly eight times higher in 1990 than they were in 1965. By 1992, GNP per capita was $US2,790 (the second highest figure in Africa, after Gabon), and Botswana was one of the few

African countries to have graduated from the least developed and low-income to the middle-income group of countries (World Bank, 1994).

On the basis of successive national development plans, the government invested much of the country's resources in establishing basic physical and social infrastructure throughout the country, building public institutions, and directly supporting improvements in social welfare through provision of health, education, and other social services and development programmes. The associated growth in demand for goods and services directly supported growth in public- and private-sector employment. The resulting improvements in physical and social infrastructure also had important indirect employment impacts by removing some of the basic constraints to economic activity, especially private enterprise. Employment and income growth were seen as the main ways to spread the benefits of Botswana's diamond revenues more widely among the population.

Relevance of Botswana's experience

The immediate reason that Botswana's experience in social development may be of interest is that it experienced large improvements in social indicators over the last thirty years. On this basis alone, Botswana's experience may offer lessons for policy-making, institutional development, and resource allocation. The broader historical context of Botswana's development experience also suggests a series of other significant features that contribute to its relevance to other developing countries:

• A rare democratic venture: Botswana has been an open and democratic society, largely comprised of a single ethnic group, the *Batswana*, that enjoyed considerable social harmony long before independence. With no major divisions in society there was general consensus in government planning and in the wider society that everyone should enjoy the benefits of the country's development (even if, in practice, everyone did not benefit equally).

• Social development challenges of a mineral-rich developing country: Botswana's experience provides an example of social policy choices and development performance in mineral-rich developing countries. One of the key problems faced by such countries is how to distribute the benefits of development widely among the population, since capital-intensive mining industries tend to have a narrow employment base and hence directly improve the incomes of only a small proportion of the population. In Botswana's case the government was the major recipient of revenues from the diamond-mining enclave (in the form of taxes and royalties), which meant that government had to take a commanding role in determining how the country's resources would be used for development.

• A long-term national development strategy that was actually implemented: With its stable political situation and record for sound economic management, Botswana provides a rare example of a country that was able to pursue the same set of principles and objectives for development over a period of more than twenty-five years and to evolve and implement what amounted to a long-term national development strategy. It did so with a considerable measure of consistency, commitment, and prudence.

• Having to start social development from 'scratch': Partly as a result of previous colonial neglect, Botswana had to establish modern social infrastructure and institutions—and educate its population in order to do so—virtually from scratch. Faced with the enormity of this task, and beginning from a position of considerable poverty, Botswana's route to development combined enlightened overall ideals and objectives with a cautious and pragmatic approach to implementation.

• Addressing the special challenges of a sparsely populated country: Botswana's case also illustrates some of the practical problems and policy choices available to countries with small, scattered populations that make infrastructure and service provision more difficult and costly to provide, e.g. national settlement policy; addressing the needs of people living in remote areas; and trying to operate rural extension services efficiently.

The objective of this chapter is to analyse the reasons for successful social development, particularly with respect to policy-making, institutional reform, and budget allocations. By taking stock of the current social situation the review also seeks to indicate key strengths and weaknesses in current policies.

While the reasons for Botswana's rapid economic development have been well documented, less attention has been given to its performance in social development. In particular the chapter seeks to provide some answers to broad social-development questions regarding how and why social conditions have improved, how equitably the benefits have been shared within society, and whether communities and ordinary people have been able to share along with government in the decisions and responsibilities for social development.

Economic background: the impact of diamonds

Botswana was clearly fortunate in the discovery of large diamond deposits soon after independence, making it one of the world's major diamond producers and exporters. Diamonds now account for around 80 per cent of export earnings; most of the rest is derived from copper-nickel matte and beef, so Botswana is, like many developing countries, heavily dependent upon primary-commodity exports. However, there are a number of important contrasts between Botswana's experience and those of other mineral and primary commodity exporters. First, Botswana has avoided the temptation to borrow internationally against expected future diamond revenues, and so the country has no debt problem and it is less vulnerable to changes in international commodities prices. Secondly, Botswana has not experienced a secular decline in its terms of trade, a problem which afflicts most primary-commodity exporters. It has benefited from the success of De Beers diamond cartel, which generates monopoly profits for producers and stabilizes prices.[2] Furthermore, most of Botswana's exports are denominated in US dollars, while its imports (which are mostly from neighbouring South Africa) are in rands. With the steady decline of the rand against the US dollar, Botswana has experienced improving terms of trade.

A further characteristic of mineral economies is the large rents which are typically generated by the production and sale of minerals. Rather than attempting to secure such rents through nationalization of mining companies, as was commonly the case elsewhere, Botswana has relied upon taxes, royalties, and free equity shares for the government, while leaving the operational control of mining companies in private hands. This strategy, which has been in place for a quarter of a century, resulted in joint ventures rather than state-owned firms and provided the private mining companies with an adequate rate of return on their capital and sufficient incentives to maintain and improve efficiency. Botswana's diamonds are produced by Debswana, a company owned 50:50 by De Beers of South Africa and the Botswana government. However the government's share of profits is between 75 and 80 per cent, and as Botswana is a large-scale, low-cost diamond producer, these profits are extremely large.[3] Diamond revenues have enabled the government to finance massive increases in social spending, especially on health and education, over the past twenty-five years.

Such a mechanism of redistribution is important; although the mineral sector accounts for over one-third of GDP, it tends to operate as both a physical and economic enclave with few direct links to the rest of the economy. The direct employment effect of mining is small, and there is little use of local inputs or processing of outputs.[4] Government is therefore the main linkage between the mineral sector and the rest of the economy. A key task has therefore been to ensure that these revenues are spent in ways which bring about sustainable and widely distributed benefits.

Substantial diamond revenues have been combined with prudent economic management and an absence of inefficient and unproductive spending, which ensured that Botswana did not suffer the same fate as some of the more profligate mineral exporters. Furthermore, Botswana has been characterized by macroeconomic stability—low and stable inflation, a strong currency, balance-of-payments surpluses, rising foreign exchange reserves, and government budget surpluses. In a further contrast with the rest of Sub-Saharan Africa, Botswana has avoided the conditionalities often associated with borrowing from the World Bank and the IMF.

Botswana's economic position has also been influenced by its membership in the Southern African Customs Union (SACU), along with South Africa, Lesotho, Swaziland, and Namibia. Whether SACU membership has yielded net benefits in economic terms is a debatable issue, but it has made major contributions to government revenues which were especially important in the early 1970s when the diamond industry was in its infancy. Botswana has enjoyed more economic independence from South Africa than do the other smaller members, especially since leaving the Rand Monetary Area in 1976, and has also experienced less of the desta-bilization (political, economic, and military) which South Africa inflicted on many countries in southern Africa during the apartheid years.

Improvements in social indicators

Table 4.1 summarizes overall trends in Botswana's economic and social indicators between 1970 and 1990 and compares these with the performance of Sub-Saharan Africa (SSA) over the period.[5] Botswana's rapid economic improvement was accom-panied by rapid social gains. Rapid growth in public spending supported the expan-sion of public-sector employment and there was associated growth in private employment, mainly in activities such as construction, trade, and services which were needed to spend the diamond revenues. Formal sector employment rose from 25,000 in 1965 to 230,000 in 1991. In tandem with rapid economic growth between 1970 and 1990 the under-5-mortality rate (U5MR) and the infant-mortality rate (IMR) were halved, life expectancy rose from 46 to 63 years, and adult literacy rates and primary school enrolments doubled. By the end of the period Botswana's U5MR of 56 per 1,000 live births was the second lowest in Sub-Saharan Africa. The crucial breakthrough period for both health and education—the achievement of almost universal primary education and of the most dramatic improvements in health indicators—appears to have been the first half of the 1980s, some fifteen years after major public investment programmes in these areas had begun.

According to the Human Development Index, Botswana ranked in seventy-sixth position in 1992 (UNDP, 1995), placing the country towards the top of the 'medium' Human Development category, the highest for any country in Sub-Saharan Africa. A particularly relevant comparison is with Gabon, a relatively rich oil producer with a population similar to Botswana. Gabon has been much less suc-cessful in translating its mineral wealth into social development, and achieves an HDI rank of 114 in the world.

Botswana's economic indicators confirm the significance of its plentiful financial resources in supporting development and providing financial stability. Between 1970 and 1990 there was a twentyfold increase in per capita government expendi-ture (in $US terms), much of which was for social provision. Over this period Botswana also received among the highest per capita levels of foreign aid in the world. As finance became less and less of a constraint over the course of the 1970s and early 1980s, the pace of development became limited by lack of absorption capacity due to shortages of qualified personnel. Botswana was still trying to catch up in terms of human resource development, as the impacts of efforts to expand education were only beginning to feed through in terms of an expanded, better-qualified human resource base. Having observed that spending in excess of absorp-tion capacity would lead to inflationary 'bottlenecks', government planners deliberately moderated the rate of development expenditure in relation to expected

TABLE 4.1. Selected economic and social indicators, 1970–1990

Indicator	Unit of measurement	Botswana			SSA average	
		1970	1980	1990	1970	1990
Foreign aid per capita	$US	15	68	129	—	32
Debt service ratio	debt servicing as % exports	1	2	4	5	14
Mineral revenue	% total govt revenue	0	34	54	—	—
Govt. expenditure per capita	% of per capita GDP	24	35	55	—	—
Under-5-mortality rate	mortality per 1,000 live births	147	109	56[e]	261	180[e]
Infant-mortality rate	mortality per 1,000 live births	100	71	43	144	103[e]
Life expectancy at birth	years	46[a]	56	62.5	41[a]	51[e]
Male adult literacy rate	% of adults	37	61	84	34	64
Female adult literacy rate	% of adults	44	61	65	17	44
Population	million	0.6	0.9	1.3	378[b]	510
Population growth rate	% per annum	3.1	3.7	3.5	2.7	3.0
Population density	persons per sq.km.	1	2	2	15	21
Total fertility rate	% per annum	6.9	7.1	5.3	6.6	6.5
Urbanization	% living in designated urban areas	11	18	24	16	28
Child immunization	% immunized at 1 year (measles)	<10[c]	56[c]	78	<10[c]	46
Secondary school enrolment	% of age-group (net)	7	16	43	6	17
Female primary education	female enrolment per 100 males	112	120	107	60	81
Female secondary education	female enrolment per 100 males	97	128	111	40	64
Under-5-malnutrition rate	% suffering from malnutrition	—	28	15	31[d]	31

Notes: [a] 1965 data; [b] 1973 data; [c] 1974; [d] 1975 data; [e] 1991 data

Sources: Republic of Botswana (1985, 1991); CSO (1991, 1994); CSO (various years), *Statistical Bulletin*; UNICEF (1991, 1993a, 1993b); World Bank (1993)

implementation capacity, contributing to substantial budget surpluses throughout the 1980s. The government's cautious approach to managing the budget led to a high level of savings and the accumulation of considerable international reserves; as a result Botswana experienced none of the debt service problems that constrained development in many African countries.

It is difficult to distinguish the relative importance of having sufficient financial resources and being able to put these resources to good use. Both factors represent necessary conditions for long-term success in development and both were generally fulfilled in Botswana's case. Elsewhere in Sub-Saharan Africa, the 1970s and 1980s were characterized by serious shortages of financial resources and/or by problems of weak, inefficient, and sometimes corrupt administrations. While Botswana was in a position to chart a path towards major and widespread social improvements, many of the other countries in Sub-Saharan Africa were not.

The country's rapid development also set in motion a series of social transformations, some that were anticipated by government development planning and some that were not. Rapid urbanization was among the most fundamental of these changes. At independence nearly all Botswana lived in rural areas, but by 1991 some 24 per cent lived in towns and a further 19 per cent lived in major villages of more than 10,000 persons. Such villages have become increasingly urban in character and are likely to be designated as towns in the near future. The concentration of formal sector jobs and social services in the capital, Gaborone, and in other emerging urban centres, was the main reason for rapid rural–urban migration. Gaborone grew from a population of less than 10,000 at independence to around 133,000 in 1991 (more than 10 per cent of the country's population).

While Botswana has performed considerably better than the rest of Sub-Saharan Africa in many aspects of economic and social development, the living standards of nearly half the population are still below the poverty line. Although child malnutrition was halved over the early 1980s, there was little additional improvement over the rest of the decade, and the national prevalence rate for moderate malnutrition continues to be about 15 per cent.

Recent research by UNICEF has suggested that, in spite of the enormous gains, Botswana could have accomplished even more in terms of improving child survival, maternal mortality, and other key social indicators. Based on observed historical relationships between economic growth and improvements in social indicators for all nations, it has been calculated that by 1992 Botswana's U5MR should have fallen to 33 per 1,000 live births instead of the level of 58 that was actually recorded (UNICEF, 1994a). The general lack of improvement in maternal mortality was also cited among the weaknesses in Botswana's performance. While this analysis suggests that Botswana has no grounds for complacency, it may also reflect some of the special difficulties associated with social development, not least the practical problems and higher provision costs associated with providing infrastructure in a vast, sparsely populated country with one-tenth the average population density of Sub-Saharan Africa. A further explanation may be that, the diamond windfall provided no automatic mechanism for distribution of benefits through mass participation in the country's new prosperity—as would have been the case if agriculture had provided the basis for growth (agriculture's share of GDP declined from 33 per cent in 1970 to only 5 per cent in 1990). This could only be achieved gradually through a combination of government interventions and through the indirect and lagged improvements in employment and incomes associated with rising demand for goods and services from government and eventually from the emerging private sector.[6]

A further threat to past achievements comes from AIDS. By 1993 it was estimated that some 92,000 people—or one person in six of Botswana's sexually active population—are infected with HIV. When the impact of AIDS on children and other dependants is taken into account, it is already certain that a substantial proportion of the population will directly experience loss and suffering due to AIDS. The situation is projected to worsen drastically over the remainder of the decade.

Expansion of social services

The improvements in social indicators were closely linked with its success in establishing basic social infrastructure and social services throughout the country. At independence there was a general lack of social services, both public and private. Most villages lacked basic social amenities such as schools, health facilities, and safe water supply. The lack of good roads and communications facilities represented a major obstacle to the provision of social services and limited the scope of economic activities that could be undertaken. After independence each of the country's development plans recognized that the provision of infrastructure and social services was of fundamental importance—both so that the benefits of development could be shared equitably among the population and because such provision was a prerequisite for development and diversification of the rural economy. From a political perspective, the provision of infrastructure and services was seen as an essential part of nation-building.

In view of the general lack of social provision at independence the task was necessarily slow, especially during the 1970s and early 1980s when shortages of qualified manpower represented a major implementation constraint. Nevertheless, over the course of two decades a network of broadly uniform social provision was established throughout the country. By 1990 nearly universal provision had been attained or virtually attained for access to safe water, health facilities, and primary education, while access to secondary education had risen rapidly. This was made possible because much of Botswana's development programme was devoted to construction of new facilities and establishing and expanding the institutional capacity to deliver services and manage the facilities. Table 4.2 provides a profile of how social infrastructure was transformed between 1970 and 1990. Hundreds of schools, health facilities, and village water supplies were built and put into operation. By 1990, nearly 3,000 km. of bitumen roads had been built, with the result that the country's national road network was more or less completed. A digital national telecommunications network system was in place, providing high quality links serving all the towns and larger villages.

The pattern of social investments suggests that, in overall terms, the government has attempted to improve social conditions for *all*. The society was comparatively free of ethnic and other divisions that might have led to social provision being manipulated in favour of certain groups.[7] Since most people lacked social services at independence it would have been difficult to justify providing for some and not for others. Furthermore, the rural power base of the ruling party has meant that the worst excesses of urban bias have been avoided.

In spite of the general intention to spread social services evenly throughout the country, recent studies have shown that the poorest and worst-off in society have experienced greater difficulty in taking advantage of these. Disaggregated data from the 1991 national census show that key problems such as child and maternal

TABLE 4.2. Improvements in social infrastructure

	Units	1970	1980	1990
Education				
Primary schools	number	282	415	602
Secondary schools	number	13[a]	38	143
Health				
Health posts	number	—	200[c]	308
Clinics	number	—	123[c]	170
Transport				
Roads—bitumen	km '000s	<0.1	1.1	2.7
Motor vehicle ownership	'000 vehicles in use	6	32	81
Communications				
Telecommunications	'000s of connected subscribers	—	6.5	22
Postal offices and agencies	number	33[b]	—	165
Power				
Electricity consumption	kwh millions	39[a]	473	990

Notes: [a] 1971 data; [b] 1957 data; [c] 1972 data

Sources: Republic of Botswana (1985, 1991); CSO (1991); CSO (various years), *Statistical Bulletin*

mortality and failure of children to attend school are more prevalent in poorer, more remote areas. The existence of such problems suggests that even a well-intended strategy of universal provision will eventually experience limitations unless special efforts are made to address the special problems of the worst-off.

Economic growth created the capacity for the State to expand its budgets to meet the demand for social services. However, the mere availability of finance does not explain Botswana's success in expanding social infrastructure and service provision. At least as important was the system of national development plans and budgetary control, under the auspices of the ministry of finance and development planning (MFDP), that provided a strong framework for ensuring that expenditure proposals were consistent with long-term objectives; and that they were individually scrutinized and controlled. This led to a general pattern of well-chosen strategic investments based on a system of planning targets that were regularly reviewed and updated.

There can be little doubt that only the government could have had the resources and institutional capacity to provide basic public social services for all. At independence people's incomes were so low that most could not afford to pay more than a token amount towards social provision. For this reason there was little private market for social services and there were few competent private service providers.

By the 1980s and 1990s rising incomes, as was seen over a similar period in Mauritius and parts of South-East Asia, had given rise to sharp growth in discretionary spending and a related emergence of private-sector suppliers of goods and services. By 1990 the wealthier part of society could usually choose between using public services or paying for private-sector provision. The most notable examples were in health and education, where there was a proliferation of private schools and private health care. Private provision represents a widening of choice and can contribute in terms of setting standards of efficiency and reducing dependency upon government over the longer term. However, since private provision is generally both of high cost and high standard compared with the public social services, it also highlights the inequalities between the rich who can afford these and the poor who cannot.

Poverty in Botswana

The results of two large-scale Household Income and Expenditure Surveys in 1985–6 and 1993–4 (Central Statistics Office, 1988 and 1995; BIDPA, 1996) provide evidence regarding poverty and income distribution in Botswana (key results are summarized in Table 4.3). The more recent survey found that poverty remains widespread, in that 38 per cent of households had incomes below the poverty line,[8] and that these households contained 47 per cent of the population. Furthermore, most of these poor households were severely poor, in that their reported incomes did not even cover the food component of the poverty line. Nationally, 23 per cent of households and 30 per cent of individuals fell into this category of severe poverty. Despite rapid urbanization, and concerns about rising unemployment, poverty in Botswana remains a largely rural phenomenon. Poverty affected 48 per cent of rural households and only 23 per cent of urban households, with the large 'urban villages' falling in between.

The two surveys do show, however, that that there has been a significant improvement in the poverty situation between the mid-1980s and the mid-1990s. Both household and individual poverty rates have declined by about 12 per cent. Furthermore, this decline has mostly been amongst very poor rural households. As this is the largest single poverty group in Botswana (in terms of numbers of households and individuals), this result is encouraging, as it suggests that the policies and economic processes that have caused the decline in poverty have been well targeted. Urban poverty remained largely unchanged, and much less severe than rural poverty. The survey data also indicate that female-headed households are more prone to poverty than male-headed households, and that this is due to the former having more dependants, less access to paid employment, and greater dependence upon remittances and transfers.

Income distribution data tells a similar story: inequality remains high, but is declining. The national Gini coefficient (on a per person basis) was 0.56 in 1993–4, compared to 0.54 in 1985–6. In 1993–4, the richest 20 per cent of the population received 59 per cent of total disposable income, whereas the poorest 40 per cent

TABLE 4.3. Botswana Poverty rates: headcount ratio, 1985–86 and 1993–94

	Total poor		Poor[a]		Very poor[b]	
	1985–6	1993–4	1985–6	1993–4	1985–6	1993–4
A. Households						
Urban	23	23	15	16	7	7
Urban villages	49	36	17	14	31	22
Rural	60	48	16	16	44	33
Total	49	38	16	15	33	23
B. Individuals						
Urban	30	29	20	19	10	9
Urban villages	58	46	20	17	38	29
Rural	68	55	17	16	51	40
Total	59	47	18	17	41	30

[a] Poor: income below the PDL; [b] very poor: income below the food component of the PDL

Source: BIDPA (1996)

received only 12 per cent of income. These income shares are comparable with those in Zimbabwe, and slightly more equal than those in South Africa, Tanzania, and Kenya.

One compensating factor for the poor is the relatively high level of 'social provision' including education, health care, and clean water available to virtually all of the population either free or heavily subsidized. In 1993 government social spending averaged approximately P5,300 ($US2,300) per family. This social income (which does not include expenditure on roads, water supplies, etc.) is very high relative to the income (cash and in kind) of the poor.[9] Although social spending is not distributed equally across the population, it can be safely assumed that it is distributed much more equally than incomes generally.

Nevertheless, the level of poverty remains high for a country which has experienced such economic success, and it would be fair to conclude that Botswana's development strategy has proved more effective in improving services and general conditions than in alleviating poverty. Experience between 1966 and 1990 lends some weight to the proposition that developing countries—especially those with mineral-dependent economies—tend to become more unequal before they become less unequal (Lewis, 1981). Although government has invested considerable resources in rural areas—particularly in health, education, infrastructure provision, and various subsidy schemes—this has not prevented the growing disparities in incomes and living standards between the poorer rural areas and the increasingly prosperous urban areas. Poverty remains widespread in rural areas, primarily as a result of the limited ability to generate adequate incomes from arable agriculture in the face of recurrent drought. But there is also a lack of alternative sources of earned income. Many rural areas where three-quarters of the population lived in 1990, are remote from the major population centres, which reduces the potential for alternative forms of economic activity. Essential infrastructure such as electricity and telephones is only slowly being extended to rural areas, and there is also a lack of raw materials on which to base productive activity. As a result, many rural households are increasingly dependent upon remittances from relatives in towns and on government transfer payments.

While sustainable means of alleviating poverty have so far proved elusive, the government can claim credit for having established a fairly comprehensive system of drought monitoring and drought-relief programmes that have helped to ensure that nobody dies of starvation during drought. During the drought of the mid-1980s, more than half of the population was assisted through drought-relief programmes, including universal food rations and widespread labour-intensive works programmes providing cash-earning opportunities. Food rations were distributed to all children, pregnant and nursing mothers, and other vulnerable groups through schools and clinics, such that during the 1992 drought year, 464,000 people—out of a population of 1.3 million—were being fed daily. In addition, some 63,000 people were employed by district councils on public-works projects such as the maintenance of rural roads. The aim (largely achieved) of these drought-relief schemes was to counteract the negative impact of subsistence crop failure on household food supplies and to provide some income to rural families so that replacement food supplies could be purchased. Over the course of the 1980s and early 1990s the drought-relief programmes seem to have become established on a more-or-less permanent basis and may increasingly represent Botswana's social safety net in all but name. Although such programmes have been largely successful in preventing starvation and keeping malnutrition to low levels, they have had the unfortunate impact of generating a high level of dependence upon government welfare provision.

Sectoral Policies

Health

Primary health-care
Public health has been one of the main focuses of social development and social investment in Botswana. At independence, the small hospital-based health service was incapable of serving more than a tiny minority of the population. In 1973 the government adopted a primary health care (PHC) strategy based on establishing decentralized provision through a countrywide network of clinics, health posts, and mobile stops, supported by hospitals and other tertiary-level health ser-

vices.[10] This emphasized equity, intersectoral collaboration, and community involvement, and provision of health services which were appropriate, accessible, and affordable. By 1978 a basic network was in place; by the early 1980s the objective of having a health facility in every village of more than 500 people was close to being met; by 1985 more than 80 per cent of the population was within 15 km. of a health facility.

Once the basic PHC network was functioning, the emphasis of further improvements in public health necessarily shifted towards sustaining the existing health system, overcoming existing weaknesses and gaps, and improving its quality. In the Seventh National Development Plan the government adopted health for all (HFA) by the year 2000 as its overall objective for the health sector. HFA sets a new and higher target for public health, seeking not merely to provide services but to assure every Batswana of the 'level of health that allows him/her to lead an economically and socially productive life' (Republic of Botswana, 1991).

While three decades of rapid development have been sufficient to establish a wide coverage of adequately resourced health facilities, it has taken longer to establish sufficient human resources to enable more rapid improvements in the quality of health services. In many instances, it has also proved easier to invest in expansion than to bring about the changes in people's knowledge, attitudes, and practices about health and hygiene services that are fundamental to the prevention of health problems and if people are to make good use of health services.

Child health has benefited from the general expansion of health services, as well as the continuous drought-related monitoring of the nutritional status of the under-5s. Nevertheless, child-mortality rates in rural areas are significantly higher than in urban areas, partly reflecting the greater difficulty associated with improving health among and within the more remote and disadvantaged portion of the population. By the early 1990s it was becoming evident that Botswana needed to develop more sophisticated approaches to identifying and assisting the worst-off, since it was clear that they were not benefiting as much as others from the general improvements in public health.

The growth in health services around the country enabled Botswana to rapidly expand immunization of children and to achieve universal child immunization during the mid-1980s (80 per cent coverage of all children against six diseases). By the early 1990s, concerns over child immunization focused increasingly on future sustainability. The expanded programme on immunization (EPI) during the 1980s had required a considerable multisectoral effort, particularly to identify those children who had not been immunized. This effort will have to be continued and expanded in the future if the growing numbers of additional children requiring immunization are to be reached. In spite of ongoing training and staff development activities there were concerns that implementation capacity may be strained in the future.

AIDS

The government's main response to the AIDS pandemic has been through the national AIDS control programme (NACP), established in 1987. The NACP serves as the lead agency for managing AIDS control and prevention activities, and is run by the ministry of health. In addition, NGOs such as the YWCA and the Botswana Red Cross have been involved in AIDS activities since the late 1980s. In spite of the increasingly vigorous and professionally run public-education programmes, the task of promoting changes in sexual attitudes and practices has proved to be difficult and slow, and the rate of HIV transmission is alarming. In 1993 some 90 per cent of people were believed to be aware of how HIV is transmitted, but this knowledge about AIDS had not led to widespread adoption of safe-sex practices. With a substantial proportion of the population already infected with HIV, Botswana is clearly entering a period of human and economic catastrophe. In order to deal with this catastrophe and contain the spread of AIDS, government and the wider society face an enormous and urgent challenge to bring about changes in sexual attitudes and practices.

Water and sanitation

Because of its scarcity, water supply is of particular significance to most aspects of human survival, settlement, and economic activity in Botswana. At independence there was a lack of hydrological information and limited capacity for drilling boreholes. No major dams had yet been developed. As a result, water development was given early priority, both as a basic means of improving living standards and as a necessary enabling investment to support other development. A major programme of groundwater drilling provided the means of providing water supply in rural areas. Major dams were developed to provide safe water supplies as an integral part of the development and expansion of urban centres.

By the early 1990s the task of providing universal access to safe water had been largely completed; 89 per cent of the country's population had access to safe water from piped supplies, boreholes, and wells, with 77 per cent coverage in rural areas and 100 per cent coverage in urban areas. The task of pioneering new water resources was by then giving way to the challenge of running the existing water supplies effectively and efficiently, expanding these in response to population growth, and trying to address the remaining gaps in rural provision. To try to guide these efforts the government prepared a National Water Master Plan in 1991 which sets out an overall framework for the water sector well into the next century. One key problem is that the existing gaps in rural provision mainly concern smaller, more remote settlements where the costs of provision are much higher and where there are sometimes risks that expensive investments may become underutilized or redundant through future migration to larger villages and towns. The option of encouraging people to settle in larger settlements has been pursued through the

National Settlement Policy, which sought to limit social-infrastructure investments to villages of at least 500 persons. But according to current trends in population and settlement there can be little doubt that many smaller, more remote settlements will remain for many years.

In comparison with the water sector, the task of increasing access to adequate sanitation was started later and proved to be slower. Between 1981 and 1991 the proportion of households with access to sanitation rose from 36 per cent to 55 per cent, increasing from 79 to 91 per cent in urban areas and from 25 per cent to 41 per cent in rural areas. The relatively high standards adopted for the new urban areas ensured virtually universal access to sanitation in urban areas. However, it was not until the late 1970s that the government began to develop a programme to improve rural sanitation, focusing on the construction of latrines by rural households on a subsidized, self-help basis. Recent studies suggest that the programme has not been particularly effective, and that the initial emphasis on subsidized latrine construction was flawed. The levels of subsidy were high and there were various technical and organizational problems with taking direct government intervention to the level of construction at household level. Moreover, subsidies did little to encourage people to use latrines properly or to adopt the health and hygiene practices needed if latrines are to make a contribution to improved public health. Because of these problems, government has been revising its strategy for rural sanitation, with the intention of concentrating greatest resources on health education in order to assist people to adopt sound health and hygiene practices and to encourage people to provide their own sanitation facilities with some technical advice from the government (along with limited subsidized provision for the worst-off). This strategy appears to have better prospects for widening sanitation coverage but may initially prove difficult to implement, not least because it will take time for councils to make the major change from running a household-level construction programme to providing community-level health education.

Education

In 1966 about 75,000 or half of Botswana's children of primary-school age were enrolled at school. The quality of education was poor and most children did not complete primary level. Secondary education had commenced only two decades previously and there were but 1,531 students enrolled in secondary schools. Faced with an acute shortage of people to run the civil service, government briefly gave greater priority to secondary education in the late 1960s. But by the early 1970s the expansion of primary education became top priority. By providing primary education in all parts of the country, the government sought to assure all children an equal start in life. By 1979 government adopted the overall objective of reaching universal primary education (UPE). With considerable support from foreign donors, government undertook major primary school construction programmes during the 1970s and 1980s. Enrolment was further boosted by the decision to cut primary school fees by half in 1973 and then to abolish them in 1980. By the late 1980s considerable progress had therefore been made toward UPE, although a minority of children were still not enrolled.

Education development shifted towards the expansion of secondary education during the early 1980s, in order to deal with the problem of low progression rates from primary schools. The number of junior secondary schools was rapidly expanded, and secondary-school fees were abolished in 1988. By 1991, the transition rate from primary school to junior secondary was 65 per cent, and Botswana was well on the way towards attaining the objective of providing nine years of basic education for all children (seven years of primary and two years of secondary).

To provide for equality in primary and secondary education a broadly uniform standard for government schools was established throughout the country, and the government retained centralized control over the allocation of teachers to ensure that more remote schools received their fair share of trained teachers. Government also supplied teachers and recurrent funding support to non-government, community-based junior secondary schools in order to raise standards of teaching to be more comparable with government schools. Most barriers to access were removed by making education free for all Botswana up to tertiary level. In 1990, the government directly financed 568 of the 636 primary schools and 169 of the 170 secondary schools, as well as most tertiary-level education, vocational training, and teacher training.

Another important accomplishment is the high level of female participation in primary and junior secondary schools. In terms of total enrolment girls now outnumber boys, with the balance expected to shift towards equal numbers of boys and girls over the next decade. The main explanation for the high female enrolment is probably that the main agricultural activity—cattle-rearing—is an exclusively male preserve, and young males are often kept out of school in order to work as herdboys. Although arable agriculture tends to be the responsibility of women, this sector is rapidly diminishing in importance. With free education, there is no reason for female children to be kept out of school.

In spite of its success, the rapid expansion of education coverage also placed considerable strain on the capacity of the education system and has given rise to blindspots in coverage and weaknesses in quality. Problems with the quality of basic education were the major focus of the 1993 National Commission for Education (Republic of Botswana, 1993).

Among the most critical quality problems are: problems associated with the language of instruction, particularly for minority groups for whom Setswana is not the first language; problems with the quality of teaching, including shortages of qualified teachers, the low entry requirement for teaching (especially at primary-school level), the relevance of existing teacher training, and problems of attitudes and motivation among some teachers.

The other major problem is the children who stay out of school. In 1991 some 17 per cent of children aged 7 to 13 years were still not attending school. Certain disadvantaged groups faced greater problems of access and others had special problems that caused them to drop out. These included children living in more remote areas, children from urban poor communities, and children who drop out of school for various reasons (this group includes teenage mothers and street children).

Improved access to education has been an important factor in improving the status of women in Botswana society. While adult female literacy is still below that of males, the gap is narrowing; and women comprise an estimated 62 per cent of participants in adult-education programmes. At the primary and secondary school levels, Botswana is one of the few countries where female enrolment exceeds male enrolment: as a percentage of male enrolment, female enrolment is 106 per cent at primary-school level and 109 per cent at secondary-school level. At that point, however, female enrolment drops sharply. The number of women receiving tertiary education is only 58 per cent of the number of men—with obvious implications for women's ability to reach higher positions in public and private employment. One of the main reasons for lower participation is pregnancy. Another reason is poor school performance, especially in mathematics and science. As a consequence, women are grossly underrepresented among science and mathematics teachers at the secondary level and in technology/science-based employment. The roots of gender bias in education are probably in the home, where the socialization process patterns the child to accept gender stereotypes, and are reinforced at the community and school levels.

Nutrition and household food security

Nutrition

Improving the nutritional well-being of its people has been a fundamental concern of the government. Investments in health facilities throughout the country provided the basic means for trying to identify and address nutrition problems. The establishment of the National Nutrition Surveillance System (NNSS) in 1978 introduced regular monitoring of the nutritional status of pre-school children attending clinics, thereby enabling rapid and representative nutritional assessments to be carried out, particularly as part of the early-warning system for drought. During drought, people's nutritional well-being was protected by a blanket supplementary feeding programme. The under-5-malnutrition rate fell from 28 per cent in 1980 to 15 per cent in 1990.

Food security

Botswana's problems of food insecurity are inherent in its poor potential for agriculture. Food crop production is limited to the four main crops of maize, sorghum, millet, and beans/pulses. Altogether, these food crops account for less than one-third of total agricultural output—with livestock accounting for two-thirds. Even in years of good rainfall, Botswana is able to produce less than half of the food needed, and in drought years this can fall to 10 per cent or less. Food self-sufficiency has never therefore been a realistic policy, and the emphasis is on achieving food security at both the national and household level.

The food-grain shortfall has been met from commercial imports and from food aid, with the latter gradually declining in importance as the economy prospered. The improvements in roads and other infrastructure and the growth of a relatively well-developed retail network has helped to ensure most parts of the country with a reliable supply of food commodities. In addition government has progressively established a network of strategic grain reserves to ensure timely availability of food in more remote areas at times of drought emergency.

While national food security has been assured by Botswana's wealth, this has not solved the problem of household food insecurity. It is common for rural households to produce inadequate amounts of food for their own needs—even during non-drought years—and poor families may lack the money to obtain their remaining needs through purchases. No estimates are available of the precise extent of household food insecurity in Botswana but, given the fact that almost half of the population falls below the poverty line, a large number of households are likely to be food insecure, particularly in the rural areas.

Drought

Drought years have been common since independence, with drought declared in 1968–70, 1974–5, 1979–80, 1981–7, and 1990–4. Despite (or perhaps because of) the frequency of drought, Botswana has been successful in protecting vulnerable groups during drought periods. The government's contribution towards the cost of drought-relief and recovery programmes over the 1981–7 period was P440m., equivalent to between 3 and 4 per cent of GDP. This was matched by a considerable contribution from foreign donors. In a decade of almost continuous drought, no one was believed to have died from starvation or lack of water. A permanent and effective supplementary-feeding scheme successfully stabilized nutritional status, and government-financed labour-intensive public-works schemes (such as rural road maintenance) aimed to replace lost agricultural income.

The evaluation study of the drought-relief and recovery programme between 1981–2 and 1987–8 was a major turning-point in terms of policy, planning, and implementation of drought-relief activities in Botswana. The policy directions that have guided the current relief.programme seek to incorporate drought preparedness into the long-term development programme, thereby reducing the need to mount a separate large-scale relief programme in the event of drought. But much needs to be done to improve targeting—particularly in the selection of participants in the labour-intensive public works and in the provision of subsidies for agricultural relief—in order to improve programme effectiveness in addressing the needs of the poor.

Although the drought-relief programmes have succeeded in keeping people alive, there has been little success with programmes aimed at permanently reducing future vulnerability to drought. Most of the beneficiaries of drought relief return to a life of poverty when the drought ends and drought-relief programmes are stopped, and indeed many now live under worse conditions in non-drought years. There is evidence that the poor are actually becoming more exposed to drought in that losses of cattle during drought years have been concentrated among owners of small herds. The livelihood of hunter-gatherers and poor communal farmers has been further marginalized by the problems of land degradation and desertification which have been associated with drought and are often linked with inadequate range-management practices and encroachment on to communal lands by commercial cattle farmers.

The 1990 evaluation of drought relief found the effects of drought on the poor and the ramifications of poverty to be intimately related in that the poorest are the most vulnerable to drought and least able to recover from it afterward (Food Studies Group, 1990). It is also recognized that, in order to limit the dimensions of dependency on government and encourage self-reliance wherever possible, drought relief should generally be provided in the form of employment-based schemes, such as labour-intensive public works rather than 'hand-outs'. In the long term, only the diversification of income-generating opportunities in the rural areas will reduce the impact of recurring drought.

Politics, Institutions, and the Policy Framework

Politics, culture, and development

Botswana's political history since independence has been somewhat exceptional by African standards. In common with most countries, independence was preceded by a multiparty election and a Western-style constitution, but it is more unusual that these are retained after that time. The political process in Botswana has been for the most part democratic, with regular free elections and a range of political parties both within and outside parliament. There is a reasonably free and independent press, no political prisoners, and in general a culture of openness and consultation, albeit with some shortcomings. The society is also relatively free of corruption.

The political scene is dominated by the Botswana Democratic Party (BDP), which has won every election since 1964. General elections are held every five years, and although there have been some instances of electoral irregularities, these have been relatively minor and the electoral process is accepted as being generally free and fair. Certainly the continued domination of the BDP appears to reflect the popular will, in that it has consistently won an absolute majority of the vote.

Nevertheless its share of the vote has been falling consistently, and in the most recent elections (October 1994) the main opposition party—the Botswana National Front (BNF)—made substantial gains.

Botswana's political stability has enabled the implementation of a consistent set of development policies over a long period of time. The open political process, coupled with a tradition of consultation and the securing of a consensus for major decisions, has also contributed to continuity and stability, and a relative lack of corruption. Botswana's general legal framework draws upon the broad democratic culture, emphasizing the rule of law, delegation of authority, freedom of speech, and the right to own private property. This was an essential foundation for the growth in private investment, including investment in the health and education sectors.

Although there are clear positive links between the nature of Botswana's political process and its relatively successful economic and social development, the question naturally arises as to why Botswana's experience differs so much from most of the rest of Sub-Saharan Africa. Below we attempt to identify some of the complex interrelationships which have contributed to the sustainability of Botswana's political economy.

Traditional society in the region now comprising Botswana was organized around a system of tribal chieftainship which incorporated both democratic and authoritarian elements. Although chiefs wielded considerable power, major decisions were taken by the *kgotla*, a meeting of all men (later extended to include women) in the community. The system incorporated both local government, through the ward system within settlements, and centralized authority at the level of the tribe and its senior chief. There was no national authority, but a number of Batswana tribes in the region fringing the Kgalagadi shared a common Setswana language and culture, into which a number of smaller, non-Batswana tribes had been incorporated over time. Relations between the Batswana tribes were largely harmonious, although members of some of the minor tribes occupied a socially inferior status to their Batswana overlords. This social harmony has largely persisted through to the present day, with Botswana emerging from the colonial period as a nation based around a single language and ethnic group, providing the foundation for a general consensus in government planning and in the wider society that everyone should enjoy the benefits of the country's development.

An important factor contributing to post-independence stability has been the dominant role of the ruling BDP, which enjoyed support throughout the country under the leadership of Botswana's first president, Sir Seretse Khama. Given its widespread support, and its ability to win democratic elections with ease, it had no real need to embark upon the kind of repressive policies followed by governments elsewhere in Africa in order to maintain its dominant position. The BDP drew much of its support from the traditional system and the chiefs (*dikgosi*). Besides enabling it to draw upon the democratic elements of the traditional system and the respect which *dikgosi* enjoyed among the population, this also meant that its policies were based more upon pragmatism than those of some of the more radical nationalist and socialist parties which came to power in other African States and which also competed for power in the pre- and post-independence elections in Botswana.

The small size and underdeveloped state of the private sector in Botswana at independence meant that the government had to play a leading role in a wide range of activities, including not just the provision of economic and social infrastructure (roads, water, health services, education, etc.) but also stimulating the development of productive activities in agriculture, manufacturing, and mining. Due to the lack of skilled personnel and resources, this had to be done in partnership with the private sector, and more specifically with foreign companies. Instead of nationalization, Botswana aimed to attract private foreign investment, if necessary through joint ventures (for instance with the state-owned Botswana Development Corporation). Even in joint ventures the private partner retained operational control, and in general the economic and legal environment was one where private companies could operate reasonably freely, with, for instance, few restrictions on the repatriation of profits overseas.

Given its origins, the BDP had (and still has) most of its power base in the rural areas, and to a certain extent amongst the new élite of the public and private sectors. An important component of its power base are the large-scale cattle-owners, a group which includes many government ministers, senior civil servants and businessmen, as well as professional farmers. As a consequence of the BDP's rural power base, the rural areas have not been unduly excluded from the overall process of allocation of developmental resources—indeed, in many respects they have benefited from social and economic investment at a much higher cost per capita than have those living in the urban areas. Government policies have not therefore exhibited the urban bias apparent in many developing countries, which is the cause of much economic and social insecurity in rural areas.

The lack of skills at independence also meant that the country was heavily reliant upon expatriates to carry out key roles in both the public and private sectors. Subsequent heavy investment in education and training has rapidly increased the supply of skilled citizen personnel and enabled significant localization, but rapid economic growth and hence expansion of the economy has also meant that the number and range of skilled personnel required has continued to rise sharply. As a result there remains a significant number of posts occupied by expatriates. While the absolute number of expatriates has continued to rise (12,500 non-citizens were employed in 1992, compared to 5,300 in 1973), their proportion of the employed labour force has fallen steadily, from 12 per cent to 6 per cent, over this twenty-year period. Although localization has been an important component of Botswana's overall development strategy, it has been an important principle that localization does not occur until a suitably skilled or experienced citizen is available.

It is also important to acknowledge the inevitable impact of the racist policies pursued in neighbouring South Africa. Many Batswana were educated and worked in South Africa, and given their experiences there it is probably not surprising that Botswana's leaders were opposed to racism and discrimination of any type. Their development philosophy was based on the principles of democracy and social justice for all people, regardless of race, class, or ethnic background. Owing to the mistrust that they had of their neighbours in both the south and the north (the former Rhodesia), they also espoused the objectives of economic independence and self-reliance which they perceived as key vehicles for developing Botswana's political identity and sustaining a multiracial society. The details of each of these goals were worked out and refined in successive national-development plans. Moreover, in a small ethnically homogeneous population it is easier both to generate a consensus and to be responsive to the range of needs and demands which are articulated. Secondly, as the proceeds of a given mineral wealth (i.e. the value of Botswana's diamonds) have to be shared among a small population, on a per capita basis, mineral revenues are relatively great. A related point is that although some special-interest groups with influence in government—most notably cattle farmers—have arguably benefited from government spending to a greater extent than could be justified in economic terms, the cost of this has still been small in relation to the total amount of resources available and has not led to *serious* inefficiencies.

Finally, it is worth noting that as a result of living on the margins of a desert with all of the climatic and ecological uncertainties that accompany such an existence, many aspects of people's behaviour in Botswana are highly risk-averse. This is evident at an individual level, where much of the rural population has diversified its income sources in response to endemic drought, so as to reduce the risk associated with dependence upon unreliable agriculture. It is also evident at a national level, where macroeconomic policy has been to conserve mineral revenues rather than spend them at all costs, thereby building up savings (in the form of foreign exchange reserves) which can therefore cushion the inevitable fluctuations in earnings which result from such a high degree of dependence upon a single primary commodity export.

Social policy framework

At the broad level, government is guided by four objectives in planning national development (Republic of Botswana, 1991): sustained development; rapid economic growth; economic independence; and social justice. The need to devote substantial resources to social spending in order to pursue these objectives has long been recognized, especially given the lack of social investment prior to independence. Translating these broad needs into specific projects and expenditure proposals takes place within the framework of national-development plans (NDPs). These have been in operation since independence (the current NDP is the seventh); each lasts six years, with a midterm review after three years. Linking the broad national development objectives with the NDPs are a number of policy frameworks which set out broad priorities and plans over a longer period than individual NDPs.

These policy frameworks address specific areas, such as education, rather than social policy as a whole. Social development has generally been based on either sectoral and subsectoral policies or on simple and often pragmatic sets of principles or aims such as the adoption of a primary health-care strategy, universal primary education, and universal access to health facilities and safe water (in settlements over 500 persons). During the 1970s and early 1980s the task of establishing basic levels of social provision throughout the country was enormous in relation to annual implementation capacity, so that for many years the emphasis of sectoral policies was on expansion of coverage.

The absence of an overall social policy often meant that social development was shaped by a series of weakly co-ordinated programmes of expanding provision and has sometimes suffered from the lesser attention given to issues of quality and strategy. In education, considerable emphasis was given to educating people to reduce national shortages of qualified and trained people and to reduce the need to employ expatriates. Apart from the non-formal education programme (which has been under-resourced and did not commence until the late 1970s), education's social value was not the subject of much debate within the government. Education came to be seen as the route to formal sector employment by both government and society.

However, by the late 1980s and 1990s the long struggle towards universal basic provision had been accomplished in most social sector activities. In the absence of a solid framework of social policies this meant that government was suddenly beset with problems over the nature, quality, and effectiveness of the basic services it was providing. Since most people now had access, there was a gradual shift in popular demands from quantity to quality—particularly in education and health—and in many instances quality was found to be wanting.

Financing Social Development

Introduction

Botswana's achievements in the field of social development have been facilitated by rapidly growing government revenues over the past twenty years, which have in turn enabled significant increases in public expenditure. At independence, however, the budgetary position was highly unfavourable. The whole of development expenditure, and a half of recurrent expenditure, was dependent upon British aid, and the general assessment of poor economic prospects for the country suggested that there was little prospect of any significant improvement in the budgetary situation in the short to medium term (UK, 1960; Republic of Botswana, 1966). In the first five years after independence, the emphasis of public spending was on infra-structure and development of newly discovered mineral resources (not the social sectors), reflecting both the urgent need to promote economic growth and the interests and influence of aid donors.

From the early 1970s, the situation was transformed following improvements in the government's revenue position, resulting from the renegotiation of the Southern African Customs Union Agreement in 1969, the development of the minerals sector, and successful efforts to attract aid from a wider variety of bilateral and multilateral sources. These factors enabled a balancing of the recurrent budget by 1972[11] and an overall budget surplus by 1983. They also enabled much greater resources to be devoted to social provision.

Public revenue and expenditure[12]

The ratio of public expenditure to GDP is often taken to indicate the magnitude of the State's role in the economy. In Botswana it has fluctuated around an upward trend, reaching 44 per cent in 1992 compared to 31 per cent in 1976, and averaging 35 per cent over the twenty years from 1976 to 1995. This is a relatively high figure by both global and African standards. It partly reflects Botswana's status as a mineral-led economy, in which a high proportion of GDP represents mineral rents accruing to the government. Public spending has grown faster than the economy as a whole, as indicated by its rising share in GDP. Whereas the average annual rate of economic growth over the period 1976 to 1991 was 10.7 per cent, public spending grew on average by 13 per cent a year in real terms.

Allocation of public expenditure

Real expenditure on health and education was roughly constant between 1967 and 1971, and falling as a share of total government expenditure.[13] From 1972 on, however, expenditure on health and education began to rise sharply in real terms, and their combined share of total public spending rose from 10 per cent in 1972 to 22 per cent in 1976.

Between 1976 and 1995, the broad pattern of public expenditure has remained fairly consistent, although there have been substantial fluctuations from year to year. General services and defence account for some 25 per cent of the total, social services around 35 per cent, and economic services just over 30 per cent. However, some trends can be detected: a steady increase in the share accounted for by defence spending, a small increase in that of social spending, and a fall in the shares of general services and economic services.

Social expenditure[14] (see Figs. 4.1 and 4.2, and Table 4.4) has accounted for between 30 and 40 per cent of total public spending, and has on average grown by 11 per cent a year in real terms, slightly faster than public spending as a whole. By 1995 total social spending was more than seven times higher in real terms than in

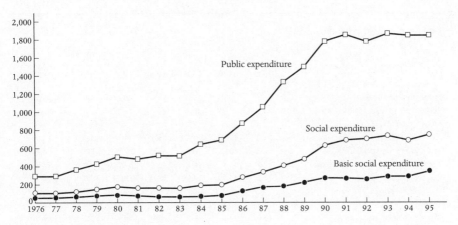

Fig. 4.1 Real expenditure, Botswana

Source: MFDP

1976. This increase has been much faster than the rate of population growth (approximately 3.4 per cent a year during the 1980s) and therefore the level of real social expenditure per capita has risen sharply—from P130 per person in 1976 to P486 in 1995 (at 1985 prices). Although this represents an average figure and not all families benefit to the same degree, the distribution of social income is more equal than that of wealth or cash income. Given the relatively high penetration of education and health services into the rural areas, social spending does make a significant difference in the quality of life of those who are otherwise below the poverty line. Social expenditure in Botswana accounts for over 17 per cent of GDP, a relatively high figure by international standards.

Allocation of social expenditure

Education has consistently accounted for the largest single share (typically between 45 and 55 per cent) of total social spending, and a very large share (around 17–18 per cent) of total public spending. This reflects a number of factors, including the lack of pre-independence educational development, a severe shortage of skilled personnel and resulting dependence on expatriates, and the desire to enhance citizens' opportunities for employment or self-employment.

Health has accounted for between 10 and 20 per cent of social spending and between 4 and 5 per cent of total spending. These proportions are not unusual by international standards, but because public spending in Botswana is so high, the result is very high levels of education and health spending per person ($US290 in 1994), far exceeding the level found in most other developing countries.

Total spending on schools, hospitals, and clinics—directed to improving the basic health and education aspects of quality of life—can be classified as basic social

TABLE 4.4. Social expenditure ratios

	1976	1980	1985	1990	1995	Average 1976–95	1985–MR[a]
Social exp./public exp.	36.4	34.4	30.6	35.9	40.6	35.0	36.2
Health and ed. exp./public exp.	23.3	23.4	20.3	20.6	28.1	22.5	22.4
Public exp./GDP	30.8	35.3	29.7	42.1	—	35.5	39.0
Social exp./GDP	11.2	12.2	9.1	15.1	—	12.3	14.0
Health and ed. exp./GDP	7.2	8.2	6.0	8.7	—	7.8	8.4
Basic social exp./total social exp.	48.7	50.0	48.0	43.8	46.7	46.9	44.7
Basic social exp./public exp.	17.7	17.2	14.7	15.7	19.0	16.0	16.1
Basic social exp./GDP	5.5	6.1	4.4	6.6	—	5.7	6.1
Health/total social exp.	15.9	13.3	14.5	11.3	12.7	13.8	13.2
Education/total social exp.	48.0	54.6	51.6	46.0	56.4	50.5	49.0
Housing/total social exp.	29.6	27.0	21.8	38.2	25.1	27.3	29.1
Other social exp./total social exp.	6.4	5.2	12.0	4.5	5.7	8.3	8.8
Per capita expenditure, real growth (%)							
Public expenditure		15.4	4.4	14.9	−3.0		
Social expenditure		16.1	2.7	25.9	4.3		
Basic social expenditure		13.4	16.1	14.9	18.0		

[a] MR: most recent

Source: Ministry of Finance and Development Planning (MFDP)

spending.[15] Between the mid-1970s and the late 1980s this accounted for around 50 per cent of total social expenditure and 17 per cent of public spending, reflecting the intense effort devoted to ensuring that all of the population had access to basic education and health care. Most of this expenditure went towards the construction and staffing of primary schools, clinics, and health posts. Now that the great majority of the population has access to such facilities the proportion of basic social expenditure is expected to fall.

In recent years, the allocation of social spending has shifted towards the provision of housing and the development of infrastructure in towns and major villages, the latter reflecting a renewed emphasis on the need to enhance income-generating opportunities. As a result, housing and urban development have accounted for well over 30 per cent of social spending since 1990, compared to an average of less than 25 per cent prior to this date (see Table 4.4).

Since 1991, the rate of growth of real public spending has been declining, reflecting the ending of rapid mineral-led growth. Nevertheless, the real per capita level of social spending has been maintained and the share of total public spending devoted to the social sector has actually increased.

Defence expenditure

The proportion of total public spending allocated to defence, and the ratio of defence spending to total social spending, are sometimes taken as reflections of a

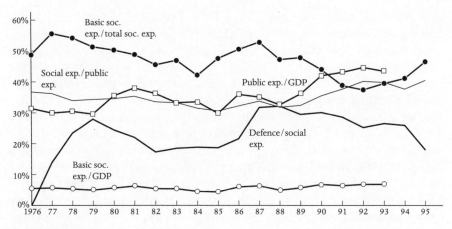

Fig. 4.2 Expenditure ratios, Botswana

Source: MFDP

nation's priorities in resource allocation. Spending on defence has increased significantly since the mid-1980s, and at around 10 per cent it now accounts for a relatively high proportion of public expenditure. While this may have been justified in the often tense regional security environment of the 1980s, the situation no longer applies, and there will increasingly be a trade-off between defence and other types of spending. Nevertheless, there is no evidence yet that defence spending has been at the expense of social provision, and the ratio of defence to education plus health spending has been falling steadily since 1987 (see Fig. 4.2).

Role of foreign aid

Botswana's democratic politics and its precarious geopolitical position adjacent to hostile racist regimes in South Africa and the former Rhodesia, as well as its good record of economic management, were the main reasons why it attracted consistently high levels of foreign aid on a per capita basis. During the 1960s and 1970s foreign aid was needed to meet most of the costs of its development budget (aid represented 100 per cent of development expenditure in 1969 and 80 per cent in 1976).[16] With the build-up of diamond revenues over the 1980s, the significance of foreign aid as a source of investment capital declined, to 45 per cent of development expenditure in 1986 and 16 per cent in 1990[17] (Dahlgren *et al.*, 1993). By 1994 several long-standing donors, including the USA, Norway, and Germany, had curtailed their aid programmes in Botswana, having concluded that Botswana no longer needed concessionary assistance.

Various studies have shown that Botswana's success in making good use of foreign aid owed much to its strength in national development planning (Stevens, 1981; Harvey and Lewis, 1990). The NDPs set out the overall development strategy and overall budgetary plan, defined all projects that were authorized, and outlined their indicative phasing and expenditure ceilings. Through its dialogue with donors Botswana consciously sought to match donors to its projects and programmes, rather than vice versa. It thereby retained control over priorities, spending guidelines, and the nature and scope of the individual development projects, and avoided many of the problems of inappropriate use of aid and poor donor co-ordination that have reduced the effectiveness of aid in other countries.

Since most donors attached overall priority to assisting the poor and meeting 'basic needs', there was considerable donor interest in providing support for social development in Botswana. Virtually all of the major expansions in social provision during the 1960s and 1970s—including roads, schools, and health facilities—were financed largely from donor sources. Even during the 1980s, when finance was no longer a major constraint, the donors continued to finance a considerable proportion of social development. However, most donors progressively shifted their support from 'hardware' to 'software', recognizing that Botswana's greatest needs were now for technical assistance, capacity building, training, and the empowerment of worse-off groups rather than budgetary support.

Having established an effective way of involving donors in implementing the national development plans, Botswana had little to fear from them and much to gain from their international experience and their access to specialized technical knowledge and expertise. This was particularly beneficial to social development,

TABLE 4.5. Government spending structure

	1976	1980	1985	1990	Average 1995	Average 1976–95	1985–MR[a]
Total	100	100	100	100	100	100	100
Economic services	35.0	33.6	33.6	30.7	23.2	33.3	27.8
Unallocated expenditure	5.1	5.5	9.0	7.4	9.7	6.5	8.8
General Services	23.4	18.1	20.3	14.5	19.2	19.9	17.1
Defence	0.1	8.3	5.7	10.7	7.4	6.2	9.7
Total social services	36.4	34.4	30.6	35.9	40.6	33.8	36.2
Of which: education	17.5	18.8	15.8	16.5	22.9	17.6	17.7
of which: schools	12.6	12.8	10.5	11.9	14.4	12.1	11.7
health	5.8	4.6	4.4	4.1	5.2	4.9	4.7
hospitals, clinics, etc.	5.1	4.4	4.2	3.9	4.6	4.5	4.4
food and social welfare	0.2	0.6	2.5	0.5	0.6	1.3	1.7
housing, urban dev., etc.	10.8	9.3	6.7	13.7	10.2	8.7	10.7
housing	5.1	3.8	2.5	5.6	3.9	3.3	4.2
local and reg. dev.	2.0	2.2	2.1	2.2	4.8	2.4	3.1
urban infrastructure	3.7	3.3	2.1	5.9	1.5	2.9	3.4

[a] MR: most recent

Source: MFDP

since Botswana began with little technical capacity for social infrastructure provision and virtually no experience of providing and running social services such as health and education. For example Botswana's impressive gains in immunization were partly due to the ongoing technical advice and support provided by donors. Using donors as its 'window to the world', Botswana was quick to embrace such concepts as primary health care, universal primary education, and safe water for all. Co-operation with donors also performed an important role in establishing an effective capacity for dealing with drought emergencies.

Private spending on health and education

Although the government has accepted the primary responsibility for providing health and education services throughout the country, a subsidiary but important role is envisaged for non-government provision. In education, there are significant numbers of private English medium-primary schools, as well as private education facilities at other levels of the system. Much of pre-school education is at present provided by non-government organizations, and there are also many colleges offering professional training in spheres such as computing and bookkeeping. Private provision probably plays a greater role in health, with three hospitals run by mining companies, a major private hospital in Gaborone, and numerous private medical and dental practitioners. Such provision is seen as a way of broadening the variety of health-care facilities, sharing the cost of providing national health care, reducing pressure on the government health budget, and enabling government to enhance the quality of its own services (Republic of Botswana, 1991:374).

At present it is not possible to accurately assess the magnitude of private health and education expenditure as data on these are not centrally compiled. This particularly applies to education, where the private system is fragmented and spread across a large number of educational facilities of different types. However, it is estimated that private expenditure on health care was approximately P60m. in 1993.[18] This is much smaller than total government spending of P230m. in 1993–4, but is nevertheless significant; approximately 20 per cent of total health-care spending in the country is currently private. This share is likely to increase over time with rising real incomes; for example, BOMAID (a private health insurer) anticipates a 10 per cent per annum growth in membership in the medium term. While real government spending on health will probably continue to grow (health tends to receive a higher proportion of public expenditure in richer countries), it is unlikely to match the rapid growth of private health spending.

Lessons from Social Development in Botswana

In social and economic development there is no substitute for sound overall economic management. Botswana's system of national development planning and budgetary control (with a single ministry responsible for both finance and development planning) offers important lessons for other developing countries.

Botswana's experience suggests that until basic social services have been developed throughout the country there may be no need for defining an elaborate social policy. A set of simple, well-chosen principles and goals at sectoral level—the low-cost provision, for example, of universal primary education and primary health care—may provide a more efficient way of guiding social development during this stage. However, once all people have access to basic services, the policy choices over what to do next become more complex. By that time there may also be accumulated problems of cost-effectiveness and efficiency in the existing services; weaknesses in co-ordination between different sectoral-level service delivery activities; and the persistence of inequity between rich and poor, which may become more transparent. It would seem that, eventually, a more elaborate social policy does become necessary, to reconcile past efforts and provide new direction and clear priorities for the future.

A social development strategy that involves providing universal access to government services can offer an effective means of spreading the benefits of social provision as widely as possible. As is evident from the impressive improvements in Botswana's social indicators, the benefits of universal coverage can be enormous. However, there is a danger that rapid quantitative expansion of social services may undermine the quality of provision. Therefore, if the investment is to be worthwhile, it is important that expansion of coverage takes place while basic minimum standards are maintained. When widespread service coverage has been attained, the strategy needs to shift towards steadily improving the quality of the existing services and reaching out to include those who have been left behind.

Botswana's experience shows that community participation and individual responsibility may be weakened under a process of rapid government-led expansion of service delivery. This not only creates a dependency on government, but may also downplay or diminish the importance that people attach to understanding and adopting the better practices needed if social services are to be effective. In Botswana such problems have been evident in many aspects of social provision, including child nutrition, children's and women's health, and rural sanitation. So far Botswana offers few answers regarding how to revive the role of the community and the individual.

Sustained economic growth will eventually give rise to the expansion of privately provided services, offering an alternative to the public social services, and removing some of the burden from universal public service provision. Government's role may gradually shift from universal provider to regulator and provider of last resort for basic services.

Botswana's impending AIDS catastrophe shows the dismal truth that countries cannot predict or plan for all eventualities. Botswana's considerable success in economic and social development—and its impressive machinery for national development planning and economic management—have provided no defence against the AIDS pandemic. The scale of HIV infection is already so great that in the future AIDS threatens to reverse some of the gains in Botswana's social indicators, including life expectancy and child and maternal mortality.

Lessons for Botswana

After nearly thirty years of independence, Botswana's social development experience stands out as one of the more successful in the developing world, and especially in Sub-Saharan Africa. During this time some useful lessons have been learned which offer insight into the origins of the problems which social development addresses, and into the means by which Botswana's successes can be sustained and developed in the future.

One of the key lessons is that the benefits of economic growth do not automatically spread throughout the population, and that some form of social policy is necessary to protect the weaker and more vulnerable members of society.

As a result of rapid quantitative expansions, basic social services are now available throughout the country. However, disaggregated data on social indicators show that certain groups of people and geographical areas continue to lag behind in terms of improvements in social conditions. These include women, female-headed households, remote area dwellers, the illiterate, and the disabled. The single factor that is generally common among these groups is their poverty. At the same time, some better-off people can now afford to pay for social services and are also able to obtain privately provided services. It would therefore be more equitable and more efficient for government to target social spending towards the worse-off, give greater priority to services needed disproportionately by the worse-off, and require the better-off to meet an increasing proportion of the cost of the social services they consume.

Other inequities are apparent. There is a considerable gap between the prosperity in Botswana's towns and larger villages and the persistence of poverty in many rural areas. Such structural poverty increases vulnerability to drought, and there is a case for reorienting or augmenting the existing drought-relief machinery to provide some form of poverty relief or social security in both drought and non-drought years, and to support a considerably expanded programme of longer-term interventions with the aim of alleviating poverty. In parallel with the reorienting of drought-relief, Botswana needs to reassess its social welfare policy and consider the options for formalizing the social safety net; defining minimum standards of social security would depend on what was efficient, equitable, and affordable. A first step would be to conduct preliminary investigations into the different options in terms of social welfare provision and poverty alleviation programmes, their costs, and their overall affordability. The government also needs to do much more to encourage the development of NGOs and to provide a framework for their effective participation in social development activities.

A further inequity is that women have not benefited as much as men from Botswana's economic growth. Greater equality will not be possible until existing legislation that discriminates against women is amended. In view of the entrenched position of men in politics and in most senior decision-making positions in the civil service, a commitment to gender equality may require greater use of affirmative action.

All of the above issues need to be addressed at a time when the rapid economic growth of the past thirty years appears to be slowing. This has implications for two key elements of past strategy of spreading the benefits of mineral-led growth— employment generation and social provision. With slowing economic growth, Botswana's overall strategy of spreading the growth in income through growth in employment may be reaching its limits at a time when only about half of the population is above the poverty line. If these limitations materialize, a major rethinking of government's approach to ensuring social justice and to sharing the benefits of economic growth will become necessary.

With regard to social service provision, now that universal access has been achieved for many basic social services, it may be expected that further improvements will depend largely on improving recurrent service provision. To support such improvements there is a need to strengthen the systems of recurrent budgeting and recurrent service management.

Greater efficiency in recurrent service provision is absolutely essential given that the government's future budgetary position is likely to be much less favourable than it has been in the past. Budget deficits have been forecast from 1998 onward due to a combination of static diamond revenues and the rising recurrent spending implications of past social investments, and there will be added pressure on social-services spending from the rising costs of dealing with AIDS. Unless greater efficiency is achieved, there must be some doubt about the capacity of the State to maintain the existing level of social-service provision in the face of these budgetary constraints. This is not to suggest that Botswana's 'miracle' is likely to collapse, simply that a change of strategy is now required to consolidate and extend past gains in new economic circumstances. Current strategy is to encourage diversification of economic activity and revenue sources so as to ensure a smooth transition to reduced dependence upon mineral revenues—a task which will be made easier by the present resurgence of economic activity in southern Africa following the transition to majority rule in neighbouring South Africa. At the same time, government needs to restrain the growth rate of its own spending, a task which will not be easy given the high degree of dependence upon government provision which has built up over the past twenty-five years. Botswana is, however, in a fortunate position in that many of the problems, needs, and constraints facing the country have been identified in good time, and are already impacting on the development planning process. What is not clear is whether the restraints and tough choices which are necessary given lower economic growth rates will be politically feasible in an environment where inequality remains very high and where expectations are slow to adjust.

Notes

1. To be precise, it was the fastest-growing country for which the World Bank reports data; this excludes small countries (with populations of less than 1m. in 1992) and non-members of the World Bank, such as Taiwan and Brunei.
2. The cartel (through the London-based Central Selling Organization) has been in operation for sixty years and is the only long-term successful commodity stabilization 'agreement' in the world. It controls about 80% of the world's supply of rough diamonds, and stabilizes prices through a buffer stock arrangement.
3. It is estimated that production costs account for only 20% of the selling price of diamonds.
4. In 1993 mining (including diamonds and copper-nickel matte) accounted for around 10,000 jobs, less than 5% of formal-sector employment. In recent years two diamond-cutting operations have been established.
5. Due to limitations in the collection of social and economic statistics prior to independence, most of the statistical comparisons in this chapter were limited to the twenty-year period from 1970 to 1990.
6. During the 1980s the government used the arguments of low population density and lack of economic diversification to downplay the country's comparative prosperity in terms of GDP per capita and to persuade donors to continue their aid programmes on concessional terms.
7. During the 1970s it became apparent that some groups of remote area dwellers (RADs) had been left out of Botswana's development. These people were neither Batswana nor Setswana-speaking, and their nomadic existence in the Kgalagadi Desert had little in common with Setswana custom. During the 1980s, many RAD settlements were provided with basic social services (water, education, and health care), but despite this they remain economically and socially marginalized. Efforts to assist them to integrate with the rest of society have been difficult and at times controversial.
8. The relevant poverty-datum line is derived from the cost of purchasing the minimum consumption basket necessary to maintain 'physical health, personal hygiene, legality and decency' (CSO, 1991).
9. The minimum wage in the formal sector is currently around P250 ($US90) per month, or P3,000 ($US1,100) per year. Since this does not apply to agriculture, domestic service or the informal sector, about one-third of the work-force receive incomes below this level.
10. This was some six years before wider international recognition of the importance of primary health care through the Alma Alta Declaration in 1978.
11. All years refer to financial years, beginning 1 April.
12. The analysis of public and social expenditure mainly covers the period from 1976 onward, when a functional classification of expenditure was introduced.
13. This was mainly due to large government expenditures associated with the establishment of the Selebi-Phikwe copper-nickel mine which involved the provision of physical infrastructure (including construction of a new town).
14. Following international conventions, social spending here includes: education, health, food and social welfare programmes, housing, urban and regional development, and other community and social services. Note that this excludes some economic services which have a major social component, such as the provision of water supplies.
15. Note that this does not exactly accord with the UNICEF definition of basic social spending

(i.e. spending on basic education, primary health-care, family planning, water, sanitation, and nutrition) which cannot be derived from Botswana government data.

16. It was not until 1972 that Botswana was able to finance its recurrent budget without foreign aid (from Britain).
17. Unfortunately, data are not available on the proportion of spending in different sectors financed by aid inflows.
18. Based on figures provided by the two major private health-insurance schemes.

References and Selected Bibliography

BIDPA (1996), Study of Poverty and Poverty Alleviation in Botswana, Gaborone: Botswana Institute for Development Policy Analysis.

Brown, C. (1983), *The Institutions Research Project: Summary of Resource Management Issues*, Gaborone: Applied Research Unit, Ministry of Local Government and Lands.

Colclough, C., and McCarthy, S. (1980), *The Political Economy of Botswana: A Study of Growth and Distribution*, Oxford: Oxford University Press.

CSO (Central Statistics Office) (1976), *Rural Income Distribution Survey in Botswana, 1975/75*, Gaborone: Govt. Printer.

—— (1988), *Household Income and Expenditure Survey, 1985/86*, Gaborone: Govt. Printer.

—— (1989), *A Poverty Datum line for Botswana*, Gaborone: Govt. Printer.

—— (1991), *Education Statistics*, Gaborone: Govt. Printer.

—— (1994), *1991 National Census*, Gaborone: Govt. Printer.

—— (1995), *Household Income and Expenditure Survey, 1993/94*, Gaborone: Govt. Printer.

Dahlgren, S., Duncan, T., Gustavsson, A., and Molutsi, P. (1993), *SIDA Development Assistance to Botswana, 1966–93: An Evaluation of 27 Years of Development Co-operation*, Stockholm: Swedish International Development Authority.

Danevad, A. (1992), *Economic Policy in a Democratic Context: Development Planning & Multi-party Politics in Botswana*, unpublished thesis, University of Bergen, Norway.

Dow, U., and Mogwe, A. (1988), *The Convention on the Rights of the Child and the Legal Status of Children*, Gaborone: UNICEF.

Duncan, W. (1988), *School Dropout in Botswana: Gender Differences at Secondary Level*, Institute of International Education, University of Stockholm.

Edwards, E. O., Aman, H., Frankenberger, T. R., and Jansen, D. (1989), *Agricultural Sector Assessment*, Gaborone: Govt. Printer.

Egner, B. (1979), *Review of Socio-Economic Development in Botswana, 1966–79*, Stockholm: Swedish International Development Authority.

—— (1987), *The District Councils and Decentralisation, 1978–1986*, Stockholm: Swedish International Development Authority.

Food Studies Group (1990), *Report on the Evaluation of the Drought Relief and Recovery Programme, 1982–1990* i–iv, Gaborone: Govt. Printer.

Government of Botswana, UNDP, and UNICEF (1993), *Planning for People: A Strategy for Accelerated Human Development in Botswana*, Gaborone: MFDP.

Granberg, P., and Parkinson, J. R. (1988), *Botswana Country Study and Norwegian Aid Review*, Bergen: Chr. Michelson Institute.

Harvey, C. (1981), *Papers on the Economy of Botswana*, London: Heinemann.

—— and Lewis, S. (1990), *Policy Choice and Development Performance in Botswana*, London: Macmillan.

Hitchcock, R. R., and Smith, M. R. (eds.) (1982), *Settlement in Botswana*, Gaborone: Botswana Society.

Kann, U. (1986), *The Missing Children*, Gaborone: National Institute for Development Research and Documentation.

—— (1989), *Education, Gender and Employment*, Gaborone: National Institute for Development Research and Documentation.

Kerapeletswe, C. K. (1991*a*), *Nine Years of Arable Lands Development Programme, 1982–1991*, Gaborone: Ministry of Agriculture.

—— (1991*b*), *Report on Model 1 Female-Headed Household Study*, Gaborone: Ministry of Agriculture.

Lewis, S. R. (1981), 'The Potential Problems of Diamond Dependent Development', in C. Harvey, *Papers on the Economy of Botswana*, London: Heinemann.

Maendeleo (Botswana) (1991), *National Rural Sanitation Strategy*, Gaborone: Ministry of Local Government and Lands.

—— (1992*a*), *Review of the Self-Help Housing Agency*, Gaborone: Govt. Printer.

—— (1992*b*), *Study of Women and Cattle in Botswana*, Caborone: CORDE.

MFDP (Ministry of Finance and Development Planning) (various years), *Financial Statements*, Gaborone: Govt. Printer.

Molutsi, P. P. (1988), *Botswana: Strengthening Local Education Capacity through Community Involvement*, Gaborone: USAID.

Nopen, D. (1982), *Consultation Non-Commitment: Planning with the People in Botswana*, Leiden, Netherlands: African Studies Centre.

Nyati-Ramahobo, L. (1992), *The Girl Child in Botswana: Educational Constraints and Prospects*, Gaborone: UNICEF.

Oomen, M. A., Inganji, F. K., and Ngcongco, L. D. (eds.) (1983), *Botswana's Economy Since Independence*, Delhi: Tata McGraw-Hill.

Parson, J. (1984), *Botswana: Liberal Democracy and Labour Reserve*, Boulder, Colo.: Westview Press.

Picard, L. (1987), *The Politics of Development in Bostswana: A Model for Success?*, Lynne Reiner Publishers.

Republic of Botswana (1965), *Transitional Plan for Social and Economic Development*, Gaborone: Govt. Printer.

—— (1966), *The Development of the Bechuanaland Economy, Report of the Ministry of Overseas Development Survey Mission*, Gaborone.

—— (1985), *Sixth National Development Plan*, Gaborone: Govt. Printer.

—— (1991), *Seventh National Development Plan (1991–97)*, Gaborone: Govt. Printer.

—— (1992), *A Draft Report on the Human Development Initiative for Botswana*, Gaborone.

—— (1993), *Report of the National Commission on Education* (Gaborone: Govt. Printer).

Schapera, I. (1993), *The Tswana*, London: International African Institute.

SIAPAC (1991), *Effects of Gender on Access to Credit and Grants in Botswana*, Gaborone: SIAPAC.

Stevens, M. (1981), 'Aid Management in Botswana: From One to Many Donors', in Harvey (1991).

Tsimako, B. (1991), *The Tribal Grazing Land Policy Ranches Performance to Date*, Gaborone: Ministry of Agriculture.

UK (1960), *Basutoland, Bechuanaland Protectorate and Swaziland: Report of an Economic Survey Mission*, London, HMSO.

UNDP (1995), Human Development Report, New York: Oxford University Press.

UNICEF (1991), *Challenges for Children and Women in the 1990s: Eastern and Southern Africa in Profile*, Nairobi: UNICEF Eastern and Southern Africa Regional Office.

—— (1993a), *Progress of Nations 1993*, New York: UNICEF.

—— (1993b), *The State of the World's Children 1993*, New York: UNICEF.

—— (1994a), *The Progress of Nations 1994*, New York: UNICEF.

—— (1994b), *The State of the World's Children 1994*, New York: UNICEF.

—— Botswana (1993), *Situation Analysis of Children and Women in Botswana*, Gaborone: UNICEF.

Women and Law in Southern Africa Research Project (1992), *Maintenance Laws and Practices in Botswana*, Gaborone: WLSA.

World Bank (1993), *World Development Report*, Washington, DC: World Bank.

—— (1994), *World Development Report*, Washington, DC: World Bank.

World Conference on Education for All (1990), *World Declaration on Education for All and Framework of Action to Meet Basic Learning Needs*, New York: UNICEF.

5

Mauritius: The Roots of Success
1960–1993

EDWARD AND BRIDGET DOMMEN

Overview

The island of Mauritius has achieved, within the short space of one generation, remarkable social and economic progress, as Table 5.1 indicates.[1] This progress has gone hand in hand with firmly rooted and lively democracy.

Mauritius approached independence (1968) with at least five trump cards, cards which it played to good advantage in the development game over the next thirty years.

The ace of trumps was a well-rooted commitment to democracy, based on concern for the disadvantaged and respect for minorities. This has taken the form of respect for democratic institutions, including liberty of the media, the construction of a welfare state, and more recently the provision of safety nets for those with special needs. The universal provision of welfare-state benefits went hand in hand with competitive labour costs, a key element of Mauritius's economic performance.

Next, the plural society, so often a cause of internal strife elsewhere, was composed of so many groups and subgroups, cutting across both class and geographical divisions, that none could impose its will on the rest.

The stability of Mauritius, resulting from these first two trumps, has been a boon to the population and an enticement to investors, first in industrial production for export and tourism, and now in other services.

The diversity of ethnic origins dealt another valuable card to Mauritius's hand: her openness to the outside world. Her special ties with Britain and France, and her links with India and with Chinese communities, have stood her in good stead time and again when economic opportunities were to be seized.

Fourthly, although entrepreneurship was at first latent in Mauritius, every section of society was historically rooted in the monetary economy and the capitalist system. Trading with the rest of the world has always directly or indirectly involved most people on the island.

TABLE 5.1. Some indicators of success

	Then (1960–2)[a]	Now (1990–2)
Adult literacy: male	65	87
female	51	77
% population 5 years and over who have never attended school	52	11
Life expectancy at birth: male	59	66
female	62	73
Maternal-mortality rate (per 100,000 live births)	150	70
Population–doctor ratio	4,968 (1959)	1,210
Daily calorie consumption per capita	2,330	2,887 (1989)
Real expenditure on[b]: education	1.6 (1964)	2.0
health	2.4 (1964)	3.4
social security	2.7 (1964)	3.9
Gini coefficient	0.42 (1975)	0.38

[a] Figures for 1960–2 except where stated otherwise; [b] as % of GDP

Source: Dommen and Dommen (forthcoming)

Lastly, the very compactness of the island was an advantage. A dense, evenly spread population facilitated the provision of economic infrastructure, basic services, and communications to all.

The pages which follow explain the importance of these cards and show how they have been sagaciously played.

Two missions visited Mauritius in 1960. One, led by James Meade, published a report on the economic prospects of the country; the other, led by Richard Titmuss and Brian Abel-Smith, published one on social policy (Meade, 1961a; Titmuss and Abel-Smith, 1961). This chapter takes those studies as its starting-point.

Population Growth

The decline in population growth

The annual rate of population growth started falling in the 1950s, from 4.1 per cent in 1951 to about 1 per cent by the mid-1980s. This early release from the pressure of population growth has been a crucial factor in explaining Mauritius's success. If the birth rate had continued to climb at 1950 rates, the population in 1982, according to Titmuss's projections, would have been nearly 1.4m. In fact, it was not quite a million (Titmuss and Abel-Smith, 1961: 64–5).

Numerically, 400,000 fewer people represented a crucial reprieve for individual families, not only in terms of the household budget, but also because the smaller number of pregnancies contributed to an enormous improvement in maternal and child health. On a national level, falling population growth rates have enabled the government to improve services such as health, education, and social welfare, rather than just maintain them in the struggle to keep up with the population.

Changing dependency ratios, brought about by the declining birth and death rates, have also worked in favour of recent economic growth: dependency due to the large and expensive child population has fallen drastically, and although it has been accompanied by an increase in dependency among the even more expensive elderly, numbers in the over-60 age-group have so far been sufficiently small not to represent a significant financial burden. At the same time, the population bulge of the 1950s and 1960s has been entering the active population just at the moment when a plentiful supply of labour suited the economy's needs (see Fig. 5.1).

By the beginning of the next century this bulge will start swelling the dependent population again as it reaches retirement age. Advances in life expectancy mean that the over-80 dependency ratio is growing. This group of the population can be particularly expensive, not only on account of pension payments and increasing health needs, but also because non-medical care on a daily basis becomes necessary for the increasing number of dependent old people unable to cope on their own. In years to come, the question of how to care for the elderly may well be as preoccupying as was birth control policy a generation ago.

Why population growth declined

Several interwoven factors can be linked to the decline of the population growth rate: the decline in infant mortality, the family-planning campaign, abortion, emigration, economic progress, and rising aspirations.

Infant mortality

Death rates which had plummeted since 1945 (due mainly to the eradication of malaria) were quickly followed by declining birth rates. The parallel decline in these two rates continues throughout the period up to the late 1980s.

'In evidence we have received from doctors, chemists, nurses, midwives, probation officers, social welfare workers and members of the public, and from investigations we and others have made, we believe that there is a substantial number of parents in all classes of the community who wish to avoid the birth of further children', said the Titmuss report (Titmuss and Abel-Smith 1961: 63). Fig. 5.1 shows that parents had started to limit their fertility in the 1950s, well before the official family-planning programme started in 1966, when the decline accelerated.

The ensuing effect on the birth rate, taken together with the downward trend in the infant-mortality rate (see Fig. 5.2), supports the 'insurance strategy' theory which maintains that families will voluntarily limit their pregnancies when they are convinced that the children they do bear are likely to survive.

The high birth rates experienced in the decade after the Second World War followed two decades of increasing infant mortality (although part of the high birth

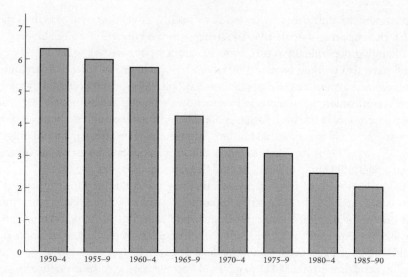

Fig. 5.1 Total fertility rate, 1950–1990

rate immediately after the war has also been ascribed to the return of Mauritian troops from abroad). The trend patterns of birth and infant-mortality rates are very similar, but declines in the birth rate follow those of the infant-mortality rate after a lag of a few years:

Improvements in child survival, which increase the predictability of the family building process, trigger the transition from natural to controlled fertility behaviour. This in turn generates the need for family planning. Until this transition effect occurs, the implementation of family planning programmes cannot precipitate significant changes in fertility behaviour, and thus cannot play an important role in the improvement of child health. (Lloyd and Ivanov, 1988: 141)

The success of Mauritius's family-planning programme, introduced in 1966, after the transition period, can perhaps best be evaluated in this context.

The family-planning campaign

Introduced in 1966, after several years of stormy debate, the effect of the new birth-control policy was to unleash a flood of latent family-planning users (see Fig. 5.3). By 1975, 64 per cent of ever-married women under 50 had used contraceptives at some time (Hein, 1977: 318). Although fertility had started falling in the early 1950s, the decline between 1966 and 1974 was at a rate 'unequalled for any population of substantial size' (Brass, 1976). Family size fell from an average of six children at the beginning of the 1960s to three (Titmuss's ideal) by 1973. Although part of this dramatic fertility fall could be attributed to an increase in the age at marriage, never-

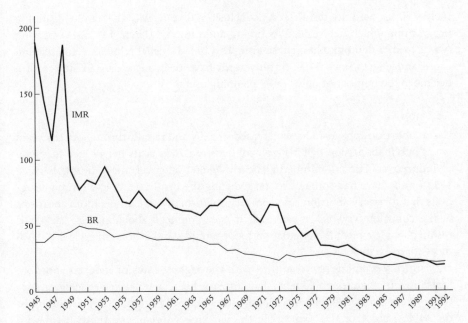

Fig. 5.2 Infant-mortality rate and birth rate, 1945–1992

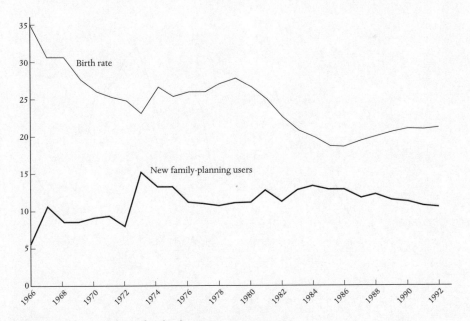

Fig. 5.3 Birth rate and new family-planning users, 1966–1992

theless 'it is hard to dismiss the conclusion that it was the family planning programme which determined its timing and rapidity' (Hein, 1977: 318)—strong words from a demographer, considering this breed's usual reluctance to attribute cause and effect. Since 1989, fertility rates have been increasing in step with a decline in the number of new family-planning users.

Abortion

Use of abortion appears to have increased steadily and rapidly throughout the years when public discussion of birth-control questions was at its height (see Fig. 5.4).

Induced abortions—numbering nearly 70,000 at government hospitals since 1960—must have had some effect on reducing the birth rate. A low estimate suggests that for every abortion case admitted to hospital there are six more abortions in the community, which means that if every induced abortion since 1960 had resulted in a live birth the population today would stand at something like 400,000 more than it actually is.

Mauritius is among the countries with the highest rates of induced abortion, indicating that although family planning has been a remarkable achievement, the services offered no longer respond entirely to needs, particularly, according to the MFPA, those of the unmarried, the working woman, and the couples who have completed their desired family size (Mauritius Family Planning Association, 1993).

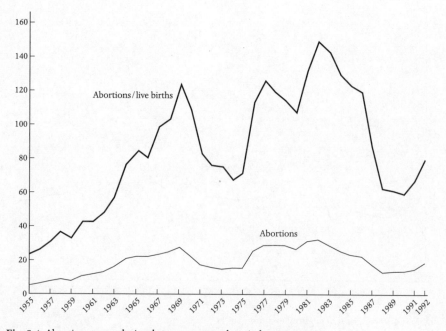

Fig. 5.4 Abortion cases admitted to government hospitals, 1955–1992

The toll taken by illegal abortion is heavy: over half the maternal deaths since 1982 have been due to complications following such abortions (MoH, 1988).

Emigration

Although erratic, net emigration has at times been substantial and has contributed in a small way to restraining the rate of population growth. On the whole, however, emigration has played a different role. At the time of independence, emigration may well have contributed to the political harmony of the country even if the numbers concerned were small: at this decisive moment a fair proportion of the hard-liners who were unwilling to accept life under an independent and multiracial government decided to leave. Their absence probably made it easier for their relatives who remained to fit into, and indeed contribute to strengthening, the balance which has since served the country so well. Apart from this special period, there appears to be little relation between emigration and economic or political conditions within Mauritius. One wonders whether pull factors abroad may not be as influential as push factors at home.

Economic progress

Between 1960 and 1991, whenever real GDP per capita fell, birth rate fell. Furthermore, within this simple trend the birth rate fell most sharply when income was falling, as in the late 1960s, or during the period of gloom cast by the IMF–World Bank structural-adjustment programme (1979–86). During the prosperous period of the early 1990s, both income and the birth rate rose. All this supports the argument that an educated population in a highly monetized economy will be responsive to economic conditions in planning their families.

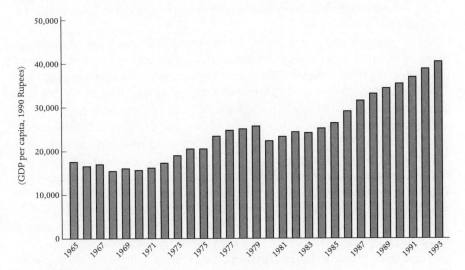

Fig. 5.5 Real GDP per capita, 1965–91

In a broader perspective, falling fertility rates coincided with the coming of a new optimism for the future, related to the beginning of suffrage in 1948 and more generally to opportunities for social mobility and hence rising expectations, particularly among the Indian population.

Economic Development

The phases of economic development

The Meade report stated that 'if the population continues to increase there is a real danger not merely that the standard of living will not rise but that it will actually decline' (Meade, 1961*a*, para 2 : 3). The evolution of the economy since the Meade and Titmuss reports can be divided into four periods. The first covers the years 1960–8. The second begins with independence in 1968 and the turn-around, with the formal establishment of the export processing zone (EPZ), until the end of the sugar boom 1975. The third period includes the aftermath of the sugar boom and the years of the IMF–World Bank structural-adjustment programme. Finally, the economy entered smoother waters again a couple of years after the 60–0 election of 1982,[2] and its course seems to have been set fair since then.

Real GDP per capita tottered about until 1964–5 when it went into a decline which lasted until after independence (see Fig. 5.5).

Looking at the GDP figures without hindsight, one could be excused for thinking that decline had at best turned into stagnation during the years 1968–72. If total employment was already on the steady upward march that was to characterize it through the 1970s, in 1971 this was due to a substantial increase in public-sector employment which turned out to be a flash in the pan. In fact, the other key sectors, the EPZ and tourism, were already on the go. The sugar boom boosted the economy and actually helped its diversification away from sugar, but was not the sole cause of its performance.

In the wake of the sugar boom the government decreed substantial wage increases in the EPZ (Hein, 1988: 45). These measures dampened the enthusiasm of investors in the EPZ, undoubtedly contributing to its relative stagnation until 1983.

While GDP continued to rise throughout the rest of the 1970s, clearer signs of trouble were already emerging in the form of a rapidly deteriorating balance of visible trade. This provoked the IMF economic and financial stabilization programme and the World Bank structural-adjustment programme which lasted from 1979 to 1986. That it corresponded in its early stages to a decline in indicators like GDP per capita or car ownership seems normal. Tourism arrivals and revenue stopped growing also during these years, but this was due to the sudden rise in world oil prices rather than to domestic policy. The fall in employment, which is often decried as a perverse effect of structural-adjustment programmes, was, in Mauritius, the consequence of the long-term decline in employment in sugar. The stabilization of public-sector employment, a common requirement of structural-adjustment programmes, has proved more durable in Mauritius: numbers remained more or less constant up to the end of the 1980s. Unlike other countries subject to a structural-adjustment programme, Mauritius did not suffer a decline in average nutrition standards during the period. The policy of free health services and free education in the public sector were maintained in the face of pressures from the IMF and the World Bank: the government remained true to its traditional concern for social justice (with the exception of housing policy).

Structural-adjustment policies tend to increase inequalities, and Mauritius was not exempt from that effect (Lamusse and Burn, 1991: 114). However, the strategy which Mauritius chose, based on the energetic growth of the EPZ, involved a rapid expansion of employment. Indeed employment creation has constantly been a top priority of government policy until full employment was officially considered as actually achieved, in 1990. It was above all the spread of productive jobs which ensured that the income of the population at large, and thus social justice, were maintained during the period of structural adjustment.

If the growth in employment has slowed since 1988, this is largely due to the fact that all those who wanted work were now beginning to find it.

Labour costs and social justice

The main economic problem of Mauritius at the time of the Meade report was the same one which plagues Europe today: unemployment. The solution in a liberal economy requires that the factor in oversupply—labour—be cheap relative to the scarce factors, i.e. that wages be low while rents and profits be high. The inequality of income which follows is, however, widely perceived as unfair, resulting in pressure for higher wages at the expense of property income.

On two occasions Mauritius responded to this pressure to such a degree that the appearance of greater equity was achieved by putting the prospects of improving overall prosperity at some risk. The first occasion was during the years of political emancipation. Between 1956 and 1959 the wage rate in the sugar industry (which sets the pattern for the rest of the island) went up in real terms by some 45 per cent. 'The sugar industry was certainly very prosperous in the sense that the big sugar estates were making very good incomes from rent and profits, and the political awakening of the underdog in Mauritius has not unnaturally been associated with aggressive trade-union action' (Meade, 1961b: 525). The second occasion was again one in which the profits of the sugar industry were high due to the exceptional prices of 1973–5. These resulted in substantial wage and bonus awards at the instigation of the government (Hein, 1988: 6). On both occasions, the consequences were unfavourable for the economy. Apart from these two deviations, the Mauritius government has been remarkably successful in maintaining low wages while guaranteeing standards of living.

First, property owners have been encouraged to invest their income, rather than consume or export it, in such a way as to create more jobs at home. The incentives offered under the system of Development Certificates, which functioned from 1962 on, stimulated by the introduction of exchange control in 1966 and then the creation of the EPZ in 1970, achieved this effect.

Secondly, the government has taxed property income, using the revenue to support the needs and prospects of the working class in several ways:

- by investing in the infrastructure: roads, electricity, water supply, the port, the airport, and, in due course, telecommunications;

- by improving the future prospects of the working class, particularly through health, education, and the encouragement of family planning. One result was that by the end of the 1960s Mauritius could offer not merely plentiful labour but lively and intelligent people whom employers were glad to engage;

- by developing social security, including 'relief works', 'travail pour tous', or 'development works'; food subsidies provided both by government and by the World Food Programme; and pensions: households were relieved of exclusive dependence on the job market for meeting their needs.

Where economic efficiency requires low labour costs, the welfare state becomes indispensable if the population at large is to be assured a fair share of the economy's output. That this was well understood in Mauritius is illustrated by the way in which the Meade and Titmuss reports were seen as closely related and given equal status. Reaching the key objective of full employment was a major element in the success of this combined policy.

The end result has been an improvement in the distribution of income. The Gini coefficient, which stood at 0.42 in 1975, fell to 0.38 by 1991–2. In facing the demands of efficiency without sacrificing those of social justice, in running a liberal economy with a human face, Mauritius has been ahead of many of the world's developed countries and has proved that this combination can establish both prosperity and growth.

The dynamic role of the sugar industry

Ever since 1825, when Mauritian sugar was first granted access to the British market on favourable terms, the government has continually striven to maintain preferential terms for sugar exports. By the end of the 1960s it was apparent to Mauritius that in Europe the economic powerhouse was going to be the European Common Market, and that Britain's economic future was less certain if not less rosy. Mauritius therefore leaned on the cultural links it enjoyed with France in order to establish a privileged relationship with the Common Market. As a result, Mauritius was, in 1972, the first Commonwealth country to acquire associate status. The continuation of a preferential market for sugar was thus ensured once Britain joined the Common Market and the Commonwealth Sugar Agreement came to an end.[3]

This protection for the industry has provided a source of rent crucial to the social and economic development of the country. By astute mobilization of this rent it has been possible on the one hand to finance investment in diversification and on the other to provide basic services to the population independent of wage rates. It should be stressed that while new export sectors have grown, the sugar industry has not shrunk.

In 1960 the Mauritius economy was based on sugar, which accounted for 99 per cent of Mauritian exports. Even if sugar accounted directly for only 35 per cent of GDP and employment, the rest of the economy was by and large confined to a quartermaster function, providing wage goods and services to sugar workers, and inputs into or support for the sugar industry (Dommen and Hein, 1985: 152). Sugar directly or indirectly funded virtually all the infrastructure which Mauritius was to use as a springboard for its economic development after independence.

Capital was accumulated not only in the hands of the sugar sector; within the quartermaster sector the traders supplying the local community also accumulated capital to invest. The availability of capital within all the various communities was soon to be important in the diversification of the economy. Since the 1930s and especially the 1940s, Indian planters had been investing in the higher education of their children, encouraging them to take up professions like medicine or law. While in the first instance the professions served the quartermaster sector, in the end they helped open the way out of sugar.

A sugar export tax, adopted in response to the Meade report, became a major source of government revenue and means of financing the welfare state and the infrastructure for the diversification of the economy.

The sugar industry has directly invested in the dynamic new economic activities like tourism, the EPZ enterprises, and industrial estates on their land to serve the EPZ. During the years 1970–84, sugar companies directly contributed 19 per cent of the estimated total equity capital, or 43 per cent of the local equity capital, in the EPZ (Lamusse, 1989: 24).

The new sectors which are at present decisive for Mauritius's prosperity undoubtedly generate little in the way of rent. Textiles produced in the EPZ enjoy protected access to the European Community market, but even so they face stiff competition. Other EPZ products, along with tourism and offshore banking must compete unprotected on the international market. In these sectors the policy of skimming profits which are high relative to wages in order to meet social needs is now running up against the constraint that profits are not markedly higher in Mauritius than elsewhere.

The development of Mauritius still depends therefore to a significant degree on maintaining the viability of the sugar industry and delicately juggling the share of the surplus left to the industry for use according to its own search for profit; the share recycled to the rest of the private economy, especially through the banking system; and the share claimed by the government for general social and economic objectives.

Domestic savings have accounted for the bulk of domestic capital formation. Over the past two decades, foreign direct investment has by and large amounted to

5 per cent of gross domestic fixed-capital formation. In the years immediately prior to independence, capital inflow was important. The decline in domestic savings after a peak during the sugar boom of 1973–5 was cushioned by capital inflows which remained large though also falling.

Infrastructure

In 1960 international experts considered the demographic prospects terrifying. None the less, although the *rate* of population growth was certainly a major problem, its *density* had advantages, for roads, electricity, and water were relatively easy to bring within reach of all, the more so as the population was fairly evenly spread over the island. Mauritius came to independence with extensive road, electricity, and water networks, key elements for both the social and the economic development which followed.

The road network was more or less complete by the time of independence, partly as a result of major investments in the 1960s, thanks to the needs of the sugar industry. The extent of paved roads was 1,593 km. in 1970, about 0.85 km. of road for every sq. km. of land. This figure suggests that roughly speaking, everyone lived within 500 metres of a paved road. The network has been improved and upgraded, but its extent rose only to 1,700 km. by 1989.

Rural electrification was a high priority in the 1960s, and the dilapidated water system in existence in 1960 has been vigorously tackled since the 1970s. Water supply has since then been reliable, though increasing demands resulting from rising standards of living and the development of tourism have put pressure on treated supply.

Infrastructure and social development

Given the quality of the road network and of the bus services which made good use of it, virtually everyone was within reasonable reach of facilities like primary schools and health centres. Electricity brought light, and thus the ability to read and study at night; it operated the range of equipment essential to the functioning of health services. Clean water, proper disposal of human waste, and hygienic housing conditions made a vital contribution to the control of disease and the reduction of mortality (see Table 5.2).

Improvement in standards of housing in the 1960s and 1970s came largely in the wake of cyclones, rather than as a premeditated housing or health policy. The Central Housing Authority was set up after the onslaughts of Alix and Carol in 1960, and had built 13,000 houses by 1970. The cyclone Gervaise was responsible for the implementation of an emergency programme in 1975 which led to the construction of another 7,500. But the result was that the new dwellings were vastly superior, from the sanitary and hygienic point of view, to the previously prevailing 'tin shacks' (Titmuss and Abel-Smith, 1961: 7). However, the housing sector was the

TABLE 5.2. Water, sanitation, housing, 1962–1990

	1962	1972	1983	1990
Dwellings with: (%)				
piped water	59	99	99	96
flush toilet	21	34	49	65
pit latrine	63	61	50	35
pail or no WC system	13	5	2	1
Houses constructed in: (%)				
cement, concrete, stone	27	37	66	79
wood, iron, and other	73	63	34	21

Source: Dommen and Dommen (1995)

hardest hit victim of structural adjustment; practically no low-cost housing loans were provided in the 1980s and old stock was poorly maintained, with the result that not only are housing aspirations frustrated, but areas where poor housing conditions threaten health still exist. The programme launched in 1992 by the newly created National Housing Development Company aims to make up for lost time, although its priority is for middle-class housing. Pockets of dramatically poor housing still exist—in Port Louis, for example.

Infrastructure and economic progress

The widespread availability of transport, electricity, and water played a key role in the development of the EPZ. Factories could be established anywhere in the country. Government policy was quick to exploit this asset (Bheenick, 1990: 224). Locating jobs close to the people instead of expensively shuttling people to jobs avoided congestion. It also made factory work more accessible and hence attractive to the women who constitute the bulk of the EPZ labour force (Hein, 1988: 15). It discouraged the poaching of skilled workers which had occurred in the early days when the factories were concentrated in a few areas. Last, but not least, it has mitigated the social and environmental problems which accompany urban drift.

The leaps which telecommunications technology have made are recent, and can still be improved, but the government was quick to realize that the arguments which applied to roads, water, electricity, radio, and television were also valid for these services. Television was introduced in 1965 and was immediately available to all throughout the island in village centres. Along with the radio, it has from the outset played an important role in getting messages of public interest, concerning health for instance, to people wherever they live, regardless of whether they read newspapers.

Now, telephones are not only available throughout the country—indeed, by

1989 there was a telephone for every fifteen inhabitants—but they provide a reliable service. Mauritius changed over to electronic exchanges in 1978–9, only six months after they were introduced in metropolitan France.

Thus, hotels and enterprises in the EPZ, wherever they are located in the country, can communicate effectively with the rest of the world (Seetohul, 1992: 89). That is an essential requirement for their type of business and equally so for the development of new service activities, like offshore banking. Indeed, telecommunications are becoming an essential element in the competitiveness of an increasingly high-tech economy.

Human Development

Education

The Ten-Year Development Plan approved in 1946 under the British Colonial Development and Welfare Act of 1945 gave priority to 'an attack on the Mauritian people's two great handicaps—ill-health and inadequate education' (Colonial Office, 1951, para 8). With respect to the latter, the aim was to democratize education, to 'enable the young Mauritian to grow up a responsible and useful citizen' (ibid., para 45). Widespread basic education has been decisive for Mauritius's lively democracy, which is in turn one of the foundations of the country's success. Furthermore, the development of the economy since the 1960s has been based on the EPZ and tourism. The employment these activities created tended to require basic literacy and numeracy rather than particular craft skills.

As the economy has become more sophisticated—and more prosperous—not only has the quality of education improved, but the range of education and training offered has expanded. It has in particular been brought more functionally into line with the needs of imaginative economic enterprise.

Primary education has long been free, and gross enrolment has been over 100 per cent for boys since at least 1950 and for girls since around 1970 (see Fig. 5.6). Secondary education became free in 1976 in private as well as in government schools. This had the effect mainly of enabling female enrolment to catch up with male, and to encourage both to continue growing steadily (see Fig. 5.7). It is to the government's credit that during the period of structural adjustment it 'resisted pressure from international agencies for reducing expenditure on education and for charging school fees' (MoES, 1993). Fees for tertiary education ended in 1988. Public schooling is thus at present free at all levels from primary up. It does not follow that indirect costs are not borne by households. Private tuition, books, and transport are among the main elements of cost (Joynathsing *et al.*, 1988: 3, 25).

In 1993 primary education became compulsory, to discourage drop-outs. Education remains extremely competitive, putting enormous pressure on both pupils and parents.

Special efforts are now being made to reduce differences in life opportunities by

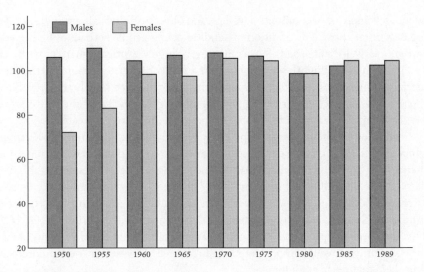

Fig. 5.6 First-level GER by gender, 1950–1989

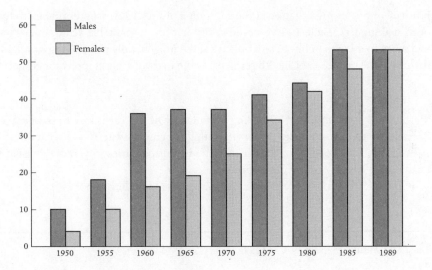

Fig. 5.7 Second-level GER by gender, 1950–89

improving standards in low-achieving primary schools, and by measures such as ensuring access to secondary schools for two pupils from any school from which no child otherwise qualifies (MoES, 1993: 34).

The enterprise culture of Mauritius is one of the assets on which its development has been built since the 1960s. It is not only that Mauritius uses legal and accounting norms familiar world-wide, but that in the 1960s it already had an adequate supply of accountants, lawyers, and other professionals at the disposal of the new enterprises. The tradition of sending young people abroad for higher education was well established. It was, however, largely a private matter (with rare exceptions like the English scholarships). As a result, higher education and the more lucrative professions for which it opened the way remained largely the preserve of those whose families were sufficiently well off. The foundation of the University of Mauritius in 1967 was therefore a step to further democratize education.

Finally, led by the initiative of private associations but with some government support, education is being developed downward into pre-primary education. More than 85 per cent of children age now attend pre-primary schools, though the standards are very variable and no compulsory registration or standards have yet been introduced (MoES, 1993: 4). Government is gradually providing classrooms in primary schools for pre-primary classes in disadvantaged areas (MEPD, 1993: 10.7). This improves the prospects of income-earning among the mothers who need it most urgently, as well as improving the educational prospects of their children and thus their chances in adult life.

Health

From an unpromising situation at the beginning of the 1960s, progress in health has been striking (see Table 5.3). It would seem that this remarkable achievement has had more to do with public health policies and with generally rising living standards than with the provision of health services, as the following paragraphs suggest.

Primary health care

Mauritius has a tradition of providing ambulatory health care close to the people. In response to overcrowding in hospitals, the dispensary system was set up in the 1930s. By the Second World War, thirty-nine dispensaries covered the island, forming the base for future development.

In pursuit of Titmuss's recommendation, government health policy has concen-

---

TABLE 5.3. Health progress, 1970 and 1991

	1970	1991
Still birth rate	70[a]	18
Deaths per 100,000 from:		
infectious diseases	123	14
perinatal conditions	138	35

[a] 1961

Source: Dommen and Dommen, forthcoming

trated on increasing the number of primary health service points, first, by a series of rationalizations and restructurings, which included the integration, from 1972, of the MFPA family-planning clinics and the estate hospitals into the ministry of health system; and secondly, by a programme of construction of health centres in the 1970s and 1980s. By 1985, people had access to primary health-care service points within a radius of three miles from their homes or within thirty minutes by public transport (WHO, 1986). Mobile units served remote areas. The main problem of physical access that remains concerns ambulance service—it is limited almost exclusively to interhospital transport, and only those with private means of transport can get to a hospital in an emergency.

In spite of an energetic policy of giving priority to the construction of health centres rather than to providing hospital beds (see Fig. 5.8), a number of features of the health picture suggest that delivery of services has not kept pace with the creation of centres.

For instance, child immunization coverage, already above 80 per cent in 1974, hardly changed between 1974 and 1991[4] (with the exception of measles vaccination, which was started only in 1982), apart from a slight and short-lived boost given by the expanded programme on immunization launched in 1981 (see Fig. 5.9). Yet infant and child mortality have continued to fall rapidly since 1974.

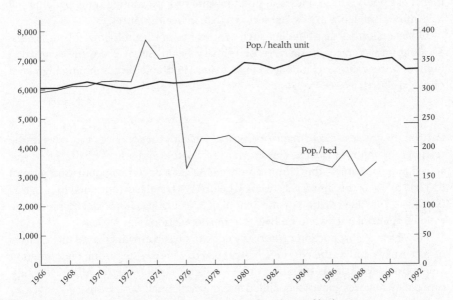

Fig. 5.8 Population per primary health service unit and per hospital bed, 1966–92

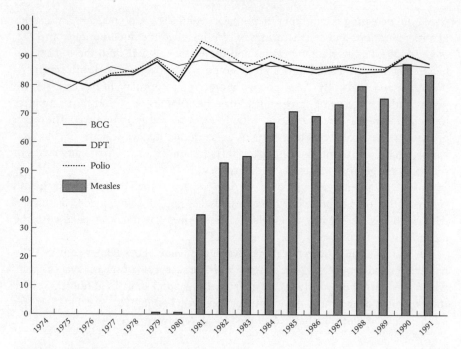

Fig. 5.9 Immunization coverage, 1975–92

Similarly, the hoped-for reduction in attendance at hospital outpatients' departments has not occurred, indicating that in spite of long waiting time, patients still have more confidence in hospital services than in health centres.

Other indicators that building such centres has not been followed by a corresponding improvement in delivery of primary health services are the stagnating number of new family-planning acceptors since 1985 and the continuing high level of illegal abortions (see Fig. 5.4).

Manpower

Part of the modest performance of primary health-care services can perhaps be related to manpower trends. The shortage of doctors and nurses of the 1960s was solved in record time—the Titmuss report aimed at a doctor-to-population ratio of 1 : 3,000 by 1980; this figure was reached before 1974, and has continued to progress (see Fig. 5.10). The creation of the School of Nursing also improved markedly the ratio of qualified nurses and midwives to the population.

However, the proportion of nurses to doctors has hardly increased in a quarter of a century—rather the contrary has occurred. This is a surprising phenomenon where primary health is supposed to be a priority, for an effective primary health-care policy requires above all qualified nursing personnel.

Inadequacy of trained management seems also to have been a continuing weak-

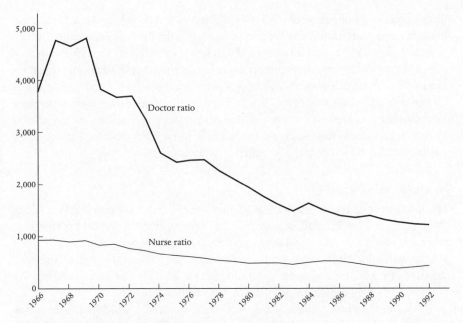

Fig. 5.10 Population per doctor and per nurse ratios, 1966–92

ness in the health service. Decentralization, adopted in the 1990s as a result of a review of the health sector, remains more a paper concept than a real delegation of responsibility, and health services seem still, as they were in 1988, to be dominated more by bureaucratic procedures and inertia than by innovation or the pursuit of efficiency.

Nutrition

Shortage of food has never been a serious problem in Mauritius. Successive household budget surveys have evidenced the increased share of meat, fish, fruit, and vegetables in food expenditure as incomes have risen. The total share devoted to food in family budgets has declined as people have become better off, motivating both the World Food Programme and more recently the government to phase out subsidies for food.

Studies on anaemia carried out in the Second World War and the mid-1960s had shown that iron-deficiency anaemia, often associated with hookworm infestation, was common. The Titmuss report recommended wearing shoes to school. This practical suggestion was followed, shoes were distributed free to schoolchildren, and hookworm has virtually disappeared. Other kinds of worm, and anaemia, continue to be a problem, however (UNICEF, 1994, sect. 4.18).

More recently, fears have been expressed that nutritional standards are threatened by the appearance of fast-food caterers and changing dietary patterns. However, anaemia among schoolchildren has regularly diminished since 1976 and a survey on diet, health, and lifestyle of youth found in 1988 that the typical meal of the 18–24-year-olds was more than adequate. It is true that the national nutrition survey of 1985 revealed some undernutrition among pre-school children, but this was associated with low income, low level of mother's education, water supplied from a public fountain, and absence of flush toilets. Mortality and morbidity caused by diabetes and heart disease are on the increase, but it is not clear how much this is due to nutritional factors and how much to other causes.

New health problems

Much has been made of the increasing incidence of non-communicable diseases (NCDs), such as heart and cerebrovascular disease, diabetes, and hypertension, related to new lifestyles typical of the more affluent. But a part of the increase can also be attributed to the changing age structure: the death rate from diseases of the circulatory system has increased by 50 per cent in the last twenty years, but the population over 50 has increased by a similar percentage.

Whatever the causes, these NCDs are also the conditions which led to pressures for costly, high-tech medicine. The introduction of Health Development Certificates to investors in order to encourage the provision of private health facilities is the government's answer to meeting this expensive demand without losing control of the quality of supply. At the same time, private companies have been setting up health insurance schemes for their employees. This policy of encouraging the private sector in the area of high-cost, curative medicine is seen by some as a means of relieving pressure on government health services and making those who can afford to pay for 'luxury' surgery do so; it is seen by others as opening the door to a two-track health system. Problems which were not priority targets in the first phase of development are now receiving more attention: alcoholism, physical and mental handicaps, and geriatrics. Mental illness remains a regrettable exception.

Social security

From rudimentary arrangements up to the mid-1960s, a comprehensive set of social security provisions was introduced gradually, the timing of implementation reflecting economic feasibility. Thus, the only scheme introduced immediately following the Titmuss report was the modest and relatively inexpensive family allowance (but without Titmuss's somewhat draconian proviso of limiting allowances to families of three or fewer children—a wise decision, as it turned out, as the population problem disappeared by other, less harsh, means). It was not until fifteen years later, in the wake of soaring sugar prices, that a comprehensive pension scheme was introduced in 1976.

The welfare state

Since the 1960s, government spending per capita and in real terms has increased by about 160 per cent for education, 180 per cent for health, and 190 per cent for social security. However, Figure 5.11 shows that the government's commitment to the welfare state, though strong, has nevertheless been subject to the vagaries of the economy. The leap forward in 1976 was due mainly to the introduction of free education at the secondary level and of the national pension scheme, at a time when high sugar prices seemed to make anything possible. With the notable exception of social security—social insurance was even extended in 1982 by the introduction of benefits for unemployed workers with dependants, and in 1986 by a benefit for severely handicapped invalids and old people—the welfare state did take a little buffeting from structural adjustment, especially in low-cost housing. Nevertheless, over the thirty years under consideration, the share to education and health have been approximately maintained.

Now it is the new social-welfare payments which are maintaining government expenditure on the social sector at high levels. As a result, a more selective approach to the welfare state has been adopted in the last decade. Interest in vulnerable groups and in targeting has emerged. In line with this new attitude, the ministry of

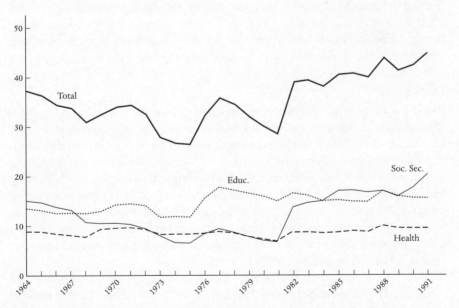

Fig. 5.11 Share of government recurrent expenditure on education, health, and social security, 1964–91

social security and national solidarity initiated programmes in favour of the elderly, the disabled, and abandoned children in the 1980s. In 1988, the Employment of Disabled Persons Act came into force. Universal subsidies on basic foodstuffs were replaced in 1993 by selective provision for the poor.

The role of non-governmental organizations

Whether by their pioneering efforts in the face of official inertia and even down-right hostility (as in the case of the MFPA in the late 1950s and early 1960s), or their consciousness-raising activities campaign by the Mauritian Action for the Promotion of Breast-Feeding and Nutrition or their provision of services to groups not otherwise served (dozens of voluntary associations provide institutional or day care for the disabled, the orphaned, and the pre-school age-group), non-governmental bodies have made a vast contribution to social welfare. It is to the credit of the government that it has been sensitive to the signals sent out by the NGOs. The various co-ordinating bodies—such as the National Children's Council, National Women's Council, and National Council for the Rehabilitation of Disabled Persons—created in the last few years are proof of the official desire to hear public opinion.

Women, Children, and the Family

Women

Perhaps the greatest change in Mauritian society over the last generation has been the transformation of the status of women—in the home, in the work-force, and in their contribution to national affairs. The causes of this metamorphosis were new employment opportunities, smaller families, and better education.

Employment

Before the 1970s, when women were employed outside the home, it was largely in sugar and domestic services. Few other opportunities were available. It was the opening up of the labour market with the creation of the EPZ in 1970 that provided the impetus needed to modernize the role of women. Pioneer firms had led the way in the 1960s in demonstrating the advantages of employing women, especially since they were in good health and sufficiently well educated to meet industrial demands. They were also less well paid and considered more docile than male workers. Women were not slow to respond: the percentage of females over 14 years old participating in the labour force increased from 20 per cent in 1972 to 28 per cent in 1983 and to 44 per cent in 1990.

The share of women in employment has, as a result, risen in all sectors except 'Community and Social Services', although the EPZ was responsible for most of this increase (see Table 5.4).

The new economic status and freedom of women was in sharp contrast to their subservient position in the home, particularly in marriage and parenthood. Indeed,

TABLE 5.4. Female employment by sector

Female employment as % of employment in:	1952	1962	1972	1983	1991
Agriculture	23	19	23	24	33
Manufacturing	14	8	15	42	56
Commerce	7	9	14	19	30
Transport, storage, and communications	1	2	3	4	9
Finance and business services	—	—	19	26	27
Community and social services	39	44	35	32	32
Total	20	18	20	26	35

Source: ILO (1945–89, 1988, 1992)

it was this subservience that employers appreciated. But it was against the background of the opening up of the labour market for women that the foundation stone of women's advancement in Mauritius was laid, by the amendment of the marriage legislation of the Napoleonic Code in 1980 and 1981. From then on, married women were guaranteed equal rights in conjugal and parental decisions, and in professional and economic life.

Family size

The stage was already set for the grand entry of women into the labour force by the previous advances in health and education. Indeed, without these underpinning improvements, neither the demand (employers appreciated the healthy, literate girls they hired) nor the supply conditions would have been right for the spurt forward in women's employment.

Smaller family size gave women more time, and also, due to fewer and better-spaced pregnancies, more energy, to participate both in paid employment outside the home, and in activities to promote the status of women. Moreover, the very use of contraceptive methods such as the pill and the IUD contributed directly to the strength of women inside the family, by giving wives the power to control their fertility independent of their husbands' intentions.

Women have certainly benefited more than men from improvements in health (see Table 5.5). The constantly rising gap between male and female life expectancy is due to the decline in maternal mortality and the fact that NCDs take a heavier toll among men.

Education of Girls

In 1950 it was mainly boys who went to school at all levels. At the primary level, the gap had almost closed by 1960: virtually all the children of both sexes in the relevant age-group were in some sort of school (see Fig. 5.6).

TABLE 5.5. Life expectancy at birth by sex, 1961–1991

	Male	Female
1961–3	58.7	62.3
1971–3	60.8	66.4
1982–4	64.4	71.7
1989–91	65.6	73.4

Source: Dommen and Dommen (1995)

At the secondary level, the enrolment ratio of girls caught up with that of boys only at the end of the 1980s, after secondary education became free (see Fig. 5.7). More progress remains to be achieved: the ratio of men to women in tertiary education was still 2 : 1 in 1989, which probably explains in part why, in spite of constituting over a third of the labour force, women are notably sparse among the higher professional echelons. Inequalities which still exist (for example, according to the census of 1990 70 per cent of those whose educational attainment was nil or pre-primary were women) need to be addressed not only in the context of women's rights, but in the pursuit of overall development.

Children

The children of Mauritius were among the main direct beneficiaries of the welfare state developed in the twenty years after 1960, particularly in the health and education fields.

Once the basic targets relating to maternal and child health were reached, the government turned its attention to more specific questions of child development, in many cases after prompting from the NGOs. Its increasing commitment to children was manifested by the adoption of a series of organizational, administrative, and legal measures: ratification of the Convention on the Rights of the Child; signature of the World Summit for Children Declaration; the addition in 1986 of child development to the ministry of women's rights; the creation of a National Adoption Council in 1987 to prevent some of the growing abuses in this area; the establishment in 1990 of a National Council for Children.

Children and the family[5]

Children are thought to be among the groups most vulnerable to the negative aspects of rapid economic development. In the aftermath of the fast rate of industrial growth experienced since 1984, much alarmism has been spread about its nefarious effects on family life and child care. However, allegations that with more mothers going out to work there has been a deterioration in health and nutritional standards of both women and children, and that children are being neglected and suffering from family breakdown, do not appear to be substantiated by the evidence so far.

A survey on breast-feeding in 1983 showed that malnutrition of babies was related mainly to poor education of the mother, and somewhat to low-income level, but not to employment of the mother (UNICEF, 1986: 22); the national nutrition survey of 1985, detecting some undernutrition among pre-school children, confirmed this conclusion.

On the second question—that of possible child neglect as a result of women working—some light is shed by changes in the age of female labour force participation. Whereas in 1952 the proportion of employed women went up after the age of 45 (Titmuss and Abel-Smith, 1961: 127), i.e. at the end of the child-bearing and child-rearing age, by 1982 it was precisely the opposite (Yin *et al.*, 1992: 42). Working mothers of small children have resorted to well-worn solutions, such as help from non-employed female members of the family and placing children in day-care centres and pre-primary schools. Resistance to compulsory overtime is another.

Complaints by women of violence in the home have become more numerous in the last decade, but professionals interpret this as one effect of women becoming more vocal and assertive as they claim their new right to autonomy within the marriage, rather than as a sign of family conflict really being more common. The increasing divorce rate, also often cited as an indicator of family breakdown, is so far no more than a juridico-statistical construction. It results from the fact that since 1981 religious marriages have legal status, with the result that what was previously an unreported separation now appears as a divorce.

That family life seems to be as intact as it ever was is borne out by at least one study, which found that 93 per cent of the 8–14-year-olds and 81 per cent of the 15–24-year-olds were spending almost all or a lot of their leisure time with their family members (MoH, 1988: 7).

Whatever future monitoring may reveal as regards the social effects of industrialization, it is undeniable that for thousands of Mauritian households, increased family incomes resulting from the recent boom years have made the difference between abject poverty and a decent standard of living. The pattern of increased indebtedness of households since the mid-1980s, committing them to regular payments over periods of up to thirty months per consumer durable purchased, has induced increased work effort and a pressing need not to put one's own employment at risk (Lamusse and Burn, 1991: 85, 115).

However, it seems that those who have suffered the most from the long hours of work put in by women in the EPZ are the women themselves. In a survey conducted in 1990, many women referred to the fatigue caused by factory work, and the majority admitted that long hours worked in the EPZ affected family life.

The Root Causes

A democratic society

Democracy has played a major role in the economic success of the country. What needs to be stressed here are the deep and spreading roots of what in so many other countries is a fragile plant.

The Labour Party, founded in 1936, was the country's first real political party (Simmons, 1982: 63), and it played a pivotal role in Mauritian politics until 1982. Even after the general election of that year, in which the coalition parties lost all sixty seats to the Mouvement Militant Mauricien (MMM), its successors in power maintained the style it had set. On core issues (religious and linguistic tolerance, parliamentary democracy, and a development strategy based on a mixed economy but with concern for all) there has been an enduring national consensus (cf. Bowman, 1991: 101).

An integral part of the democratic game everywhere is to make attractive offers on the eve of elections. In Mauritius the offers take the form of actual realizations. Thus relief works were introduced at the time of the campaign for the independence elections (British funds were involved). A number of major social measures were introduced on the eve of the 1976 elections: the thirteenth month and the national pension scheme, free secondary schooling, and reduction of the voting age to 18. These significant innovations were not just a gimmick, however; they were retained as lasting elements of social policy.

Consensus

The time and effort for consultation, both inside and outside government, when new solutions are to be found or decisions to be made, have become characteristic of the Mauritian way, especially since 1982. In the 1960s relations between the government and the private sector, in particular the sugar industry, were distant. The need at the time was to insist on altering the balance between the economic power of the plantocracy and the new popularly elected political power. Now that this has been achieved, the government's objective is to operate by consensus. The standard method with respect to any particular issue is to bring the interested parties together to work out an agreement. Once they have succeeded, the government adopts it as policy. Evidence of the method lies in the alphabet soup of committees, subcommittees, councils, associations and such, often established at government instigation or with official support.

One social category remains on the fringe of this process: the workers. Trade unions represent only certain sectors and by and large only one sex. In the East Asian style, employers in the new sectors—EPZ and tourism—have a strong preference for docile workers. The dispersion of industry throughout the island, while bringing the benefits outlined above, also has the effect of making trade-union recruitment harder.

A vigorous press

In Mauritius, a lively, outspoken, and free press plays a major role in keeping government action under public scrutiny, thereby giving the authorities a powerful incentive to honesty and democracy.

In the 1960s there were twelve dailies fuelling lively political debate. Absolute circulation numbers were lower in 1988 than in 1965 even though literacy had spread and population was greater. Readership fell substantially in the decade after 1965, i.e. after the introduction of television. There are now only two major dailies.

Although there is a loss in the diversity of opinions expressed in the media, both papers need to offer broad and objective coverage rather than colourful polemic to attract a wide range of readers.

Liberalism with leadership

Since 1982 the aim of government has been 'to implement a liberal, dynamic and competitive economic strategy on the lines of that followed with such eminent success by the East Asian NICs' (Lamusse, 1989: 32).

There is an element of *dirigisme* in East Asian liberalism. In the same spirit, government has been willing to take initiatives in pointing directions for the private economy. The EPZ had been legally established in 1970, following a lead set by private enterprise. It was in 1985 that government took a more active role by founding MEDIA to promote the EPZ among foreign investors (Lagesse, 1988: 221).

The creation of the Mauritius Freeport Authority in 1993 owes much to government initiative. Government is also playing more of a leadership role in Mauritius's current efforts to diversify into offshore financial services. Government is using state enterprises or parastatals either to provide services to the private business sector or to goad it through competition to more innovative, efficient, or socially desirable behaviour.

No army

Mauritius is one of about twenty-five countries in the world which has no army (this section succinctly reflects the conclusions of Dommen and Maizels, 1988). This can be considered a factor of political stability since it excludes the possibility of military intervention in the political process as has occurred in so many other countries (Hein, 1989: 50). Furthermore, the government budget is relieved of what elsewhere can be a significant burden; it can concentrate more single-mindedly on development and welfare.

Future Problems

The preceding account is not to deny that Mauritius has had its share of difficulties: there *have* been race riots and labour unrest; there *is* some poverty and inequality;

deviations from the institutions of democracy *have* occurred. The way such tensions have been dealt with in the past is nevertheless a cause for optimism in the future, where several subjects need to be addressed: how to juggle the sugar rent between other sectors; what can take the place of the sugar rent or complement it; competition in export markets: how to maintain it if wages rise; inequality of income: poverty and class beginning to coincide with race and religion (the *malaise créole* is a symptom); policy towards immigrant workers; signs of corruption; some of the highest abortion rates in the world; changing costs of the welfare state with an ageing population; stress of modern post-industrial life: new dangers to health and families; democracy, a delicate plant, needing to be continuously nurtured; and the role and functioning of public administration.

Democracy, social justice, and the multicultural society all currently support each other in an intricately inseparable way. The confrontation of this subtle structure with the harsh ideologies which at present constitute the accepted wisdom throughout the world may be the greatest source of precariousness in Mauritius's development prospects today.

Notes

1. The social, political, geographic, and economic make-up of Rodrigues is quite distinct from that of the main island. Rodrigues and the other islands constituting the State of Mauritius are therefore not included in this study.
2. For a description of the 60–0 election, see section on 'A Democratic Society'.
3. Association with the Common Market was also of great importance to ensuring access to the European Market for the products of the EPZ.
4. A survey conducted in 1993 indicates that coverage was some 10% higher than officially reported, perhaps because immunizations performed at private institutions may be under-reported (UNICEF, 1994: sect. 4.38).
5. This section draws heavily on Lamusse *et al.*, 1990; Lamusse and Burn, 1991; Maxwell Stamp, 1992; and University of Mauritius, 1993. For easier reading, the sources have not been attributed to each point made in the text.

Bibliography

Beller, W., d'Ayala, P., and Hein, P. (1990), *Sustainable Development and Environmental Management of Small Islands*, Paris: UNESCO.

Bheenick, Rundheersing (1990), 'Sustainable Development and Environmental Management in Mauritius—or a Tale of Two Birds', in W. Beller, P. d'Ayala, and P. Hein (1990).

Bowman, Larry W. (1991), *Mauritius: Democracy and Development in the Indian Ocean*, Boulder, Colo.: Westview Press.

Brass, W. (1976), 'Impact of the Family Planning Programme on Fertility in Mauritius', *IPPF Medical Bulletin*, 4.

Colonial Office (1951), 'British Islands in the Southern Hemisphere 1945–51', London: HMSO, Cmd. 8230.

Dommen, B. and Dommen, E. (1995), *Mauritius. The Roots of Success*. London: Zed Books.

Dommen, Edward, and Hein, Philippe (1985), *States, Microstates and Islands*, Beckenham: Croom Helm.

—— and Maizels, Alfred (1988), 'The military burden in developing countries', *Journal of Modern African Studies*, 26/3.

Hein, Catherine (1977), 'Family Planning in Mauritius: A National Survey', in *Studies in Family Planning*, 8/12.

—— (1988), 'Multinational Enterprises and Employment in the Mauritian Export Processing Zone', Working Paper 52, Geneva: ILO.

Hein, Philippe (1989), 'Structural Transformation in an Island Country: The Mauritius Export Processing Zone (1971 to 1988)', *UNCTAD Review*, 1/2.

ILO (various years), *Yearbook of Labour Statistics*, Geneva: International Labour Office.

Joynathsing, M., Manssoy, M., Nababsing, V., Pochun, M., and Selwyn, P. (1988), *Private Costs of Education in Mauritius*, University of Mauritius, School of Administration.

Lagesse, Marcelle (1988), *150 Années de Jeunesse: Histoire de la Mauritius Commercial Bank*, Port Louis: Editions la Caravelle.

Lamusse, Roland (1989), 'Adjustment to Structural Change in Manufacturing in a North-South Perspective: The Case of the Clothing Export Sector in Mauritius', International Employment Policies Working Paper 27, Geneva: ILO.

—— and Burn, Nalini (1991), 'Structural Adjustment, Employment and Poverty in Mauritius', final draft submitted to ILO/JASPA.

—— Joynathsing, M., Kalasopatan, S., and Essoo, N. (1990), 'Study on Absenteeism among Production Workers in the Mauritius Export Processing Zone', School of Law, Management and Social Studies, University of Mauritius.

Lloyd, C. B., and Ivanov, S. (1988), 'The Effects of Improved Child Survival on Family Planning Practices and Fertility', *Studies in Family Planning*, 19.

Mauritius Family Planning Association (1993), *Research Report on the Use of Induced Abortion in Mauritius*.

Maxwell Stamp PLC (1992), *Study of the Social, Economic and Environmental Impact of Industrialisation and Strategy Formulation*, final report and appendices.

Meade, James E. (1961a), *The Economic and Social Structure of Mauritius*, London: Macmillan; reprinted Frank Cass, 1968.

—— (1961b), 'Mauritius: a case study in Malthusian economics', *Economic Journal*, 71/283.

—— (1993), *Liberty, Equality and Efficiency*, London, Macmillan.

MoED (Ministry of Economic Planning and Development) (1988), *National Development Plan 1988–1990*.

—— (1993), *National Development Plan 1992–1994*.

MoES (Ministry of Education and Science) (1993), *Citizens of Tomorrow: Education in Progress*, 83–93.

MoF (Ministry of Finance) (1988), *Health Sector Review: Main Report*.

MoH (Ministry of Health) (1988), *Survey on Diet, Health and Lifestyle of Youth in Mauritius*.

—— (various years), *Health Statistics Annual*.

Seetohul, Brijlall D. (1992), 'Transports et télécommunications à l'île Maurice, Mémoire pour la maîtrise de géographie', Université de Bordeaux III.

Simmons, Adele Smith (1982), *Modern Mauritius*, Bloomington, Ind.: Indiana University Press.

Titmuss, Richard M., and Abel-Smith, Brian (1961), *Social Policies and Population Growth in Mauritius*, London: Macmillan; reprinted Frank Cass, 1968.

UNICEF (1986), *Breast-Feeding and Infant Health in Mauritius*, Port Louis.

—— (1994), *Situation Analysis of Women and Children in Mauritius 1994*, Port Louis.

University of Mauritius (1993), *Study on the Evolution of the Status of Women in Mauritius 1968–1992*.

WHO (1986), *Weekly Epidemiological Record*, 11.

Yin, Pierre, Ha Yeung, Donald, Kowlessur, Deshmuk, and Chung, Mirella (1992), *L'île Maurice et sa zone franche*, Port Louis.

6

Rapid Social Transformation despite Economic Adjustment and Slow Growth: The Experience of Zimbabwe

RENE LOEWENSON AND MUNHAMO CHISVO

Introduction

Zimbabwe is a good case-study for examining the relationship between social and economic development, both because of the stark differences between pre- and post-independence policy and practice and because of the significant social gains made in the 1980s, despite its low-income status and relatively weak economic growth. This chapter discusses the social and economic policy trends in three periods, focusing on social development in health, education, and population: in (a) the pre-independence phase, before 1980; (b) the post-independence phase in the 1980s, and (c) the phase of structural adjustment starting in 1991.

The experiences of British colonialism, of the liberation war, and of the conditions after independence have produced stark contrasts. The settler white population systematically undermined peasant agriculture and mining, expropriated black land, and used black labour from Rhodesia (as it was known prior to 1980) and the neighbouring countries to build up a base of large-scale farming and mining, and, in the mid-1900s, a manufacturing sector. African nationalism increased in the 1960s. The liberation struggle caused an increase in military expenditures and disrupted rural production at a time when economic stagnation had begun to set in. From 1975 onward, the country shifted to a war economy.

In mid-1979, a Commonwealth initiative led to an agreement at Lancaster House in London on a Westminster-type constitution (with protection of land and property rights and reserved white seats), and universal elections in February 1980. Despite an overwhelming majority in the elections for Zimbabwe African National Union (ZANU) (PF), in a policy of 'reconciliation' the new government, led by Robert Mugabe, invited the participation of senior members of Zimbabwe African People's Union (ZAPU) and of the white community. At the time of independence in 1980, the government inherited a contradictory situation: extreme inequalities in incomes, assets, and access to education, housing, and health care, together with a diversified economy including industry, agriculture, and services, an excellent formal sector infrastructure, and an apparently good potential for growth. This inequality coexisted with huge expectations that the government would immediately address the inherited inequalities, with respect to both economic and social opportunities.

Trends and Factors in Social Development

Since 1980, the government has been a multiparty democracy, with elections every five years. Government followed first a 'socialist' agenda, then a mixed social demo-cratic agenda, and finally, in the 1990s, a classical World Bank structural-adjustment programme. There has been significant social progress in Zimbabwe, particularly over the decade 1980–90, despite a relatively sluggish economic performance placing the country generally ahead of other Sub-Saharan African countries and developing countries in social progress.

Policy support for social-sector development

There were three clear policy shifts in the three periods under discussion, pre-1980, post-1980 to 1990, and 1990 onward. Pre-1980 policy promoted a racially divided social system with a fragmentation of service provision based on race, income, and geographical area. After 1980, policies emphasized reconstruction, equity, and redistribution in social development, with a deliberate focus on the non-racial expansion of services to cover the whole population and a more limited set of policy initiatives to allocate resources according to need. In the third phase, post-1990, the policy of structural adjustment introduced new criteria of efficiency and cost-sharing into the social sector, reducing the emphasis on equity. Policies in the 1980s encouraged community participation leveraged by state resource support and organized through state structures. Post-1990 structural-adjustment policies also placed emphasis on public input, but through more individual measures of cost recovery and with a lesser degree of state input. These policy changes, and their consequent impact on resource allocation in the social sector, are exemplified in health and education.

Pre-independence health policy was not clearly articulated: in practice, services were divided and segregated by rural/urban, socio-economic, and racial groupings. As independence drew closer, efforts were made by the government to articulate a health policy that would not be racially based, but that would preserve economic privilege in the health sector, i.e. access by wealthier groups to a high-cost private medical sector and by the poor to cheaper and less well-resourced public services (Gilmurray *et al.*, 1979).

In 1980, the new government made health a focal area of change. Its health policy aimed to ensure that every citizen would have access to the necessities for basic health and thus stressed positive discrimination in health care; the abolition of racially discriminatory laws; reconstruction and rehabilitation of rural health services; establishment in policy of an integrated public health infrastructure from community to quaternary health facilities; restriction of private-sector expansion; post-training bonding of health workers to the public sector and barring of immigrants to private practice; and incorporation of the traditional health sector, establishment of an essential drugs list, and a unified health insurance scheme. These policies were articulated in 'Planning for Equity in Health' (1984). Central to health policy in 1980 was the primary health-care approach, aimed at providing accessible frontline health care and involving communities in the planning and development of health activities. These policies were sustained through the 1980s, but after the introduction of structural adjustment, the budgetary dimension to policy was given a more central focus. The 1992 ministry of health *Corporate Plan* reflected a shift from proactive measures that focused on equity in the early 1980s towards reactive measures that dealt with fiscal and economic policy constraints.

Education policy similarly underwent a major change in 1980. Education policy prior to 1980 was tailored to suit the racially divided system of skills development and production in Zimbabwe. The economic structure of black labour and white management was supported by the education system. Education thus became one of the key elements of the liberation struggle. Post-independence education policy emphasized that education was the birthright of every citizen and that the State would ensure, at all costs, equal educational opportunity for all. Education policy abolished racial discrimination, provided for free and compulsory primary education for all children, made provisions for post-primary education, provided state support for informal and adult education, and aimed to bring the majority of the black population into the mainstream of development. The commitment to educate the population has been one of the most persistent policies in Zimbabwe.

These social-policy changes were supported by and reflected in economic policy. In the 1980s, the government explicitly and clearly articulated social policy in all areas, including the implications for economic and budget policies through the 'Growth with Equity' strategy and Transitional National Development Plan (1992). These development policies used public-sector expenditure and revenues from growth to effect social change, leaving the private sector essentially unchanged. Economic policy measures created an enabling environment for social policy by supporting the expansion of the public sector as a key area of economic growth and investment. In its five-year Transitional Development Plan, the government set an ambitious growth rate target of 8 per cent and emphasized redistribution of the outcomes of growth as a way of achieving social development.

During the 1980s, the economy expanded by about 3 per cent per annum. Considering the weakness of the world economy, declining terms of trade, and the periodic occurence of drought, this was a relatively good performance, especially when compared with the regional average. Unfortunately, the high population growth eroded the benefits in terms of per capita income gains.[1] Despite the difficult international economic environment and the high population growth, the country managed to maintain its level of per capita income, a respectable achievement indeed. The economy's investment ratio was high, at an average about 20 per cent, indicating that the efficiency of investments was low.[2]

Economic factors in the sustainability of social investments

Investment in social development peaked in the early 1980s, reinforced by external borrowings and donor assistance. Budgets were also reorientated, with shifts within sector budgets and between sectors, as outlined earlier. By the end of 1985, the government seemed to have responded effectively to the new demands and difficult circumstances of the post-independence period, and to have made progress towards long-term development needs. The damaged transport and power infrastructure had been effectively rehabilitated and the basis for the country's social infrastructure had been laid. Priority investment in agriculture yielded an increase in marketed output while the largely inward-oriented manufacturing sector also began to find external markets. The economy had a relatively large contribution from the manufacturing sector, although the major growth over the 1980s was in the service sector.

Growth in formal-sector employment mainly occurred in the service sector. The share of manufacturing in output actually fell while its share in employment remained the same. In 1980, out of a labour force of 2.5m., 1m. people were in formal wage employment, while the remainder were either in informal-sector employment where incomes are much lower, or unemployed. By 1990 the ratio had changed to 1.25m. employed out of a labour force of 4m. (ILO, 1993). While the estimates on unemployment vary, the ministry of finance estimates that it may be as high as 1m. workers (Govt. of Zimbabwe, 1991a).

Through the 1980s it became evident that the economic policy assumptions of growth and particularly of investment were not being achieved to the extent needed to sustain the high levels of social expenditure, increasing borrowings, and shifting economic preoccupations to fiscal policy issues. Investment (GFCF as a percentage of GDP), particularly in the productive sectors, became sluggish in the 1980s. In addition, to deal with the budget deficet, import restrictions and cut-backs in foreign exchange allocations reduced the volume of imports to a level inadequate to permit the efficient functioning of the economy, while export growth was slow. Given the need for investment, with the extremely old capital stock and the lack of domestic investment, stimulating investment and reducing the deficit, rather than redistributing wealth, became a key policy issue of the mid-1980s.

Given these economic problems, the government embarked on a structural-adjustment programme (ESAP) in late 1990 with the support of the World Bank and the IMF. However, the supply response to those reforms has been relatively weak, and was further undermined by drought in 1992 and 1995. Although some aspects of economic liberalization have been successfully implemented, especially in the areas of foreign-exchange management and international trade, economic growth has remained anaemic. The expected rapid recovery from the 1992 drought did not materialize. The fiscal deficit remains as large as in the pre-ESAP period, if not larger, because of the weak revenue collection, faltering parastatal reforms, and a rising debt burden. The combination of a tight monetary policy with a relatively lax fiscal stance forced the government to rely more on domestic commercial borrowing to finance the budget deficit at an average interest rate of close to 30 per cent p.a.

As a result, debt service charges absorbed nearly 40 per cent of the budget in 1995, up from 20 per cent in the pre-ESAP period. The country's external debt stock has skyrocketed to approximately 80 per cent of GNP in 1993, up from about 50 per cent in the second half of the 1980s. Principal and interest payments to multilateral creditors alone rose tenfold from $US18m. in 1985 to $US176m. in 1994. In relative terms, they increased from 0.4 to 3.1 per cent of national income (UNICEF, 1996).

The persistently large fiscal deficits fuelled inflation. The rate of inflation actually rose to over 20 per cent per year in 1994 and 1995. In a liberalized financial market, this limited the prospects for a reduction in the interest rate, a precondition for a gradual reduction of the share of the fiscal revenue that needed to be set aside for (domestic) debt servicing. Weak economic growth, high inflation, and falling discretionary budgetary expenditure rapidly jeopardized the social achievements of the 1980s.

Based on the 1990–1 household income and expenditure survey, the World Bank estimates that 31 per cent of the rural population and 10 per cent of the urban residents live below the poverty line. Since those figures relate to the pre-ESAP and pre-drought period, the poverty assessment further admits that:

it seems likely that poverty has become more common since 1991, especially in urban areas. Reasons cited include, slow growth in employment opportunities, sharp increases in prices, reduction in real wages, and retrenchments in the public as well as private sector. Programs set up to help alleviate these transitional problems have not been as effective as planned. The large increase of street kids roaming Harare is one indication of this. (World Bank, 1995)

In short, the economic structural adjustment programme—which was interrupted by severe drought in 1992 and again in 1995—has had mixed results. Some reforms have yielded encouraging results, especially the loosening of the regulations on foreign exchange, imports, and investments, but the overall supply response has been disappointing. The country's social progress has been seriously jeopardized while its economic performance has not improved. On balance, the majority of the population have paid a relatively high social cost for the very limited economic benefits that have resulted from the reforms (see later discussions). Indeed, some of the reforms were quite intrusive in the sense that they had a direct impact on the daily life of almost every Zimbabwean child.

Health

The main health indicators over the period prior to independence and up to 1990 are shown in Table 6.1. In the 1960s and 1970s, the highest levels of ill health were in women and children. Mortality differed by race, class, and geographical area, with a 1 : 3.5 : 10 ratio in infant-mortality rates between whites, urban blacks, and rural blacks in 1980, corresponding to a 39 : 5 : 1 ratio in incomes (MoH, 1984a). The IMR for the black majority was estimated at between 120 and 300 per 1,000. The disease pattern in the high-income white population groups was similar to that of industrialized countries, while that of the black majority was a combination of nutritional and communicable diseases and problems associated with pregnancy. Maternal undernutrition contributed to low birth weight in 10–20 per cent of births (Loewenson and Sanders, 1988). Common diseases included measles, pneumonia, tuberculosis, diarrhoea, malaria, meningitis, and neonatal tetanus. Occupational lung diseases, high blood pressure, pesticide intoxication, schistosomiasis, mental illness, liver diseases and other alcohol-related problems, and STDs were also common in the adult population.

The health-care system did not address this unequal health pattern: health services were inadequate and inequitable, based on racial division. By 1980, the predominantly white, health-insured population using urban private services had a health expenditure per capita of $Z31, while the rural black population, who depended mainly on mission and lower-level public services, had a health expenditure per capita of $Z4. In fact, only districts surrounding urban areas or the large mines and agricultural estates had hospitals: in 1980, 44 per cent of the health budget went to the urban-based sophisticated central hospitals serving about 15 per cent of the population, while only 24 per cent went to the primary- and secondary-level facilities that served the majority (MoH, 1984a).

After 1980, the policy of enhancing equitable access to health services had an observable impact on health status. Infant mortality, and particularly neonatal mortality, fell steadily up to 1990 (GoZ/UNICEF, 1994). The most marked decline in IMR was in rural areas, where it fell from about 140 per 1,000 to about 73 per 1,000, with rural–urban differentials reduced to about half. Over the 1980s measles declined substantially as a cause of mortality, while respiratory and intestinal infection and nutritional deficiencies remained important causes (GoZ, 1991b). By 1990, pneumonia and diarrhoea together were consistently responsible for nearly 40 per cent of deaths annually. However, by 1991 HIV-related deaths had become the single leading cause of death responsible for over 20 per cent of mortality in the City of Harare (City of Harare, 1990–2).

One of the key aspects of the health sector contributing to the positive changes in maternal and child health post-1980 was the expansion of primary health care (PHC). PHC was introduced into the health-care system as the first basic level of health care, with an emphasis on the horizontal integration of the various pro-

TABLE 6.1. Health indicators

	Pre-1980	1980	1985	1990
Life expectancy yrs	50 (1970)	55	60	64
Infant mortality/1,000	120–50	88	79	61
Under-5 mortality/1,000	—	104 (1978–82)	—	87
Maternal mortality/100,000	—	150	87 (1987)	80
Immunization coverage (%):	—	(1982)	(1984)	
BCG		59	87	76
OPV		31	61	75
DPT		32	66	72–8
Measles		51	53	72–6
Tetanus toxoid		—	—	51
Births attended by health personnel (%)	—	—	63 (1983–8)	74
Population with access to safe water (%)	—	—		
rural			35	74
urban			100	100
Access to sanitary disposal (%)	—	4	7	21
rural				
urban		100	100	100

Sources: World Bank (1992, 1994); Govt. of Zimbabwe (n.d.), *Estimates of Expenditure, 1980–90*, Harare, and data obtained from the Central Statistical Office

TABLE 6.2. Health input indicators

Indicator	Pre-1980	1980	1985	1990
Doctors/1000	0.102 (1970)	0.143	0.144 (1986)	0.147
Nurses/1000	0.89 (1979)	0.98	1.06 (1986)	1.4
Nurses/doctor	6.58 (1979)	6.39	7.30 (1986)	9.5

Sources: World Bank, (1988, 1994); data obtained from the Central Statistical Office, Ministry of Health, 1987, 1989

grammes (immunization, nutrition, family planning, etc.). The main cause of the reduction in immunizable diseases has been the successful expanded programme on immunization (EPI) that at its peak covered over three-quarters of Zimbabwean children (see Table 6.1). The EPI led to an increase in the number of children between 12 and 23 months fully vaccinated in rural Zimbabwe, from 25 per cent in 1982 to 80 per cent by 1988. By 1988, coverage began to plateau at a time when government aimed to take over from the largely donor-assisted nature of the programme while facing cuts in the real per capita allocations to the ministry of health. Not surprisingly, therefore, since 1988, reported coverage for all antigens has registered a steady decline. In 1989–93, 5–10 per cent of infants annually dropped out before receiving their second dose of OPV and DPT, and a further 5–10 per cent dropped out before receiving their third dose (GoZ, 1995).

In 1980, the ministry of health significantly expanded maternal health services and in 1988 increased maternal health coverage rates (see Table 6.1). Antenatal care (ANC) rates rose to 90 per cent and above, with a reduction in the rural–urban differential in ANC (96 per cent coverage in urban areas, 90 per cent in communal areas, and 94 per cent in large-scale farm [LSF] areas) (MoH, 1988a). By 1988, 92 per cent of urban women, 64 per cent of communal area women, and 56 per cent of LSF women delivered at a health facility, and nearly 80 per cent of women surveyed in 1991 delivered in a health facility (clinic, rural health centre, or hospital).

An important aspect of PHC has been the interface between the community and the health services. The village health worker (VHW) was initiated in the liberation struggle. The concept was adopted in national policy in 1980, and by 1984 over 7,000 VHWs were involved in the promotion of primary health care. VHWs were issued bicycles and later given allowances by the ministry of health, together with basic drug packs (analgesics, antimalarials, etc.). In the early 1980s, VHWs shifted from being community-based workers (elected, paid by, and responsible to the community) to being the lowest arm of the ministry of health at the community level. In the late 1980s, the VHW was transferred to the then ministry of community development and co-operatives, where they became the village community worker (VCW), supporting both community development and PHC activities as extension agents of government, a fundamental shift from the original concept of community mobilizer/organizer and teacher on health issues (Loewenson et al., 1989–90). The role of such community-based workers revived again in the early 1990s as the health sector faced the problems of meeting health-care needs. For example, overstretched by the demands of the AIDS epidemic, the Bulawayo City Health Department initiated, with the co-operation of the residents' associations and community groups, a home-based programme on AIDS, working with community activists. These promoters also cover primary health care, working closely with local civic groups on health needs.

The expansion of primary health care in the 1980s was backed by a significant thrust to spread access to primary and secondary levels of curative care, particularly in the underserved rural areas. Following the policy of developing a comprehensive health service outlined earlier, in 1980 the sector was reorganized into a four-tier system of service delivery: rural health centres, fifty-six district/rural hospitals, provincial hospitals, and quaternary central hospitals. The government built or upgraded rural health centres and district hospitals, repealed the laws that governed the racial division of hospital services, shifted budgets towards rural, preventive, and primary-care facilities, targeted donor and NGO support on previously underserved, rural, primary-care needs, and implemented massive training and deployment programmes of health personnel, upgrading equipment at primary- and secondary-care facilities. By the late 1980s, 85 per cent of Zimbabwe's population lived within 8 km. of a health unit (CSO, 1989), with 927 health centres in 1992. The government also established and implemented an essential drugs list and a system for drug procurement.

The expansion in programmes and services after 1980 led to a rapid expansion of new and existing personnel (see Table 6.2). The number of registered nurses increased from 1981 to 1989 by 656 SRNs and 2,082 SCNs, the former being concentrated at central (urban) facilities and the latter at primary care centres and rural/district hospitals. New personnel were added, including rehabilitation assistants and community health workers. This expansion, driven by the expansion in training, was counterbalanced by loss of personnel, particularly high-cost professional personnel, from the public sector to the private sector and through emigration to better-paying countries in Southern Africa, as well as by concentration of highly skilled personnel in urban, central facilities, and by their lack of willingness to work in rural areas (Loewenson *et al.*, 1989–90). The number of registered doctors increased from 1,159 in 1981 to only 1,290 in 1989 (i.e. an increase of 131), despite 462 local doctors graduating in the period and an annual employment of about seventy-five expatriate doctors. Less than 15 per cent of doctors were in government service five years after graduating, with about 60 per cent of doctors working in the private sector and 70 per cent in urban areas.

The policy commitment to health led to a growth in health-sector financing from a per capita value of $Z9.87 in 1979 to $Z11.49 in 1988, measured at constant 1980 prices. Most of this growth was concentrated in the first years of independence, with a small decline after 1986. The health expenditure over the 1980s rose to about 2.5 per cent of GDP and about 5 per cent of the government budget (see Table 6.3). The main providers of health care in 1986–7 were the public sector (55 per cent of health financing) and the private sector (25 per cent) (World Bank, 1993). Between 1980 and 1988, equity measures included a reduction in the medical care services allocation (90 per cent to 82 per cent) and a doubling in the preventive services share (7 per cent to 14 per cent). The share of salaries, wages, and

TABLE 6.3. Allocations to health

Indicator (%)	Pre-1980	1980	1985	1990
Share of health exp. in govt. expenditure	4.6 (1979)	5.4	4.9	5.3
Health expenditure to GDP	—	2.4	2.4	2.5
Share of donor funding to health expenditure	—	8 (1982–3)	49	75

Sources: World Bank, *Public Sector and Poverty Reduction Options*, Harare, 1994, mimeo; Govt. of Zimbabwe, 1980–1990 *Estimates of Expenditure*, Harare; World Bank, *Zimbabwe: A Review of Primary and Secondary Education*, Washington, DC, 1992; data obtained from the Central Statistical Office

allowances also increased in the period from 26.3 per cent in 1980–1 to 44.7 per cent in 1986–7, while grants and loans to local authorities and missions were initially increased at the expense of the central hospitals, and then later reduced.

Some issues remained difficult to resolve despite the policy emphasis on equity: inequity between private and public health systems and their clients and between central urban care and rural primary care; ineffective functioning of the referral system; and resistance in doctors to work in rural areas or to stay in the public sector. Hence, inequity was not eliminated in facility provision: problems in the referral system persisted, with patients using the closest facility, meaning that higher-income groups used the much more costly quaternary facilities for sec-ondary care, using greater resources to manage a similar range and severity of ill-nesses (Loewenson *et al.*, 1989–90).

The HIV / AIDS epidemic has posed a huge challenge to health in the 1990s. The first AIDS cases were confirmed in 1985. By 1992 official estimates put countrywide infection with HIV at 800,000 persons (Wilson *et al.*, 1993*a*), extensive in both rural and urban areas. It is estimated that by the year 2000 AIDS will lead to the deaths of 1 million Zimbabweans (780,000 adults and 220,000 children) and to 600,000 orphans, putting a heavy burden on the already weakened extended family, as well as on severely strained social services (ibid.).

While the post-1980 changes narrowed the wide gap that existed between rural and urban income groups and between high- and low-income groups in access to health care, this plateaued in the late 1980s, and in the 1990s there was a reversal in many of the positive health-care coverage gains, in poorer communities.

Indeed, basic social services were not immune to fiscal austerity. Between 1990 and 1995, public spending on preventive health care dropped by over 40 per cent in real per capita terms. The government's real recurrent per capita expenditure on health declined from $Z16.50 in 1990–1 (1980 dollars) to $Z10.92 in 1993–4, barely above its 1980–1 level (Chisvo, 1993, 1994). Such dramatic reductions nullified most of the progress made during the 1980s. In some instances, real per capita expendi-tures have fallen below their level at independence in 1980. As a result, several social indicators have deteriorated in the early 1990s. Although only a few social statistics are available for the early 1990s, they all indicate a reversal of the progress made during the 1980s. Maternal mortality and malnutrition have risen, while female enrolment ratios have started to decline, especially at the secondary level. Although it is difficult to isolate the impact of the drought, it can be ascertained that the reduction in budgetary expenditure on basic social services has compounded the vulnerability of the poor in recent years.

• Bed occupancy at Harare central hospital declined by 17 per cent between December 1990 and December 1991, with a shift in admissions toward more emer-gency procedures (Renfrew, 1992).

- The proportion of babies born before arrival increased, with a greater proportion dying before or at the neonatal unit, indicating barriers in access to maternity services (ibid.).

- Nurses per 100 people in government service fell by 10 per cent between 1991 and 1992 and a further 3 per cent by 1993; the real value of the government medical stores drug fund fell by 13 per cent from 1991–2 and the nominal value of the drug fund declined from 50–100 per cent of annual turnover between 1980 and 1989 to about 30 per cent in 1992–3, while inflation reduced the real values of drugs supplied by 22 per cent between 1990 and 1993 (Chisvo, 1993, 1994).

- Condom distribution declined by 43 per cent (see earlier discussion), as did STD treatments by 5 per cent between 1991 and 1993.

- Central hospital maternal mortality rates rose from 73 to over 200 per 100,000 (ibid. 1993);

By 1991, the rural–urban differentials had widened again: while 90 per cent of urban women delivered in a health facility, only 60 per cent of women living in rural areas did so. Surveys have found that early attendance at ANC and delivery at a health facility were affected by access to services and socio-economic status (Mash East PMD, 1987, 1988; Fawcus *et al.*, 1989). A large proportion of women in a 1992 survey said they attended ANC late because they could not afford the fees introduced at the health facilities (MoH, 1992*b*).

Food security and nutrition

Before 1980 'food security' was interpreted to mean national, rather than household, self-sufficiency. State control in maize marketing was implemented to protect the interests of white farmers from black peasant/smallholder competition. The methods used included forced removal of black farmers from the majority of the country's high-potential farming land to the less-productive 'communal areas' that had poor infrastructure and access to markets; taxes on black households to increase the incentive for wage labour; investment exclusively in markets for white large-scale production; more favourable prices for the same crops from white large-scale farms through the marketing boards; and restrictions on grain movement from peasant areas into towns, mines, and other demand centres where African production could otherwise compete against European-produced goods (1934 up to 1993). These policies eroded peasant-marketed production: in 1975–6 smallholders accounted for only 4.9 per cent of total Grain Marketing Board (GMB) maize intake. They shifted consumption away from indigenous staples towards maize meal, undermining food security in the poorest rural households, while subsidizing urban staple food prices so that food security did not fuel urban unrest.

Nutrition data gathered from eighteen nutrition surveys undertaken at various times and seasons between 1980 and 1982 found 21 per cent of the under-5-year-old population with second- or third-degree malnutrition based on weight for age, 28 per cent with stunting, and 9 per cent with wasting (World Bank, 1983). In 1981–2, under-5 malnutrition was greatest in large-scale commercial farming (LSCF) areas, followed by communal areas and mines, with urban areas having the least malnutrition (World Bank, 1983). Responding to the nutritional deprivation caused by war and underdevelopment, the government sponsored a child supplementary feeding programme (CSFP) in November 1980, providing a daily, energy-rich supplementary meal to over 250,000 children in over 8,000 communal area feeding-points. This programme, together with the drought relief programme, undoubtedly mitigated nutritional deterioration among the poorest and established a basis for nutritional improvements (MoH, 1985). The State mobilized resources, including tax levies, channelling these to households in need on an aggregate community basis.

The government also re-established and enhanced peasant production through the expansion of GMB buying points into communal areas (GMB, 1987), an increase in real producer prices for maize, and increased disbursement of agricultural credit to peasants. This resulted in a dramatic rise in GMB intake from the smallholder sector, from 86,000 tons in 1980–1 to 654,000 in 1989–90 (ibid. 1991). The incentives were mainly to increase production, and marketing policies continued to channel this food to urban area industrial millers for sale with relatively subsidized prices in urban areas (Jayne and Chisvo, 1991).

Peasant grain sales became the major food supplier to the nation by 1985. However, as the policies did not address retention of and access to these food outputs, household-level data indicated the coexistence of food insecurity even in high food output areas, and hence sustained rural undernutrition after an initial improvement in the early 1980s (Rohrbach, 1989; Stack and Chopak, 1990; Sunga *et al.*, 1990; Jayne and Chisvo, 1991). Grain supplies were siphoned out of rural areas, and industrial urban millers had a monopoly on maize distribution into grain-deficit areas, inflating consumer grain prices and reducing food purchasing power among rural consumers by as much as 30 per cent (Jayne and Chisvo, 1991).

In the ministry of health, a nutrition unit was established; it oversaw a programme of nutrition surveillance that included use of a growth chart, the children's supplementary feeding programme (CSFP), and the supplementary food production programme. By 1986, over 90 per cent of 1-year-old children possessed a growth card. Discussion on nutrition began to deepen in the late 1980s towards identification of programmes that supplement pre-harvest food supplies, when food stocks were low, or the identification of early harvesting forms of food crops. In 1980 and again in 1985 the ministry of health called for a national co-ordinating body, based on the recognition that food insecurity was not a product of overall lack of food production, but of factors affecting access to food, such as incomes, access to land and agricultural investment, food prices, food distribution networks, and access to means of food storage.

Between 1980 and 1983–4, levels of undernutrition appear to have declined significantly, although there is less firm evidence of any decline thereafter. In 1980, undernutrition among under-5-year-olds ranged from 50 per cent in large-scale farm areas (Chikanza *et al.*, 1981), to 22 per cent on mines (Sena *et al.*, 1982), and 6–10 per cent in urban areas (Loewenson *et al.*, 1989–90). By 1988, national levels of child malnutrition were 11.5 per cent weight/age (<2 standard deviations (SD) from the mean), 29 per cent stunting (height/age <2 SD mean), and 1.3 per cent wasting (weight/height <2 SD mean). In other words, while stunting had not declined compared to the early 1980s, second-degree malnutrition and wasting had fallen sharply. Rural levels of underweight and stunting remained approximately double those in urban areas (MoH, 1986; Loewenson, 1988; Mazur and Sanders, 1988; Interministerial Committee, 1993*a*).

The introduction of structural adjustment added a new dynamic of market liberalization. Many food commodity prices were decontrolled and subsidies removed. Between 1991 and 1992, food prices for lower-income households rose by 53.4 per cent as against 47 per cent for their total spending, indicating far greater stress in meeting food needs (ILO, 1993).

In June 1993, the government eliminated the subsidy on commercial roller meal, decontrolled maize-meal pricing, and eliminated most controls on private maize movement. Responding to price increases, consumers switched to more nutritious but cheaper straight-run hammer-milled meal (MLAWD-USAID, 1993). This may account for the absence of a severe decline in urban nutritional status after the removal of subsidies in urban Zimbabwe.

While measures were being taken to liberalize the marketing system, the social policy response to deal with the consequences came in two forms: food assistance through the social dimensions fund (SDF), mainly in urban areas, and supplementary feeding through drought relief, mainly in the rural areas.

These two programmes were markedly different in their approach: food assistance through SDF operated 'exclusively', i.e. was specific in its criteria for qualification and demanded proof of eligibility to subsidize individuals for maize-meal costs. The programme was difficult to access and had extremely low coverage, despite obvious need (MPSLSW, 1993–5).

In contrast, the 1991–2 drought-relief exercise was an example of an extremely successful and effective programme. The government imported 208,000 tons of maize as food aid and used an 'inclusive' mechanism of food distribution: Where over 15 per cent of children were malnourished using mid-upper-arm circumference (MUAC), *all* children under 5 in the area were fed. School meals were provided to the first three grades of primary-school children in selected schools, covering one-fifth of the 5–9-year age-group. Adults were targeted through village development committees, over 75 per cent of rural people receiving an average of 5 kg.

rations per month. The 1992–3 child supplementary feeding programme covered 1 million children at 21,595 feeding-points by March 1993, and reversed a deterioration in nutrition from a 59 per cent increase in the monthly caseload of under-5 malnutrition cases in 1991–2 to 19 per cent from June to December 1992 (ILO, 1993). The worsening of undernutrition in urban areas, and containment of undernutrition in rural areas through the drought-relief exercise, indicate the contrasting effectiveness of two strategies in the same period.

Education

In education, Zimbabwe achieved the transformation of education from a racially divided, fragmented education system that enrolled less than half the potential primary-school enrolment, to a non-racial, free, and state-supported primary education system in the 1980s, with 100 per cent enrolment of eligible children and reorientation of the curriculum towards national culture and development concerns. Table 6.4 highlights key indicators of changes in education over the period covered.

Prior to independence, as indicated earlier, education was structured on racial, geographical, and social-class lines. Among the poorest schools were the unregistered schools on the large-scale farms, which often pooled children into an accessible group of child labour. Many areas had inadequate facilities, so that many children did not attend school at all, with only 819,586 enrolments in primary school by 1979 out of an eligible population of about 2m.

After independence, the government was faced with the task of unifying and reorganizing the inherited school structure. Racial segregation was abolished,

TABLE 6.4. Key education indicators

Indicator	1980	1985	1990
Adult literacy rate			
Male	—	70	74
Female	—	55	60
Total	50	—	63
GER in primary school	42 (1983)	124	107
Transition rates Grade 7–form 1	—	—	69
Primary enrolment	1,236,694		2,120,565
No. of primary schools	3,161		4,565
No. of primary teachers	18,483		60,886

Sources: Govt. of Zimbabwe, *National Action Plan for Children*, Harare, 1992; ILO, *Structural Change and Adjustment in Zimbabwe*, ILO, Geneva, 1993

though the fees charged by élite schools impeded full integration. Primary-school fees were abolished, which massively increased enrolment. Many new schools were built, often with community contributions, often in previously unserved areas, and existing schools were expanded. To meet the massive increase in the volume of education demands, pupil–teacher ratios were allowed to rise and a large number of unqualified and expatriate teachers were hired. The expansion in the system is evident in the share of GDP and government expenditure devoted to education (see Table 6.5).

Primary-school expansion was the most strongly emphasized area of develop-ment of education in the 1980s, as witnessed by the large proportion in the share of GDP it commanded. Figure 6.1 shows how this share began to decline in the 1990s, under structural-adjustment policies.

Looking at the years from 1979 to 1989, primary-school enrolment peaked in 1981, declined in 1985, and then began to rise again, probably reflecting the 'catch-up' in the early years of independence in enrolment of those children whose educa-tion had been disrupted by lack of facilities or by war, together with the enrolment of those children of Grade 1 age (MoEC, 1989). In later years, as costs of education began to increase for households (uniforms, levies, books, and materials), some children would be held back until the money had been found, making them late

TABLE 6.5. Allocations to education (%)

	Pre-1980	1980	1985	1990
Education expenditure / GDP	—	7.5 (1982–3)	8	9
Education expenditure / Govt. expenditure	—	14.5	16	18

Source: World Bank, *Public Sector and Poverty Reduction*, Harare, 1994, mimeo

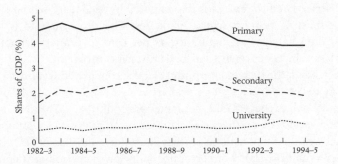

Fig. 6.1 Public expenditure on educational subsystems

Source: World Bank (1994)

entrants in a different year and inflating the enrolment for that year. The gross primary-school enrolment rate exceeded 100 per cent by 1990.

This expansion in primary-school enrolment in Zimbabwe was the highest in the decade in southern Africa. This had obvious implications for longer-term capacity of the population for skilled and semi-skilled production, social mobilization, informed participation in social development, and in development in general. It also, however, provided pressure for a similar expansion in economic opportunity to avoid a growing gap between skills and employment—an expansion that did not occur, leading to frustration. This was particularly the case for females for whom employment opportunities have been and continue to be worse than for males.

Between 1979 and 1989 there was a 161-per cent increase in the number of male pupils and a 195-per cent increase in female pupils. The system redressed the previous gender bias in education and led to parity between males and females at primary level. Drop-outs from primary school have been a growing phenomenon in recent years, particularly since fee-charging in 1991, but it is still a marginal phenomenon. For example, only 72 per cent of those who entered grade 1 in 1987 finished grade 7 in 1993. Many households have reported having to use and deplete family savings to finance school fees, indicating the high value placed on education. There has thus been a steady increase in those not attending school, from 7 per cent in 1992 to 13 per cent in 1993 and 32 per cent in 1994 (GoZ/UNICEF, 1994).

Similar gains were made post-1980 in secondary education. Laws limiting the entry of African children into secondary education to 12 per cent of all post-grade 7 pupils were removed. Between 1979 and 1989, the number of secondary schools rose by 749 per cent while total enrolment rose almost tenfold. There was an increase in the proportion of female enrolment, although the male–female ratio is still not at parity (1.3 : 1) indicating continuing barriers to female enrolment in secondary schools. Enrolment in secondary schooling (form 1) increased after 1980, and the overall drop-out rate to form 4 remained relatively low over the 1980s. The significant drop-out rate was thus from grade 7 to form 1 (e.g. 314,629 grade 7s in 1988 falling to 206,531 form 1s in 1989 or a 34 per cent reduction). This indicates that the barrier to education, probably imposed by secondary-school fees, strikes about one-third of primary-school graduates. The drop-out rate is higher for female children: females accounted for 49 per cent of primary-school places in 1986, but less than 25 per cent of the total university enrolment.

The increase in the demand for primary and secondary education was matched by an increase of 215 per cent in primary-school teachers and 603 per cent in secondary-school teachers (MoEC computer printout, 1989). The joint demand for training and service of teachers was achieved through in-service training such as the Zimbabwe integrated national teacher education course (ZINTEC). This made the teacher a full-time classroom practitioner during the period of training, resulting in over 4,000 trained teachers, supported by an additional 20,000 untrained teachers, by 1987. Enrolment in teachers' colleges rose from 2,824 in 1980 to

15,780 in 1988. So rapid was the rise in the number of teachers, in fact, that the pupil–teacher ratios fell in primary schools from 43 : 1 in 1980 to 39 : 1 in 1989. Urban high-density schools had much higher-than-average pupil–teacher ratios and had to resort to methods like 'hot seating,' repeating classes in morning and after-noon rotations. While it was projected that an additional 7,579 teachers would be required in 1994, the personnel and funds to pay them were not readily available, even though salaries by 1992 took 95 per cent of the ministry of education budget, up from 92.7 per cent in 1988–9. In the context of increasing needs and declining available resources, problems of inflation and low wage increments have led to declining real take-home pay for teachers. Reduced allocations for non-wage resources have undermined access to other items that support teachers in the class-room. Increasingly, schools were pressured to find their own funds (i.e. to levy parents) to acquire textbooks and paper, or do without. Hence, by 1990, only 40 per cent of schools had achieved a ratio of one textbook for every four pupils and only 5 per cent of schools had a functioning library. Only 60 per cent of schools had a chalkboard in every classroom and sufficient chairs and desks for all pupils and teachers (GoZ, 1992*b*).

The allocation of resources to education in the 1980s, from both government and parents, has also been enormous. The education ministry has had the largest allocation of all the ministries since 1980, or 18 per cent of the government budget. Added to this, communities have contributed household labour school construc-tion costs, levies, materials, uniforms, and examination fees. Education expansion has incurred huge costs: the nominal costs of sustaining the teaching force alone is estimated to be $Z418.8m., compared to $Z59.5m. in 1981–2. The education vote rose by 53 per cent from $Z120m. in 1979–80 to $Z184.7m. in 1988–9. Real per capita expenditure on primary education rose in the first three years after independ-ence from $Z20.15 to $Z26.06 in 1990–1 (Chisvo, 1994), and total real per capita spending on education peaked at $Z42.25 in 1990–1.

The introduction of structural adjustment reduced real budget allocations for health and education. Government spending on education, and particularly primary education, has also fallen since 1990–1, with the projected real per capita spending on primary education in 1993–4 at $Z17.71, its lowest level since independence (Chisvo, 1993, 1994). As in the health sector, by the end of the 1980s coverage had greatly expanded, but the quality of service was coming under scrutiny more and more; lack of resources was becoming a major constraint on quality education. Low pass rates at key transition points such as the end of form 2 and O levels were an indication of problems with quality, explained in part by the high pupil–teacher ratio and lack of trained teachers outlined earlier. In the 1991 Zimbabwe junior certificate (ZJC) examinations, the average pass rate was 16.1 per cent, while those for 1992 O levels ranged from 18 per cent to 64 per cent (MoEC Examinations Branch, 1993). This poor return made the issue of effective resource allocation a more pressing one.

Analysis of the problems in the quality of education have focused attention on the level of training and the skills of teachers, the availability of good learning materials, the teaching skills of those in higher education, and the availability of basic teaching hand-outs and support materials. There has also been discussion on directing curricula towards improved technical and vocational training, although approaches that build technical skills are still not well integrated into the academic syllabus. Departures from traditional curricula and development of vocational education have demanded a higher level of interaction between the educational systems and the productive sectors than exists at present.

Population

These social development changes are confronted by a population growth that generally exceeds economic growth. With a relatively large population of 11 million, a high dependency ratio, and a growth rate of 3.13 per cent, there has not been substantial change in demographic indicators since the 1970s, as indicated in Table 6.6 (CSO, 1993). It is notable, therefore, that Zimbabwe achieved a high level of social progress in the 1980s without evidence of undergoing change in demographic indicators or a demographic transition.

Despite the sustained high growth and fertility rates, there has been a significant change in fertility regulation, in both policy and practice. Pre-1980 policies of population control viewed a growing black population as a political threat, while post-independence policies of child-spacing and fertility regulation were more widely supported, leading to a contraceptive prevalence rate that is one of the highest in the region (38 per cent in 1985 and up to 48 per cent in 1992). Gender and religious issues continue to limit contraceptive use, and adolescent pregnancy remains a substantial problem. By 1989, 16 per cent of female teenagers were already mothers and a further 4 per cent pregnant with their first child (CSO, 1989).

Hence, while Zimbabwean fertility-regulation programmes are among the most successful in Africa (with a decline in total fertility rate from 6.2 in 1980 to 5 in the

TABLE **6.6.** Key population indicators

Indicator	Pre-1980	1980	1985	1990
Population growth rate	3.27 (1962–9)	2.93 (1969–82)	2.76 (1985–90)	2.64 (1990–2)
Total fertility rate	6.4 (1969)	5.1 (1982)	—	5.5 (1988)
Contraceptive prevalence rate (% married women using contraceptives)	—	—	38 (1984)	43 (1988)

Sources: Govt. of Zimbabwe, *National Action Plan for Children*, Harare, 1992; data obtained from the Central Statistical Office

early 1990s, the slow decline in population growth makes demographic issues important factors in the sustainability of social services and social progress).

Conclusions

Zimbabwe became a success story in the ten years following independence in 1980. A close focus on the common aspects of social development in this period provides an insight into key aspects of social development and key issues in the relationship between social and economic development. Some of the factors that enabled social progress to occur included:

- the clear policy support for social development, reinforced by economic policies that identified redistribution with growth as clear policy objectives;

- allocation of substantial public-sector resources towards social services, while also internally reallocating budgets to priority areas of spending, such as primary education, primary health and medical care, and rural social services;

- targeting of international funds to key areas of social development outlined in social policy, while also leveraging community contributions through labour, organization, community health workers, etc.;

- using social sector inputs to offset poverty and slow changes in income, and also initiating steps towards redistribution of land and income.

The first section also outlined some of the constraints these investments faced, including the slow economic growth limiting finances available for social expenditure, poor progress in addressing economic equity and growth in household incomes limiting the possibility of household contributions to social development, and the strong dominance of the public sector in social services limiting contributions from private-sector sources to public health. These constraints contributed to the 'turn-around' in 1990 and the introduction of the economic structural-adjustment programme that shifted the policy concerns from equity and redistribution as a means to growth to market reforms and international competitive advantage as the basis for growth, and from demand-driven social policy to services based on sustainable financing and efficiency.

Changes in social-sector inputs alone are able to achieve only a limited outcome in terms of social status changes, both in the capacity to deliver adequate services and in the capacity of the household to use these services. This is demonstrated, for example, in the health sector, where non-health-sector inputs like income and employment become more critical determinants of health changes once service provision has been achieved. It is testimony to the Zimbabwean commitment to social development that poor households did contribute huge amounts to education, health, and other areas, through voluntary labour, building materials, and costs.

The pressure to sustain social expenditures under stagnant economic growth led to the accusation of social expenditures' 'crowding out' productive sector investments and slowing growth, although growth was in fact impeded by many other factors, factors exogenous to the economy, such as drought, the global recession, and unfavourable export markets, as well as internal structural distortions and lack of real investment of private domestic capital.

Most critically, Zimbabwe's social investments in human resources were made while not developing an economic model that would explicitly reward use of these investments, as through labour-intensive production. Hence, economic and social investment became viewed as contradictory. In the absence of effective productive use of these social investments, borrowing has been used as a means of financing social development. Hence, in Zimbabwe, investment in education and health was not wrong, but was not supported by other factors of production becoming available, including access to credit, capital, land, and other investment resources.

It is also apparent that policies of redistribution, such as those involving land and financial capital, should be viewed as instruments for social development since, by relieving land pressures and increasing access to capital, they provide the landless and the poor with livelihood. The resettlement programme, for example, the main instrument for redressing inequities in land distribution, was slowed in the late 1980s and early 1990s, as the government ran out of money to buy land and as the land prices skyrocketed and domestic financing was not forthcoming.

Peace

Peace was a key factor in success. In a continent plagued by war and civil strife, the impact of peace in 1980, and the relatively sustained nature of that peace (without denying periods of regional dispute, or the impact of South African destabilization), and Mozambian refugees, allowed for over a decade of social progress in Zimbabwe. Defence expenditure as a percentage of total expenditure fell from 23 per cent in 1979–80 at the end of the liberation war to an estimated 7 per cent in 1994–5. The peace dividend in Zimbabwe has been an important factor in social and economic development.

Public-sector capacity

The huge expansion and capacity building in the public sector in the first half-decade of independence coincided with and supported the expansion of social services, while committing government to large manpower expenditures. The more complex environment that emerged in the late 1980s demanded capable, adequately resourced (and paid), and stable public-sector management. This has made the erosion of salaries, public-sector cut-backs, and a declining resource base in the early 1990s a more unacceptable experience. As the public sector is eroded, donor co-ordination becomes more problematic and donor dependency can grow (particularly as senior civil servants move to higher-paying jobs in the donor agencies).

Social organization for social sector development

During the liberation struggle, new forms of social organization emerged that encouraged popular participation under the auspices of the liberation movements. After independence popular participation was mobilized, channelled by party and central-government programmes and structures. Over the 1980s, this increasingly shifted to more bureaucratic forms of participation in response to central-government policy, as described earlier.

In the ESAP period, the experience has been of a more stagnant, difficult, or even oppositional climate created by the social fragmentation, marginalization, and difficulties of structural-adjustment policies. In fact, the latter phase has also seen the development of more civic and consumer groups, as the protection of social and human rights and concerns around access to social security and wealth have become more prominent. These include residents' or ratepayers' associations, human rights groups, women's groups, housing groups, trade unions, school development committees, and other producer or economic lobby.groups. This coincides with a weakening of the perceived role and capacity of the State (through public-sector cut-backs, liberalization).

The emergent organizations are, however, poorly articulated into national central-government policy discussions, thus making them often oppositional or marginalized. It has, however, emerged as critical that social organization, particularly of the poor, is an important force for the advocacy and protection of basic social rights.

An international commitment to social development

The experience of Zimbabwe provides evidence of the positive potentials for interaction with the international community and also some of the negative consequences. Zimbabwe benefited greatly from the wealth of experience of post-independent countries and the international community in models of primary health care, primary education, and other areas of social development, as well as from international financial support for its social and economic programmes. At the same time, points of contradiction between national goals and international conditions emerged—some caused by markets, others caused by extra-market pressures—in the recession and increasingly unfavourable terms of international markets, and in the conditions placed on loan agreements. It is necessary to address, at international level, the challenges made by international trade and finance institutions, and the pace and nature of reforms, so as to allow for both investment in human resources and harmony between economic policies and social development.

Notes

1. It should be noted that the total fertility rate fell from 6.2 in 1980 to about 5 in the early 1990s, which was in itself a major success.
2. The incremental capital–output ratio (ICOR) was about 7.

Bibliography

Chidzero, B. (1991, 1993), *Budget Statement*, Harare: Government of Zimbabwe.

Chikanza, I., Paxton, D., Loewenson, R., and Laing, R. (1981), 'The health status of farm-worker communities in Zimbabwe', *Central African Journal of Medicine* 27/5: 88–91.

Chisvo, M. (1993), 'Government Spending on Social Services and the Impact of Structural Adjustment in Zimbabwe', report produced for UNICEF, Harare.

—— and Munro, Lauchlan (1994), 'A Review of the Social Dimensions of Adjustment in Zimbabwe', report produced for UNICEF-Zimbabwe, Harare.

City of Harare (1990–2), *Annual Reports of the Harare City Health Department*.

Crowther, C., and Brown, I. (1986), 'A Review of Perinatal Mortality in an Urban Situation in a Developing Country', *Journal of Perinatal Medicine*, 14.

CSO (Central Statistical Office) (1982–8), *Quarterly Digest of Statistics*, Harare: Government Printers.

—— (1984), *1982 Population Census: A Preliminary Assessment*, Harare: Government Printers.

—— (1987, 1989), *Statistical Yearbook*, Harare.

—— (1989), *Demographic and Health Survey*, Harare.

—— (1992a), *Census 1992: Zimbabwe Preliminary Report*, Harare.

—— (1992b), *Combined Demographic Analysis, iii: Raw Data*, Harare.

—— (1993), *Census 1992: Provincial Profile Mashonaland Central*, Harare.

—— Westinghouse Institute for Resource Development (1988–9), *Zimbabwe Demographic and Health Survey*, Harare: Government Printers.

Fawcus, S., Crowther, C., and van Baelen, P. (1989), 'Booked vs. Unbooked Deliveries at Harare Central Hospital: Maternal Characteristics and Fetal Outcome', paper presented to the *IEA Africa Regional Conference*, Harare, August.

Gilmurray, J., Riddell, R., and Sanders, D. (1979), *The Struggle for Health*, The Struggle for Health from Rhodesia to Zimbabwe Series, Gweru: Mambo Press.

Goldman, R., and Block, S. (eds.) (1993), Proceedings from the Symposium on African Agricultural Transformation in Africa, APAP Technical Report 137, Agricultural Policy Analysis Project, Bethesda: Abt Associates.

GoZ (Government of Zimbabwe) (1982), *Transitional National Development Plan*, Harare: Government Printers.

—— (1986), *First Five Year National Development Plan*, Harare: Government Printers.

—— (1991a), *A Framework for Economic Reform 1991–1995*, Harare: Government Printers.

—— (1991*b*), *The Social Dimensions of Adjustment and Social Development Fund*, Harare: Government Printers.

—— (1992*a*), *Land Acquisition Act (1992)*, Harare: Government Printers.

—— (1992*b*), *National Programme of Action for Children: Our Second Decade of Development and Progress*, Harare.

—— (1992*c*), *Rural Development in Zimbabwe: A Conference Report*, Harare.

GoZ/UNICEF (1994), *Children and Women in Zimbabwe: A Situation Analysis Update*, Harare: UNICEF.

—— (1995), *Situation Analysis of Women and Children in Zimbabwe*, Harare: UNICEF.

Grain Marketing Board (GMB) (1987–92), Routine Data 1987–1992, Harare, unpublished.

Hongoro, C., and Chandiwana, S. (1994), *Effects of User Fees on Health Care in Zimbabwe*, Blair Laboratory/MoHCW, Harare, mimeo.

ILO (1993), *Structural Change and Adjustment in Zimbabwe*, Occasional Paper 16, Geneva: ILO.

—— (1994), *Seminar on Structural Change and Adjustment in Zimbabwe: Rapporteur's Report*, Harare: ILO.

Interministerial Committee on SDA Monitoring (1992), *Findings and Recommendations from the First Round of Sentinel Site Surveillance for SDA Monitoring*, Harare: Government of Zimbabwe and UNICEF, mimeo.

—— (1993*a*), *Findings from the Second Round of Sentinel Surveillance for SDA Monitoring*, Ministry of Public Service, Labour and Social Welfare.

—— (1993*b*), *Findings from the Third Round of Sentinel Surveillance for Social Dimensions of Adjustment Monitoring*, Ministry of Public Service, Labour and Social Welfare, Harare.

Jayne, T. S., and Chisvo, M. (1991), 'Unravelling Zimbabwe's Food Insecurity Paradox', *Food Policy*, 16/5.

—— —— (1992), 'Zimbabwe's Grain Marketing Policy Challenges in the 1990s: Short-run vs. Long-run Options', paper presented at the Seventh Annual Conference on Food Security Research in Southern Africa, 28–30 Oct. 1991, Makasa Sun Hotel, Victoria Falls.

Kaseke, Edwin, and Ndaradzi, Maxwell (1993), 'A Situation Analysis of the Social Development Fund', study report for the Government of Zimbabwe and UNICEF, Harare.

Loewenson, R. (1988), 'Labour Insecurity and Health', *Social Science and Medicine*, 27/7: 733–41.

—— and Sanders, D. (1988), 'The Political Economy of Health and Nutrition', in C. Stoneman (ed.), *Zimbabwe's Prospects*, London: Macmillan.

—— —— and Davies, R. (1989–90), 'Equity in Health in Zimbabwe—a Post Independence Review', report prepared for the Ministry of Health, Harare: Government of Zimbabwe, mimeo.

Mash East PMD (1987, 1988), Provincial Directors' Reports, Marondera, mimeo.

Mazur, R., and Sanders, D. (1988), 'Socioeconomic Factors Associated with Child Health and Nutrition in Preurban Zimbabwe', *Jo Ecology of Food and Nut*, 22.

MLAWD-USAID (1993), 'Consumer Maize Preferences in Zimbabwe: Survey Results and Policy Implications', report prepared for MLAWD and USAID/Harare by Lawrence Rubey, University of Zimbabwe.

MoEC (Ministry of Education and Culture) (1989), Computer Statistics.

—— (various years), *Report of the Secretary for Education and Culture*, Harare.

—— (various years), Unpublished examination results data, Examinations Branch, Harare.

—— (various years), Unpublished enrolment data.

MoH (Ministry of Health) (1980–5), *Annual Reports of the Secretary for Health*, Harare: Government Printers.

—— (1984a), *Planning for Equity in Health: A Sectoral Review and Policy Statement*, Harare: Government Printers.

—— (1984b), The Evaluation of the Child Supplementary Feeding Programme, Harare, mimeo.

—— (1985), Report of the MCH workshop, Nyanga, mimeo.

—— (1986), Baseline Survey for the Family Health Project, Harare, mimeo.

—— (1986–7), *Health Information Updates No. 1, 2, 4*, Provincial Medical Director of Mashonaland East Province, mimeos.

—— (1987), *Primary Health Care Review 1987*, Harare: Government Printers.

—— (1987–92), *MCH Annual Reports*, mimeo, Harare.

—— (1988a), *Report on PHC/MCH/EPI Surveys*, Harare, mimeo.

—— (1988b), *Summary of Nutrition Surveys Carried Out Since 1980*, Harare, mimeo.

—— (1988c), *Summary Statistics from the Health Information System 1988*, Harare, 1988, 1990, 1991, 1992, mimeos.

—— (1991a), Department of Maternal and Child Health, unpublished routine data, Ministry of Health and Child Welfare, Harare.

—— (1991b), Report on the MCH Household Survey, Harare, mimeo.

—— (1992a), *Corporate Plan*, Harare: Government Printers.

—— (MoHCW) (1992b), 'Zimbabwe NCH/FP Coverage Survey 1001', National MCH/FP Co-ordinating Committee, Harare, mimeo.

MPSLSW (Ministing of Public Service, Labour and Social Welfare) (1993–5), Reports of the Interministerial SDA Monitoring, Rounds 1–5, Harare: Government Printers.

—— (1994), 'The Impact of Maize Market Liberalisation in Zimbabwe's Urban Areas', Harare.

Renfrew, A. (1992), *ESAP and Health*, Gweru: Mambo Press.

Rohrbach, D. D. (1989), 'The Economics of Smallholder Maize Production in Zimbabwe: Implications for Food Security', *International Development Paper*, 11, East Lansing: Dept. of Agricultural Economics, Michigan State University.

Sena, A., Zengeya, S., Zanza, J., Loewenson, R., and Laing, R. (1982), 'The health status of mineworker communities in Zimbabwe', CAJM, 28/7: 155–69.

Stack, Jayne, and Chopak, Charles (1990), 'Household Income Patterns in Zimbabwe's Communal Areas: Empirical Evidence from Five Survey Areas', in T. S. Jayne, J. B. Wyckoff, and M. Rukuni (eds.), *Integrating Food, Nutrition and Agricultural Policy in Zimbabwe*, Harare: UZ/MSU Food Security Research Project, Dept. of Agricultural Economics and Extension, University of Zimbabwe.

Sunga, E., Chabayanzara, E., Moyo, S., Mpande, R., Mutuma, P., and Page, H. (1990), Farm extension base-line survey results, Harare: Zimbabwe Institute of Development Studies, mimeo.

UNICEF (1996), 'Influencing Policies in Favour of Children: An Evaluation of UNICEF's Experience in Zimbabwe', New York, mimeo.

—— (1993), An Evaluation of the Child Supplementary Feeding Programme, report by R. Ewbank, UNICEF-Zimbabwe, Harare.

Wilson, David *et al.* (1993*a*), *Zimbabwe AIDS Prevention and Control Project, ii, Social Soundness Analysis*, report prepared by Diana Patel, IRT/Speciss Consulting Services for USAID, Harare.

—— (1993*b*), *Zimbabwe AIDS Prevention and Control Project, iii, Institutional Analysis*, report prepared by IRT/Speciss Consulting Services for USAID, Harare.

World Bank (1983), *Nutrition in Zimbabwe*, Washington, DC: World Bank.

—— (1985), *Zimbabwe Country Economic Memorandum Performance, Policies and Prospects*, Country Programs Department 1, Eastern and Southern Africa Regional Office.

—— (1986), 'Poverty and Hunger', in *Issues and Options for Food Security in Developing Countries*, Washington, DC.

—— (1991), *Zimbabwe Agriculture Sector Memorandum*, Report No. 9429-ZIM, ii, Southern Africa Dept. Agriculture Operations Division, Washington, DC.

—— (1992), *Zimbabwe: A Review of Primary and Secondary Education from Successful Expansion to Equity of Learning Achievements*, Washington, DC.

—— (1993), 'Investing in Health', *World Development Report*, Washington, DC.

—— (1994), *Zimbabwe: Country Economic Memorandum*, Washington, DC.

7

The Route to Social Development in Kerala: Social Intermediation and Public Action

T. N. KRISHNAN

Introduction

The high level of social development achieved by Kerala State[1] has by now become legendary (United Nations, 1975). This has even provoked the question: is there a Kerala model of development? (Franke and Chasin, 1992; Jeffrey, 1992; George, 1993). Attempts to prove or disprove the existence of a Kerala model of development are misplaced since most authors who discuss this question do not state explicitly their concept of the model of development. Their conclusions appear also to be based on an inadequate understanding of the social and economic processes at work in this State. A Kerala model of development has a great deal of relevance if the definition is restricted to social development. On the contrary, if economic growth is also considered a constituent of the model, then no Kerala model of development exists. The critical question is: Can social development take place in a milieu of and in spite of low levels of per capita income? The answer would be in the affirmative if we analysed the Kerala experience. Can high income growth promote or accelerate social development? The answer would be rather inconclusive. It *should*, but there might exist a substantial time-lag before the social transformation manifests itself. While private initiative may raise growth rates of income, the trigger for social development is invariably public action. A comparative study of the levels of social development among the Indian States makes this proposition quite apparent. Increase in per capita income alone is inadequate for accelerating the rate of social development. The early history of social development in Kerala indicates that vigorous public action could indeed transform the level of social development and cause major improvements in social indicators even at low levels of per capita income. Further, the recent history of Kerala provides evidence in support of the view that modest-to-high rates of increase in per capita income might hasten this process of social development. What is important is to realize that the complementarity between income growth and social development is probably weak at low levels of per capita income. But it could be compensated by adequately strong public action. At high levels of income the need for strong compensatory public action may be lower since there would be sufficiently strong incentives for private initiative in developing the institutional infrastructure necessary for social development. At low levels of income, the weakness of private initiative might account for the lag in social development, in the absence of public action.

The significance of the Kerala story becomes obvious only in the context of a comparative setting. One of the smaller States in the Indian Union, Kerala surpasses all other states in levels of human development. Kerala's HDI (Human Development Index) is estimated to be 0.775 compared to 0.744 for Punjab, while its per capita State domestic product is less than half that of Punjab's. The access to education and health care is primarily responsible for this result. The female literacy rate increased from 38.9 per cent in 1961 to 86.9 per cent in 1991. The corresponding change in Punjab is from 14.1 to 49.7 per cent. Life expectancy at birth is estimated at 67.6 years for males and 73.8 years for females for 1988–91 in Kerala, and 65.6 and 65.3 in the Punjab. The infant mortality rate is 17 in Kerala compared to 61 in Punjab. Data given in Table 7.1 provides a comparative position of Kerala among the major States in India with respect to some of the key economic and social parameters of development.

A unique feature of Kerala among the Indian States is its gender ratio, which is quite favourable for women. While there are only 927 females for every 1,000 males in India as a whole, Kerala boasts 1,036 females (Samuel, 1991). Kerala also reports the lowest birth, death, and infant-mortality rates in India. The birth and infant-mortality rates are 18.4 and 17 in Kerala compared to 31.1 and 86 for India in 1992. These in turn have resulted in a life expectancy of around 71 years compared to about 59 years for India. The census of 1991 also recorded a literacy rate of 90 per cent for Kerala compared to 52 per cent for India (see Table 7.1).

Kerala ranked eleventh from the top in per capita state income in 1992. While Kerala ranked twelfth in per capita consumer expenditure in 1973–4, this improved dramatically and now Kerala occupies the fourth rank from the top. In 1973–4, 59.71 per cent of Kerala's population was estimated to lie below the poverty line, but this declined to 32 per cent in 1987–8 (Planning Commission, 1993). In terms of the size of the poverty ratio, Kerala ranked the fifth highest in 1973–4, but moved down to twelfth in 1987–8. Since poverty is measured in India on the basis of the distribution of per capita consumer expenditure, the decline in poverty in Kerala is a direct reflection of the improvement in per capita consumer expenditure. During this period, a large number of Kerala workers migrated to the Gulf countries and their remittances were primarily responsible for this rise in per capita consumption. An interesting and important fact is that neither a high level of poverty nor a low level of per capita income has stood in the way of improvements in literacy rates or in mortality levels in Kerala.

The present Kerala State was constituted by integrating Malabar district with Travancore-Cochin State in November 1956. Since Malabar had been under the

TABLE 7.1. Some key parameters of development

	Birth rates rural 1990-2 (per 1,000)	Infant-mortality rates rural 1990-2	Life expectancy 1988-91 Male	Life expectancy 1988-91 Female	Literacy rates Male 1961	Literacy rates Male 1991	Literacy rates Female 1961	Literacy rates Female 1991	Human development index	Per capita SDP, current prices 1991-2 (Rs)	Persons below poverty line (%) 1973-4	Persons below poverty line (%) 1987-8
Andhra Pradesh	25.9	76	59.10	62.23	30.2	56.2	12.0	33.7	0.361	5,570	49.25	27.20
Assam	31.1	79	55.74	55.23	37.3	62.3	16.0	43.7	0.256	4,230	51.23	36.84
Bihar	32.7	74	58.21	57.00	29.8	52.6	0.7	23.1	0.147	2,904	61.78	53.37
Gujarat	29.2	74	58.34	61.49	41.1	72.5	19.1	48.5	0.566	6,425	47.21	32.33
Haryana	33.8	75	63.41	61.97	a	67.9	a	40.9	0.624	8,690	35.24	16.63
Himachal Pradesh	28.5	72	—	—	27.2	74.6	0.6	52.5	0.425	5,355	26.40	15.46
Jammu and Kashmir	—	—	—	—	a	a	a	a	0.109	4,051	42.59	23.20
Karnataka	28.1	83	62.15	63.31	36.1	67.3	14.2	44.3	0.502	5,555	54.34	38.14
Kerala	18.4	17	67.60	73.80	55.0	94.5	38.9	86.9	0.775	4,618	59.71	32.08
Madhya Pradesh	37.4	118	56.24	54.71	27.0	57.4	0.7	28.4	0.196	4,077	61.90	43.40
Maharashtra	28.2	67	62.00	64.30	42.0	74.5	16.8	50.5	0.655	8,180	52.94	40.10
Orissa	29.6	124	57.13	55.15	24.7	62.4	0.9	34.4	0.224	4,068	66.24	55.61
Punjab	28.4	61	65.61	65.30	33.0	63.7	14.1	49.7	0.744	9,643	28.08	12.70
Rajasthan	35.7	88	57.80	58.69	23.7	55.1	0.6	20.8	0.246	4,361	46.33	34.60
Tamil Nadu	21.2	67	60.85	60.80	44.5	74.9	18.2	52.3	0.508	5,078	56.51	45.13
Uttar Pradesh	37.4	103	54.14	49.64	27.3	55.4	0.7	26.0	0.110	4,012	56.98	41.99
West Bengal	30.0	71	59.95	59.53	40.1	67.2	17.0	47.2	0.436	5,383	63.39	43.99
India	31.1	86	58.1	59.10	34.4	63.86	12.9	39.42	—	5,596	54.93	39.34

Notes: [a] Some of the figures for these states are not available due to reorganization of states according to present classifications

Sources: Economic and Political Weekly, 39/21; Report of the Expert Group on Estimation of Proportion and Number of Poor, Perspective Planning Division, Planning Commission, Government of India, New Delhi, July 1993

direct rule of the British for a long time, the education and health indicators here were comparable to the rest of India in the mid-1950s. Therefore, Malabar significantly lagged behind Travancore-Cochin (which had never been directly ruled by the British) in literacy levels and in access to health care. The history of social development since the formation of Kerala State is really a story of how these differentials were eliminated or narrowed and what policies and programmes were adopted for this purpose within the span of two generations. The basic strategy was the same: extension to Malabar region of the policies and programmes followed earlier in Travancore and Cochin. This was a combination of public and private investment in education and health, and provision of financial incentives for the private sector to establish and operate educational institutions. The private sector has also played a major role in health-care delivery, especially since 1975, but there were no financial or other incentives in this case. A larger share of investment in education and health was earmarked for the Malabar region, so that over the years the disparities in the number of public institutions between the two regions would considerably narrow. The result of these developments in the building up of social infrastructure was that literacy rates and infant mortality rates in Travancore-Cochin and Malabar regions have now converged. Kerala demonstrates that a comparatively high level of social development can be achieved within a single generation. At first this might appear to be a false proposition since social development in Travancore and Cochin took nearly a full century. The extension to Malabar of policies and programmes which succeeded in Travancore and Cochin produced similar outcomes within a span of thirty-five years. The wide differentials in literacy, birth, death, and infant-mortality rates have almost disappeared since the integration of the two regions. This was the result of a conscious policy aimed at eliminating such disparities between the two regions, and is a clear demonstration that deliberate and targeted social policy can indeed lead to significant improvements in levels of human development even in situations where per capita incomes are low. If such policies are complemented with moderate increases in consumption levels, the results can be quite impressive. In the case of Kerala such moderate increase in per capita consumption was made possible by migrant workers' remittances.

The Beginnings: Social Intermediation and Public Action

The level of human development (as measured by the UNDP Human Development Report) achieved by a society depends principally on its achievements in education, health, and the level of per capita income. In the case of Kerala, its per capita income is not only low compared to many low-income countries, but is even low compared to most States of India. Therefore Kerala's relatively high level of human development is largely the outcome of the State's achievements in education and health. The social conditions in India during the colonial and the immediate post-independence period, unlike those in many developing countries today, blocked any rapid or drastic improvements in the prevailing social situation for a large group of the population. A singular factor responsible for this, if one might identify a major cause, was the hierarchical caste structure. Kerala was no exception in this matter. In fact, the denial of opportunities for human development based on caste considerations was the severest in Kerala till the beginnings of the present century. Upper castes who had easy access to education and health care constituted less than 20 per cent of the total population of the State.

Human development can take place only if the following conditions are satisfied simultaneously:

• Changes occur in social and behavioural attitudes that promote rather than suppress human development. These changes will increase the demand for education and health care, and were achieved in Kerala through a process of social intermediation.

• Institutional structures for promoting human development which represent a supply response to rising demand are created. In this regard, the role of the government is critical in education and health.

• There is willingness and ability to commit resources, especially financial resources, for enhancing human development. Such commitment is required by public authorities as well as the public. Though education and health are flows of services, the level of services is determined by the volume of assets which in turn depends on the accumulation of social capital (Murray and Chen, 1990).

The history of the development of education and health in Kerala would show that all three factors operated simultaneously. But for their mutual interactions and complementary natures, the level of human development achieved by Kerala probably would have remained no different from those of other States in India. Most States in India have yet to create the necessary preconditions for human development.

Kerala overcame the caste impediments to social progress through a process of *social intermediation*. By *social intermediation* we mean, in the context of human development, interventions at different levels of the society by various agents to change the social and behavioural attitudes within the then-prevailing social environment to achieve desired social outcomes (Kabir and Krishnan, 1992). Progress in education and health not only requires changes in social and behavioural attitudes but those attitudes also change with advances in education and health. In fact, Caldwell describes health transition as a process that includes 'the social and behavioural changes that parallel the epidemiological transition and may do much to propel it' (Caldwell *et al.*, 1989). This at once implies that the health outcome in a society is not a function of health technology alone but very much depends also on social changes. This is equally true for education. While analysing the health transition of Kerala in its historical context (Kabir and Krishnan, 1992), we proposed a distinction between 'social and behavioural attitudes' and 'social and behavioural environment'. Normally, 'social and behavioural changes' are a consequence of changes in the 'social and behavioural environment'. The caste structure in nineteenth-century Kerala was a bulwark against any changes in the social and behavioural environment. The caste hierarchy determined the access to education and health care since 'social distance' was a key weapon utilized by the upper castes to deny access to these facilities to the depressed castes. The backward communities and depressed castes constituted nearly half the population of Kerala, and without them, the level of human development achieved by the State would have been distorted and incomplete. It is not only important that high levels of human development are desired but also that the fruits of human development are equitably distributed among all sections of the society (Sen, 1993). One of the reasons for the low levels of human development in some States in India today is the high degree of inequality in the distribution of the benefits of human development. It was in this context that we emphasized the importance of the process of social intermediation in the health transition of Kerala that made possible a more equitable distribution of health care among the severely deprived and denied sections of society. The 'concept of social intermediation has relevance beyond the health field and it was equally important in the spread of education in Travancore. We shall indicate (later) how education of the lower castes along with other economic changes altered the social environment itself whereby the attitudes of the lower castes began to change towards access to health, education and public employment' (Kabir and Krishnan, 1992). By generalizing the concept of social intermediation, we are able to provide a framework of analysis which endogenizes the process of human development in Kerala.

The rigidity of the caste system in Kerala froze the social environment, and there was strict adherence to 'social distances', which also meant keeping physical distances between persons of various castes (Rao, 1981). Though the hierarchical caste structure was a descending continuum with increasing 'social distances', broadly the population could be aggregated into three groups. The top group enjoyed unrestricted access to all private and public facilities; the middle group, consisting of backward communities, had partial access; and the bottom group, consisting of depressed classes, were denied access to all public facilities. Since the Christian and Muslim communities were outside the caste structure, they did not fall under the purview of 'social distance'. Thus, as far as access to educational and health facilities are concerned, they were on a par with the top group. Till the middle of the nineteenth century, many in the bottom group were 'agrestic slaves' thus lacking even some basic personal freedoms, like the freedom of their women to cover the upper part of the body (Sivanandan, 1989). The history of the development of education and health in Travancore and Cochin is the story mainly of the mutual interactions between the State and the society and the responses of the State and caste-based communities to social intermediation.

Education and Social Intermediation

The beginnings of modern education in Travancore are attributed to the famous proclamation of Rani Laxmi Bayi in the year 1817; it spoke of the need for universalization of education and the responsibility of the State to defray the costs of such education. This policy was not seriously implemented for nearly a century. In the first half of the nineteenth century, this new policy was confined to the opening of a Rajah's free school and a few English schools in district headquarters, and encouraging the missionaries to open and operate schools. Since admissions to the government schools were restricted to the upper castes only, there was no way by which education could be universalized. However, the missionaries seized this opportunity to convert the depressed classes to Christianity by admitting poor children to their schools. Thus, the missionary schools filled an important vacuum in the early phase of the educational development of Travancore by providing an institutional structure for the spread of English-language education. Further, this education inculcated values of equality and social justice and thus planted the seeds of the social revolution yet to take place in Travancore society.

However, missionary-led educational efforts did not contribute to large-scale expansion of education in the State for three important reasons. First, the State itself withdrew its support for such activities fearing large-scale conversion of Hindus to Christianity. Secondly, and for the same reason, upper-caste children were not sent to missionary schools. Thirdly, the indigenous Christian population also resented the missionary educational efforts fearing that it would undermine their traditional values and culture (Gopinathan Nair, 1989; Joseph, 1990).

The real development of education in Travancore began in the second half of the nineteenth century when an integrated and well-thought-out educational policy was articulated and put into action. This educational policy had three aspects: (1) expansion of government educational institutions; (2) encouragement of vernacular schools whose medium of instruction was Malayalam as opposed to English; and (3) provision of financial incentives to the private sector to establish schools.

While these measures were intended to create the necessary infrastructure to increase the supply of educated persons, a series of institutional and economic reforms undertaken during this period also led to an increase in the demand for educated manpower. The prescription of minimum educational qualifications for entry into government service and the expansion of the government sector provided strong incentives to continue one's education and to obtain the minimum qualifications required for entry into government service. This period also saw expansions in trade and commercial activities, and the setting up of manufacturing facilities, where a minimum level of education was found to be of great help either in carrying on those vocations or in securing jobs in such fields.

The expansion in demand for 'educated' persons encouraged the establishment of new schools in the private sector and the switch-over of the traditional vernacular schools to the new system of education. The offer of financial incentives in the form of grant-in-aid encouraged this process. Much before the establishment of English schools, Travancore, Cochin, and Malabar had a well-established system for imparting vernacular education. This was organized at the village level on a 'Gurukula' basis by an 'Ezhuthachan', i.e. instruction for small groups in reading and writing Malayalam, conducted by a single teacher at his own residence. Therefore, when the government offered grant-in-aid for the expansion of vernacular schools, a number of these traditional establishments converted themselves to vernacular schools by adopting the new structure of education and adding more classes and teachers.

Another group that took advantage of grant-in-aid happened to be the local Christian community belonging to the Catholic faith. They had earlier resisted the spread of English education among their followers, but the provision of financial incentives encouraged them to establish schools. They opened a large number of schools especially in those areas where there was a significant Catholic population. These schools should be distinguished from those of missionaries whose primary purpose in establishing educational and health care institutions was proselytization. As a result of these developments, there was a significant increase in the number of schools as well as in the numbers attending by the last decade of the nineteenth century. The number of aided private schools (vernacular) rose from 20 in 1873–4 to 440 in 1882–3 and to 1,388 in 1894. The total number of students attending these schools rose from 9,637 to 57,314 in 1881 (Gopinathan Nair, 1981).

During this period the forces of social intermediation were gathering momentum, and by the last decade of the century they were being fully articulated. The result of such articulation was not only the rapid expansion in educational and health facilities but, by the early decades of the present century, the removal of most of the impediments against the use of these facilities by the backward and depressed castes and classes. The ruling élite of Travancore State perceived a potential threat to their dominance in the large-scale conversion of the depressed classes to Christianity through the route of education (and also through the route of health care, as we shall soon note) and therefore wanted to create alternative avenues for educating them and retaining them among the Hindu-fold. Even though government and private schools were, in principle, accessible to all castes from 1894–5, in reality the depressed castes were kept out of educational institutions till the beginning of the second decade of the present century.

In initiating the process of social intermediation, the Ezhava community, the most numerous among the backward castes, played the pioneering role. This was possible for two reasons. First the land reforms of the 1860s and the prosperity of the State during this period improved the economic conditions of this community, and instilled in them an urge for improvement in their social status, too. By a strange coincidence of circumstances, a social reformer and spiritual leader, Narayana Guru, emerged from this community during the same period. Narayana Guru's ideas on social reforms were extraordinarily revolutionary for his times. For the uplifting of the poor and the downtrodden, he advocated combining spirituality with material well-being. He saw that lack of education and poor hygiene were responsible for the practice of 'social distance' and the observance of pollution. While he advocated 'one caste, one religion, one God', he was extremely sensitive to Indian cultural traditions. The core of the philosophy of 'social distance' and of the observance of caste pollution was that the backward and depressed communities were denied entry to Hindu temples. Narayana Guru saw this as the denial of a basic human right (and also one of the reasons for conversion) and consecrated a Hindu temple in 1888 where anyone was allowed entry for worship. This was an act of major defiance against the existing social and religious order, but the upper castes found themselves in no position either to challenge or to punish him (Pillai, 1994). It was a turning-point in the history of social development in Kerala. By this time, a number of persons from his community had received education and drew inspiration from Narayana Guru to press for further changes in social order. Narayana Guru provided them with the moral authority to demand education, health care, and other social improvements, and encouraged them to organize themselves for achieving these objectives. Later, the same degree of moral authority was provided by Mahatma Gandhi to the Indian movement for independence. Inspired by the actions of Narayana Guru, another reformer, Ayyankali, belonging to the depressed Pulaya community and a leader of the depressed castes, found the courage to articulate the demand for education and health care for members of all depressed communities. This became possible because the Travancore government permitted a limited degree of democracy by establishing a 'Peoples' Assembly' to which representatives of these communities were also nominated.

The forces of social transformation began to consolidate their positions, and in 1903, the Ezhava community formed the Sree Narayana Dharma Paripalana Sanghom (Sree Narayana Society for the Protection of Rights). The avowed objectives of the society were the promotion of education, hygiene, and industry. The favourable popular response which the society received encouraged other communities to constitute societies of their own, two of the notable ones being the Sadhu Jana Paripalana Sabha (Society for the Protection of the Poor People) established in 1907 and the Nair Service Society started in 1914. The relentless fight which the SNDP and the SJPs waged within the legislature and outside finally bore fruit in 1911–12 when all barriers on admission to government schools based on caste and sex were totally removed. The result of this was a doubling of school attendance within a decade leading to the rise in literacy rates between 1911 and 1921 as indicated in Table 7.2.

TABLE 7.2. Percentage of literates to total population by sex and caste in Travancore, 1891, 1911, and 1921

Castes	% of total population in 1901	1891		1911		1921	
		Male	Female	Male	Female	Male	Female
Forward community							
Nairs	17.7	37.5	6.9	46.7	9.7	61.2	32.4
Backward community							
Ezhavas	16.7	12.1	0.1	21.2	1.9	36.4	9.5
Depressed community		0.0	0.0	1.4	0.2	3.5	1.0
Kuravas	1.8	0.4	0.0	1.8	0.1	4.0	1.4
Pulayas	7.0	2.9	0.3	2.8	0.3	10.9	5.5
Parayas	2.4						

Source: P. R. Gopinathan Nair, 'Universalization of Primary Education in Kerala', in P. R. Panchamukhi (ed.), *Studies in Educational Reforms in India*, ii. 271, Himalaya Publishing House, 1989

While the forces of social change were similar and parallel in many respects in Travancore and Cochin, in Malabar, under direct British rule, the continuation of the feudal structure of the society and the prevalence of a high degree of inequality in land and wealth distribution weakened the forces of social intermediation and stifled progress. While various social movements did create popular demand for education and health care, the effective demand for these was confined to a few belonging to the upper castes in Malabar. These interregional differentials within the area persisted till the formation of Kerala State in 1956. By that time, however, the social environment of Kerala had undergone complete transformation. The social intermediation process begun by Narayana Guru with the consecration of a temple in 1888 culminated in the famous Temple Entry Proclamation of 1936 by the Maharajah of Travancore, by which all the temples were thrown open for worship to all communities. This proclamation heralded a new social environment in Kerala in which caste hierarchy no longer determined or even dominated one's social position. Since then, social status of a person gets determined by his economic position. Caste has yielded to class, even though caste has assumed a new role among the erstwhile 'oppressed' communities as a claim for preferential treatment in education and employment.

Women and Education

Numerous studies have commented upon Kerala's notable efforts at women's education and the role of women in Kerala's social development (Jeffrey, 1992). Social barriers to women's education continue to be important factors preventing female literacy levels from rising in many parts of India. These barriers began to crumble in Travancore and Cochin in the second half of the nineteenth century. Again, the forces of social intermediation played an important role in this. While the first girls' schools in Travancore were opened on the initiative of missionaries, in Cochin it was local efforts which pushed for women's education. Initially, separate schools for girls were established to overcome social resistance, but ultimately coeducational schools began to outnumber them. As a result of all these measures, the female literacy rate, while lower than that for males, was highest in Travancore and Cochin by the turn of the century.

Literacy rates among women in 1891 indicate that it was highest among Brahmins, Nairs, and Christians. The Brahmins constituted a minuscule proportion of the total population. Numerically, Nairs, Christians, Ezhavas, Muslims, and depressed classes make up the rest of the population. Therefore, the history of female literacy and women's education is really the story of how these groups responded to the schooling of girls.

Upper-caste women, especially among the economically better-off Nair community, had a long tradition in functional literacy since they wanted to read religious works like Ramayana and Mahabharata in the Malayalam language. Thus, girls from these families were allowed to learn to read and write under the tutelage of the village 'teacher'. When the indigenous schools were converted to vernacular schools, girls from the upper castes continued to attend schools. Their attendance was also encouraged by opening separate girls' schools.

Nair girls were in an especially good position to attend schools because of the prevalence of the matrilineal system which enabled them to move outside their homes freely and independently. Since Nair women enjoyed a higher status within the family, and a girl child was necessary for the continuation of the family line, girl children enjoyed considerable social freedom within the family, and there were no cultural or social barriers to their attending schools.

Though the matrilineal system was a factor in the rapid spread of literacy among Nair women, Christians closely followed their example. The establishment of a large number of schools under the grant-in-aid scheme by the indigenous Christian community opened the doors of education to Christian girls who had also enjoyed a freedom of mobility similar to the Nairs within society. Christian women too prized functional literacy since it enabled them to read the Bible. The Church enjoined on the Christian families to send their girls to school. They also set up separate girls' schools run by nuns under the management of the Church. Literacy rates among Christian women were equal to or exceeded those of Nairs by 1941. In fact, the highest female literacy rates in 1991 are in those districts where the Christian population is concentrated.

With the abolition of caste barriers, the Ezhava girls also began attending schools in large numbers. A section of the Ezhavas also practised matriliny but it would be wrong to attribute the progress of female literacy largely to this factor. Kerala women belonging to all castes, except Namboodiri Brahmins and Muslims, did not practise the custom of purdah[2] and thus enjoyed some measure of freedom of movement outside their homes. The tradition of Purdah is considered a powerful barrier against raising the literacy levels as well as the status of women in the backward Hindi-speaking states (Minturn, 1993). Comparatively high female literacy rates among the southern States might be partly due to the absence of the Purdah tradition in this part of the country.

The Route to Total Literacy

The basic strategy for human development adopted in Kerala was to ensure access to education and health to every individual. Access to education, in this context, meant locational, economic, and social access. Locational access implied the availability of schools within walking distance from homes. Economic access was ensured by making education progressively free up to and including high school. Later, needy children were also provided noon meals at the schools. Social access was vital to ensure that children of backward and depressed communities were not denied enrolment in schools. It was the question of social access which was basically solved through the process of social intermediation. These policies had been followed in Travancore and Cochin since the early decades of this century with the result that these two regions were already ahead of Malabar when Kerala State was constituted in 1956.

Another important policy was the integration of the private sector in the mainstream of education. During the 1860s, when a large number of public (government) schools were opened in Travancore and Cochin States, the governments realized that they would not have enough resources to build schools for all the school-going children in their territories. The mechanism of grant-in-aid to private schools was devised to take care of this resource constraint. The grant-in-aid would go only towards meeting the recurrent cost of running schools, while the capital cost of land and buildings had to be provided by the private agency concerned. Thus, half or more of the capital formation in the education sector was contributed by the private sector. As mentioned in the previous section, the provision of grant-in-aid was a powerful incentive to various communities for starting schools.

After the unification of the Travancore and Cochin States in 1949, this policy was modified under pressure from teachers' unions. The system whereby private schools transferred 80 per cent of fees collected to the government and paid their teachers different wages was eliminated. It was replaced by one in which tuition fees were eliminated and the salaries of teachers in government and private schools were unified and the private-school teachers were entirely paid by the government. This is an important factor in the high proportion of current expenditure on education in Kerala.

The situation in Malabar at the time of the integration of the States was very different. The number of government schools was few, and the grant-in-aid scheme was not as comprehensive as in Travancore and Cochin. When Kerala was constituted in 1956, Malabar lagged behind the southern region in regard to number of schools and access to schools for children in different parts of the district. The first priority was, therefore, to redress the imbalance in the regional distribution of educational facilities by opening a large number of government schools in Malabar. The government also extended all the other facilitating measures, such as payment of salaries to private-school teachers and the noon meal programme, to the Malabar region. In 1955–6, Malabar had only 90 primary, 25 middle, and 11 secondary schools operated by the government, but in 1960–1 their numbers were 1,083, 248, and 100 respectively. In 1990–1, Malabar had a total of 5,477 schools of which 1,866 were government schools. It is also clear that the gap in literacy levels between males and females has declined over this period.

In April 1991, Kerala achieved the unique distinction of becoming the first State in the country to be declared totally literate. This achievement was the culmination of an experiment at total literacy launched in the Ernakulam district by voluntary agencies, the success of which led to the formulation and implementation of the Total Literacy Programme in the State.

A One-Day Literacy Survey conducted to identify all the illiterates in the State revealed that they numbered about 2.85m., constituting 9.6 per cent of the total population. The 1991 population census estimated the literacy rate to be 90.6 (6 years and over) which is consistent with the figure obtained in the Literacy Survey.

The total literacy campaign in Kerala was a co-operative venture by government, political parties, a large number of NGOs, and individuals. It involved the free services of about 400,000 volunteers to teach the illiterates (State Planning Board, 1992). Thus, the programme for the eradication of illiteracy in Kerala represented the *summum bonum* of the process of social intermediation begun during the closing decades of the last century. Later, the National Literacy Mission and the various States adopted the Kerala approach in their own literacy campaigns.

Enrolment and Drop-out Rates

By 1990, Kerala had one school for every 2,400 people. The regional disparity in access to schools has been completely eliminated. Almost all children in the 5–15 age-group attend schools in all the districts of Kerala.

Kerala's performance in education can be fully understood only if we compare the results with those of other States in India (see Table 7.3). The lower enrolment rates in most States were due to low enrolment of girls. For example, in Rajasthan only 47 per cent of girls in the 6–11 age-group were enrolled, while the rate exceeded 100 per cent in Himachal Pradesh, Kerala, Maharashtra, Tamil Nadu, and West Bengal. The total enrolment rate at the lower primary stage varied from a low of 75 per cent in Uttar Pradesh to a high of 132 in Tamil Nadu. The rate was 108 for Kerala.

TABLE 7.3. Gross enrolment ratio and drop-out rates in major States (%)

	Enrolment 1987–8						Drop-outs 1986–7 Classes I–V General
	Classes I–V (6–11 years)			Classes VI–VIII (11–14 years)			
	Boys	Girls	Total	Boys	Girls	Total	
Andhra Pradesh	118.2	88.5	103.5	61.6	34.8	48.0	59.6
Assam	112.2	98.8	105.7	60.2	44.8	52.8	64.2
Bihar	107.2	53.8	80.8	49.7	17.1	33.6	65.4
Gujarat	128.1	99.9	114.3	68.4	44.8	56.9	44.5
Haryana	97.6	72.8	85.4	81.3	44.1	63.7	29.3
Himachal Pradesh	121.6	104.6	113.2	108.9	76.4	92.9	31.6
Jammu and Kashmir	101.3	66.9	84.6	71.2	39.7	55.9	39.2
Karnataka	113.0	96.2	104.7	63.0	45.1	54.1	56.0
Kerala	109.1	107.0	108.1	98.0	95.7	96.9	0.4
Madhya Pradesh	119.5	78.2	99.5	71.1	29.0	50.5	42.4
Maharashtra	130.7	112.2	121.7	82.20	55.8	69.2	42.1
Orissa	112.4	83.6	98.1	51.4	28.4	39.9	51.3
Punjab	97.7	91.8	94.9	67.0	56.5	62.1	39.4
Rajasthan	110.0	47.2	79.6	63.9	17.0	41.2	51.1
Tamil Nadu	139.6	123.8	131.8	97.2	71.0	84.3	22.3
Uttar Pradesh	93.9	53.3	74.7	64.4	24.5	45.7	45.8
West Bengal	134.9	101.0	118.1	72.7	57.6	65.2	62.7

Source: State Planning Board (1992)

In all States, excluding Punjab, Haryana, Himachal Pradesh, Jammu and Kashmir, Tamil Nadu, and Kerala, drop-out rates exceeded 40 per cent of those enrolled in classes I to V in 1987–8. The drop-out rate in Kerala was negligible, only 0.4 per cent; in Bihar it was 65 per cent (State Planning Board, 1992).

In Kerala the enrolment rates are similar for boys and girls in the 6–11 age-group throughout the period beginning 1960–1. While 99 per cent of the 5–9 age-group were enrolled in schools, the enrolment rate at the next age-group, 10–14, was as high as 94 per cent. This is largely the result of a new policy on promotion which limits the failures in each class to 10 per cent or less of the number of students attending that class. While this policy has drastically reduced the number of drop-outs, one outcome of the policy has been a low percentage of passes at the high school examination. The policy raises some important questions regarding the quality of education, but there is no doubt that the social and cultural impact of a longer period of schooling is significant for the society.

The achievement of total literacy, continuous rise in mean years of schooling, and the elimination of gender differentials in education in Kerala have their origins in the closing decades of the last century. The policies initiated at that time have proved to be unerring in their objectives and have continued to guide the develop-ment of education to this day in the State. With the formation of Kerala State, these policies were extended to Malabar. By this time, the social conditions in Malabar had undergone a drastic change, and the dominance of the caste hierarchy were on the wane.

Health and Social Intermediation

There is some indirect evidence for advancing a hypothesis that health conditions had begun to improve in Travancore and Cochin by the end of the nineteenth century. The evidence is provided by the respective growth rates of population in Kerala and India. During 1901–10, Kerala's population growth rate was 11.75 per cent, compared to 5.75 per cent for India. During the decade 1911–20, when India's population growth rate fell below zero (−0.31 per cent) due to the great influenza epidemic, Kerala still had a growth rate of 9.16 per cent. Kerala had a higher popu-lation growth rate till 1971, at which time the rate began to decline. These growth rates imply that by the end of the nineteenth century, mortality rates in Kerala had begun to decline at a faster rate than the decline in fertility rates. These facts also show that mortality rates were probably lower in Kerala than in any other part of India. However, this decline in mortality was probably not continuous, but rather exhibited a fluctuating pattern.

These fluctuations reflect the effect of differential policy initiatives and also the impact of Malabar. The mortality rate was higher in Malabar in the 1970s and the early 1980s, but by the end of the 1980s, the differentials between Malabar and Travancore-Cochin areas had almost vanished. We shall indicate later the factors that brought about this convergence.

Also, it must be remembered that a substantial part of the success of the mater-nal and child health programmes must be attributed to the better status enjoyed by women in Kerala. The prevalence of matriliny among a large section of the popula-tion and the encouragement of schooling of girls, first among the Christian com-munity and later by all, conferred substantial autonomy to women in household decision-making. Matriliny and its influences also created a social situation where female children are as preferred as male children, or at least are not discriminated against. These factors make Kerala unique among the States in India because it is the only State in which the gender ratio is in favour of women. These elements cannot, by themselves, explain the favourable health outcomes observed in the State, and the difference in pace during different periods. However, they are the foundation on which health (especially mother and child) policies are based. They are the core of social intermediation in this area.

Kerala has the lowest infant-mortality rate among all the States in India. In 1992, Kerala's infant mortality in the rural sector was about one-fourth India's. Orissa had recorded an infant-mortality rate of 126 compared to 17 for Kerala in 1991 (see

Table 7.1). Infant mortality is a key factor in the health transition of a population, as the life expectancy at birth and the general mortality rate are dependent on its level. Historically, it appears from the population census estimates that infant mortality in Kerala declined from 220 in 1921–30 to 120 for the decade 1951–1960.[3] Panikar has attributed the decline in mortality rates during this period to preventive measures, such as the spread of smallpox and cholera vaccinations, improvement in sanitation, and the extension of drinking-water schemes. Impressive as this reduction in half in infant-mortality rates is, during the following thirty years, it was reduced to slightly above a tenth of its 1960 level. How this result came about is discussed in the next section.

Health Transition: Factors in Convergence

Life expectancy at birth in Kerala is fifteen years longer than it is in India. The death rate in rural Kerala is half that of rural India, and infant mortality is only one-sixth that of rural India. The instruments and policies which achieved the transition from a relatively high mortality region to a low mortality one within a span of thirty-five years and the lessons that Kerala can offer to societies with similar levels of income are discussed.

The health status of a population at any particular moment in time is a result of multiple interactions and feedbacks among a number of factors—socio-economic as well as biologic (Mosley and Chen, 1984; Caldwell, 1986). While the socio-economic factors determine the intensity of desire and the ability to seek health care, the biologic factors interacting with the quality of health care determine the outcome of the actions taken in response to illnesses. We are primarily concerned with the socio-economic factors that have aided and accelerated the process of health transition in Kerala.

The infant-mortality rate since the formation of Kerala State in 1956 has declined rapidly (see Table 7.4). A closer analysis indicates that this decline has

TABLE 7.4. Changes in infant mortality in rural Kerala

Year	Infant-mortality rate	Percentage decline
1951–60	120	
1966	68	43.33
1976	55	19.12
1986	27	50.90
1992	17	37.04

Sources: Sample Registration in Kerala, Rural *Annual Reports*, 1980 and 1988; *Sample Registration Bulletin*, 1994

occurred in three stages. During the first decade after the formation of Kerala State, between 1956 and 1966, the infant-mortality rate declined by about 43 per cent; it appears to have slowed down until 1976, when the decline again accelerated. It declined by 69 per cent between 1976 and 1992, the corresponding figure for India being around 39 per cent.

A substantial part of this reduction can be attributed to the improvement in Malabar and its convergence towards the levels observed in Travancore-Cochin. It was estimated that in 1956 the death rate in Malabar was probably twice the rate prevailing in Travancore-Cochin (United Nations, 1975). These differences probably arose from the differentials in health-care facilities between the two regions. For instance, in 1956–7 the population : bed ratio was 3,125 persons in Malabar, and 1,282 persons in Travancore-Cochin, compared to 1,021 and 642 persons respectively in 1989–90. After the formation of the State, the government placed greater emphasis on the expansion of health-care facilities in the Malabar region in order to reduce the inequality in the availability of health care between the two regions. The reduction in death rate and in infant mortality in the Malabar region must be partly attributed to this factor (see Fig. 7.1).

Locational and economic access are equally important in health care for the lower-income groups. If health-care centres are located far from home, additional costs must be added to the direct cost of medical care. In this matter Kerala stands apart from the other States in India. The population : bed ratio may be considered a good indicator of the overall availability of health care. Kerala not only has the

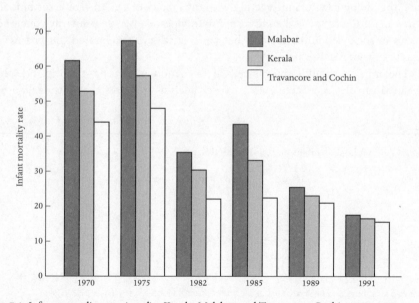

Fig. 7.1 Infant-mortality rate (rural)—Kerala, Malabar, and Travancore-Cochin, 1970–1991

lowest ratio among all the States in India, but the facilities are almost evenly divided between rural and urban areas. The distribution of hospitals and dispensaries, as well as beds, in rural and urban areas of different States in India, clearly shows their unequal distribution in all States except Kerala. Rural populations are close to 80 per cent of the total in most States, but in the majority of States, less that 20 per cent of the hospital beds are located in rural areas. These figures include only partial data for the private health sector. If the private-sector facilities were also considered, the disparities would be much larger. In the case of Kerala, nearly 55 per cent of total hospital beds are in rural hospitals and clinics.

Recent data indicate that the cost of treatment is closely related to access to health care. Kerala reports the lowest cost of treatment among all the major States in India. Besides, the burden of treatment—the ratio of the total cost of illness (direct plus opportunity cost) to the income of the individual—is also one of the lowest for the poorer income groups in Kerala (Krishnan, 1994).

Data on causes of death for all ages indicate major shifts in the causes even between 1959 and 1965. Smallpox accounted for 1.9 per cent of reported deaths in 1959, but declined to 0.1 per cent in 1965. The number of deaths due to diarrhoea, respiratory diseases, and fevers declined from 27.8 per cent of the total in 1959 to 16.0 per cent in 1965. Based on these findings, we may conclude that the expansion of health-care facilities, especially in the Malabar area, and the vaccination programmes against infectious diseases, have been the main factors responsible for the rapid decline in mortality rates and the increase in the expectation of life during the first phase of the health transition. Although these policy initiatives are not radically different from those applied in Travancore-Cochin since the 1920s, in Malabar they were implemented faster and on a larger scale, thus their results seem more dramatic.

Maternal and Child Health

Before we discuss the reasons for the slowing down of the mortality declines during the second phase, let us discuss the third phase of the transition, during which these rates again accelerated. We attribute this phase of the transition mainly to the emphasis placed on maternal and child health during this period. The maternal and child-health programmes begin with antenatal care and include paediatric care, the institutionalization of childbirths, and the immunization of children, among other things. While information on the extent of antenatal care is not available for various periods and years, we may safely conclude that it would have risen with the institutionalization of childbirths.

The data presented in Table 7.5 on the percentage distribution of births in rural Kerala by type of medical attention received show that the percentage of births taking place in institutions rose from 26 in 1973 to 91.5 in 1991. Only about 3.5 per cent of childbirths were attended by untrained and non-professionals in 1991,

TABLE 7.5. Percentage distribution of births in rural Kerala by type of medical attention received, 1973, 1978, 1988, and 1991

Year	Institutional	Trained professional	Untrained professional	Non-professional
1973	26.0	20.0	36.6	17.4
1978	40.8	16.4	40.6	2.2
1989	86.0	5.6	6.8	1.5
1991	91.5	5.0	3.5	0.0

Source: Sample Registration in Kerala, *Annual Reports*; *Sample Registration System*, 1991

whereas it was nearly 54 per cent as recently as 1973. This explains why, as late as 1980, no deaths were reported from complications arising from childbirth. Infant deaths due to malposition, cord infection, or malnutrition were also not reported in 1980. This result could be attributed to the extension of antenatal care of pregnant women. Various enquiries have shown that the extent of coverage of tetanus toxoid immunization of pregnant women is almost universal in all parts of Kerala.

Of the 29 million people treated by the public allopathic system in 1987–8, women and children constituted 42 per cent and 29 per cent respectively. We have no data on the number of persons treated by the private health-care system, but given its size, the numbers might be even larger. The immunization survey indicated that nearly one-third of the total number of child immunizations and over half the number of TT immunizations were given by private physicians. A 1993 survey on immunization indicates that immunization rates vary between 70 per cent and 90 per cent in all districts except Malappuram, Palghat, and Trichur. These rates will be much higher if we consider only DPT immunizations.

In light of the data presented above, it is clear that a major factor, besides the expansion of health-care facilities, in the decline in infant and child deaths since 1976, is principally the extension of maternal and child health. Kerala introduced the expanded programme on immunization in 1978, and the entire State came under the programme in 1982. These factors essentially explain the acceleration in the rates of mortality decline during the third phase.

We may now attempt an explanation for the deceleration in mortality decline between 1966 and 1976. First, the immunization programme probably reached a plateau by 1966 and did not increase very much until the programme was strengthened in 1978. Secondly, the rapid expansion of health facilities in the Malabar region that had taken place since the formation of the State, in order to reduce the disparities within the State, had largely achieved its objectives by 1976, and there was a slowing down in the expansion of health facilities during the second phase. Thirdly, during this period the country passed through a difficult phase in its economic performance, which considerably affected the planning process.

Demographic Transition

Since the story behind Kerala's demographic transition is well known, it is not discussed in any great detail here (Krishnan, 1976; Zachariah, 1984; Mari Bhat and Rajan, 1990; Zachariah *et al.*, 1994). In Kerala, the birth rate declined by more than half between 1966 and 1991, from 37 to 18 per 1,000 population. While it is a matter of concern that the decennial population growth rate for India has only marginally declined from 24.7 per cent during the decade 1971–81 to 23.5 per cent during the decade 1981–91, Kerala has recorded the lowest decennial growth rate (13.98 per cent) among all the States in India. In fact, the district-wise population growth rates during this decade lend further support to the finding that in large parts of Kerala the birth rate has declined below the replacement level. The lower fertility and mortality rates in Kerala, compared to the rest of India, have also altered the age distribution of the population in Kerala. Kerala now reports the highest proportion of 60+ in its population among the States in India (Irudaya, Rajan, Misra, and Sarma, 1993).

There existed wide differences in fertility levels between Travancore-Cochin and Malabar at the time of the integration of these two regions to form Kerala State (see Fig. 7.2). Our estimates indicate that the rural birth rate in Malabar was about

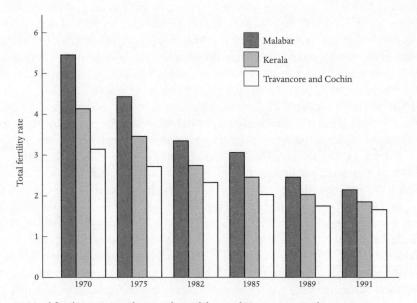

Fig. 7.2 Total fertility rate (rural)—Kerala, Malabar, and Travancore-Cochin, 1970–1991

42 per 1,000 compared to 33 per 1,000 in Travancore-Cochin in 1966, ten years after the integration of these regions. By 1991, the birth rate declined to 18.4 per 1,000 in rural Kerala. Similar differences are also seen in total fertility rates. It is estimated at 5.6 for Malabar compared to 3.3 for the Travancore-Cochin area in 1969. The total fertility rate had fallen below the replacement level by 1991 to 1.9. While this figure is 2.1 for Malabar, the corresponding level is 1.8 in the Travancore-Cochin area. A combination of factors led to this decline. A rise in the age at which women married (thanks to more years of schooling), greater acceptance of contraception by married women in the 25–30 age-group, and a decline in infant-mortality rates, have been identified as the principal factors of this demographic transition. The important fact that needs reiteration here is that the extension of the same social programmes which were already in force from Travancore-Cochin to Malabar accelerated the pace of this transformation.

The decline in the total fertility rate cannot be attributed to the success of the official population programme. The contraceptive prevalence rate is in no way greater than some of the other States where birth rates are much higher than in Kerala (see Table 7.6). The fertility rates in Kerala indicate that the actual use of family planning is presumably greater than is officially reported. While two-thirds of tubectomies are performed on women aged 30 and above in most States, in Kerala the same proportion is performed on women below 30. Therefore, the impact of the official programme will also be the greatest in Kerala.

As a consequence of the social developments discussed earlier, Kerala presents a singular case of a contemporary developing society where the health and demographic transitions were achieved within a single generation—in a period of about thirty-five years. An important lesson on Kerala's health and demographic transitions for the poorer countries is that health improvements and fertility declines can be 'de-linked' to a large extent from increases in per capita income and that these two transitions can be not only complementary but also contemporaneous.

The per capita income of Kerala is one of the lowest among the developing countries, but life expectancies, mortality rates, and even the pattern of morbidity correspond to observed figures of other nations with much higher levels of per capita income. The situation in Kerala as regards per capita food intake, the availability of protected public water supply, and the availability of improved sanitary facilities is not significantly better than in other States in India. Per capita daily calorie intake is lowest in Kerala and more than half of its cereal consumption is met through the public distribution system (United Nations, 1975; Krishnan, 1992). While the record is marginally better than other States in the matter of sanitation, it is not so in the case of protected water supply. Zachariah and Patel found that there was no statistically significant relationship between infant mortality on the one hand and landownership, sources of water supply to the house, toilet facilities, and per capita household expenditure on the other.[4] They found that both neonatal and

TABLE 7.6. Effective couple protection rates due to all family-planning methods, 1970–1990 (%)

	1970	1975	1980	1985	1990	Average annual increase in CPR	
						1970–80	1980–90
Andhra Pradesh	9.4	18.4	25.6	32.0	42.9	1.6	1.7
Assam	6.1	9.3	19.3	24.9	28.2	1.4	0.9
Bihar	4.8	7.3	12.4	17.2	26.3	0.8	1.4
Delhi	16.1	23.8	34.8	35.6	41.7	1.9	0.7
Gujarat	11.0	20.8	31.3	45.5	56.5	2.0	2.5
Haryana	11.2	21.3	29.1	45.8	58.9	1.8	3.0
Himachal Pradesh	8.5	9.1	24.4	35.7	50.1	1.6	2.6
Jammu and Kashmir	7.0	8.7	11.0	15.6	21.7	0.4	1.1
Karnataka	9.2	12.3	22.3	32.8	46.0	1.3	2.4
Kerala	13.9	20.8	28.9	38.1	54.4	1.5	2.6
Madhya Pradesh	9.2	13.4	21.7	29.5	39.4	1.3	1.8
Maharashtra	14.6	25.8	34.5	51.8	54.4	2.0	2.0
Orissa	12.3	17.8	26.9	32.8	40.7	1.5	1.4
Punjab	17.2	20.9	23.5	48.9	73.2	0.6	5.0
Rajasthan	4.9	6.9	13.3	19.8	30.0	0.8	1.7
Tamil Nadu	12.5	20.7	28.2	36.1	57.1	1.6	2.9
Uttar Pradesh	5.5	7.5	11.5	17.1	33.3	0.6	2.2
West Bengal	9.5	11.5	21.4	27.3	33.1	1.2	1.2
India	9.4	14.8	22.3	32.1	43.3	1.3	2.1

Sources: *Family Welfare Programme in India*, Year Book 1987–8, table E-3, Ministry of Health and Family Welfare, Dept. of Family Welfare, Govt. of India, New Delhi; *Analytical Review of Couple Protection Rates, 1990*, Evaluation and Intelligence Division, Ministry of Health and Family Welfare, Govt. of India, New Delhi, 1991

infant mortality were inversely related to the level of the education of the mother. Thus, educational achievement (especially female education which, in turn, depends on the status enjoyed by women) is a fundamental pillar of the health and demographic transitions. The other pillar is public financing of services.

Financing human development

The achievements of Kerala in human development would not have been possible but for the commitment of financial resources by the government. Travancore and Cochin were already devoting a large share of public expenditure for social development before independence and this trend proved socially and politically irreversible afterwards.[5] Therefore, the five-year plans allocated the largest share of expenditures to social services in Kerala's plans. The cumulative plan (i.e. capital) expenditure from the first plan (1951–6) to the seventh plan (1985–90) formed 23.9 per cent of total outlay for social services compared to 19.5 per cent for energy and 10.5 per cent for industry. The picture is similar when we examine the current expenditure of the government. Expenditure on social and development services have averaged 55 per cent of total current expenditure throughout the period since 1960–1 (Govt. of Kerala, various years).

Education had received the largest share of public expenditure from very early times in Travancore and Cochin. This trend has continued since independence. Expenditure on education rose from about 36 per cent of total current expenditure in 1960–1 to about 40 per cent in 1975–6 from whence it began to decline, falling to 26 per cent by 1992–3. Expenditure on education constituted about 3.75 per cent of the state domestic product in 1960–1 but rose to 6.36 per cent by 1990–1. However this increase is somewhat misleading since there was a decline in the growth rate of SDP after 1974–5.

There are wide variations in the share of total current expenditure devoted to education among the different States in India (see Table 7.7). Tilak has shown that these disparities have increased during the past thirty years. Tilak's data show that Kerala is one of the two or three States that spend the highest proportion of total current expenditure on education. This is also true in terms of per capita current

TABLE 7.7. Proportion of educational expenditure to total budget of the States (revenue account only)

State	1960–1	1970–1	1975–6	1980–1	1990–1
Andhra Pradesh	23.2	20.9	27.0	25.7	24.5
Assam	21.1	20.8	26.8	29.0	25.5
Bihar	18.9	19.5	29.9	26.5	28.1
Gujarat	23.4	20.2	25.9	23.6	24.3
Haryana	[b]	19.8	20.0	21.2	18.6
Himachal Pradesh	—	24.5	27.0	25.7	22.6
Jammu and Kashmir	16.3	13.4	14.6	19.3	17.0
Karnataka	21.2	21.3	24.6	22.3	22.1
Kerala	36.0	35.7	39.7	35.5	30.4
Madhya Pradesh	24.2	24.2	21.7	21.4	24.2
Maharashtra	25.2	21.3	24.7	24.0	21.1
Orissa	12.8	16.8	24.0	22.8	24.2
Punjab	20.6[a]	22.1	26.2	29.3	22.7
Rajasthan	24.5	18.9	24.7	26.0	26.5
Tamil Nadu	23.4	22.5	23.6	24.3	22.7
Tripura	—	30.7	28.5	19.4	23.5
Uttar Pradesh	14.5	18.2	29.9	22.0	24.0
West Bengal	37.1	23.0	24.9	24.2	30.4
India	22.5	21.4	25.8	23.8	25.4
Coefficient of variation	4.4	22.0	18.9	15.5	13.9

[a] Including Haryana; [b] Included in Punjab

Source: Tilak, May 1995, p. 32

expenditure (Tilak, 1995: 32). According to his calculations, government funds formed over 80 per cent of total funding for education in India (ibid. 17).

Current expenditure on education at 1980–1 prices grew at 4.63 per cent during the entire period. When this is broken into two subperiods, 1960–1 to 1974–5 and 1974–5 to 1990–1, the rates of growth are almost identical. Therefore, the decline in the share of total current expenditure should not be construed as indicating a decline in the rate of growth of educational expenditure.

The bulk of educational expenditure is devoted to primary education, constituting 52 per cent in 1982–3. In that year the combined expenditure on primary and secondary education constituted 81 per cent of the total. The proportion of expenditure on primary education has been declining marginally since then and was 49 per cent of the total in 1991–2.[6]

While public funding provided nearly 80 per cent of the total expenditure for education, it is estimated that about 75 per cent of health expenditure in India is attributed to private household spending (Berman, 1995). Berman has estimated that in India total public and private health expenditure amounts to 7 per cent of its GDP (ibid.). Though this figure is similar to the share of health expenditure in some developing and a large number of developed countries, the quality and access to health care in India are considered poor in comparison, and the efficiency of health expenditure is believed to be low. One of the reasons for this situation may be the low share of *public* expenditure on health care, around 2 per cent of GDP compared to 5 per cent or more in many developed countries. The high dependence on private spending to secure health care has not only put a disproportionately high burden on poorer households, but is also the cause of the poor quality of health care (Krishnan, 1994).

As provision of health care is mainly the responsibility of state governments, the critical element is the amount of local public resources devoted to this sector. Expenditure by States on health-care provision constituted between 1 and 3 per cent of state income. Kerala was one of the States which spent close to 3 per cent and thus belonged to the upper end of public expenditure on health. The backward States like Bihar and Madhya Pradesh spent even less than 1 per cent of state income's public expenditure on health care. What is surprising is that a relatively affluent State—Punjab—also belonged to this group. During the 1980s and 1990s this situation changed, and there was an increase in public expenditure on health care, but it still fell below 3 per cent in most States. Kerala, however, raised this proportion to over 3 per cent.

The higher share of health expenditure as a proportion of state income in Kerala is a reflection of the higher proportion of total public expenditure devoted to health care. Total health expenditure (including medical and public health, family welfare, water supply and sanitation, nutrition, and child and handicapped welfare) has varied between 12 per cent and 15 per cent of total government expenditure. Per capita health expenditure is also larger in Kerala. Kerala ranked number one in terms of real per capita health expenditure in the 1960s and early 1970s. There are a few States whose per capita levels of expenditures are close to that of Kerala, but now the health outcomes are much lower than that of Kerala.

Household Expenditure on Health

While government expenditures on health are available, information on household expenditures is not generally available. Some sporadic data on household health expenditures are available through limited enquiries. The seventeenth round of the National Sample Survey collected data on medical expenditure for the year 1961–2. The highest per capita expenditure recorded among all the States was for Kerala both for the rural and the urban sectors. At that time, per capita spending in urban areas in health was 20 per cent higher in Kerala than in the rest of India. In rural areas it was more than double. Kerala is the only State in which there is practically no differential in health expenditures between the rural and urban sectors, even going as far back as 1961–2. Expenditure on health care constituted 3.25 per cent of total household expenditure that year.

A survey on the utilization of remittances in Kerala conducted in 1987 indicated that the annual per capita expenditure on health by households receiving remittances from the Gulf countries was 5.8 per cent of per capita total expenditure, and for households which did not receive such remittances it was 6.2 per cent of per capita total expenditure. However, in absolute value the latter were spending slightly more than half the former. We estimated the rates of growth of public and household expenditure separately for the period before and after the start of labour migration to the Middle East. While the rate of growth of government expenditure is almost identical in both periods, that of personal expenditure rose from 4.21 per cent during 1961–2 to 1973–4 to 6.52 per cent during 1973–4 to 1986–7.

The analysis of Kerala's health transition clearly showed an acceleration from 1975. The acceleration in the decline in infant mortality, the expansion in private provision of health-care facilities, and the increase in the expenditure on health all occurred during this period. This period also coincided with the outflow of Kerala workers to the Middle East giving rise to a substantial inflow of remittances. Households which received remittances spent 76 per cent more on health than households which did not receive any (Dept. of Economics and Statistics, 1987). A larger share of remittances was probably received by the population residing in the northern region of Kerala since a majority of the migrants were from this region. It was pointed out earlier that the differential in the utilization of health care had considerably narrowed between the southern and northern regions and that infant mortality rates were similar in the two regions.

A major contributing factor for this convergence might have been a relatively higher increase in per capita income arising from remittances to the population of the northern region thus enabling them to spend larger amounts on health care. Therefore, the role of income in hastening the health and demographic transitions should not be entirely dismissed in the Kerala case. An increase in disposable income of the households led to an increase in effective demand for health care.

Economic Constraints and Sustainability

The impressive gains in social indicators achieved by Kerala took place in an economic environment where per capita State income grew at an unimpressive rate of less than 1 per cent for the entire period since 1961. From the mid-1970s, the annual growth rate of state income decelerated. In fact, the per capita state income for every year from 1980–1 to 1987–8 was below that of 1980–1.

Consistent with these trends, the State ranked tenth in per capita consumer expenditure in 1972–3, below the all-India average. However, by 1983 the State had moved to the fourth position in terms of consumer expenditure behind Punjab, Haryana, and Himachal Pradesh. Kerala has retained this rank ever since. Thus, Kerala's per capita state income hides the true level of income in the State as it excludes the earnings remitted by Kerala workers employed in the Middle East. But consumer expenditure reflected the magnitude of remittances since it is determined by the level of disposable income. It is a matter of great concern that the remittances failed to raise the growth of state income and that this period witnessed a decline in the growth rate of output.

An examination of the sectoral growth rates provides a clearer understanding as to how this decline in growth rates occurred. The agricultural sector (including forestry and fishing) had a negative growth rate from 1975; similarly, the growth rate of unregistered manufacturing also declined. The latter reflects to a large extent the decline of employment and output in traditional industries of Kerala. Table 7.8 shows the sectoral growth rates for the two periods.

The migration of construction workers to the Gulf region combined with a boom in construction activity also triggered a rise in the wages of construction workers in Kerala. This increase in construction wages seems to have triggered a rise in the wages of agricultural labourers which possibly resulted in the decline in agricultural output (Kannan and Pushpangadan, 1988; Krishnan, 1992). There is reason to believe that the decline in the output of traditional industries and that of the unregistered sector of manufacturing are also related to similar wage increases. Our analysis of the earnings of workers in these sectors shows that they have risen substantially since 1975. Possibly this was the result of implementing stringently the notified minimum wages in these industries. The traditional industries like coir and cashew call for very little investment in machinery and equipment, and their output is almost exclusively due to employment of labour. Since there is a physical limit to the amount of output that can be raised by manual labour alone, the increases in wage rates cut into the profits of the manufacturer. When this happens,

TABLE 7.8. Sectoral growth rates (compound) of state domestic product at 1980–81 prices: 1960–1 to 1989–90 (revised series)

Sector	1960–1 to 1974–5	1974–5 to 1989–90
Agriculture	2.00	0.78
Forestry and logging	5.73	−12.05
Fishing	6.11	−3.51
Mining and quarrying	−4.68	6.91
Primary sector: Total	2.19	0.03
Manufacturing	6.67	3.13
Manufacturing: registered	6.60	5.01
Manufacturing: unregistered	6.77	0.62
Construction	8.61	−2.58
Electricity, gas, and water supply	3.98	3.81
Secondary Sector: Total	6.22	2.94
Tertiary Sector: Total	5.15	3.85
Net state domestic product	3.91	2.08

Source: Calculated from *Economic Review* (various years), Kerala State Planning Board, Trivandrum

the industrialists look for other locations where wage rates are still considerably lower than in Kerala. It appears that the functioning of the labour market affects crucially the performance of the Kerala economy.

Though Kerala's economy is fully integrated with that of India, many features of Kerala's labour and commodity markets are quite distinct from the pattern prevailing in the rest of the country. The relationships and interlinkages between the rural labour, land, and credit markets in different regions of India as envisaged in the relevant literature are almost non-existent in Kerala. This is the result partly of extensive reforms in landownership and tenancy and partly due to the political and organizational mobilization of labour. This mobilization of labour led to the rapid growth of trade unionism not only among agricultural, industrial, and public-service employees, but has now spread to the informal labour sector as well. The rapid growth of labour unions among labourers in the informal sector is a consequence of the substantial increase in the size of the non-agricultural labour force, especially since 1975. Perhaps Kerala represents one of the few regions where workers in the informal sector are organized and unionized; this fact cannot but have important repercussions on the economy. Unionization was aided by the high literacy levels of the Kerala labour force; literacy also helps to transmit labour market information rapidly.

Nominal wage rates in Kerala have risen without any interruption during the period under analysis for all categories of labour almost at the same average annual rate. Money wage rates in 1989 were about twelve times higher than in 1963. While the cost-of-living index also rose dramatically, especially after 1974, real wage rates more than doubled during this period. Kerala happens to be the only State in India where real wages have nearly doubled between 1960 and 1990, and this is particularly significant in light of the observation made earlier that the Kerala economy had practically remained stagnant after 1975.

These wage increases have also been aided by the periodic revision of minimum wages that took into account increases in the cost of living. Kerala is perhaps the only State in India where the minimum wage notifications are effective and operational. The notification of minimum wages also provided a valid argument for the trade unions to demand wage revisions.

A question that is often raised is why Kerala did not raise its growth rate in spite of large inflows of remittance incomes? The answer is a complex one. Kerala is an integral part of the Indian economy and there is free trade within the borders of the country. Three-quarters or more of the commodities consumed in Kerala are imported from outside. Kerala has a deficit of 50 per cent in its requirements for food consumption which is largely made good by the public distribution system. Therefore, the multiplier effects of the remittance incomes are widely dispersed among the different States in India which supply the requirements of Kerala.

Another factor appears to be that the rate of savings in the Kerala economy did not rise commensurately with remittances. Households which received remittances mostly belonged to the semi-skilled and unskilled workers' families, and the immediate impact of remittances was an increase in their consumption levels. Most of these families had also incurred debts to finance the migration which meant that the immediate post-migration remittances were also utilized to repay the loans. For all these reasons, the marginal rate of household savings did not rise sharply in the economy. The savings of the households which received remittances were invested in house construction. During this period, savings of government and public enterprises also began to decline or even became negative. Kerala produced only a very small proportion of building materials and the rest were imported from outside the State. Therefore the multiplier effects of construction activity too were elsewhere and not within the State itself.

The only sectors which grew were the service sectors. But commodity production suffered, affecting the overall growth rate of the economy.

Conclusion

Kerala's achievements in the field of social development provide some important lessons for other States in India, and also for other developing countries. It shows that social development is a complex process and that without the participation of the people it will be difficult to achieve. Education and health provide both private as well as public benefits. Thus they are ideal for co-operative development. Thus private investment made good the lack of public resources in establishing the infrastructure for education. Presently, the private sector is also a major player in the health field. This is largely because the demand for health care in Kerala has out-stripped the public facilities in this sector. Kerala also demonstrates that once social development takes place, the process of demographic transition inevitably follows. There is no need to use pressure for the adoption of a small-family norm.

While the pace of social development was gradual and slow but steady in Tra-vancore and Cochin, the transformation was fast and dramatic in Malabar. While it took more than one hundred years to achieve this transformation in Travancore and Cochin, the period was compressed to less than thirty-five years in the case of Malabar. This was possible because the social intermediation process had already taken place in Malabar; what was lacking was investment in education and health care. With the formation of Kerala State, this situation was corrected with larger resources being diverted to the Malabar region.

The Kerala 'model' does not provide any evidence for the view that one could have high development in a context of low and stagnating per capita income. What it shows is that a high degree of social development is achievable in a context of low per capita income if sufficient resources are devoted to 'social capital formation'. At the same time, if a conscious policy of 'social capital formation' is pursued along with growth in per capita income, clearly there will be an acceleration in the process of social development. This is precisely what has happened in Kerala since 1975, when Gulf remittances began to flow into the State. In recent years, a rise in per capita disposable income is as much a factor as the role of the State in the social transformation of Kerala State.

Notes

1. Kerala State, a narrow strip of land about 600 km. long and between 110 and 120 km. wide, is situated on the south-west coast of India. The 1991 census estimated Kerala's population to be 29.098m., forming 3.44% of India's population. These figures indicate a high density of 749 persons per sq. km.
2. This practice involves a range on limitations of women and girls. It ranges from a certain dress code to restrictions on movement outside the home without male escort.
3. This was substantially lower than in the rest of India.
4. On the other hand, child (as opposed to infant, i.e. under 1-year-olds) mortality was strongly associated with sources of water supply and sanitary facilities (Zachariah and Patel, 1982).
5. As it was mentioned in the introduction, it must be recalled that in Travancore and Cochin, these decisions were taken locally with no interference from the British.
6. Due to the low fertility rate prevailing in the State, this decline does not imply a reduction in the emphasis on primary education.

References

Berman, Peter (1995), 'Financing of Rural Health Care in India', paper presented at the International Workshop on Health Insurance in India.

Caldwell, John C. (1986), 'Routes to Low Mortality in Poor Countries', *Population Develop-ment Review*, 12/2.

—— and Findley, Sally (eds.) (1989), *What We Know About Health Transition: The Cultural, Social and Behavioural Determinants of Health*, i and ii, Canberra, Australia: Australian National University.

Dept. of Economics and Statistics (1987), 'Report of the Survey on the Utilisation of Gulf Remittances in Kerala, Government of Kerala', Trivandrum.

Franke, R. W., and Chasin, Barbara H. (1992), *Kerala: Development Through Radical Reform*, New Delhi: Promilla & Co.

George, K. K. (1993), 'Limits to Kerala Model of Development—An Analysis of Fiscal Crisis and Its Implications', Trivandrum: Centre for Development Studies.

Gopinathan Nair, P. R. (1981), *Primary Education, Population Growth and Socio-Economic Change, A Comparative Study with Particular Reference to Kerala*, Allied Publishers Private Ltd.

—— (1989), 'Universalisation of Primary Education in Kerala', in P. R. Panchamukhi (ed.), *Educational Reforms at Different Levels, Studies in Educational Reform in India*, ii, Himalaya Publishing House.

Govt. of Kerala (various years), *Budget in Brief*.

Irudaya, Rajan, Misra, and Sarma (1993), 'Ageing in India: A Demographic Assessment of Past and Future', background chapter prepared for the India Case Study of Ageing, Centre for Development Studies, Trivandrum and Social Development Section, UN, Bangkok.

Jeffrey, Robin (1992), *Politics, Women and Well Being: How Kerala Became 'A Model'*, Oxford: Oxford University Press.

Joseph, Thomas A. (1990), 'Educational Development in Kerala', Government College, Nattakam, Kottayam.

Kabir, M., and Krishnan, T. N. (1992), 'Social Intermediation and Health Transition: Lessons from Kerala', Working Paper 251, Trivandrum: Centre for Development Studies.

Kannan, K. P. *et al.* (1991), 'Health Status in Rural Kerala: A Study of the Linkages Between Socio-Economic Status and Health Status', Integrated Rural Training Centre, Kerala Sastra Sahitya Parishad.

—— and Pushpangadan, K. (1988), 'Agricultural Stagnation in Kerala', *Economic and Political Weekly*, Review of Agriculture.

Krishnan, T. N. (1976), 'Demographic Transition in Kerala: Facts and Factors', *Economic and Political Weekly*, 11/31 (Special no.).

—— (1992), 'Population, Poverty and Employment in India', *Economic and Political Weekly*, 27/46.

—— (1994), 'Access to Health and Burden of Treatment in India: An Inter-State Comparison', Discussion Paper Series 2, Project of the United Nations Development Programme, Centre for Development Studies.

Mari Bhat, P. N., and Irudaya, Rajan (1990), 'Demographic Transition in Kerala Revisited', *EPW*.

Minturn Leigh (1993), *Sita's Daughters Coming Out of Purdah*, New York: Oxford University Press.

Mosley, Henry W., and Chen, Lincoln (1984), 'An Analytical Framework for the Study of Child Survival in Developing Countries', *Population and Development Review*, Suppl. 10: 25–45.

Murray, Christopher J. L., and Chen, Lincoln (1990), 'A Conceptual Approach to Morbidity in the Health Transitions', Working Paper 2, Cambridge, Mass.: Center for Population and Development Studies, Harvard University.

Office of the Registrar-General of India (1991), *Sample Registration System, Annual Report*, New Delhi: Ministry of Home Affairs

—— (1994), *Sample Registration Bulletin*, 28/2, New Delhi: Ministry of Home Affairs.

Panikar P. G. K., and Soman, C. R. (1984), 'Health Status of Kerala: The Paradox of Economic Backwardness and Health Development', Trivandrum: Centre for Development Studies.

Pillai, Govinda P. (1994), *Malayala Manorama Daily*, 31 May.

Planning Commission (1993), 'Report of the Expert Group on Estimation of Proportion and Number of Poor', Perspective Planning Division, Government of India, New Delhi.

Rao, M. S. A. (1981), 'Changing Moral Values in the Context of Social-Cultural Movements', in Adrian C. Mayer, *Culture and Mortality*, New Delhi: Oxford University Press.

Samuel, N. M. (1991), Census of India: Kerala, Series 12, Paper 2, Population Totals, Kerala.

Sen, Amartya (1994), 'Life Expectancy and Inequality' in *Development and Change* (edited by Pranab Bardhan, Mrinal Dutta-Chaudhari, and T. N. Krishnan), Bombay: Oxford University Press.

Sivanandan, P. (1989), 'Caste and Economic Opportunity: A Study of the Effect of Educational Development and Land Reforms on the Employment and Income Earning Opportunities of the Scheduled Castes and Scheduled Tribes in Kerala', Ph.D. thesis, University of Kerala.

State Planning Board (1992), *Status Paper on Literacy in Kerala: A Regional, Gender and Social Analysis, Social Service Division*, Government of Kerala.

Tilak, Jandhyala B. G. (1995), 'Costs and Financing of Human Development in India: A Review of Issues, Problems and Prospects, Studies on Human Development in India', Discussion Paper Series 5, Trivandrum.

United Nations (1975), 'Poverty, Unemployment and Development Policy: A Case Study of Selected Issues with Reference to Kerala', New York.

Zachariah, K. C. (1984), 'The Anomaly of the Fertility Decline in India's Kerala State', World Bank Staff Working Papers 700, Washington, DC.: World Bank.

—— and Pate, Sulekha (1982), 'Trends and Determinants of Infant and Child Mortality in Kerala', World Bank, Population and Human Resources Division, Discussion Paper 82–2.

—— (1994), 'Demographic Transition in Kerala in the 1980s', Trivandrum: Centre for Development Studies.

8

Social Policies in a Slowly Growing Economy: Sri Lanka

PATRICIA ALAILAMA
AND NIMAL SANDERATNE

Attainments in Social Indicators

Sri Lanka's social indicators are impressive for a poor country with a per capita income of around $US700 in 1995. In 1991, Sri Lanka's crude death rate was 6 per 1,000; the expectation of life at birth was 72.5 years; infant and maternal mortality rates were 17.5 and 4 per 1,000 live births respectively; adult literacy stood at 87 per cent (1981); and secondary school enrolment at 72 per cent. There were virtually no gender differences in either literacy or school enrolment. About 90 per cent of children had been immunized. The progressive decline in maternal and infant mortality are captured in Fig. 8.1.

Although economic policy and strategy have seen reversals, successive governments have consistently supported social development over the last five decades. The first section discusses the origin of this commitment and how it has been maintained within the framework of the political, social, and economic changes that took place in the country. The next section discusses the sectoral policies and strategies in health and education, while the third section examines the resource mobilization for each sector over the 1950–90 period. The final section attempts to draw the lessons from Sri Lanka's experience.

The pre-independence period

The social-welfare provision in Sri Lanka evolved from schemes designed to protect a particular occupational group, i.e. the indentured labour brought from India to work on the plantations (Indian Tamils). It was gradually extended to cover other parts of the population on the basis of socio-political considerations engendered by the spread of democratic socialism from Britain to its colonies, the growth of an indigenous middle class centred on services to the plantation sector, and the colonial administration and its push for social and administrative reform.

Significant political gains were made when universal adult franchise was introduced in 1931 under the Donoughmore Constitution. This made the government

responsible to the people and raised the number of voters. In the competitive electoral politics which emerged, the role of the dynamic Marxist opposition was also
significant in spurring the government to improve social conditions and adopt an
egalitarian approach.

The spread of health and education services throughout the country was
financed by surpluses generated by the plantation sector and came to be seen as an
instrument for broadening the distribution of benefits from export production. It
picked up momentum after the general elections of 1931 and 1936 (Figs. 8.1 and
8.2). In particular, the State assumed much more responsibility for the provision of
education, which had hitherto been provided by religious denominations, mainly
Christian. The medical services were already the most highly developed of the
social services, but were concentrated in urban and estate areas.

Between 1935 and 1947, about 2.5 per cent of GDP was spent on rapidly increasing health facilities and personnel (see Table 8.1). The number of health centres
increased very sharply between 1930 and 1945 concentrating attention on antenatal
and postnatal health. Declines in infant mortality and death rates accelerated in the late 1930s and 1940s, but those of the estate population remained
better than the all-island averages up to the end of this period. About half the
total number of births was cared for by field midwives or in hospitals and nursing
homes.

State intervention to maintain minimum consumption levels was started in the
1940s. The most significant measure was the attempt to relieve food shortages
during the war by the creation of the Department of Food Supply in 1942 whose
purpose was to purchase rice (local and imported) and distribute it to the whole
population on a ration. After the war food shortages eased, the scheme was carried
on as a means of stabilizing the cost of living. Retail prices of rice, wheat flour,
bread, and sugar continued to be partially or completely controlled after the Second
World War. Subsidized rice on the ration was distributed to consumers through co-
operative retail and wholesale outlets and licensed private dealers through the
department. Every person in the population, except children under 1 year, was entitled to ration books containing coupons for rationed rice and other commodities,
as designated by the government from time to time.

Three important documents set the stage for the state-based universalistic
welfare model in the post-independence period. The Kannangara Report (Sessional
Paper XXIV of 1943) recommended a national system of free education as a means
of ensuring equality of opportunity for all. The Cumpston Report (Sessional Paper
III of 1950) argued for a full and efficient free health service for every citizen as a
matter of right; the development of concurrent preventive and curative services;
and the abolition of private practice for government doctors. The Jennings Report
(Sessional Paper VII of 1947) on social assistance refrained from recommending a
system of social insurance, but settled for the provision of a provident fund; cash
benefits covering ill health and unemployment for the employed population; the

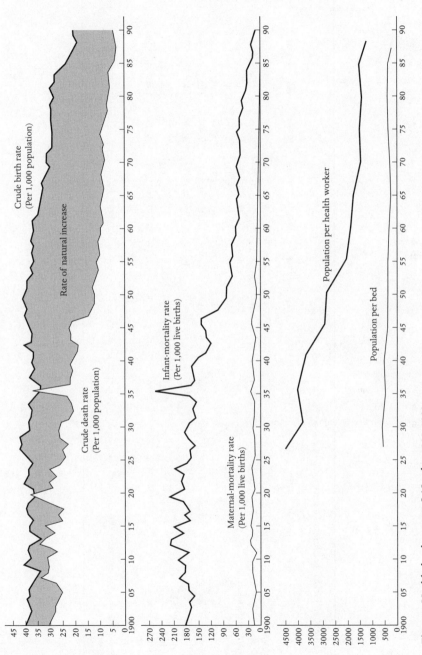

Fig. 8.1 Health development, Sri Lanka, 1900–1989

Table 8.1. Health Facilities and Personnel in Public Sector 1930–1990

	1930	1935	1940	1945	1950	1955	1960	1965	1970	1975	1980	1985	1990
Hospitals[a]	112	112	126	153	263	274	289	296	326	345	380	397	417
Beds	9,477	11,893	11,992	15,650	19,959	24,321	29,816	35,167	37,735	39,518	42,275	45,211	41,416
Maternity homes	—	—	12	38	107	107	108	72	82	103	104	93	85
Central dispensaries	595	632	632	260	240	283	283	292	332	355	339	338	278
Doctors[b]	341	339	404	514	674	952	1,173	1,494	1,932	2,118	2,055	2,239	2,440
Asst. medical practitioners	409	416	469	548	676	990	1,107	1,242	1,205	1,068	1,018	984	1,074
Nurses	605	618	744	1,165	1,387	2,210	3,232	3,642	5,542	5,685	6,834	8,091	8,957
Population per:													
bed	554	472	534	425	385	359	332	317	332	342	349	355	371
health worker[c]	3,876	4,084	3,693	2,986	2,805	2,100	1,795	1,750	1,442	1,522	1,489	1,509	1,406

[a] excludes maternity homes; [b] in the Dept. of Health; [c] doctors, nurses, and assistant medical practitioners

Sources: Health Administration Reports quoted in Gunatilake (1984); Dept. of Census and Statistics (1987); Central Bank of Sri Lanka, Economic and Social Statistics of Sri Lanka (various issues)

extension and improvement of free health services throughout the country; state-funded assistance to orphans, the aged, the blind, and the unemployed not covered by insurance; and a poor law system as a residual service.

In addition, labour legislation on minimum wages, and conditions of work, formation of trade unions, and the like, which was passed during the Depression, remains in force today and continues to be administered by the Labour Commissioner, with amendments from time to time.

Consolidation of basic service network after independence

The Second World War marked a turning-point for Ceylon's economy. The supply of cheap labour from India became limited. Further tracts of land for the plantations could be provided only with difficulty and at increased expense. Private international capital flows dried up and were only fractionally replaced by foreign aid. However, the export sector surpluses, which previously had furnished a principal source of investment, remained. Large reserves (over three times budgeted government expenditure in 1945–6 and mostly in sterling), which had been built up during the war, were available at the time of independence; these were further reinforced by the boom in rubber prices during the Korean War in the early 1950s (Snodgrass, 1966).

Till the mid-1950s the balance of payments was strong, external reserves were high (about 8–9 months of imports), and both debt servicing and defence expenditures were negligible. The government was able to respond to the popular demand generated through the democratic system by taxing the export crops and devoting as much as 32 per cent of its expenditure (about 7.5 per cent of GDP) to the welfare package. The total expenditure on health, education, welfare payments, and food subsidies increased to 9.9 per cent of GDP during the 1960s (35 per cent of total expenditure). Education expenditure predominated and accounted for almost half the social expenditure in the 1950s and 1960s.

This period was also characterized by major population increases from 6.6m. in 1946 to 10.5m. in 1963. Rapidly declining death rates and a slight increase in birth rates up to the early 1960s resulted in high rates of natural increase. Birth rates started declining in the early 1960s, prior to the advent of the family-planning programme, stimulated by better education and health levels; this slowed population growth in the subsequent periods to 19 per cent in the 1960s and 17 per cent between 1971 and 1981. The fall of death rates, mainly for infants, had an immediate impact on the numbers of children.

· The social infrastructure expanded significantly after independence in 1948. Between 1950 and 1960 the expansion of health facilities and personnel kept well ahead of population growth. The number of doctors in the Department of Health Services increased by 74 per cent, assistant medical practitioners by 63 per cent, and nurses more than doubled (241 per cent) (see Table 8.1 and Fig. 8.1).

The control of malaria in the 1940s had consequences far beyond the major fall in mortality. It resulted in an overall improvement in health conditions and enabled the setting up of settlements in the malaria-prone dry zone which covers two-thirds of the island.

The quantitative expansion of education facilities also accelerated in the 1950s and 1960s (Table 8.2 and Fig. 8.2). Between 1945 and 1965 the number of schools increased by 67 per cent, teachers by 259 per cent, and enrolment by 195 per cent. Secondary and university enrolment showed the fastest rates of expansion as facilities for these levels had been completely neglected earlier. The school system absorbed the impact of the population bulge so that its effects on the labour market began to be felt only in the late 1960s.

The improved availability of food after the war and the fairly stable price level contributed to an improvement in the nutrition of the poor. The network of co-operatives throughout the country continued to implement the food subsidy and make available essential food items. Welfare provision was further extended with the nationalization of private bus services in 1959. Transport (rail and bus), together with utilities (electricity, water, and sanitation), continued to be provided over the next four decades at subsidized rates.

The government's commitment to maintaining per capita expenditure on the social services petrified during the prosperous 1950s, and by the time the pressure of the sudden population increase was felt, it was politically explosive to attempt any modification. Caught between rising service bills and the relative inelasticity of government revenues, increasingly large overall budget deficits appeared. Government investment suffered and the rate of expansion of the social services slowed down. A continuous deterioration in the balance of trade, with unrestricted imports and a net outflow of long-term capital, contributed to persistent and increasingly large deficits in the basic balance of payments. Import restrictions were imposed and import-substitution became the main economic strategy.

The seeds of the current ethnic violence were sown during this period with the introduction in 1956 of a bill making Sinhala the official language, without safeguarding the use of Tamil as the language of the courts in the Tamil-speaking northern and eastern provinces and elsewhere. This squeezed the traditional avenue of employment for Tamils—the public service—as knowledge of Sinhala became mandatory for public servants. Negotiations and peaceful demonstrations were carried out by the Tamils to obtain a devolution of power and some degree of autonomy for Tamil areas to resolve their educational, linguistic, and employment problems. However, the Tamils became increasingly disillusioned when informal pledges and settlements negotiated between the Tamil political parties and both the SLFP (the Bandaranaike–Chelvanayakam Pact in 1957) and the UNP (the Senanayake–Chelvanayakam Pact in 1965) were eventually reneged on, in the face of severe criticism from whichever Sinhala party was in opposition at the time.

TABLE 8.2. Growth of educational facilities and literacy, 1900–1992

	1900	1910	1920	1931	1935	1945	1950	1955	1960	1965	1970	1975	1980	1984	1988	1992
Schools, total ('000)	3.9	4.2	4.3	4.2	4.2	5.7	5.4	7.0	8.0	9.5	9.9	9.6	9.7	9.9	10.2	10.5
Government	0.5	0.7	0.9	1.3	1.5	2.4	3.2	3.6	4.3	8.3	8.7	8.6	9.1	9.5	9.7	10.0
Assisted (1)	1.3	1.9	2.1	2.8	2.7	3.3	3.2	3.2	3.6	1.0	1.0	1.1	0.6	0.3	0.4	0.4
Unaided (2)	2.1	1.5	1.3	—	—	—	0.06	0.06	—	0.1	0.8	0.04	0.03	0.05	0.06	0.07
Students, total ('000)	204.2	336.3	397.9	557.2	670.5	867.2	1,366.7	1,665.8	2,301.5	2,455.6	2,716.1	2,560.4	3,389.7	3,635.4	4,083.7	4,198.2
Government	48.6	96.6	131.2	216.0	274.5	378.8	690.7	863.8	1,332.9	2,383.9	2,550.1	2,431.6	3,280.7	3,539.2	4,000.8	4,155.0
Assisted (1)	120.7	203.0	238.9	341.1	396.0	488.3	669.2	785.6	968.6	11.1	109.1	84.1	54.0	26.9	37.8	43.2
Unaided (2)	34.8	36.7	27.7	—	—	—	6.7	16.2	—	60.5	56.8	44.7	54.9	69.3	82.9	87.0
Teachers, total ('000)	—	—	—	18.2	19.2	25.5	39.2	50.1	69.6	91.9	96.4	104.4	141.1	141.6	147.5	182.5
Government	—	—	—	—	—	10.3	18.5	24.1	38.9	85.9	90.6	99.04	136.7	136.4	141.2	175.6
Assisted (1)	—	—	—	—	—	15.2	20.3	25.2	30.7	3.1	3.4	2.1	2.1	2.3	3.3	3.6
Unaided (2)	—	—	—	—	—	—	0.3	0.7	—	2.9	2.6	2.0	2.2	2.8	3.0	3.2
Literacy rate, total	26.4	31.0	39.3	—	—	57.8	—	65.4	71.6	—	78.5	—	87.2	—	—	86.9
Male	42.0	47.2	56.4	—	—	70.1	—	75.9	79.3	—	85.6	—	91.1	—	—	90.0
Female	8.5	12.5	21.2	—	—	13.8	—	53.6	63.2	—	70.9	—	82.2	—	—	83.8

Notes: (1) from 1961 onwards this category includes only estate and pirivena schools; (2) from 1961 onwards this category includes private fee levying and non-fee-levying schools

Sources: Data on schools, students, and teachers up to 1955 was obtained from the Administrative Reports, and thereafter, from the Statistical Abstracts of the Dept. of Census and Statistics; literacy and participation rates from 1963 onwards were obtained from the population Census reports of the same Dept.; participation rates for 1990–5 are estimated; literacy figures for 1991 are taken from the 1990–1 Household Income and Expenditure Survey, Dept. of Census and Statistics

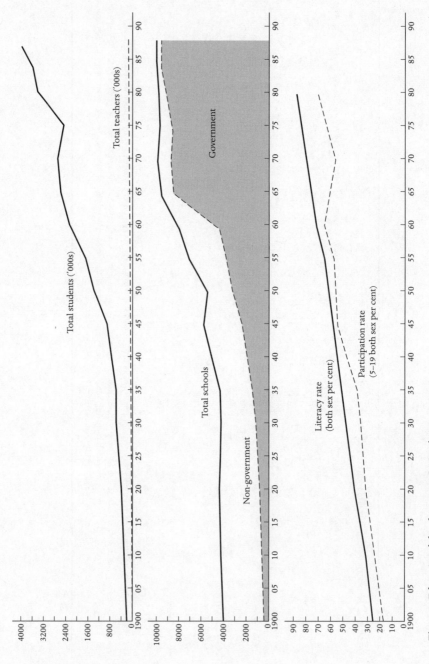

Fig. 8.2 Educational development, Sri Lanka 1900–1989

Interventionist social policy, 1970–1977

Awareness among the lower-income groups of the Sinhalese that they had been benefiting little from the growth in rice production and industry in the late 1960s, aggravated by unemployment, culminated in the insurgency of Sinhala youth in 1971. Although the insurgency lasted only three months, it exposed the extent of the dissatisfaction of a substantial part of the population with the existing socio-economic structure and the type of development that had been taking place. More direct action was therefore initiated to bring about a major and rapid social transformation.

Social development came to be regarded in a much wider sense as including not only improvement in standards of living through the provision of services and maintenance of minimum consumption levels; but also the use of fiscal and economic initiatives to achieve social objectives such as income distribution, changes in social institutions and attitudes, government reforms, and public participation in development activity. Wide-ranging land reforms, a ceiling on housing property, and the nationalization of various production activities characterized this period. By 1975, the public sector accounted for 30 per cent of GDP, more than half of total export earnings and one-quarter of total employment.

To reduce the alienation of educated Sinhala youth, the government also experimented with various formulae to ensure that a politically acceptable proportion of Sinhala students would be admitted to university, particularly for the professional courses of medicine and engineering; and made a determined effort to implement Sinhala as the sole official language.

The rise of the militant Tamil youth movement may be traced to the disgruntled youth who saw their traditional avenue to betterment and future prospects severely limited by these moves. They spurred the Tamil political parties to form an alliance, the Tamil United Liberation Front (TULF), with a common manifesto demanding 'an independent, sovereign, secular, Socialist State of Tamil Eelam that includes all the geographically contiguous areas that have been the traditional homeland of the Tamil-speaking people in the country' (TULF manifesto, 1977, quoted in Jayantha, 1985: 71). Thereafter, the competition for resources was translated into ethnic terms, on a rising tide of violence.

Between 1971 and 1976 there was a decline in Sri Lanka's rate of economic growth. From an average of 4.6 per cent per annum in the 1960s, GDP growth dropped to 2.3 per cent per annum in the 1971–7 period. The net deterioration in the terms of trade which averaged 4 per cent in the 1960s accelerated to 6.5 per cent between 1968 and 1972 and 15 per cent per annum between 1972 and 1975. Increasingly stringent balance-of-payments constraints restricted capital creation and capacity utilization. The situation was aggravated by successive droughts, high food prices on international markets, and the disruption of export-crop production subsequent to the land reforms. Unemployment continued to grow and affected over 20 per cent of the labour force in the mid-1970s.

The government's responsibility for generating economic growth escalated as a result of increased state ownership. However, the inability of public enterprises and nationalized plantations to generate adequate surpluses and the ineffective implementation of some revenue-augmenting measures resulted in the government being unable to meet its obligations on the economic as well as the social front (Jayasundera, 1986). Capital expenditure was financed out of local and foreign borrowing, as was some part of current expenditure. Although food subsidies were maintained in real terms, education and health expenditures declined by 1.6 per cent and 1.3 per cent per annum respectively.

Between 1965 and 1975 there was hardly any expansion in educational facilities, and participation rates declined between 1963 and 1971 (see Table 8.2). The decline in the mortality rates slowed down as well (see Fig. 8.1).

Impact of structural adjustment since 1977

The change of government in 1977 resulted in a reversal of the earlier economic policy, a change in priorities for government expenditure, and the elimination of subsidies, particularly on food. The development strategy adopted placed primary emphasis on increasing investment and rehabilitating the country's infrastructure and supporting services so as to lay the basis for more rapid growth in output and employment. Economic growth would generate incomes which would enable the people to meet their basic needs. Public-sector investments were concentrated on three 'lead' projects, i.e. the multipurpose Mahaweli River power, irrigation and land settlement scheme; urban development (including housing, water supply, and sanitation); and export-promotion zones offering attractive incentives.

All available policy instruments were mobilized to stimulate the economy and increase production. The exchange rate was allowed to float and imports liberalized with the support of IMF credits and substantial foreign aid so as to attain full utilization of existing capacity, boost output and investment. Interest rates were increased to stimulate domestic savings. Food prices rose as domestic prices began to approach world prices. Combined with favourable weather conditions, these measures stimulated domestic rice production. GDP growth rates increased to 4.2 per cent in 1977, 8.2 per cent in 1978, 6.3 per cent in 1979, and 5.8 per cent in 1980. Unemployment fell to 18 per cent in 1981. However, the terms of trade continued to decline, as did the production of Sri Lanka's main exports, i.e. tea, rubber, and coconut products. In terms of SDRs, imports doubled but exports increased by only 50 per cent so that the current account deficit trebled by 1982.

The basic features of the free education and health services remained intact, but other policies affected the poor adversely. In September 1979 the universal food subsidy was eliminated and a food stamps scheme targeted to the poor and defined in terms of family income was substituted. The number of beneficiaries increased progressively to include over 40 per cent of the population, but the real value of the food stamps decreased significantly as the money value was kept constant while prices rose sharply. This, combined with poor targeting, made it ineffective as a consumption safety net. Boosted further by a huge devaluation of the currency, the prices of basic foods rose threefold between 1977 and 1985 (Sanderatne, 1985).

The population had reached 14.8m. by 1981, but population growth rates have been below 1.5 per cent per annum since 1983 and were down to 1.2 per cent in 1993, due mainly to a rapid decline in fertility and high out-migration. Increase in the age at marriage (to an average of 25 years for women in 1993) and significant declines in marital fertility were the main causal factors in declining fertility. Fertility decline accelerated during the 1980s, with the total fertility rate reaching 2.3 during 1988–93. Net migration had averaged 5.6 per cent during the 1971–81 period when large-scale repatriation of stateless Indian workers was taking place. It continued at a high level (2.7 per cent) during the 1981–91 period due to labour migration for employment, mainly to the Middle East. Sri Lanka, with a population of 17.9m. in 1994, is now well into a demographic transition, with declining pre-school and young child cohorts and increasing numbers reaching retirement and the over-65 age-group.

Despite the favourable economic and demographic changes, the decade of the 1980s was marked by civil strife. By 1981, the Sinhalese constituted 74 per cent of the population, the Ceylon Tamils (located mainly in the north-east) 12.6 per cent, and the Indian Tamils (working mainly on the plantations) 5.5 per cent. In 1983, an attack on Sinhala soldiers in the north precipitated ethnic riots, followed by increasing violence in the northern and eastern provinces; by 1987 this had reached the level of a civil war, although fighting was confined to these provinces. In June 1987, the government signed the Indo-Sri Lanka Agreement, under which Indian troops were brought in to control these militant groups. This sparked off the simmering dissatisfaction of the Sinhala youth in the rest of the country, and developed into another insurgency during the 1987–9 period. The economy, services, and public administration were seriously disrupted before it was put down. The loss of lives and the destruction of property in the northern and eastern provinces continued after the Indian Army withdrew in March 1990. Defence expenditure, which was below 1 per cent of GDP prior to 1984, had escalated to 3 per cent by 1985, and 3.4 per cent by 1993.

A second round of reforms was launched in 1989 intent on stabilizing the economy, rationalizing the public sector, and introducing a more effective welfare package targeted at the poor. The reforms were successful in reducing the budget deficit to 7.1 per cent of GDP in 1993 (from 16 per cent in 1988) and the balance-of-payments current account deficit to 4.1 per cent of GDP in 1993 (from 7 per cent in 1989), the latter being facilitated by a 28 per cent growth in the volume of merchandise exports. Aided by good weather and an improved security situation in most parts of the country, economic growth increased to 6.2 per cent in 1990, 4.6 per cent in 1991, 4.3 per cent in 1992, 6.9 per cent in 1993, and 5.6 per cent in 1994, from the depressed levels of 1.4 per cent in 1987, 2.7 per cent in 1988, and 2.3 per cent in 1989.

The growing realization that income inequality and poverty were becoming serious, the insurgency of 1987–9, and the presidential election strategy on poverty alleviation resulted in the introduction of the extravagant Janasaviya Programme. This programme, which promised all those receiving food stamps Rs. 2,500 per month, was implemented in phases and in a modified form. Several other welfare programmes were also introduced, i.e. a free midday meal and free uniforms for school children.

However, during the 1980s the overall impact of the structural-adjustment strategy on the poorest quintile turned out to be negative in income terms. In contrast to the high-income groups, the poorest quintile showed a decline in real income and income share in the early 1980s and some recovery in the late 1980s. For the decade as a whole the poor experienced a decline in real income (Table 8.3).

Income distribution data indicate that disparities increased in the post-1973 period (see Table 8.4). Between 1985–6 and 1990–1, however, the rate of increase in income concentration slowed down. In contrast, expenditure data show a decline in concentration in the period from 1985–6 to 1990–1 (World Bank, 1994*b*).

However, it is clear that all ethnic communities have participated in and benefited from the gamut of social services provided, as well as higher employment levels. In contrast to the Ceylon Tamil community, who do not show deprivation in terms of education or unemployment (see Table 8.5), the Indian Tamils and Moors, who have the lowest attainments in literacy, education, and health, have not taken

TABLE 8.3. Per capita income at constant prices by decile

Deciles	Per capita income at 1980–1 prices			% Increase at constant prices		
	1980–1	1985–6	1990–1	1980/1–85/6	1985/6–90/1	1980/1–90/1
1	51	48	55	−12.6	6.3	−7.1
2	81	80	82	−2.7	1.3	−1.5
3	105	102	100	2.5	2.9	5.5
4	128	123	118	4.0	4.1	8.2
5	152	146	139	4.7	4.1	9.0
6	179	175	163	7.4	2.3	9.9
7	213	213	192	11.0	0.0	11.0
8	264	372	235	58.4	−29.0	12.4
9	359	344	309	11.3	4.4	16.1
10	873	1,134	646	75.4	−23.0	35.1

Sources: Dept. of the Census, 1987, 1993

TABLE 8.4. Income distribution

	Monthly income received (as % of total income)					
	1953	1963	1973	1978–9	1981–2	1986–7
Lowest 20%	5.20	4.45	7.17	6.26	5.72	5.06
Lowest 30%	9.30	8.45	12.77	10.94	10.03	9.15
Lowest 40%	14.50	13.66	19.29	16.64	15.25	14.14
Top 20%	50.38	52.31	42.95	48.94	51.96	52.30
Top 20% to lowest 40% ratio	3.71	3.83	2.23	2.94	3.41	3.70

Sources: Dept. of the Census 1987, 1993

TABLE 8.5. Education and unemployment by community, 1953–1981/2

	Mean years of schooling			Unemployed workforce (%)			
	1963	1973	1981–2	1953	1963	1973	1981–2
Sinhalese (Kandyan)	3.07	3.71	4.60	18.9	17.5	30.1	14.6
Sinhalese (Low Country)	4.00	4.57	5.06	15.6	12.8	23.0	11.3
Ceylon Tamils	3.56	3.52	4.80	8.4	11.7	17.1	6.7
Indian Tamils	1.68	1.89	2.28	17.8	6.7	12.3	4.9
Moors	2.80	3.23	3.73	15.9	4.6	21.3	10.9
Malays	4.62	5.66	6.16	[a]	2.8	43.5	22.6
Burghers	6.82	6.64	7.03		21.9	21.3	28.6
Others	—	4.74	6.83			28.6	0
All communities	3.94	4.52	4.62	16.6	13.8	24.0	11.7

[a] included under Moors

Note: More recent data not available

Source: Central Bank of Sri Lanka, *Consumer Finances Survey Reports* 1953, 1963, 1973, 1981–2.

to violence. The explanation for Sri Lanka's ethnic violence therefore lies in a complex of historical, linguistic, and political factors, rather than in deprivation in terms of human development.

Sectoral Analysis: Reasons for Success

The paradox of Sri Lanka is that relatively good social indicators have been achieved at an early stage of development. They have continued to improve (or been maintained) during the 1970s and 1980s, despite adverse economic conditions, rising civil unrest, expenditure cut-backs, the shrinking purchasing power of the poor, and increasing inequality of income distribution. The factors responsible are discussed below.

Health strategy

A primary health-care package, which was very similar to that recommended and adopted in the Alma Ata Declaration of 1978, was already the basis of health-care service development in the pre-independence period in Sri Lanka. Preventive health care had been institutionalized with the start of the Health Unit system in 1926; Health Unit areas were specified and paramedical personnel were made responsible for the health status of the population (about 40,000) in each area. In the campaign against malaria in the 1930s and 1940s, field medical officers were appointed to cover the whole country, strengthening the supervision of all services; and the Health Unit system was expanded. A team of paramedics, i.e. the assistant medical practitioner (AMP), the public health inspector (PHI), and the public health midwife (PHM), were used to provide preventive, promotive, and curative care under the supervision of a doctor at the peripheral level and linked to the inter-mediate institutional level for more specialized services (Vidyasagara and de Silva, 1985).

The number of public health midwives increased rapidly from 70 in 1933 to 765 in 1937 and 918 in 1948. Institutional deliveries were still low (17 per cent in 1950) but home deliveries were attended by trained personnel, contributing to the rapid decline of MMR from 26.5 to 16.5 per 1,000 and IMR from 263 to 140 per 1,000 live births between 1935 and 1945. The antenatal, postnatal, and child-care pro-grammes and the supplementary feeding programmes for mothers, infants, and school children were expanded, and a limited school health programme reached about 25 per cent of students (Gunatilleke, 1985: 10).

The decline in infant mortality and crude death rates which had been accelerat-ing in the late 1930s and early 1940s for the island as a whole (see Fig. 8.1) showed a spectacular fall between 1946 and 1947; they continued to fall at a slower pace in 1948 and thereafter. The use of DDT in the antimalaria campaigns of 1946–8, and significant declines in other causes of death with the use of newly developed anti-biotics throughout the spreading health-care system, are generally recognized as being the main factors in this remarkable improvement (Newman, 1965; Gunatilleke, 1984). The provision of health personnel, more than the availability of beds, was closely associated with the improvements in health indicators which took place up to the time of independence and beyond (see Fig. 8.1).

In the post-independence period the improvement in health indicators contin-ued, but at a slower pace, and the integrated structure of the curative and pre-ventive health services developed earlier was continued and expanded. The number of Western-type health institutions, bed strength, and the major categories of health personnel increased rapidly. Out-patient services in the traditional Indian system of medicine of Ayurveda were also provided in a small way by government in the late 1960s with the provision of 238 clinics throughout the country in conjunction with local governments. Today, the public sector concentrates mainly on Western medicine and provides virtually all the preventive health services, most of the in-patient treatment, and about half the out-patient treatment in the country. In the private sector, Ayurveda medicine has far more practitioners than Western medicine, but in-patient facilities are almost entirely Western. The problem of accessibility to health services virtually does not exist in Sri Lanka (Simeonov, 1975: 178).

The strategy of using a team of paramedics was modified with the substitution of doctors for AMPs; but the doctors found conditions uncongenial in the remote areas and a massive exodus of doctors took place from the early 1970s on. Despite continuous expansion in medical training and the sanctioning of private practice for government doctors, the number of doctors in public service in 1991 still had not exceeded the 1972 level of 2,398. Subsequent training of AMPs has been sporadic, dependent on whether it was felt there was a 'surplus' of doctors. The public health inspector cadre has also been allowed to run down. However, there has been a major expansion in the number of public health midwives with each midwife now covering a population of only 3,000–4,000 and being given the broader jurisdiction of family health, in view of the increase in institutional deliveries and declining birth rates. A further innovation has been the introduction of a voluntary health worker under the PHM who communicates with a family cluster on basic health concepts and simple health problems.

According to the Sri Lanka Demographic and Health Survey (1987), effective prenatal care was provided for 96.6 per cent of all mothers giving birth during the previous five years, 87.3 per cent received assistance at delivery from a doctor, nurse, or midwife, and 73 per cent had received two doses of tetanus toxoid. This survey also found that mothers' education has a significant effect on the usage of the available MCH services as well as the health status of the children. On average about 77 per cent of children under 5 years of age had a health card, and of these 98 per cent had been covered by BCG vaccination and 80 per cent by three doses of DPT and the polio vaccine.

The poor also derive substantial benefit from the health services, since they are provided free by the government and are easily accessible. Although the data available do not distinguish between in-patient and out-patient treatment, 60 per cent of the poor sought treatment in government facilities (Western and Ayurveda) in the early 1970s, with a decline to 50 per cent in 1978–9 and a recovery to 56 per cent in the 1980s (see Table 8.6). However, there is increasing concern about the quality of care provided by government institutions: curtailed recurrent expenditures and an imbalance in the distribution of resources in favour of larger institutions and tertiary-level care and the demoralizing effect of doctors' private practice are contributory factors.

TABLE 8.6. Distribution of the poor and non-poor seeking treatment by source of treatment

	1969–70		1978–9		1981–2		1986–7	
	Poor	Non-poor	Poor	Non-poor	Poor	Non-poor	Poor	Non-poor
Ayurveda Govt.	5	5	2	2	2	2	2	2
Ayurveda Private	17	16	16	16	12	12	13	13
Western Govt.	55	45	48	39	54	40	54	39
Western Private	16	30	27	39	25	41	27	44
Other	7	7	7	4	7	5	4	2
Total	100	100	100	100	100	100	100	100

Notes: The 'poor' are defined as those in the bottom 35% of households classified according to total household income

Sources: Dept. of Census and Statistics (1974), Special Tabulations; Central Bank of Ceylon (1983), pt. 1, table 37; (1984) pt. 1, table 3.34; Special Tabulations (1990)

Public investment was directed into the water supply and sanitation sector in a substantial way only in the post-1977 period. Government has been providing piped water supply services and grants for installation of water-seal latrines. It is estimated that in 1990, 12 per cent of the urban population was still dependent on unprotected water supplies and 19 per cent did not have either flush, water-seal, or pit latrines. One-third of the rural and estate populations were without access to safe and adequate water supplies and sanitation facilities. Service levels and quality of water supply are also highly variable, with the average unaccounted for water as high as 35 per cent.

That there was an epidemiological transition taking place became evident in the post-1977 period with the emergence in many areas of morbidity and mortality patterns that prevail in developed countries (and require high-cost interventions). At the same time, there were areas, e.g. the estates, where the dominant problems were still infectious diseases, high perinatal mortality, avoidable deaths, and morbidity in the middle-age groups due to inadequate environmental sanitation, education, and social development.

For the country as a whole the two patterns overlap, i.e. while mortality from heart disease is rising, there are still a large number of preventable deaths from diarrhoea and infectious diseases. The leading causes of hospitalization, outdoor treatment, and death can be traced to poor environmental sanitation, especially unsafe water supply, sewage disposal, and vector control. Substantial increases in in-patient morbidity rates for intestinal infections, malaria, hypertension and heart disease, and abortions have been recorded over the last two decades, while helminthiasis immunizable diseases and (to a lesser extent) malnutrition have registered declines. This suggests that although curative interventions have succeeded in reducing mortality due to certain diseases, the preventive aspects of health care have not received sufficient emphasis to have an impact on reducing morbidity, other than in immunizable diseases.

Education strategy

The thrust of the post-1931 education strategy was to make educational facilities available throughout the country through a rapid expansion of government schools and teachers. However, two clearly demarcated classes of schools persisted. There were the free Sinhala- and Tamil-language schools dispersed throughout the country, whose aim was only to provide literacy in these languages; they had poor buildings and facilities, and catered to about 95 per cent of the school-going population. In contrast, there were the predominantly urban, English-language schools which charged fees and were liberally assisted by state grants; they provided good facilities and a range of subjects and activities for their students. To combat this inequality in educational opportunity, the free education scheme proposed by the Kannangara Committee was given legal sanction in 1945. The regulations governing free education also stipulated the use of the mother tongue of the pupil as the medium of instruction in primary classes. Assisted denominational schools were given the option of either joining the scheme and receiving increased state assistance, or remaining outside the scheme and levying fees, with no state aid.

Heavy investment in educational facilities increased the number of schools, with the fastest increase taking place in the 1950–65 period (see Fig. 8.2). An island-wide system of scholarships enabled poor children from remote areas to attend the best schools. The government also sought to increase the number of English-type senior schools and Central Schools as fast as teachers and facilities could be provided, to promote quality secondary education throughout the country, and to improve the access of the poor to university. Free schooling and easy geographical access to education encouraged parents to send children of both sexes to school. As there were no barriers for girls, by 1981 the participation of girls almost equalled that of boys of the 5–9 and 10–14 age-groups, and for the 15–19 age-group female rates were higher. Government has maintained and promoted the policy of equalizing educational opportunity by way of a near-monopoly on the services provided at primary, secondary, and tertiary levels. Public schools and non-fee-levying private schools are allowed to charge only the small 'facilities fee' set by the Education Ministry.

Financial considerations governing access have been further reduced by subsidies on transport (bus and train fares) for schoolchildren, free textbooks since 1980, a school biscuit programme from 1974 to 1986 and a midday meal programme since 1989, and a free school uniform for every child since 1990. Altogether these

TABLE 8.7. Participation rates[a] of the poor[b] and non-poor in education by age, 1969–70, 1980–1, 1986–7

Age-group	1969–70			1980–1			1986–7		
	Poor	Non-poor	All	Poor	Non-poor	All	Poor	Non-poor	All
05–09	68	78	74	71	77	74	79	86	83
10–14	73	83	79	80	85	83	88	93	91
15–19	29	43	39	40	50	46	43	59	54
20–4	3	9	7	5	11	8	4	10	8

[a] the number declared as 'students' taken as a percentage of the total population in that age and income group. The age of entry into school was 5 years in all years; [b] the poor are defined as the population living in the poorest 35% of households classified according to total household income.

Sources: Dept. of Census and Statistics (1974), Special Tabulations; (1983), Special Tabulations; Central Bank of Ceylon (1990), Special Tabulations

welfare measures accounted for about 35 per cent of the annual recurrent budget for general education in the 1990s.

Special tabulations of students by household-income group obtained from the 1969–70, 1980–1, and 1986–7 sample surveys show that in the course of the general improvement in participation in education, the participation of poor children improved substantially between 1970 and 1987 (see Table 8.7). The rates for the poor for the 5–9, 10–14, and 15–19 age-groups increased faster than for the non-poor, thereby narrowing the disparity that existed in 1970. Further, despite highly restricted entry into the university system, children from poor families are also obtaining admission on a substantial scale. At least 50 per cent of university students come from families at the lower end of the income scale, i.e. where the guardian is an urban worker (including skilled and unskilled), a small farmer/fisherman, or retired/unemployed.

The high rate of school enrolment in Sri Lanka is not due to compulsory primary education but rather due to a cultural reverence for education and the easy accessibility of free facilities. Although the 1939 Education Ordinance provided for regulations to be made to enforce compulsory attendance at school, such regulations were not formulated. Awareness that 10 per cent of the school-age population continue not to attend school and that child labour and child prostitution may be increasing has brought out the need for legislation to make education for the 5–14 age-group compulsory.

Further, due to resource constraints, the quality of education provided across the system is quite uneven. Schools have undergone a stratification over time where the lowest stratum consists of poor, ill-equipped schools, located in urban slums, remote villages, and areas with a large plantation sector. These schools have relatively high drop-out rates, low student literacy and numeracy levels, and poor student performance at GCE O level and A level examinations. The 'good' schools keep expanding in response to pressure from parents who want their children to gain admission; they attract the more affluent, and are able to maintain and expand their facilities through parental support.

Nutrition strategy

Sri Lanka's food supply is still significantly dependent on imports, though this dependence has been decreasing. From an import dependence of over 52 per cent in the 1960s and 47 per cent in the 1970s, it fell to 39 per cent in 1979 and 33 per cent in 1993. The main decrease has been in rice imports which were nearly 50 per cent of total rice supply in the 1960s and had declined to 11 per cent in 1993. The dependence on wheat imports has, however, increased, with wheat contributing 24 per cent to total cereal availability in 1993, compared to 12 per cent in 1960 (Alailima and Sanderatne, 1982).

Government intervention to maintain minimum consumption levels and stability in the availability of the most important foods consumed in Sri Lanka in aggregate terms has been a significant feature of the post-independence period. A complex system of subsidies and controls was developed over the three and a half decades prior to 1979. Three types of subsidies were used: first, the control of rice prices through the Guaranteed Price Scheme as a means of providing an incentive price to the producer and assisting consumers; secondly, the provision of a free ration of rice and subsidized quantities of rice, flour, sugar, and other foodstuffs on the ration, as determined from time to time, to provide a minimum food consumption basket; and thirdly, the provision of a general subsidy on selected items freely available in the open market.

This strategy was generally successful in maintaining a consumption safety net, except in the period 1973–5 when successive droughts reduced local domestic production and a severe decline in the country's terms of trade constrained the country's capacity to import food. The food ration and subsidy programme played an important role during this period, increasing its contribution to total calorie consumption of the poor from 21 per cent in 1970 to 44 per cent in 1973 (Alailima, 1988). However, the shortages of food and high rates of unemployment at this time resulted in high levels of malnutrition and re-emergence of diseases associated with acute malnutrition.

The liberalization of the economy in the post-1977 period, accompanied by good paddy harvests and large flour imports, improved food availability. By 1978–9, per capita calorie consumption for the non-poor had reached 2,692 calories per day, but for the bottom two quintiles it was still as low as 1,710 calories (Alailima, 1988). Subsidies on rice, flour, milk, and kerosene were removed in January 1980, and food stamps were substituted. Those who did not receive food stamps were seriously affected by the price increases generated. Those who did receive food stamps were not fully compensated for the movement from ration rice to open-market rice between 1979 and 1980, for the ration rice provision was much cheaper (Alailima and Sandaratne, 1982).

Nutrition levels became more dependent on income levels after the removal of the food ration and subsidy programme. By 1981–2 the consumption of the lowest decile had fallen further to 1,181 calories per person per day. 'Most households in the bottom three deciles were unable to recover from the impact of price changes that occurred during 1979–80, while about 70 per cent of the households improved their calorie consumption' (Edirisinghe, 1984: 40). In fact, between 1978–9 and 1981–2, the lowest quintile experienced a decline in the quantities of the staple foods rice, wheat flour, bread, sugar, and coconut, which they consumed (Alailima, 1985).

Despite rapid economic growth between 1980–1 and 1985–6, the incomes of the poor were not able to keep up with price increases. Wage rates, which had kept ahead of price increases between 1977 and 1980, lagged behind during most of the decade and caught up only towards the end. Very high levels of malnutrition among pre-school children were evident in the early 1980s. A nutrition survey conducted in 1980–2 found that wasting was 15.9 per cent and stunting 30.5 per cent among children 6–36 months; low-income households had relatively larger proportions of malnourished children, i.e. 49 per cent in the lowest per capita income quintile were chronically malnourished and 15 per cent acutely malnourished; in the highest quintile the proportions were 22 per cent and 9 per cent respectively.

The non-price-indexed food stamps became increasingly ineffective in providing a consumption safety net for the poor; and the effects of declining real wages were compounded by the social disruption of the 1987–9 insurgency which reduced the workdays available to the poor. Consequently, 1988–9 showed an increase in the incidence of malnutrition (both stunting and wasting) to 51.4 per cent among this age-group. Between 1988–9 and 1993, however, there was a substantial improvement in both indicators, individually and together, to levels below what they were in 1980–2, i.e. 36.3 per cent reflecting the improvement in general economic indicators and real wages of the poor.

The bun and milk provided to schoolchildren in the post-independence period up to 1971 was succeeded by a school biscuit programme in 1974. Beneficiary levels peaked at 1.25m. in 1978, but the programme was subsequently phased out and terminated in 1986. A school midday meal programme was started in 1989 which provided Rs. 3 to each child who brought a wholesome meal from home. The coverage of the midday meal programme increased from 1.78m. children in 1989 to 2.8m. in 1990 and 1991. The nutritional impact of the school-feeding programmes has not been assessed, but it has been observed that they may provide an incentive for very poor children to attend school.

Intersectoral impacts

Sri Lanka's major social programmes have always been designed and implemented along sectoral lines. However, they have had substantial intersectoral impact because of their near-universal accessibility and coverage. In particular, the basic food consumption basket provided under the ration and food subsidy programme ensured a minimum nutrition level, which improved health and participation in education. In turn, increasing education levels helped mothers make use of the available health services and adopt health practices (including family planning) which improved the health status of their children. Thus Sri Lanka has been able to benefit from the reinforcing linkages between the major sectoral social programmes and is now seeing the second- and third-order effects of the earlier accumulation of social capital.

Even in very poor villages, where basic infrastructure such as roads, post office, health clinics, etc., are non-existent, there is generally a primary school. State-funded welfare schemes, e.g. food stamps, school midday meal, and Janasaviya are important in supporting a minimum consumption level and amount to about 16 per cent of income. The pervasive influence of the free education and health services over the last forty years is evident in that the proportion of women getting married while under 15 years is only 3 per cent for the poorest women, 2 per cent for 'other poor' women, and 2 per cent for non-poor women; marriages in the age-group 15–19 years take place for 42 per cent of poor women (poorest as well as 'other poor') and for 35 per cent of non-poor women. Literacy is 74 per cent among the poorest, 81 per cent among the 'other poor', and 89 per cent among non-poor women (CENWOR 1992*a*, 1992*b*).

However, the weakness of the sectoral approach is now becoming evident, particularly in dealing with cross-sectoral problems such as malnutrition and poverty. Intersectoral co-ordinating mechanisms are poorly developed and ineffective, and links with community organizations and their participation in government programmes are weak.

Resource Mobilization for Social Development

The government's political commitment to social development and an extensive welfare programme consisting of food subsidies, free health, free education, and a number of other social services implied a very large government expenditure on social development. The social development expenditure components as a percentage of GDP are given in Table 8.8.

The trend in expenditure on social development indicates differing emphases in policy and the availability of funds. From 1948 till 1965 there was a strong commitment to welfare policies. The food subsidy, and the expansion of health and education facilities, resulted in increased expenditure. In the 1965–70 period there was an

TABLE 8.8. Public social development expenditure as percentage of GDP, 1951–1990

	1951–6	1956–60	1961–5	1966–70	1971–5	1976–80	1981–5	1986–90
Social development expenditure of which:	7.1	8.1	10.5	9.0	9.9	9.1	5.5	8.0
Food subsidy	2.4	2.1	3.7	2.7	4.3	3.4	0.2	1.1
Education	—	3.3	4.0	3.6	2.9	2.3	1.9	2.6
Health	—	2.0	2.0	1.8	1.5	1.2	1.0	1.6
Other social services	0	0	0.1	0.2	0.2	0.2	0.1	1.9

Sources: Jayasundera (1986); Central Bank, Annual Reports

attempt to curtail some of the welfare expenditures, especially the food subsidy, partly owing to the growing economic crisis and partly due to a shift in policies to increase investment for economic growth.

In the 1970–7 period there was still a strong commitment to welfarism, overall social welfare expenditure rose despite very difficult economic conditions (Table 8.8). The food subsidy increased as a percentage of the government budget from 9 per cent in 1969–70 to 17 per cent in 1975 and as a proportion of GDP. However, the allocation for education fell below 3 per cent of GDP for the first time since independence. The curtailed expenditure was adequate to meet only the essential recurrent expenditures such as teachers' salaries and the cost of expansion of schools necessitated by increased school enrolment, but quality suffered. Health expenditure, which was around 2 per cent of GDP in the 1950s and 1960s, declined drastically in the 1970s to 1.5 per cent in the first half and 1.2 per cent in the second half.

Social-sector allocations in general have shown a decline from 1979 till the mid-1980s, both as a percentage of government budget and of GDP, due to a change in policy which emphasized investment in economic growth and a curtailment in social expenditure. Priority was given to the three 'lead' projects up to the mid-1980s and to the burgeoning defence expenditure thereafter. While the most significant decline was the reduction in the food subsidy and the targeting of the food stamps programme to the poorer half of the population from 1979 onward, health and education also registered consistent declines in the early 1980s.

Funds became more readily available for new infrastructure projects or proposals to rehabilitate existing infrastructure, but recurrent expenditures were restricted. The emphasis in funding within the social sectors changed in favour of capital-intensive and more sophisticated services. Higher education increased its share of the education budget from 7 per cent in 1977 to 17 per cent in 1993. Within the health budget, patient-care services increased their share from 62 per cent in 1977 to 74 per cent in 1983 and fell back to 66 per cent in 1993. There were also very substantial increases in expenditure on water supply and housing; on capital account in 1984 these totalled Rs. 110 per capita compared to Rs. 38 per capita for education and health. Housing expenditure plateaued after 1984 but per capita capital expenditure on water supply continued to climb and had reached Rs. 172 by 1992, compared to Rs. 115 on health and Rs. 170 on education.

Substantial flows of foreign aid came into the social sectors in the 1980s as awareness grew about the cumulative effects of neglect over the previous decade and as the 'lead projects' were completed. By 1989, foreign aid amounted to 34 per cent of health capital expenditure and 12.5 per cent of the education capital budget, starting from almost zero in 1980. The private sector was also encouraged to become more active in the provision of social services, and private organizations in the education and health sectors have received increased direct support as well as some easing of restrictions on their activities.

There was a decrease in current expenditure on health, particularly in the period after 1978 when it was around 5–6 per cent of total current expenditure. On the other hand, capital expenditure on health increased noticeably in some years in the 1978–92 period. It grew from 9 per cent of the health budget in 1977 to an average of 19 per cent during 1978–82. In 1983 it grew sharply to 36 per cent. The construction of new buildings and sophisticated equipment absorbed significant sums of money. Equipment purchases quadrupled between 1979 and 1982. Building activities also shifted from provincial and base hospitals in the mid-1970s to teaching hospitals in the 1980s.

The increase in capital expenditure and the tendency towards purchasing higher-cost, sophisticated health technology combined with the reduction of recurrent expenditure all contributed to difficulties in maintaining buildings and equipment and supervising service delivery and to falling service standards. A World Bank *aide-mémoire* of 1983 observed that 'only about 0.6 per cent of the replacement cost of equipment was budgeted for maintenance and repairs, in contrast to a requirement of at least 4 per cent', and went on to say that 'Taking past capital expenditure into account, the 'underfunding' of the health services may now be in the region of 20 per cent of existing budget approvals' (World Bank, 1983 quoted in Alailima, 1985: 32).

Although the Presidential Task Force Report on Health (1992) assessed the needed expenditure on health to be 3.5 per cent of GDP, it was only 1.6 per cent of GDP between 1986 and 1990, or slightly higher at 1.8 per cent of GDP in 1987–92. Per capita real expenditure on health declined from Rs. 148 in 1987 to Rs. 134 in 1992, reaching a low Rs. 100 in 1988 (Ernst and Young, 1994: 6). The reduction in state expenditure on health, despite a professed commitment to free health services, has resulted in a shortage of drugs at government hospitals. In fact, patients pay for both drugs and doctors' fees (Ernst and Young, 1994: 25).

Expenditure on education as a proportion of GDP increased till the mid-1960s and declined thereafter. In the first half of the 1960s educational expenditure reached a peak of 4 per cent of GDP (see Table 8.8). This was UNESCO's upper target of expenditure at that time. After that expenditure fell, and in 1981–5 it was less than 2 per cent of GDP. Since 1986 it has risen to 2.6 per cent of GDP.

The expenditure on education increased over time mainly to finance the expansion of schools to accommodate the increasing numbers of students. In the allocation of expenditure for education, essential recurrent expenditure, such as that for teachers' salaries, was protected, but there was a tendency to cut other supporting expenditures when there is a shortage of funds. In the 1960s, 64 per cent of the expenditure was on teachers' salaries; in the 1980s they accounted for about 75 per cent of educational expenditure.

In terms of the relative expenditures by level of education, a recent estimate is that 38 per cent is for primary education, 52 per cent for secondary education, and 10 per cent for university education (World Bank, 1994a: 69). In 1980 the ratios were 64, 28, and 8 respectively, for primary, secondary, and tertiary education. While the expenditure on primary and secondary education is higher than for many low-income countries, the expenditure on university education is low (Educational Consultants India Ltd., 1989: 242). Another characteristic of educational expenditure is the wide disparity among the different types of schools. The small rural schools and estate schools get much less than the larger urban schools. Reflecting this condition are the much poorer facilities in the small schools and estate schools (UNICEF 1991: 87–90).

Welfare expenditure on transfer payments increased after the institution of the Janasaviya and midday meal programmes in 1989, though conventional health and education expenditures remained more or less static. Expenditure on the food stamps programme, which had declined to 0.9 per cent of GDP by 1988, was supplemented by the new Janasaviya and midday meal programmes after 1989. Together, the food stamps and Janasaviya programmes accounted for 19 per cent of social expenditure by 1993. Education and health also showed a slight increase in their shares of GDP, and the government budget after devolution split these budgets between the centre and the provinces from 1989 on.

Responsibility for providing a large range of education and health services was devolved to the provinces in 1989 under the 13th Amendment to the Constitution which aggravated the shortage of finances to institutions in the periphery. Only 50 per cent of education expenditure was going to the provinces in 1993 (down from 58 per cent in 1990) to run about 9,800 schools; recurrent expenditure accounted for 91 per cent of the provincial education budget and was barely sufficient to cover the salaries of teachers. The devolution of expenditure in the health sector was even less, with 60 per cent retained by the centre (down from 63 per cent in 1990) and recurrent expenditure accounting for 88 per cent of the total. The inadequacy of the capital budgets for maintaining the large number of devolved institutions has resulted in the deterioration of these facilities and a clamour from the public for the centre to take them back, particularly key hospitals in the health sector.

Cost recovery on any significant scale has not been regarded as a feasible option in either the education or health sectors due to the commitment of successive governments over the last five decades to the provision of free services and to the principles of equality of access and opportunity. For this reason there has been an inbuilt incentive in both systems to reduce costs and provide an acceptable service within the funds available. In 1993 the island-wide education services were costing government annually just $US18 per capita and the health services $US8.50 per capita.

Lessons of Experience

A massive expansion of health and education services took place throughout the country in the 1950s and 1960s and these were maintained with difficulty in the 1970s and 1980s. Due to the small size of the country, a good road network, and subsidized transport services, the free education and health services were readily accessible in physical as well as financial terms. The cultural attitude to female autonomy and the value placed on literacy and education reinforced accessibility and resulted in a high level of participation of both boys and girls in the education services. Declining rates of population increase from 2.2 per cent in 1970 to 1.5 per cent in 1989 have been accompanied by an epidemiological transition.

The accumulation of social capital over five decades continued to provide second-generation benefits in the 1970s and 1980s. Even though the purchasing power of the poor was shrinking, social indicators continued to improve due to the provision of free services, the density of service provision, the type of service package developed and the efficiency of its delivery, and the demands from an educated and mobile population.

The impact of a social programme in each micro-area was enhanced and reinforced by the other welfare policies, since the services were so widespread that they were almost universally accessible. Food subsidies played an important role in ensuring minimal nutritional levels of the poor, and this in turn contributed significantly to improved health conditions. Similarly, improved health conditions would have enhanced learning ability. The food subsidy and the free midday meal contributed to school enrolment and educational attainments. The expansion of primary education and the high rate of literacy improved the awareness of public hygiene, the ability to communicate health instructions, the effectiveness of immunization programmes, the improvement of prenatal conditions, and the widespread use of maternity hospitals and midwives at childbirth. The equality of access to schooling for most women and their increasing educational attainment was another important factor in ensuring the success of health programmes.

Average social indicators, however, tend to mask deterioration in quality and geographical disparities in service provision. There are also internal contradictions in intrasectoral policy which have been exacerbated by continued underfunding. For instance, when resources are limited, the pursuit of free access and the equitable provision of services to different groups and geographical areas militates against the promotion of relevance and excellence in education, and against the demand for high-tech equipment to treat degenerative diseases.

Nutrition-related programmes have not enjoyed the same degree of consistent support that the education and health sectors have. Nutrition status became far more sensitive to declines in real income after the non-price-indexed food stamps programme was substituted for the quantity-based ration programme and food subsidies were removed in the early 1980s. The lack of an effective consumption safety net in the face of high inflation rates and declining real wages resulted in high malnutrition rates in the 1980s; these started to decline in the 1990s, but still remain high.

Water and sanitation quality and access to public facilities and programmes in these areas is dependent to a large extent on the ability to pay for services provided by government. The income effect is reduced only to the extent of the subsidy provided and obtained by the household. The access of the poor is limited by the size of the initial outlay required and the very poor are generally excluded (Alailima, 1988). However, the propagation of good hygienic practices can offset to some extent the lack of safe water supply and sanitation facilities. For example, the use of boiled water, safe disposal of faeces, and use of soap, as well as the recent promotion of oral-rehydration salts and home-based mixtures, have played an important role in reducing mortality from diarrhoeal diseases.

There are areas in Sri Lanka's experience from which useful lessons may be drawn by other developing countries. First, the importance of the mutually reinforcing effects of investments in the social sectors must be recognized and exploited. By providing a range of basic services in one place, the impact of these linkages can be maximized and a greater degree of social development achieved than by geographically scattered investments. Secondly, a certain degree of substitutability is possible between social-sector investments, when simultaneous investment in all sectors is too costly. Concentration on education (especially of women) and health is likely to be most beneficial and can compensate to some extent for the lack of provision in other sectors, e.g. quality water supply and sanitation facilities.

Sri Lanka's experience in the 1970s and 1980s illustrates the vulnerability of social development programmes to the vicissitudes of economic change which have been experienced by other poor and dependent economies; and the susceptibility of these programmes to cuts when pitted against major investments in economic infrastructure or in defence. Whether Sri Lanka achieved high levels of human development at the expense of economic growth is still a debatable issue. Undoubtedly, poor economic performance did aggravate the competition for resources and this was translated into ethnic terms on a rising tide of violence. Hence, as in other countries, inadequate economic growth and the ongoing diversion of resources to military expenditure are the biggest stumbling-blocks to the achievement of still higher living standards.

Bibliography

Alailima, P. J. (1985), 'Impact of Social Programmes and Service Delivery', in UNICEF, 1985: 24–40.

—— (1988), 'The Impact of Public Policy on the Poor', Ph.D. thesis, University of Bradford, UK.

—— and Sanderatne, N. (1982), 'Trends and Future Prospects for Food Supply and Consumption: Implications for Food Policy in Sri Lanka', mimeo.

CENWOR (Centre for Women's Research) (1992*a*), 'Baseline Survey of Sellankandal in Puttalam District', Colombo, memo.

—— (1992*b*), 'Baseline Survey of Divulwewa in Puttalam District', Colombo, memo.

Edirisinghe, N. (1984), *The Food Stamp Scheme in Sri Lanka: Costs, Benefits and Options for Modification*, Research Report 58, Washington: Food Policy Research Institute.

Education Consultants India Ltd. (1989), *Education and Training in Sri Lanka*, i–iv, New Delhi, n.d.

Ernst & Young (1994), *Current Financing of Health Care and Implications*, Colombo, mimeo.

Gunatilleke, G. (1984), 'Health and Development in Sri Lanka: An Overview', paper presented at the Inter-Regional Seminar on Health for All, Colombo, mimeo.

—— (1985), *Health and Development in Sri Lanka*, paper presented at the Rockefeller Foundation conference on Good Health at Low Cost, Bellagio, Italy.

Jayantha, D. (1985), 'Sri Lanka: The Political Framework, 1947–84', Washington, DC.: World Bank, mimeo.

Jayasundera, P. B. (1986), 'Fiscal Policy in Sri Lanka', in W. Rasaputra, W. M. Tillekaratne, S. T. G. Fernando, and L. E. N. Fernando (eds.), *Facets of Development in Independent Sri Lanka*, Ministry of Finance and Planning Colombo, pp. 43–82.

Newman, P. (1965), *Malaria Eradication and Population Growth—with Special Reference to Ceylon and British Guyana*, Ann Arbor, Mich.: University of Michigan Press.

Sanderatne, N. (1985), 'The Effects of Policies on Real Income and Employment', in UNICEF, 1985: 11–24.

Simeonov, L. A. (1975), *Better Health for Sri Lanka*, New Delhi: WHO-SEARO.

Snodgrass, D. R. (1966), *Ceylon; An Export Economy in Transition*, New Haven: Yale University.

Vidyasagara, N. W., and de Silva, A. V. K. V. (1985), 'Health Care Delivery System in Sri Lanka for PHC with Specific Reference to the Expanded Programme of Immunization (EPI) and the Control of Diarrhoeal Diseases', Colombo: WHO.

PUBLICATIONS OF GOVERNMENT AND INTERNATIONAL AGENCIES

Central Bank of Ceylon (1954), *Survey of Ceylon's Consumer Finances 1953*, Colombo.

—— (1964), *Survey of Ceylon's Consumer Finances, 1963*, Colombo.

—— (1974), *Survey of Sri Lanka's Consumer Finances, 1973*, Parts I and II, Colombo.

—— (1983), *Consumer Finance and Socio-Economic Survey 1978/79 Sri Lanka*, Parts I and II, Colombo.

—— (1984), *Report on Consumer Finances and Socio-Economic Survey 1981/82, Sri Lanka*, Parts I and II, Colombo.

—— (1990), *Report on Consumer Finances and Socio-Economic Survey 1986/87, Sri Lanka*, Part II, Colombo.

—— (various issues), *Review of the Economy* and *Annual Report*.

Dept. of Census and Statistics (1974), *Socio-Economic Survey of Sri Lanka 1969/70*, 2 vols., Colombo.

—— (1976), *Census of Population, 1971*, 2 vols., Colombo.

—— (1983), *Labour Force and Socio-Economic Survey 1980/81, Sri Lanka*, Colombo.

—— (1986), *Census of Population and Housing 1981*, 2 vols., Colombo.

—— (1987*a*), *Labour Force and Socio-Economic Survey 1985/86, Sri Lanka*, Colombo.

Report of the Special Committee on Education, Sessional Paper XXIV–1943, Colombo: Government Press.

Report of the Commission on Social Services, Sessional Paper XXIV–1947, Colombo: Government Press.

Report on the Medical and Public Health Organizations of Ceylon, Sessional Paper III–1950, Colombo: Government Press.

Report of the Presidential Task Force on Formulation of a National Health Policy for Sri Lanka, Sessional Paper No. II–1993, Colombo: Government Press.

UNICEF (1985), *The Social Impact of Economic Policies in the Last Decade*, Colombo.

—— (1991), *Children and Women in Sri Lanka, A Situation Analysis*, Colombo.

World Bank (1994a), 'Sri Lanka Education and Training Sector Strategy Review,' vols. 1 and 2, Washington, DC.

—— (1994b), *Sri Lanka Poverty Assessment*, Report No. 13431–CE Washington, DC.

9

Social Policies in a Growing Economy: The Role of the State in the Republic of Korea

SANTOSH MEHROTRA,

IN-HWA PARK, AND HWA-JONG BAEK

Introduction

In the post-Korean war period, the Republic of Korea (hereafter Korea) has succeeded in sharply reducing absolute poverty through labour-absorbing economic growth, which has been rapid and sustained. At the same time, the improvement in certain indicators such as life expectancy, infant mortality, nutritional status, coverage of piped water supply, and school enrolment rate, demonstrate the broad benefits of development over the past three decades (see Tables 2.1 and 2.2 in Chapter 2). Korea has been one of the top ten performers in human development, measured by a composite of three indicators: longevity, knowledge, and per capita income, during 1960–92 (UNDP, 1994).[1]

The Korean State single-mindedly pursued the goal of economic growth from the early 1960s onward. There was no special effort made to advance the health status of the population for nearly thirty years following independence from Japanese rule in 1945. However, two of the most significant developments which laid the foundations of subsequent economic growth and human development—investments in primary and secondary education and land reform—occurred early after independence at the instance of the State. During this period, US assistance was critical to the survival of the Korean State. The role of the USA in both land reform and educational investment was also significant, as we will discuss later. The US role began with the US Military Government (1945–May 1948), and continued in the form of US forces through the Korean War (1950–3) and since, and in the form of massive economic and military assistance.

Three distinct stages can be discerned in Korea's social-welfare policies: the 1950s to the mid-1970s, the late 1970s to the mid-1980s, and the late 1980s to the present. Each period is classified by the relative importance of government intervention.

The 1950s to the mid-1970s

Starting with the First Five-Year Plan (in 1961) Korea's national development strategy focused on economic growth rather than social equity. The government was very effective in achieving economic growth based on exports; real wages increased and the unemployment rate was substantially reduced. Welfare was basically the responsibility of the people themselves during this period. But three programmes undertaken by the government during this period were crucial to both economic growth and social development: investment in education, land reform, and family planning.

The late 1970s to the mid-1980s

While economic growth remained a dominant concern of policy-makers in the late 1970s, the issue of social welfare received increasing attention. The underprivileged exhibited greater discontent as accelerated urban–rural, interclass, and regional income disparities accompanied the process of rapid industrialization; this deepened social conflict and emerged as a major bottleneck to further development in the 1980s (Yeon, 1989). Concerns surfaced during the fourth plan period, leading to the health insurance scheme being introduced for large organizations, and gradually spread to cover the entire population. Later the government's commitment to social policy became evident in what came to be called the Fifth Five-Year Economic and *Social* Development Plan (emphasis added).

The late 1980s to the present

Beginning with the Sixth Republic (1988–92), the issue of welfare policy came to the forefront of national politics. Following a reassessment of national priorities, the government adopted a strategy to pursue social-welfare policies in conjunction with stabilization, liberalization, and structural adjustment, which were deemed to be of greater short-term significance for the nation's growth. Nevertheless, the government has initiated and expanded several important welfare programmes.

Under the Seventh Five-Year Plan period (1992–6), the government enacted various programmes to improve social welfare, to resolve regional and sectoral imbalances, and to improve the quality of life. This approach emphasized economic efficiency and qualitative development rather than economic growth *per se* as pursued in the past. This chapter is largely devoted to a discussion of the first two periods.

In the next section, the foundations of social development and the linkages between social and economic development during the first period are discussed. Following that, the means by which population growth was controlled and a demographic transition achieved by the end of the second period are examined. Next, the factors underlying overall social development—as represented by selected indicators of health, nutrition, and education—are analysed. The development of major national social-security programmes (which occurred mostly during the second period) and resource allocation to social development is also discussed. The chapter concludes by highlighting the key features of Korea's social development.

Roots of Social and Economic Development

In 1945, Korea was largely a traditional, closed agrarian economy just emerging from thirty-five years of colonial status. As the Japanese surrendered at the end of the Second World War, the US Military Government took over the administration below the 38th parallel. The beginnings of development, initially under the US Military Government and then, from 1948, under Korea's first elected government, were sharply interrupted by the Korean War. The first fifteen years of independent Korea were characterized by slow recovery assisted by massive grant aid from the USA. In fact, the slowness of the recovery led the US government to wonder if Korea was not, in fact, a 'basket case', which will be forever dependent on US assistance (Mason *et al.*, 1980).

However, the roots of rapid economic growth, which began from 1961, were laid in this early period by the State with two measures: land reform and the investment in education.

Asset and income distribution

One of the most significant policy interventions of the US Military Government, with far-reaching social and economic consequences, was the distribution of Japanese-owned land followed by the land of large Korean landowners. This distribution led to a demand from peasants for all tenanted properties and the government established a limit on the possession of farmland by promulgating the Land Reform Act in 1949.[2] Consequently, the proportion of tenant farmers decreased from 42.1 per cent of the farm population in 1947 to 5.2 per cent in 1964. Although the economic merit of parcelling agricultural land into submarginal pieces was widely questioned, this measure of distributing the sole kind of meaningful asset in the pre-industrial stage turned out to have an important social effect in creating a threshold of industrial take-off. In other words, given that the majority of the population was employed in agriculture, it accounted for a substantial part of the improvement in living standards. Above all, it gave Korea an advantage compared to the vast majority of developing countries in both South Asia and Latin America by laying the basis of a relatively equal distribution of assets right at the outset of the development process.[3]

Birdsall *et al.* (1995) presented cross-economy evidence that low inequality stimulates growth (independent of its effect on education, as we discuss below). Specifically for Korea, they argue on the basis of econometric analysis, that if, in 1960, Korea had had Brazil's level of inequality, Korea's predicted growth rate over the following twenty-five years would have been reduced by 0.66 percentage points per year, implying that after twenty-five years, GDP per capita in Korea would have been nearly 15 per cent lower. This captures the direct effect of inequality on economic growth. (In addition to its direct effects, an indirect effect of high inequality is that it appears to constrain growth by constraining investment in education.)

The literature cites several reasons why lower inequality may stimulate growth, on the basis of the East Asian case. Adelman argued, on the basis of the experience of countries combining income increases of the poor with rapid growth, for (i) tenurial reform before implementing policies to increase agricultural productivity; and (ii) large investments in education before rapid industrialization. Such an asset-distribution strategy sets in motion a virtuous circle whereby greater equity engenders and sustains faster economic growth. How may this happen? Several components of the interacting causation are identified here, though any of them on their own may not be sufficient. First, greater equality in the distribution of assets leading to higher income for the poor will increase their savings and investments. It will increase investment in education by easing liquidity constraints of the poor. Moreover, as the health and nutrition status are positively correlated with the level of income, greater income equality stimulates growth through enhanced productivity. Thus, even though the marginal propensity of the rich to save is higher than that of the poor, the quality of the human capital resulting from the poor's greater savings and investment in human capital may offset the reduction in savings of the non-poor.[4]

Second, lower inequality will stimulate growth through political and macroeconomic stability (Birdsall *et al.*, 1995). Low inequality can reduce the risk of fiscal prudence being sacrificed for populist reasons. Thus, limited state resources in education were not devoted in Korea to higher education, which benefits the children of the élite—as was the case in most of Latin America (Mehrotra and Pizarro, 1996). Lower inequality can also contribute to macroeconomic stability by avoiding exchange-rate overvaluation. Overvaluation will reduce the price of imports (consumed by the well-off) at the expense of agriculture, where the poor are employed, and export-oriented sectors, thus worsening external imbalances—as has been the experience of the majority of developing countries. On the other hand, Korea has maintained realistic and stable exchange rates over the last three decades. Moreover, in the case of an external shock, lower inequality will ensure that the burden of adjustment on the domestic economy will be shared more equitably. Thus, the first oil shock did not lead in Korea to an absolute decline in wages, only to a sharp reduction in the growth rate of wages, and the government was able to adjust domestic absorption by reducing consumption but protecting investment—while most developing countries undergoing adjustment have been unable to protect either wages or investment. In spite of the absence of political democracy, the lower inequality in Korea helped legitimize the government and minimized alienation of the poor.

Third, lower inequality raises the efficiency of workers in both industry and agri-culture. Thus, in industry, Korea was characterized by relatively narrow income differentials between managers and workers. Amsden (1992) argues that the work-force in most late-industrializing countries has been subjected to more political repression than in the first and second Industrial Revolutions (in Europe and North America). The demoralizing effects of this phenomenon may be lessened by a better income distribution, and the motivation of the work-force, productivity and quality improved. In agriculture, it is well established that labour intensity and yield are inversely related to size of landholdings (see Bharadwaj, 1962; Berry and Cline, 1979), and the land reforms in Korea improved output and demand for labour.

Finally, lowering income inequality by raising rural incomes has considerable demand as well as multiplier effects on the economy leading to industrial growth.

The investment in education

The other major intervention by the Korean State, with widespread social and economic consequences has been the investment in education. Confucianism, historically the state philosophy of Korea, places great emphasis on the benefits of education, and has always been the route to government office. Thus, demand for education has always been high in Korean society. After independence, educational facilities expanded greatly, and enrolment in the formal education system increased rapidly at all levels. Local communities generally provided the facilities for schooling, and the US Military Government covered about two-thirds of operating costs and also provided teachers to replace the departing Japanese teachers.

The USA again provided assistance in the rebuilding of schools in the aftermath of the destruction of the Korean War. From 1945 to 1960, elementary-school enrol-ment increased 265 per cent, while that in institutions of higher education increased twelvefold (from about 8,000 to 100,000). One result was that the illiter-acy rate decreased from 78 per cent to 28 per cent during that period. In fact, so rapid was the increase in educational opportunities that serious rates of unemploy-ment emerged among college graduates during the 1950s. Approximately 20 per cent of them were unemployed, a situation that underscored the need to rebuild the nation's industrial base as a source of jobs.

Education contributed to Korea's economic growth. Birdsall et al. (1995) predict that with Pakistan's low 1960 enrolment rates, Korea's growth would have been considerably slower, resulting in a per capita GDP for 1985 that is nearly 40 per cent lower than the one Korea actually attained. Thus the relatively equal income distri-bution in Korea not only benefited growth directly, but also indirectly by enabling households to invest in education.[5]

Economic growth and its social consequences

Since Korea's development strategy focused on economic growth rather than welfare, it is necessary to briefly examine the nature of growth and its social ramifications. Between 1953 and 1962, Korean GNP grew at only 4.1 per cent per annum, and gross domestic investment was barely 10 per cent of GNP, 70 per cent of it financed by foreign savings. From the mid-1960s onward, domestic savings have financed 70–80 per cent of gross fixed capital formation, but until then foreign assistance was critical to economic growth. From 1953 to 1962, foreign aid, 95 per cent of which came from the USA, accounted for 8 per cent of Korean GNP, 77 per cent of fixed capital formation, and some 70 per cent of the financing of imports. The high level of foreign assistance for a decade after the war probably accounted for the 'difference between some (1.5 per cent per annum) and no growth in per capita income' (Mason *et al.*, 1980). It has been suggested that without this growth, the living conditions would have been very difficult, political cohesion would have been affected adversely, and the foundations for later economic growth would not have been laid. While aid was critical to the survival and growth of the state for twenty years until the mid-1960s, between 1965 and 1975 it added barely 1 per cent to the already high growth rate and was not so significant (ibid.). It is also important to note that until 1965 all US assistance was in the form of grants. Hence, when Korea later found it necessary to enter international capital markets to borrow, it had no significant burden of foreign debt to cope with.

With the commencement of development planning in 1962 began the period of rapid economic growth (see Table 9.1). The First Five-Year Economic Plan (1962–6) established as its primary objective export-oriented industrialization and growth, and this objective has dominated all subsequent plans. According to Kuznets (1966), in today's industrialized countries the growth in the share of industrial output in GDP was 1 to 6 percentage points per decade. On the other hand, Kuznets notes that in Korea industry's[6] share of GDP increased about 10 percentage points per decade during the 1960s and 1970s. In 1960, industry's share of GDP was 20.1 per cent. By 1970, it was 29.2 per cent and by 1980 it reached 41.3 per cent. After 1980, however, the industrialization process slowed down, the share of industry reaching 43 per cent in 1987. In 1963 the share of employment in primary and secondary sectors were 63.1 per cent and 8.7 per cent respectively. By 1977, the initial year of the Fourth Five-Year Plan, the share of employment in the secondary sector reached 22.4 per cent, about half the level of the primary sector, which was 41.8 per cent. In terms of the structure of employment, Korea was predominantly a rural agricultural country through 1955, but over the following twenty years, the urban, industrial, and service workers came to equal in number their rural, agricultural counterparts.

TABLE 9.1. Major indicators of the Korean economy

	1965	1970	1975	1980	1985	1990	1994
GDP per capita (1990 Won: '000)	730	1050	1468	1950	2728	4187	5307
GDP per capita avg. annual growth rate (%) (for half-decade ending)	—	7.55	6.94	5.84	6.94	8.95	6.57[a]
% of people below poverty line	40.9	—	14.8 (1976)	9.8	—	—	3.9 (1993)
GINI coefficient	0.344	0.332	0.391 (1976)	0.389	0.345	0.336 (1988)	—

[a] for the 5-year period 1989–94

Sources: IMF, *International Financial Statistics Yearbook*, 1995; KEDI (1993); MOL, *Monthly Labour Survey*; NSO (1970–94).

Table 9.2 presents the contributions of sectoral growth to the overall growth rate. The highest contribution to growth throughout the period came primarily from the secondary and tertiary sectors. The most rapidly growing sector of manufactured output was production for export.

Apart from the structural transformation of the economy in terms of output and employment, by 1991 Korea had become the eleventh largest trading nation in the world. As trade grew faster than the economy as a whole, trade dependence, or the ratio of total trading volume to GNP, increased dramatically. Export dependence rose from 2.4 per cent in 1962 to 11.6 per cent in 1971. In the 1980s this ratio reached and stayed well over 30 per cent. At the same time, a five-year average for the import–GNP ratio remained at over 30 per cent throughout the 1970s and 1980s.[7]

These three structural changes—the transformation of the structure of production in the economy, of the structure of employment, and of the role of foreign trade—were the outcome of the development strategy of labour-intensive export-oriented industrial growth. The industrialization process began in the fifties with light manufacture (mainly textiles, especially spinning and weaving), but switched in the 1960s to synthetic fibres, and between 1972 and 1978 to chemicals and heavy industries. The share of heavy and chemical industries was 40 per cent in manufacturing output (and 14 per cent in merchandise exports) in 1971 but 62 per cent in 1984 (60 per cent in exports). Simultaneously the share of light industry fell from 60 per cent (86 per cent in exports) to 38 per cent (40 per cent for exports) over the same period. The labour surplus (in the Lewisian sense) in the economy disappeared by 1980.

While an educated work-force was essential for growth, economic growth also stimulated investment in education, by raising the individual's returns to education—thus setting in motion a virtuous cycle (see Chapter 15 for further discussion). The high growth led to a high demand for labour. In particular, the export

---

TABLE 9.2. Average sectoral contribution to GNP growth, 1962–1991 (%)

	1962–6	1967–71	1972–6	1977–81	1982–6	1987–91	1962–91[a]
Agriculture, forestry, and fishery	32.1	4.5	15.7	−5.1	6.5	−1.4	8.8
Mining and manufacturing	20.5	33.8	43.7	47.2	39.8	34.0	36.7
(Manufacturing only)	—	—	—	32.7	38.5	30.8	—
Others	47.4	61.7	40.6	57.9	53.7	67.4	54.5

[a] data for 1991 are preliminary

Source: NSO (1970–1992)

orientation of the economy resulted in a skill-demanding growth path. The East Asian exporters shifted into more technologically sophisticated and more capital- and skill-intensive goods, as rising wages of unskilled labour eroded international competitiveness in labour-intensive manufacturers.

While Korea was a low-wage economy in the 1950s, the rapid absorption of the surplus labour force had a major social consequence. Manufacturing wages (the size of the manufacturing work-force was the same as that of agriculture by 1975) grew at an average annual rate in real terms of 9.8 per cent between 1965 and 1973, 5 per cent in 1974–5, and 18–20 per cent between 1976 and 1979, before the growth rate fell (until the mid-1980s) to the trend of the 1965–73 period. By 1980 the unlimited supply of agricultural workers for manufacturing industry had come to an end. This process was aided by the Middle East boom, which resulted in able-bodied males migrating in unprecedented numbers (as they did from Sri Lanka and Kerala State, India). Between 1977 and 1979 about 292,600 male workers migrated overseas, i.e. almost 27 per cent of the male manufacturing work-force (Amsden, 1987).

Inflationary pressures built up as nominal wages in the late 1970s rose faster than productivity. Towards the end of the 1970s, Korea had no choice but to shift to an alternative strategy for sustained growth and development. The State launched a phase of stabilization. The previous development strategy of 'growth at any costs' was replaced by the strategy of 'stability at any price'. The government tried to restrain its own budgetary expansion through 'zero-based budgeting', wage-earners were urged to accept smaller wage increases, farmers were to accept fewer subsidies, businesses were to refrain from price increases, and households were to spend less and save more. An important reason why the government was able to make both capital and labour share the costs of adjustment was that income distribution was relatively equal in the country. In fact, it is striking that other countries in this volume (especially Costa Rica, Cuba, and Malaysia) too have attempted unorthodox ways of stabilization and adjustment.[8]

It has been argued that 'the more equal the distribution of income economy-wide, the higher the quality of government intervention and, hence, the faster the rate of growth of manufacturing output and productivity' (Amsden, 1992). As indicated earlier, land reform in Korea was an important factor underlying relatively equal income distribution, which in turn was a positive factor for growth. In an economy where the income distribution is skewed, a small class of landowners, financiers, and industrialists has the power to manipulate the State, weaken its authority, and maintain an economy founded on its own private rent-seeking activity[9]—thus hampering growth. In an economy where income distribution is relatively equal, the State disciplines not just labour (as it does in an economy characterized by inequality) but also capital—thus the quality of government intervention is superior.

In all late-industrializing economies, the State has played an extensive role with highly active industrial policies. Subsidies have been a necessary condition for industrial development in the absence of pioneering technology (which provided the competitive edge to firms during the first two Industrial Revolutions). However, a major difference between the slow- and fast-growing late industrializers has been the principles governing subsidy allocation. In slow-growing countries, e.g. India, no performance standards have been imposed on subsidy recipients, and subsidies have been allocated on the principle of give-away, which raises the total production costs of the economy and makes it necessary to have even higher subsidies to offset inefficiency. In the fast-growing countries, like Korea, subsidies have been allocated in exchange for concrete performance standards with regard to output, exports, product quality, investments in training, and, recently, R and D. Amsden has argued that a relatively equal distribution of income is a necessary condition for late industrialization because it 'empowers the state to discipline business (and not just labour) and facilitates the state bureaucracy's monitoring of the disciplinary process'. Reinforcing but further this argument, Evans (1995) shows that the Korean State was not just a 'strong' or 'autonomous' bureaucracy but also had formal and informal ties to private firms. These ties, combined with the fact that the State had more capital to invest than private firms, allowed the State to forge a symbiotic relationship with private firms rather than being subservient to them, as in many countries.

Population Control and the Growth Strategy

From the beginning of the 1960s, the Korean government saw population control as a significant component of its growth strategy—again with significant social consequences. In other words, while no particular attention was paid to public health measures, family planning was actively supported by the State. Along with land reform and the investment in education, family planning became a third plank of social policy, with major implications for the growth process as well as social development.

Trends in Population Growth

Due to a high level of fertility Korea experienced a high population growth rate before 1960. The population growth rate of Korea decreased from 3 per cent in 1960 to 0.95 per cent in 1990. The total fertility rate of Korea also decreased significantly from 6 in 1960 to 2.7 in 1980, and dropped below the replacement rate of 2.1 during the mid-1980s. It further decreased to 1.75 in 1993 (KIHASA, 1994). Clearly, Korea achieved a demographic transition very rapidly and early in its development.

Korea's population structure in 1960 was typical for a country with high birth and death rates. By 1990, the population pyramid had been transformed into a more rectangular shape, due to fertility and mortality reductions. The child population—the future source of new labour—decreased not only relatively but also in absolute numbers. The young population aged less than 15 years accounted for 42.3 per cent of the total population in 1960; it decreased to 25.6 per cent in 1990 and is expected to be 21.2 per cent in the year 2000. On the other hand, the proportion of the old population to total population was maintained at about 3 per cent until the 1970s. The proportion will slowly increase to an expected 6.8 per cent by 2000. Accordingly, changes in age composition are reflected in the decrease in dependency ratio from a level of 82.6 per cent in 1960 to 44.6 per cent in 1990 (see Table 9.3). A very low dependency ratio could be greatly advantageous in accelerating economic growth. Korea is expected to enjoy 'a golden period' of lower-age dependency ratio, below 50, for the thirty-five years from 1990 to 2025. Owing to strong government population-control measures and improved health conditions, Korea was able to achieve its demographic transition within a relatively short period.

Factors underlying the rapid demographic transition

The death and destruction caused by the Korean War was followed by the spread of education and urbanization and the expansion of health services in urban areas. As a result, the death rate fell from 33 per 1,000 during the years 1950 to 1955 to 16 per 1,000 from 1955 to 1960. A simultaneous rise in the birth rate occurred in a post-war baby boom, and the population grew by 3 per cent per annum. This caused considerable concern among policy-makers. The removal of President Synghman Rhee, who had opposed institutionalized family-planning programmes, allowed family planning to emerge in the policy dialogue. Soon, family planning became one of the seven key programmes for promoting economic development adopted by the government in 1961.

As part of its Five-Year Economic Development Plan, in 1962 the government started providing free contraceptive services, assuming that the availability of contraceptives would help the motivation for family planning.[10] In the initial stage of

---

TABLE 9.3. The demographic transition

	1960	1966	1970	1975	1980	1985	1990
Total fertility rate	6.0	5.4	4.3	3.5	2.8	1.7	1.6
Total dependency ratio	82.6	88.0	83.8	72.5	60.7	52.5	44.6

Sources: NSO (1981–93)

the programme, the main emphasis was placed on the provision of family-planning services in rural areas. In the 1970s, with urbanization occurring rapidly with industrial growth, the main focus of the programme switched from the rural to urban areas, with provision of services for the urban poor and the industrial workers. Particularly in the mid-1970s, it was highlighted by the introduction of social-support measures, numerous incentive schemes that included reduced child-delivery charges for those who wanted sterilization after the first or second childbirth, priority in allotting public housing to those who accepted sterilization and had no more than two children, and income-tax exemption to families with up to two children. These population policies were formalised in a presidential decree issued in 1981. Thanks to the decree, there was a strong political commitment to family planning and active participation of the ministries concerned. This unusual concern by the government was one of the major factors contributing to rapid changes in fertility levels and contraceptive prevalence rates in the 1980s (Lee and Cho, 1992: 27).

Governmental implementation and evaluation of the family-planning programme were supported by the Korea Institute for Family Planning, the Korea Institute for Health and Social Affairs (KIHASA) and activities of NGOs such as the Planned Parenthood Federation of Korea (PPFK). In particular, the high acceptance of family-planning programmes was attributed to integration of Family Planning Mothers' Clubs with the community developmental programme of the Saemaul Undong (new village movement) under the slogan 'industriousness, self-reliance, and co-operation' during the 1970s and 1980s.

According to quantitative analysis of factors accounting for fertility decline, the decline for those in their early and mid-twenties was mainly due to the rise in age at marriage. Thus, the much increased urban employment opportunities for women, made possible by their high and rising educational levels, resulted in their delaying marriage, and in limiting the number of children once married. For those aged 30–34 years, 85 per cent of the decline was due to the increase in contraceptive practice and induced abortion rates (Lee and Cho, 1992: 27–66) (see Table 9.4). The contraceptive programme was a public–private well-funded effort concentrating on educating women in contraceptive techniques. It reached rural and urban women, and women of all educational levels. While the fertility rate declined from 6 in 1960 to 3.5 in 1975, over roughly the same period (1961 to 1973) there was a rise in the abortion rate from 0.7 to 2.1. Although abortion rates and fertility rates are not directly comparable because women may have more than one abortion per year, the rising abortions explained a large part of the decline in fertility.[11] The government did not oppose abortions and generally overlooked a law prohibiting them; the law was finally abolished in 1973. In addition, the government fully supported the privately run contraception programme and approached it 'like a military campaign'.[12]

The poor usually have a higher fertility rate than the well-off. In other words, a relatively equal distribution of income (when overall incomes were rising) would

TABLE 9.4. Contraceptive rate of eligible women by method (%)

Year	Contraceptive practice rate (total)	Temporary method	Sterilization (female)
1970	24.4	21.1	3.3 (—)
1976	44.2	35.9	8.3 (4.1)
1979	54.5	34.1	20.4 (14.5)
1985	70.4	29.9	40.5 (31.6)
1991	79.4	32.1	47.3 (35.3)
1993	77.4	37.2	40.2 (28.6)

Sources: KIFP (1978a); KIHASA (1992, 1994)

contribute to a low fertility rate. In other words, land reform and the relatively egalitarian pattern of Korean development were factors contributing to the fertility decline.

Thus, apart from activist government policies (like free contraceptive means), structural factors like the rise in the marriage age (consequent upon a rising female labour force participation rate) and a low inequality of income combined to hasten Korea's demographic transition.

Social Development

Health

Of all the countries examined in this book, Korea is unique in being the only one which did not have a government-financed public health system worth the name— except a family-planning programme—till thirty years after independence. Nevertheless, the general health status of the people has improved greatly in the past three decades, as borne out by the changes in indicators, such as prolonged life expectancy, decreased infant and maternal mortality, improved daily dietary intakes, and improved conditions of water supply (see Table 9.5).

Male life expectancy at birth increased from 51.1 in 1960 to 67.7 in 1991, which is a 17-year extension of life in thirty-two years, and for females, from 53.7 to 75.7, a 22-year extension of life. From 1960 to 1992, the infant-mortality rate decreased from 69 to 12.8, a drop of more than 80 per cent. Also, the maternal-mortality rate fell from 88 in 1965 to 30 in 1992. How was this achieved?

Health resources and major health policies

As discussed earlier, the Korean State was not welfare-oriented until the mid-1970s, and a medical insurance system with limited coverage began operation only in 1977. Until the mid-1970s, pharmacists (i.e. prescribing druggists) and private

TABLE 9.5. Changes in major health indicators, 1960–1993

	1960	1965	1970	1975	1980	1985	1990	1993
Life expectancy at								
birth (years): Male	51.1	58.1	59.8	—	62.7	64.9	67.7	—
Female	53.7	64.7	66.7	—	69.1	73.3	75.7 ('91)	—
Infant-mortality rate (per 1,000 live births)	69.0	61.8	53.0	41.0	17.3	13.3	12.8	12.8 ('92)
Maternal-mortality rate (per 100,000 live births)	—	88	83	56	42	34	30	26
Immunization coverage								
BCG	—	6.1	38.3	48.2	49.8	65.9	78.4	98.5
Polio	—	—	—	—	—	—	93.0	99.5
Pregnant women who received pre-natal care(%)	—	—	—	57.2 ('77)	69.3 ('82)	90.0	95.1 ('91)	99.2
Births attended by health personnel(%)	—	—	—	35.8 ('77)	69.3 ('82)	90.0	95.1 ('91)	98.8
Population with piped water supply(%)	16.9	21.2	32.4	42.4	54.6	66.6	78.5	81.1

Sources: KIFP (1978b); KIHASA (1992, 1994); KIPH, *A Survey on Immunization Status of Infants and Young Children in Korea*, 1989; MOC *Statistical Yearbook on Construction*; MoHSA (1994); NSO (1993, 1994)

clinics were the major providers of health services in the country. In the rural areas in particular, where trained health professionals were limited, the major providers were pharmacists and herb doctors (providing traditional medicine). Although the number of medical professionals was expanding, they tended to be concentrated in urban areas. In 1975 only one-third of all births were attended by health personnel (see Table 9.5). Not surprisingly, infant-mortality rate was quite high (53 in 1970 and 41 in 1975). Yet at the same time, life expectancy had risen considerably from 51 years for males and 54 years for females in 1960 to nearly 60 and 67 respectively in 1970, largely as a result of rising incomes and high levels of education which ensured high utilization of private facilities, and rising nutrition levels (discussed later).

In 1973, life expectancy (about 65 years on average) was higher in Korea than in Malaysia or Thailand (59 years), but the infant-mortality rate was actually higher as well. This is a reflection of the fact that preventive and public health measures had not received much priority by the Korean government. Malaysia and Thailand had made a conscious effort to expand health services to the rural areas (see Chapter 10), which Korea had not. Table 9.6, on the growth in the number of health facilities between 1955 and 1975, shows how limited the publicly funded facilities were.

Among the hospitals and clinics, privately owned facilities represented 99 per cent of the 6,255 institutions and 73 per cent of the 41,000 beds in 1975. The government established health centres, which grew rapidly after 1962 (the Health Centre Law) and were scattered throughout the country. But public expenditure on health was very low even after the mid-1970s, and was negligible earlier (less than 20 per cent of that of Malaysia in 1973 in per capita terms). This is reflected in the utilization rate by type of facility (see Table 9.6). Thus, in 1973 six out of ten patients used a pharmacy, while three out of ten used a private clinic. The rest of the patients were divided among hospitals, herb doctors, and health centres, in that order.

Table 9.7 presents the growth in health personnel. The number of licensed health personnel increased dramatically until the mid-1970s. However, in 1975 about one-third of the physicians and nearly half the licensed nurses were actually working overseas. As a result, the number of pharmacists, whose number had increased from barely 200 in 1955 to about 20,000 in 1975, became the largest group of health professionals actively practising in Korea, accounting for over one-third of the total (Mason *et al.*, 1980). Secondly, these health professionals were heavily concentrated in the cities, particularly in the two largest ones (Seoul and Pusan). Thus, between 55 and 60 per cent of the physicians, dentists, nurses, pharmacists, and herb doctors were actually located in these two cities, and even 40 per cent of the midwives were in the urban areas.

The government gave low priority to the provision of health services, including the improvement of water supply and sanitation. The Korean tradition of using human waste (night soil) for fertilizer implied that cities grew without a sewage system for removal of such waste, and building such systems into existing cities raised costs. By 1980, 90 per cent of Seoul's residents were served by central sewage and water-supply facilities. However, only one-third of the population had piped-water supply until 1970 (see Table 9.5), and just over half by 1980.

While public health was generally not a major area of government concern until the mid-1970s, it became one in the latter half of the decade, as exemplified by the

TABLE 9.6. Health facilities and their utilization

	1955	1965	1975	Utilization, 1973 (%[a])
Hospitals	90	200	168	8.0
Clinics	2,800	5,002	6,087	30.0
Health Centres	16	189	198	0.5
Herb Clinics	1,284	2,247	2,367	3.5
Pharmacies	—	—	—	58.0

[a] distribution of patients among the different kinds of facilities

Source: Mason *et al.* (1980: 402–4)

TABLE 9.7. Health input indicators

	1960	1965	1970	1975	1980	1985	1990	1993
Total population ('000s)	24,989	29,160	31,435	34,679	37,407	40,420	43,390	44,056
No. of hospital beds	—	11,610	16,538	21,242	38,096	74,363	99,843	126,126
No. of doctors (physicians)	7,765	10,854	18,184	19,588	22,564	29,596	42,554	51,518
No. of nurses	4,836	8,898	17,958	23,632	40,373	59,104	89,032	107,883
Hospital beds per 1,000 persons	—	.398	.526	.612	.999	2.052	2.329	2.863
Doctors per 1,000 persons	.311	.372	.578	.565	.603	.732	.981	1.169
Nurses per 1,000 persons	.194	.305	.571	.681	1.079	1.462	2.052	2.449
Nurses per doctor	.623	.820	.988	1.206	1.789	1.997	2.092	2.094

Note: population in 1960–90: census data; population in 1993: estimate of mid-year population

Sources: MoHSA (1970–94); NSO (1994)

flurry of state interventions. Social tensions were beginning to emerge in an economy growing at an unprecedented rate. After the oil crisis (1973), inflation which had been under 15 per cent through the 1960s, suddenly jumped to over 25 per cent in 1974 and 1975, and remained over 20 per cent until 1980—leading to 'institutional wear and tear that was socially destabilizing' (Amsden, 1987). The expression of discontent was greatest among the educated and the higher-paid workers.

In July 1977, Korea embarked on a new medical insurance programme designed to improve national health and to enhance social security by facilitating easier access to medical care. Initially, the new law established a two-tier programme including: (i) a plan requiring employers with 500 or more workers to provide speci- fied medical insurance benefits for their employees and their dependants, and (ii) a voluntary community-based plan providing medical insurance for all others. Insur- ance was also available, on a voluntary basis, to firms employing fewer than 500 workers. The medical insurance system was expanded substantially in 1988 to include self-employed farmers and fishermen who were not covered previously, and the coverage was extended throughout the nation in 1989 (see Table 9.8). Thus the Korean system is a network of 'sickness funds'—300 independent insurance funds—covering all occupational and regional groups. As in the past the country's health providers are still largely private, and are paid on a fee-for-service basis. This form of organization—72 per cent of physicians and 80 per cent of hospital beds are private—has meant there is little incentive to control costs. Total health expen- diture was 6.6 per cent of GDP in 1990, the highest in the region, three-fifths of which was private expenditure (World Bank, 1993c).

TABLE 9.8. Beneficiaries of national medical security by programme (as % of population) and their distribution

		1978	1980	1985	1990	1992
Medical assistance		5.6	5.6	7.9	9.2	6.1
of which (%):	Class I	21	30	20	18	26
	Class II	79	70	80	50	65
	Class III	—	—	—	32	9
Medical insurance		10.5	24.2	44.1	93.7	94.7
of which (%):	Industrial workers	99	58	68	40	39
Govt. employees and private-school teachers		—	46	23	11	11
Self-employers and others		2	1	9	48	50
Total covered		16.1	29.8	52.0	102.9	100.8

Note: difference exists between the total population and the medical security beneficiaries due to dual qualification

Sources: KFMI (1990–1993); MoHSA (1993)

Since 1978 the government has also strengthened the supply of health resources in rural areas. These efforts include (1) establishment of private medical institutions with financial incentives such as long-term, low-interest loans, (2) expansion of public health centres to hospital-level ones, (3) construction of primary health care posts operated by community health practioners (CHP) who are qualified nurses or midwives, and (4) supply of public health doctors, designated to serve in doctorless areas in place of their military duty.

To cover the poor, in 1977 a medical-assistance programme was established to provide medical services under social security for those unable to pay for medical care (see Table 9.8). As a result of this programme, all medical services are provided free to those who are below the poverty line and unable to work (Class I). For those low-income persons able to work (Class II), the programme pays 80 per cent of hospital costs and all out-patient expenses. Moreover, the government provides low-interest loans for the remaining 20 per cent of hospital costs exceeding 100,000 Korean won. For quasi-low-income persons able to work (Class III), the programme pays 56 per cent of outpatient expenses, and 80 per cent of hospital costs (MoHSA, 1993). Overall the government's subsidy to the insurance system is progressive, as it contributes 30 per cent of national social insurance funding on behalf of low-income households.

Utilization of health services

The introduction of the health-insurance programme has played a key role in enhancing the utilization of health services and raising the health status of the people. The number of medical cases treated per 100 insured persons increased from only 75.6 in 1978 to 393 by 1991. In other words, during this thirteen-year span, there was a 5.2-fold increase in the average number of medical cases treated per 100 insured persons. Particularly, the service utilization directly related to maternal and child health has indicated great progress since the late 1970s. The proportion of pregnant women receiving prenatal care rose to 99.2 per cent in 1993 from 57.2 per cent in 1977. Likewise, 98.8 per cent of deliveries occurred at medical institutions in 1993 (see Table 9.5). All these improved health services combined with others have brought a significant decline in the infant- and maternal-mortality rates.

Nutritional improvement

Rising nutrition levels went hand in hand with rising incomes, and in the early decades accounted for improving health status, despite the limited public-health services. Calorie and protein supplies per capita have shown considerable improvement since the 1970s. Though the daily calorie supply per capita was less than 2,000 kcal in 1962, by 1965 it was already at 2,200—the recommended level—and 2,400 by 1970 (Table 9.9). By the mid-1970s the World Bank was already reporting

TABLE 9.9. Changes in major nutrition indicators

	1962	1965	1970	1975	1980	1985	1990	1991	1994
Daily calorie supply per capita (kcal)	1,943	2,189	2,370	2,390	2,485	2,687	2,858	2,883	—
Daily calorie intake per capita (kcal)	—	—	2,150	1,992	2,052	1,936	1,868	1,930	—
% of energy from cereal	—	—	81.2	82.5	77.4	61.9	65.8	—	—
Daily protein supply (per capita: g)	53.2	57.7	65.2	71.1	73.6	86.6	89.4	89.7	—
Daily protein intake (per capita: g)	—	—	64.6	63.6	67.2	74.5	78.9	73.0	—
% of protein from animal source	—	—	14.7	20.6	28.7	41.7	39.8	—	—
Low birth-weight babies	—	—	—	—	—	—	—	—	7.1[a] (1993)
Breast-feeding ever-practice rate (%)	—	—	—	94.4 (1974)	—	—	—	—	—
Median duration of breast-feeding (months)	—	—	—	19.2[b]	—	—	—	—	—

[a] based on 4,320 births delivered at 39 medical facilities in 1993; [b] mean duration

Sources: EPB and KIFP (1977); KREI (1992); MoHSA (1991); Park and Hwang (1993, 1994)

(based on budget studies and nutritional surveys) that Koreans suffer 'little gross undernutrition' and that 'real nutrition does not contribute significantly to disease' (World Bank, 1977).[13] In 1992, the average calorie supply totalled 2,815 kcal, 1.5 times higher than that of the early 1960s. Meanwhile, the calorie intake trend shows a decreasing pattern since the 1980s, accompanied by the falling tendency of re-commended dietary allowances, reflecting a reduced physical activity associated with lifestyle changes. The daily calorie intake per capita fell from 2,052 kcal in 1980 to 1,930 kcal in 1991 (see Table 9.9). Contrary to the calorie intake, protein intake, which implies the quality of diet, indicated an increasing trend in the past twenty-year period. As a result, the nutritional status of children has manifested itself in considerably improved height and weight.

The overall status of nutrition in Korea will no longer pose a question of sur-vival. But there are other problems related to nutrition e.g. overnutrition. Another key issue is that nutrition programmes have not been actively pursued due to a lack of understanding among policy-makers and the general public. These problems are reflected in the fact that the breast-feeding practice rate has declined during the last twenty years. In 1994, the breast-feeding practice rate was no higher than 72.5 per cent and only 55.6 per cent of newborns were exclusively breast-fed during the first month of life (Park, 1994). As against the limited concern for nutrition services in the health sector, school lunch programmes have been actively executed by the ministry of education.

Expansion and improvement in education

Beginning with the 1950s, but especially in the 1960s and 1970s, there was a rapid quantitative expansion in the education sector with economic growth. As the six-year plan for the provision of compulsory education was implemented, all school-aged children were enrolled in primary school, and hence secondary-school enrolment increased threefold (see Table 9.10).

As indicated in Table 9.11, the adult literacy rate reached 97 per cent in 1992. The average years of educational attainment increased nearly 4.5 years during the past twenty-five-year period, from 5 years of schooling in 1965 to 9.5 years in 1990 (Table 9.10). Likewise, nearly half of the population aged 6 years and over attained high-school and above levels of education in 1990, compared with only 15 per cent in 1970. The transition rate to college and university from high school increased to 40 per cent for boys and 37 per cent for girls in 1993, as the opportunities for higher education expanded, when compared with the 27 per cent and 29 per cent level respectively, in 1966.

For 6–11-year-olds, the Republic of Korea had achieved 100 per cent enrolment by 1970. Most importantly, the growth of enrolment was not accompanied by fiscal pressures experienced in other countries. The explanation lies in the internal and external efficiency of the Korean educational system, the nature of the

TABLE 9.10. School gross enrolment rate by school level (%) and educational attainment

	Primary school[a]			Middle school[b]			High school[c]			Educational attainment[d]		
	Total	Male	Female	Total	Male	Female	Total	Male	Female	Total	Male	Female
1960	90	—	—	29	—	—	17	—	—	—	—	—
1966	98	98	97	41	51	31	26	35	19	5.03	6.19	3.97
1970	101	103	100	51	65	41	28	37	22	5.74	6.86	4.72
1975	105	103	105	72	81	63	41	51	33	6.62	7.61	5.70
1980	103	101	104	95	96	93	63	74	56	7.61	8.67	6.63
1985	100	102	101	100	99	100	80	88	76	8.58	9.66	7.58
1990	101	100	103	98	99	97	88	97	85	9.54	10.55	8.58
1993	101	101	102	96	96	97	90	90	89	—	—	—

[a] no. of students/population aged 6–11 years;
[b] no. of students/population aged 12–14 years;
[c] no. of students/population aged 15–17 years;
[d] average years of education of those who have left school

Sources: EPB (1980); KEDI (1993); NSO (1960–90)

TABLE **9.11.** Adult literacy rate

	1945	1955	1960	1970	1992
Adult literacy rate (%)	22	71	72	88	97
Females as % of males	—	—	—	86	95

Sources: MoE (1980); UNDP (1994)

private–public mix in financing, and the role of foreign assistance. In addition, there were factors outside the educational system which helped reduce the number of school-age children through a reduction in fertility. An important reason for the internal efficiency was the low cost per pupil, which was in turn the outcome of very high pupil–teacher ratios at the primary level: nearly 66 in 1952, 59 in 1960, and by 1975 dropping only to 52. This ratio seems particularly high, given that educators believe that the maximum pupil–teacher ratio at the primary level should be about 45, especially in a resource-constrained economy. On average, pupil–teacher ratios of 35 are common in many developing countries.

As in Zimbabwe and Malaysia, there was substantial double- and triple-shift teaching, and thus a high utilization rate of existing facilities (this tended to fall as the number of classrooms increased). In the initial stages of educational investment in a resource-poor country, such efficient utilization of existing school buildings can keep total costs down. Costs per pupil were also kept low by reducing drop-out rates. This was done (as in Zimbabwe and Malaysia later) by offering automatic promotion from grade to grade. As a result, not only did the mean years of schooling increase constantly, but the transition rate from primary to secondary level was very high. This has avoided the wastage that is common through high repetition and drop-out rates in most developing countries.

Moreover, the cost per pupil was kept low by keeping teacher salaries low. Given that throughout the developing world teacher salaries account for nearly 90 per cent or more of current educational expenditures, especially at the primary level, this fact deserves special mention. However, the initial investment in education in the early stages of development enables a rapid accumulation of human capital to occur, increasing the supply of teachers, thus mitigating the pressure for teacher salaries to rise. Thus, the impact of rising wages on the cost of education and hence on enrolments is diminished. In Indonesia and Malaysia the annual earnings of primary-schoolteachers are around 2.4 times per capita GNP (World Bank, 1993*a*). In Sub-Saharan Africa, however, where human capital is scarce, that ratio is much higher. In South Korea, the earnings of primary-school teachers are currently 3.9 times per capita GNP, but on account of higher pupil–teacher ratios the unit-operating cost per pupil is not much different from Malaysia or Indonesia.

Another major factor that kept the education costs to the government low is the manner in which different levels of education were financed. Almost all primary-school children (99.5 per cent in 1965 and 98.5 per cent in 1975) were in publicly funded schools. But in 1965 only 55 per cent of lower-secondary (59 per cent in 1975) and 42 per cent of higher-secondary (39 per cent in 1975) schoolchildren were in public schools. In other words, at the secondary-level private financing of schooling was and still is much more important, while all primary education is financed publicly. At college and university level, the share of students in public schools was only 27 per cent in 1965 (and the same in 1975).

Defence expenditures, largely paid for by the USA, accounted for the largest share of government expenditure in the 1950s and 1960s, followed by economic development; the third place was occupied by education (averaging around 15 per cent over 1965–75). While the government spent under 1 per cent of GNP on education in 1954, by 1960 it had risen to 2.5 per cent and was within the range of 2.2 to 3 per cent of GNP between 1965 and 1975—a level lower than that in other countries that have undergone comparable enrolment expansions. Since 1978, government expenditure on education as a percentage of GDP has remained around 3 per cent—much lower than other countries in this book, mainly on account of the low and falling fertility rate. However, almost three-quarters of that expenditure in the earlier decades went to primary education.

Perhaps an important reason why the government was able to maintain low levels of public expenditure was that private households paid about two-thirds of direct costs of education (which include in-school as well as out-of-school expenditures) (Mason *et al.*, 1980). Private educational expenditures took various forms. In the elementary school, it was customary to supplement budgetary expenditure with parental contributions made through the Parent-Teacher Association. In-school private expenditures covered fees, school-support funds, and experimentation and practical training expenses. Between 1966 and 1975 in-school expenditures accounted for 20–30 per cent of total educational expenditures, with some 40 per cent being accounted for by out-of-school expenditures. Out-of-school expenditures included the normal cost of books (most elementary-school students must buy their own), school supplies, transportation, extracurricular activities, and after-school tutoring.

Another important factor which explains Korea's expansion of educational enrolment, especially in the early years, was foreign assistance, especially from the USA. Over 1945–8, while the Koreans generally provided the facilities, the US Military Government covered two-thirds of operating costs at the primary level (Mason *et al.*, 1980). After the Korean War (1950–3), US assistance to education expanded enormously. Between 1952 and 1956, foreign assistance to Korea for education came to about $100m. (approximately 1,000m. won per annum at 1958 exchange rates)—which was 200 per cent of government expenditure in 1954 and about 30 per cent of it in 1957. These sums were spent on classroom construction; secondary, vocational, and higher education; and teacher training.

A final reason for the educational achievement in Korea (and in other East Asian economies) was that it moved to a demographic transition before other regions, which reduced the growth rate of the number of children of school-going age. The number of school-going children actually declined between the mid-1960s and 1989. As a result, the country was able to keep its educational expenditure share constant, while the number of children fell. In South Asia or Sub-Saharan Africa, rising expenditures are necessary even to maintain the current enrolment ratio.

Women and children

At independence, sexual discrimination against women dominated all aspects of women's lives—consistent with Confucian traditions. The constitution of Korea, promulgated in 1948, guaranteed respect for the dignity of individuals and equality between men and women as a fundamental principle. Based on this principle, various legislative reforms have been implemented, and the status of women in Korea has undergone enormous changes. While the primary enrolment ratio for girls was already 94 per cent in 1960, the push from parents for enrolling girls in secondary school came when employment expanded rapidly with economic growth.

The proportion of women engaged in the primary sector has sharply declined in recent years in contrast to an increase in secondary and tertiary sectors (see Table 9.12). Following Sen, we have argued in Chapter 2 that where women engage in work outside the home and earn an independent income, the well-being of women

TABLE 9.12. Labour force participation of women

Year	Male	Female	Female/male participation rate (male = 100)	Distribution of women working in:		
				Agriculture[a]	Industry[a]	Services[a]
1965	76.6	36.5	47.7	69.6	6.4	24.0
1970	75.1	38.5	51.3	61.5	12.9	25.6
1975	74.5	39.6	53.2	59.9	14.7	25.4
1980	73.6	41.6	56.5	58.8	16.8	24.4
1985	72.3	41.9	57.9	46.5	21.9	31.6
1990	63.9	47.0	63.6	27.7	23.3	49.0
1993	75.4	46.3	61.4	20.4	28.1	51.5

[a] as percentage of total women working

EPB (1960–90, 1983); id. *Social Indicators in Korea* (1981, 1987); NSO (1994)

is positively affected. Women were the key behind the initial spurt of rapid economic growth in the East Asian countries. As we suggested earlier, this was achieved through labour-intensive export industries, such as textiles. Up to 80 per cent of employees in such industries were women, especially those who were young and single (a phenomenon similar to that found in Mauritius). However, women wage rates were 10 to 20 per cent lower than those of men (Wee and Heyzer, 1995).

Women's labour-force participation increased enormously but discrimination exists not only in wage rates. Due to inheritance laws, women own less than 5 per cent of agricultural land. Non-ownership of land also means that women do not qualify for credit.

The supply of public child-care facilities for children of low-income female workers falls short of the sharply growing demand due to the continuously increasing trend of married women participating in economic activities. The more women engage in occupational activities, the more the responsibilities of protecting and nursing children are shifted from family to society. The ministry of health and welfare (MoHW) promulgated the Child Day Care Act in 1991 for the purpose of systematizing and increasing the facilities for protecting and nursing infants and young children. As of December 1993, there were 153,270 children accommodated at 5,490 day-care centres, which accounts for only 15.2 per cent of those who need child care. Therefore quality child-care is a problem as well, although the government is planning to help low-income families by supporting child-care centres.

The Social Security Programme and Social-Sector Financing

The social security programme

During the last three decades, rapid economic growth created many job opportunities that in turn led to the significant alleviation of poverty. Absolute poverty dropped from 40.9 per cent in 1965 (55 per cent in urban areas, 36 per cent in rural) to 9.8 per cent in 1980, with a poverty line of 121,000 won in constant 1981 prices for a household of five persons (Suh *et al.*, 1981). By 1984 the incidence of poverty was reduced to 4.5 per cent of the population (5 per cent in urban areas, 4 per cent in rural)—and even further to 3.9 per cent in 1993.

Given that the poverty incidence was still around 10 per cent at the end of the 1970s, starting then the Korean government became active in the area of safety nets with both social insurance and public-assistance programmes—during what we called the second period in the evolution of social welfare policies. This concern surfaced with the Fourth Five-Year Economic Development Plan and resulted in the creation of an active social security system.

Social insurance: the National Pension Programme

The National Pension System is the only universal social security system, while others are occupational pensions. The National Pension Programme was enacted in 1988 for workers at workplaces with ten or more employees. The coverage of the programme was enlarged in 1992 to include firms with between five and nine workers. The National Pension System is being expanded to cover farmers and fishermen and its coverage will be widened further to include the urban self-employed in 1998. Then the National Pension System will achieve nationwide coverage.

Public-assistance scheme

Public-assistance programmes are based on the notion that every human being has the fundamental right to the necessities of life guaranteed by the government. Among these, the Livelihood Protection Act, medical assistance, and anti-poverty programmes deserve special mention.

- Livelihood Protection Act

The Livelihood Protection Act was enacted in 1982 in order to guarantee a minimum standard of living to those lacking the means to live without any help, and could be of three kinds: home care, institutional care, and self-support care.

- Anti-poverty Programmes

Government policy to alleviate poverty focuses on how to enhance the poor's self-reliance. There are two types of strategies for poverty alleviation. One is direct government intervention: (i) Cash assistance is provided to two types of extremely poor, one accommodated in public facilities and the other remaining in private homes. They are paid in kind with rice and in cash to buy food. (ii) Public works schemes for low-income labourers, who can participate in environment-improvement and village-development projects which are closely related to residents' lives. However, payment is very low compared with wages in the labour market. Hence, the beneficiaries are mainly the old who cannot join the labour market.

The other is an indirect approach to enhance their income-earning capacity involving vocational training and subsidies: Government subsidizes tuition and living expenses for the period of training. Training preparation and job-search expenses are also paid by the government. The poor can, therefore, concentrate on training without being a burden to their family. Loans are offered to the poor for small business activities and housing at low interest rates with a long redemption period.

Public expenditure on social development

Government expenditure on social development has steadily increased since the 1970s.[14] The share of central government outlays going to social development,[15]

TABLE 9.13. Government expenditure by function (general account) (%)

	1965	1970	1975	1980	1985	1990	1993
National defence	11.9	12.7	11.3	9.7	10.7	10.2	12.0
Social development[a]	8.1	4.9	6.7	6.4	6.8	8.9	9.2
Education	15.5	17.3	12.7	17.7	20.1	20.4	19.8
Economic development	19.8	20.6	26.7	21.5	16.1	14.1	20.7
Others	11.7	22.0	13.8	9.1	15.7	21.4	13.7
Total	100.0	100.0	100.0	100.0	100.0	100.0	100.0

[a] includes expenditure on health, social security, housing and community development, and others

Sources: EPB (1965, 1970); NSO (1994)

broadly defined, rose from 23.6 per cent in 1965 to 29.0 per cent in 1993 (see Table 9.13). As a percentage of GDP, social-development expenditure rose from 2.5 per cent in 1965 to 4.1 per cent in 1993. Efficiency, however, remained the Korean government's primary objective during the period from the 1970s to the mid-1980s. This focus is clear from the fact that, in terms of both the share of total spending and the absolute level, government spending on social development in Korea is still relatively low by international standards.

The detailed breakdown of public expenditure shows that most of the social-development expenditure has been directed to education,[16] which has been related to productivity, while only a small portion has been directed to health and social welfare. Between 1965 and 1993, the share of education in total government expenditure rose from 15.5 per cent to 19.8 per cent.

Although the share allocated to national defence has declined gradually since 1980, its level remains high due to the strained relationship with the Democratic People's Republic of Korea, and restricts the expansion of social welfare.

Conclusions

Korea appears to offer a route to a high level of human development despite rather limited public action. It seems to be—and has often in the past been presented as —a case where economic growth resulted in the drastic reduction of poverty and an increase in the level of human development. However, this growth was itself dependent on three pillars: educational expansion (especially at the base of the system), land reforms, and an adequate supply response when the demand rose for the means of birth control. The State (albeit with US assistance) had an important role in all three areas even before growth accelerated. Economic growth thus was not automatic nor the result of a free play of market forces, but essentially state-led. The initial conditions (an educated population, relatively equal asset distribution, and slowing population growth) helped to reinforce growth. A virtuous circle was set in motion, which further improved income equality.

Only later did the State explicitly focus on the health sector, women's issues, and a social safety net. When the State did intervene in the health sector, it accelerated improvements in an already high health status.

Although there was no publicly provided health system worth the name until the mid-1970s and the State was not welfare-oriented, a relatively equal distribution of income, rising incomes with economic growth, and improving nutrition levels ensured rapidly rising life expectancy. Although the infant-mortality rate was relatively slower to fall on account of the absence of public provision of health services, rising incomes and high education levels, especially of women, ensured constant improvements in health status. But when the State gradually introduced compulsory medical insurance from the mid-1970s onwards, the health status improved further. Meanwhile, rising female participation in the labour force, rising incomes, and rising marriage age led to a demand for contraception. The State supported family-planning services from the early 1960s, and created the incentive structure to ensure high utilization of those services. Equitable distribution of income also contributed to low fertility.

Thus, a high level of human development was based not only on unprecedented growth but also state action. As a result, Korea not only managed to achieve rapid rates of economic growth, nutritional improvements, and educational development, but a rapid decline in the incidence of poverty. Few countries can claim to have achieved poverty-reducing growth and social development to the same extent. With Malaysia and Mauritius, Korea exemplifies best the synergies within social development, and between social development, poverty-reduction, and macro-economic growth (that are discussed further in Chapter 15), which lie at the heart of this volume.

Notes

1. The five countries showing the largest absolute increases in Human Development Index (HDI) were Malaysia (+.463), Botswana (+.463), Korea (+.462), Tunisia (+.432), and Thailand (+.424).
2. The reform was implemented without much political resistance because about one-fifth of the land farmed by tenants was owned by Japanese landlords who left Korea in 1945. As for the Korean landlords, they were in a politically weak position because they carried the taint of collaboration with the Japanese.
3. Land reform may temporarily have reduced productivity per unit of land, but this was offset by political and social benefits. The temporary fall in output prompted large aid-financed imports of fertilizers from the USA.
4. The point here is that while the investment of the poor will be in human capital, that of the rich will be largely in physical capital—the complementarity between the two will favour growth.

5. The effects will be not merely additive, as Birdsall argues, but multiplicative, as suggested in Ch. 15.
6. Notice that Kuznets's industry classification includes not only mining and manufacturing but also the construction, light and power, gas, water, transportation, communication, and agricultural sectors (see Kuznets, 1966: 92).
7. In the 1960s and early 1970s 70 to 75% of total exports went to the major trading partners: the USA and Japan. While these two countries are still major trading partners today, the share of exports going to them has steadily decreased, as Korea has diversified exports to Europe, the Middle East, and other Asian countries. The import share of these two major partners dropped from nearly 80% in 1965 to around 50%.
8. For a discussion of a case where the adjustment has involved major social costs, see Ch. 6.
9. India, with widespread poverty and a relatively unequal income distribution, exemplifies the case of rent-seeking activity—encouraged by the State—run rampant, with the result that industrial growth is hampered.
10. The State provided a family-planning education programme to change individual fertility behaviour, an incentive and disincentive programme to lead directly to contraceptive practice, and encourage induced abortion, in addition to an organized emigration programme to export surplus population. But the private sector played a key role. Cigarette-booth sales of condoms were permitted in every village. Beauty-aids salespersons, who were mostly women and had easy access to housewives, were enlisted to increase contraceptive distribution (Hong, 1978).
11. In 1973 the rate of abortions among rural women (2) was about as high as that of urban women (2.2), but the rural fertility rate (4.7) was still higher than the urban one (3.3) (Mason *et al.*, 1980).
12. National and local targets were set for adoption of various types of contraceptives, and the performance by targets was monitored at the national level. In India, a similar approach of target-setting and incentives for achieving targets has been adopted for family-planning programmes during the last decade, and has come under severe criticism for the abuses and misreporting it leads to (which was the case in Korea as well). See Dreze and Sen (1995).
13. This was accomplished while Korea was becoming, from being a major rice exporter in the 1930s, an increasing importer of grain in the 1960s and 1970s. While overall agricultural growth was rapid (see Ch. 15), most of the agricultural growth in the 1950s and 1960s was accounted for by non-grain crops, because PL 480 imports from the US were used to suppress grain prices (Mason *et al.*, 1980).
14. Although general government outlays consist of the central and local governments' contributions, this study concentrates on the central government's expenditures, due to the centralized nature of the Korean government. For reference, as of 1990, the ratio of the central to local budget was 7 : 3, and share of social welfare and public benefit (regional development, culture, and sports) was 57.7% of total local government expenditure (NSO, 1993).
15. This included government expenditures on health, social security, housing and community development, education, and others.
16. For this reason, education expenditure is classified as a separate item, rather than being included in the social-development expenditure of the Korean budget.

References

Adelman, Irma, and Robinson, Sherman (1988), 'Income Distribution and Development,' in H. Chenery and T. N. Srinivasan, *Handbook of Development Economics*, ii, Amsterdam: North-Holland.

Amsden, Alice H. (1987), *Republic of Korea*, Stabilisation and Adjustment Policies and Programmes, WIDER Country Study 14, Helsinki.

—— (1992), 'A theory of government intervention in late industrialisation', in L. Putterman and D. Reuschemeyer (eds.), *State and Market in Development; Synergy or Rivalry?*, Boulder, Colo. and London: Lynne Rienner Publishers.

Balassa, Bela (1988), 'The Lessons of East Asian Development: An Overview', *Economic Development and Cultural Change*, 36/3 (suppl.).

Bark, Soonil, *et al.* (1993), *Causes of Poverty and Policy Measures in Korea*, KIHASA.

Berry, R., Albert, and Cline, William (1979), *Agrarian Structural Productivity in Developing Countries*, Baltimore: Johns Hopkins University Press.

Bharadwaj, Krishna (1962), *Production Conditions in Indian Agriculture*, Cambridge: Cambridge University Press.

Birdsall, N., Ross, D., and Sabot, D. (1995), 'Inequality and Growth Re-considered: Lessons from East Asia', *World Bank Economic Review*, 9/3.

BoK (Bank of Korea), *Economic Statistics Yearbook*.

—— *National Accounts.*

Bruno, Michael (1988), 'Opening Up: Liberalization with Stabilization,' in Rudiger Dornbusch, F. Helmers, and C. H. Leslie (eds.), *The Open Economy*, EDI series in Economic Development, London: Oxford University Press.

Choo, Hakchung (1992), *Income Distribution and Distributive Equity in Korea*, Seoul: Korea Development Institute, mimeo.

Dreze, J., and Sen, A. K. (1995), *India: Economic Reforms and Social Opportunity*, Oxford: Oxford University Press.

EPB (Economic Planning Board, Republic of Korea) (1960–85), *Population and Housing Report.*

—— (1960–90), *Population and Housing Census.*

—— (1965), *Summary of Budget for Fiscal Year.*

—— (1970), *Summary of the First Supplementary Budget for Fiscal Year.*

—— (1980), *Handbook of Korean Economy.*

—— (1983), *Report on the First Employment Structure Survey.*

—— (1983–90) *Annexe to Summary of Budget.*

—— (1990), *Annual Report on the Economically Active Population Survey.*

—— KIFP (1977), *The 1974 World Fertility Survey: Korea.*

Evans, Peter (1995), *Embedded Autonomy: States and Industrial Transformation*, Princeton: Princeton University Press.

Federation of Korea Medical Insurance Societies (1985–92), *Medical Insurance Statistics Yearbook.*

Han, Sung-Hyun, and Cho, Nam-Hoon (1987), 'Changes in Induced Abortion and Their Impact on Fertility', *Fertility Changes in Korea*, KIPH.

Hong, Sawon (1978), *Population Status Report: Korea*, Seoul: Korea Development Institute.

IMF (1993), *Government Finance Statistics Yearbook.*

KEDI (Korea Education Development Institute) (1990), *The Analysis of Total Educational Expenditures in Korea*, Research Report 90-13.

—— (1993), *Educational Indicators in Korea.*

KFMI (1992), *Medical Insurance Statistical Yearbook.*

KIFP (Korea Institute of Family Planning) (1978a), *Population and Family Planning Statistics.*

—— (1978b), *Statistics on Population and Family Planning in Korea.*

KIHASA (Korea Institute of Health and Social Affairs) (1992, 1994), *The National Fertility and Family Health Survey Report.*

Kim, Kwang Suk (1985), 'Lessons from South Korea's Experience with Industrialization', in V. Corbo, A. Krueger, and F. Ossa (eds.), *Export Oriented Development Strategies: The Success of Five Newly Industrialized Countries*, Boulder, Colo.: Westview Press.

Kim, Kwanyoung, and Kim, Wonshik (1990), *Alternative Social Development Policy and Planning Scenarios Towards the Year 2000 and Beyond: The Case of Korea*, KDI Working Paper 9014.

—— (1989), *Journal of Population and Health Studies.*

—— (1989), *A Survey on Immunization Status of Infants and Young Children in Korea.*

KIPH (Korea Institute of Population and Health) (1992), *National Family Health Survey Report.*

KREI (1992), *Food Balance Sheet.*

Krueger, Anne O. (1979), *The Developmental Role of the Foreign Sector and Aid*, Cambridge, Mass.: Harvard University Press.

—— (1974), 'The Political Economy of the Rent-Seeking Society', *American Economic Review*, 64/3.

Kuznets, Simon (1995), 'Economic Gross and Income Inequality', *American Economic Review.*

—— (1966), *Modern Economic Gross*, New Haven: Yale University Press.

KWDI (Korean Women's Development Institute) (1991), *White Paper on Women.*

Kwon, Soonwon (1989), *Review of Current Social Development Policy and Planning*, KDI Working Paper 8930.

Lee, Hung-Tak and Cho, Nam-Hoon (1992), 'Consequences of Fertility Decline: Social, Economical and Cultural Implications in Korea', *Impact of Fertility Decline on Population Policies and Programmes Strategies: 27–66*, KIHASA.

Leipziger, Danny M., and Petri, Peter (1989), 'Korean Incentive Policies Towards Industry and Agriculture', in Jeffery G. Williamson and Vadiraj R. Panchamukhi (eds.), *The Balance Between Industry and Agriculture*, New York: St Martin's Press.

McGinn, Noel F., Snodgrass, D. R., Kim, Yung Bong, Kim, Shin-Bok, Kim, and Quee-Young (1980), *Education and Development in Korea*, Council on East Asian Studies, Harvard University.

Mason, E. R., Kim, M. J., Perkins, D. H., Kim, K. S., and Cole, D. C. (1980), *The Economic and Social Modernisation of the Republic of Korea*, Harvard University Press.

Mehrotra, Santosh, and Pizarro, Crisostomo (1996), 'Social Policies in Chile, Costa Rica and Mexico: An Inter-regional Perspective', in UNICEF (1996).

MoE (Ministry of Education) (1980–92), *Statistical Yearbook of Education.*

MoF (Ministry of Finance) (1980–92), *Government Finance Statistics in Korea.*

MoHSA (Ministry of Health and Social Affairs) (1993), *Major Indicators on Health and Social Affairs.*

—— (1970–94), *Yearbook of Health and Social Statistics*.

MoL (Ministry of Labour), *Monthly Labour Survey*

NFMI (1990–3), *Medical Insurance Statistical Yearbook*.

Noland, Marcus (1990), *Pacific Basin Developing Countries: Prospects for the Future*, Washington, DC: Institute for International Economics.

NSO (National Statistical Office) (1970–94), *Major Statistics of Korean Economy*.

—— (1994), *Population Projection by Province: 1960–2000*.

—— (1991), *Population Projection in Korea: 1990–2021*.

—— (1981–93), *Social Indicators in Korea*.

Papanek, Gustav (1988), 'The New Asian Capitalism: An Economic Portrait', in Peter L. Berger and Hsin-Huang M. Hsiao (eds.), *In Search of an East Asian Development Model*, New Brunswick: Transaction Books.

—— (1994), in Hwa and Hwang, Na-Mi, *Patterns of Breastfeeding and Policy Measures in Korea*, KIHASA.

—— (1993), *Policy Issues and Development Strategies of MCH Services in Korea*, KIHASA.

Park, Yung Chul (1986), 'Foreign Debt, Balance of Payments, and Growth Prospects: The Case of Korea, 1965–88', *World Development*, 14/8.

Sakong, Il (1993), *Korea in The World Economy*, Washington, DC: Institute for International Economics.

Seoul City Government (1989), *A Study on Realities and Counter-Measures of the Poor in Seoul*.

Suh, Sang Mok (1992), 'Korea's Welfare Policies and Future Direction', International Conference on Social Welfare State: Present and Future', *Korean Academy of Social Welfare*, September.

—— Park, Fun-Koo, Kim, Jong-Gie, Choi Il Sup, Lim, H. S., Lee, Y. H., and Kim, S. S. (1981), *Patterns of Poverty and the Anti-Poverty Program for Korea*, Korea Development Institute.

UNDP (1991, 1994), *Human Development Report*.

UNICEF (1996), *Social Development in the Nineties: The Case of Chile, Costa Rica and Mexico*, Planeta, Bogotá.

Wee, V., and Heyzer, Noeleen (1995), *Gender, Poverty and Sustainable Development*, Engender and UNDP.

Westphal, Larry E. (1990), 'Industrial Policy in an Export-Propelled Economy: Lessons from South Korea's Experience', *Journal of Economic Perspectives*, 4:41–59.

World Bank (1977), *Growth and Prospects of the Korean Economy*, Washington, DC.

—— (1987), *Managing the Industrial Transition*, i and ii (The Conduct of Industrial Policy and Selected Topics and Case Studies), Washington, DC: World Bank.

—— (1993a), *The East Asian Miracle: Economic Growth and Public Policy*.

—— (1993b), Office of the Vice-Presidents, East Asia and Pacific Region, *East Asia and the Pacific Regional Development Review: Sustaining Rapid Development*.

—— (1993c), *World Development Report 1993*, Washington, DC.

Yeon, Hacheong (1990), 'Inter-Generational Economic Security in Asian Countries', *Asian Development Review*, 8/1.

——— (1991), *Prospects for North-South Korean Economic Relations and the Evolving Role of Korea in Continental Northeast Asian Economic Development*, in Jang-Won Suh, (ed.), *Northeast Asian Economic Cooperation*, Seoul: Korea Institute for International Economic Policy.

——— (1989), *Social Development in the Republic of Korea: Considerations of Equity versus Efficiency Issue in Policy-Making*, KDI Working Paper, 8906.

10

Malaysia: Social Development, Poverty Reduction, and Economic Transformation

LEONG CHOON HENG AND TAN SIEW HOEY

Introduction

Malaysia has recorded impressive achievements in both social and economic development, especially when seen in relation to the situation at the time of independence in 1957. The country then was beset with deep communal and religious differences and wide economic disparities, which divided its population and threatened the viability of the new nation. The major ethnic groups were the Malay (Bumiputra or indigenous) population (49.5 per cent), Chinese (37.2 per cent), and Indian (11.7 per cent).[1]

A major task of social development was to integrate the population, especially the indigenous segment, into the modern economy as quickly as possible. This was seen as a *sine qua non* for nation-building. Part of the efforts involved redistributing the wealth of the nation, through rapid economic growth rather than through outright expropriation of assets. A comprehensive programme also had to be developed to deliver essential social services, such as primary health care and education, to the population, especially those living in the rural areas.

Throughout its history, Malaysian planners have successfully sequenced a mix of policies to meet these challenges. This chapter is an attempt to piece together the Malaysian experience in its efforts to attain social and economic goals simultaneously. This is done by looking at the successive education policy reforms, the organization of rural health-service delivery, and the integration between these two and rural infrastructure development.

Steady Economic Transformation (1957–1990)

From 1960 to 1990, real GDP growth averaged slightly more than 6 per cent a year in Malaysia. Correspondingly, real per capita GNP growth averaged 4 per cent, resulting in almost a tripling of real per capita income over the period (see Table 10.1). In the process, the economy was steadily transformed from one based on agricultural production and mining to one in which manufacturing became predominant. The share of agriculture declined from 40.7 per cent of GDP in 1960 to less than 20 per cent by 1990 (see Table 10.1).

The transformation of the economy since independence can be divided into four phases:

1. In the first phase (1957 to 1970) the government laid the foundation of a rural development programme. Industrialization was limited to a few import-substituting industries. The economy was kept relatively open with little government intervention in the industrial sector.

2. The second period (1971 to 1984) began with the implementation of the New Economic Policy (NEP) in 1971 which signified the beginning of long-term planning over a twenty-year period. Government intervention became pervasive, extending into the non-agricultural sector. An affirmative action programme was designed to increase Malay (Bumiputra) participation in employment and equity ownership in the modern sectors of the economy. This strategy was interrupted by the recession beginning in 1984.

3. The third phase was a process of economic adjustment and reform prompted by the recession of 1984. In 1985, the economy recorded a growth rate of minus 1 per cent. The unemployment rate rose from 5.8 per cent in 1984 to 8.3 per cent in 1986. This period saw the introduction of stabilization and market reform policies.

4. The period after 1987 has been one of uninterrupted economic growth, averaging more than 8 per cent a year. This growth is partly the result of high levels of foreign investments.

The success of Malaysia's industrialization policies in generating employment and output had a profound impact on social development as industrial employment helped to raise the income of the population. Much of the industrial growth has been due to an increase in investments rather than productivity, as noted by a World Bank study (*The East Asian Miracle*). This strategy was appropriate to the needs of the 1970s and 1980s, i.e. to facilitate the shift away from rural employment to indus-

TABLE 10.1. GDP growth and composition

	1960	1965	1970	1975	1980	1985	1990
GDP growth rate (%)	6.0	6.0	8.2	0.8	7.9	−1.0	9.7
Sectoral composition of GDP							
Agriculture	40.7	31.5	30.6	27.7	23.8	21.0	19.4
Manufacturing	8.5	10.4	13.1	16.4	18.6	19.8	26.5

Source: Ministry of Finance Malaysia, *Economic Report*, various issues

trial employment and fulfil the objectives of the NEP. The recession of 1984 to 1987 also focused concerns on increasing investment inputs. It was only with the rise in labour costs in the 1990s that there occurred a policy shift to introduce measures to increase the productivity and international competitiveness of Malaysian industries.

Although industrialization was crucial to Malaysia's economic growth, rural development and agricultural growth helped to raise the incomes and standards of living of the rural population. The focus on the rural sector was imperative in the 1960s. The majority of the Malay population lived in the rural areas and provided the political support for the ruling party. Thus, the first three five-year plans concentrated on improving economic opportunities in the rural areas.

Rural Development and Income Generation

The rural development strategy emphasized crop diversification, opening and cultivation of new land, and productivity enhancement through the adoption of new agricultural technology. The economic problems besetting the rural population had been the lack of employment opportunities and low levels of productivity both of which resulted in low incomes and poverty. The strategy adopted to combat these problems tended to be commodity-specific and consisted of the provision of both 'hard' and 'soft' inputs:

1. Drainage and irrigation works; development of rural roads and bridges; expansion and improvement of rural schools and health facilities; and provision of water and electricity supplies.

2. Institutional provision of agricultural research and extension; credit and marketing; and organization of producers' associations.

3. Enhancing the incentive structure through tariffs and subsidies.

4. Rehabilitation of existing agricultural areas.

5. Opening of new land for development.

Through these means, both output and equity goals were achieved in the first two decades of agricultural development. Crop diversification into oil palm and to a lesser extent cocoa, for instance, helped to raise as well as stabilize rural incomes. For areas under existing cultivation, such as rubber and rice areas, a commodity-specific approach was undertaken. The main method relied on an extension programme to reach out to and persuade farmers to adopt new technology to increase yields.

Also, the emphasis on rural schools and health centres as part and parcel of the rural development strategy should be highlighted.

For rubber smallholders, the key responsible agency is the Rubber Industry

Smallholders' Development Authority (RISDA). RISDA manages replanting grants for smallholders, defined as those owning rubber holdings of less than 100 acres (40 hectares). Complementing the efforts of RISDA is the Federal Land Consolidation and Rehabilatation Authority (FELCRA) which is responsible for consolidating small, fragmented units of land into larger units and rehabilitating the land with high-yielding crops to make cultivation more efficient. This strategy is fully backed by a research and development programme undertaken by the Rubber Research Institute (RRIM). Palm oil holdings are supported by the Palm Oil Research Institute of Malaysia (PORIM).

Intervention in the rice-growing areas, on the other hand, involves instituting price support and subsidy schemes to ensure a minimal level of income to the farmers. The state marketing board also plays a role in guaranteeing the purchase of the output of the farmers. Besides improving existing cultivated land, the rural-development programmes also include the clearing, cultivation, and settlement of new land. These land-settlement schemes are undertaken by the Federal Land and Development Authority (FELDA).

The income-generation and poverty-reduction programmes in the rural areas tend to the comprehensive and include community-development programmes, adult literacy programmes, advice on child care, nutrition, and sanitation, and efforts to reorient the attitudes and values of the rural population. Such community-development programmes are implemented through autonomous institutions such as FELDA, FELCRA, and RISDA. The approach is to work through the traditional institutional structure in order to gain peasant confidence in the programmes.

There is no denying that government policy has brought about a transformed rural economy. The 'conscription' of the target groups into the process of modernization brought with it access to other facets of well-being such as improved sanitation in their surroundings (access to piped water and electricity), awareness of the value of education for their children, and socialization into the norms of modern living conditions. The initial emphasis on a rural development programme also prevented a premature rural–urban migration with all its attendant effects, a condition which seems to afflict many basic cities of the developing world.

Poverty Reduction and Equity Issues

The success of the rural development programmes can be judged by the degree to which they have helped to reduce poverty and promote equity. With regard to poverty reduction, the impact of government intervention varies according to the type of crop grown. In the paddy sector, the outcomes have not been encouraging on grounds of both efficiency and equity, but the new land-settlement programme of FELDA has been relatively more successful. On the whole, the impact of the FELDA programme on rural development and income generation has been greater as it covers larger tracts of land and there is greater commercial demand for the crops grown.

Compared to new land schemes, areas under existing cultivation eventually have to face the problem of population pressure. The size of holdings eventually imposes limits to poverty-reduction efforts, especially in the rice sector. Farm size becomes critical to those practising monoculture. With fixed farm sizes, it is difficult for a family to subsist on paddy farming without ever-larger subsidies from the government. With hindsight, it can be said that policy-makers missed the opportunity to oblige settlers owning small parcels of land in their place of origin to give them up in exchange for larger landholdings in the new land schemes. This being the case, assistance to the rice sector today resembles an income-maintenance programme that enables farmers merely to stay above the poverty line.

Tan (1989) estimated that in 1985, the fertilizer and price subsidies together accounted for 69 per cent of income derived per hectare. Based on the prevailing costs and the poverty-line income in 1982, a paddy household would need 1.7 hectares to cross the poverty threshold. Higher and higher levels of subsidies would be needed to maintain farm incomes. Fortunately, the presence of off-farm income opportunities could help to reduce the dependence of household income on land size. The implication here is that solutions to the poverty situation cannot be based strictly on a commodity approach.

Despite the above limitation, the rural-development programmes involving land settlement, rehabilitation and consolidation, crop diversification and improvements, agricultural extension work, price and input subsidies, and provision of rural amenities have helped to reduce the incidence of rural poverty. The incidence of rural poverty dropped from 58.7 per cent of rural households in 1970 to 19.3 per cent in 1990 (see Table 10.2). The bulk of the reduction in rural poverty however occurred after the mid-1970s, following the introduction of the New Economic Policy with its objective of restructuring economic imbalances in the society and eradicating poverty.

Urban poverty also declined from 21.3 per cent in 1970 to 7.3 per cent in 1990, resulting largely from employment generated by the government and by the industrialization programmes of the 1970s and 1980s. However, certain poor groups continue to persist and have not been affected by the income-generation programmes. This has prompted the government to formulate a special programme in the Sixth Malaysia Plan (1991–5) to target specifically the hard-core poor in order to totally eradicate poverty.

It should also be borne in mind that a reduction in poverty is often construed as an improvement in equity in the Malaysian context. This need not necessarily be the case, as a reduction in the number of poor can be achieved from growth without any improvement in the distribution of income, particularly in the case of income distribution within an ethnic group.

The mean and median incomes of the population have improved substantially

TABLE 10.2. Incidence of poverty by sector (% of total households)

Sector	1970	1975	1980	1985	1990
Rural	58.7	54.1	29.2	24.7	19.3
Urban	21.3	19.0	12.6	8.2	7.3
Total	49.3	43.9	29.2	18.4	15.0

Source: Ministry of Finance Malaysia, *Economic Report*, various issues

TABLE 10.3. Peninsular Malaysia: mean and median incomes (in *ringgit* per household per month in 1970 prices)

		1970	1979	1984	1987	1989	Growth rates (%)			
							1970–9	1980–4	1985–7	1988–9
Bumiputra	Mean	172	296	382	381	389	6.2	5.0	0.0	1.0
	Median	120	197	261	269	—	6.7	6.0	1.0	—
Chinese	Mean	394	565	674	628	662	4.1	4.0	−2.1	3.0
	Median	268	373	460	448	—	3.7	4.0	−1.0	—
Indian	Mean	304	455	491	478	503	4.6	2.0	−1.0	3.0
	Median	194	314	347	355	—	5.5	2.0	0.8	—
Others	Mean	813	1,147	1,101	1,267	1,442	3.9	−1.0	5.0	7.0
	Median	250	331	518	283	—	3.2	9.4	−18.2	—
All races	Mean	264	417	494	472	487	5.2	3.4	−1.5	1.6
	Median	166	263	325	324	—	5.2	4.4	0.0	—
Urban	Mean	428	587	691	645	—	3.6	3.3	−2.2	—
	Median	265	361	461	441	—	3.5	5.0	−1.5	—
Rural	Mean	200	331	370	375	—	5.7	2.3	0.4	—
	Median	139	222	267	276	—	5.3	3.7	1.1	—
Gini coefficient		0.513	0.508	0.480	—	0.445				

Sources: 4th and 5th Malaysia Plans and Mid-Term Reviews

during the years of economic development. Over the period from 1970 to 1979, government statistics show a very rapid growth in the mean and median incomes of the indigenous (Bumiputra) population, averaging 6.2 per cent and 6.7 per cent per year respectively (see Table 10.3). The growth rates were higher than for the other ethnic groups. This trend continued into 1984. The recession years from 1985 onward, however, put a damper on income growth. Growth resumed after 1988, but this time it was higher for the non-indigenous ethnic groups, possibly reflecting a holding back of affirmative action programmes which had played a big role in boosting indigenous incomes.

Despite the various government programmes, income distribution, as measured by the Gini ratio, did not narrow as significantly as in the Republic of Korea and Taiwan over the last two decades. The Gini ratio declined from 0.51 in 1970 to 0.44 in 1989 (see Table 10.3). The emphasis of the economic-growth programmes in the NEP period was similarly to eradicate poverty and redress ethnic economic imbalances. The objective of tackling the issue of overall income distribution was only of secondary importance. Equity was attained as an after effect of income generation and affirmative-action policies. Even though the distribution of wealth remained inequitable, the population, especially the lower-income groups, were able to enjoy steady improvements in the standard of living as a result of the social policies carried out by the government. As the provision of social services was independent of individual income, large sections of the population could access social services much earlier than they would have been able to do on the basis of their own income. Thus, universalization of social services not only improved their standard of living but also promoted equity.

Steady Progress in Social Development

The country has experienced almost forty years of steady improvement in social services. Health standards improved significantly and education has been expanded to a near-universal level. Life expectancy, for example, increased for males from 56 years in 1957 to 69 years in 1990, and for females from 58 years to 74 years. A significant proportion of this increase was experienced quite soon after independence in 1957. By 1970, male life expectancy had reached 64 years and female 68 years. Many middle-income countries had not reached this level by the early 1980s (see World Bank Report 1985, table 1). Accompanying the increase in life expectancy was a marked decline in infant mortality. Infant mortality rates dropped from 76 per 1,000 live births in 1957 to 13 per 1,000 in 1990. Again the drop was experienced quite early on.

Achievements in education were equally impressive. By 1990, almost every child between 6 and 11 years of age was enrolled in a primary school (see Table 10.4). In fact, the gross enrolment ratio exceeded 90 per cent by the end of the first decade of independence. This rate was comparable to those found in many of the middle-income countries in the mid-1960s.

It is important to note that despite the remarkable advances made in health and education, the rate of population growth remained rather high, at an average of 2.5 per cent per year. There was no dramatic slow-down in population growth in line with the normal demographic transition. The expanding economy has made the limit on population growth less urgent. In the 1980s, in fact, the prime minister came out against efforts to curb population growth and envisaged a target of 70m. people by the year 2100, up from a population of around 15m. in 1980. It must be remembered that the population density of Malaysia is not only one of the lowest

TABLE 10.4. Age-groups enrolled in assisted schools (%) and transition rates

School level	Age-group	1967	1970	1975	1980	1985	1990
Primary education	6+ to 11+	91.0	88.2	96.0	93.6	95.4	99.8
Lower-secondary education	12+ to 14+	52.0	52.2	69.5	79.9	84.3	83.0
Upper-secondary education	15+ to 16+	16.0	20.1	32.7	38.1	47.9	49.1
Transition rates (%):		1970–1	1974–5	1980–1	1984–5	1989–90	
From primary to lower-secondary		68.6	82.3	87.5	90.2	86.7	
From lower-secondary to upper-secondary			65.0	64.9	65.2	67.2	

Source: *Educational Statistics of Malaysia*, various years

in the world (61 inhabitants per sq.km.) but also about half of that of its neighbours Thailand (114) and Indonesia (106). Nevertheless, in terms of arable land its density is not as low (470 inhabitants per sq.km.)[2] which means there are limits to the natalist policy.

The steady expansion of health and educational services, especially in the first two decades after independence, has made it possible for the increased population to have access to these services. By the 1990s, the principal diseases, such as malaria, tuberculosis, and diarrhoea, and causes of morbidity, such as poor sanitation and malnutrition, which are associated with poverty and underdevelopment, had been replaced by illnesses associated with affluence, such as cardiac problems and hypertension.

Provision of Essential Social Services

Improvements in social services have been more a result of social policies than economic growth which increased the purchasing power of the population. Raising income and hence demand is not a guarantee that a population, especially those living in the rural areas, will have access to adequate social services. Accessibility is as crucial as affordability. The government played an active role in delivering such essential services as health and education directly to the people.

One cannot underestimate the contribution of the education and health investments in the 1950s and 1960s, prior to and (later on) contemporaneous with growth and industrialization. It is important to understand how these two sets of policies were implemented simultaneously.

Delivery of Primary Education[3]

The achievements in primary-school enrolments must be seen in relation to the inadequate system of primary education which existed under the colonial government. At that time, the provision of primary education in the vernacular languages, i.e. Chinese and Tamil, and Islamic education were the responsibility of respective ethnic communities. In the urban areas, the governments, together with Christian missions, offered schooling in English and, in the rural areas, only a rudimentary form of primary education was offered to the Malays in the Malay language (Barnes Report, 1951).

Early on, it was recognized that universal education was necessary to forge a nation out of the disparate elements of the newly formed Malay Federation. Also, by redressing the low education level of the Malay community, it would be able to empower itself. These were the views of Tun Abdul Razak, who was the Minister of Education during this early period. Thus, the objective of ensuring 'a place in a school for every child born in the country' (Razak Report, 1956: 28) was seen by Razak as an integral part of the effort to uplift the standard of living of the rural, and largely Malay, population. His proposals attained remarkable results as the government backed its support with substantial resources to the Education Ministry.

After independence, the government embarked on a massive effort to unify the system and at the same time to create the necessary infrastructure to deliver primary education to the entire population, targeting especially the rural population. By 1967, slightly over ten years after the Razak Report drafting the plan of action, 91 per cent of all primary-aged children were enrolled in school in Peninsular Malaysia (see Table 10.4).

The increase in primary enrolment was, nevertheless, not dramatic but rather steady, as can be seen from Table 10.4. Between 1956 and 1960, enrolment increased by about a third. Subsequently, the increase for every five-year period was about 12 per cent to 17 per cent, up to the mid-1970s. Progress was gradual because there often exists a time-lag between a policy initiative and its implementation, hence producing a gradual course. Also, additional initiatives and the staggered implementation of policies described in the Razak Report helped to sustain the momentum of steady improvement.

The Razak Report laid the basis for the successful establishment of a unified national system of education in a multi-ethnic society with the absence of severe interethnic conflicts while ensuring universal primary education. A national system using Malay as the main language of instruction out of a disparate system based on four different languages used by the different ethnic groups could be attributed to the way in which the policies presented in the Report were formulated and implemented. The process involved the state-led standardization and Malayanization of the school system—the curriculum, syllabus, timetable, language of instruction, organization, and funding of schools—as well as of the teaching profession.

The desire to minimize interethnic conflicts was in the minds of policy-makers from the beginning. The sensitivities of the various ethnic communities were considered in the formulation of policies. The Razak Report proposed 'to bring together the children of all races under a national educational system in which the national language is the main medium of instruction, though we recognize that progress towards this goal cannot be rushed and must be gradual' (p. 3).

Each racial group had expressed a strong desire to have their children educated in the mother tongue. Parents wanted the freedom to choose the medium of education for their children. So instead of converting all schools into ones using the national language, the government only made it compulsory that Malay be taught in all government-assisted schools up to the secondary level. Along with this, the government undertook the task of converting government Malay primary schools into standard (later national) schools (Razak Report, 1956: 3 and 10). Non-Malay schools using English, Chinese, or Tamil as the medium of instruction and receiving government assistance would be converted into standard-type (later national-type) schools. Standard-type or national-type schools were schools which taught the national curriculum using English, Chinese, or Tamil instead of the national language. Independent primary schools in the various communal languages continued to be allowed to operate without government assistance. In this way, parents were free to choose the medium of instruction they wished their children to be educated in. The gradual approach of establishing and converting existing schools into standard national schools using the national language eased the transition and aided acceptance of these schools by the non-Malay communities.

The Malayanization and standardization of the teaching curriculum was also carried out in various ethnic languages. Common syllabuses and timetables were promulgated for use in all schools. Thus, whatever language was used, all pupils learned the same things in the same way. This task was by and large completed by 1960.

The government, through the Ministry of Education, was clearly the main force in the increase in primary enrolment. The government stepped up its expenditure on education and allocated a substantial portion of its development-plan budget to it (see Table 10.5).

The privately funded and partially government-funded schools did not have the resources to cater for the rapid rise in the demand for education. Eventually, almost all of these schools, in order to receive government funding, converted to national-type schools, i.e. schools following the national curriculum (even if the medium of instruction was Chinese or Tamil).

The supply of teachers was crucial to the success of the universal education programme. Only the government could undertake the task of supplying the large number of teachers needed on a nationwide scale. This involved the setting up of training institutes and programmes to train primary-school teachers. The number of students attending teacher-training centres and colleges increased by two and a

TABLE 10.5. Sectoral breakdown of development expenditure, 1966–1990 (%)

Sector	First Five-Year Plan 1956–60	Second Five-Year Plan 1961–6	First Malaysia Plan 1966–70	Second Malaysia Plan 1971–5	Third Malaysia Plan 1976–80	Fourth Malaysia Plan 1981–5	Fifth Malaysia Plan 1986–90
Economic			63.3	50.6	54.4	60.5	76.2
Agriculture and rural development	22.6	17.6	26.3	18.3	18.7	16.3	16.0
Others	52.8	48.9	37.0	31.9	35.4	44.3	60.3
Social	13.8	15.6	17.7	13.1	14.6	21.5	7.6
Education and training	6.0	8.9	7.8	7.1	6.2	10.1	5.1
Health	1.3	3.8	3.5	1.9	1.2	1.6	0.4
Housing, social services and others	6.5	2.8	6.5	4.2	7.1	9.8	2.1
General administration	6.5	6.3	3.3	1.5	1.9	1.8	1.6
Security	4.3	11.6	15.7	10.4	14.2	16.2	5.0
Total	100.0	100.0	100.0	100.0	100.0	100.0	100.0

Note: there are changes in the categories especially after the first two five-year plans

Sources: for 1st and 2nd Five-Year Plans figures: 1st MP; Table 2.6; for First Malaysia Plan figures: 2nd MP, 1971, Table 2.4; for Second and Third Malaysia Plans figures: 4th MP, 1981, Table 6.2; for Fifth Malaysia Plan figures: Mid-term Review of 5th MP, 1989, Table 5.3

half times from 1957 to 1960 (Ministry of Education Malaysia, various years). With the government in control of the profession, teachers could be sent to serve in rural and remote areas upon completion of training as a way of fulfilling their contracts.

Another major task was to build schools to accommodate a larger enrolment. The government was directly involved in the construction of Malay primary schools which were considered government-standard schools. Whether the schools were government-run or privately run, they received financial assistance from the government (Chew Tow Yow, 1973: 105). The Chinese, Tamil, and Christian mission schools, for example, were given grants to expand by themselves.

Another policy initiative found in the Razak Report which helped to raise primary-school enrolment was the guarantee of automatic promotion from one year to another. This encouraged students to stay in school. In 1960, the Education Act was introduced to formalize the effort of providing universal primary education. However, education continued to be voluntary and not compulsory.

The Rahman Talib Report (1960) signified another policy breakthrough by making primary education free in all fully assisted schools beginning in 1962. In the early years, the effort to promote universal primary education was constrained by the existence of school fees. Before the Rahman Talib Report, students had to pay a fee of RM2.50 a month in fully assisted primary schools and RM4 in partially assisted, i.e. English and Chinese primary schools (Rahman Talib Report, 1960: 23). Schooling was free in Malay-medium and Tamil-medium schools. As a result, only about half of all primary-school pupils had been receiving free education.

Following successes in primary education, there were pressures to expand secondary education. The Rahman Talib Report of 1960 also recommended efforts to increase the level of education, turning government's attention to secondary education. It stressed that 'the first priority in the development of our educational system must be the raising of the school-leaving age and that the target must be to raise it to 15' (p. 19). The government introduced automatic promotion from primary to secondary school in 1964, thus allowing every primary-school student to move into secondary school. This policy breakthrough was carried out by abolishing the Malayan secondary-schools entrance examination which until then had served to screen out about 70 per cent of primary students from access to academic secondary education (Ministry of Education Malaysia, 1970: 73; Wong and Ee, 1971: 99).

As a result, enrolment in secondary education increased by 146 per cent from 1960 to 1965. The transition rate from primary to secondary education, however, improved more gradually, as can be seen from Table 10.4. It was not until the 1980s that the transition rates exceeded 85 per cent.

The expansion of secondary education required increases in budget allocations. The biggest increase came after 1969 when several new universities were set up. In the 1970s and 1980s, the government spent between 12 per cent and 20 per cent of its total expenditure on education.

Another major achievement was in gender equality. The ratio of male to female in primary enrolments dropped from 1.55 in 1956 and 1.31 in 1960. Improvements continued to be made so that enrolments of both sexes were on par by the late 1970s. The same was achieved for secondary enrolment. There was no policy aimed specifically at increasing female enrolment. The increase came naturally in response to policies which were gender-neutral.

Pragmatic concerns outweighed idealistic, nationalist considerations in the early years of educational reform. It was felt to be more important to put every child in school regardless of the medium of instruction than to ensure that they be taught in the national language. In order to achieve the goal of universal primary education, all existing schools in different languages had to be enlisted. In this way, enrolment was not adversely affected by the programme to establish a national system of education using the national language.

Later, government grants were used as an incentive to get schools to convert to national or national-type. The government also attempted to increase enrolment in national schools by building more facilities and raising their standards to make them attractive to children. By 1960 nearly half of all primary students were in such schools (Rahman Talib Report: 4–5), attesting to the success of this non-coercive method of establishing national primary schools. Another inducement involved making education free in national primary schools. The Malaysian experience points to the importance of a clear political will and political sensitivity to guide the process of delivering a national system of primary education to a multi-ethnic population.

Delivery of Rural Health Services[4]

As with primary education, the Malaysian government has been successful in delivering health services to the population, especially those living in the rural areas. The life expectancy for males and females has increased gradually over the years while the various mortality rates have dropped substantially (see Table 10.6). Improvements in the health status of the population came about steadily. Although there were no discernible turning-points in health achievements, significant policy breakthroughs were made which fuelled the process of steady improvement in various areas.

The first policy initiative came as early as the mid-1950s under the colonial government. Following a study by the World Health Organization, the Development Plan of 1954–6 formulated a national rural health programme to redress the unequal distribution of health services in the country. Seventy per cent of health services were concentrated in urban and semi-urban areas around 1957 (Abdul Majid Ismail, 1971: 1). Many rural areas had little or no medical or health service. The rural population had to go to clinics in small towns and hospitals in the larger towns to seek treatment for their illnesses, but often did not have the resources to make the trip.

The major policy development came with the setting up of the Rural Health Ser-

TABLE 10.6. Health indicators for peninsular Malaysia

	1947	1957	1960	1967	1970	1975	1980	1985	1990
Life expectancy									
Male	—	55.8	—	—	63.5	—	66.7	67.9	69.0
Female	—	58.2	—	—	68.2	—	71.6	73.0	74.0
Infant-mortality rate	102.0	75.5	69.0	45.0	40.8	33.2	24.0	17.0	13.1
Maternal-mortality rate	700	280	240	170	150	80	60	40	20

Note: 1975 CBR and CDR figures are for 1974

Source: Ministry of Health Malaysia, *Annual Report*, various years

vices Scheme to deliver health services directly to the rural population (Abdul Majid Ismail, 1971: 1). A three-tier system was developed consisting of a health centre, health subcentres, and midwife clinics, which together formed a rural health unit to deliver services to the rural areas.

A strong political will was the driving force for the scheme. In the 1960s, there was close co-operation between rural health planning and the planning for rural development under the deputy prime minister, Tun Razak. As described by Jayesuria (1967: 4):

The planning of the Rural Health Units was co-ordinated in each State by the Chief Medical and Health Officer with the State Rural Development Committee while the Medical Officer of Health would co-ordinate with the District Rural Development Committee at each district level. At the village or 'kampong' level, the Medical and Health Officer in charge of the Rural Health Unit or his representative would co-ordinate with the Village or Kampong Development Committee.

The integration of health planning into overall rural development planning was crucial to ensure that funds were appropriately apportioned to finance the building of rural health facilities. The importance of this integration is twofold. On the one hand it allowed the emergence of complementarities among education, health, and economic development outcomes to arise. On the other hand, it facilitated planning the location of primary health-care units as described below.

The government spent a substantial portion of its total expenditure on health. In 1961, 8 per cent of total expenditure was for health, amounting to 2 per cent of GNP (see Table 10.7). Rural health services received about a fifth of the development expenditure for health for each five-year-plan period (see Table 10.8).

The success of the scheme, however, was not entirely due to budgetary commitments. In the early years, most of the health services were delivered through low-cost measures in the form of makeshift facilities and mobile units. Much of the success therefore was owed to the efficiency of the organizational set-up and the commitment of the personnel involved.

The Rural Health Services Scheme had to tackle a root cause of the poor state of rural health, i.e. the inaccessibility of the health facilities to the rural population. An extensive network of rural health units was set up that could bring health care right to the village level. The structure of each health unit is depicted in Fig. 10.1. The health subcentres and midwife clinics were to be sited peripherally and radially from the main health centre and away from one another to increase their coverage of the rural population.

Planning of the health units was based on the size of the population to be served. Each unit was intended to serve a population of 50,000. So each health centre of the unit would serve 10,000 people. Each had one midwife located within it together with four other midwife clinics linked to it. In this way, there would be five midwives for a population of 10,000 and 25 for 50,000, with each subcentre or midwife in the main centre serving 2,000. Each midwife clinic was to have one trained midwife.

The rural health units served as outposts of hospitals located in towns and cities and were linked to them through a referral system offering out-patient services (in-patient services were referred to hospitals). Doctors in the health units would first diagnose the rural patients and then refer them to hospitals for more specialized treatment. Another way of reaching the rural population was through home visits by health personnel, such as doctors, nurses, and midwives, from the health units. Other approaches included relying on travelling dispensaries, mobile teams, flying doctors, and rail ambulance service. All these were measures aimed at making

TABLE 10.7. Total government expenditure on education and health

	1961	1965	1969/70	1975/76	1980	1985	1990
Education							
% of total gov. expenditure	—	—	—	20.3	12.4	15.4	18.3
% of GNP	—	—	4.0	5.5	5.0	5.9	5.9
Health							
% of total gov. expenditure	8.0	5.9	5.6	5.8	5.3	4.3	5.5
% of GNP	2.0	1.9	1.5	2.4	3.5	2.2	1.7

Notes: secondary schools refer only to academic secondary schools data before 1980 for Peninsular Malaysia; data from 1980 onwards for Malaysia. 1975, 1980, and 1985 data on grants to primary and secondary schools refer only to development expenditures

Sources: *Educational Statistics of Malaysia*, various years; Ministry of Health Malaysia, *Annual Report*, various years

TABLE **10.8.** Distribution of development expenditure for health and population programmes by plan period (actual and estimated expenditures %)

	1st MP (1966–70) Actual	2nd MP (1971–5) Actual	3rd MP (1976–80) Estimated	4th MP (1981–5) Estimated	5th MP (1986–90) Actual
Programmes					
Public health services	16.1	20.7	21.0	25.0	—
of which:					
Rural health services	13.6	20.1	20.8	24.6	19.4
Control of communicable diseases	2.5	0.6	0.2	—	—
Distribution					
Patient-care services	75.4	60.3	52.9	60.7	73.3
Dental health services	—	1.3	1.3	0.5	0.6
Training programmes	—	9.5	5.1	2.4	1.2
Applied food and nutrition	—	—	2.3	1.8	1.1
Other health programmes	8.5	7.1	9.3	3.5	3.3
Population and family health	—	1.1	8.1	6.0	1.1
Total	100.0	100.0	100.0	100.0	100.0

Sources: Malaysia Plans, various years

health services accessible to the rural population, especially those in remote parts of the country.

Besides being extensive in its operation, another important feature of the rural health units was the comprehensive health care they provided. Services ranged from maternity and child health care, medical care, dental care, immunization, family planning, applied nutrition, school health, communicable disease control, environmental sanitation, health education, laboratory service, and data collection (MMA, 1980: 44). The health unit was oriented towards improving the entire health of a targeted rural community consisting of a cluster of villages.

The emphasis was on the maternal and child-health component of the service. This was crucial as adequate care for mother and child helped to reduce drastically infant- and maternal-mortality rates. Another important service provided by the health units was midwifery. Infant-mortality rates were correlated with home delivery (Chee Heng Leng, 1990: 38–40), and by making trained midwives available, the risks associated with deliveries at home were greatly reduced. Maternal and child care was comprehensive and included antenatal as well as postnatal care and home visits by nurses and midwives.

Much of the improvement in the health of the rural population was also due to preventive health services, such as immunization and disease control, undertaken

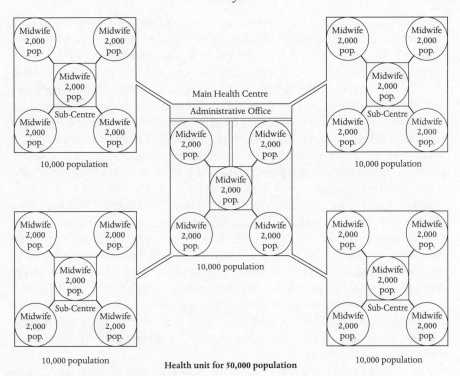

Fig. 10.1 Rural health-services scheme

by the health units while providing curative care. The drop in mortality and morbidity rates and the decline of such diseases as cholera, tuberculosis, malaria, and
typhoid, could not have been achieved without successes in public health and preventive work. Although a large part of the work in the health centres was preventive, initially few rural dwellers would take the initiative to come to the clinics to
receive preventive care for such diseases as tuberculosis and whooping cough. So
the curative component in the health centre functioned as an enticement to get the
rural villagers into the habit of seeking medical help from professionals, into the
habit of coming to health centres. Over time, the health workers were able to gain
the villagers' trust and therefore their willingness to take part in preventive health
care.

Rural health services have been virtually free which partly explains their success.
According to Meerman's estimate (1980: 139), two-thirds of hospital in-patients and
three-quarters of out-patients at government facilities in the country did not pay a
fee.

Periodic upgrading of the system was another factor accounting for its success.
Throughout the 1960s, the three-tier system for delivering health services was

gradually expanded to cover larger areas. Although this mechanism had proven effective it was not regarded as final. Efforts were undertaken to improve on it. A decision was made in the Mid-Term Review of the Second Malaysia Plan in 1973 to upgrade the system by converting it to a two-tier system (*Third Malaysia Plan*, 1976: 409). To achieve this, health subcentres would be upgraded to health centres and midwife clinics to multipurpose rural clinics. A health unit in the two-tier system would comprise one health centre for every 15,000–20,000 people and four rural clinics (*klinik desa*), each serving 3,000–4,000 people. This increased the population which could be served. Each upgraded health centre would have a resident doctor and dental team. The upgraded rural clinic would have two multidisciplinary rural nurses (*jururawat desa*) upgraded from the unidisciplinary midwives.

Another reason for the success of the Rural Health Services Scheme lies in the effective training and deployment of health personnel, especially the paramedical staff. Midwives received two years of training. Nurses who would be sent to the rural areas, in addition to their normal training, would receive one more year of rural health training and preferably another year of midwifery. Nurses involved in public health work had to undergo five years of training altogether. Health inspectors who were responsible for environmental sanitation work and for helping to control communicable diseases were trained for three years at the Public Health Institute. Given the long duration of training, the rural health units were generally staffed with well-trained people.

The government also continuously set up and upgraded training institutes to increase the number of health personnel. Table 10.9 shows a steady improvement in the ratios of health personnel to population in the country. In fact, in the first decade after independence the doctor–population ratio increased by a third, the nurse–population ratio by two and a half times, and the midwife–population ratio by twenty times. By 1980 for instance, 82 per cent of deliveries were attended by trained health personnel.

After receiving their training, the health professionals were sent to serve in the rural areas as part of their service. In the early 1970s, a law was introduced that

---

TABLE 10.9. Population per health personnel ratio in Malaysia

Population per	1947	1957	1967	1976	1980	1985	1990
Doctor	17,361	7,352	4,855	4,132	3,800	3,174	533
Medical assistant	48,309	5,397	—	5,063	—	—	—
Nurse	—	3,891	1,626	976	716	—	—
Midwife	—	20,408	3,952	2,597	878	—	—
Dentist	—	—	—	—	19,892	15,059	12,075

Sources: Ministry of Health Malaysia, *Annual Report*, various years; Chee Heng Leng (1990), Table 3.7; MMA (1980), Table 3.17

required all medical-degree holders to undergo three years of compulsory service with the government. This enabled the government to post doctors to the rural areas where few would go on their own, as most preferred instead to practise in the urban areas. This legislation did help to increase the number of doctors in the rural areas.

Immunization, disease control, and improvements in sanitation also played an important role. Immunization coverage was high by the standards of developing countries in 1980, and rose sharply in the 1980s. The percentage of children below the age of 1 year that were immunized for common diseases such as tetanus, polio, and hepatitis (but not for measles), was over 80 per cent by 1990. Ninety-five per cent of them received BCG vaccination in 1985. The immunization programme has also eradicated smallpox.

Along with rural health units, credit must also be given to what were called vertical programmes for helping to reduce the incidence of communicable diseases. The control and eradication of certain common diseases such as yaws, tuberculosis, and malaria were carried out through vertical programmes, the earlier of which started in the 1950s. Vertical programmes were directed from their central headquarters all the way down to the district level, with each programme focusing on a particular disease. Each programme has its own organization, hierarchy, and personnel (Abdul Majid Ismail, 1971: 7–9). The vertical programmes were necessary because the rural health units did not have the personnel and expertise to deal with the diseases targeted. Once the capability at the rural health units improved, the vertical programme could be integrated into the normal functions of the units.

Improvements in sanitation, i.e. water supply and sewage disposal, also helped to raise the health standard of the population. Safe-water coverage was very high in urban areas by 1980, but only two out of five households were covered in rural areas. However, the health service delivery system, declining poverty, and very high access to education more than compensated for any weakness in this area.

Complementary Social and Economic Policies: The FELDA Experience

The Malaysian experience in health highlighted the importance of tying health programmes to the overall effort of rural development. The above analysis hinted at the complementary nature of Malaysia's social and economic development policies. This complementarity is most visible in the FELDA experience, which is a land-development scheme aimed at alleviating rural poverty and equipping the settlers in the schemes with a comprehensive set of social services.

By 1990, a total of 119,300 households had been settled in the land schemes, comprising 715,800 people or 3.3 per cent of total households in the country.[5]

These people were settled into communities and provided with a host of amenities and services like housing, health, sanitation, education, and training pro-grammes aimed at preparing them to meet the demands of modern economic activities.

Households are grouped into economic sizes of about 400 families per 4,500 acres of land. Such a settlement size would mean a population of at least 2,000 which makes it eligible for such essential services as a midwife's clinic, a primary school, and a police post. Such a population size would also justify the costs of pro-viding piped-water supply and the construction of village and access roads. It would also be adequate to support the development of a small commercial centre to service the settlers.

The core approach to this settler and community-development programme is training, both formal and informal, which starts from the time of entry into the scheme. Through training sessions, settlers acquire technical skills in taking care of the crops as well as managerial and decision-making skills, and also learn about the daily responsibilities and obligations of working and living in a community. Settlers are also taught to participate in entrepreneurial activities and are exposed to the potentially captive businesses which emerge in the schemes. In response to settler enthusiasm, FELDA established a RM2m. fund in 1974 to provide loans to settler co-operatives to purchase vehicles for transporting their fruit, replacing private con-tractors. A management committee composed totally of settlers would run the business profitably. Similarly, settlers also bought shares in FELDA's Shop Corpora-tion. Such activities enhanced the income of the settler household.

Through the process of socialization, settlers become aware of the value and importance of education for their children. While primary and secondary educa-tion are provided free by the government, settler commitment to education is indi-cated in their willingness to contribute to pre-school education in the schemes. Settlers themselves contribute to the costs of constructing the school building, helped in part by a grant from FELDA. Daughters of settlers with the necessary qualifications are hired as teachers after intensive training. Students can go on to secondary education in selected schools in the cities. Practical training is given to out-of-school youths who are inclined towards agriculture through the Youth Works Brigades introduced in 1970.

Women play a critical role in the scheme in facilitating changes in values and atti-tude. Extension work is conducted through the Women's Institute Scheme and covers such aspects as home management and family and community living. The women's institute and its counterpart, the resident settler development assistant at the authority level, are in charge of all women's activities. The main approach used by the extension workers is the individual home visit. Among the subjects taught and discussed during such visits are child development, nutrition, sanitation, family budgeting, and family development.

The success of the schemes cannot be measured in economic terms alone.[6]

Their ability to deliver the rural population from poverty, induce self-reliance as well as prepare them for economic opportunities outside the schemes cannot be overstated. No doubt the FELDA approach is a very expensive one and it is doubtful whether many other developing countries possess the financial resources to undertake such an experiment. By 1985, the cost per settler on an oil-palm scheme totalled RM53,000[7] of which only RM28,000 was charged to the settlers in the form of a long-term loan payable over fifteen years at the rate of 6.5 per cent per annum.[8] Nevertheless, the FELDA experience provides useful lessons on how a government authority can provide a comprehensive package of economic and social incentives to tackle the problem of rural poverty.

Financial Support

The above analyses point to the importance of policy breakthroughs and the creation of appropriate institutions for successful social development. Another key factor is the availability of financial resources. In the 1960s and 1970s, the revenue came largely from export taxes on tin and rubber. Beginning in the early 1980s, export taxes on oil palm became a major source of revenue. Another important source of revenue for the government was petroleum. From the mid-1970s onward, petroleum accounted for around 10 per cent of total revenue, increasing to close to 20 per cent in the 1980s (Ministry of Finance, *Economic Report*).

The availability of revenue was matched by a commitment to social services. Although the bulk of government expenditures on development has gone to the economic sector, the social sector received between 13 per cent and 22 per cent of total expenditures for each of the five-year plans up to 1985 (see Table 10.5). In the economic sector, the commitment to agriculture and rural development is also evident. Between 17 per cent and 27 per cent of government expenditures have been allocated to this sector. In terms of social development, education and training received the largest share, averaging between 7 per cent and 8 per cent for all the plan periods. Health, however, has consistently received less than 4 per cent.

Such investments in education and health have complementary effects on economic growth.[9] In view of this, the high growth rates observed after 1988, could be attributed to the release of human potential that have accumulated over many years of investment in human resources through the social programmes.

Although the government has been the main source of investment in education and health services in the country, private-sector financing has also played a complementary role. Data on the extent of private financing is not directly available. However, some indication can be glimpsed from the growing presence of private health and education institutions since the late 1980s. The strong performance of the economy has produced a relatively affluent middle class that is willing to pay for private educational and health services.

The largest number of private-education establishments cater to the pre-school level. In recent years, however, an increasing number of private schools and colleges providing primary, secondary, and tertiary education have been set up to meet the demand for quality education. Yet, the number enrolled in such institutions still represents a small proportion of the total.

There has also been a rise in the number of private hospitals in the country, catering mainly to the wealthy and the middle class. Private clinics run by physicians or consortia of medical practitioners have always been in existence in the urban areas to complement the services of public clinics and hospitals. The fees charged in private clinics have always been within the reach of the average wage-earning person. The most foreboding trend is the pending privatization of government hospital services throughout the country. On the whole, with increasing affluence, there has been a tendency to move away from government to private financing of social services.

Growth with Social Cohesion

Economic and social policies in Malaysia have to be carried out in ways that would minimize ethnic conflicts. Often it means accommodating the differing interests of the various ethnic communities. At the same time, the policies have to promote economic growth and interests tied to national identity. Several strategies were undertaken. The tremendous efforts put into developing health services in the rural areas helped to redress the uneven distribution of health care which otherwise would have gravitated in favour of the urban non-Malay areas at the expense of the rural Malay areas.

In education, the process of creating a national system based on the Malay language took place gradually. Primary education is allowed to be taught in several languages to address the needs of every ethnic group. Secondary education is conducted in the national language to meet national objectives. Even here, private secondary schools outside the national language are allowed to exist.

The main mechanism for ensuring ethnic equity in economic development was the New Economic Policy (NEP) which was introduced after the racial riots of 1969. Underlying this strategy is the principle of gradually redistributing wealth out of growth rather than outright expropriation, so as to 'eliminate the identification of race with economic function'.[10] The indigenous population was targeted to own at least 30 per cent of the corporate wealth and account for a similar proportion of modern-sector employment by 1990. This affirmative action programme would be implementated in such a way that 'no group would feel any sense of deprivation'. A twenty-year period was given to private enterprise to fulfil the restructuring objectives.

The wealth and employment-restructuring objectives were implemented through the Industrial Co-ordination Act (ICA) under which companies with shareholders' funds of above RM2.5m. would have to allocate 30 per cent equity to the Bumiputra population. To speed up Bumiputra participation in the commercial sector, the government set up state enterprises which provided employment opportunities at every level. Small and medium-sized non-Bumiputra enterprises were basically unaffected by the ICA and left to proliferate. The long time-frame, gradual approach, and presence of escape routes for non-Bumiputra businesses helped to limit ethnic animosity towards the policy.

Conclusion

The Malaysian experience demonstrates it is possible to balance economic and social goals. Economic growth policies, especially industrialization policies, worked hand in hand with redistribution policies, such as the NEP, to achieve growth with interethnic equity. Poverty was reduced as a result of the economic policies which created employment in both the urban and rural areas. Economic development in turn generated revenue for the government to finance the provision of social services, such as health and education. In the rural sector, social services were provided as an integral part of agricultural development programmes. This could be seen in the FELDA schemes as well as the organizational set-up of the planning machinery for rural development.

Rents were available first in the form of tin and rubber export earnings, then oil-palm and later petroleum revenues. The rapid human capital formation enabled the country to rapidly scale up the skill-intensity of exportables. The rapidity of the economic growth in fact has enabled Malaysian policy-makers to be relatively unconcerned by demographic pressure. Population growth rates are much higher than in most neighbouring countries, and there is active encouragement of a policy of population growth—unlike most other developing countries.

Notes

1. Bruton (1992: 187).
2. All these figures are from UNFPA (1993: 11).
3. This analysis of the educational experience would not have been possible without the valuable information provided by Mr Kum Boo who, in various capacities, played an important role in helping to promote universal primary and secondary education in the country.
4. This section owes a great deal to Dr Lim Ewe Seng who provided useful information on many of the health programmes. Dr Lim served in the health profession in various capacities, as a public health officer, and medical planner.
5. See *Sixth Malaysia Plan, 1991–1995*, p. 100.
6. Various estimates of the social rate of return to land settlement have been made. Despite being sensitive to interest rates and price level chosen, the estimated rates exceed 10%. See Lim, 1973: 194.
7. From the *Fifth Malaysia Plan, 1986–1990*.
8. See Shamsul Bahrin and Perera, 1977.

9. Bhalla and Kharas (1992) found that the return to investment in physical capital in the country was about 11% whereas the social rate of return to education was 11.5%.
10. See *Second Malaysia Plan, 1971–1975*.

Bibliography

Abdul Majid Ismail (1971), *Rural Health*, Kuala Lumpur: Ministry of Health, Malaysia.

Ahmad Idriss (1990), *Malaysia's New Economic Policy*, Kuala Lumpur: Pelanduk Publications.

Anand, S. (1983), *Inequality and Poverty in Malaysia: Measurement and Decomposition*, Washington, DC: Oxford University Press.

Bhalla, Surjit, and Kharas, Himi (1992), 'Growth and Equity in Malaysia: Policies and Consequences', in Hoe Yoke Teh and Kim Leng Goh (eds.), *Malaysia's Economic Vision: Issues and Challenges*, Kuala Lumpur: Pelanduk Publications.

Bruton, Henry J. (1992), *Sri Lanka and Malaysia: The Political Economy of Poverty, Equity, and Growth* (A World Bank Comparative Study), Washington, DC: Oxford University Press.

Chee, Heng Leng (1990), *Health and Health Care in Malaysia: Present Trends and Implications for the Future*, Kuala Lumpur: University of Malaya.

—— (1992), 'Changing Patterns of Physical Health in Malaysia: Implications for the Health Care Sector', in *Caring Society: Emerging Issues and Future Directions*, Kah Sin Cho and Ismail Muhd. Salleh (eds.), Kuala Lumpur: Institute of Strategic and International Studies Malaysia.

Chew, Tow Yow (1973), 'Primary Education in Malaysia,' *Bulletin of the Unesco Regional Office for Education in Asia*, 14 (June).

Cho, Kah Sin, and Salleh, Ismail Muhd. (eds.) (1992), *Caring Society: Emerging Issues and Future Directions*, Kuala Lumpur: Institute of Strategic and International Studies Malaysia.

Choo, Keng-Kun (1989), 'Modernisation and Social Development in Malaysia,' in *Regional Development Dialogue*, 10/2 (Summer).

Demery, David, and Demery, Lionel (1992), *Adjustment and Equity in Malaysia*, Paris: Development Centre of the Organisation for Economic Cooperation and Development.

Esman, Milton (1972), *Administration and Development in Malaysia: Institution Building and Reform in a Plural Society*, Ithaca: Cornell University Press.

Fong, Chan Onn (1986), *Technological Leap: Malaysian Industry in Transition*, Singapore: Oxford University Press.

Gan, Wee Beng (1988), 'Macroeconomic Policy, Real Exchange Rate and International Competitiveness—the Malaysian Experience during the 1980s', Kuala Lumpur: Faculty of Economics and Administration, University of Malaya, mimeo.

ISIS Malaysia (1986), 'ISIS First National Conference on Poverty,' 6th and 7th January 1986, Institute of Strategic and International Studies, Kuala Lumpur.

Ismail Muhd. Salleh, and Meyanathan, Saha Dhevan (1993), *Malaysia: Growth, Equity and Structural Transformation* (The Lessons of East Asia Series), Washington, DC: World Bank Publication.

Jayesuria, L. W. (1967), *A Review of the Rural Health Services in West Malaysia*, Kuala Lumpur: Ministry of Health (for the National Health Council).

Jenkins, Glenn P., and Lai, Andrew (1989), *Trade, Exchange Rate and Agricultural Policies in*

Malaysia (A World Bank Comparative Study on the Political Economy of Agricultural Pricing Policies, Washington, DC: Johns Hopkins University Press.

Jomo, K. S. (1990), *Growth and Structural Change in the Malaysian Economy*, London: Macmillan Press.

Khan, M. Adil (1991), *Initiatives in Efficiency: Experience of Malaysia in Monitoring and Evaluation* (A Report commissioned by the Central Evaluation Office [CEO]), UNDP, CEO Evaluation Studies, no. 2/91.

Lim, Sow Ching (1976), *Land Development Schemes in Peninsular Malaysia: A Study of Benefits and Costs*, Kuala Lumpur: Rubber Research Institute of Malaysia.

MacAndrews, Colin (1977), *Mobility and Modernisation: The Federal Land Development Authority and Its Role in Modernising the Rural Malays*, Gajah Mada: Gajah Mada University Press.

MMA (Malaysian Medical Association) (1980), *The Future of the Health Services in Malaysia* (A Report of a Committee of the Council of the Malaysian Medical Association), Kuala Lumpur: Malaysian Medical Association.

Meerman, Jacob (1980), 'Public Services to Meet Basic Needs', in *Malaysia: Growth and Equity in a Multiracial Society*, Kevin Young, Willem C. F. Bussink, and Parvez Hasan (eds.), Baltimore: Johns Hopkins University Press.

Mohd. Yaakub Johari (1991), *Issues and Strategies in Rural Development*, Kota Kinabalu: Institute for Development Studies (Sabah).

Rampal, Lekhraj, Oothuman, Pakeer, and Nagaraj, Shyamala (1988), *A Study on the Health Care Delivery System in Plantations in Peninsular Malaysia*, Kuala Lumpur: Malaysian Medical Association.

Shamsul, Bahrin and Perera, P. D. A. (1977), *FELDA: 21 Years of Land Development*, Kuala Lumpur: FELDA.

Snodgrass, Donald R. (1980), *Inequality and Economic Development in Malaysia*, Kuala Lumpur: Oxford University Press.

Tan, Siew Hoey (1989), *Government Interventions in the Padi and Rice Industry of Malaysia* (Report prepared for the Economic Planning Unit and World Bank Rice Industry Restructuring Project), Kuala Lumpur, mimeo.

UNFPA (United Nations Population Fund) (1993), *Family Planning and Population: A Compendium of International Statistics*, New York.

University of Malaya (1990), *Issues and Challenges for National Development* (selected papers presented during the 21st Anniversary Conference of the Faculty of Economics and Administration, Kuala Lumpur).

Wong, Francis Hoy Kee, and Ee, Tiang Hong (1971), *Education in Malaysia*, Kuala Lumpur: Heinemann Educational Books.

World Bank (1977), *Appraisal of the National Small-Scale Irrigation Project: Malaysia*, Report No. 1523, Washington, DC: World Bank.

—— (1983), *Incentive Policies in Agriculture: Sector Report on Malaysia, vol. ii, Main Report*, Washington DC: World Bank.

—— (1987), *The Jengka Triangle Projects in Malaysia: Impact Evaluation Report*, Washington, DC: World Bank.

—— (1989), *Malaysia: Matching Risks and Rewards in a Mixed Economy* (World Bank Country Study), Washington, DC: World Bank.

GOVERNMENT PUBLICATIONS

Bank Negara Malaysia, *Annual Report*, various issues.

—— *Quarterly Economic Bulletin*, various issues.

Malaysian Industrial Development Authority (MIDA), *Annual Report*, various years.

Ministry of Education Malaysia (1970), *Education in Malaysia*, Kuala Lumpur: Dewan Bahasa dan Pustaka.

—— (1985), *Report of the Cabinet Committee: To Review the Implementation of Education Policy*, Kuala Lumpur: Dewan Bahasa dan Pustaka.

—— (various years), *Educational Statistics of Malaysia*.

Ministry of Finance Malaysia, *Economic Report*, various years.

Ministry of Health, *Annual Report*, various years.

Report of the Committee on Malay Education (Barnes Report) (1951), Kuala Lumpur: Govt. Press.

Report on the Economic Aspects of Malaysia (1963), by a Mission of the International Bank for Reconstruction and Development under Jacques Rueff, Federation of Malaya: Govt. Printers.

Report of the Education Committee 1956 (Razak Report) (1966), Kuala Lumpur: Govt. Printers.

Report of the Education Review Committee 1960 (Rahman Talib Report) (1960), Federation of Malaya: Govt. Printers.

The Second Outline Perspective Plan 1991–2000 (1991), Kuala Lumpur: Govt. Printers.

GOVERNMENT FIVE-YEAR PLANS (CHRONOLOGICAL ORDER)

First Five-Year Plan 1956–60 (1956), A Plan of Development for Malaya. Kuala Lumpur: Economic Secretariat.

Second Five-Year Plan (1961), Kuala Lumpur: Govt. Printers.

Interim Review of Development in Malaya under the Second Five-Year Plan (1964), Kuala Lumpur: Govt. Printers.

First Malaysia Plan 1966–1970 (1965), Kuala Lumpur: Govt. Printers.

Mid-Term Review of the First Malaysia Plan 1966–1970 (1969), Kuala Lumpur: Govt. Printers.

Second Malaysia Plan 1971–1975 (1971), Kuala Lumpur: Govt. Printers.

Mid-Term Review of the Second Malaysia Plan 1971–1975 (1973), Kuala Lumpur: Govt. Printers.

Third Malaysia Plan 1976–1980 (1976), Kuala Lumpur: Govt. Printers.

Mid-Term Review of the Third Malaysia Plan 1976–1980 (1979), Kuala Lumpur: Govt. Printers.

Fourth Malaysia Plan 1981–1985 (1981), Kuala Lumpur: Govt. Printers.

Mid-Term Review of the Fourth Malaysia Plan 1981–1985 (1984), Kuala Lumpur: Govt. Printers.

Fifth Malaysia Plan 1986–1990 (1986), Kuala Lumpur: Govt. Printers.

Mid-Term Review of the Fifth Malaysia Plan 1986–1990 (1989), Kuala Lumpur: Govt. Printers.

Sixth Malaysia Plan 1991–1995 (1991), Kuala Lumpur: Govt. Printers.

11

Barbados: Social Development in a Small Island State

MYRTLE D. BISHOP, ROSALYN CORBIN,
AND NEVILLE C. DUNCAN

Introduction

The World Summit in Copenhagen in March 1995 defined social development as the improvement and enhancement of the quality of life for all people, requiring democratic institutions, respect for human rights and fundamental freedoms, increased and equal economic opportunities, the rule of law, promotion of respect for cultural diversity and rights of persons belonging to minorities, and an active involvement in civil society. It is manifested in the active involvement of all members of society in the affairs of the communities in which they live; gender equality and equity in all economic, social, and political activities; full access to education, health-care services, and decision-making processes; productive employment; recreational enjoyment, and spiritual expression.

Barbados is considered to have performed remarkably well in the area of social development. In 1993 it was ranked twentieth in the UNDP's Human Development Index, and first among the developing countries.

Ironically, Barbados is currently experiencing the symptoms of social decay which can be found in many other so-called 'developed' countries. These include drug abuse; chronic 'lifestyle' diseases including heart disease, cerebrovascular disease, and diabetes mellitus; and escalating crime, especially robberies and the growth of gangs. When coupled with increasing unemployment and declining food and agricultural production, the nature of social development in Barbados, as elsewhere, becomes an issue for debate, since truly holistic social development, as defined earlier, should promote community health and harmony.

This chapter analyses some of the trends in the development of primary and secondary education and in health in Barbados. The bulk of it is based on the role which has been played by the State in the development of these two sectors.

Trends in Social Indicators

This section examines trends in education and health indicators, highlighting the periods when significant expansions in enrolment occurred, and when there was a dramatic decline in the infant-mortality rate (IMR).

School enrolment and literacy

The information available is too sparse to facilitate the identification of the exact period in which there was rapid acceleration in the primary enrolment ratio. The first school for the education of the sons of slaves was established in 1818. By 1938, there was a net enrolment ratio of 88 per cent. This compared favourably with Jamaica and Trinidad and Tobago where rates were about 80 per cent. The enrolment ratio for Barbados was remarkable, since Barbados, unlike the other islands, did not have any form of compulsory attendance (e.g. West India Royal Commission, 1945).

Up to the early 1950s, the places in secondary schools were limited, after which they expanded rapidly. During the 1960s, enrolment ratios increased from 17 per cent to 69 per cent (Massiah, 1981). The data in Table 11.1 show that there was no significant difference between enrolment ratios for females and for males. The net enrolment ratios at both the primary and secondary levels exceeded 80 per cent.

Due to the expansion in enrolment, the literacy rates in the 1946 and 1970 censuses were 93 per cent and 99 per cent respectively. If one uses data on years of schooling as an indicator of very basic literacy, then Table 11.2 reveals levels exceeding 90 per cent from 1960 onwards.

TABLE 11.1. Enrolment ratios, 1970, 1980, 1990

Year	Sex	First level		Second level	
		Gross	Net	Gross	Net
1970	MF	102	86	69	—
	M	103	87	68	—
	F	101	85	70	—
1980	MF	100	97	90	87
	M	100	96	91	87
	F	100	97	90	86
1990	MF	114	97	87	80
	M	114	98	90	85
	F	113	96	83	75

Sources: UNESCO, *Statistical Yearbook*, 1970, 1980, and 1990

TABLE 11.2. Mean years of schooling by sex (15-year-olds and over, in %)

Years of schooling		1960	1970	1980	1990
Male	less than 5	6.7	7.8	2.1	1.2
	5 and over	93.3	92.2	97.9	98.8
Female	less than 5	8.6	9.8	2.6	1.5
	5 and over	91.4	90.2	97.4	98.5

Sources: Census 1960, 1970, 1980, 1990

TABLE 11.3. Infant-mortality rates per 1,000 live births

	1930	1950	1960	1970	1980	1990
Barbados	251	125	60	46	22	15
Guyana	146	—	—	79	67	45
Jamaica	141	78	51	32	12	24
Trinidad and Tobago	127	81	45	35	34	20

Sources: West India Royal Commission Report; Chief Medical Officer, Annual Reports

Mortality and life expectancy

Prior to the 1960s, IMRs in Barbados were considerably higher than in other Caribbean countries, but this changed significantly between 1950 and 1960 when the rate was halved, falling from 125 deaths to 60 deaths per 1,000 live births (see Table 11.3). The success achieved in reducing the IMR in the 1950s gained international recognition for the country. By 1992, the IMR had fallen to 13 per 1,000 live births. As a consequence of this declining rate of mortality, life expectancy at birth was 77.2 years for women and 72.9 years for men in 1990, representing an increase of 9.5 years in life expectancy for both sexes since 1960 (see Table 11.4).

There was a steady decline in the mortality rate for children 0–4 years from 1960 to 1990 and the maternal-mortality rate was low (see Table 11.4). During this period, the crude death rate ranged between 8 and 9 per 1,000 population. The principal causes of death in the early 1990s were heart disease, malignant neoplasm, cerebrovascular disease, and diabetes mellitus. This shows that non-communicable chronic diseases are assuming priority in the country's morbidity picture and mortality profile, a situation which is typical of most developed countries.

TABLE 11.4. Demographic indicators

	1960	1970	1980	1990	1992
Life expectancy, males	63.4	65.8	70.2	72.9	—
Life expectancy, females	67.7	70.9	75.2	77.2	—
Crude death rate	8.8	8.7	8.1	8.8	8.8
Under-5 (0–4) mortality rate (per 1,000 population)	17.3	10.5	5.2	4.4	3.3
Maternal-mortality rate (per 1,000 live births)	2.2	1.4	0.2	0.9	0.7
Total population	232,327	235,229	244,228	260,491	—
Population density (per sq.km.)	538	545	565	603	—
Dependency ratio (0–14)	69	68	49	38	—
Dependency ratio (65+)	12	15	17	19	—

Sources: CMO, Statistical Dept.; Census 1960, 1970, 1980, 1990

Facilitating Factors

The improvements which Barbados has recorded in the development of the health and education sectors have been heavily influenced by the implementation of programmes by the government. This section examines some of the factors which prompted the government to take action, as well as those which facilitated the development of public-sector programmes.

Physical features

By the end of the seventeenth century, an island-wide road system with the main arteries radiating from Bridgetown (the capital city and main port) had been established to cater to the needs of plantations and sugar factories. The small size of the island and the flat topography has facilitated delivery of goods and services throughout the country in a cost-effective way. In other island States, mountainous terrain has multiplied considerably (by as much as seven times) the cost of roads, international airport runways, pipe-borne water systems, electricity grids, schools, health facilities, and centres for the delivery of government-provided services. Although significant financial allocations have been made in these countries for health and education, the realized value had been significantly lower than in Barbados.

Early development of primary education

Public interest in elementary education in Barbados in the early 1800s was kindled primarily by contemporary developments in England, as well as by the fact that the emancipation of slaves, which occurred in 1838, was imminent. Whereas education for the slaves had been seen previously by the plantocracy as an aid to rebellion, it came to be regarded as a means of maintaining social control and preserving law and order.

The high enrolment ratio in the 1930s indicates that there was a desire for education; that facilities were available for the provision of education; and that parents took advantage of the educational opportunities to ensure that their children obtained at least an elementary education. In a presentation to the West India Royal Commission (Moyne Commission),[1] the then secretary of the Board of Education attested to the fact that Barbadian parents were exceedingly keen on getting an education for their children. This desire was no doubt governed by the notion that a sound education would open doors to improved standards of living for the family and create opportunities for social mobility. Although slavery had been abolished, children were still employed in child gangs in the fields; and therefore many parents, however poor, saw education as a means of escape from the rigours of the plantations.

The Church played an important role providing educational facilities. Two differing views have been advanced to explain this phenomenon. One suggestion is that the Church was prompted by humanitarian and philanthropic motives. The other view is that the schooling which the Church offered reflected its teachings and served to reinforce obedience and servitude. Whatever the reason, the disadvantaged black population benefited from this activity.

Demographic factors

Barbados has one of the highest population densities in the world. In the 1960 census, the population was just over 230,000 with a population density of 538 per sq. km. By 1990, the population had risen to about 261,000 and the population density was 603 per sq. km. (see Table 11.4). Barbados recorded an average annual growth rate of less than 1 per cent, the lowest rate in the Caribbean, during each of the three decades between 1960 and 1990, as a result of migration and birth-control policies. Barbados is considered to have entered an advanced stage of demographic transition.

Although Barbados has not developed a population policy, in terms of clearly defined roles, institutions, and resources focused specifically on population issues, the government has been actively involved in programmes—first for emigration and then for birth control—which influenced population growth.

Since emancipation, emigration has had an impact on population growth in Barbados. During the period 1861–91, emigration was instrumental in curbing population growth, and in the period 1891–1921, emigration flows were large enough to result in declining populations (Massiah, 1981). Since the late nineteenth century, migration has resulted from both government-sponsored schemes and individual initiatives. Up to the end of the Second World War, emigrants were mainly males. Since then females have constituted a higher proportion than in previous years.

Emigration flows have contributed to economic growth through remittances. At the same time, it has been argued that the loss of important adult figures has had a destabilizing effect on family life in some instances.

Since 1960, the main contributing factor to population stability has been declining fertility. Compared with other countries of the region, Barbados recorded high levels of use of birth control. The total fertility rate declined by just over 60 per cent from 1960 to 1980; the birth rate in 1992 was 16 per 1,000 population, representing a decline of 50 per cent from 1950. The data available indicated that women using contraceptives increased from 47 per cent in 1980 to 55 per cent in 1988.

Four factors have been identified as being responsible for motivating the population to expand the use of contraceptives. These factors are rising income levels and the attendant increases in consumption; increased levels of educational attainment by women; the gradual shift in female employment from low-productivity to high-productivity occupations; and the Information, Education and Communication (IEC) programmes of the Barbados Family Planning Association.

The distribution of the population by broad age-groups shows that the 0–14 age range fell steadily from 1960 to 1990 both in absolute terms and proportionately. The 15–64 age-group increased after 1970, while the population 65 years and over rose to 11.9 per cent in 1990. As a result, there was a significant decline in youth dependency while the dependency ratio of the elderly increased over the period (see Table 11.4). It must be noted that expansion of the older population, with a decline in the youth, is an observed feature of 'developed' countries.

Growing demand

The changing expectations of the population, and the attendant increase in demand for services, have played an important role in motivating the government to implement social programmes. The mid-1940s marked the start of a period of significant developments. The population had been agitating for social change since the beginning of the century. Serious discontent had resulted from a combination of factors: a steady increase in the population; a depressed economy severely affecting the poor, particularly those who worked as agricultural labourers; very unsatisfactory living, housing, and sanitary conditions for many people; and the desire for more adequate and satisfactory education. The demand for improved conditions resulted in the riots of 1937 (Hoyos, 1974). The riots jolted the Colonial Office out of its complacency and prompted emergency action in the form of the Moyne Commission. The clamour for social change gained impetus from the publication in 1940 of the report of this commission, which recommended a comprehensive programme of social welfare reform. Action on the recommendations was delayed until after the Second World War.

Long before the international electronic media came into their homes, Barbadians were becoming increasingly aware of the facilities and services available in developed countries. This knowledge was acquired largely through contacts with nationals who had migrated to the UK, the USA, and Canada.

Political commitment

During the 1940s, the lower and middle classes in Barbados benefited from greater representation in the House of Assembly. This political development enabled leaders, who were not only aware of the needs of the population but were also agitating for economic and social reform, to enter Parliament. Then, in 1946, the governor of the colony announced that the composition of the Executive Committee, the policy-making body, would more clearly reflect the representation in the House of Assembly. Furthermore, the members of the committee would be asked to assume responsibility for the general policy relating to particular departments of the government. In other words, there was a significant move toward 'responsible government' (Hoyos, 1974).

Since 1951, when elections were first held under universal adult suffrage, the political scene in Barbados has been dominated by two political parties. Successive regimes have been committed to a policy of ensuring the availability of quality health care and educational facilities. The provision of more and better services in these sectors became the key factors in partisan competition, and ensured that significant budgetary resources were always committed.

During different phases of social development, governments, colonial and local, have worked together with the Church, concerned citizens, and, more recently, special groups and associations to resolve problems during times of crisis. The establishment of a 'social contract' between the State, labour, and capital in August 1995 symbolizes, more formally, this consensus.

Social stability

During the period between the mid-1800s and the late 1930s, the Barbadian society was held together by economic dependence on wage labour, the desire for education, and social mobility. In addition, Christianity and education contributed by emphasizing a value system of conformity and respect.

Following the publication of the Moyne Commission, the demands of the population were integrated, and institutionalized within a formal political and trade union structure, led by British educated intellectuals with the respect and backing of the working class. This process has continued up to the present time.

Role of women

The improvement in the health status of the population can be attributed partly to women in their roles as nurturers of children and managers of households. During the past two decades, the government has taken active steps to enhance women's capacity to perform these tasks efficiently.

Women have benefited from improvements in health services, and they have equal access to educational and training facilities. The authorities have enacted legislation designed to guarantee women's rights and eliminate discrimination. Women have equal access to productive resources and the inequality in the sharing of power and decision-making has narrowed. In 1990, they formed 48 per cent of the total labour force. In addition, the government of Barbados has ratified the Convention on the Elimination of All Forms of Discrimination against Women, which came into force in 1981.

In spite of these developments, there are areas of concern. Many women, who are engaged full time in productive activities, are still performing most of the household tasks. This means that women, more so than men, are likely to be overburdened by the workload associated with their combined reproductive and productive roles. In addition, the tasks of coping with the problems resulting form economic hardship, fall largely on the shoulders of women in both female- and male-headed households.

Macroeconomic trends and social development

Economic conditions in Barbados in the 1930s were depressed largely because of a crisis in the sugar industry, which at that time dominated the economy, and because of the world Depression. However, the resurgence of the sugar industry after the end of the Second World War led to a period of buoyancy in the economy in the 1950s and early 1960s.

At no time since 1946 has the Barbadian economy experienced a sustained period of very high growth. Since the total population hardly grew by 12 per cent between 1960 and 1990, slow GDP growth (averaging 1.5 per cent per annum over the three decades) was still reflected in rising standards of living.[2] Emigration was a major reason for the slow growth in the population (apart from the falling TFR), while remittances from emigrants helped raise the standard of living. In spite of the 1973–4 oil-price shocks and the accompanying stagflation, the Barbados economy never descended into unmitigated disaster. Indeed, by 1976, the economy was in an upward phase based upon good tourism-sector performance (Jamaica's disaster, Barbados's boon). This was supported by the growing capacity of the economy to contain its oil bill and a modest improvement in the manufacturing sector (sugar, rum, electronic components, etc.) during the 1973–80 period. Indeed, the balance of payments went into the negative only once, in 1977.

Sectoral Analysis

This section examines the processes which led to the significant increase in enrolment in schools and the decline in the infant-mortality rate. The mechanisms, which have been instituted to develop and expand facilities for primary and secondary education and primary health care, are also discussed.

Education

School enrolment and literacy

Between 1834 and the end of the century, education for the masses was financed by the central government, local authorities, private humanitarian organizations, and the Church. Education was also provided privately. The first grant from the legislature for popular education was made in 1846 (MoE, 1960). By the end of the century, the government was financing the entire cost of education provided in Church-run schools, while the Church was responsible for administration. This relationship between church authorities and the State was unique. In other Caribbean countries, there were two types of arrangements: in one situation, the State assumed full responsibility for both costs and administration; in the other, the religious denominations were responsible for administration, while expenditure was financed partly by contributions from communicants and partly by grants from state funds (West India Royal Commission, 1945). The unique arrangement in Barbados worked adequately until the 1950s when the State deemed it necessary to take full responsibility for all aspects of primary and secondary education.

Up to the 1950s, the secondary schools catered primarily for whites and middle-class browns and the children of the comparatively small black professional population. Government programmes of free education after 1960 provided the opportunity for the majority black population to aspire to upward social mobility through education.

The expansion in enrolment in secondary schools was initiated during the 1950s, with the construction, by the government, of four secondary modern schools for both boys and girls. The total enrolment of the first two schools which were constructed was 1,500 in their first year of operation, compared to an enrolment of about 3,000 in the eight existing government-aided secondary schools. The programme of expansion intensified during the 1960s. The new schools, which were located in both urban and rural areas, were designed to provide technical and vocational education as well as traditional academic studies.

The important developments that have occurred in primary and secondary education since 1960 include:

- the abolition of tuition fees in government secondary schools;[3]

- the passing of legislation making education compulsory between the ages of 5 and 16;[4]

- the enactment of legislation providing for education of children of compulsory age, who require special education;[5]

- the implementation of a programme to ensure that girls have equal access to secondary schools;[6]

- the introduction of termly reports for students in primary schools;[7]

- the implementation of the Programme of Assistance to Approved Independent Schools.[8]

The current educational system is structured into tiers, with some overlapping, comprising early childhood (3–5 years), primary (5–11 years), secondary (11–16 years), and tertiary. Education at primary and secondary levels is provided mainly in government schools. Over the years, enrolment at government schools has expanded to such an extent that the private primary and secondary schools account for less than 5 per cent of total enrolment.[9]

(a) Access to schooling

There is universal access to primary and secondary education, including private institutions. A number of programmes have been designed to enable all students to benefit from the educational services and facilities available:

- subsidized school meals are provided for primary-school students;

- under the school's medical service, ophthalmic and dental services are provided free of charge, mainly to primary-school children, at the polyclinics;

- under the textbook loan scheme, students in government and approved independent schools are issued textbooks on the payment of a nominal annual rental fee;[10]

- subsidized bus fares;

- provision is made for female students of compulsory school-age who become pregnant to resume their education after confinement.

The ministry of education has developed programmes to deal with a variety of problems that can have an adverse effect on the performance of students and on their preparation for the world of work. These mechanisms include: the guidance and counselling programme and the provision of psychological services; the establishment of the school attendance section; and the establishment of the drug education programme.

(b) Quality and efficiency of education

Successive governments have had the conviction that teachers are the primary source of instruction and that they have the most direct impact on quality. To this end, various programmes have been instituted to improve the quality of instruction and teaching with emphasis being placed on the provision of training in specialized areas such as remedial education and early childhood education. Educational institutions have access to appropriate instructional and educational materials through the services provided by the Audio Visual Aids Department of the ministry of education. Data on teacher–student ratios at the primary level reveal relatively low ones of 1 : 29 and 1 : 18 for the years 1980 and 1990 respectively. However, the ministry of education is seeking to achieve cost-effectiveness in the delivery of services by reducing the number of small schools which are very uneconomical to operate.

(c) Automatic promotion, repetition, and drop-outs

The ministry of education employs a procedure of automatic promotion in primary schools. Emphasis is placed on moving children through the various stages, so that at the age of 11 years they are in their final year at primary level and are appropriately placed to take the secondary-school entrance examination. This system has been criticized widely, primarily because it does not give enough consideration to the readiness of the child to move on from one stage to the other and it ignores the various and varying learning abilities of children.

The system of automatic promotion has virtually eliminated repetition in primary schools. As a result, repetition occurs only in those situations where a child is working above his/her age-group, and must repeat a year at some time or stage. In most primary schools, a homogeneous grouping system is employed where children are grouped and taught according to age and learning abilities.

Data on completion rates are scarce, but it is understood that the number of drop-outs is low. It would appear that the monitoring mechanisms employed by the school attendance section and other programmes which have been designed to enable students in straitened circumstances to benefit from the educational services and facilities have contributed to the low figure.

(d) Remedial education

In an effort to ensure that the rate of illiteracy does not increase through complacency or negligence, the ministry of education has initiated several programmes to counter problems in reading experienced by primary-school students. These include the introduction of: an in-service training programme in the teaching of reading and remedial methods of reading; the implementation of a remedial programme in each primary school and in selected secondary shools; and the appointment of a peripatetic teacher to provide on-site guidance and support to teachers in this programme.

(e) Decentralization

Decentralization in the public sector has been limited. A system of local government which was in existence up until the 1960s was abolished. Under the provisions of the Education Act of 1981, the boards of management of government secondary schools are responsible for the management, control, operation, and maintenance of these schools. Moreover, the ministry of education has identified the Parent Teachers' Association (PTA) as the organization which will facilitate the enhancement of the relationship between the school and the community (Barbados,

Development Plan, 1988–93). All secondary schools and the majority of primary schools have PTAs. However, at this time, neither the boards nor the PTAs really have the power or authority to carry out these tasks, and the provisions remain in name only.

Constraints

Barbados has recorded much progress in education since 1960. However, there are a number of factors which can have a negative impact on the ability of the education sector to 'develop the people's potential to the fullest . . . stimulate creative and innovative solutions to problem-solving and prepare citizens for successful living in a technological age' (MoE, 1993). Notwithstanding this recognition, there are inadequate signs of urgency in achieving these objectives, especially in the presence of reduced real financial resources.

Although the government has repeatedly promoted the importance of early childhood education, there has been limited expansion by the government in this area. A lack of appropriate facilities and trained personnel have often been cited as the main reasons.

A number of weaknesses have been identified in the primary education system:

• Teachers require additional training in order to effectively diagnose and address learning difficulties.

• There is a shortage of school-based library resources.

• There is growing recognition that the secondary school's entrance examination has an adverse effect on curriculum, instruction, pupil achievement, and, ultimately, quality of education. The results of this examination tend to determine the type of secondary school to which a student gains admission. As a consequence, preparation for the examination tends to be associated with restrictive teaching methodologies; a disproportionate time being allocated to the teaching of mathematics and English; neglect of students with learning difficulties; and the limiting of the creative potential of students (MoE, 1993).

The main issues which have a bearing on the provision of quality secondary education relate to:

• the method of selection of students, which gives rise to the perception, in the minds of the public, that there are prestigious and non-prestigious schools;

• the fact that there are few teachers adequately trained to teach technical and vocational subjects;

• limited certification of student achievement; and

• restricted opportunity for progression in technical and vocational education programmes (MoE, 1993).

The inadequate level of functional literacy and numeracy manifested by many school-leavers and the weak performance of many students who take the approved English-speaking Caribbean Certificate examinations are also matters which suggest the need for deep reform in the educational system. The ministry of education has failed to reduce élitism in the school system significantly, to provide more adequately in each school for technical and vocational education, or to provide wider opportunities for professional achievement and certification in technical and vocational education. These have occurred in spite of the fact that schools have been provided with trained, graduate teachers, allowing for a generalized equality of conditions. The system of allocating the best students to the traditionally better schools and the mind-set which permits this continuation are probably at the root of the difficulty.

Despite the growing global recognition that mentally and physically challenged children would learn best when integrated into the classroom with children without disabilities, this is not attempted in Barbados. Basic provisions for wheelchairs and walkers are only now making an appearance in educational institutions. Teachers and administrators continue to discriminate against these persons, and there are instances where they are unwilling to permit them into their institutions.

Health

Infant-mortality rate

The high IMR in the first half of this century in Barbados was caused by a number of factors, including inadequate maternity services, even at hospitals; inadequate knowledge of basic principles of child care; and shortages of medical officers of health who would have provided highly technical public services such as maternal and child welfare, the control of communicable diseases, school medical work, and health education (Barbados, 1945). In addition, the proportion of government expenditure devoted to health was one of the lowest in the English-speaking Caribbean (West India Royal Commission, 1945).

The report of the Moyne Commission contained recommendations which had a positive influence on developments in the health sector. Some of these recommendations had been made earlier by medical personnel but hardly any action had been taken by the House of Assembly (Ramsey, 1979). Some sections of the decision-making community displayed ignorance by arguing that the high IMR was due to overpopulation while others even held the view that the high IMR was a safety valve which helped to keep the population down (Barbados, 1945). At that time, health services in the public sector were provided partly by the central government and partly by the vestries, which, *inter alia*, were responsible for sanitation. The chief medical officer acted in an advisory capacity with respect to sanitation, without any power to ensure the adoption of regulations by the parochial boards, whose members were appointed by the vestries.

The establishment of the Department of Medical Services in 1947 marked the first step towards organizing a cohesive medical system, while the Public Health Act of 1954 contained the first comprehensive public-health code, with provisions for the development of an institutional framework and for the establishment of health centres and subclinics (Massiah, 1981).

During the 1950s, the government established three health centres which were strategically located to facilitate access by both urban and rural communities. The health centres provided maternal and child health services and conducted STD clinics.[11] These developments in the post-war period represented a fundamental change in government policy, when 'the State assumed a proactive leadership role in public health with the creation of health centres and a vigorous community health service run essentially by a dedicated corps of public health nurses' (Alleyne, 1991). These policy changes were related to the rise of trade unionism, mass political parties, and the beginning of the transfer of political authority to the majority black population.

The authorities were convinced that the health education and immunization programmes, provided at the health centres, contributed in a meaningful way to the fall in the infant-mortality rate in the 1950s (Ramsey, 1979). However, the work of public-health inspectors, proper garbage collection and disposal, the provision of potable pipe-borne water, better personal hygiene, the use of pit latrines and water cabinets, and the reduction in the widespread exploitation of workers and general poverty probably had a greater impact. The already high rate of literacy among women enabled them to use the best available health practices, as well.

The data on causes of infant deaths indicated that deaths from nutrition-related diseases fell by 70.2 per cent during the period 1955–60. The improvements also resulted from the application of weaning habits and feeding practices which were learned through the health education programmes.

The achievement of better health occurred at a time when the entire population already had easy access to potable water, either through connections to private property or through public standpipes. The first significant intervention by the government, with respect to domestic sanitation facilities, came in 1959, when the government, with the assistance of UNICEF and WHO, implemented an environmental project to provide pit latrines for households, by which time considerable progress had already been made in reducing the IMR.

Primary health-care since 1960

For the purpose of this analysis, two categories of health care are identified—the delivery of personal health services and the implementation of public-health programmes.[12]

(a) Personal health services

The developments in the provision of primary health care in the 1960s included the expansion of facilities providing maternity services and the establishment of out-patient clinics mainly for pensioners and patients on welfare. However, the major health programme centred around the expansion of curative services, with the opening of the new government acute general hospital (CMO, 1991–2). During this period, there was a deceleration in the decline in the IMR when compared to the 1950s. Ramsey, while not asserting that there was a causal relationship between the deceleration and the nature of government expenditure, nevertheless draws attention to the fact that the 1950s had witnessed an expansion of public-health services and preventive medicine, while the 1960s saw the development of curative services (Ramsey, 1979).

Polyclinics: Up to the 1970s, persons seeking free medical (primary) care either visited the emergency ward of the government acute general hospital or were seen by district medical officers, after having been declared eligible for such assistance by the relevant authority. The situation changed when the government embarked on a programme which was centred around the establishment of polyclinics and aimed at decentralizing the delivery of medical care. The process of decentralization was designed to limit the incidence of the inappropriate use of tertiary services and to contain the cost of providing primary health care to the patient.

There are eight polyclinics which provide promotive, preventive, curative, and rehabilitative services free of charge. They are strategically located across the island and serve catchment areas, ranging from 20,000 to 50,000 persons. These institutions differ from the health centres which were established in the 1950s by the services which they provide. The specific services available are: maternal and child health services; family-life development programmes including family planning; ophthalmic and dental care primarily for children; general medical care, with clinics for hypertension, diabetes, and STDs; laboratory, radiological, and pharmaceutical services; nutrition services; community mental health services; and environmental health services.

The referral system between the polyclinics, district hospitals, and the government hospital, and vice versa, operates reasonably well, yet there are complaints that the general hospital emergency services are being preferred by some patients, and for the elderly the clinics are used for social intercourse.

There are several factors which can affect access to the services provided by the polyclinics. Two of these factors can lead to the utilization of the facilities at the acute general hospital for the delivery of primary health-care. The polyclinics have limited hours of operation while the hospital is open twenty-four hours per day. Moreover, there will be persons who have more confidence in the services the hospital offers than in those provided by the polyclinics. An examination of data on out-patient attendances at the hospital for the years 1980, when the polyclinic system was in its early stages, and 1991 reveal that the number of attendances in 1991 was only 17.5 per cent lower than in 1980. The data suggest that the services of the acute general hospital are still being preferred.

A third factor can arise in cases where there is a stigma attached to the utilization of the services provided in the polyclinic, thus leading to a demand for services in the private sector. Such a situation is a matter for concern when it relates to low-income persons who should be taking full advantage of the services available in the polyclinic.

Maternal and child health services: The government has developed a comprehensive maternal and child-health programme within the polyclinics. All pregnant women are encouraged to attend clinics before the twelfth week of gestation, and the authorities have set a target of 100 per cent attendance by the year 2000. For many years, all deliveries have taken place in health institutions and, as long ago as 1975, the proportion was 99 per cent. Health sisters are required to visit all mothers within ten days of delivery to ensure that lactation is established and to encourage mothers to breast-feed exclusively. However, this target is not always achieved. Infants and children, up to 5 years old, are monitored at all polyclinics where their nutritional status is assessed. Their mothers are advised on feeding methods and routine immunizations are performed. The authorities are making a determined effort, through increased community visits by health sisters, to identify children who do not attend child-health clinics.

Barbados Drug Service: The establishment of the Barbados Drug Service (BDS) in 1980 was regarded as a significant achievement in the delivery of health services. The objectives of this institution are, *inter alia*, to prepare, maintain, and update the Barbados national drug formulary; to make arrangements for the selection, procurement, distribution, and utilization of formulary drugs free of cost, at point of service, in both the public and private sectors; to provide a continuous supply of formulary drugs to all government health-care institutions and the private sector; and to rationalize the use of formulary drugs and reduce their cost to the public.

Under the special benefit service of the BDS, the following are eligible to receive drugs free of cost, at point of service: persons 65 years and over; children under 16 years of age; persons who receive prescribed formulary drugs for the treatment of hypertension, diabetes, cancer, epilepsy, and asthma.

Cost containment is an important objective in the operations of the BDS, and a number of measures have been adopted to achieve this goal. The organization tries to limit expenditure on salaries and overheads to 12 per cent of its budget. There is an agreed pricing formula for drugs purchased by persons not included in the special benefit service. Limits are placed on the supply of medication for particular ailments, where it is felt that prolonged use of the drugs is not necessary, with provisions being made for exceptional cases. The BDS calculates the cost per month of a range of drugs for selected ailments and makes this information available to doctors and pharmacists to assist them in prescribing drugs in a rational manner. The operations of the BDS are computerized so that it can monitor the utilization of drugs by individuals. In recent years, the BDS has paid close attention to the new area of managed health care. The underlying premiss is that the skilful use of drugs at the primary-care level can lower the demand for tertiary-care services by reducing admissions to hospitals and by limiting the length of stay of persons who have to be admitted.

During the period 1983–93, the proportion of the current health budget devoted to supplying drugs to all patients in the public sector and the majority of those in the private sector was less than 10 per cent.[13] The operations have been internationally recognized, and in 1983 WHO designated the BDS a WHO Collaborating Centre for Drug Supply Management. In addition, the organization has provided technical assistance to other CARICOM member States.[14]

The operations of the BDS have been adversely affected by a number of factors. The budgetary constraints, which were imposed after the economic crisis in the early 1990s, were felt by the organization. There is a need to enhance the institutional capacity of the BDS through the training of the staff, and the activities of the organization are hampered by the absence of facilities for marketing its services. In addition, there has been constant conflict between the medics and administrators about the purpose and decisions of the BDS.

(b) Public health programmes

Immunization: Since 1970, the government has intensified its effort to control diseases which are preventable by vaccination. Fig. 11.1 shows that in 1990, immunization coverage exceeded 80 per cent.[15] The Expanded Programme on Immunization (EPI) was introduced in 1974. However, there has been complete coverage of 5-year-olds against diphtheria, pertussis, tetanus, poliomyelitis, and measles since 1971, when legislation was passed providing for compulsory immunization of children entering school for the first time.

The immunization programme is fully integrated into the primary health-care programme, and immunizations are performed routinely at child-health clinics, at the government polyclinics, and by pediatricians in the private sector. Immunization against tuberculosis is provided in schools and is also administered to those

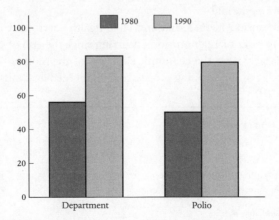

Fig. 11.1 Immunization coverage: percentage of children less than 1 year old

persons who show a negative reaction to tuberculin. The Ministry of Health anticipates that it will achieve 100 per cent immunization coverage of children less than
1-year-old through the health-promotion activities of medical personnel who
undertake community visits.

Nutrition: Data on health outcomes relating to nutrition are scarce. The proportion of infants with low birth weight was 10.3 per cent in 1993. The information
which is available suggests that the nutritional status of children under 5 years is a
matter for concern. The malnutrition ratio was 2 per 1,000 in 1980, but the degree
of malnutrition today is not known. However, the results of a pilot survey on the
nutritional status of children in this age-group conducted in polyclinics during the
early 1990s, revealed that both malnutrition and obesity were prevalent (CMO,
1991–2). Table 11.5 indicates that there was a steady increase in per capita daily
calorie and protein supply.

A supplementary feeding programme for schoolchildren has been in existence
for more than fifty years. Substantial improvement in this feeding scheme came in
the early 1960s when the school meals programme, which placed emphasis on
nutritional value, was introduced with the assistance of the World Food Programme.

During the period 1967–78, two programmes embracing continuity of care were
implemented in an effort to deal with the problem of the high incidence of protein-
energy malnutrition (PEM) in preschool children from low-income groups
(Ramsey, 1979). Investigations had revealed that the pediatric problems in the government hospital centred around long-stay patients with PEM, complicated by
gastroenteritis and respiratory-tract infections and by overcrowding and cross-
infection on the ward. The researchers were satisfied with the results of the two
programmes and concluded that the statistics on mortality suggested that during
the 1960s and 1970s, malnutrition was a problem of diminishing severity and magnitude and that the health profile of Barbadian preschool children registered a
marked improvement (ibid.).

With the expansion in maternal and child-health services, it is reasonable to
assume that any cases of malnutrition occurring since the end of the 1970s would
have resulted largely from the economic situation of the mother rather than from
lack of knowledge of the weaning process and infant-feeding habits.[16]

TABLE 11.5. Per capita food supply

	1962	1970	1980	1987
Daily calorie supply per capita (units)	2,602	2,890	3,120	3,193
Daily protein supply per capita (grams)	68.7	79.5	86.4	99.1

Source: Ministry of Agriculture, 1989

The National Nutrition Centre, which was established in 1972, has decentralized its activities by assigning community nutrition officers to polyclinics. These officers are responsible for the implementation of nutrition programmes in the polyclinics and catchment areas.

The National Nutrition Survey, which was conducted in 1981, revealed that, *inter alia*, the incidence of obesity, hypertension, and diabetes was high, and a number of recommendations were made in respect of the findings. Two programmes relating to these recommendations have been initiated in recent times. The Ministry of Health has developed a policy on breast-feeding, with basic guidelines that are being enforced in its health-care institutions. A second programme is being implemented by the National Nutrition Centre which is seeking to establish a nutrition surveillance system for children under 5 years, with the assistance of Pan-American Health Organization.

During the past two decades, the public has become more conscious of nutrition and the importance of proper dietary habits as a result of the intensification of the information, education, and communication (IEC) programmes relating to nutrition. However, in view of the fact that a National Nutrition Survey has not been conducted since 1981, questions can be raised about the capacity to make a meaningful assessment of the extent and degree of improvement in the health and nutritional status of the population.

Water: There has been a significant increase in the proportion of dwelling units with piped water on the premises, with the figure reaching 94 per cent in 1990 (see Fig. 11.2). During the period under review, the principal task of government has been to provide an adequate supply of water to meet the increasing needs of domestic, commercial, and industrial consumers, as well as those of the agricultural sector. There are four main factors which can have an influence on the ability of the authorities to satisfy the demand for water. These are the quantity of resources, the extent to which water conservation measures are applied, pollution of groundwater, and the increase in demand for water. There is also a seasonal problem when a period of drought leads to a fall in the groundwater level.

Barbados obtains practically all of its water from underground aquifers, but the time is fast approaching when the country will have to identify supplementary sources of water. With respect to water-conservation measures, IEC programmes are being used to persuade consumers to use water wisely. However, reports in the press suggest that the government corporation responsible for providing the population with water has not been operating efficiently. The coral limestone which comprises sixth-sevenths of the surface of Barbados acts as a filtering process, but there are potential sources of pollution of groundwater. The mechanisms which are currently being employed to protect the potable water supply are the identification of water protection zones with varying levels of control for development activity and sewage management; the adoption of WHO guidelines; the introduction of waste-water disposal systems; and the monitoring of the quality of potable water.

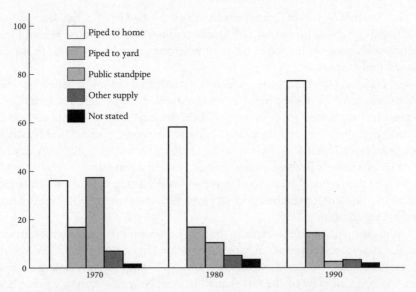

Fig. 11.2 Type of water supply, Barbados 1970–1990: percentage distribution of dwellings

Sources: 1970, 1980, 1990, Censuses

The demand for water for non-domestic purposes has increased considerably with the expansion of industrial and commercial activity and the development of tourism. Generally, the quality of drinking-water in Barbados meets the criteria set out in the WHO guidelines, except for the level of nitrates.

The costs of providing potable water from alternative sources are expected to be considerably higher than the costs currently incurred in treating groundwater. Therefore, the probability that there will be a substantial increase in water rates when water is provided from alternative sources cannot be ruled out. Such an increase would cause concern, particularly to low-income consumers.

Sanitation: The rise in the proportion of dwelling units with water cabinets was paralleled by a decrease in the proportion of dwellings units with pit latrines. The proportion of dwelling units with WCs rose from 27 per cent in 1970 to 66 per cent in 1990 (see Fig. 11.3). The project which was initiated in 1959 to provide low-cost sanitary conveniences for households is still in operation, and these units are provided, free of charge, to old-age pensioners and needy persons on the recommendation of the Welfare Department. There have been considerable improvements in the situation relating to domestic sanitation. However, persons living in some low-lying areas can experience problems during periods of heavy rainfall when flooding may result in the overflow of wells.

At the national level, the country is experiencing severe difficulty in locating suitable sites for disposal of solid waste. As a result, urgent attention is being paid to the

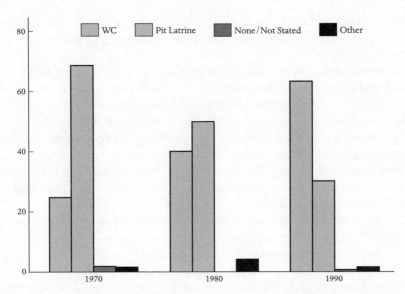

Fig. 11.3 Type of toilet facilities, Barbados 1970–1990: percentage distribution of dwellings

Sources: as Fig. 11.2

matter of solid-waste management. In the case of liquid waste, inappropriate methods of disposal along heavily populated coasts can have an adverse effect on the marine and coastal environment as well as on the tourism industry. This problem is being addressed through the installation of sewage treatment systems.

Family planning: The health sector in Barbados has developed the capacity to deliver services which can be effectively used to avoid fertility-related health risks. These services include the provision of information relating to the spacing of pregnancies and effective methods of contraception, mechanisms to ensure availability of contraceptives, and measures to facilitate access to safe abortion when necessary.

Family-planning activities were initiated by the Barbados Family Planning Association (BFPA) in 1955. This quasi-non-governmental organization was established in 1954 as a result of a recommendation made by a committee consisting of members of Parliament, which had been appointed to examine the question of overpopulation in Barbados. Successive governments have supported the activities of the BFPA, which are partly funded by an annual grant from public revenue, but the formal involvement of the public sector in family-planning activities started in the 1980s when a programme was launched at the polyclinics. Family-planning services are also provided in the private sector.

Over the years, the BFPA has sought to develop programmes which respond to the needs of the public. Such programmes include the Family Life and Peer Counselling Course which provides training for persons from 13 to 30 years—the system whereby contraceptives can be obtained from commercial outlets (mainly pharmacies) located throughout the country; and the provision of clinical services to its clients at the workplace.

The collaboration which takes place between the BFPA and the Ministries of Health and Education demonstrates how the public sector and NGOS can enter into effective and meaningful relationships. Nurses/midwives from the BFPA provide services at the government institutions where women attending antenatal and postnatal clinics are counselled. In addition, nurses from the ministry of health are assigned to the BFPA's clinic to gain practical experience in family-planning activities and to be exposed to family-planning administration. In the education sector, the BFPA, as well as the polyclinics, provide assistance in the delivery of 'Health and Family Life Education'.

The Medical Termination of Pregnancy Act, which was passed in 1983, provides for the termination of pregnancy where there is a grave injury to the physical and mental health of the woman and where there is risk of life. Written consent is required at all times. Data available from the government hospital indicate that there has been no significant increase in the number of pregnancies which have been terminated at that institution since the legislation was introduced. Data on the increase in abortions undertaken by private medical practitioners are not available.

HIV/AIDS: The first HIV/AIDS case was diagnosed in 1984 and since then there has been a steady increase in the number of reported cases. Data on the cumulative number of AIDS cases, which were reported up to the end of 1994, show that females account for just under one-quarter of the total, while children less than 15 years old represent 5 per cent. In the early years of the epidemic, homosexual males accounted for the majority of the cases, but the incidence of heterosexual transmission is rapidly increasing.

The HIV/AIDS prevention programme is implemented within the framework of a national policy, which is consistent with that of the Global Programme on AIDS of the World Health Organization (GPA/WHO). This programme is well established in the primary health-care system. In antenatal clinics, tests for HIV/AIDS are optional and are performed only after the mothers-to-be have been counselled and have given signed consent. It should also be noted that guidelines have been developed for dealing with HIV/AIDS cases in schools. The Ministry of Health has found that the level of sympathy among members of the public for HIV/AIDS patients has increased considerably (CMO, 1991–2).

The AIDS epidemic has the potential to lead to serious health and social problems if attempts to curb the spread of the disease are not successful. The authorities could find it extremely difficult to satisfy the demand for health care for AIDS patients, while at the same time meeting the needs of other patients.

Decentralization: The Ministry of Health is committed to the strategy of decentralization of primary health-care services with wide community participation in the promotion of health and the prevention of disease (Ministry of Health, *Develop-*

ment Plan, 1993–2000).[17] However, the process of achieving meaningful community participation in health management is still to be developed. It was only in 1993 that a pilot project was initiated at one polyclinic with the establishment of a district health management committee.

Trends in Government Revenue and Social Allocation

Revenue increased at an average annual rate of 12.9 per cent in the period 1960–90. An examination of the relationship between revenue and nominal GDP reveals that in the 1960s the ratio moved upward from 20 per cent to about 27 per cent, and after 1969 it tended to fluctuate between 27 per cent and 34 per cent.

During the period 1960–90, total government expenditure grew at an average annual rate of 13.0 per cent. In the 1960s, the ratio of government expenditure to nominal GDP fluctuated between 25 per cent and 30 per cent and for the next two decades it did not fall below 30 per cent.

During the period 1960–90, government expenditure on social sectors (education, health, housing and community activities, and other community and social services) accounted for more than 40 per cent of total expenditure except during the first two years of the 1960s (see Fig. 11.4). Government expenditure on education represented 20 per cent or more of the total for most of the period, while expenditure on health generally ranged between 13 per cent and 16 per cent.

In 1960, expenditure on the social sectors was equivalent to 8.2 per cent of GDP, while the corresponding ratios for health and education were 2.5 and 3.4 per cent

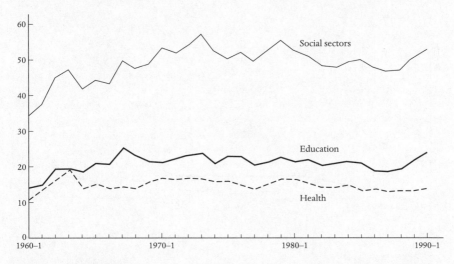

Fig. 11.4 Government expenditure, Barbados 1960–1990: education and health as percentage of total government expenditure

Source: Central Bank of Barbados

respectively (see Fig. 11.5). By 1970, the ratios had doubled. The data on health and education expenditure per capita reveal a trend upward in the period 1970–80 (see Fig. 11.6).[18]

The data in Tables 11.6 and 11.7 indicate that the proportions of government expenditure devoted to education and health respectively, have tended to be higher in Barbados than in Guyana, Jamaica, and Trinidad and Tobago. Furthermore, Table 11.7 shows that per capita health expenditure in Barbados during the period 1970–90 was considerably higher than in Guyana and Jamaica. However, the data in Table 11.8 reveal that the share of current expenditure on education devoted to the primary level in Barbados tended to be lower than in the other three Caribbean countries.

Financing from non-public-sector sources

Health care in the public sector is financed primarily from general revenue. User fees are also collected by the government general hospital from patients who opt to pay for medical services rendered, while revenue is collected by the Barbados drug service from pharmacies in respect of the sale of drugs.

Currently, user fees constitute a very small proportion of the operating costs of the hospital. It is projected that in 1995, the revenue earned by the hospital will be the equivalent of 7 per cent of operating costs. User fees, collected by the hospital, and fees for services provided in the private sector, are made directly by clients or through insurance schemes. It is estimated that private expenditure on health in

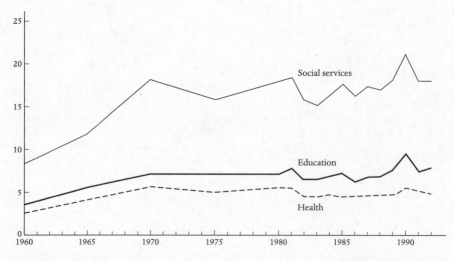

Fig. 11.5 Government expenditure, Barbados 1960–1990: education and health as percentage of GDP

Source: as Fig. 11.4

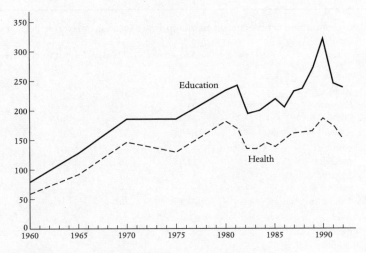

Fig. 11.6 Real expenditure per capita, Barbados 1960–1990

Source: as Fig. 11.4

TABLE 11.6. Central government expenditure on education as % of current expenditure

	1970	1975	1980	1985	1990
Barbados	23.2	24.9	23.5	23.8	23.1
Guyana	13.2	14.9	15.2[a]	13.0	5.2
Jamaica	—	16.0	19.4	15.8	17.1[b]
Trinidad and Tobago	16.0	17.7	17.6	18.3[c]	13.5

[a] 1979; [b] 1989; [c] 1987

Sources: Central Bank of Barbados (1992); UNESCO, *Statistical Yearbook*, 1983, 1990, 1993

TABLE 11.7. Central government expenditure on health: % of total central government expenditure

	% of total government spending					Per capita in 1988 $US				
	1970	1975	1980	1985	1990	1970	1975	1980	1985	1990
Barbados	16	16	16	13	14	110	149	245	208	232
Guyana	7	5	7	4	—	26	27	45	29	22
Jamaica	9	8	9	9	—	51	62	62	36	—
Trinidad and Tobago	—	7	4	7	—	—	68	117	196	178

Sources: Central Bank of Barbados, *Annual Statistical Digest*; *Health Conditions in the Americas*, i, 1990 edn., PAHO-PASB Regional Office, WHO

TABLE 11.8. Central government current expenditure on education by level (percentages)

	First level	Second level	Third level	Other types[a]
1970				
Barbados	34.7	33.9	13.0	18.3
Guyana	46.5	34.4	14.7	4.3
Jamaica	44.7	35.6	8.8	10.8
Trinidad and Tobago	52.5	24.0	13.9	9.5
1980				
Barbados	32.0	32.0	18.1	17.9
Guyana[b]	41.6	33.1	15.2	10.2
Jamaica	34.7	36.9	19.2	9.3
Trinidad and Tobago	46.9	34.9	10.2	8.0
1990				
Barbados	37.5	37.6	19.2	5.7
Guyana	—	—	—	—
Jamaica	37.4	33.2	21.1	8.3
Trinidad and Tobago	42.5	36.8	11.9	8.9

[a] not distributed; [b] relates to 1979

Source: UNESCO, *Statistical Yearbook*, 1983, 1993

1988–9 was the equivalent of 16 per cent of total government expenditure on health.[19]

Primary and secondary education is financed largely by the government. Tuition is free at government primary and secondary schools and post-secondary institutions including the Cave Hill (Barbados) Campus of the University of the West Indies (UWI).[20] The government also provides financial assistance to approved private secondary schools. There are a number of private-sector institutions and civic organizations which provide post-secondary education and training in academic, technical, and vocational studies. Private expenditure on education in 1988–9 was the equivalent of 5 per cent of total government expenditure on education.[21]

Funds for both education and health programmes are also provided by the donor community. However, detailed information on the extent of donor financing is not available.

Economic Crises

Fiscal and balance-of-payments problems

In 1981, Barbados experienced severe balance-of-payments pressure as a result of disappointing performances from the three major productive sectors, significant outflows for interest payments and non-trade transactions, and a sharp increase in public-sector expenditure which was not matched by growth in revenue. Stabilization measures were implemented in 1982 and official financing was obtained from international banks and the International Monetary Fund (IMF) to maintain adequate foreign exchange reserves (Central Bank, 1982; Worrell, 1987; Howard, 1989).

Despite the economic recovery in 1983, there were further disturbing trends during the rest of the decade and, in the period 1990–2, the economy contracted by about 12 per cent. In 1991, the country was again faced with serious domestic and external imbalances which necessitated the introduction of a stabilization programme, with the assistance of the IMF. The programme included contractionary fiscal and monetary measures which led to a reduction in public-sector employment and a high rate of unemployment generally. The stabilization measures were successful in reducing the imbalances, but total capital expenditure declined by about 50 per cent in 1991–2 compared to that of the previous year.

Effects on government expenditure

Government expenditure on education and health declined, in real terms, during the 1980s. In 1981, total government expenditure on the social sectors was equivalent to 18.5 per cent of GDP (see Fig. 11.5). This was followed by a steep decline in 1982. After fluctuating between 15.3 per cent and 17.7 per cent during the period 1982–8, the ratio again reached the 1981 level in 1989. Similar trends were experienced in regard to total expenditure on education and health. Total expenditure on education was equivalent to 7.8 per cent of GDP in 1981. The ratio then fluctuated between 6.4 per cent and 7.3 per cent during the period 1982–8. With respect to total expenditure on health, the ratio declined from 5.5 per cent in 1981.

During the period 1982–8, per capita expenditure on education fluctuated below the level of 1981 (see Fig. 11.6). After registering increases in 1989 and 1990 it declined in 1991. Per capita expenditure on health followed the same general pattern as education expenditure, during the period 1981–9, falling below the level of 1980.

The programmes of the Ministries of Education and Health were affected by the reduction in expenditure. In the education sector, the financial constraints imposed by the government in the early 1990s curtailed the development of the programme for early childhood education, led to restrictions in the procurement of textbooks, and resulted in interruptions in the construction of schools and other facilities (MoE, 1993). With respect to the ministry of health, work on the construction of polyclinics was suspended or deferred and the sanitation service authority received a reduced subvention (MoH, Development Plan, 1993–2000).

Although health and education outcome indicators were not affected as a result of the compression of social expenditures, other problems remain.

One major disappointment concerning the modernization of the economy is the fact that the level of open unemployment has been relatively high. Manufacturing, the most labour-intensive of the productive sectors, was unable to generate any meaningful increases in employment. The information available for the period since 1975 suggests that the unemployment rate did not fall below 10 per cent and was, for most of the time, higher than 15 per cent. Up to 1991, female unemployment rates were noticeably higher than those for males.

During the 1980s, it became clear that Barbados was losing its competitiveness in the manufacturing and tourism sectors. As a result, it is generally felt that emphasis must be placed on the establishment of high value-added and knowledge-intensive industries and on achieving increases in productivity if there is to be a resurgence in economic activity. This is particularly important in view of the fact that a decision has been made to reduce the level of protection provided to domestic industries. There are a number of issues relating to the implementation of this development strategy. These concern the ability of persons from low-income households to acquire requisite skills and training; the ability of industries to create sufficient employment opportunities which can have a significant impact on the level of unemployment; and the capacity of government to provide an adequate safety net during periods of severe dislocation.

Finally, the incidence of poverty appears to have increased in the 1980s. In one study, which sought to assess poverty head-count levels, it was estimated that the proportion of the rural population in poverty increased from 10.5 per cent in 1980 to 21.1 per cent in 1989, while the corresponding figures for urban poverty were 4.9 per cent and 2.3 per cent respectively (Psacharopoulos, 1993). More recently, it was estimated that approximately 8 per cent of the population was living in poverty (IDB, quoted in Dellimore, 1995). An analysis of the performance of the economy suggests that there has been an increase in economic hardship since the beginning of the last decade and particularly since 1989. Indications are that there has been a noticeable increase in the number of men seeking assistance from the welfare department. This development can be viewed as an indicator of the existence of a serious problem, since it is known that Barbadian men are usually reluctant to turn to the welfare department for help and, in any case, do this only as a last resort.

Conclusions

The study has revealed that:

- The gains in social development which Barbados experienced during the past four decades were due largely to the initiatives taken by the government in response to the demands for social services by the population. However, the implementation of the various programmes in health and education were facilitated by a combination of demographic factors, assisted by the physical characteristics of the country.

- One significant feature of the early development of primary education was government financing of the entire cost of primary education at the turn of the century. This allowed parents to send their children to school in the absence of legal obligations.

- The deliberate action by the government to initiate preventive health care programmes resulted in a dramatic reduction in the IMR in the 1950s.

- Considerable improvements in the health status of a population can be achieved through efffective IEC programmes.

- There is hardly any targeting based on socio-economic factors or the application of a means test. In the education sector, tuition is provided free of charge at government institutions from primary to tertiary level. Since the late 1970s, targeting in the health sectors has tended to be based on demographic and epidemiological characteristics.

- The economic problems experienced in the early 1980s and 1990s did not influence government to change its policies in regard to the provision of free services in education and health.

- In the absence of natural resources of any significant commercial value, governments have placed great emphasis on human-resource development.

The analysis has revealed some critical areas which could have serious implications for future development:

- There is a scarcity of data which can provide information on the quality of life of different segments of the population in the income distribution. There is a need to create an environment for elderly persons in which their health, nutritional, and housing needs, including relief from loneliness, can be met.

- The high unemployment rate among the economically active population in the 15–29 age-group can lead to frustration which in turn can result in deviant behaviour—crime, delinquency, and substance abuse.

Without resumption of sustained macroeconomic growth many of these objectives will remain unfulfilled. The government and the opposition have ruled out any meaningful cost-recovery system and continue to outbid each other in offering more to the electorate. Without fundamental public-sector reform and without a similar change in the medical/public health system, no real advance above the current level is anticipated.

Notes

1. The Moyne Commission had been established by the UK government in 1938 to investigate social and economic conditions in the West Indian colonies following disturbances and unrest in a number of colonies.

2. Per capita GDP increased by 23% and 3% in the 1970s and the 1980s respectively, compared to a decline of 5% in the 1960s.
3. This provision was implemented in 1962.
4. The Education Act, 1975.
5. The Education Act, 1981.
6. This programme was intensified during the 1970s.
7. This programme was implemented in 1985.
8. The Programme of Assistance to Approved Independent Schools was instituted in 1965.
9. The decline in enrolment in private secondary schools is due to a combination of two factors: the expansion of facilities in government schools and the abolition of tuition fees in these schools.
10. Currently, parents and guardians of primary-school children have to provide textbooks. However, the ministry of education will distribute textbooks to primary schools starting in the 1995–6 academic year.
11. It should, however, be noted that the first public-health centre in Barbados, which was staffed entirely by volunteers, had been established 1943.
12. There are two points which must be made here; it is acknowledged that these categories are not mutually exclusive and it is debatable as to what should be the minimum components in each group.
13. The ratio fluctuated between 5.7% and 9.9%. This is considered to be a significant achievement since, according to the BDS, both the World Bank and WHO recommend that a minimum of 10% of current health expenditure should be devoted to the procurement of drugs for the public sector.
14. The Caribbean Community (CARICOM) is an arrangement among thirteen English-speaking countries designed to achieve economic and functional integration.
15. The information on immunization coverage prior to 1980 is not disaggregated according to age.
16. It should, however, be noted that the National Nutrition Survey which was conducted in 1981 revealed that the proportion of infants being breast-fed at six months was only 17% compared to 52% in 1969.
17. It has already been noted that there are no local government authorities in Barbados.
18. Details of the ratio of expenditure on education and health to GDP and of per capita expenditure, during the 1980s, are provided in the next section.
19. These estimates are based on information from the Household Budget Survey.
20. Students at the three UWI campuses in the Bahamas, Jamaica, and Trinidad and Tobago pay part of the economic costs of tuition.
21. These estimates are based on information from the Household Budget Survey.

Bibliography

Alleyne, George (1991), *Health and Politics: A Public Lecture*, Nation Publishing Co. Ltd.

Alleyne, Yolanda (1993), *Management of Groundwater Resources in Barbados: The Environmental and Planning Issue*, Paper Prepared for the Third International Environmental Management Seminar, Canada.

Arthur D. Little, Inc. (1963), *Industrial Development for Barbados*.

Barbados, *Development Plan*, 1960–5, 1962–5, 1965–8, 1969–72, 1988–93.

—— *Population Census*, 1946, 1960, 1970, 1980, 1990.

—— (1945), *A Ten Year Development Plan for Barbados: Sketch Plan of Development 1946–1956*, Advocate Co. Ltd.

Barbados Drug Service (1987–93), *Report on the Operations of the Barbados Drug Service For Fiscal Years*.

Barbados Family Planning Association, *The Barbados Family Planning Association*.

—— *History of BFPA*.

Bureau of Women's Affairs (1994), Report to the United Nations Fourth World Conference on Women, Barbados.

CARNEID, *Profiles of the Organisation and Administration of Educational Systems in Caribbean Countries*, Caribbean Network of Educational Innovation for Development.

Central Bank of Barbados (1992), *Annual Report*.

CMO (Chief Medical Officer) (1990, 1991–2), *Annual Report*, Ministry of Health, Barbados.

Dellimore, Jeffrey W. (1995), *An Approach to the Challenge of Poverty Alleviation and Reduction*, mimeo.

Director of Medical Services, *Annual Report*, 1956–7, 1957–8, 1960.

Howard, Michael (1979), *The Fiscal System of Barbados, 1946–1965*, Occasional Papers Series, No. 12, ISER, Cave Hill, Barbados: University of West Indies.

—— (1989), *Dependence and Development in Barbados 1945–85*, Bridgetown, Barbados: Carib Research & Publications, Inc.

Hoyos, F. A. (1974), *Grantley Adams and the Social Revolution*, Macmillan.

Hunte, Keith (1991), *Twenty-Five Years of Education in an Independent Barbados: A Critical Review and the Future Analysis*, mimeo.

Lewis, W. A. (1950), 'Industrialisation of the British West Indies', *Caribbean Economic Review*, 2/1.

Massiah, Joycelin (1981), 'The Population of Barbados: Demographic Development and Population Policy in a Small Island State', Ph.D. thesis, University of the West Indies.

Miller, Beverley (1990), 'The Polyclinic Services', *Barbados Drug Service, 10th Anniversary 1980–1990*.

MoE (Ministry of Education), *Report*, 1957–60, 1960–3, Barbados.

—— (1990), *Education in Barbados, Information Handbook*.

—— (1993), *Education Sectoral Plan, 1993–2000*, Barbados.

MoH (Ministry of Health), *Development Plan*, 1960–5, 1962–5, 1965–8, 1977–82, 1983–7, 1988–93, 1993–2000, Barbados.

National Report on Population (Barbados) 1994 (1994), Prepared for the International Conference on Population and Development, Cairo, Egypt.

Psacharopoulos, George (1993), *Poverty and Income Distribution in Latin America: The Story of the 1980s*, World Bank.

Ramsey, Frank C. (1979), *Protein-Energy Malnutrition in Barbados: The Role of Continuity of Care in Management*, Josiah Macy, Jr., Foundation.

UNESCO (1978), *Prospects for Educational Development*, UNESCO, Paris.

Walker, Cyril V. (1990), *Basic Education in Barbados: An Illustrative Case Study*.

West India Royal Commission Report (1945), London: HMSO.

World Bank (1993), *World Development Report, 1993*, Oxford: Oxford University Press.

Worrell, DeLisle (Ed.) (1982), *The Economy of Barbados 1946–80*, Central Bank of Barbados.

—— (1987), *Small Island Economies—Structure and Performance in the English-Speaking Caribbean Since 1970*, New York: Praeger.

—— (1990), *Barbados at 25: The Economy*.

12

Costa Rica: Social Development and Heterodox Adjustment

LEONARDO GARNIER, REBECA GRYNSPAN,
ROBERTO HIDALGO, GUILLERMO MONGE,
AND JUAN DIEGO TREJOS

How has a small country like Costa Rica, with an economy that fits the model of peripheral capitalism, been able to attain social indicators that are closer to that of an industrialized country, despite being a lower-middle income country?[1] This is the main question addressed in this chapter.

Located on the Central American isthmus, with an area of 51,000 sq.km. and a population of 3m., Costa Rica is one of the smallest countries in the Western hemisphere. The country has two ecosystems: the Central Valley, accounting for 15 per cent of the national territory, is home to two-thirds of the population, where most of the nation's advances are concentrated; and the coastal regions.

Costa Rica is rapidly becoming an urban economy. Half of the population, however, still lives in rural areas, and one-quarter of the working population is engaged in agriculture. The country is also known for its social and cultural homogeneity, political stability, and democratic traditions, and the fact that its constitution stipulates that it shall have no army.

Direct provision of social services has been a long-standing tradition for the Costa Rican State. Its social policy was instituted during the 1940s, although at that time it dealt mainly with legal issues, and coverage was restricted to wage-earners and their families.

Indicators of Social Progress

Several decades of steady growth

Between 1950 and 1990, per capita income more than doubled, life expectancy at birth increased by 20 years, and the average level of schooling increased by more than two years (see Table 12.1).

Between 1950 and 1990, the infant-mortality rate was reduced by 84 per cent and illiteracy was reduced by 67 per cent. Other indicators that have been available only

TABLE 12.1. Indicators of social development, 1940–1990

Indicator	1940	1950	1960	1970	1980	1990
Economic						
Gross domestic product (GDP), per capita (1970 dollars)	286	347	474	656	876	809
Labour force employed in agriculture (%)	66	63	59	49	35	33
Education						
Illiteracy (%, ages 15 and over)	27	21	16	13	10	7
Years of schooling (population: aged 25 and over)	n.a	4.1	4.4	5.5	6.7	6.5
Health						
Life expectancy at birth (years)	46.9	55.6	62.5	65.4	72.6	75.6
Infant-mortality rate (per thousand)	137	95	80	67	21	15
Nutrition						
Malnutrition (% of children under age 6)	—	—	14	12	4	4
Development						
Human development index	—	—	0.550	0.647	0.746	0.848
Poor families by income (percent)	—	—	50	29	19	19
Houses with electricity (%)	—	40	51	65	79	93
Telephones per 1,000 pop.	7	11	12	23	79	103

Sources: Rosero (1985); UNDP (1994); Trejos *et al.* (1993); Miranda (1994); and National Population Censuses

since 1960 show similar improvements. Malnutrition declined by 71 per cent, and whereas poverty had afflicted half of the country's families in 1960, in 1990 only one-fifth were poor. According to the human development indicators developed by UNDP, Costa Rica's level of human development rose from medium to high during the 1980s (UNDP, 1994) (see Table 12.1).

Costa Rica as compared with other countries

A comparison between Costa Rican development indicators and its standard of living and those of economically more advanced countries brings to light several features. In 1992, Costa Rica's infant-mortality rate was 14 per 1,000, compared to 13 per 1,000 in the industrialized countries; the mortality rate for children under age 5 was 16 per 1,000, compared to 15 per 1,000 in the industrialized nations (UNDP, 1994). Life expectancy at birth in Costa Rica was 76 years—a figure equal to or greater than the figure for industrialized economies. Adult literacy in Costa Rica is 93 per cent; in the most advanced countries, it is 99 per cent (UNICEF, 1994) (see Table 12.2).

Costa Rica's success becomes clearer when these figures are contrasted with those for the other Central American countries, which have similar geographic features and economic models. In those countries, life expectancy is 65 years, infant

TABLE 12.2. Human development in Costa Rica and other countries, 1960–1992

Indicator	Costa Rica	Rest of Central America[a]	Latin America and Caribbean	Developing countries with high HDI	Indus- trialized countries
Life expectancy at birth (years)					
1960	61.6	47.3	56.0	58.5	69.0
1992	76.0	64.8	67.7	70.5	74.5
Infant mortality (per thousand live births)					
1960	85	135	105	83	35
1992	14	52	47	30	13
Mortaliy—under age 5 (per thousand live births)					
1960	112	207	157	115	43
1992	16	69	50	26	15
Access to potable water (% of population)					
1975–80	72	44	60	68	—
1988–91	92	62	79	86	—
Malnutrition (% of children under age 5)					
1975	10	25	17	14	—
1992	8	22	10	10	—
Adult illiteracy (% of population aged 15 or over)					
1970	88	50	76	83	—
1992	93	66	86	92	—
Total enrolment (% of population aged 6–23)					
1980	55	43	59	64	—
1990	56	47	62	66	79
Per capita real GDP (PPA in dollars)					
1960	2,160	1,441	2,140	3,140	6,280
1991	5,100	2,545	5,360	7,290	19,000

[a] Includes Guatemala, El Salvador, Honduras, and Nicaragua

Sources: UNDP (1994); UNICEF (1994)

mortality is over 52 per 1,000, and adult literacy is barely 66 per cent (see Table 12.2).

It should be noted, moreover, that a comparison of ninety-four developing countries shows that in the late 1980s, only two (Cuba and Singapore) had better under-5 mortality than Costa Rica, none surpassed its life expectancy at birth, and only four (Argentina, Chile, Cuba, and Trinidad and Tobago) had a higher adult literacy rate. In all of these cases, the countries which surpassed Costa Rica had a higher per capita income (Trejos, 1991).

How was this achieved?

The rest of this introduction examines some of the features of Costa Rica's polity and society. The next section offers an interpretation of each of the successive stages of development identified in the chapter. The final section deals with the economic basis of Costa Rican social policies. The last part discusses the prospects for sustainability of the social model over the next few years, emphasizing the institutional, financial, and socio-political aspects.

During the thirty years following 1948, the State became the motivating force for national development, as it took on new roles in the social and economic spheres, and created most of the existing institutions. The governing junta that took over after a year and a half of civil war (which had started in 1948), under the leadership of Jose Figueres, an agricultural entrepreneur, launched the country on a process of rapid transformation.[2] Figueres provided both the framework for national development and the political leadership that were needed to carry out these far-reaching changes. His social policies were taken up by the *Partido Liberación Nacional* (National Liberation Party—hereinafter referred to as PLN), the political party created under his leadership by the winners of the 1948 civil war. PLN administrations have been instrumental in bringing about the changes that have taken place in Costa Rican society since the 1950s;[3] political developments and struggles between the various social forces in the country made this possible (Rovira, 1982). Figueres, who was president of Costa Rica on two occasions and who played a leading role in PLN, was the main driving force behind these changes.

Over three decades, public employment rose from 6 per cent of the work-force to nearly 20 per cent. The State has proven itself functional thanks to three factors. In the first place, there is a clear-cut separation of powers (executive, legislative, and judicial). In the second place, the various social groups enjoy broad representation in state institutions. In the third place, efforts to modernize the State and upgrade the professional qualifications of public officials have been relatively successful (Garnier and Hidalgo, 1991).

The political system was developed along democratic lines. The abolition of the army allowed the country to avoid authoritarian regimes and the interference of military élites in an essentially democratic political playing-field. That kind of situation has occurred frequently in a majority of the countries throughout the region, and has introduced formidable obstacles to political stability and social development. Furthermore, public resources that would have been assigned to the armed forces were available to finance social programmes.[4]

The political system was also strenghthened by 'the freest and fairest electoral machinery of any country in the world' (Ameringer, 1982), which means that, since

1948, every administration has come to power through popular elections and the parties have alternated in office. Voter turnout at these elections has been close to 80 per cent in recent decades.

Economic reforms furthered the expansion and diversification of Costa Rica's structure of production. This was achieved by a number of measures, such as the nationalization and strengthening of the country's banking system (a measure which greatly increased general access to credit), development of the infrastructure that is crucial to economic modernization, and implementation of aggressive social policies aimed at building up human resources. The average growth rate of the Gross Domestic Product (GDP) over the last forty years is evidence: at approximately 5 per cent per year, this growth rate has truly set a record for the Latin American region (Rama, 1994: 12).

This process of far-reaching social change provided the framework for a unique model of social development. Many clues may be found in this model to explain the remarkable contrast between Costa Rica's economic output, which is modest, and its level of social development, which is high. In the Costa Rican model, social development is interpreted as a process which must be promoted by social as well as economic policy. It is perceived as a prerequisite for, rather than a result of, economic growth (Garnier and Hidalgo, 1991).

Stages in the Implementation of Social Policy

During the three decades following the 1948 revolution, economic policy was guided by a philosophy that overcame the idea that social development is merely an outcome of economic growth. Instead, social development was viewed as a prerequisite for economic growth; what is more, social development became the key element of development *per se*. To a certain extent, social policy began to take on the functions of economic policy, since data on social aspects were used as a guide for the allocation of national resources to allow for adequate funding of social development programmes. The social sectors account for close to 45 per cent of total public spending.

Social policy went hand in hand with a policy aimed at increasing real wages; thus, real minimum wages grew at an annual rate of 2.1 per cent between 1950 and 1969, and 0.8 per cent between 1970 and 1980. Public spending was supplemented with private spending, leading to a rapid improvement in living standards. The wage policy was an especially powerful tool when it came to reducing poverty, especially in light of the fact that wage-earners account for a very high percentage of the country's work-force, which has continued to increase (as the population growth rate has been high, though slightly lower than the regional average). At the same time the share of the population employed in agriculture consistently declined (see Table 12.1), as did the share of output contributed by agriculture (see Table 12.3). The most significant impact of the increasing wage on the income of

TABLE **12.3.** Economic trends, 1940–1990

Indicator	1940	1950	1960	1970	1980	1990
Agricultural/GDP (%)	33.5	38.5	29.7	25.1	19.2	15.8
Industrial/GDP (%)	13.2	11.6	12.5	15.2	16.9	19.4
Exports/GDP (%)	25.9	26.2	21.8	26.4	22.5	30.0
Growth rate–real GDP[a]	—	4.5	5.8	6.1	5.6	2.4
Growth rate–per capita GDP[a]	—	2.0	2.4	3.3	3.1	−1.1

[a] yearly average during decade ending that year

Sources: Rosero (1985); National Population Censuses; Mideplan/UNDP (1994); Bulmer Thomas (1989)

the poorest groups occurred in the rural areas. Additionally, the expansion of public services in rural areas led to strong upward social mobility, in so far as the inhabitants had broader access to health, education, housing, electrification, telephones, and potable water, among other things (see Table 12.1). These changes, as well as others, explain why social development could occur in the countryside, in spite of the fact that the country's land is highly concentrated, similar to many countries throughout Latin America. In the Costa Rican countryside, it was possible for economic inequality to coexist with high levels of cultural and social equality, which can be illustrated by the fact that the children of the agricultural labourers went to the same schools and to the same health clinics as a majority of the children of the owners of the farms on which their fathers worked.

Since the 1950s, this wage policy has also been viewed as an incentive to improving the productivity of the work-force, and hence as a means for achieving modernization and industrialization. As early as 1949, Figueres had expressed the view that experience had shown that 'everywhere in the world, and especially in Latin America, unless pressure was exerted—either by organized labour or by progressive governments—to increase daily wages, nations tended to adopt inefficient work methods, which only achieved well-being for a few people, through the work of many.'[5]

Poverty (understood here as low income) had been reduced to the point where it affected 20 per cent of the country's families at the end of the 1970s, whereas it had affected 50 per cent in 1960. The inequality in family income distribution was also reduced (Fields, 1980).

The middle class grew quickly, more than doubling its share in the population between 1950 and the mid-1970s; around 1980, it accounted for nearly one-quarter of the economically active population. In addition, the rural lower class and the upper class both diminished in their share of the population, altering the composition of Costa Rican society (see Table 12.4).

The large population increase highlights, even more, the magnitude of the

TABLE 12.4. Costa Rica: Trends in social structure

Social strata[a]	1950	1963	1973	1984	1988
Total active population (thousands)	264	384	565	794	1,006
Relative structure					
High-income groups	13	4	2	4	7
Entrepreneurs	11	3	1	3	5
Managers	2	1	1	1	2
Middle class	11	18	22	26	27
Small business owners	1	3	4	5	5
Professionals and technicians	3	6	8	8	9
White-collar workers	7	9	10	13	13
Overall low-income groups	76	78	76	70	66
Urban low-income groups	28	31	39	43	41
Microentrepreneurs	3	4	4	7	7
Proletariat-industry	15	16	21	20	21
Proletariat-services	10	11	14	16	13
Rural low-income groups	48	47	37	27	25
Small farmers	14	21	15	9	10
Proletariat-agriculture	34	26	22	18	15

[a] These are very broad categories and are not intended as precise classifications

Source: J. D. Trejos, 'La política social y la valorización de los recursos humanos', in L. Garnier *et al.*, *Costa Rica entre la ilusión y la desesperanza: Una alternativa para el desarrollo*, San José, C. R.: Ediciones Guayacán, 1991

improvements in standards of living during this period. The nation's population increased two and a half times, with growth rates high when compared worldwide. The natural growth rate of the population was 26 per 1,000 during the 1950s, when both the birth and death rates were already very high; this later climbed to a maximum of 38 per 1,000 at the beginning of the 1960s (see Table 12.5).[6] Population growth was significantly curtailed during the 1960s, to the point that during the 1970s it returned to the levels found twenty years earlier, while the demographic transition advanced towards the current pattern of moderate birth rates[7] and low mortality rates (see Table 12.5).

The country's achievements in the reduction of poverty are all the more remarkable considering that during this period, the bulk of the population lived in rural areas, 67 per cent in 1950 and 57 per cent in 1980 (see Table 12.5). Because of their low population density and limited social infrastructure, rural areas pose a greater problem than urban areas in the fight against poverty. Another development was also taking place between 1950 and 1980: social services were becoming more and more concentrated in urban areas, owing to the fact that the urban population tripled during this period.

The government's commitment to its social policy resulted in a steady and

TABLE 12.5. Population trends, 1940–1990

Indicators	1940	1950	1960	1970	1980	1990
Total population (millions)	0.6	0.9	1.2	1.7	2.3	3.0
Birth rate (per thousand)	45	44	48	33	31	27
Overall mortality rate (per thousand)	23	18	10	7	4	4
Natural growth rate (per thousand)	22	26	38	26	27	23
Final descendants per couple (children)	6.6	7.0	7.6	5.0	3.4	3.2
Population under age 15 (%)	42.1	43.5	47.4	46.1	38.5	36.2
Dependent pop. to pop. aged 15–65	—	1.1	1.0	1.0	1.4	2.5
Urban population (%)	—	33.5	35.0	38.0	43.0	47.0
Population density (per sq.km.)	12.9	16.9	24.6	34.0	44.8	59.1

Sources: Rosero (1984, 1985); UNDP (1994); Miranda (1994); and National Population Censuses

marked increase in spending on social programmes during the 1950s, 1960s, and 1970s, both in terms of overall government spending and of GDP. Social spending rose from 9 per cent of the GDP in 1950 to 24 per cent in 1980 (see Table 12.8). The availability of financial resources to achieve these social gains could be assured, thanks to the country's expanding economy, buttressed by a growing world economy, the ability to obtain abundant foreign resources for investment in its economic and social infrastructure, contributions to the government's social programmes from civil society,[8] and low unproductive expenditures (the military was abolished in 1948). Thus, the financing of social policy was not at odds with the attainment of economic growth; in fact, the two complemented each other.

The social policies implemented during this thirty-year period may be clearly divided into two different stages, as discussed below.

Social development: 1948–1969

The first stage comprises the two decades which followed the 1948 civil war. During this period, social policy was aimed at improving social conditions and expanding the middle class. Whereas the emphasis during the 1940s had been on helping wage-earners and their families, the focus now shifted to the population as a whole. The objective was to ensure that the population as a whole benefited from and participated in the development process. From the economic standpoint, this stage coincided with the application of the import-substitution model designed to encourage industrialization within the framework of a regional market. Production expanded at mean annual rates of 7 per cent, and per capita production grew by 3.3 per cent per year.

The scope of social policies was greatly broadened during this stage. The foundations were laid for the national health system that was to take shape over the next

TABLE 12.6. Health services, 1940–1990

Indicator	1940	1950	1960	1970	1980	1990
Inputs						
Per capita expenditures—health (1970 dollars)	14.6	7.7	14.2	36.7	65.3	56.5
Doctors (per 10,000 population)	2.7	3.1	2.8	5.6	7.8	8.0
Hospital beds (per 1,000 population)	5.6	5.1	4.6	4.1	3.3	2.3
Access or coverage						
Out patient care (per capita)	—	—	1.1	2.0	2.9	2.3
Hospital discharges (per 1,000)	—	95	101	111	117	100
Deliveries in institutions (%)	—	20	49	70	91	95
Population covered by health insurance (%)	0	8	15	39	78	84
Active population covered (%)	0	23	25	38	64	68
Population with piped water (%)	—	53	65	75	84	93
Population with toilets or latrines (%)	—	48	69	86	93	97
Outcomes						
Life expectancy at birth (years)	46.9	55.6	62.5	65.4	72.6	75.6
Infant mortality rate (per 1,000)	137	95	80	67	21	15.3
Undernutrition (% children under 6)	—	—	14	12	4	4

Sources: Rosero (1985); UNDP (1994); Trejos *et al.* (1993); Miranda (1994); and National Population Censuses

ten years. Universal health-care coverage was included in the nation's constitution, and efforts to modernize and expand hospital services were begun. The School of Medicine was created; from its very inception, it worked in close collaboration with the nation's hospitals. The School of Medicine provided the institutional base that would make it possible to train the professionals needed to expand the nation's health services. In addition, wage-earners with medium-to-high incomes were included in the obligatory social security system (including health insurance), thus strengthening and broadening its financial base. Consequently, per capita spending on health care rose at a yearly rate of 8 per cent (Rosero, 1985). As a result of these changes, the percentage of the population covered by social security rose from 8 per cent in 1950 to 39 per cent in 1970 (see Table 12.6).

The nation's first community health programme was begun during the early 1960s; at its peak, it covered seventeen areas throughout the country. It operated through mobile units manned by medical personnel and health specialists who provided communities with medical care and advice on health-related issues; in addition, they provided support for local health committees. Also during this period, a very successful campaign against malaria was conducted. Vaccination campaigns were suspended during the mid-1960s, in order to give way to permanent and universal vaccination programmes (Miranda, 1994).

More than the health services, the 1950s and 1960s were the period of rapid expansion in educational coverage. The government throughout its history has given priority to strengthening the educational system. In 1869 the grammar school was declared free and compulsory. The University of Costa Rica was closed at the end of the nineteenth century by the General Law of Common Education in an effort to allocate more resources to strengthen the primary- and secondary-school systems.

However, at the beginning of the twentieth century Costa Rica still had a low level of education: 55 per cent of adults were illiterate in 1910. But half of the 7–14-year-olds were registered in primary schools at the time (Mata and Rosero, 1988). At the beginning of the century the State spent about 10 per cent of the national budget on education, which increased to 15 per cent over 1930–50, with the result that illiteracy had declined in 1940 to just over a quarter of the population.

After the civil war educational expenditure expanded sharply in per capita terms, partly because the per capita GNP rose, partly because the share of the national budget in GNP rose, and partly because the proportion of the national budget allocated to education increased.

Over 90 per cent of the country's children were enrolled in elementary schools in 1960; by the end of the decade, the figure had risen to 100 per cent of school-age children. The drop-out rate at the primary level was barely 7 per cent in 1960 (see Table 12.7). Access to secondary education, however, was relatively limited: high-school enrolment rose from 15 per cent in 1960 to 24 per cent in 1970. These

TABLE 12.7. Educational services Costa Rica 1940–1990

Education	1940	1950	1960	1970	1980	1990
Inputs						
Per capita expenditures on education (1970 dollars)	7.1	6.3	19.3	35.1	73.4	57.3
Students/teachers—primary	—	—	26	30	28	29
Students/teachers—secondary	—	—	20	17	19	21
Access or coverage						
Enrolment—primary and secondary (as %, ages 5–19)	31	39	52	62	63	60
Enrolment—pre-school (as %, ages 5–6)	—	—	12	14	39	62
Enrolment—primary (as %, ages 7–12)	—	—	93	110	106	103
Enrolment—secondary (as %, ages 13–18)	—	—	15	24	61	51
Drop-out rate—primary (% of enrolment)	—	—	7	4	4	2
Repeaters—primary (% of enrolment)	—	—	19	11	8	12
Outcomes						
Illiteracy (%, ages 15 and over)	27	21	16	13	10	7
Women completing primary education (%, ages 20–34)	14	22	28	43	66	83
Years of schooling (population 25 and over)	—	4.1	4.4	5.5	6.7	6.5

Sources: Rosero (1985); UNDP (1994); Trejos *et al.* (1993); Miranda (1994); and National Population Censuses; World Bank (1987)

improvements were supported by the increase in real per capita public spending on education, which rose at an annual rate of 9 per cent (Rosero, 1985).

Government institutions designed mainly to assist the poor were created. A building and subsidized credit programme for housing was begun for medium- and low-income sectors (1954). An ambitious programme was created for the purpose of distributing land to landless rural families (1962). The government created a specialized institution to handle the country's potable-water supply (1961), and another to train a skilled work-force (1965). In addition to the interventions in health and education (see Tables 12.6 and 12.7), improvements were also made in living conditions and access to basic services such as water and electricity. Between 1950 and 1970 the percentage of the population that had running water rose from 53 per cent to 75 per cent; the percentage that had a water cabinet or latrine rose from 48 per cent to 86 per cent (see Table 12.6), and the percentage of homes with electricity increased from 40 per cent to 65 per cent (see Table 12.1).

The 1970s: Broadening the scope of social programmes

The 1970s ushered in the second stage in the implementation of social policies. From the economic standpoint, it became evident that the import-substitution model had become obsolete; the situation was further aggravated by the energy crisis, and the debt crisis eventually contributed to its demise. Nevertheless, the boom in coffee prices during the second half of the decade enabled the economy to grow at a reasonable rate—5.6 per cent per year and 2.7 per cent per capita— though not as fast as it had during the previous stage.

At the beginning of the decade, the country's political leadership realized that twenty years of social development had not sufficed to benefit the entire population. This was especially true for the people who lived in the more remote areas, who were also the poorest. A qualitative change was made in social policy in order to remedy this situation. While continuing with the expansion of national programmes, the government also embarked on a policy of targeting social spending on specific areas (Trejos, 1991). This reform was begun during Jose Figueres's third administration (1970–4) under the slogan of conducting a 'war on poverty'. In 1971, the Instituto Mixto de Ayuda Social (a social-assistance institution better known by the acronym IMAS) was created to deal directly with poverty-related problems.

The *Fondo de Desarrollo Social y Asignaciones Familiares* (Social Development and Family Allowance Fund—FODESAF) was created in 1975, as a supplement to IMAS, for the purpose of financing programmes for the poor. Thus, targeted spending was not achieved at the expense of the middle class, as has been suggested by some international agencies, and as was indeed the case in other countries, such as Chile (Raczinsky, 1994).

Nearly 1.5 per cent of the country's GDP was channelled into FODESAF, which since 1975 has mobilized close to $US1bn. towards selective programmes designed to supplement social policies of universal scope. During this period, FODESAF was able to implement primary health-care programmes and extend them to the general population, and nutrition programmes for both pre-schoolers and elementary-school children were strengthened.

Within the government's programmes to fight poverty, nutrition programmes have played a supporting role. The main effect of the government policy to improve nutrition among the poor has been through increasing wages. It is interesting to note that while the social advances of the 1970s were taking place, the country did not experience an increase in nutritional intake. Between 1966 and 1978, caloric intake increased by only 7 per cent in the rural areas, and actually declined by 16 per cent in the urban areas (Mata and Rosero, 1988). This confirms that the relation between nutrition and health occurs not only through the supply of food, but also through the availability of a more ample menu of health services (Drèze and Sen, 1989).

FODESAF preceded the social emergency funds and the social investment funds of the mid-1980s by more than a decade. It also differs from them in several respects; for example, FODESAF is funded with revenues from specific taxes that remain relatively stable over time, and thus does not compete for resources assigned to universal programmes. Another practice that makes FODESAF different is that of channelling its resources into existing government institutions. This enables it to avoid the duplication of effort and the waste that occurs when the State creates social infrastructure which it cannot adequately handle (Trejos *et al.*, 1994*a*).

The universalization of health care and social security continued during this period (see Table 12.6). In 1975, the health-insurance coverage provided by the *Caja Costarricense de Seguro Social* (Costa Rican Social Security Fund, hereinafter referred to as CCSS) was expanded to cover non-wage-earning workers who wished to join the programme on their own account; in addition, CCSS began providing free state-subsidized care for the indigent. A genuine national health-care system was established, using the guidelines for the First National Health Plan begun in 1970. All public hospitals and clinics were brought into a unified system administered by CCSS. They were modernized and expanded so as to provide the infrastructure necessary to effectively implement the mandate to universalize the country's health services. In order to guarantee funding for the national health system, a payroll tax was instituted to finance CCSS (Miranda, 1994) (see later discussion on financing the social sector).

Primary health care took a quantum leap forward. In 1973, the rural health programme was established, and in 1976, the community health programme. They were both staffed by basic teams of doctors and auxiliary health personnel assigned to health centres throughout the country; they also made house calls in the communities. These programmes included activities such as immunization, distribution of milk to poor pregnant women, family planning, building of latrines, and environmental sanitation (Miranda, 1994).

By the end of the 1970s, the rural health programme covered 60 per cent of the rural population, and the community health programme covered 60 per cent of the urban population (Miranda, 1994). The health centres were established using geographic targeting criteria, since priority was given to the country's poorest communities. These programmes have also benefited the populations served by integrating them into the national health system through patient referral to medical services in the CCSS clinics and hospitals. The programmes had a significant impact, not only in reducing infant mortality, but also in reducing the gap between the poorest and the most prosperous zones. It is very significant that during the 1970s, the cantons with a rural and community health coverage of 75 per cent or more showed a decline in infant mortality from 80 to 17 per 1,000, while in the cantons where this coverage was almost non-existent, the change during the same period was from 49 to 21 per cent 1,000.

The success of the primary health-care programmes was reflected in relative reductions in some components of curative health programme costs. In fact, hospital bed density decreased from 5 per 1,000 in 1950 to 3 per 1,000 in 1980, as hospitalization became more infrequent.

During the 1970s, epidemiological information began to be used systematically as a criterion for decision-making in public health (Pfeffermann and Griffin, 1989). Obligatory notification of causes of disease and death was established for the whole country, thus providing a source of reliable information. An elaborate system of nutritional information was also set up.

The country's most dramatic gains in the health sector took place during the 1970s. Life expectancy rose by almost 8 years, mainly as a result of the decrease in the infant mortality rate, which dropped by 70 per cent during a single decade, reaching 20 per 1,000 in 1980. This appears to be an all-time world record, which is even more impressive if one also takes into consideration the fact that infant mortality at the beginning of the 1970s was already quite low (Drèze and Sen, 1989). Thus, during the 1970s, Costa Rica broke away from the regional pattern of slight reductions in infant mortality, and progressed in one leap from a rate typical of an underdeveloped country to one typical of a developed country. It also broke with another regional pattern, that of the sharp differences in mortality among different socio-economic groups (Rosero, 1985). It has been estimated that 41 per cent of the reduction in infant mortality that was achieved during the 1970s may be explained by the expansion of primary health care, 32 per cent by the expansion of secondary care,[9] and the remainder by overall social and economic progress (22 per cent) and the decline in fertility (5 per cent)[10] (Rosero, 1985).

The 1970s was also the period when the secondary-school system in rural areas expanded. Secondary-school enrolment rose from 24 per cent in 1970 to 61 per cent in 1980 (see Table 12.7). In other words, it was in the 1970s that the country was able to provide access to secondary schooling to a majority of children.

Crisis, adjustment, and social compensation

The 1980s began with an economic crisis without precedent. The crisis in the three-year period between 1980 and 1982 brought the country's previous development style to a halt. Real production showed a cumulative decline of 9 per cent, real wages lost close to 40 per cent of their purchasing power, and rates of unemployment and underemployment doubled. This increase in poverty affected one-third of the country's families. The flow of real resources to government institutions waned considerably. Between 1980 and 1982, spending on social programmes fell at an annual rate of 18 per cent; total public spending dropped at a yearly rate of 9 per cent, and the GDP fell at an annual rate of 5 per cent. In practice, this contraction did not do as much to reduce the extent of the state's social services as it did to reduce the quality (Sanguinetty, 1988a, 1988b; World Bank, 1990).

However, PLN administration took office in 1982, and began to implement an unconventional stabilization process. Macroeconomic equilibria were restored. At the same time, policies were implemented that were designed to benefit the poor and increase domestic demand, with a view to reactivating production, curbing the deterioration of real wages, and improving overall employment. As this stage drew to a close, a number of programmes for the poor were created within the framework of the *Plan de Compensación Social* (Social Compensation Plan).

Under this plan, external and domestic resources were obtained to fund a temporary food aid programme, an employment subsidy programme, and other programmes designed to promote production among the poor. The production incentive programmes were aimed both at the informal urban sector (providing credit and training) and the rural small-farmer sector (providing credit and food). Mechanisms for indexing wages were also introduced, in order to curb their decline, and a *Plan de Salvamento de Empresas* (Business Rescue Plan) was also introduced to protect jobs, among other goals (Villasuso, 1992).

These measures made it possible to reverse the impoverishment process, stabilizing the economy and expanding real wages and employment. The stabilization process was aimed at maintaining public employment and reducing the fiscal deficit, not only by reducing spending but also by increasing tax revenues. This enabled the government to provide financial support for its social institutions, especially CCSS in the health sector, the *Instituto Nacional de Aprendizaje* (National Vocational Training Institute—INA) in the job-training sector, and FODESAF in matters pertaining to programmes for the poor. The strengthening of these institutions went hand in hand with improvements in the efficiency of state institutions. Thus, social policy underwent no major conceptual or practical changes (Trejos, 1991).

The PLN remained in power for the remainder of the 1980s. The emphasis on economic policies centred on structural change. Special attention was given to strengthening the export sector, particularly to promoting the sale of non-traditional products outside the Central American region. With regard to social policy, the government continued its efforts to improve the efficiency of its social institutions.

Two programmes for the poor which featured substantial participation by the private sector in their implementation were created during this period. The first one, the *Bono Familiar para la Vivienda* (Family Housing Voucher—BFV), consisted of subsidized, long-term credit for low-income housing. Private and public financial institutions were responsible for supervising the housing projects and selecting beneficiaries. Private companies were in charge of actual building.

The second programme, the *Programa de Informática Educativa* (School Computer Programme—PIE), was created to improve the deteriorating quality of the country's primary education and reduce the gaps among different income groups. Its implementation was entrusted to a private foundation organized for this specific purpose (Fonseca, 1991). With regard to employment, job subsidies were reactivated, following more traditional procedures, and the Ministry of Labour initiated a credit programme for micro-enterprises in the informal sector (Trejos *et al.*, 1994b).

Spending on social programmes was clearly a significant component of the adjustment policies implemented during the 1980s. This was evident in the recovery which began in 1983; spending on social programmes grew at an average annual rate of 12.4 per cent up to 1986, when it surpassed 1980 levels, both in real terms and as a share of overall public spending. Social expenditures then remained stable in real terms—growing at an average rate of 3.8 per cent—until 1989, when strong action was being taken to restore fiscal equilibrium.

During this period, the economy grew at an annual rate of more than 4 per cent. Relative poverty levels remained virtually unchanged, thanks to an increase in employment, and in spite of the application of a restrictive wage policy under which real wages fell slightly (Trejos *et al.*, 1994b). Within the prevailing framework of compensation, the overall results may be considered satisfactory. Despite the seriousness of the crisis, a temporary increase in the poor population, and the sharp reduction of resources available to state institutions, the social indicators did not seem to deteriorate, and, for the most part, continued to improve, albeit at a slower pace (see Table 12.1).

Costa Rica was a pioneer among Latin American countries, in the sense that it was the first to show concern for the social cost of adjustment. Thus, it was able to implement far-reaching adjustment and stabilization measures without provoking the popular backlashes in other countries, such as Argentina, Brazil, the Dominican Republic, and Venezuela.

Although the government's emphasis on social compensation may be considered a step backward in the evolution of social policy, the magnitude of the crisis, as well as its social repercussions, clearly made it inevitable. It is also clear that the Costa Rican concept of compensation was an unconventional one. The Costa Rican State intended to accomplish two things through compensation: on the one hand, it sought to alleviate the more severe symptoms of the crisis, and on the other, it endeavoured to promote policies designed to address the structural adjustment that had to be made, and to distribute the social cost of adjustment more equitably. This was to be done while preserving the state institutions charged with executing social policy (Garnier and Hidalgo, 1991).

This has been recognized by a number of international agencies. For example, the ILO (PREALC, 1990) has pointed out that

[T]he crisis of the 1980s clearly demonstrated the importance of a number of state institutions that make Costa Rica different from the other countries of the region, and have enabled it to effect a rapid and profound economic stabilization with minimum social cost. This cost has been distributed evenly among the country's main social groups. The state spends a great deal on education, health care, housing, employment, and social security.

In contrast to social indicators, however, the composition of society underwent significant changes that were not always for the better. The expansion of the middle class and the low-income urban groups came to an abrupt halt (see Table 12.4). The middle class—especially professionals and technical workers—saw their purchasing power plummet (PREALC, 1990). This group seemed to have become fragmented, and the gap between it and the upper class widened. Among the low-income groups, the slowing down of the economy led to a significant increase in poverty, at least temporarily (Sauma and Trejos, 1990). Low-income groups in rural areas were the losers in the face of the ongoing process of urbanization and modernization. For these groups, temporary impoverishment was added to the structural poverty which already characterized many of their members. In urban areas, the income of the poorest quartile declined by a quarter over 1980–8, while that of the richest 10 per cent of the population increased by 4 per cent (ECLAC, 1994).

The high-income strata continued to grow, increasing the concentration of income and property ownership as upward mobility declined. The implementation of a set of policies aimed at promoting change in the country's structure of production through substantial subsidies to exporters of non-traditional products and other support measures may be creating new patterns of wealth which, because of their magnitude and forms of ostentation, do not fit traditional moulds. It would appear that the groups at the top of the social pyramid are distancing themselves from the rest of society, in an unprecedented 'divorce' that could even jeopardize the success of the social development attained thus far.

Temporary implementation of orthodox approaches

The 1990s began with the coming to power of the political party that was the PLN's main opponent. This party adopted a neoliberal approach. In economic matters, this meant the acceleration of reforms aimed at achieving structural change. Social policies were no longer given priority, but rather were viewed as secondary to economic policies. Welfare programmes were increasingly used as a means to fight poverty, and the private sector was given a greater role in the provision of social services.

In terms of macroeconomic policy, the former practice of a gradual application of adjustment policies ended, resulting in a deterioration of fiscal and external equilibria and the implementation of drastic 'shock' stabilization measures. This in turn led to a slowing down of growth and an increase in poverty. According to the household survey, the percentage of poor families rose from 20 per cent in 1990 to 24 per cent in 1991, and then fell to 22 per cent in 1992. In absolute terms, these percentages mean that nearly 20,000 families, approximately 100,000 more people, became poor during those two years (Trejos *et al.*, 1994*a*).

As far as institutions are concerned, emphasis was placed on reducing the size of the State, and not on increasing the efficiency and quality of its services. This approach was reinforced by the government's preoccupation with balancing the fiscal budget. The resulting cut-backs in resources for institutions in the social sector caused their services—particularly those pertaining to primary health care, nutrition, and housing programmes—to deteriorate. In addition, transferring money to the poor was given priority over providing services for them, even though the government assigned a smaller proportion of the overall budget to them than previous administrations had. A food voucher (*Bono Alimentario*) was instituted. The family housing voucher (*Bono Familiar para la Vivienda*) was changed from a subsidized credit to a gift. A school voucher (*Bono Escolar*) was instituted; this consists of a cash sum given to families in order to help pay for school supplies and uniforms. All of these measures were part of an approach that was new to the Costa Rican experience, i.e. the idea that spending on social programmes should be targeted solely on the poor.

Resources for Social Development

The magnitude and evolution of social spending

In 1992, spending on social programmes accounted for 19 per cent of GDP and 44 per cent of total public spending. Per capita spending amounted to $US390.[11] The State's role in financing social programmes grew during the three decades immediately preceding the 1980 crisis. During the 1950s and 1960s, public spending on social programmes rose, not only because overall public spending increased, but also because the social sector represented a larger share of the overall budget. This increase in social spending was financed, in part, with resources that became available after the abolition of the army in 1948.[12] In the 1970s, the increase in government spending on the social sector was proportional to the increase in overall public spending (Table 12.8).

The education sector increased its share of the budget during the three decades

TABLE 12.8. Costa Rica: Trends in public spending for social programmes, 1950–1990

Indicator	1950	1958	1971	1980	1990
Total public spending (TPS)					
% GDP	25.8	28.9	37.6	54.3	43.4
Total spending—Social programmes (TSS)					
% GDP	8.6	8.7	16.4	23.6	20.7
% TPS	33.3	30.2	43.5	43.5	47.6
Total spending—Education					
% GDP	1.5	2.6	5.2	6.2	4.9
% TPS	5.9	8.9	13.9	11.4	11.4
% TSS	17.7	29.5	32.0	26.3	23.9
Total spending—Health					
% GDP	6.5	4.9	6.1	8.7	8.4
% TPS	25.3	16.9	16.1	16.1	17.7
% TSS	76.2	55.7	37.0	36.9	37.2

Sources: Contraloría General de la República (Office of the Comptroller General) (1971); Trejos, *et al.* (1994*b*)

mentioned above. The health sector's share underwent a relative decline during the 1950s, and then speeded its growth during the following years, at a rate similar to that of total public spending (see Table 12.8).

Statistics for the 1980s illustrate the impact of the crisis and the adjustment measures. The figures for the public sector as a whole show a decline; despite efforts to protect the budget for social programmes, it represented a smaller share of the GDP. The health sector maintained its share, but the education sector shrank (see Table 12.8).

A drastic reduction of public social spending took place during the crisis of the early 1980s, both in real terms and in terms of GDP and overall public spending—a sharper drop than in overall public spending and in GDP.

Recovery began in 1983. Spending on social programmes rose at an annual rate of 12.4 per cent up to 1986, when it surpassed its 1980 level, both in terms of actual spending and in proportion to overall public spending. It remained stable in real terms up to 1989, when strong measures were taken to balance the budget. Judging by the comeback which it made from 1983 onward, spending on social programmes seems to have played an important role in the adjustment policies of the early 1980s. In 1990, however, this pattern was broken. Within a context of economic growth, the government began to apply drastic fiscal-adjustment measures, which had a disproportionate effect on social expenditure. By the end of 1992, per capita spending on social programmes was 20 per cent lower than it had been twelve years earlier (see Table 12.9).

When per capita spending on social programmes is broken down by sectors, it

TABLE 12.9. Costa Rica: Trends in per capita spending on social programmes, 1980–1992[a]

Item	Median yearly variations					Sectoral distribution 1992
	1981–2	1983–6	1987–9	1990–2	1980–92	
Total spending on social programmes	−20.9	3.9	1.1	−4.6	−1.9	
Education	*−20.3*	*5.7*	*−2.7*	*4.4*	*−1.6*	*100.0*
General	−22.6	4.9	−4.0	7.7	−1.8	59.8
Pre-school	−12.1	12.0	−2.4	13.7	4.3	4.0
Primary	−22.5	5.6	−3.5	8.3	−1.3	35.8
Secondary	−23.6	3.0	−5.0	8.7	−3.4	20.0
Vocational training	−23.1	14.3	10.2	−0.1	2.5	7.7
University	−15.9	5.7	−3.3	0.3	−1.8	32.5
Health	*−22.3*	*8.7*	*3.8*	*−5.1*	*−1.8*	*100.0*
Primary care	−22.8	2.0	−12.2	−9.9	−9.0	10.0
Curative services	−22.7	8.9	9.1	−3.5	−0.2	81.9
Water and sewerage	−17.6	22.2	−5.4	−12.8	−1.3	8.1
Social security	*−16.6*	*11.0*	*−6.8*	*−3.8*	*−2.2*	*100.0*
Retirement plans	−20.0	17.3	−8.1	3.8	0.4	65.4
Support for vulnerable groups	−13.6	5.2	−5.2	−13.7	−5.6	34.6
Housing	*−33.2*	*17.6*	*25.0*	*−19.9*	*−1.3*	*100.0*
Management and financing	−33.7	15.9	11.8	−42.1	−12.0	8.9
Direct subsidies	−40.1	91.9	133.3	−24.0	31.6	39.4,
Urban/Rural organization	−32.7	15.7	−0.6	−4.1	−2.9	51.7
Other social services	*−10.0*	*7.1*	*−12.8*	*−10.8*	*−5.6*	*100.0*

[a] Data for subsectores are relative to the total for the sector concerned

Note: Social expenditures are deflated by the consumer price index

Source: Fiscal statistics provided by the Ministry of Finance and the Second Committee on State Reform

will be noted that the health and education sectors fell by 20 per cent between 1980 and 1992, while the social security sector declined by 24 per cent. The sharp drops in spending on secondary education (which has a serious problem with insufficient coverage) and social security programmes for vulnerable groups are particularly worrisome. The health sector's losses were concentrated mainly in primary health care. This could explain the reappearance of several diseases in the late 1980s; these were diseases that had already been eradicated, and could have been prevented either by immunization campaigns or by environmental sanitation programmes. In contrast, housing programmes were more successful during the 1980s, thanks to direct subsidies, particularly the family housing voucher (see Table 12.10).

Private health and education services

Data concerning private services are very scarce. With regard to the health sector, it is a well-known fact that CCSS is responsible for providing almost all the hospital care in the country. In 1991, it accounted for 96 per cent of all hospital discharges. A 1988 study (Kleysen, 1988) shows that private spending on health care was equivalent to 25 per cent of public spending in that sector. Similar figures may be obtained from the *Encuesta Nacional de Ingresos y Gastos* (National Survey of Income and Expenditures), conducted in 1988, which shows that 23 per cent of all spending on health care came from private sources (Sáenz and León, 1992).

There are no studies on private spending in the education sector. Only 8 per cent of the country's educational centres are private; they account for 6 per cent of all enrolments. The highest private coverage is at the pre-school level, where it accounts for 11 per cent of total enrolment.

The progressive nature of social spending

From the 1980s to the present, the poor seem to have received a share of social expenditure that is commensurate with their share in society as a whole. Social policy is clearly limited in that it has not succeeded in allocating a greater share of that spending to the poor. This would appear to be borne out by Table 12.10, which shows estimated spending on social programmes for the poorest quintile. Subsidies come mainly from universal health and education programmes, and represent an in-kind income which is equivalent to 80 per cent of the average autonomous income received by the poor. Programmes designed to fight poverty—especially the family housing voucher—have not substantially increased the share of social expenditure allotted to the poor, but at least they have stopped it from shrinking (Trejos, 1990; Taylor-Dormond, 1991).

Public spending on health care has increased gradually. In 1986, 46 per cent of all subsidies provided by health-care programmes went to rural areas, and 54 per cent

TABLE 12.10. Costa Rica: Estimated spending on social programmes for the poorest 20 per cent of the population, by subperiods

Social sector	Percentage of social expenditures received in			Distribution of social expenditure	
	1980–2	1984–6	1989–91	1980–2	1989–91
TOTAL	23.1	20.3	20.7	100.0	100.0
Education	18.6	18.7	17.1	21.2	18.9
Health	29.4	24.5	25.3	47.1	46.3
Social security	20.2	16.6	15.8	24.3	19.4
Housing	17.7	20.3	23.1	5.5	14.0
Other sectors	23.3	23.3	23.6	1.9	1.3

Note: Households are organized according to per capita

Source: Trejos *et al.* (1994*a*)

to urban areas. This shows a slight bias in favour of rural areas, which accounted for 48 per cent of the country's population. The bias is even more pronounced in the area of preventive health services—with over 60 per cent going to rural areas—and curative medical services, 52 per cent of which went to rural areas (Rodríguez, 1986).

Three-fourths of the families benefited by these services belong to the poorest 60 per cent of the population; only one-fourth belong to the wealthiest two quintiles. The poorest quintile accounts for 28 per cent of families benefiting from government health services, while the richest quintile accounts for only 11 per cent. The poorest 20 per cent of the country's families receive 22 per cent of out-patient medical care, 28 per cent of preventive medical services and hospital care, and 39 per cent of food and nutritional services. This spending pattern has had the effect of promoting redistribution, as evidenced by the fact that the poorest 10 per cent of the population received 17 per cent of the subsidies, while the wealthiest 10 per cent received 9 per cent of the subsidies (Rodríguez, 1986).

In contrast to the situation with respect to public spending in the health sector, private health spending is strongly regressive. A breakdown of the distribution of expenditures on health care by social class shows that the wealthiest quintile accounts for more than half of that expenditure, while only 4 per cent is accounted for by the poorest quintile. This contrast is especially noticeable in regard to diagnostic and specialized services: in these two fields, the poorest 20 per cent of the population accounts for less than 2 per cent of private spending, whereas the richest 20 per cent accounts for 80 per cent of spending (Sáenz and León, 1992).

In the education sector, the increase in public spending has also been progressive. In primary education, the poorest 40 per cent of the population receives 57 per cent of public spending in that sector, while the wealthiest 40 per cent receives 21 per cent. At the high-school level, spending distribution is slightly progressive, with spending on the poorest 40 per cent being only slightly larger than spending on the wealthiest 40 per cent (Sauma and Trejos, 1990).

In contrast, private education in general has been quite exclusive. At the grade-school and high-school levels, it is generally the domain of the highest-income sector. The cost of private education rose rapidly during the 1980s. In recent years, a new type of school has appeared on the scene, i.e. schools that are actually run as businesses, rather than the traditional religious, non-profit educational centres (Trejos *et al.*, 1994*a*).

The financing of social expenditure[13]

Tax revenues constitute three-quarters of the financial resources for social expenditures. Among these, direct taxes represent almost one-half (see Table 12.11). Since this type of tax tends to be progressive, it could be argued that the financial basis for social spending deepens the redistributive effect of the State's social programmes,

TABLE 12.11. Costa Rica: Financing of spending on social programmes, 1992

	Social programmes	Education	Health	Social security	Housing	Others
Total income	100.0	100.0	100.0	100.0	100.0	100.0
Current income	99.8	99.9	100.0	100.0	98.6	100.0
Tax revenues	*76.4*	*90.6*	*89.5*	*68.5*	*41.5*	*83.4*
Direct	47.9	23.2	82.0	47.4	23.8	16.6
Payroll tax	42.2	11.2	80.7	43.7	14.9	6.2
Income tax	4.4	11.1	1.2	3.4	0.6	9.7
Property tax	1.3	0.9	0.1	0.3	8.3	0.7
Indirect	28.5	67.4	7.5	21.1	17.7	66.8
Goods and services	20.0	46.5	4.8	14.4	16.4	41.3
Foreign trade	7.9	20.1	2.1	6.2	1.2	21.1
Others	0.6	0.8	0.6	0.5	0.1	4.4
Non-tax revenues	*23.7*	*8.8*	*10.5*	*31.5*	*56.3*	*14.7*
Sales of goods and services	12.5	2.7	6.5	15.9	36.4	8.8
Rent-factors	8.3	4.7	3.2	11.5	17.6	4.4
Others	2.3	1.4	0.8	4.1	2.3	1.5
Transfers	*0.3*	*0.6*	*0.0*	*0.0*	*0.8*	*1.9*
Capital earnings	0.2	0.1	0.0	0.0	1.4	0.0
Deficit or surplus (% of total spending)	11.5	−5.0	−4.2	49.2	9.4	3.1

Sources: Ministry of Finance, Technical Secretariat of the Budget Office

or at least does not revert it. This structure varies from that of the central government, which depends to a greater extent on indirect taxes. This majority contribution to social spending by direct taxes is due in the most part to payroll taxes collected on the health and social security sectors. This can be seen more clearly when the overall financing of the social sector is contrasted with that of the education sector. The latter depends almost exclusively on the resources provided by the central government and thus reproduces its financing structure.

Table 12.11 shows the role played by payroll taxes in overall financing and, in particular, in the health sector. In 1970, the payroll tax to finance CCSS accounted for about one-third of the sector's resources; in 1980, it covered almost one-half, and in 1990 it provided 69 per cent of all resources for the sector (Güendel and Trejos, 1994). This type of tax, which is unpopular because of its potential negative effect on the Costa Rican labour market and competition, has in fact allowed for the strong growth and consolidation of the health sector.

It could be argued that it was this type of financing that made it possible, during the 1970s, to transform the health sector into a genuine national health system, and to shield it from the impact of the difficulties faced by the economy during the 1980s. Overall, the social sector shows a surplus. That statement, however, should be modified to take into account the fact that health and education, the two most important sectors, and the ones that mobilize the most resources, show a deficit. On the other hand, the social security system, although showing a considerable surplus, involves specific pension systems for different groups of government employees. These special systems are generating disequilibria in government accounts. If corrective measures are not taken, the combined deficits could soon threaten the sustainability of social expenditures as a whole.

The role of international co-operation[14]

During the second half of the century, international technical and financial co-operation have played a crucial role in the country's effort to modernize the society and establish a network of modern state institutions. Figures provided by the Organization for Economic Co-operation and Development (OECD) show that net external resources received by the country between 1970 and 1992 amounted to $US3.413bn., which is almost equivalent to the current foreign debt. Seventy-eight per cent of those resources were received from 1981 onward, i.e. during the financial crisis. It should be noted, however, that a very substantial part of the educational breakthrough and the health transition had occurred during the 1970s.

The increased influx of external resources did play an important role during the economic crisis of the 1980s. During the period 1970–80, aid represented 1.4 per cent of GDP, and during the period 1981–92, this proportion increased to 4.5 per cent. This increase did not represent foreign debt, since the country's access to new loans was frozen during the 1980s, as Costa Rica's foreign debt rose to 120 per cent of GDP, causing the country to lose its borrowing capacity. Rather, it was due to an increase in donations, which represented more than half of all the foreign aid received between 1981 and 1992. More than 60 per cent of these donations came from the government of the USA. These exceptional contributions from that government took place within the framework of the US's geopolitical strategy towards Central America. During the 1980s, there was a civil war in neighbouring Nicaragua, and the USA had a special interest in buttressing the socio-political stability of Costa Rica for the duration of this economic crisis (Rovira, 1989).

Most of the foreign resources received during the 1980s were destined to stabilize the balance of payments. From a social policy perspective, this provided a cushion against the pressures for contraction of social expenses during the economic crisis.

Central Bank figures show the magnitude of the economic co-operation received during the 1970–80 period by the health, education, and housing sectors. This amounted to $US328m. and accounted for 16 per cent of all external credit received between 1970 and 1980. Between 1981 and 1992, economic co-operation for these sectors declined to $US114m., and represented only 4.4 per cent of all external credit received.

Above and beyond the actual amount of the foreign aid received by the social sector, its contribution has played a key role in enabling Costa Rican political leaders and technical experts that conceived and directed social policy to be fully aware of what is being done in their fields in other parts of the world.

Some Lessons and Future Options

The development style that arose in Costa Rica after mid-century received its initial push from a fractured political situation, the civil war in 1948, which catalysed the historical traits of the country in favour of general welfare. Those traits, *inter alia*, are a social and cultural homogeneity, a liberal democratic regime, relative man-power scarcity which placed a limit on inequality in the social and economic structure, and a long tradition of social service provision by the State, including the decision made over 100 years ago, when the country was still rural and dominated by small farmers, to universalize basic education. From 1948 on, several processes made it possible for social and economic growth to occur, and indeed to last until the end of the 1970s. The action programme of the party which came to power at the end of the 1940s conceived of social welfare and economic modernization as two sides of the same coin. The armed forces were abolished, so that their allocations could be reoriented to social services and a source of political instability could be avoided. Within a context of economic growth, the structure of production was modernized, but, nevertheless, it continued to be typical of a peripheral capitalist economy. The institutional apparatus modernized, to conform to a complex Welfare State, wherein social policy held a preferential seat. Community participation grew to solve collective problems, frequently with government partnership. And finally, it was possible to create a broad national consensus around a basic political project.

Several traits of this national experience offer useful lessons. In this case, social policy concentrated on direct state provision of basic services, such as education, health, housing, or environmental sanitation, to a majority of the population. These services were complemented with other, more sophisticated ones, such as high technology, institutionalized medicine, or the training of skilled workers, which are also the means adopted for successful insertion into international markets. In a parallel manner, there were policies targeted on the most vulnerable groups. These had the peculiarity of being initiated during periods of growth—and of growing resources—not during periods of adjustment, when there was a risk of reduced public expenditures. Furthermore, they were designed to incorporate the targeted social groups into the universal social policies, from which they had been excluded. In this sense, the social programmes have been complementary and have not acted to substitute economic policies.

Social policy has shown its potential to promote human development, not only at times of economic growth, but also in the crisis and adjustment of the 1980s. In spite of the deterioration in public finance, the institutions in the social sector made the difference between a weak and restricted social compensation and one that was truly effective and broad-ranging. In these circumstances, social policy created social, political, and economic conditions to accelerate the economic recovery.

The Costa Rican experience has also shown that what a country needs is not so much high income levels, but rather growing levels of resources and the political will to assign them to goals with high social returns. Economic growth was not the only way to transfer resources to social programmes. Among others, a reallocation of expenses within the State was paramount, as well as its broadened participation within the economy. This is also a case where the thesis of congenital inefficiency in the public sector cannot be confirmed by the facts. The almost exclusive public provision of services was highly effective in terms of the results achieved. Instead of incorporating market mechanisms to achieve efficiency, the 'voice' mechanism (Hirschman, 1977) was chosen, as well as the accountability permitted by the electoral system.

Currently, the country faces a transitional period to another developmental style, whose basic traits are still being defined. An essential task for this period is that of reforming the social development model, to maintain and extend its achievements. It is true that the success of this reform depends on the country's general progress in the economic and political realms, but it is also true that it can be undertaken at once, and that its outcome will have an impact on the general direction taken by national development.

There is scope to raise the effectiveness of social expenditures. Some of the mechanisms that would be helpful include: strengthening government control over social programmes in order to provide clearer guidelines for, and improve co-ordination among, the agencies concerned with the social sector; shutting down or redesigning institutions and programmes; community participation at the grass-roots level, in order to exert pressure on institutions to improve their efficiency; applying worldwide advances in technology, in order to improve the quality and coverage of services and reduce costs; implementing more effective and progressive tax reforms; improving eligibility guidelines for selective programmes, in order to ensure that all those entitled to benefits do indeed receive them. The transformations that are currently being promoted in the social sector point precisely in this direction.

Notes

1. Costa Rica's per capita GDP is similar to the average GDP of the Latin American region, and about one-third lower than the GDP of developing countries with a high Human Development Index (HDI) (see Table 12.2).
2. The war, in which there were 2,000 casualties, broke out in an atmosphere of unrest caused by evidence of corruption within the government and electoral fraud.
3. PLN and the opposition have taken turns running the country every four years, except in two instances—once during the 1970s and once during the 1980s—when PLN remained in power

for two consecutive terms. PLN also consistently retained control of the legislative assembly until 1990. This legislative control enabled it to follow through with Jose Figueres's policies.

4. The absence of armed forces also allows savings on other types of costs. In Costa Rica, institutional solutions for a majority of social conflicts have been provided, thereby reducing the costs that these conflicts inflict on citizens and businesses (Garnier and Hidalgo, 1991).

5. Radio address delivered by Jose Figueres, the president of the *Junta Fundadora de la Segunda República* (Founding Junta of the Second Republic) on 2 Nov. 1949 (Figueres, 1986).

6. This high a figure, rarely reached in other countries, may be influenced by improvements in vital statistics registrations, but it also expresses a reduction in mortality and an increase in fertility rates, as a result of improving maternal-health conditions (Gómez, 1994).

7. The birth rates remained moderately high, in spite of a substantial decline in fertility, due to an increase in women in the fertile ages, caused by the heavy population growth of the 1960s.

8. We refer here to voluntary contributions from neighbourhood associations for different types of health and education programmes in their communities, such as the donation of land, building materials, or labour for school construction, new classrooms, or health centres, or the donation of foodstuffs and voluntary labour for school-meal programmes. Although there are no studies to quantify these contributions, it is evident that they have been significant and, at times, have had a synergistic effect on the State's resources assigned to the communities.

9. If one considers that primary care was responsible for increased access by the population to secondary care, an indirect impact can also be estimated for primary care in the reduction in infant mortality; it could then be added to the direct impact calculated in this study.

10. In spite of the noteworthy reduction in the fertility rate, which declined from 7.6 children in 1960 to 3.4 children at the end of the 1970s, there continues to be a wide variance according to the socio-economic status (SES) of the mother. According to data from 1993, the fertility rate was 33% higher among lower SES mothers than those in the middle levels, and 87% higher than those of the highest SES (Achío, 1994). These differentials favour increased growth among the population trapped by poverty. The increased fertility in the poorest strata helps to explain the reduced impact of the fall in total fertility rates on the decline in infant mortality.

11. It is very difficult to develop an accurate estimate of the trends in public spending for the social sector. Table 12.9 represents an effort to trace the evolution of such spending based on the most reliable sources available, despite the obvious limitations of such data.

12. Military expenditures in Latin American and Caribbean countries tend to be very high. In a group of twenty-four countries in the region, military expenditures as a share of GDP (over 1990–1) was more than 3% in half of these countries, including four of the seven Central American countries. Furthermore, military expenditures were higher by 30% than spending on health and education in fifteen of these countries; in nine—four of which are Central American—this percentage was higher than 60% (UNDP, 1994).

13. Given the complex nature of the state apparatus, which calls for a large number of intrasectorial transfers, it is difficult to consolidate spending figures and to reconstruct the composition of financing. The estimates shown in Table 12.11 are based on the assumption that transfers from central government to institutions responsible for executing social programmes reflect the same income structure as that of central government. Under the accounting procedures applied, credit is not listed as income but rather as financing of the deficit, and therefore is not shown as capital income.

14. Statistics on this point were provided by ATD Consultores (1994).

Bibliography

Achío, M. (1994), 'La fecundidad en Costa Rica.' in CCSS (ed.), *Encuesta Nacional de Salud Reproductiva. Fecundidad y Formación de la Familia*, San José, Costa Rica: Caja Costarricense de Seguro Social.

Ameringer, C. D. (1982), *Democracy in Costa Rica*, Stanford: Praeger; cited in Drèze and Sen (1989).

ATD Consultores (1994), *Costa Rica. Perfil de la ayuda externa. Periodo 1970–1992*, San José.

Bulmer-Thomas, V. (1989), *La economía política de Centroamérica desde 1920*, San José, Costa Rica: EDUCA, for the Central American Bank for Economic Integration.

Drèze, J., and Sen, A. (1989), *Hunger and Public Action*, Oxford, Clarendon Press.

ECLAC (Economic Commission for Latin America and the Caribbean) (1994), *Social Panorama of Latin America*, Santiago.

Fields, G. (1980), *Poverty, Inequality and Development*, New York, Cambridge University Press.

Figueres, J. (1986), *Escritos discursos, 1942–1962*, San José, Costa Rica: Editorial Costa Rica.

Fonseca, C. (1991), *Computadoras en la escuela pública costarricense. La puesta en marcha de una decisión*, Serie Educación e Informática 1, San José, Costa Rica: Fundación Omar Dengo.

Garnier, L., and Hidalgo, R. (1991), 'El Estado necesario y la política de desarroll', in L. Garnier, R. Hidalgo, G. Monge *et al.*, *Entre la ilusión y la desesperanza: una alternativa para el desarrollo de Costa Rica*, San José, Costa Rica: Ediciones Guayacán.

Gómez, V. (1994), 'La transición demográfica en Costa Rica', in CCSS (ed.), *Encuesta Nacional de Salud Reproductiva. Fecundidad y Formación de la Familia*, San José, Costa Rica: Caja Costarricense de Seguro Social.

Güendel, L., and Trejos, J. D. (1994), *Reformas recientes en el sector salud de Costa Rica*, Serie Reformas de Política Pública, 18. Santiago, Chile: ECLAC.

Hirschman, A. (1977), *Voz, Salida y Lealtad*, México: Fondo de Cultura Económica.

Kleysen, D. (1988), *Private Expenditures on Health Care*, San José, Costa Rica: Instituto de Investigaciones en Ciencias Económicas.

Mata, L., and Rosero, L. (1988), *National Health and Social Development in Costa Rica: A Case Study of Intersectoral Action*, Washington, DC.: Technical Paper, 13, Pan American Health Organization.

MIDEPLAN/UNDP (1994), *Costa Rica en cifras: 1950–1992*, San José, Costa Rica: Ministerio de Planificación Nacional y Política Económica.

Miranda, G. (1994), *La seguridad social y el desarrollo en Costa Rica*, 2nd edn., San José, Costa Rica: EDNASSS-CCSS.

Pfeffermann, G., and Griffin, C. (1989), *Programas de nutrición y salud en América Latina. Enfoque en los gastos sociales*, Washington, DC.: World Bank, in co-operation with the International Center for Economic Development.

PREALC (1990), *La deuda social en Costa Rica*, San José, Costa Rica: Guadiseños Ltda. para el Programa Mundial del Empleo de la OIT.

Raczynski, D. (1994), 'Estrategias para combatir la pobreza en Chile: programas, instituciones y recursos', Documentos de trabajo, Washington, DC.: Banco Interamericano de Desarrollo.

Rama, G. (1994), *A la búsqueda del siglo XXI: Nuevos caminos de desarrollo en Costa Rica. Informe de la Misión Piloto del Programa Reforma Social del Banco Interamericano de Desarrollo*, mimeo.

Rodríguez, A. (1986), *El gasto público en salud y su impacto en la distribución del ingreso familiar*, Documento de Trabajo 100. San José, Costa Rica: Instituto de Investigaciones en Ciencias Económicas, Universidad de Costa Rica.

Rosero, L. (1983), *Social and economic policies and their effects on mortality: the Costa Rican case*, Seminar on Social Policy, Health Policy and Mortality Prospects, Paris: International Union for the Scientific Study of Population.

—— (1984), 'Las políticas socio-económicas y su efecto en el descenso de la mortalidad costarricense', *Mortalidad y Fecundidad en Costa Rica*, San José, Costa Rica: Asociación Demográfica Costarricense.

—— (1985), 'Determinantes del descenso de la mortalidad en Costa Rica', in Asociación Demográfica Costarricense (ed.), *Demografía y epidemiología en Costa Rica*, San José: Asociación Costarricense de Demografía.

Rovira, J. (1982), *Estado y política económica en Costa Rica: 1948–1970*, San José, Costa Rica: Editorial Porvenir.

—— (1989), *Costa Rica en los años 80*, San José, Costa Rica: Editorial Porvenir.

Sáenz, L., and León, M. (1992), 'Gastos de los hogares en servicios de salud privados en Costa Rica durante 1987–1988', San José, Costa Rica: Caja Costarricense de Seguro Social, Mimeo.

Sanguinetty, J. A. (1988a), *La educación general en Costa Rica. La crisis y sus posibles soluciones*, San José, Costa Rica: Development Technologies, Inc.

—— (1988b), *La salud y el Seguro Social en Costa Rica*, San José, Costa Rica: Development Technologies, Inc. and Pragma Cooperation.

Sauma, P., and Trejos, J. D. (1990), 'Evolución reciente de la distribución del ingreso en Costa Rica. 1977–1986. Documento de Trabajo 132', San José, Costa Rica: Instituto de Investigaciones en Ciencias Económicas, Universidad de Costa Rica.

Taylor-Dormond, M. (1991), 'El Estado y la pobreza en Costa Rica', CEPAL Review, 43, Santiago, Chile.

Trejos, J. D. (1990), *Pobreza y política social en Costa Rica*, Documento 1, Proyecto Regional para la Superación de la Pobreza en América Latina (RLA/86/004), San José, Costa Rica: Ministerio de Planificación Nacional y Política Económica.

—— (1991), 'La *política social y la valorización de los recursos humanos*', in L. Garnier, R. Hidalgo, G. Monge *et al. Entre la ilusión y la desesperanza: una alternativa para el desarrollo de Costa Rica*, San José, Costa Rica: Ediciones Guayacán.

—— (1994), *La pobreza en Costa Rica. Una síntesis cuantitativa*, mimeo.

—— Garnier, L., Hidalgo, R., and Monge, G. (1994a), 'Enhancing Social Services in Costa Rica', in C. Aedo and O. Larrañaga (eds.), *Social Service Delivery Systems: An Agenda for Reform*, Inter-American Development Bank, Washington, DC.: Johns Hopkins University Press.

—— Picado, X., Rodríguez, A., and Sáenz, I. (1994b), *Estrategias para combatir la pobreza en Costa Rica: Programas, instituciones y recursos*, Serie de Documentos de Trabajo, 192, Washington, DC.: Inter-American Development Bank.

UNDP (1994), *Informe sobre Desarrollo Humano 1994*, Mexico City: Fondo de Cultura Económica S.A.

UNICEF (1994), *Estado Mundial de la Infancia, 1994*, Barcelona, Spain: J y J Asociados for UNICEF.

Villasuso, J. M. (1992), 'Fondos y programas sociales en Costa Rica durante los ochenta', in PAHO/WHO (ed.), *Fondos y programas de compensación social. Experiencias en América y el Caribe*, Programa de Desarrollo de Políticas de Salud. Washington DC.: Pan American Health Organization, World Health Organization.

World Bank (1983), *World Tables*, ii: *Social Data*, 3rd edn., Baltimore, Maryland: Johns Hopkins University Press.

—— (1990), *Costa Rica. El gasto público en los sectores sociales*, Informe 8519-CR Washington, DC.: World Bank.

—— (1992), *Informe sobre el desarrollo mundial, 1992. Desarrollo y medio ambiente*, Washington, DC.: World Bank.

13

Human Development in Cuba:
Growing Risk of Reversal

SANTOSH MEHROTRA

Cuba is a small, very open economy, and has been so since before the Cuban revolution. Its dependence on trade for both consumption and output has not diminished since the revolution, so that it remains highly vulnerable to external shocks. For thirty years after the revolution it faced a relatively stable external environment, and within the limits of the structural constraints of being a small, open economy, output grew at a remarkable pace, even over the 1980s, when the rest of Latin America faced negative growth. Social indicators improved dramatically. However, whenever external shocks have occurred, output has been adversely affected throughout this century, and the experience of the 1990s has not been contrary to the historical experience of many other small, developing economies. This fact should be constantly borne in mind while analysing the Cuban experience.

This chapter is in two sections. Section 1 analyses mainly social (but also economic) development in Cuba during the period between 1960 and 1989, i.e. between the revolution and the collapse of the Soviet Union and the Council of Mutual Economic Assistance (Comecon). The section begins with an analysis of initial conditions in 1960. Most of it is, however, devoted to an analysis of how and why Cuba's social indicators improved so dramatically to become not only the best in Latin America, but in some cases comparable to those prevailing in the industrialized countries. It also discusses the linkages between social development and growth, and the weaknesses and strengths of the growth process. During the 1989–94 period, the weaknesses of that process were manifested in the economic decline resulting from the collapse of the Soviet Union and the intensified US economic embargo on Cuba, and in the growing risks of reversal of the social gains made over the preceding three decades—although no actual reversal has in fact occurred. Section 2 is devoted to an analysis of these effects on the collapse of Comecon and that of the US economic embargo on Cuba.

Social Development and Economic Growth, 1960–1989

In terms of the rate of growth of output, Cuban history over the last three and a half decades can be broken into three periods: the 1960s, when the institutional restructuring of Cuban society was taking place and growth was slow (negative in 1966–70); the 1970s until the mid-1980s, when growth was rapid; and the mid-1980s to the present, when slowing growth with the exhaustion of the extensive model of growth was followed by the collapse of output, resulting largely from the collapse of trade ties with Comecon. Dramatic social changes in the 1960s had laid the foundations of rapid economic growth in the later period. But the sustainability of growth was crucially dependent upon Soviet aid, and stability in the international trading system within Comecon which accounted for most of Cuban trade, which in turn accounted for a very substantial share of Cuban output.

Initial conditions

Both measured by real per capita income as well as some social indicators, Cuba was not one of the least developed of the Latin American countries in 1959. In the mid-1950s, the Cuban GNP was estimated to be $361 (in current US dollars), putting it fourth after Venezuela, Uruguay, and Argentina (Brundenius, 1984).[1] Both the under-5-mortality rate (U5MR) and the infant-mortality rate (IMR) were also well below the regional average in 1960: 87 in Cuba for U5MR (157 in the region) and 62 for IMR (against 105 in the region).

However, despite the relatively high level of average income, the economy was characterized by widespread poverty, open unemployment (16 per cent in 1956–7), and an unequal distribution of income. In 1961, nearly one-quarter of the adult population was illiterate, and malnutrition, especially in large rural families, was widespread. The unequal distribution of income was largely a reflection of the unequal ownership of land, given that most of the population was rural. Two-thirds of the landowners, with nearly as high a proportion of the total farms, occupied only 7 per cent of the cultivated area. At the same time, 9 per cent of the owners (who accounted for 8.5 per cent of the farms) held 73 per cent of the cultivated area.[2]

Apart from the highly unequal distribution of income (not unlike the rest of Latin America), the economy had two other characteristics: a very high dependence on one primary commodity (sugar), and a deep penetration of the economy by the USA, processes which were encouraged by the War of Independence against Spain (1895–8). The USA intervened in the war and accelerated Spain's defeat, then followed by the military occupation of the country, intermittently, until 1908.

Cuban sugar output expanded dramatically in the first two decades of the century, from 5 per cent of world output in 1901 to 22 per cent in 1918. Sugar cultivation grew along with the growth of the *latifundios*. The expansion of sugar cultivation took place at the expense of land devoted to other crops (especially coffee).

The reciprocal trade agreement reduced the duty on Cuban raw sugar in the US market while it increased the duty on refined sugar, thus hindering industrialization. US investments gradually replaced British and Spanish investments in the country. In 1929, US investments in Cuba were the largest in any Latin American country, accounting for just over one-quarter of total US investment in the region. About two-thirds of the US investment was in sugar-mills or other agricultural assets; and the banking sector was largely in the hands of US interests. Apart from sugar and tourism (the benefits of the latter also went to foreign interests or the domestic élite), there was little dynamism in the economy.

In 1960, less than two years after the revolution, Cuba began to establish trade ties with economies located thousands of kilometres from its shores, initially with the Soviet Union and subsequently with the rest of the countries of Eastern Europe, despite the fact that it was not the natural geographic region for Cuba's economic integration. The establishment of these ties was directly related to the economic blockade decreed by the USA which also put pressure on the rest of Latin America not to trade with Cuba. These relations led to a growing process of economic integration, and Cuba's admission to the Council of Mutual Economic Assistance in 1973. Within this framework, the country took on the role of supplying mainly sugar, as well as nickel, and other minor traditional Cuban products as the focus of its economic strategy, given the high prices and safe markets offered by that community.

The strategy pursued also included investments to expand the productive infrastructure: to modernize and expand agriculture and the capacity of traditional industries like sugar and nickel, as well as citrus fruits. In addition, new industrial capacity was created in the machine industry, construction materials, chemicals, the food industry, pharmaceuticals, textiles, and fishing.

Output grew slowly during the 1960s. Total material product may have declined during the second half of the decade of the 1960s. In fact, rapid growth in output began only in the early 1970s. This period of rapid economic growth was preceded by a series of measures which redistributed both assets and income. First, land reform occurred in 1959, and tenants of smallholdings became owners. Two *caballerias* (or 27 hectares) was fixed as the minimum farm size. The maximum was fixed at 30 *caballerias* in 1959, and the rest were taken over by the State (if not distributed). In 1963 this limit was reduced to 5, and all land above that limit was taken over by the State, affecting about 24 per cent of owners. Urban rents were cut in half in 1960, and within ten years tenants could become owners. Second, income was distributed in several ways. Wages were increased, with minimum wages becoming about 100 pesos. For management staff salaries were reduced, with most around 300 pesos; thus, the spread between minimum and maximum salaries was only 3 to 1.[3] In addition, piece-rates and other incentive payments were abolished in the latter half of the 1970s. There was particular emphasis on moral incentives as opposed to material ones.[4] Finally, health services and education were made free, and charges were also done away with for water, school meals, entrance to sporting events, and local telephone calls. Basic foodstuffs were also placed on ration and their prices as well as those for bus trips were kept low.

The 1960s in Cuba had some similarities to the 1950s in the Republic of Korea, in that social development during the period laid the foundations of future economic growth. First, land reforms laid the basis of an equitable distribution of income, so that when rapid economic growth began in the early 1970s, a virtuous circle of growth and improving equality was set in motion. Second, a large investment was made in education before rapid economic growth began. Later in this section we examine the strengths and weaknesses of this growth process, but first we turn to why and how health and education indicators improved so sharply.

Public health

After the revolution, in parallel with the nationalization of the means of production, there occurred a gradual nationalization of private health entities and institutions. The turning over of health-care services to the State was accelerated by the permanent exit from the country of the owners of private clinics and other health institutions. This gradual process culminated in 1970 with the integration of all the mutual aid institutions into the ministry of public health. This transformation guaranteed that the decisions made at the ministerial, territorial, and governmental levels were quickly put into effect. This is the only country studied in this book in which the health system has for the last quarter century been entirely in state hands. In this respect it is at the opposite end of the spectrum in organizational terms from the Republic of Korea, although the outcomes of the two systems were similar.

The 1960s were a period of reconstruction for the health services. The first migratory wave in 1959 and the early 1960s had left the country with half of its doctors (about 3,000). As Table 13.1 shows, the number of inhabitants per doctor actually increased from 1958 to 1965 and even up to 1970. Only by the early 1970s did the number of inhabitants per doctor drop below the 1958 level. Infant mortality did not decline for several years, and may have increased until about 1968. Clearly, the shortage of doctors resulting from the exodus following the revolution had its consequences.[5] Moreover, the stagnation of output in the 1960s was reflected in the production of necessities, especially food. From 1962 to 1968–9, non-sugar agricultural output fell by 18 per cent and supplies of consumer goods were tighter. However, the introduction of rationing in 1962 ensured that basic necessities were made available to the entire population. A comparison of nutritional surveys in 1967 with those made a decade earlier showed 'a definite improvement' in the state of nutrition (Navarro, 1972).

The development of primary care was, from the very beginning, one of the priorities of the revolutionary government. The shortage of doctors in the country

Table 13.1. Health input indicators

	Inhabitants per doctor	Inhabitants per dentist	Hospital beds per capita	Children born in health institutions (%)
1958	1,076	27,052	4.3	63
1965	1,252	6,508	—	73
1970	1,389	6,256	5.0	91
1975	997	4,010	—	98
1980	638	2,667	4.2	98
1985	441	1,893	—	99
1990	274	1,524	5.2	100
1994	203	1,242	—	100

Sources: Mesa Lago (1997) and Ministry of Public Health

and their concentration in the cities led, in January 1960, to the Rural Medical Service Law being passed, stipulating that recent graduates of medical schools had to do one year of service in rural areas. Later, the length of rural service was doubled. Health care was to be provided free of charge. In addition to free medical care, there had been active mobilizations of the population to increase immunization, donate blood, clear garbage dumps, and organize other similar activities, in most cases organized by the Committees for the Defence of the Revolution. With the first division of the national territory into health-care regions, the population began to have total access to medical services, including those in the rural areas. This and the fact that these services were provided free of charge constitute two major aspects of the Cuban concept of health care.

By the early 1970s primary care was being provided by a system of integral polyclinics, rural hospitals, dental clinics, and hygiene and epidemiology centres. Secondary care is given basically by municipal and provincial hospitals, while tertiary care is provided by national hospitals. Ten years of experience with integral polyclinics culminated in the application of a model of community medical care. The most important aspects of that evolution were: care provided by sector, which means that the doctors and health workers in charge of primary care take responsibility for the health conditions of a given number of inhabitants; and constant follow-up of patients and continuous attention to families.

This model served as the basis of the family-doctor programme, which began in 1984 in the jurisdictions of urban polyclinics and rural hospitals, with the general goal of caring for 120–40 families per family-doctor's office, the equivalent of 600–700 persons. The family doctor plan is aimed at offering high-quality preventive and curative care, to follow-up on the chronically ill, to treat all the population in their homes if necessary or advisable, and to reduce the demand for hospital and polyclinic services. But the essential concept permeating all the family-doctors' actions is watching over the population's health. This means that before going into details—which are so central to the specialist—the family doctor takes into consideration the factors of the environment, local culture, educational characteristics, and family living patterns. In late 1993, Cuba had 22,000 family doctors covering 90 per cent of the total population. Children are one of the main focuses of the family-doctors' attention.[6]

With the assistance of the Soviet Union and the East European countries, Cuba was able to set up a pharmaceutical manufacturing industry. During the 1980s, the pharmaceutical industry was able to meet 85 per cent of the country's needs in this field, although pharmaceutical production is highly dependent on the international market for raw materials. Continuing along this path, the first steps were taken to set up scientific complexes, bringing together resources from various institutions to carry out research.[7]

Along with the extension and quality of primary care, modern diagnostic and therapeutic equipment has been introduced at the higher levels of service. Tertiary care utilizes the latest in diagnostic and treatment technology—services matched only in the most developed countries. These include the generalization throughout the country of diagnostic ultrasound, CAT scanning and magnetic resonance imaging, *in vitro* fertilization, hyperbaric oxygenation, the development of organ and tissue transplants, and the establishment of pediatric intensive care units. Not surprisingly, per capita public health spending rose from 48.4 pesos in 1981 to 80.0 pesos in 1989, and given that inflation was almost non-existent, the real increase was substantial. This increment can be explained by the expansion of the family doctor system and the increased use of more modern and costly equipment in hospitals and institutes, as well as inefficiency in the use of human and material resources. But the State is now focusing its attention on economic efficiency in the design and use of health services.

The major difference after the revolution was that the number of rural facilities, and doctors located there, increased. The great demand for doctors in those years led to the creation of new medical schools, and today there are twenty-three such institutions in the country. As a result, the country went from 9.2 doctors per 10,000 inhabitants in 1958 to 33.1 doctors in 1989 and 46.7 in 1994 (currently there may be a glut of doctors). Four dental schools were also created, the number of nursing schools went from six to twenty, and thirty-two polytechnic health institutes were founded. A component of preventive care was the training of nutritional hygienists, sanitary engineers, and epidemiologists.

The immunization programme, founded in 1960, was carried out by specialized personnel with the support of the health and education sectors. As the doctor population was restored and the vaccination programme expanded, many diseases were entirely eradicated, including malaria and poliomyelitis, and mortality rates as a result of diseases such as tuberculosis, diphtheria, and intestinal parasites were sharply reduced. Table 13.2 shows how rapidly immunization coverage increased, and how high it was already in the 1970s. Table 13.3 shows the results of immunization for the whole population. Incidence of vaccine-preventable diseases had fallen to negligible levels by the early 1990s.

Organizations of civil society were critical to the public health effort. Various social organizations (like the Federation of Cuban Women) work voluntarily and free of charge at the grass-roots level in support of the primary-care system. This was a decisive element in the oral polio vaccine campaign and in the promotion of voluntary blood donations. In fact, the support brigades for public health comprise more than 61,000 women committed to helping the Ministry of Public Health in the areas of immunization, cancer detection, and prenatal and postnatal care.

One of the most powerful reasons for the drop in the infant-mortality rate is the sustained increase in hospital births. The share of children born in health institutions was already quite high in 1958 (63 per cent, see Table 13.1). This share increased very sharply to 73 per cent in 1965 and 91 per cent in 1970. Within fifteen years of the revolution nearly all children were being born in health institutions. In order to increase the number of hospital births, during the second half of the 1960s maternity homes were established, in the beginning to house pregnant women who lived far away from the hospitals. In the 1980s these institutions also started to receive women from urban areas with high-risk pregnancies.

Infant mortality dropped from almost 40 per 1,000 live births in 1960 to 10.2 in 1992. This figure puts Cuba in seventh place in the world and among the lowest in Latin America and the Caribbean (UNICEF, 1994). Table 13.4 shows infant-mortality rate (IMR) according to cause of death, in the first and last years of the period under analysis.

TABLE 13.2. Immunization rate, 1965–94

Vaccine	1965	1970	1975	1980	1985	1990	1993	1994
DPT: under 1 year old	—	46.6	71.5	66.8	91.2	95.6	98.5	104.6
DPT: 1–4 years old	—	—	—	—	90.83	83.4	94.5	94.3
PSR: under 1 year old	—	—	33.3[b]	48.2[b]	85.0[b]	94.9	92.9	99.8
Tuberculosis: under 1 year old	65.6	73.5	92.5	99.3	97.5	97.2	97.2	99.4
Polio: under 1 year old	86.2	87.8	100.0	101.9	86.7	96.0	96.9	96.0
Meningococcal[a]	—	—	—	—	—	—	84.3	102.1
Hepatitis B[a]	—	—	—	—	—	—	84.3	98.1

[a] not included in PAI; [b] only anti-measles

Source: Ministry of Public Heath

TABLE 13.3. Incidence in total population of some diseases preventable by vaccination

Disease and year vaccinations began	First year	1993
Poliomyelitis (1962)[a]	0.6	0.0
Typhoid fever (1970)	4.9	2.3
Tuberculosis (1965)	63.5	7.2
Diphtheria (1965)	8.0	0.0
Whooping cough (1965)	26.6	0.1
Tetanus (1965)	6.5	0.0
Neonatal tetanus (1965)	1.3	0.0
Meningococcal meningitis (1984)	9.0	0.8
Rubella (1989)	1.8	0.1
Mumps (1989)	0.6	0.1[b]
Measles (1986)	32.5	0.1[b]

[a] polio's elimination in Cuba was certified by the Commission of Experts headed by the PAHO-WHO in 1994; [b] data from 1992

Source: Statistics Dept., Ministry of Public Health

Infant mortality by cause has undergone very significant modifications. During this whole period, perinatal problems, although still playing a dominant role, have been substantially reduced, while congenital defects have become more statistically preponderant, and infectious and immunopreventible diseases have lost prominence. This panorama is similar to that of industrialized countries. As with IMR, the under-5-mortality rate went from 50 in 1960 to 12.2 in 1993, one of the world's lowest figures for this indicator. In the 1–14 age-group, in fact, the biggest cause of death is accidents. Not surprisingly, at the end of the period under discussion, life expectancy at birth stood at 75 years (Lage, 1994: 10).

Maternal-mortality rates, which are among the lowest in the world, were another outcome of Cuba's system of pre- and post-natal care and hospital births. It decreased more than fourfold in the period, from 118 deaths per 100,000 live births in 1960 to 27 in 1993 (Table 13.5). The legalization of abortion played an extremely important role in lowering maternal mortality during the period. The introduction of this practice in Cuban hospitals in 1965 offered the safety of the health-care system to women and lowered maternal mortality caused by illegal abortions.[8]

While in 1960 Cuba was already ahead of most other developing countries in health indicators, these further declines (from IMR of 65 to 10 in 1991) are the most difficult to achieve.[9] The two other countries in Latin America that had 1960 rates near Cuba's have not achieved the advances that Cuba made. Argentina, which began 1960 with IMR and U5MR of 59 and 70 respectively, progressed only to 22 and 24 in 1991. Uruguay advanced from 51 and 57 to 21 and 24 in 1991. These advances have been made, and maintained, despite a per capita income in 1990 one-

TABLE 13.4. Principal causes of death among infants (per 1,000 live births)

Causes	1960[a]	1993
Perinatal problems	15.2	3.6
Enteris and other diarrhoeal diseases	9.4	0.4
Influenza and pneumonia	3.9	0.7
Congenital defects	3.5	2.5
Accidents	2.8	0.3

[a] figures with omissions

Source: Statistics Dept., Ministry of Public Health

TABLE 13.5. Health outcome indicators

	U5MR	Life expectancy	Maternal-mortality rate per 100,000
1960	49.5	60	118
1965	—	—	107
1970	41.5	65	70
1975	—	—	68
1980	25.5	71	53
1985	—	—	31
1990	12.9	75	32
1993	10.3	—	27
1994	—	—	44

Source: Ministry of Public Health

half that of Argentina and Uruguay and one-twentieth that of the USA (where the indicators are comparable with those in Cuba). So successful has Cuba's health system been that the country sends large numbers of health workers to other countries. During the 1980s, between 2,000 and 3,000 health workers were sent each year for two-year periods to over thirty-six countries on three continents (Kuntz, 1993).

However, Cuba's health sector suffers from all the same inefficiencies that characterize many East European economies in transition. In 1988 the rate of hospital bed occupancy was 76.9 per cent, the average length of hospital stay was 9.9 days, and the average number of consultations was 4.4 per year (Mesa-Lago, 1996). By international standards, the first rate is low while the other two are high. If the average length of stay was reduced, the hospital occupancy rate would fall even further. The challenge facing the country is how to reduce costs without at the same time adversely affecting the health outcomes.

It is difficult to assess what the role of water and sanitation interventions was in the health transition, on account of the sparseness of the data. According to the 1981 census, half of all homes in Cuba lacked indoor plumbing: in rural areas 91 per cent of homes lacked that facility and in urban areas 33 per cent. But as Table 13.6 points out, by 1990 safe water and sanitation coverage were very high, though sanitation coverage was less than complete in rural areas.

The role of nutritional interventions in the health transition, however, cannot be denied. The measures soon after the revolution to alter the distribution of assets and income and the restructuring of public expenditure took care of the inequality in consumption. With a view to guaranteeing a minimum ration to all citizens, a strict rationing system was introduced in March 1962, and was rapidly expanded to cover most consumer goods by 1970. Calorie intake (in terms of kcal) was adequate on average in 1965 (see Table 13.7). Estimates suggest that the per capita availability of food and beverages increased by about 50 per cent between 1963 and 1980 (Brundenius, 1984).[10] What is remarkable, however, is that while calorie intake and protein intake increased, and the percentage of children born with low birth weight declined, the import-dependence on staples (see Table 13.13) is very high. It has not declined since the revolution. Thus, in the 1940s, 95 per cent of the rice consumption was met by imports.

A major outcome of the remarkable health transition during the three decades after the revolution was that the demographic transition was hastened. The total fertility rate fell below 2 in 1978 (see Fig. 13.1)—well below what is normal for Latin

TABLE 13.6. Coverage for safe water and sanitation services (%)

	1990	1995
Safe water		
Urban, total	83.6	98.0
domestic connection	83.0	85.0
public service	—	8.0
easy access	0.6	5.0
Rural, total	77.8	89.7
domestic connection	29.9	37.0
public service	27.9	35.0
Basic sanitation		
Urban, total	96.1	99.0
sewer system	39.1	42.0
septic tanks and latrines	57.0	57.0
Rural, total	68.2	81.0
sewer system	3.2	7.0
septic tanks and latrines	65.0	74.0

Source: Ministry of Public Health

TABLE 13.7. Nutrition indicators

	Low birth weight (%)	Calorie Intake (kcal)	Protein intake (gr)
1965	—	2,552	66.4
1970	—	2,565	68.8
1975	11	2,622	71.6
1980	10	2,867	75
1985	8	2,929	79
1990	8	2,726	74
1993	9	1,863	46
1994	9	—	—

Source: Ministry of Public Health

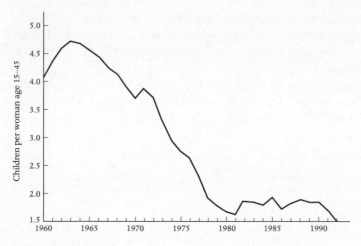

Fig. 13.1 Fertility rate, 1960–1992

Source: Ministry of Public Health

America, even for the high achievers in the region. Although Cuba has one of the highest population densities in Latin America, it has achieved one of the lowest fertility rates in the region, despite never having established an explicit population policy to control population growth. The rise in women's educational levels, the significant increase in women's participation in the work-force, and the profound transformation of their role in the family and society all played decisive parts in lowering the fertility rate. By the end of the 1960–93 period, there were about 60 per cent fewer births than at the beginning of the period (State Committee on Statistics). The reduction in fertility and mortality rates since the early years place the country in an advanced stage of demographic transition. Average family size has dropped from 4.9 members in 1953 to 3.8 in 1990.

Other determinants in Cuba's decrease in fertility are contraceptive use and abortion (Pérez Izquierdo, 1989, González Quiñones, 1994). Among women of reproductive age, 70 per cent used contraceptives in 1987–92, and abortion services have been available on request. Starting in 1989—the year which marks the loss of Cuba's international trade framework and the beginning of severe contractions in family budgets—family considerations concerning daily difficulties have also played a major role in regulating births.

Education

Fertility, health service utilization, and health-related behaviour is heavily influenced by the level of education, especially of women (as discussed in Chapters 2 and 3). By Latin American standards, the revolutionary State inherited not only a relatively high standard of living, but a relatively well-educated population. In 1953 enrolment in public schools as a percentage of the relevant age-group (i.e. the net enrolment ratio) was 58 per cent in primary schools, 19 per cent in secondary schools, and 5.5 per cent in universities. These figures were among the highest in Latin America, and similar to educational levels in Central America (other than Costa Rica) twenty years later. Before the revolution, Cuba had a relatively small proportion of illiterate adults (12 per cent in urban areas, 42 per cent in rural areas, and 23.6 per cent overall in 1953). Its labour force was unusually well organized, even in rural areas, by Latin American standards, and had a high level of schooling (about 75 per cent had at least completed primary school) (Carnoy and Samoff, 1989). Above all, there was no male–female differential in primary enrolment rates in 1960, and no differences in the literacy rate of men and women in 1970.

However, access to education was unequally distributed and the education ministry was characterized by considerable corruption.[11] Four statistics reflected the conditions prevalent in 1958: there were still one million total illiterates, over a million semi-illiterates, 600,000 children without schools, and 10,000 unemployed teachers (Castro, 1976). Access to higher education was restricted to the offspring of wealthy families. This explains why the first steps taken by the revolutionary government were oriented towards overcoming social exclusions.

From the very beginning of the revolutionary process, education was declared to be everyone's right. A key law, decreed on 6 June 1961, nationalized education, and defined education as being free of charge. The education process now aimed to redefine citizenship in collective terms and nationalism in international revolutionary terms. Schooling was to develop a motivation for collective rather than individual material success (in the productive sphere, a debate between material vs. moral incentives raged constantly), and a sense of belonging to Cuba as a revolutionary society.

Starting in 1960 several aspects of the educational system changed drastically. First, there was a nine-month campaign to make adults literate. Second, there was a move to eliminate inequality of access to education, implying a shift in emphasis from urban to rural children and adults, from universities to primary and secondary education, and from academic to vocational training. The latter required changes in curriculum. For primary and secondary schools this implied that manual work was an integral part of the school curriculum, and for university students it meant part-time work while attending university (Carnoy and Samoff, 1989).

The commitment also implied a very substantial allocation of resources. Education expenditure increased rapidly in the 1970s. As the material product increased, social spending increased even more rapidly. During the 1960s, Cuba spent around 4.2 per cent of GDP, rising in the 1970s to 7 per cent (in 1979), which is nearly twice the average of 4 per cent that UNESCO set as a goal for developing countries. Education spending per pupil by level is remarkably equitable, as Table 13.8 shows. In 1966, while expenditure per primary pupil was 65 pesos, for secondary pupils it was 305. If anything, the ratio became even more equitable later, with 210 pesos being spent per pupil at primary level, 451 pesos at secondary level (1 : 2 : 1), and 576 pesos (1 : 2 : 7) at the university. By contrast, in Sub-Saharan Africa, expenditure per pupil at the higher level as a multiple of the primary level is 33 on average, and 9 in Asia in 1992 (Mehrotra and Vandemoortele, 1996).

In the 1960s, the emphasis was on primary education and on adult literacy. There were 7,500 primary schools, with about 700,000 children enrolled in 1958–9. Within the first year after the revolution this number increased to one million. By 1975, there were almost 13,000 primary schools in rural areas and 2,800 in urban areas, and a total of 1.8m. children were enrolled (see Table 13.9). As total fertility fell, total enrolment declined from the late 1970s onward. Within twenty years of the revolution all children were going to school.

Table 13.8. Education spending per student by level of schooling, 1961–90 (pesos)

Year	Primary	Basic secondary	Total secondary	University
1961	54	—	177	—
1965	69	—	278/318	—
1966	65	—	305	—
1980	210	535	451	576
1982	244	671	565	891
1983	274	660	610	923
1990	335	—	633	966

Sources: Carnoy and Samoff (1989) and UNESCO (1994)

In 1961, Cuba captured the world's attention by carrying out a nine-month literacy campaign in which the government mobilized over 100,000 secondary-school students and other volunteers to teach 707,000 adults from all over the country to read and write. The illiterate adults had previously been identified through a census. At that time 23.6 per cent of Cuban adults were illiterate. The literacy campaign brought the revolution to the most isolated members of Cuban society, and connected the urban, educated groups, especially youths, to the rural poor and illiterate.

On the completion of the literacy campaign, formal education classes for adults began in early 1962. The classes were for those who had become literate during the campaign and for those who never finished primary school. In striking contrast with Kerala where a similar literacy campaign was organised in the late 1980s, one aspect of the Cuban government's effort was that when the literacy campaign ended, a programme to elevate the educational level of the people was launched, and primary and secondary schooling was offered in farms, factories, offices, and night schools.[12] According to a national survey in 1979, Cuba had been able to reduce the illiteracy problem to only 3.9 per cent. By the mid-1970s the number of adults registered in these classes had dropped sharply (see Table 13.9). In 1990, illiteracy had been reduced to 0.2 per cent (Govt. of Cuba, 1993) for the population ages 15 and older. Two new types of adult education began in the late 1960s: lower-secondary schools for adults, and worker-peasant faculties to prepare adults for entering university. From 1962 to 1989, 1.5m. adults finished 6th grade and 900,000 finished 9th grade.

With the advent of moral incentives in the mid-1960s, school curricula increasingly emphasized the relation of schools to work. The need for agricultural labour and the development of the 'socialist man' required a new experiment of moving 'schools to the countryside'. Beginning in 1966, teachers and students would live and work together in the countryside for about seven weeks. This not only provided additional labour at sugar-harvest time, but had as an objective the elimination of the difference between town and country. 'Schools to the countryside' is still a feature of secondary schooling in Cuba. Students from urban areas continue to go to rural areas for thirty to forty-five days a year to do agricultural work. By the late 1970s, though, such work was more for consciousness-raising than for its contribution to agricultural output.[13]

After 1970 'schools to the countryside' was replaced by schools in the countryside. Educational opportunities expanded, particularly in the rural areas. Before 1959 there were no secondary schools at all in the rural areas, and even in 1970 gross enrolment ratio at the secondary level was only 25. Secondary enrolment expanded very rapidly in the 1970s (see Table 13.9). Since then, a very substantial effort has been made to construct boarding-schools in the rural areas, which are based on the principle of half-time work and half-time study. By the end of the 1970s such

TABLE 13.9. Enrolment level ('000s)

Year	Pre-school	Primary	Secondary	Adult	University	Special	Craft schools	Others	Total
1958–9	92	626	88	0	2	0	0	4	811
1965–6	90	1,242	232	574	26	4	0	1	2,169
1975–6	127	1,796	629	595	85	12	23	1	3,267
1980–1	124	1,469	1,146	277	152	29	15	2	3,213
1985–6	109	1,077	1,157	185	235	46	20	3	2,833
1988–9	144	900	1,127	142	251	49	22	1	2,636
1989–90	145	886	1,073	142	242	54	20	1	2,563
1990–1	166	888	1,002	133	242	59	20	0	2,511
1991–2	148	918	912	129	225	63	22	0	2,416
1992–3	162	942	820	119	198	60	30	0	2,332
1993–4	165	983	726	114	166	57	29	0	2,241

Source: Govt. of Cuba, National Statistical Office

schools accounted for a quarter of total secondary enrolment. By the end of the 1980s secondary education was practically universal—in contrast to the rest of Latin America where the secondary-school enrolment ratio was under 50 per cent at the same time (UNICEF, 1996).[14]

Most students at these schools came from urban areas, boarded at the school, and spent the weekends with their families. But the schools were built around agricultural production plans and combined work and study throughout the year. However, although it was estimated that the work of the schoolchildren would cover operating costs of the school and even some of the capital costs incurred in building such schools, that objective was not realized. The schools proved to be an expensive solution to the secondary-schooling problem (Carnoy and Samoff, 1989).

Enrolment in universities declined after 1959 until 1965, as the government shifted policy emphasis to first primary and then secondary education. However, as economic growth increased after 1970, university enrolment was able to expand along with the resources available to the economy. The expansion of university enrolment was also part of the shift in economic strategy. After 1970, the growth strategy was to focus on centralized, technocratic planning, with decentralized decision-making at the factory level. Thus, growth was to be based on a substantially larger number of highly trained decision-makers.[15] For the same reason, the early 1970s was the period when the construction of élite secondary vocational schools began. These schools focus on technical and scientific subjects, are well equipped, employ highly skilled teachers, and take only the best students. In fact, Carnoy and Samoff argue that these schools are 'the evident manifestation of the shift in policy from building socialist consciousness [dominant in the 1960s] to focusing on immediate development of the structure of production and capital accumulation'.

At the beginning of this period, the organization and preparation of teaching personnel was an extraordinary task. For this purpose, rural primary-school teachers were first trained. Later, in the early 1970s, junior high-school students and high-school graduates were mobilized to work as teachers. Those who expressed a desire to become educators were grouped together into pedagogical detachments, in which the idea of combining work and study constituted a new educational concept. By 1980 the pupil–teacher ratio at the primary level was 20, a very favourable ratio from the viewpoint of the quality of learning. Since then it has decreased to 16 (1993–4). In the 1980s, efforts continued to improve teacher training, and out of this came the first university graduates in primary education. The goal now is for all those who impart basic education on a regular basis to have an undergraduate degree in education.

Overall the results have been remarkable. The average level of schooling in 1953 was less than 3rd grade, but today is close to 9th grade. By 1979 the share of the population with at least six years of schooling had increased from one-fourth in 1953 to almost two-thirds. Currently the average Cuban has almost a 9th-grade education. This has made it possible to extend the age to which education is compulsory to 9th grade, but steps are being taken to extend it to 12th grade.

Providing for children of pre-primary age has been a concern throughout the period. Before 1960, thirty-eight day nurseries and one charity home cared for some of the children in need of public assistance. In 1960, the revolutionary government assigned the recently founded Federation of Cuban Women the task of organizing institutions to care for the small children of working women, using state funds. In 1993 there were 1,154 of these institutions in the country, under the direction of the Ministry of Education. A significant proportion of all children who enter primary school have been to pre-primary schools in Cuba, more than in most other developing countries.

Table 13.10 gives a sense of the magnitude of the Cuban achievement in social development. Although income levels are much lower than in the formerly centrally planned economies of Eastern Europe, in 1990 social indicators in Cuba were at least comparable, if not superior. Thus, infant mortality rates are the lowest, and life expectancy the highest in Cuba, as are the number of physicians per 10,000 population. Adult illiteracy is comparable, and secondary-school enrolments are among the highest. Even tertiary-level enrolments are close to the highest levels found in Eastern Europe.

Women in Cuban society

Male–female differentials in educational indicators were never really a serious problem in Cuba. As educational opportunities, especially in rural areas, expanded for the entire population, women also started completing secondary education in large numbers by the 1970s. The female work-force more than doubled during the 1970s from 482,000 to more than one million, as against an estimated female labour force in 1960 of 300,000 (then only 13 per cent of the labour force). By the mid-1980s, more than one-third of the labour force consisted of women, similar to the ratio found in developed countries. Of total women of working age (minus full-time students), economically active (or occupied) women rose from 25 per cent in 1970 to nearly 48 per cent in 1980 (Brundenius, 1984). What is significant is that almost two-thirds of the new members of the labour force entered the service sector and only one-third joined the other sectors, and of those entering the services the largest increase was in social services, i.e. health and education.

Women have been a potent force in the mass mobilizations in the health and education sector. The Federation of Cuban Women, created in 1960 to organize, educate, and mobilize women from all parts of Cuban society, grew from 400,000 in 1962 to 3.2m. in 1990. The federation influences policy at all decision-making levels of society. It is supported by dues from members and subsidies from government, and has good access to media and to the facilities of government departments. The federation has been closely involved in improving the education of

TABLE 13.10. Social indicators in Cuba and other centrally planned economies

	Infant-mortality rate (1990)	Physicians per 10,000 inhabitants (1984)	Life expectancy at birth (1990)	Total adult illiteracy (1990)	Gross secondary enrolment (1990)	Armed forces as a % of teachers (1987–90)
Albania	31	—	72	15	79	140
Bulgaria	14	36	73	7	73	213
China	30	10	70	27	48	39
Cuba	11	37	75	4	90	124
Czechoslovakia (former)	11	37	72	1	83	184
Hungary	15	32	71	1	81	106
Poland	16	21	72	2	83	112
Romania	27	18	71	4	92	122
USSR (former)	23	37	71	1	94	135
Yugoslavia (former)	20	18	73	7	80	124

Sources: UNICEF, *State of the World's Children*, 1992; Mesa Lago (1997)

rural women. One of its wings, the Contingent of Militant Mothers for Education, with 1.4m. members, is helping to raise the education of all workers to the 6th-grade level. Similarly, the support brigades for public health consist of more than 61,000 women committed to helping the ministry of public health in such areas as immunization, cancer detection, and prenatal and postnatal health care. Women make up nearly half of all physicians and occupy about half of the directorships of hospitals and polyclinics. Of the 12,000 family doctors in the country, three-fifths are women.

It is not surprising, therefore, that women's political representation in Cuba is the third highest in the developing world. In 1994, nearly a quarter of parliamentarians were women, having fallen from constituting one-third of the parliament (UNDP, 1995). Thus, while in almost all the countries discussed in this book the indicators of discrimination against women were nearly eliminated and women's economic activity rate increased, in Cuba women have been even more successful in establishing what Sen has called 'women's agency', thus ensuring not only their own well-being but that of their entire families.[16]

Social expenditures

The social achievements of Cuba were not only the result of mass mobilization, but of government commitment reflected in social allocations which were very high in comparison with the rest of Latin America. Although there are some difficulties in comparing Cuban figures with those in other Latin countries (on account of the different systems of national accounts and material product), Cuban social expenditures (as percentage of Gross Social Product) compared with Latin American averages (as percentages of GNP) at the end of the 1980s were: almost twice as large in education, 2.6 times in health, and 3.8 times in social security (Mesa-Lago, 1994b). Mesa-Lago's comparison of the structure of public social expenditures in the former centrally planned economies of Eastern Europe in 1987 demonstrates that Cuba's shares of education (37 per cent) and health (21 per cent) were respectively the highest and second highest in a list of seven countries (Cuba, the USSR, Poland, Hungary, Czechoslovakia, Bulgaria, and East Germany). The high education expenditures are due to Cuba's having one of the youngest populations in the ex-Comecon countries, and to the high priority accorded to health care. However, given the lower level of income in Cuba compared to the other former centrally planned economies, there is scope for arguing that there may have been some over-investment in the health sector in Cuba.

As Table 13.11 shows, the share to education, health, and social security has tended to increase consistently over the last three decades. While education's share in GSP was 4 per cent in 1969, by 1990 it had risen to 6.8 per cent. Similarly, while health's share in GSP was 2.9 per cent in 1969, in 1990 it stood at 4.7 per cent. What is more remarkable is that their share has probably risen since the economic crisis

TABLE 13.11. Education and health expenditure

	Share of gross social product (%)				Share of total social spending (%)		
	Education	Social security	Health care	Total	Education	Social security	Health care
1959	—	—	—	—	35.2	52.8	12.0
1969	4.0	5.5	2.9	12.4	32.5	44.0	23.5
1979	7.5	4.0	2.4	13.9	54.0	28.7	17.4
1990	6.8	5.3	4.7	16.8	40.5	31.4	28.0
1992	8 to 13	7 to 11	6 to 10	22 to 34	38.4	32.1	28.6

Source: calculated from data in Mesa Lago (1997)

began. That is perhaps more a reflection of the fact that GSP has fallen sharply, and not that there has been an increase in priority to the social sectors. In contrast to the vast majority of Latin American countries, which reduced their priority to social sectors during the 'lost decade' of the 1980s, Cuba did not let social allocations slip even after the crisis began.[17]

Health expenditures have been protected ever since the crisis broke, as is evident from Table 13.11 on the distribution of social expenditures between education, health, and social security. It appears, in fact, that while social security and health expenditures have remained relatively immune to the crisis, the most serious cuts within the social sectors may have occurred in education.

Like many other centrally planned economies, social expenditures are characterized by considerable inefficiencies and some wastage. As we shall see below, the economic crisis resulting from the collapse of economic ties with Comecon has forced the State to look for cost-effective ways to provide the same level of services.

The social impact of economic growth and structural change

The relative strength of the economy from the early 1970s until the mid-1980s allowed social expenditures to rise. After the slow growth over the 1960s (total material product grew 2.8 per cent per annum), the economy grew very rapidly for over a decade (7.1 per cent over 1970–81). The growth was founded on industry, and particularly capital-goods industry. Industrial growth rate increased to 8.4 per cent per annum over 1971–80, up from 3.6 per cent over 1961–70; this was much faster than agriculture, which increased its growth rate from 1.5 per cent in the first decade to 3.6 per cent in the second. The expansion of the capital-goods sector was the outcome of a planning strategy to build up a domestic resource base around agriculture. Thus, Cuba has a modest but important sector producing combine-harvesters, fertilizers, pesticides, and other inputs for agriculture (Brundenius, 1984).

Structural change in the economy was occurring simultaneously with social development. Industrial activities, defined as mining, manufacturing, electrical energy, and construction, accounted for 46.4 per cent of GDP in 1981, probably one of the highest figures in Latin America. The increase from 32 per cent in 1960 was a remarkable example of structural change within two decades, compared to other countries in Latin America.[18] Changes in the economy affected the structure of employment as well: the share of agriculture declined in both absolute and relative terms. Agriculture accounted for nearly 42 and 37 per cent of the labour force in 1953 and 1958–9 respectively, but fell to 30 per cent in 1970 and 21.9 per cent in 1979. Those employed in agriculture were typically wage-labourers, who comprised 64 per cent of the agricultural labour force, rather than subsistence farmers. In absolute terms, the number of those employed in agriculture fell from 813,000 in 1958–9 to 716,000 twenty years later. Industry and construction, which accounted for 24.8 per cent in 1958–9, employed 31.4 per cent of the work-force in 1989. There was a very substantial expansion in service-sector employment, particularly in health and education. In fact, as women began entering the labour force in the 1970s, they were absorbed mainly in the health and education sectors (a trend found in Eastern European countries as well).

Another structural change of major social significance was the government's successful effort to reduce inequalities between town and country. Although the average 1962 wage in agriculture was only 49 per cent of the average wage in industry, the difference between the two sectors had narrowed to 86 per cent in 1980. As we discussed above, health and education services were also targeted at the rural areas. Housing construction was also concentrated in the rural areas, as were installations of electricity, piped water, and sanitation facilities. These policies helped to keep rural–urban migration down, and in the early 1980s only about 20 per cent of the population was living in the large metropolitan areas—in striking contrast with most other Latin American countries.[19]

The narrowing of the wage differentials between rural and urban areas was helped by the shortage of skilled labour which developed in the economy after 1961. To meet this shortage and with the 1961–3 commitment to industrialization, the enrolment in industrial schools increased rapidly, more than tripling the 1959 number by 1963. In other words, long before general secondary schools expanded in the 1970s, technical education had expanded. Moreover, the difference between academic secondary schools and technical schools was minimal, especially in the early years of the revolution, when there was little growth in university education. In fact, much pressure was put on university students at the time to train to become secondary-school teachers, and, as we saw earlier, for secondary-school students to take on vocational tasks as a condition of continuing into higher education (Carnoy and Samoff, 1989).

From 1975 to 1985, the average growth rate of production was of the order of 6.2 per cent annually at constant prices, an enviable growth rate for Latin America in that period. However, this growth was obtained on the basis of an extensive model (based on ever-increasing applications of labour and capital), which implied an ever-greater demand for investment[20] or even decreases in labour productivity growth. The decline in productivity indicates that this model of growth had exhausted itself by the end of the 1981–5 period. Although capital investments increased consistently until 1988, productivity of capital had begun to decline earlier. The systemic inefficiencies that characterized all centrally planned economies, manifested in the falling productivity after extensive sources were exhausted, had begun to affect the performance of the Cuban economy.

Cuba's economy has always been quite dependent on foreign trade; throughout the period its import coefficient has been quite high in relation to national income (48 per cent during 1980–9). We began by saying that by any standard Cuba had a very open economy (with a high commodity concentration of exports) and hence is highly vulnerable to external shocks. In fact, Cuba's economy was one of the most open within the Comecon: reliance on imports and exports amounted to half of global social product. The Cuban economy's dependence on imports can be seen in Table 13.12, which reflects the levels of the domestic demand met from imported supply, estimated to be at approximately 51 per cent, on the average, in the 1985–9 period (National Institute of Economic Research, 1995: 7). What the table does not reveal is that Cuban dependence on imported petroleum and petroleum products is almost complete.[21]

Although Cuba's foreign trade grew by a factor of 9.7 from 1960 to 1985, industrial development was not sufficient to significantly modify the export structure,

---

TABLE 13.12. Share of imports in domestic consumption (selected goods)

	Share (%)
Food and agricultural products	
Cereals for human consumption	100
Fats and oils	98
Beans	90
Fertilizers (raw materials)	94
Herbicides and pesticides	98
Livestock feed (raw materials)	87
Textiles, footwear, and soaps	90–100
(Cotton, polyester fibres, tallow, raw materials, and other)	
Production of containers and printed matter	75–100
(Tin, cellophane, sodium carbonate, paper pulp, wood)	
General industrial operation and maintenance	60–100
(Fuels, sulphur, caustic acid, rubbers, titanium dioxide, zinc)	

Source: E. Alvarez, *La Apertura Cubana*, Institute for Economic Research

within which sugar represents 80 per cent of sales. Meanwhile, in agriculture, the production levels were generally lower than what could have been obtained with the land and available resources. Table 13.13 reflects the inefficiencies of collective or state farms, and also Cuba's specialization in the international socialist division of labour. Per capita production of some agricultural commodities like corn and rice, vegetables (beans, tomatoes, tubers), and coffee has fallen or stagnated.

Cuban trade was also highly dependent on the Comecon market. In 1989 the Comecon countries accounted for 79 per cent of Cuba's total trade (the USSR for 65 per cent), but by 1992 their share had fallen to 19 per cent, while the total value of Cuba's trade had shrunk disastrously. In addition, the Soviet supply of oil and oil by-products, which met about 90 per cent of Cuba's energy needs, fell sharply. Besides, Cuba's re-exports of refined Soviet oil was its main source of hard currency after sugar, and this too disappeared.

The external vulnerability—a combination of the openness and high commodity concentration of trade—resulted in continuous trade deficits and a burgeoning foreign debt. Cuba's trade deficit as a percentage of GSP was already 7.5 per cent in 1985, and rose to 10.1 per cent in 1989.

Thus, after growing very rapidly for one and a half decades until 1985, the economy was growing slowly thereafter, and in spite of considerable structural change, its vulnerability to external shocks was still high. Over three decades there was enormous success in mechanizing agriculture, shifting labour from agriculture to industry and services, and quadrupling the number of women in the labour force, while keeping the economy at near full employment. But precisely because of its openness, when economic ties with Comecon collapsed, output collapsed with it. Estimates vary (see Table 13.14), but economic activity may have declined

TABLE 13.13. Per capita production of selected agricultural commodities (kg.)

	1958	1986–9
Corn	33.0	3.7
Beans	5.7	1.3
Tomatoes	16.0	25.4
Tubers and root vegetables	119.7	63.5
Rice	20.7	25.7
Eggs	15.3	250.0
Coffee	6.7	2.6
Milk	61.3	100.8
Cattle[a]	0.9	0.5
Citrus fruits	9.2	83.0

[a] head per inhabitant

Source: Nova Armando, 'Agricultura cubana y las transformaciones necessarias', Institute for Economic Research, 1993

TABLE **13.14.** Estimate of decline in trade and GSP

	Foreign trade: % decline based on 1989	GSP: % decline
1990 High	13.8	7
Medium[a]	—	5
Low	11.8	1.5
1991 High	48.5	40
Medium	46.2	24
Low	44.4	15
1992 High	68.1	20
Medium	66.7	11
Low	55.6	6

[a] is both the median and the average of the different estimates

Source: Mesa Lago (1997)

by up to half from 1990 to 1994—a much larger decline than that experienced by any Latin American economy during the lost decade of the 1980s.

The Economic Crisis and its Impact

On the decline in growth trend since the mid-1980s was superimposed not only the effect of the collapse of Comecon, but in addition, the US tightening of its thirty-three-year embargo on Cuba in 1992. The economic and social consequences of the two events have been devastating.

The decline in foreign trade since 1989 had a dramatic impact on all the main economic variables—output, consumption, and investment. Cuba probably suffered more than any other economy of the Comecon in the 1990s on account of the collapse of the special trade relationships. As the Cuban economy was designed on a model of trade and specialization in production, the suddenly disappearance of the framework meant the loss of markets, sources of financing, technological integration, and preferential prices, as well as the breakdown of the development strategy the country had been following until that moment.

Gross domestic investment declined by 43 per cent between 1989 and 1991. By 1993 investment may have dropped to only 5 to 7 per cent of GSP, down from 17 per cent of GSP in 1989, which will have a considerable impact on future economic growth. An important reason was the termination by 1992 of economic (and military) assistance from the Eastern European countries. Russia may have left six hundred incomplete investment projects in Cuba, though some are being resumed (Mesa-Lago, 1994*a*). A Washington-based group backing an easing of the US embargo pointed out that, to recover its 1988 standard of living, the Cuban economy will have to grow for eight years in a row at 7 per cent (Fiddler, 1995).

The collapse of economic relations with Comecon has led to widespread shut-downs in industry and mining, a virtual halt of ground transportation, reduced energy and water supplies, and cuts in commerce, printing, and entertainment. In 1970 unemployment was only 1.7 per cent, most of it frictional. A rapidly growing work-force in the 1970s led to some open unemployment, which was 5.5 per cent in 1979 and even in 1988 was only 6 per cent. Since then figures on unemployment have not been published. But since output has been most affected in the above-mentioned areas, it is likely that unemployment is highest there (though as in other transitional economies there may be considerable labour hoarding by enterprises). The sectors least affected by the crisis are agriculture (prioritized by the Food Pro-gramme); the sugar industry (though production has been declining since 1989); social services (on account of government commitment), and tourism (which is being expanded) (Mesa-Lago, 1996).

Consumption has been affected by rising inflation. Since February 1992 the gov-ernment has been raising prices of retail foodstuffs very sharply in order to be able to cut subsidies and provide private farmers with incentives to cultivate high-value crops. Later in the year a radical reform of wholesale prices—not changed since 1981—was approved, bringing them closer to real prices of exports and imports and reflecting more closely their production costs. The number of consumer goods which are rationed was constantly increased from 1990 on, so that by 1993 virtually every consumer good was rationed. However, current rationing quotas (on the assumption that they are fulfilled in practice, which is usually not the case) cover only two weeks of minimum food needs of the population. In 1989, 57 per cent of the protein and 51 per cent of the calories consumed in Cuba came from imports. The daily calorie intake declined from 3,103 in the mid-1980s to 2,835 in 1989 and 2,000 in 1992, or below the minimum set by the WHO (Mesa-Lago, 1997).

The shortage of goods, combined with high wages, had resulted in accumulated savings and a huge monetary surplus by the end of the 1980s when the economic crisis struck—a situation in which most Eastern European economies found themselves at the time.[22] The goods shortage became worse when imports fell sharply after the collapse of Comecon. It is estimated that in Cuba the enormous liquidity which had been accumulated was comparable to the GDP in 1993.[23] This has sparked an underground economy at market prices which is characterized by galloping inflation. This underground economy, even combined with what the government offers at regulated prices, does not meet the population's needs, but has been a real alternative for acquiring essential goods. Added to this is the establishment in 1993 of a market in convertible currency. These two factors com-bined provide the setting in which the Cuban household economy functions.[24] There are risks of the re-emergence of poverty: it was announced that 20 per cent of the population is low income (*Granma*, 2 May 1994), defined as 50 pesos or less per capita, but the decisions to increase official prices and rates on selected products and services will probably result in a modification of the notion of social vulnerability.

Macroeconomic balances have been very adversely affected. As output fell, government revenues declined, but the effort to sustain a safety net meant that government expenditures had to be maintained. The government's budget deficit rose to one-third of domestic output in 1993 (though it has been slashed since then). As regards the external balance, a rising trade deficit has led to foreign debt in freely convertible currency. In 1993 the foreign debt stood at over $8bn. This figure grows systematically with the accumulation of interest, since the country has not received new credits since the early 1980s.

The government has responded by undertaking economic reforms, and it is estimated that the economy is turning around, and should grow by 2 per cent in 1995. The government says that it favours the model of economic reform combined with strong political control provided by Vietnam and China. The decisions being made imply major changes and indicate that the government has adopted a new model of development and economic policy.

Social impact of the economic crisis and embargo

Every aspect of Cuban household life has been affected by the economic crisis, but also by the embargo. The US embargo against Cuba has been the longest embargo by one State against another in modern history. Before the Cuban revolution in 1959, the US was Cuba's major trading partner, accounting for about 75 per cent of exports and imports. On account of the US economic embargo, Cuba completely shifted its trade ties to Comecon in the early 1960s. Over the past three decades these sanctions have been periodically changed to respond to evolving US objectives. In 1975, under pressure from US allies and US subsidiaries wanting to trade with Cuba, the USA lifted the ban on subsidiary trade with Cuba under specific conditions. The regulations were also revised to allow third-country ships engaged in trade with Cuba to dock at US ports. This proviso acquires significance considering that 85 per cent of Cuban trade was carried in ships belonging to other countries, mainly Comecon countries until 1990.

The Cuban Democracy Act of 1992, however, aimed to reimpose third-country sanctions that had been rescinded in 1975 (at the time the cold-war *détente* began). Once again US subsidiaries in other countries are prohibited from trading with Cuba and ships that have landed in Cuba are forbidden from docking in the USA for six months afterwards. All trade, including that in food, medicines, and medical supplies, which at the time of the legislation comprised over 90 per cent of Cuban trade with US subsidiaries was prohibited.[25] It is not always possible to disentangle the effects of the economic crisis resulting from the collapse of economic ties with

Comecon from those of the US embargo (though where it is possible we attempt to do so below).

While the previous section examined the macroeconomic effects and household-level implications of the crisis facing the Cuban economy, here we look at the sectoral impact at the household level in terms of food consumption, health services, and micro-nutrient availability, water supply, and schooling.[26] We have indicated above that food is an important component of Cuban imports. After the collapse of Comecon, Cuba substantially increased its imports of foodstuffs from subsidiaries of US corporations. From 1988 to 1990 there was a tenfold increase in the Cuban import of grain, wheat, and other consumables from US subsidiaries. According to Cuban officials, in 1991 $347m. out of $383m. in goods bought from US subsidiaries were foodstuffs.

By switching sources of supply, the country managed (between 1989 and 1992) to maintain a steady volume of grain imports, but was purchasing less expensive kinds of grains on account of a shortage of hard currency. It placed considerable priority on achieving self-sufficiency in food, but needs were far from being met. Cuban officials expect grain and foodstuff imports to continue (mainly from Western countries) (Kuntz, 1993). Agricultural production has been affected by the combined impact of the economic crisis and the high commodity concentration of trade with US subsidiaries (which was banned by the Cuban Democracy Act of 1992). About half of all proteins and calories intended for human consumption were imported in the 1980s, but imports of foodstuffs declined by about 50 per cent from 1989 to 1993. Fertilizer imports declined from 1,300 tons in 1989 to 3 tons in 1992. Cereal imports for animal consumption declined from 1.8m. tons in 1989 to half a million tons in 1992. Domestic production of meat, milk, and eggs was hampered by lack of animal feed. Petroleum imports (necessary to run the capital-intensive Cuban farms) were 30m. tons per day in the 1980s, and only 6m. in 1992. Naturally, domestic food production was impacted. From 1989 to 1992 milk production fell by 55 per cent, sugar and bean production by 30 per cent. Edible oil production was so low and imports so delayed that supplies in early 1994 were adequate only for the country's bread production. The milk ration of one litre a day provided daily to children up to age 7 was in 1994 given only up to age 5. An effort was made to spread the burden and share equally the privations faced by the population (ibid).

By limiting foreign shipping, the embargo has led since 1992 to greater reliance on the country's limited commercial shipping fleet. It was estimated that sea shipping since 1992 costs $15 per ton more, resulting in excess costs of $41m. in 1993 for importation of food. In total, Cuban imports were about $4bn. in current dollars during the last three decades; about $1bn. of that total is estimated to be excess costs associated with the embargo (Garfield *et al.*, 1994).

The decline in calories and protein poses health risks resulting from protein-energy malnutrition. But preferential rationing led only to a moderate rise in the percentage of babies born with weights under 2,500 grams, from 7.3 per cent in 1989, the lowest level reached in the 1980s, to 8.7 per cent in 1993.

Micro-nutrient deficiencies also appear to be growing. For the first time in more than a decade iron-deficiency anaemia affected 35 per cent of pregnant women and 50 per cent of infants from 6 to 12 months in 1991.[27] Vitamin A deficiency was the major risk factor associated with the epidemic of optic neuropathy (a nerve disorder that causes blurring and progressive loss of vision) which affected over 45,000 people in 1992 and 1993. However, since late 1992 the entire population has been provided periodic vitamin supplements to address the problem.

The effects of the US embargo on health services manifest themselves mainly in Cuba's access to vital medicines, supplies, and medical equipment, and to raw materials and spare parts used in local production of drugs and maintenance of equipment. While the lack of hard currency to purchase the products is central to Cuba's trade problems, even with hard currency the country cannot obtain the necessary goods at any price. While most European and Latin American countries have been trading with Cuba, foreign pharmaceutical firms (and producers of other products) cannot sell their products to Cuba if more than 10 per cent of the product is of US origin. Replacement parts and supplies for Cuba's high-technology diagnostic equipment are under US patent or are manufactured by US firms. Even when medicines and medical supplies can be obtained from other sources, the costs are much higher. In addition, there are frequent delays in transportation from these distant markets which forces bulk buying, and this ties up scarce capital.

The public-health infrastructure has also been affected. A lack of materials for water systems has caused, for the first time, a reversal of the trend towards universal access to household connections for potable water.[28] In addition, disruptions in the supply and production of the chemical industry have created serious shortages in materials for water treatment (chlorine and aluminium sulphate). Many households lack water supply during most of the day because of pump failures and fuel shortages. Garbage pick-up is less frequent. Shortages in transport for waste disposal, nutritional factors, and deteriorating housing and sanitary conditions during 1989–92 are associated with a rise in incidence per 100,000 population of tuberculosis from 5.5 to 5.8, diarrhoaeal diseases from 2.7 to 4.3, infectious and parasitic diseases from 8.6 to 10.9, and in pneumonia, asthma, and syphilis. There is a serious shortage of soap and detergents (Garfield *et al.*, 1994).

Nevertheless, the foundations of the Cuban health and nutrition system are strong enough to ensure that the infant-mortality rate and the under-5-mortality rate are being maintained—at least so far.[29] As Jolly argues (in Chapter 1) adjustment has normally affected input indicators (e.g. public expenditure on health and education) rather more than output or outcome indicators—though in areas of extreme poverty (especially in Africa) nutritional outcomes and education enrolments worsened during the 1980s. In the Cuban case, as we discussed above, the government responded to the crisis by increasing its fiscal priority to the health and education sectors—quite the contrary of what happened in the rest of Latin America in the 1980s. However, as discussed above, even in Cuba the incidence of low birth-weight babies—an important indicator of maternal nutrition—has worsened, just as the incidence of certain diseases, though the decline is rather limited. This performance is in strong contrast to the situation over 1989 to 1995 in Eastern Europe and the former Soviet Union, economies which are also undergoing major transition—but which, by and large, failed to protect social expenditures and whose economic systems imploded through 'big bang' type policies. The latter are faced with a severe welfare crisis that affects children and adolescents in particular, an increase in mortality, shocking drops in births, increases in poverty, and faltering social protection and child development programmes (UNICEF, 1993, 1994, 1995; Kaser and Mehrotra, 1996). On the other hand, Cuba (like China) has had political stability and more orderly macro-economic adjustment.

Above all, the crisis is forcing the Cuban State to take a much closer look at the efficiency of current expenditures. Medical personnel have increased home visits and are releasing patients from hospitals for follow-up care in the home. Health providers are increasingly using herbal medicines, acupuncture, and other non-Western procedures. It is felt that important advances are being made in this potentially valuable new area of alternative medicine.

Unlike the health sector, there is much less information available about the impact of the crisis on education. Availability of books is likely to have declined, as happened in the former Soviet Union after the break-up of that country. In Cuba about 30 per cent of the raw material used in domestic production of paper is wood pulp, which was imported at very low prices from Comecon countries; it is now purchased in the world market against hard currency. In the circumstances domestic production of books is likely to have suffered (Mesa-Lago, 1997).

Conclusion

Relative to other countries in Latin America, revolutionary Cuba began with a fairly high level of per capita income, and reasonably good health and education indicators. But even compared to other high achievers in Latin America, it has made remarkable progress in terms of social indicators. It now has a health profile comparable to that found in developed countries. In terms of educational development, no other Latin American country has nearly universal secondary enrolment rates, while Cuba has been able to achieve those for both males and females. This is in spite of the fact that per capita incomes in Cuba are well below those found in most of Latin America. The country is well on the way to demographic transition, unlike the high achievers in Latin America. Cuba's population growth rate (of 1 per cent per annum over 1980–90) is less than half the average of developing countries, and just over half that of Latin America. Its social indicators are even better in some respects than those of other former centrally planned economies.

Major advances were made in these indicators in the first decade of the revolution, before the period of rapid economic growth. Even after growth slowed in the mid-1980s, and output drastically declined, the outcome indicators have been maintained. In this respect as well, the Cuban experience stands in strong contrast to the experience since 1990 of Eastern Europe.

Although the economic crisis and the embargo have not so far resulted in the reversal of outcome indicators, input indicators of social-service delivery and household consumption have been affected severely. The State remains committed to containing the risk of reversal of its social achievements. Without resumed growth, and with it government revenues, the State's capacity to even sustain, let alone increase, health and education expenditures is open to question. Cuba faces strong challenges if its economy is to be integrated into the world market, as it will need to do, while keeping at bay risks of large-scale deindustrialization and substantial social costs. The challenge is to maintain current levels of industrialization, diversify further away from sugar both in agriculture and industry, sharply increase efficiency in the social sectors, all the time minimizing the social costs that will result from increased unemployment and falling social expenditures in per capita terms. Without the cost reductions that lifting the embargo will allow and additional international assistance, it will be extremely difficult to meet all of the challenges simultaneously.

Notes

1. Harry Oshima, cited in Brundenius, put the 1953 GDP at $430, or about the same as that of Puerto Rico.
2. The remaining 24% of the owners, accounting for 23% of the number of farms, occupied 19% of the area. This category owned farms between 5 and 30 *caballerias* (or 67 and 402 hectares), with the poor owning less than 5 and the rich over 30 (Brundenius, 1984).
3. Seers (1974). However, Mesa-Lago (1971) estimates the spread as being 7-to-1; see also Mesa-Lago (1981). The chapter on Korea in this book also discusses the role of limiting the differential of worker–manager salaries as an incentive.
4. For a discussion of the Soviet model adopted during 1962–5 and the Guevarist model of the 1966–70 period, see Mesa-Lago (1981).
5. Crude mortality rates may have increased in the 1960s for a number of reasons: improvement in death registration, the departure of physicians, and problems in the supply of equipment and medicines: see Seers (1974) and Brundenius (1984).
6. Along with these duties, the family doctors take specialized courses in the polyclinics, in a new academic field closely tied to the community, known as general integral medicine. For more in-depth information about these ideas, see UNICEF *et al.*, 1991. However, Mesa-Lago (1994*a*) argues that this programme was very expensive and launched at a time when Cuba was experiencing severe external constraints and significant gaps in housing, food, etc.

7. New research centres, among them the Finlay Institute, Genetic Engineering and Biotech-nology Center, and the Immunoassay Centre, have made significant contributions, such as developing the Hepatitis B recombinant vaccine, the meningitis vaccine, interferon obtained through genetic engineering, and the creation of the computerized ultramicroanalytical system, which consists of portable kits for clinical analysis that allow large groups of the population to be tested quickly and with less use of reagents. These and other research centres became interrelated during the period, until the so-called Biological Front was created for the development of multidisciplinary biomedical research, considered a top prior-ity.

8. Standards were set for aiding pregnant women and non-working mothers without family support, as well as unprotected children and adolescents. Cuban laws cover women workers' maternity benefits as well as mothers aged 15 to 17 who for exceptional reasons are autho-rized to work.

9. Chile and Costa Rica also made dramatic improvements in their health indicators over the same period, but from much higher initial levels compared to Cuba, highlighting the point that the reductions from already low levels are relatively more difficult (and costly) to achieve.

10. Per capita intake has declined since 1986, particularly in the 1990s.

11. Seers (1974) (quoting Truslow) described the Ministry of Education before the revolution as 'a principal focus of political patronage and graft . . . a cave of entrenched bandits and of gunmen and an asylum of professional highway robbers'. These words are taken from a report published under the World Bank's auspices at the time.

12. As a result of the limited follow-up activities in Kerala after the literacy campaign, many neo-literates have receded into illiteracy again. In recent years, when a non-Communist govern-ment came to power in Kerala, the political commitment to follow-up seemed to wane.

13. Mesa Lago (1981) has argued that, in spite of the cost of maintaining these children in the countryside, their net contribution to output was positive.

14. For the contrast between Latin America and the East Asian 'tigers' in terms of the quality of primary education (as reflected in completion rates) and secondary enrolment rates, and its implications for the contrasting growth experiences, see Mehrotra and Pizarro (1996).

15. Between 1959–60 and 1992–3, over half a million Cubans graduated from universities, and of that number only 3.4% studied abroad.

16. An agent, Sen (1985) argues, has an active role in pursuing whatever goals she has reasons to support and promote; in terms of objectives, the agency role can be much broader than the promotion of self-welfare.

17. For an excellent analysis of Latin American social expenditures during the 1980s, see ECLAC (1994). Countries which maintained their high levels of social expenditures are analysed in Mehrotra and Pizarro (1996).

18. Brundenius indicates that definitions of industrial activities may be somewhat broader than that used in the rest of Latin America, but despite that difference, the significant change can only be accounted for by growth in basic industry, capital goods, and the construction indus-try, especially since 1971.

19. The level of urbanization in the country is high, however, but that is because a large propor-tion of the population lives in small towns.

20. The efficiency of basic investment funds dropped from 59% in 1980 to 54% in 1985 and to 40.4% in 1988. See Rodríguez (1990).

21. At the time of the revolution, American, British, and Dutch companies had refineries in Cuba to process crude oil from their oilfields in Venezuela, paying what the Cubans considered

inflated prices, as Soviet oil could be obtained at lower world market prices. When the petro-leum companies were about to agree to refine Soviet oil, although under protest, the USA told them to reject the plan: see Brundenius (1984). For India's similar experience with the oil giants when faced with competition from Soviet oil, see Mehrotra, 1990.

22. For an analysis of similar problems during the transition in the Central Asian States of the former Soviet Union, see Kaser and Mehrotra (1996).

23. In late March 1994, liquidity stood at 11.636bn. pesos, *Granma* daily, 2 May 1994.

24. In July 1994 the dollar was worth approximately 100 pesos on the informal market. However, according to the official exchange rate both currencies have the same value.

25. In addition, there have been US efforts to put direct pressure on allies and international insti-tutions to isolate Cuba. However, European allies of the USA have resisted it. The US strat-egy has denied Cuba access to funding from international organizations—the World Bank, IMF, and Inter-American Development Bank—and limited access to funding from the Pan-American Health Organization.

26. Only certain aspects of the impact are considered here, as this chapter is restricted in scope to health and education. The reduction in the oil imports has severely restricted the number of cars on the streets, and caused periodic power shortages. The severe shortage of petrol and a lack of spare parts for automobiles and buses have led to greater use of bicycles. Since public transportation has always been seen as the main means of transportation, waiting time has increased for the few functioning buses: see Kuntz, 1993.

27. In 1994 UNICEF received a project proposal to provide iron supplements to children between the ages of 5 months and 5 years.

28. The proportion of the population with domestic water connections declined from 83 to 81% in urban areas, and from 30 to 27% in rural areas between 1990 and 1993: see Garfield *et al.* (1994).

29. Anand and Chen (1995) argue that health status is best described as a 'stock', whose level in any period depends on the volume and quality of current 'flows' of health care, income (including food), environment and behaviour, and the level of the previous period 'stock'. The reason why mortality may not rise immediately in response to large deterioration of income and other health 'flows' during macro-economic change is that the stock normally provides a margin of health reserves above the critical threshold. Decline in health flows can lead to stagnation or slow-downs—and only in the extreme, to reversals—of long-term mor-tality change.

Bibliography

Anand, Sudhir, and Chen, L. C. (1995), 'A Framework for Assessing the Health Implications of Economic Policies', New York: UNDP, mimeo.

Brundenius, Claes (1984), *Revolutionary Cuba: The Challenge of Economic Growth with Equity*, Westview Press, Boulder, Colo.

Carnoy, Martin, and Joel Samoff (1989), *Education and Social Transition in the Third World*, Princeton University Press, Princeton, NJ.

Castro, Fidel (1976), *La unión nos dió la victoria*, Edic. DOR, Havana.

Chenery, Hollis, Ahlliwalia, M. S., Bell, C. L. G., Duloy, John H., and Jolly, Richard (1974), *Redistribution with Growth*, Oxford University Press.

ECLAC (1994), *Social Panorama 1994*, Santiago.

Fiddler, Stephen (1995), 'Castro Keeps Reforms on the Leash', *Financial Times* (London), 27 Oct.

Garfield, R., Santana, S., and Fernandez, P. L. (1994), *The Health Impact of the Economic Embargo Against Cuba*, New York, mimeo.

Gonzalez Quiñones, Fernando (1994), 'Mujer, trabajo y transición de la fecundidad en Cuba', Centro de Estudio Demográficos, Folleto *Aspectos relevantes de la transición demográfica en Cuba*, Havana.

Govt. of Cuba (1993), *National Programme of Action*, Havana.

Kaser, Michael, and Mehrotra, Santosh (1996), 'The Central Asian Economies after Independence', in Roy Allison (ed.), *Challenges for the Former Soviet South*, Brookings Institution, Washington DC.

Kuntz, Diane (1993), *The Politics of Suffering: The Impact of the U.S. Embargo on the Health of the Cuban People*, Report of a fact-finding trip to Cuba by American Public Health Association, Washington, DC.

Lage, Carlos (1994), 'La Nación y la emigración'.

Mehrotra, Santosh (1990), *India and the Soviet Union: Trade and Technology Transfer*, Cambridge University Press.

—— and Pizarro, Crisostomo (1996), 'Social Policies in Chile, Costa Rica and Mexico: An Inter-Regional Perspective', in UNICEF, *Social Development in the Nineties*, Bogotá: Planeta.

—— and Vandemoortele, Jan (1996), 'Cost and Financing of Primary Education: Options for Reform in Sub-Saharan Africa', UNICEF Staff Working Paper, New York.

Mesa-Lago, Carmelo (1971) *Cuba in the 1970s: Pragmatism and Institutionalization*, Albuquerque.

—— (1881), *The Economy of Socialist Cuba: A Two-Decade Appraisal*, Albuquerque.

—— (1994a), *Are Economic Reforms Propelling Cuba to the Market?*, North-South Center, University of Miami, Coral Gables, Florida.

—— (1994b), *Breve Historia Económica de la Cuba Socialista*, Alianza Editorial, Madrid.

—— (1997), 'The Social Safety Net in the Two Cuban Transitions', in *Transition in Cuba: New Challenges for US Policies*, Florida International University, Cuban Research Institute.

National Institute of Economic Research (1995), *La Apertura Cubana*, Havana.

Transition in Cuba: New Challenges for U.S. Policies, Florida International University, Cuban Research Institute (forthcoming).

Navarro, V. (1972), 'Health, Health Service and Health Planning in Cuba', *International Journal of Health Services*.

Pérez Izquierdo, Victoria (1989), 'Aspectos para perfeccionar la metodología de planificación de las necesidades de círculos infantiles por territorio', Instituto de Investigaciones Económicas, Compendio de Investigaciones, 7, Havana.

Rodríguez, José Luis (1990), 'Los cambios de la política económica y los resultados de la economía cubana de 1986–1989', *Cuadernos de Nuestra América*, 7/15, Havana.

Seers, Dudley (1974), 'Cuba', in Chenery *et al.* (1974).

Sen, Amartya (1985), 'Well-being, Agency and Freedom: The Dewey Lectures 1984', *Journal of Philosophy*, 82.

State Committee on Statistics, *Anuario Demográfico de Cuba*, Havana.

UNDP (1995), *Human Development Report 1995*, Oxford University Press.

UNESCO (1994), *Statistical Yearbook*, Paris.

UNICEF (1993), *Central and Eastern Europe in Transition, Public Policy and Social Conditions*, International Child Development Centre, Florence, Regional Monitoring Report 1.

—— (1994), *Central and Eastern Europe in Transition. Crisis in Mortality, Health and Nutrition*, ICDC, Florence, Regional Monitoring Report 2.

—— (1995), *Central and Eastern Europe in Transition. Poverty, Children and Policy: Responses for a Brighter Future*, ICDC, Florence, Regional Monitoring Report 3.

—— (1996), *State of the World's Children 1996*, Oxford University Press.

UNICEF, UNFPA, PAHO, WHO, MINSAP (1991), *El Plan del Médico de la Familia en Cuba*, Cosolis S.A. publishers, Mexico.

Part III

Conclusion

14

Paths to Social Development:
Lessons from Case-Studies

LINCOLN C. CHEN AND MEGHNAD DESAI

Introduction

The year 1989 was historic for many reasons. It was the bicentenary of the French Revolution, an event which, more than any other, ushered in the modern era. It was also the year in which the Berlin Wall collapsed and brought to an end the cold war as well as the post-1945 settlement in Europe. Dramatic events inspire much speculation, and it was then thought that the world would enter a new phase in which market-led economic growth and political democracy were going to be the twin tracks on which the future of all countries would move forward.

Six years later and on the occasion of yet another anniversary, the UN's fiftieth year, such optimism seems to have evaporated. A 'New World Order' has not emerged. Economic transformations of a more profound kind captured by the catch-all phrase 'globalization' seem as much a threat as an opportunity to North and South alike. Unemployment is high in both developed and developing countries. In the North, recession has gripped the previously powerful economies of Germany and Japan. In the South, there is *development pessimism* or even more profound *Afro-pessimism*. There is diminishing public support for development aid funding. Themes of social exclusion on the one hand and of ethnic cleansing on the other have emerged in place of the radiant optimism of an earlier era.

Has development failed the Third World? Is there no hope of combining decent economic growth with social equity? Are we all to be plunged into a Victorian climate where economic success requires that the poor and the weak be further marginalized, where unemployment is a price worth paying, and where governments are helpless, in the face of global economic forces, to pursue social as well as economic goals?

This collection of case-studies is based on the conviction of Richard Jolly, as well as many others, that the pessimism is overstated and that there are as many good as bad cases in the annals of development. There are success stories! Countries of South-East and East Asia are enjoying a remarkable growth spurt and many have done so while also promoting social development. The ten country studies presented here are bright spots that span three continents—Asia, America, and Africa. All of the countries are characterized by high levels of health and educational achievement at their respective income levels. Painstakingly and professionally edited by Santosh Mehrotra, these case-studies offer rich materials and provide invaluable lessons for policy-makers who wish to promote social development.

It is important to underscore that although commonalities exist across the case-studies, each is also unique. Caution is thus indicated in drawing universal truths from such materials. Case-studies do not provide rigorous scientific proof, nor do they offer a blueprint. Indeed, even among these cases, generalizations encounter exceptions. Counterfactual scenarios were not considered. What would have happened if another path had been taken? Rather, these in-depth studies help us understand the diverse challenges faced, the roles of people, leaders, and institutions, the public policies adopted, and the outcomes achieved. Most useful of all, these studies help us identify key questions that can inform contemporary strategies for social development.

Even the definition of social development, and thus the selection of these cases, is ambiguous. The UNDP (1990) equates social development with 'sustainable human development', which it defines as enhancing human capabilities for enlarging human choices. The Human Development Index measures a country's combined achievements in life expectancy, education and literacy, and basic income (Haq, 1995). UNICEF (1991) focuses on children, as reflected by the child health and educational goals adopted at the 1990 Children's Summit. Multilateral banks employ a sectoral approach, viewing social development as investments in social programmes (World Bank, 1993). The 1995 Social Summit in Copenhagen prioritized three aspects—poverty, unemployment, and social integration.

Paul Streeten (1992) maps social development as a three-dimensional process: social services (health, education) and social transfers (social security, safety nets); economic access and productive returns (livelihood generation and remunerative employment); and social integration (peace, absence of violence). Every level of society is engaged—the individual, the family, the community, and the nation State. Social development is holistic, encompassing physical and psychosocial well-being, a healthy polity, and harmonious social relations—not simply the abundance of material goods.

These definitions, though different, overlap substantially. In a sense, 'we know what we mean' by social development. In any event, these case-studies span many of the issues involved in the notion of social development, though they do adopt a national perspective and concentrate more on government action than on private or community action. Three broad conclusions can be derived from these studies:

Governance. Strong and effective social policies require a stable political environment, responsive government, and consensual social values oriented towards equity.

Integration. 'Market-friendly' economic policies have to be integrated with 'socially friendly' policies since there are powerful interdependencies between the two.

Universality. Social progress depends on the universal provisioning of basic social services, financed in a responsible way and implemented efficiently and equitably by government.

Despite their apparent simplicity, each of these three propositions contains complex ideas. Indeed, the three propositions raise as many questions as they answer. In what follows, we examine some of these unresolved issues and bring out the complexities. Our aim is to further the understanding of 'how to get social policies right'.

Governance

Responsive regime

Does social development require political liberal democracy or can it be achieved in other regimes as well? A democratic system is defined here as a multiparty system with universal franchise, secret ballot, and predictably frequent free and fair elections (Putnam, 1993). Evidence from these cases, as in the larger set of information available elsewhere, is mixed in this regard. While most of these countries are at present democracies, not all have multiparty political cultures. Cuba is a one-party State, and the Republic of Korea and Malaysia are one-party-dominant polities.

The important ingredient is not, however, democracy as such but whether the regime is *responsive* or *caring*, i.e. responsive to the needs and wishes of its people (particularly in relation to economic and social dimensions), caring about their welfare in a wide sense.

In all the case-studies, government plays a crucial role in social development. In the centrally planned economy of Cuba it plays a comprehensive role, but even in market economies, there being no 'invisible hand' to look after social issues, it falls on the government to provide the safety nets for the weak and the vulnerable. The quality of a government's performance—its professionalism, pragmatism, and intolerance of corruption—is crucial if good policies are to be delivered. Some form of governmental accountability, therefore, appears to be important; political commitment or a progressive stance is not sufficient.

Accommodation

But the effectiveness of policy is also shaped by historical and cultural roots, by the degree of homogeneity, ethnic or tribal, by the willingness to accommodate multiculturalism, and by the shared notion of equity.

History has been found to be an important factor in public-policy effectiveness in developed economies, Italy being the subject of a recent study along these lines (Putnam, 1993). The fact that Sri Lanka had over 100 years of public commitment to equitable social development makes it easy to understand why it also had one of the strongest infrastructures in health and education. It also acquired universal franchise as long ago as 1931. Beginning in the nineteenth century, Kerala experienced social movements against caste untouchability, missionary work on health and education, as well as an enlightened monarchy. Christian missionaries were also important in Mauritius. Barbados launched free public services soon after independence and Cuba soon after the revolution.

It is claimed that certain cultural or religious traditions have also contributed. Confucianism in the Republic of Korea (hereafter Korea) and Malaysia accords high value to education. Primary education in Korea was privately demanded (and privately paid for) even before government schooling became widespread. It is claimed that Sri Lanka's Buddhist ethos reinforces social egalitarianism and collective responsibility to assist the poorest in society.

The countries in this volume are characterized by either ethnic homogeneity or multicultural diversity. Unlike most other Sub-Saharan African countries, Botswana consists of one dominant tribal group, 'Batswana'. Costa Ricans are mostly of European decent; indigenous groups have been absorbed and Blacks are few. Malaysia, Mauritius, Kerala, Sri Lanka, and Zimbabwe are all multicultural societies. Social and political accommodation, therefore, played important historical roles in social-policy development. Accommodation differs from the concepts of social cohesion or ethnic integration in that accommodation implies the avoidance of violence, the rule of law, and peaceful sharing or competition for resources and economic opportunities. Accommodative processes characterized Malaysia, Mauritius, Kerala, and Zimbabwe. In cases where such accommodation breaks down, as has unfortunately happened in Sri Lanka, ethnic conflict can erupt as has occurred between majority Singhalese Buddhists and minority Tamil Hindus in that country.

Equity

The process of accommodation invariably involves some form of social, economic, political, and gender equity, sometimes in access to opportunities and sometimes in outcomes. This is usually a shared notion of equity. The selected countries display a high degree of equity as reflected by social indicators. Thus, these countries all enjoy high levels of literacy and health. Gender equity also characterizes all the case countries; none of the study countries showed gross gender disparities. In some country cases, a small gender gap persists in certain social indicators, while in others women are ahead of men. Many of the social advances reported are attributed to women's agency, the action of women as proactive agents of social change, not simply women as beneficiaries of social programmes.

Interestingly, the situation of economic equity varies significantly between the case countries. Well-balanced distribution of productive assets like land characterizes Korea, Kerala, and Sri Lanka. Income distribution shows more marked variability. In low-income Botswana and Zimbabwe, income is comparatively maldistributed in comparison to the better income distribution of low-income Kerala and Sri Lanka. Among middle-income countries, Malaysia has maldistribution of personal income (though a diminished disparity in interethnic income) in comparison to the better distribution patterns of Korea, Costa Rica, and Mauritius. Poverty levels are high in all low-income countries and also high in those middle-income countries with income maldistribution.

Time-trends of income inequality are as important as cross-sectional distributive patterns. In Malaysia and Costa Rica, income distribution is worsening due in part to the effects of economic recession, private markets, and structural-adjustment programmes. Similarly, Sri Lanka had reasonably good income distribution through the 1970s, although about one-quarter of the population was below the poverty line. By the 1980s, income distribution had worsened significantly; the top 10 per cent of the population commands over 40 per cent of the income. In none of the case countries were there reports of steadily improving income distribution.

Integration

What makes for 'socially friendly' economic policies? Do some economic strategies advance social development better than others? If so, are there critical decision-making junctures? Does the timing or sequencing of social and economic policies matter? Are there trade-offs between economic and social investments?

Socially friendly economic policies, we believe, depend primarily upon prioritizing social development as an integral part of national economic strategies. Economic and social strategies are complementary, not antagonistic or one-sided, because the relationship is bidirectional. Economic growth generates the material means that can be applied to social advances. Social development is indispensable to economic progress because peace and social stability are necessary but insufficient conditions for economic development. People as human capital are critical for economic growth. Even more important, social development is not simply an instrument or outcome of economic growth, but in all the case countries, it is intrinsically valued.

While wealth is positively correlated with some developments, it does not guarantee it nor does poverty necessarily preclude social advances, as demonstrated in the country studies. Social development can be achieved at very different levels of national economic development. About half of the country cases had gross national products above and half below $2,000 per capita. Indeed, Korea's GNP is perhaps twentyfold that of Sri Lanka and Kerala. Yet all ten countries enjoy outstanding social-performance indicators.

Per capita income is, however, only one dimension. What about the total population size? Is it a burden or an opportunity? Four of the country cases have small populations; Costa Rica, Botswana, Mauritius, and Barbados have from several hundred thousand to about 3m. people. Does a small population associated with high population density, geographic compactness, road and communications penetrability, and people's accessibility to modern facilities make a difference? The case-studies do not support this hypothesis. Korea has a large population of 44.5m., and Malaysia, Sri Lanka, Zimbabwe, Cuba, and India's Kerala State have medium-sized populations of from 10m. to 30m. Bostwana's small population occupies a vast geographic space resulting in an exceedingly low population density and exceptionally difficult access and communications. Malaysia and Zimbabwe are also geographically large countries.

External contact

Rather than demography, the relevant factor appears to be national political commitment to equitable social progress coupled with outward-oriented economic strategies that exploit external markets, foreign investments, modern technology, and international opportunities for economic emigration. As described by the Dommens (Chapter 5), Mauritius illustrates how anticipating and preparing for global markets, along with strong social policies, can make a difference. After independence in 1968, Mauritius experienced a boom in sugar exports, established export-processing zones, and promoted tourism. Resource rents were invested heavily in social services. During a difficult structural-adjustment period in 1975–86, Mauritius adapted quickly and cushioned negative social consequences by maintenance of free and universal services, enabling the people and the economy to enter smoother waters in the past decade.

Like Mauritius, most of the countries in this study export primary products and services—minerals (Botswana), coffee (Costa Rica), sugar (Barbados, Cuba), tourism (Barbados, Cuba, and Costa Rica), and oil, rubber, and tin (Malaysia). Many of the countries also export human capital. Emigration of labour characterizes Kerala, Sri Lanka, Barbados, and Mauritius. In some cases, these outward economic strategies have led to reasonable economic growth—for example in Mauritius, Malaysia, Botswana, Korea, and Barbados. In other cases, like Kerala and Sri Lanka, overseas financial remittances have helped buoy up a stagnant economy. In all cases, the country's interface with the external environment has been critical to social and economic development.

Excessive dependence on the external environment obviously creates vulnerability. A hostile context can lead to reversals in economic and social conditions. This vulnerability is well illustrated by Cuba. Linked into the Soviet economic system, Cuba has experienced a dramatic erosion of economic and social gains since the collapse of the USSR in 1991. Economic devastation was brought about by the withdrawal of Soviet trade, an economic embargo imposed by the USA, and restrictive economic management by an overly controlled, centrally planned government. In a brief period of five years, Cuba has experienced an 80-per cent decline in imports, including vital medical supplies. Cuba's current situation is clearly unsustainable.

Investing in social development

Is it economically profitable to invest in social development? The answer is a resounding 'yes', whether social development is viewed instrumentally as human capital or is intrinsically valued.

Korea and Malaysia demonstrate the economic returns of social investments. As reported by Mehrotra, Park, and Baek (Chapter 9), a massive land reform and the high value people accorded to education were two bases upon which Korea's economic take-off depended. As the economy grew, Korea's social investments increased in both absolute and relative terms. Interestingly, Korea's social investments, especially in health, are still significantly lower than in comparable economies. The interaction between economic and social strategies in Korea may be viewed as a sequencing of baseline human capital formation and equitable asset distribution followed by export-oriented economic growth. With greater economic capacity, social welfare investments have increased. As described by Leong and Tan (Chapter 10), Malaysia's story follows the Korea case. Since independence in 1957, Malaysia has accorded consistently high priority to poverty alleviation, and health and educational services. These social investments were initially supported by the export of primary products and more recently export-oriented growth. Despite a difficult period of structural adjustment in 1984–7, Malaysia was able to sustain social-sector investments. The maintenance of investments in human capital has paid off handsomely; Malaysia's social rates of return to education (11.5 per cent) are even greater than the returns to investment in physical capital.

During economic expansion, investing in social development is feasible, but do social investments compete with economic priorities under stagnant economic conditions? Would any of the five poor countries with GNPs under $2,000 (Sri Lanka, Zimbabwe, Cuba, Costa Rica, and India's Kerala) have done better, economically or socially, had they invested less in the social and more in the economic sector? This line of reasoning, we argue, is a false trade-off as economic growth requires social investments. A more pertinent question, as noted by Alailima and Sanderatne for Sri Lanka (Chapter 8), is whether better social strategies would have achieved 'the same measure of social progress, as well as higher rates of economic growth'. To address this question, the effectiveness, efficiency, and equity of social strategies need to be examined, including differentiating the multiple purposes of social investments (safety net, human capital, social integration, etc.) and their linkages to economic performance.

Junctures, Timing, Sequencing

In many case-studies, critical decision-making junctures, which had profound implications for social policies, can be identified. The Cuban revolution in 1959 was one such critical time, when students and teachers were mobilized to propagate mass literacy among nearly a million adults. Malaysia's 'race riots' in 1969 resulted in the 1971 New Economic Policy by which economic growth was channelled equitably between immigrant Chinese and indigenous Malays. These policies had the dual effect of advancing the economy while advancing ethnic harmony.

Structural adjustment illustrates another critical juncture experienced by most case countries. While the timing, pace, and character of structural adjustment programmes were country-specific, most of the countries accorded high priority to maintaining public allocations to the social sector. As described for Costa Rica, the three-year economic crisis (1980–2) witnessed a fall of GDP by 5 per cent per year, and social spending fell by 18 per cent annually. The cut-backs were absorbed not through staff lay-offs but in the reported quality of services rendered. In 1982 the *Plan de Compensacion Social* was instituted, which combined domestic and foreign aid resources for food security, employment subsidy, and economic productivity among the poor and disadvantaged. Flexible social funds were established to complement and not displace customary governmental services. By 1983, social expenditures were increasing at 12 per cent annually, and by 1986, the 1980 level of social expenditures had been fully restored. Although most of the other structural-adjustment programmes (those in Korea, Malaysia, Barbados, and Mauritius) also protected social programmes, in some cases, as in Sri Lanka and Zimbabwe, the social sector was badly affected by macroeconomic policies.

In these case-studies and more generally, we understand poorly the social implications of critical decisions. Some have argued that social development has both 'stock' and 'flow' properties. Social progress in health and education is the result of sustained, long-term forces that are difficult to reverse by short-term change. Social assets—like knowledge, adaptive behaviour, and technology—do not respond quickly to short-term disruptions. Preston has shown that at any given level of economic wealth, longevity has consistently been increasing over time throughout this century, presumably reflective of the build-up of social assets. For example, basic education and the adoption of hygienic practices like hand-washing are social stocks that are not lost because of economic set-backs. This stock–flow approach to social development provides an explanation for the comparative resiliency of mortality indicators to resist sharp economic deterioration that has characterized some structural-adjustment programmes (Murray and Chen, 1993; Anand and Chen, 1996).

Also poorly explained are periods of accelerated progress ('breakthroughs') or of stagnation. It is entirely unclear what is an appropriate lag period to observe the presumed social effects of economic change. The crude death rate in Korea, for example, declined 24–33 per cent in each of the three decades after 1965. It remains entirely uncertain how many of these improvements can be attributed to economic changes in the coinciding or earlier decades.

Finally, we lack understanding of how social gains may be shifted under economic pressure. Some have argued, for example, that while secular decline of mortality may persist during periods of economic hardship, the maintenance of mortality decline is due to a disguised shift from mortality to morbidity, not easily measured by traditional indicators. Others have hypothesized that the maintenance of primary-school enrolment may incompletely capture a shift away from secondary and tertiary educational enrolment during times of crisis.

Universality

Not surprisingly, all of the countries in this study accord high priority to the universal provisioning of public social services. In many cases, public action involves engaging the broad mass of people in very simple social measures, not expensive programmes. The introduction of shoes in Mauritius, for example, contributed to the eradication of hookworm. Cuba's mass literacy campaigns after the 1959 revolution was implemented by volunteers helping people to achieve adult literacy. Gender equity accelerated in Kerala and Sri Lanka because social movements for women's participation in the society had long historical roots.

In all these countries, formal social services are provided by the government. Are such social services expensive? Can the level of public expenditures be sustained? How are the public services organized? What about people's demand, participation, and utilization? What have been the roles of the private sector?

Financing and sustainability

Although allocations for social services display great variability, all selected countries accord high priority to the public financing of social services. As a percentage of GDP, the ten countries commit about 5–8 per cent to education and health combined, levels that exceed their respective regional averages. In Botswana, the government accounts for 42 per cent of GDP, with education and health expenditures at almost 7 per cent and 2 per cent of GDP respectively. Social programmes in Costa Rica command close to 50 per cent of public expenditure, with education and health at 5 per cent and 8 per cent of government budgets respectively. In India's Kerala, health and education command almost 10 per cent and 28 per cent of state government expenditures. These social commitments translate into absolute per capita expenditures ranging from a few dollars to $175 for education and to $50 for health.

Considerable sectoral and regional diversity is displayed in expenditure patterns. For example, the highest per capita absolute expenditure in education is Korea's and in health is Mauritius's. Sri Lanka and India's Kerala had the lowest absolute educational and health expenditures. Interestingly, the Sub-Saharan African cases (Botswana, Mauritius, and Zimbabwe) are extremely high absolute investors in health and education, much higher than some Latin America cases (Costa Rica) and nearly approaching the levels of richer East Asian countries (Korea, Malaysia).

Of course, what counts is not simply the quantum of public funds, but the efficiency with which they are deployed. In some cases, decentralization in planning, management, and monitoring with people's involvement helped to enhance efficiency. In all countries, there are attempts to provide basic services with universal coverage. Primary education and health care are accorded high priority. Between one-quarter and one-half of public educational expenditures, for example, are committed to the pre-school and primary levels in these countries, and in all countries girls enjoy the same educational public benefits as boys.

With a growing economy and an expanding tax base, public expenditures can be maintained. But what happens if the economy stagnates or the tax base dwindles? The case of Sri Lanka illustrates well the challenge of fiscal sustainability. Sanderatne argues that since Sri Lanka's universal franchise in the 1930s, massive social programmes have been implemented without targeting, requiring high costs that have become fiscally unsustainable. Recent fiscal stringency has compelled the government to retrench services by slimming benefits, compromising quality, recovering costs through user charges, and targeting beneficiaries. Such belt-tightening undoubtedly reduces the fiscal burden, but sustainability must take into account not only financial viability but also human and organizational health, as well as the outputs from the systems. At the same time as these social cutbacks were implemented, the Sri Lankan government increased military spending from virtually zero to 12 per cent and debt-servicing grew to 29 per cent of total budget.

Supply and demand of social services

One strategic issue in the supply of services is comprehensiveness in terms of the type of services offered and the eligibility of the population to be served. Regarding the former, little difference can be found between selective vertical vs. comprehensive integrated services. Most of the countries studied attempt to provide basic health and education services in an integrated manner. Two countries (Sri Lanka and Mauritius), however, enjoyed success with classical vertical malaria-eradication efforts. Virtually all of the countries have had successful childhood immunization campaigns, several of which have been vertically implemented. Noteworthy in both Sri Lanka and Mauritius, however, is that the initial vertical programmes were eventually integrated into basic health-care systems.

The issue of targeting vs. universality reflects the staging of programme evolution. In most of the country cases, free and universally accessible public services are provided. Under fiscal stringency, some, like Sri Lanka and Cuba, are gradually shifting towards targeting services at the most disadvantaged. Few countries appear to have moved in the opposite direction, that is, from selective eligibility to universality. Yet, this reverse evolution from targeting to universality is extremely popular with some international agencies. UNICEF, for example, has aggressively pushed several high-priority service components: immunization, oral rehydration, basic education. The World Bank argues that cost-effectiveness analysis should be used to prioritize interventions and targeting. Unclear is the sustainability of such selective approaches. Selectivity obviously relieves fiscal burdens, but it also narrows the social and political constituency in support of social programmes. The question remains whether tightly targeted services to the most disadvantaged, who are politically weakest, can be sustained politically.

With regard to service demand, participation, and utilization, the case-studies offer a mixed picture. In Korea, it was the demand for education in a Confucian society that culturally values education for its own sake which created the broad base of educated people who participated in the economic take-off. Similarly, in Kerala and Sri Lanka, public demand for services is extremely high, forcing responsive government action. Public health clinics closed without authority when they should be open could generate a social protest in Kerala. In these cases, the people's and community's participation drives the public sector to superior performance.

In such cases, the people are proactive agents of social change, not passive recipients of government services. The Botswana case illustrates that not all government provisioning is necessarily positive. In Chapter 4, Duncan, Jefferis, and Molutsi argue that the Botswana government's provisioning of social services has made the people passive. The lack of community participation operates as a serious barrier to social-service improvements. Individual initiative and responsibility are low. The notion of whether there is sufficient or insufficient public provisioning is simplistic. Rather, social services operate in a dynamic supply-and-demand interaction to generate a strong, efficient, and equitable set of public services.

Public-private mix

All of the case-studies concentrate on public services. Comparatively neglected is the private sector. Throughout the world, the private sector is an important contributor to social-service provisioning. The private sector may be dichotomized into two types—non–profit NGOs, churches, and charities, and commercial health and educational enterprises run for profit.

In many of the countries, the private sector may be quite active. In Kerala, for example, private schools and medical facilities are abundant. Although many are operated by NGOs and religious organizations, commercial enterprises for profit are numerous. Sixty per cent of Kerala's schools, for example, are private enterprises for profit. As is the practice in some other Indian States, Kerala regulates and monitors these private schools by paying the salaries of all teachers, whether private or public, and all private schools are regulated, inspected, and monitored by the State to ensure quality and conformity to standards. Kerala also has abundant private medical practitioners and private clinics and hospitals. Again, the State plays an important regulatory role in health care. In Costa Rica, the private health sector generates a highly regressive health expenditure pattern. The wealthiest quintile of the population accounts for over half of the private health expenditure, while the poorest quintile commands only 4 per cent. This regressive pattern in health-care spending parallels similar regressive patterns in private educational expenditure.

A central challenge for all these countries is an appropriate public–private mix of social services. Private markets in social services can bring additional resources, relieve pressures on public funds, and impose fiscal discipline through price signals. However, imperfections of market mechanisms are well established in health and education. Social services driven by the profit incentives can cause waste, abuse, and inefficiencies in the absence of effective state controls. The private sector also will not venture into services or serve populations without profit incentives, thereby precluding universality. Thus, government intervention is indicated in public-service provisioning and in legislation and regulations to optimize the health and educational impact of private-sector activities. To do so, a legislative and regulatory infrastructure must be developed, as illustrated by the Kerala private school. An optimal public–private mix, therefore, is dependent upon the human and institutional infrastructure of a society as determinants of both public- and private-service performance. Whatever the public–private mix, the serious engagement of the government would appear to be critical. In attempting to determine the effects of private income and public expenditures on social outcomes, Anand and Ravallion (1992) found that whereas private incomes accounted for about one-third of health and educational advances, public expenditures accounted for two-thirds.

Conclusion

The key ingredients to successful social development appear to be responsive governance, socially friendly economic policies, and the universal provisioning of social services. In all three of these endeavours, the role of government is central. In not one case of successful social development is the government unresponsive. Although economic growth may depend upon markets, social development appears possible in either open or closed market economies. A mix of public–private service provisioning is feasible, but the role of performance of government again is central to success.

Neither defeatist pessimism nor naïve optimism is supported by these experiences. After all, only a few decades ago several of the cases reported here were considered 'basket cases'. After the devastation of war and national partition, and endowed with extremely meagre natural resources, South Korea in the 1950s was considered a hopeless development fledgling. Similar gloom also dominated thinking about other countries: Malaysia, Mauritius, and Botswana.

The studies also demonstrate that remarkable progress is feasible within the time-span of a single generation. Thirty-five years ago, the backward half of Kerala, Malabar, was merged with the more socially developed Travancore-Cochin. Unified by common social policies, both regions today enjoy similar levels of social development. In less than two decades after independence, Zimbabwe has put apartheid behind as it moves towards equitable development. Costa Rica broke away from its regional pattern twenty-five years ago to achieve near-universal literacy and high life expectancy that now parallel those of advanced industrialized nations.

Finally, the studies show that social development is neither a singular nor a linear process. The strategies pursued may be diverse, and the paths to success can be varied. Each is shaped by unique circumstances. Nor is success, or failure, guaranteed. Rather, periods of acceleration and set-backs are not uncommon. Sustaining social progress is a challenge faced by all societies. Applying lessons learned by one society from another is a worthwhile endeavour that may help avoid mistakes and may identify alternative paths to social development in the future.

References

(To this list must be added all of the individual case-study chapters in the volume)

Ahmad, E., Drèze, J. P., Hills, J., and Sen, A. K. (eds.) (1991), *Social Security in Developing Countries*, Oxford: Oxford University Press.

Anand, Sudhir and Ravallion, M. (1992), 'Human Development in Poor Countries: On the Role of Private Incomes and Public Services,' *Journal of Economic Perspectives*, 7 (Winter).

—— and Chen, Lincoln (1996), 'Health Implications of Economic Policies: A Framework of Analysis', Discussion paper series No. 3, Office of Development Studies, United Nations Development Programme, New York.

Birdsall, Nancy (1993), 'Social Development Is Economic Development', Policy Research Working Paper 1123, World Bank, Washington, DC.

Cole, D. C., and Lyman, P. N. (1971), *Korean Development: The Interplay of Politics and Economics*, Cambridge, Mass.: Harvard University Press.

Desai, Meghnad (1991), 'Human Development: Concepts and Measurement', *European Economic Review*, 35.

Dollar, David (1992), 'Outward-Oriented Developing Economies Really Do Grow More Rapidly: Evidence from 95 LDCs, 1976–1985', *Economic Development and Cultural Change*, 40.

Drèze, Jean and Sen, Amartya (1989), *Hunger and Public Action*, Oxford: Clarendon Press.

Haq, Mahbub ul (1995), *Reflections on Human Development*, New York: Oxford University Press.

Murray, Christopher, J. L., and Chen, Lincoln (1993), 'In Search of a Contemporary Theory for Understanding Mortality Change', *Soc. Sci. Med.* 36/2: 143–55.

Putnam, Robert, with Leonardi, R., and Nanetti, R. Y. (1993), *Making Democracy Work: Civic Tradition in Modern Italy*, Princeton, NJ: Princeton University Press.

Streeten, Paul (1992), 'Global Governance for Human Development', Human Development Office Report Occasional Paper 4, UNDP, New York.

Taylor, Lance (ed.) (1993), *The Rocky Road to Reform: Adjustment, Income Distribution, and Growth in the Developing World*, Cambridge, Mass.: MIT Press.

UNICEF (1991), *State of the World's Children Report 1991*, Oxford University Press for UNICEF, New York.

UNDP (1990), *Human Development Report 1990*, New York: Oxford University Press for UNDP.

World Bank (1993), *World Development Report 1993: Investing in Health*, Washington, DC: Oxford University Press for the World Bank.

The Links between Economic Growth, Poverty Reduction, and Social Development: Theory and Policy

LANCE TAYLOR, SANTOSH MEHROTRA, AND ENRIQUE DELAMONICA

1. Introduction

The overview of ten country experiences in Chapter 2 showed that while all had achieved high levels of health and educational indicators, their poverty-reduction outcomes were diverse. Even more varied was their income growth. While some had dramatically transformed their economies in terms of the structure of output and employment, in many cases there had been little evidence of a 'Great Transformation'[1]—even over a relatively long 30- to 40-year period of analysis. This variability in these aspects of development prompted the questions addressed in this chapter: what are the key links among the desired outcomes of social development, economic growth, and poverty reduction?[2]

In Chapter 2 we noted that human development or capabilities could be advanced by the State's promotion of two kinds of synergies: one, between interventions in nutrition, health, education, and fertility; and two, at a macro-level, between income growth, the reduction in the dispersion of income so that poverty declines, and social development. While the first kind of synergy has been the dominant theme of this book, the latter is the main subject of this chapter. We would like to suggest that development policy and practice could contribute much to human development if these synergies were better recognized and promoted through state action.[3]

It must be stressed at the outset that we do not view the provision of social services and poverty reduction as merely an investment with (more or less) high rates of return or as a hand-out. Although we will stress that they foster growth, they must be valued for their own intrinsic worth.

There are at least two policy implications emanating from this value judgement. The first applies to the first kind of synergy described above. Rather than seeing sectoral interventions as means which can be ranked using cost-benefit analysis and pursued independently of each other, seeing them as ends induces a more integrated and holistic approach. This leads to a substantially different approach to social policy implementation which uses scarce resources much more efficiently than has been the experience so far. Second, this value judgement also provides a framework for formulating and evaluating economic policies (e.g. macroeconomic adjustment or industrial and trade policies) through the lens of people—hence the phrase 'people-centred' development. Fiscal, monetary, exchange rate, and trade policies have equity implications, therefore they cannot be formulated without regard to their effect on income-poverty reduction and social development and their feedback from the latter into the former.[4]

The next section presents a brief review of debates about these issues in development economics. In the following section the normative stance that none of our three desired outcomes should be sacrificed for the sake of the other two is accompanied by an analysis of processes by which advances in each area reinforce progress in the others. Thus, each outcome, valuable as it is *per se*, also becomes an input in the process which furthers the other ones. This discussion is presented along with a taxonomy of countries according to their observed outcomes with respect to the three indicators, taking them two at a time. The fourth section explores the nature of economic growth required for countries to realize the synergy between health and education interventions, income growth, and poverty reductions. Some conclusions are offered in the fifth section.

Growth, Poverty, and Social Development: a Review of the Literature

Four intertwined issues are pursued in this section by tracing the evolution of the debates in development economics: the connections between growth and income-poverty, between growth and social development, between social development and income-poverty, and the role of the State in influencing each of these elements. The presentation is not thematic. It follows the debates more or less chronologically.

Classical economic theory from before the time of Adam Smith was concerned with the question of development and its effects on the standard of living and distribution of income. However, 'development economics' as currently understood took shape in the late 1940s and early 1950s. The name was inspired by Schumpeter's (1934) classic book which defined development as a disequilibrium transition from one configuration of economic balance (or 'circular flow' in Schumpeter's usage) to another. The new doctrines were heavily influenced by the positive role for state intervention advocated by Keynes (1936), and much intellectual effort was devoted to attacking the problems of planning for late industrialization (Hirschman 1981; Todaro 1982).

The arguments by Rosenstein-Rodan (1943), Nurske (1953), Prebisch (1959), and others against relying only on market forces to lead industrialization became the guiding principles for policy-makers as most countries in Africa, Asia, and Latin America embarked on import-substitution strategies (ISI). At the macroeconomic level, there was a focus on 'binding' constraints in the form of scarce produced means of production. In large economies relatively closed to foreign trade (the Soviet Union, India, China) a shortage of physical capital, e.g. 'machines to make machines', was seen as a factor holding back growth (Mahalanobis, 1953). Elsewhere, the ability to generate foreign exchange via import substitution or export promotion was seen as an essential input into the growth process. Building on ideas implicit in Prebisch's work, 'two-gap' models emphasized how additional foreign resources both complement domestic saving and add to capacity to import intermediate and capital goods (Chenery and Bruno, 1962). Such considerations remain relevant to the discussion of country growth prospects, as discussed in section 4 below.

In the 1960s and 1970s, this older tradition emphasizing the role of state direction and planning began to be challenged by another line of thought placing more emphasis on the role of markets. What separates the two camps is not whether countries should embark upon industrialization, but rather on the policies which help or hinder it. Although criticized by authors such as Lipton (1977), a pro-industry or urban bias has characterized much discussion of development questions. However, in agricultural policy there has also been a division of opinion as to whether the sector should be regulated, or ruled by free-market logic after price structures have been appropriately adjusted. Schultz (1964) was an enormously effective pamphlet in support of the latter course. (The role of agriculture is also discussed in section 4.)

It was also recognized early on that not all the outcomes of industrialization would be positive, at least in the short run. Relying on the historical experience of industrialized countries, Kuznets (1955) put forth a famous conjecture that in the early phases of growth, the distribution of income would become less equal and only later would it tend to become more equal again. His 'inverse-U' curve relied upon relatively higher income inequality in the industrial sector compared to the rural sector, and a population shift from the latter to the former. An early challenge came from Adelman and Morris (1973). Using data for less developed countries, they observed that declines in inequality as incomes rose (the pattern Kuznets found in the industrialized countries between the 1930s and 1960s) did not come about automatically and needed to be supported by appropriate policy.

This empirical debate was connected to, and thereby underlined, the theoretical argument that industrialization required large investments which required huge savings. The absence of well-developed capital markets implied that in order to generate those savings income had to shift towards the higher-income families which had a higher marginal propensity to save (Kaldor, 1957), i.e. there was supposed to exist a clear trade-off between equity and growth.

By the early 1970s the availability of data for more LDCs started to undermine the strength of this pessimistic view, with the data seeming to show that for some countries growth led to more income inequality and for others it did just the reverse! Subsequent research has further weakened Kuznets-style hypotheses (Sundrum, 1991; Anand and Kanbur, 1993) for developing economies,[5] while rising inequality over the past two decades in rich countries has transformed the Kuznets curve linking distribution and inequality into something more like a snake.

An important policy prescription resulted from all this information: average per capita income growth cannot be assumed to alleviate inequality and income-poverty automatically (Chenery *et al.*, 1974). Thus, policies which directly address income distribution are called for. Especially with skewed initial distributions of income and wealth, economic growth can have weak and delayed effects in terms of reducing income-poverty. Following a proposal by Meade (1964), the book by Chenery *et al.*, *Redistribution with Growth*, emphasized asset accumulation by the poor as a means to reduce inequality and growth. The book, however, did not have the policy impact it could have had[6] because the oil shock, the ensuing international recession, and later the debt crisis soon reoriented the priorities of countries and multilateral agencies.

These events marked the close of the post-war Golden Age of impressive and sustained output growth, both in developed and developing countries. One consequence of this historical transition was that strong theoretical voices began to be raised against the role of the State in general and the ISI strategy which had prevailed through the 1960s in particular. In the development literature, early examples are Little *et al.* (1970) and Bhagwati (1971),[7] while 'supply-side' economics was a kindred trend in the industrialized world.

In this new view the role of the State was transformed—it became part of the problem rather than a solution. Such ideas were not as readily accepted in developing countries as they were in the industrialized ones. Nevertheless, since the early 1980s more and more countries have adopted 'market friendly' policies in the aftermath of the debt crisis. In part, they had no choice because their only sources of increasingly scarce hard currency were the international financial institutions (or IFIs), whose own policy prescriptions were heavily influenced by the new orthodoxy. With the first structural-adjustment loans from around 1980, market-based reforms became tied to adjustment lending.

During the second half of the 1980s, however, the positive impact of social services (especially education) on growth was emphasized by a number of neoclassical economists. Based on the 'human capital' model developed earlier for wage differentials in the US (Schultz, 1961; Becker, 1964), Psacharopoulos (1985, 1994) measured the effect of education on wage differentials across countries. Some of these ideas have recently been rejuvenated under the New Growth Theory (NGT) label.[8] As these models are based on representative agents, the focus has shifted from earnings differentials to cross-country comparisons based on the aggregate level of education. Also, they have stressed the external effects of education, rather than those which are 'internalized' by the market through differential wages.[9] Spending on education (public or private) leads to more productive workers. Even without taking into account the positive effects of education on individuals' lives, it directly fosters growth through productivity increases.

However, learning by doing may play as large or a larger role in terms of generating productivity increases and wage differentials than formal schooling (Arrow, 1962; Mincer, 1962). This theoretical point reduces considerably the possibility of using NGT models to promote free, publicly provided basic education. Moreover, individuals maximizing their own utility would try to improve their skills by choosing to engage in education or working. This would create a demand for education which could be satisfied by the private sector. Some models stress that not all individuals can pay for their education but, within the boundaries of the model, this is a credit market imperfection which can be solved through regulation and not necessarily with publicly funded education.

Finally, note that whether it is internalized via wage differentials or is an externality, human capital is another produced means of production, akin to physical capital or foreign exchange as discussed above. An immediate planning problem arises as to which of these three inputs (if any) represents a bottleneck, and how it can be widened. This way of looking at the problem is alien to much of the recent literature stressing how markets smooth out all economic rough spots, but it is one that confronts practical policy formulation every day.[10]

On the empirical side, authors such as Behrman and Deolalikar (1988), Birdsall (1988), Birdsall and Griffin (1993), and Behrman (1995) have focused on all social services which may increase human capital (defined more broadly) and growth, e.g. health, population control, nutrition, water supply, and sanitation. They also report on the synergies among them (and between them and other sectors, e.g. population control and the environment).[11]

Another group of mainstream economists have focused their research on the relationship between income distribution and economic growth. They stress the positive effect of income equality on growth but do not explicitly deal with income-poverty reduction. The models rely on some endogenous growth mechanism or on a notion of redistributive political economy equilibrium. In the first case, education provides human capital which not only increases an individual's earning capacity but has a spill-over effect as well. If the income distribution is unequal and there are credit constraints, only those sections of the population which are better off would be able to obtain education and the size of the externality will be small. If the distribution of income is more egalitarian, or transfers can be performed from the rich to the poor, not only will there be a larger group of educated workers but the size of the externality will be larger as well. However, depending on the initial conditions, in a more egalitarian society it may be impossible to provide the transfers for everybody to attend school and the economy stagnates (Perotti, 1993).

In 'political equilibrium' models the mechanism at work is similar. In order to foster growth a subsidy (financed through general taxation) is required to equate the private to the social rate of return of capital. If the distribution of income is rather unequal and decisions are made through majority voting, most people will object to a policy which favours the capital-holding minority. Contrariwise, if the distribution of income is more even, the proportion of voters who will favour such a policy increases. Thus, the subsidy is introduced, growth ensues, and all members of the economy are better off (Bertola, 1992; Alessina and Rodrik, 1994; Persson and Tabellini, 1994). According to Alessina and Perotti (1994), the empirical evidence for these models is weak. Given their simplifying assumptions about the economy and its decision-making processes regarding taxation and subsidies, such a finding is no surprise.

NGT models, by concentrating on steady-state equilibria and the competitive mechanisms which may lead to them, fail to highlight that while education and knowledge are crucial for growth, they are not sufficient. They forget that they are looking at only one of the constraints. Thus our argument here is not so much that they are wrong (in terms of emphasizing that knowledge, education, and basic social services in general are crucial to growth), but that they are incomplete. By concentrating on a very specific link they miss the broader picture and the more interesting policy problems: how should governments allocate their resources among and within sectors in order to remove the different constraints. Put differently, other policies are also needed to spur growth.[12]

Moreover, recent authors view growth as a simple expansion of output. In contrast, 'old guard' scholars saw 'development' as a process transforming the structure of the economy as a whole (Hirschman, 1958; Chenery, 1986; Syrquin, 1988; and also see Nell (1992a) for similar concept for industrialized countries).

No variant of NGT models attempts to deal with income-poverty, whether in its broad definition or just in monetary terms. The issue of the relation between growth and income-poverty—which is absent in the NGT literature—is taken up by Ravallion and others.[13] Their findings are a pillar for recent policy recommendations by the World Bank: faster growth reduces income-poverty (World Bank, 1990). Again, however, their concept of growth is as limited as that of other neoclassical writers. Moreover, their results depend on the assumption that growth is distributionally neutral—if it is not, it may cease to be pro-poor (Lipton and Ravallion, 1994). Unfortunately for these models, growth is hardly ever distributionally neutral, in particular when growth is accompanied by fundamental structural transformations.

Moreover, there remain substantial doubts about the appropriate tools to promote growth. A 'Washington consensus' on these matters emerged in the 1980s (Williamson, 1989), prescribing a minimalist State, undistorted product, financial, and factor markets, and public provision of infrastructure. As noted above, such policies are strongly recommended by the IFIs but are not uniformly applauded in the literature (Amsden, 1989; Fanelli *et al.*, 1990; Wade, 1990). Moreover, authors such as Fanelli *et al.* (1992) and Taylor and Pieper (1996) point out that their outcomes have not been uniformly beneficial, involving in many cases slow growth (Sub-Saharan Africa), financial instability and increasing inequality (Turkey, many Latin American and East European countries), and at times virtual economic chaos (Mexico, Russia). Although everybody involved in the current discussion would argue against extremely distorted markets, 'very large' fiscal deficits (nearing or exceeding 10 per cent of GDP, say) and overly ambitious redistributive packages, they differ fundamentally about the need for active market regulation, foreign trade intervention, and expansionary macroeconomic and targeted industrial policies on the part of the State.[14]

At the same time, in true dialectical fashion neoclassical arguments for a minimalist State began to be undermined by empirically minded scholars who identified a series of crucial state interventions in the most successful developing countries, the East Asian NICs (Amsden, 1989; Wade, 1990). These writers noted that rather than allowing markets to allocate resources without guidance, East Asian economic authorities actively pursued policies to foster certain industries. These policies depended on the institutional characteristics and historical experiences of these countries and were not based on a theoretical framework which systematically suppresses such variables (Shapiro and Taylor, 1990).

Important factors highlighted by these authors are that the 'first wave' of rapidly growing East Asian economies (Japan, Republic of Korea, and Taiwan) never faced binding foreign exchange constraints and enjoyed egalitarian distributions of income and assets (mainly land) prior to their industrialization pushes. Subsequently, relatively equal savings rates across the population supported an egalitarian distribution of the growing stock of assets a la Meade and Chenery (You, 1996).

Income-poverty reduction is also associated to the provision of social services by economists of different persuasions. The concept of poverty can be expanded to include non-monetary aspects, e.g. independently of their income people who do not have access to basic services should be defined as poor (Singh, 1990; Lipton and van der Gaag, 1993). Providing social services reduces poverty in a thoroughly direct way.

This, however, is not a novel notion. Other scholars mainly outside of the mainstream tradition have discussed the connections between social services and economic growth, e.g. the ILO's basic needs approach (ILO, 1976), Streeten *et al.* (1981), Sen (1985), and the first and seventh Human Development Reports (UNDP, 1990, 1996). The thrust of these 'basic needs' and 'capabilities' approaches is that social objectives are too important to wait until countries develop before engaging in policies to satisfy them. Indeed, policies aimed at meeting social goals can contribute directly to growth (Streeten *et al*, 1981, Ch. 4). The other side of the coin is that not all countries with high per capita income growth were improving the lot of their citizens. As with distribution and income-poverty reduction, growth does not automatically foster social development, and state policies are a *sine qua non* of human development.

Thus, although a consensus on the need for policies to increase the human capabilities (health, nutrition, and more importantly education) of the poor is emerging, the elements of the consensus are disparate and not well integrated. In order to realize the synergies between interventions in basic social services higher taxes may be required, as well as for building up the government's ability to provide services more generally (as the IFIs have implicitly recognized in African 'success cases' such as Ghana and Uganda). However, the State will also need to be the catalyst for realizing the second kind of synergies, i.e. between growth, poverty-reduction, and social services. The literature reviewed in this section addresses only inadequately these links. In the next section an attempt to integrate explicitly these three elements is made. This is done by taking as given the synergies among the social services, and concentrating on the synergies between social development, income-poverty reduction, and economic growth.

Growth, Poverty, and Social Development: Exploring the Synergies

In this section the ten countries of the present volume, plus others included for comparison purposes, are classified according to their performance in terms of growth, income-poverty reduction, and social development. To simplify the exposition countries are classified by level (high and low) for two variables at a time (social development and economic growth, social development and income-poverty reduction, income-poverty reduction and economic growth).[15] The goal of the analysis is to provide the building blocks of the growth trajectories briefly formulated in section 4 by sorting out different interaction mechanisms.

The way that Tables 15.1 to 15.3 are set up means that in each case the north-east corner dominates the south-west one, i.e. the former shows positive outcomes and the latter negative ones. Comparing the south-east and north-west corners is less straightforward.

Nevertheless, and acknowledging it is only a value judgement, we believe that from the perspective of human development, the south-east corner is a superior outcome to the north-west one. This opinion rests on a ranking of outcomes where 'social' outcomes are preferred to 'purely economic' ones (such as growth). Stated differently, we prefer to live in a country which grows slowly (or not at all) but where there is no income-poverty and there is universal access to basic social services.[16] We would rather see universal access to basic social services with no increase in income than the inverse case.

A further element of 'convergence' needs to enter the discussion. From the evidence in the country studies, it seems to be the case that it is relatively easier (in some sense) to move to the north-east corner from the south-east corner than from the north-west one. In order to substantiate this claim we need to take a first cut at the underlying processes which lead to the outcomes classified above.

For Table 15.1 (where countries are classified according to outcomes in respects of economic growth and income-poverty reduction): in the absence of serious distributive biases, growth (in traditional per capita income terms or using a broader interpretation) will generally lead to income-poverty reduction. However, there are circumstances in which it is a very weak force, e.g. Brazil prior to the debt crisis.[17] When output expansion is observed in conjunction with a relatively constant proportion of the population under the income-poverty line, the growth pattern is either not incorporating the majority of households or doing so with stagnant real earnings.[18] In either case, a fundamental redirection of policy is needed to reduce income-poverty. In particular, asset or income redistribution policies may be needed. Such moves, however, can alter the growth pattern and could prompt a reduction in growth rates.[19] Unless the growth model is income-poverty-reducing to begin with, the policies needed to ensure income-poverty reduction may negatively affect output expansion.

In the case of high income-poverty reduction combined with low economic growth the situation is different. Such a combination may indicate that redistribution does not allow massive physical investment.[20] It can, however, lay a foundation for future expansion as soon as income-poverty levels are reduced. The elimination

TABLE 15.1. Poverty reduction and economic growth

Economic growth	Poverty reduction	
	Low or negative	High
High	Botswana (6.1 / 1980–92)	Korea, Rep. of (7.8 / 1965–92)
	Brazil (6.3 / 1965–80)	Malaysia (4 / 1965–92)
	Mexico (5 / 1965–92)	Mauritius (4.5 / 1965–92)
Low	Costa Rica (2.1 / 1980–92)	Cuba (1960–70)
	Sri Lanka (2.7 / 1965–92)	
	Zimbabwe (0.8 / 1965–92)	
	Sub-Saharan Africa (1.5 / 1965–92)	
	Bangladesh (0.6 / 1965–92)	
	India (2.2 / 1965–92)	
	Pakistan (2.4 / 1965–92)	

Note: Figures in parentheses refer to annual average growth rates of per capita GDP and the corresponding period. There is a dearth of long-trend comparable data on poverty. The classification in the table is based on information in Chs. 2 and 4–13. For India see Government of India (1994), for Pakistan and Bangladesh see World Bank (1990), and for Brazil see ECLAC (1994)

A negative outcome on poverty reduction implies that the incidence of poverty increased

For Cuba, see Chapter 13

Source: UNICEF, *State of the World's Children, 1995*

of income-poverty favours growth through several channels as families are in a better position to enhance their own capabilities, markets and demand are expanded (which affect both employment and the possibility of engaging in self-employment), and a more equal distribution of physical assets allows more families to pursue income-generating activities (e.g. Cuba during 1960–70).

Summarizing, although growth may lead to income-poverty reduction it depends on the kind of growth.[21] The basic questions are how the process of accumulation affects lower-income groups and if it generates numerous high-paying jobs or self-employment possibilities. If growth is not intrinsically income-poverty-reducing, attempts to help the poor may upset the model. On the other hand, increasing the income of the poor has positive effects on growth at least in the medium to long run, even if redistribution diminishes current investment in the short run. Although income-poverty reduction may not be a sufficient condition for starting a growth process, given its positive influence on accumulation it is a better base (in conjunction with other policies) than an initial situation with high levels of income-poverty and rapid growth.

For Table 15.2 (where countries are classified according to outcomes in respect of social development and income-poverty reduction):[22] first, we consider a situation with insufficient social development but a significant decrease in income-poverty. The latter can occur basically in two ways: as a consequence of very rapid economic growth[23] or as a result of a significant redistribution of physical assets among households. In the first case the situation may not be sustainable as there will be a shortage of skilled workers to sustain output expansion. In the second case

TABLE 15.2. Poverty reduction and social development

Poverty reduction	Social development	
	Low	High
High		Cuba
		Korea, Rep. of
		Malaysia
		Mauritius
		China
Low or Negative	Bangladesh	Barbados
	Brazil	Botswana
	India	Costa Rica
	Pakistan	Kerala
		Sri Lanka
		Zimbabwe
		Mexico

Notes and source: see Table 15.1

the income level (and income growth) of households who receive transfers of assets but who lack the skills to succeed in a market context will, in the medium run, stagnate or deteriorate in the absence of supplementary policies. In both cases, the reduction in income-poverty does not easily lead to enhancing capabilities and diminishes the opportunities to achieve human development. These effects could be attenuated if the reduction of income-poverty allows families to buy or get access to publicly provided basic social services. Which effect will dominate is uncertain but it does not seem likely that social development could be maintained in either scenario without public intervention to support it.

Contrariwise, a situation where income-poverty has not been reduced substantially but social development is high (e.g. several of the countries analysed in this book) could be considered to be in an unstable equilibrium where progress in income-poverty reduction is just waiting to happen.[24] Small interventions[25] in asset (or income) redistribution would easily generate household income increases which would expand demand and employment opportunities through a multiplier effect. As most households, even if they are currently poor, enjoy a high level of capabilities (due to the high level of social development) it would be within their reach to be engaged in high value-added activities. Through its effect on incomes, this would further increase demand and lead to a virtuous circle of reduction in the proportion of families below the poverty line.[26]

Briefly, then, although income-poverty reduction has a positive effect in allowing families to access basic social services, policies which only address income-poverty without providing social services would tend to be short-lived and unsustainable. However, with a solid base of social development, it is easier to reduce income-poverty.

For Table 15.3 (where countries are classified according to outcomes in respect of economic growth and social development):[27] it must be remembered that the productive transformation characterized as economic growth (development) in this chapter cannot be assumed to happen automatically or rely exclusively on market forces; public direction is needed (if only to guide, strengthen, focus, or foster the private sector). Much evidence suggests that income and asset distribution, social development, and income-poverty reduction are favourable for growth (as we argued in the previous section). However, none of these three factors by itself can guarantee that growth will occur (e.g. Barbados, Costa Rica, Zimbabwe). The role of the State is to catalyse the synergy between interventions which promote poverty-reducing growth and social development.

Nevertheless, if a country is in a situation characterized by a high level of social development but slow growth, the most difficult aspect of social development has been overcome, i.e. establishing and funding basic social services for the whole population. Moreover, our case-studies indicate that per capita income growth is not necessary for the universal provision of basic social services (Kerala, Sri Lanka, Zimbabwe). Many of the fundamental interventions are low cost.[28]

TABLE 15.3. Social development and economic growth

Economic growth	Social development	
	Low	High
High	Brazil	Botswana
		Korea, Rep. of
		Malaysia
		Mauritius
Low	Sub-Saharan Africa	Barbados
		Costa Rica
		Kerala
		Sri Lanka
		Zimbabwe
		Mexico

Notes and Source: see Table 15.

Reallocation of resources in favour of social services can be achieved even in the presence of very modest growth. High social development means that households enjoy universal (or near-universal) access to services which enhances their well-being and capabilities.[29] It is much easier to undertake a high growth strategy with such a population than with people who lack basic education and are undernourished—as the cases of the Republic of Korea and Malaysia illustrate.[30]

One difficulty is that fast economic growth does not ensure that basic social services will be provided. Policies which could direct resources to social sectors may involve allocation mechanisms which differ from those that could generate growth (whether it is led by private profitability or planned). In other words, growth is neither necessary nor sufficient for expansion of basic social services, but the latter are 'almost necessary'[31] for growth.

The next question is how the three processes are intertwined. They reinforce each other in virtuous circles, but no single one (economic growth, income-poverty reduction, or basic social services) is a sufficient condition for the others. The case-studies show substantial success in terms of providing social services but the picture is less clear regarding the reduction of income-poverty, i.e. the two processes are not causally linked.

This can clearly be seen at the household level. Individuals who are literate, live long, and whose children are well fed, are not necessarily able to find jobs or engage in self-employed income-generating activities. Self-employment can only occur if the household possesses physical capital and/or land, while wage-employment for a growing labour force can only occur in a sustainable fashion if the economy is growing and generating employment opportunities where individuals can apply their capabilities in order to add value to production.

In so far as very rapid economic growth or a drastic redistribution of assets could reduce income-poverty in the absence of enhanced longevity or knowledge, it becomes clear that for income-poverty reduction enhanced capabilities are not a necessary condition. Moreover, neither economic growth nor redistribution can be interpreted as being necessary conditions for higher levels of health and educational status in a country. Nevertheless, the presence of each of them compounds the effect of the others. Thus, if employment opportunities in value-adding sectors are increased (or physical assets are distributed), healthy and educated individuals will be better prepared to engage in those activities (or profitably use their newly acquired assets). Such actions allow them both to break away from income-poverty individually and to contribute to the growth of the economy when their increased incomes are aggregated. Although improvements in basic social services are not necessary for income-poverty reduction or economic growth, they favour or enable them.

Moreover, and to complete the virtuous circle, as families escape income-poverty they are able to obtain for themselves the means to enhance their own capabilities, and in turn contribute to economic growth. Social development, however, does not occur without direct state intervention in the provision of basic services, in part because of the characteristics of the goods involved (they are public goods with externalities and there are economies of scale in their provision by the State).

We have tried to demonstrate that policies which do not focus on at least two of the three variables (economic growth, income-poverty reduction, and social development) will have serious difficulties in realizing the desirable outcomes initially set out. In some circumstances, focusing interventions on only two of the variables can be enough. If the outcomes in just those two are above some threshold level, the synergies described above can be triggered off; thus positive processes and results can be set in motion to enhance human capabilities.

For instance, a combination of universal provision of basic social services and growth (leading to high-wage employment expansion) could achieve substantial reductions in income-poverty even in the absence of asset or income redistribution policies (as in Mauritius).[32] Policies which stimulate and sustain income-poverty-reducing growth and education of households will be mutually reinforcing even in the absence of specific public health policies (as the example of the Republic of Korea shows).[33]

On the other hand, policies which focus on social development ignoring growth and income-poverty reduction will lead to outcomes which may not be sustainable in the long run (e.g. Kerala, Sri Lanka, Zimbabwe). Policies which focus on income-poverty reduction and social development without regard to macroeconomic imbalances or constraints which limit growth (e.g. Cuba) run the risk of reversal in situations of external shocks. Policies which focus largely on economic growth without much regard for income-poverty reduction or social development (the non-success story of most of Latin America) are doomed to unequal income distribution or low levels of human capabilities which dampen economic prospects in the long run. Finally, when there is neither growth, nor social development, nor income-poverty reduction (all non-success stories in Sub-Saharan Africa or to a lesser extent, South Asia) a vicious cycle of rapid population growth, rising income-poverty, and environmental degradation results.

The above discussion suggests that the effect of interventions in one area enhances the outcomes in another area. A simple, if schematic way of visualizing this is to perform a simulation exercise comparing a 'traditional' case where there are no feedbacks and synergies among the sectors and one where they do occur.[34] Results from such an exercise are shown in Fig. 15.1. The simulations were done for a hypothetical country which starts with a level of per capita GNP of 100 and grows at 2 per cent per year. Also, 30 per cent of the population are assumed to be poor and life expectancy is 65 years.[35]

In part (a) of the figure it can be seen that when there are no synergies and inter-actions GNP per capita after ten years is 120 (bottom line). The direct effect eco-nomic growth has on reducing income-poverty and increasing life expectancy, is observed in the reduction of the income-poverty level from 30 to slightly above 27 per cent (top line, part (b)) and the almost two and a half extra years (bottom line, part (c))—from 65 to 67.5—which are added to life expectancy after ten years.

The effect of the synergies can be observed in the same graph. Two additional cases have been simulated. In the first one the synergies result in less income-poverty, higher human capabilities (here represented as longer life expectancy), and an interaction effect (income-poverty reduction times life expectancy) increasing the level of GNP per capita. After ten years the increase in per capita income is 50 per cent more (i.e. 30 as opposed to 20) than in the base case (top line, part (a)). However, it is noticeable that income-poverty reduction is greater in this case (middle line, part (b)) because of higher human capabilities and the interaction between human capabilities and higher growth. Thus the final level of income-poverty has been reduced to less than 23 per cent. Similarly, life expectancy is higher (middle line, part (c)) because of the direct effect of lower income-poverty and the interaction between reduced income-poverty and higher per capita income.

In the second simulation the rate of growth of per capita income is lower (1.5 per cent per year) but the initial level of income-poverty is also lower (25 per cent). It can be seen that in the presence of synergies and a lower initial income-poverty level the final level of per capita income is 25 per cent higher than in the absence of synergies (middle line, part (a)). This means that the lower growth rate has been more than compensated by the positive effect on growth of the initial lower level of income-poverty. In terms of income-poverty, although the final level is much lower than in the other two cases (bottom line, part (b)), the initial level was also assumed to be lower. It can be observed (top line, part(c)) that life expectancy is higher than in the base case and marginally higher than in the first simulation. This means that although life expectancy should be lower than in the first simulation because of the lower level of income (resulting from the lower growth rate), the lower level of

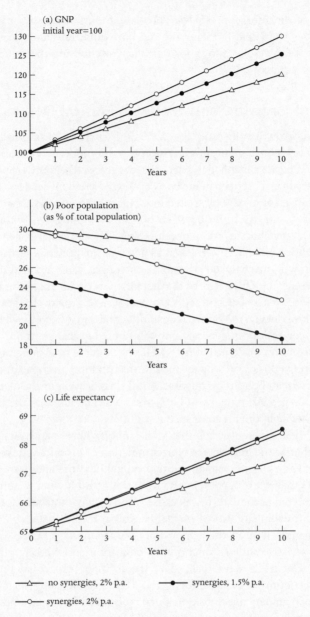

Fig. 15.1 Simulating the synergy between GNP growth, poverty reduction, and life expectancy

income-poverty enhances well-being and life expectancy, compensating for the lower level of income.

Although these results are only illustrative (as other simulations with different coefficients or initial values would give different results), they help to visualize the importance of the interaction effects. These are important for two reasons. On the one hand, they show that the synergies can have quite substantial effects. Second, the presence of synergies allows for flexibility in choosing the priority areas for policy in each country.

Patterns of Growth Consistent with Human Development

What kind of growth will ensure that a virtuous circle of social development and income-poverty-reducing output expansion is set in motion? The missing element in the preceding discussion has been the nature of the growth process. Two processes have been described in the book and in the previous section: (a) a virtuous circle among income-poverty reduction, social development, and economic growth, and (b) the synergies between policies and outcomes within the social sectors which contribute to social development. The latter have been the focus of most of the book and have been taken as given in the previous section. However, economic growth, its characteristics, and constraints, cannot be left unanalysed if we are to give a complete picture of the first virtuous circle. This is attempted in the current section. First, we discuss the sectoral nature of growth that is most likely to prove poverty-reducing and human capability-enhancing. Second, we discuss how developing economies can generate enough foreign exchange to buy key production inputs from the world economy—while at the same time integration with the global economy does not worsen income distribution to weaken the synergy between growth and poverty reduction. A full classification of the factors underlying sustainable growth remains to be formulated, but some of the points raised above help shed light on this complex question.

First, in their different ways the Mahalanobis, Lucas, and two-gap growth models emphasize the importance of accumulation of produced means of production—respectively physical capital, human capital, and the ability to earn foreign exchange to buy key production inputs from the world market. Country histories can be interpreted in these terms. Because of politically motivated foreign aid, for example, the Republic of Korea (hereafter Korea) in the 1960s was not short of foreign exchange. It used the opportunity to accumulate human and physical capital on a massive scale through public education and publicly guided private investment. The fruits were realized in the form of export-led growth which enabled the economy to evade the debt crisis. The economic bureaucracy played an essential role in guiding this transition, but it is also true that rapid employment creation and wage increases helped contain inequality.

Cuba also did not have severe foreign exchange problems until quite recently, and effectively accumulated human capital. However, its relative technological backwardness, close ties with the socialist trading bloc, and political isolation did not allow it to make an easy transition to exports for the West when its foreign inflows were cut off in the late 1980s. The island economy lacked ability to generate hard currency on a sustained basis; adjustment to its external shock had to take the form of massive output reduction to cut back on imports.

In a third example, Brazil pursued ISI to the extent that between the 1940s and early 1980s it was the fastest-growing country in the world. However, the income distribution remained highly unequal, and synergies of the sort described in previous sections could not be realized. Its rate of accumulation of physical capital was very high, but insufficient to provide a cushion against the debt crisis which forced the economy to shift from a trade deficit of several per cent of GDP to a trade surplus of equal magnitude. This macroeconomic shock led to a 'lost decade' of growth (from which it is still trying to recover), and which underlined the fact that human capital accumulation had been weak.

Elsewhere in Latin America, South Asia, and Sub-Saharan Africa the results of ISI were mixed. Colombia maintained a relatively closed economy, pursuing combined import substitution and export promotion policies with a regulated external capital market. Its fiscal balance and access to foreign exchange from primary product exports (most legal, some not) have permitted ongoing accumulation of human and physical capital and sustained growth. In this respect, its experience of growth in the 1980s contrasted dramatically with the rest of Latin America—especially the large economies of Argentina, Brazil, and Mexico—where the lack of financial intermediation prevented savings from being converted into investment, and in fact open capital markets permitted flight of capital as large as the external debt in many countries.

In the 1980s India appeared to break away from its traditional 3.5 per cent 'Hindu rate of growth', largely due to public investment in infrastructure and expansionary macroeconomic policy. A degree of trade liberalization plus currency devaluation have subsequently permitted solid export growth on the basis of capacity built up during a long period of ISI. For the moment, the foreign exchange constraint is not binding, and accumulation of physical capital and even human capital (though its distribution is still very skewed) proceeds at a steady pace. But as discussed below, economy-wide synergies have yet to appear.

Finally, in Sub-Saharan Africa, 'surplus extraction' from export agriculture to benefit urban-based industrialization was an important element of the region's development strategy after the Second World War. Although there were substantial internal resource transfers, several factors supervened to make the strategy unsuccessful. Externally, trends in the export prices for the food, beverage, fibre, and mineral exports the region produces were consistently unfavourable. Internally, lack of investment in infrastructure and technological improvement hampered agricultural output growth while industrial strategies did not bear fruit. More recently, there have been continuing adverse shifts in the terms of trade and escalating interest obligations on official debt, tightening the external constraint. Physical and (some) human capital accumulation has taken place, but has not been realized in terms of sustained output growth.

These vignettes suggest that sustained growth is not feasible over a very long run unless all three forms of 'capital'—physical, human, and the capacity to generate foreign exchange—are at hand. However, a dearth of foreign exchange may be more immediately binding than shortages of the other forms of capital as the cases of Cuba and Brazil attest. Output growth may be sustainable and physical capital may accumulate (with the help of borrowed foreign savings) for fairly long periods even if human capital accumulation is weak—India and Brazil. To complete the circle, the case of Mauritius shows that if resource rents are reinvested in social services, growth can occur without a massive build-up of physical capital, but such conditions may hold only in very small economies.

The sectoral nature of the growth process is critical to the kind of constraints which will be faced, how they could be resolved, and whether it is income-poverty-reducing or not. As income-poverty in the vast majority of countries in Asia (where most of the world's poor are concentrated) and Africa (where the incidence of income-poverty is the highest) is largely a rural phenomenon, without ensuring that rural productivity and hence incomes increase more rapidly than the rate of growth of the rural labour force, there is little prospect of eliminating income-poverty. Even in Latin America, the incidence of income-poverty in rural areas is greater than that in urban. However, the urban population exceeds the rural, and hence its share of the total poor is larger. Therefore policy must concentrate on reducing income-poverty incidence in the urban areas. At the same time, agriculture and rural development will need to play a greater part than they have in the past, in order to stem the rural–urban migration, which increases and deepens urban income-poverty (de Janvry and Sadoulet, 1995).

Historical experience from the now-industrialized countries, as well as the statistical link between agricultural and overall economic growth in developing countries, have established that development (industrialization) involves two processes; first, the share of agriculture in a country's labour force and total GDP declines as incomes per capita increase; and second, that rapid agricultural growth accompanies or precedes overall economic growth. This apparent paradox may have given rise to the impression that agriculture is unimportant, a misperception encouraged by the emphasis of most developing-country governments on ISI. This resulted in the paradigm that agriculture could be squeezed to generate a surplus for industrialization to occur. This strategy may have worked in Japan or Western Europe, where agriculture was already growing rapidly before rapid industrialization commenced or as in the USSR where agriculture started with a large surplus relative to the subsistence needs of the population (Timmer, 1988). But if agriculture started with traditional technology and productivity and incomes near subsistence, major investment in agriculture was needed if the industrial revolution was to succeed. In fact, in South Asia and Africa, and to a lesser extent also in Latin America, agricultural growth rates have been well below those found in East Asia since the 1960s.

Thus, in Sub-Saharan Africa, agricultural growth rates between 1965 and 1990 have been consistently below population growth rates (World Bank, 1990). In India per capita agricultural production growth was negative over 1961–70, 0.3 per cent over 1971–80, and 1.7 per cent over 1981–92 (and not very different in Pakistan). In Latin America per capita agricultural growth was in the range of 0.5 and 1.5 per cent between 1965 and 1990. Compared to these performances, in China per capita agricultural output grew by 3.7 per cent per annum over the 1960s, 1.5 per cent over the 1970s, and 2.5 per cent over the 1980s; in Korea by 1.8, 3.0, and 1.0 per cent; and in Malaysia by 2.8, 2.7, and 3 per cent respectively (UNCTAD, 1993).

Agricultural growth leads not only to rising incomes within the sector and released resources for industrialization, but is critically important for the reduction of income-poverty in rural areas directly and indirectly through its effect on non-farm incomes. First, briefly on the direct effects: with increasing population in most regions, technical change rather than expanding cultivated land has been the main source of output growth. But the green revolution has not been generalized in most of Sub-Saharan Africa, and even in South Asia remains restricted to a limited variety of crops and to limited regions. Rising demand for labour with technical change can raise agricultural wages, thus reducing rural income-poverty in countries where there is a substantial body of agricultural labour. But in order to improve its income-poverty-reducing impact, an equitable distribution of land (and at least secure tenancy) would have both a productivity-raising and equity-enhancing impact. Second, non-farm linkages resulting from technical change in agriculture can accelerate agricultural growth and its income-poverty-reducing impact. These non-farm linkages are both of a backward and forward nature: a growing agriculture demands non-farm production inputs and supplies raw materials to transport, processing, and marketing firms. The rural non-farm economy, contributing 25–30 per cent of rural income in Africa and 30–40 per cent in Asia and Latin America, is particularly important to the rural poor. Landless and near-landless households everywhere depend on non-farm earnings; those with fewer than 0.5 hectares typically earn over one-third of their total income from non-farm sources. In studies in India a 10 per cent increase in agricultural income will lead to an additional 6.4 per cent in rural non-farm income, and the elasticity of non-farm sector employment to agricultural income was estimated to be 1.2 (Hazell and Haggblade, 1993). Clearly, for these multiplier effects to be realized through agricultural growth, the State has to intervene with infrastructure, including roads, irrigation, research, and extension services—which suggests a 'big push' type emphasis on agriculture.

In other words, here we are not talking about emphasis on agriculture of the kind promoted by the IFIs through adjustment policies in the 1980s which justifiably intended to redress the bias against agricultural producer prices but failed to address the underlying structural constraints to agricultural output growth. In the great rush towards export-orientation in Africa in the 1980s and in South Asia in the 1990s, it has been forgotten that agriculture is one of the 'unsung heroes' of the East Asian miracle (Saith, 1996). As the Malaysian example demonstrates, land improvement and agricultural growth, combined with rural development programmes which focused on health and education, have not only led over the last four decades to income-poverty-reducing growth, but as labour transferred from agriculture to industry, created the capacity for labour skills to be constantly upgraded and the economy to move up the product-cycle ladder in the international division of labour.

It was mentioned above that in Latin America income-poverty is mainly an urban phenomenon. For countries where rural populations are still significant, effective programmes of rural development that include access to land, productivity increases for small farmers, and employment creation in agriculture and in rural non-farm activities are called for. However, for most countries economic growth needs to resume along a different path. This, in turn, is crucially dependent upon domestic savings being converted into domestic investment (rather than becoming flight capital), which requires a 'intermediation mechanism' for this conversion to occur (Fanelli *et al.*, 1990). Financial liberalization, à la the 'Washington consensus', however, is unlikely to resolve the problem of low investment rates based on low savings or ensure that domestic savings remain at home. In other words, domestic savings are the key to reducing two of the three constraints—physical capital and foreign exchange—mentioned at the beginning of this section. Given that Latin American economies are open to external capital markets, the portfolio decision between real assets and foreign financial assets (i.e. capital flight) plays a crucial role in determining the investment decision and therefore growth. Investment in physical capital financed with domestic savings, when combined with investment in human capital, can set in motion a virtuous circle.

The continued seriousness of the debt burden and import requirements of production will perforce require export-orientation of the growth strategy. However, given that the international net barter terms of trade for Latin America declined over the 1980s, the success of the export effort in mitigating the foreign exchange constraint will be dependent upon the diversification of the export mix away from primary commodities to increasing exports of higher value-added products. Taking advantage of the new opportunities of globalization and liberalization would require then a renewed investment in education, both in order to improve the quality of primary schooling so that completion rates of primary education improve, and widening access to secondary education. Without this investment, there is little likelihood of Latin America being able to replicate the East Asian miracle of skill-upgradation, combined with rapid moves up the product-cycle ladder.

We noted earlier that a shortage of foreign exchange may be more immediately binding than shortages of human and physical capital. The essential nature of foreign inputs in any twentieth- (or twenty-first-) century development process interacts with a country's economic size, measured most conveniently by population for a given per capita income level. A small country is necessarily more open to trade, and has to adjust its economic structure to pressures from the world market. In many European countries, corporatist bargaining and accommodation among labour, enterprises, and the State, along with ample provision of social services have played central roles in their capacity to adjust to changes in external markets and their growth process for decades (Katzenstein, 1985). In the developing world, prospects are more open. In other words, we do not necessarily subscribe to the logic underlying the view of the Bretton Woods institutions that countries most integrated into world trade and capital markets enjoy the fastest output growth, and conversely, countries who fail to integrate risk falling increasingly far behind (World Bank, 1996).

This is the IFI's new empirical twist to the old theoretical argument for developing countries to realign incentive structures in favour of an outward looking policy regime (which underlay stabilization and adjustment in the 1980s). It is obvious that export growth contributes to output growth as exports are part of aggregate demand and resource allocation in some sectors might improve as a result. However, in practice, these policies condemn most developing countries to maintaining a static production structure biased toward primary exports which prevents the generation of employment in value-adding activities. Middle-income countries which have already diversified their production structure face different problems. When export promotion is accompanied by too rapid or drastic import liberalization, their capacity to compete is threatened. As industrial output shrinks, urban unemployment rises.

The IFI view does not recognize sufficiently the need for policy differentiation depending on initial conditions (and levels of development). Moreover, the IFI view does not recognize that the causality may run in the opposite direction, i.e. countries which do not subscribe to the mainstream policy recommendations grow and, as their output increases, they are able to export. As output grows, the economies of scale and efficiency of local industry is enhanced and they may become competitive in world markets.[36]

In the low-income economies of Sub-Saharan Africa, Central America, the Caribbean, and parts of Asia, prospects for sustained export growth rest on primary products and cheap labour—in varying proportions. ISI is a less appealing option in small countries because limited market sizes do not favour attainment of low production costs resulting from economies of scale. The cheap, relatively skilled labour option à la Mauritius is probably more feasible in Asia due to regional agglomeration effects than elsewhere. After decades of resource 'mining' in Sub-Saharan Africa, reviving the agro-export sector will be a difficult task.

Small economies in the middle-income range typically face the problem of extending their production structures beyond natural-resource exports. Historically, some small European economies went 'downstream' in this sense, e.g.

Sweden's and Finland's transitions from exporting raw forest products through pulp and paper and on to the associated capital goods. In Asia, the model has been increasing indigenization of manufacturing assembly operations to go further down the value-added chain (Porter, 1990).

Elsewhere, some natural-resource endowments are more favourable to down-stream exploitation than others—forest products and some metals provide better prospects than sugar and bananas. Financial accumulation based on resource rents which is subsequently channelled to growth of physical and human capital—as historically happened with coffee in Colombia and Brazil, tin rubber, palm-oil and then petroleum in Malaysia, diamonds in Botswana, and more recently with tourism in Mauritius—will be essential to any growth process.

Large countries have more 'degrees of freedom' in growth strategies in so far as they can isolate large parts of their economies from world market pressures—imported automobiles were prohibited for decades in Japan and Korea as ISI permitted manufacturing capacity to be built up. But this relative isolation means that internal distributional conflicts have to be confronted directly.

In India, for example, one can imagine two alternatives. One would be an 'agriculture-first' strategy of the sort recommended by Chakravarty (1987), perhaps based on public infrastructure investment which might 'crowd in' private capital formation. Rising rural incomes could then accelerate the decline in rural birth rates, leading to a virtuous circle of per capita income growth.

Others, however, might argue for a development strategy based on an industrial push emphasizing consumer durables produced for the middle class (the richest 30m. households, say) and ultimately for export. Such an internally oriented, socially exclusive industrialization strategy kept Brazil growing very rapidly for decades. However, it also can provoke distributional tensions which can lead to inflation, high fiscal spending on palliative social welfare programmes (such as public-sector employment in Brazil), and perhaps growing external debt.

India as a nation is so diverse that perhaps both paths may be partially followed. However, its case illustrates the range of options that a large economy can follow through its agrarian transition. Social development in the countryside and patterns of rural–urban migration will influence the outcomes and help determine whether output growth and an equitable income distribution can go hand in hand.

What, in fact, are the factors that can permit such a development pattern to occur? The examples presented in this section suggest that the specific characteristics of any given economy will strongly affect its growth prospects and the policy mix which supports it. A fundamental question, for instance, is what factors in Korea's and Taiwan's long histories led to egalitarian rural property holdings when industrialization was about to begin? More importantly for the transition, what forces maintained equality as these economies' agricultural employment shares declined to levels of less than 10 per cent in the 1990s? Factors such as real wage growth and relatively equal savings rates across the classes must have entered to soften a fundamental inequality built into capitalist development—its tendency to build on the best. How such a balance of forces works out in a specific country context determines whether its social development, economic transformation, and income-poverty reduction can go hand in hand. The ultimate outcome can never be precisely foretold.

In other words, the foreign exchange constraint and the possibilities for relaxing it are different across countries. They depend on size, resource endowment, the previous industrialization experience, and the nature of the institutions regulating capital movements. Consequently, the policies which are applicable or advisable differ. In terms of the physical capital constraint, a similar situation arises. In this case, the country's size and natural endowments are less important but the historical and institutional evolution of industry (e.g. the role of multinationals, protection, labour relations, government subsidies, technological transfers, etc.) play a larger role.

Thus, in order to inform policy and analyse patterns of growth of different countries, many diverse factors (and their interaction) need to be included. This is very different from creating an artificial world populated by rational agents which can be simulated in a computer exercise. A country-specific model which incorporates the different constraints, their determinants, and their changes over time is needed so as to inform policy and evaluate the possible outcome of diverse policy packages. It is in this sense that a 'development recipe' to achieve a given outcome cannot be predetermined, unlike what is assumed by the IFIs. The two synergies discussed in this book only represent a broad outline within which country-specific strategies could be formulated.[37]

Conclusions

We have acknowledged what the mainstream literature has always argued that economic growth is essential to income-poverty reduction. The emerging consensus on the need for investment in human capital, both in the theoretical and policy literature, is more recent—coming some three decades after human capital theory emerged and some two decades after the 'basic needs' approach. We have argued that without public investment in basic health and basic education, longevity and knowledge will not be enhanced at the appropriate speed and scope, i.e. the population of developing countries cannot wait for health and education indicators to rise until per capita income rises. Thus, not only do we explicitly broaden the notion of human capital beyond that in mainstream literature to include health, but we also re-emphasize the interactive effects of health and education investments. In fact, without an investment in basic education, even the benefits of health investment will not be as rapidly realized. Our case-studies imply that policy-makers must take advantage of the potential synergies between investments in education, safe water/sanitation, nutrition, and health in order to maximize the level of social development achievable with their given resources and constraints. Besides, the case-studies suggest that when the intrinsic value of social development is addressed it generates wide political support for the required policies.

Early in the chapter we have also tried to demonstrate another kind of synergy: that a relatively equal distribution of income as well as human capital formation are conducive to economic growth. A more egalitarian income distribution not only helps income-poverty reduction directly, but also indirectly through its positive impact on growth. Improvements in health and education are not only valuable in themselves (and critical for output expansion), but also give individuals the tools with which to emerge from income-poverty.

Without a recognition of these synergies that marked the historical development of countries which experienced income-poverty-reducing economic growth and social development, policy-makers in developing countries may delay inordinately such a desirable outcome—thus extending the untold suffering of millions who currently live below the poverty line, a life which is 'nasty, brutish and short', without the benefits of longevity, knowledge, and overall well-being. However, our studies have suggested that not all investments have to be contemporaneous—nor necessarily undertaken by the State. That is, the State need not directly deliver the services as long as its policies ensure they are provided (e.g. through financing or regulation of the private sector). In fact, precisely because of the existence of synergies, private expenditures with rising incomes can also account for improving health outcomes (as the Korea example shows).

We have also tried to establish that a virtuous cycle of economic growth, social development, and income-poverty reduction cannot be set in place so long as the foreign exchange and physical capital constraints are binding. The sectoral characteristics of growth and its capacity to generate foreign exchange, therefore, will be critical to the realization of income growth which is income-poverty-reducing. When combined with appropriate investments in the health and education of the population, it can lead to a virtuous circle which is sustainable and which also, more or less rapidly, builds up the necessary physical capital. Here, again, the role of the State is critical to ensure aggregate macroeconomic consistency (i.e. that the economy works within its set of constraints) and at the same time to promote the easing of the constraints, by ensuring a sufficient level of foreign exchange and the accumulation of physical and human capital.

However, that does not mean that similar development policies can be assumed to be applicable and suitable to all countries, unlike the recommendations from the IFIs and donor governments on the role of the State, the trade and exchange rate regime, and capital market liberalization seem to imply. Initial conditions, as well as the history and institutional characteristics of countries, need to inform the content of all economic policies. Countries must explore and arrive at their own 'development recipe' rather than rely on a 'Washington consensus'.

The role of the State, we have argued throughout this chapter, is critical to the realization of the two kinds of synergies that have been the subject of this book. Asset and income redistribution will not occur automatically and growth of average income per capita in an unfettered market economy cannot be guaranteed to be distribution-neutral. Growth will not reduce income-poverty or improve human development without specific state policies directed towards those goals.

However, the State may not be willing or able (for reasons of political economy) to take policy measures which are necessary to realize these synergies. This established the critical importance of civil and political liberties and full participation of civil society in the decision-making process.[38] This is a defining criterion of human development and human capabilities (as discussed in Chapter 2). Hence, the agenda we have identified in this book relies on this participation in order to be fully realized.

APPENDIX

A simple form of the basic symbiotic model could be written as

$$\dot{x} = a1x + b1y + c1xy$$
$$\dot{y} = a2x + b2y + c2xy$$

We have expanded it to three variables and compared it to a model with no synergetic elements (the c_i's). An example of a model corresponding to our case, then, consists of three equations. It is assumed that per capita growth equals 2 per cent per year:

$$\dot{GNP}pc = 0.02$$

It is also assumed that every percentage point increase in aggregate output per capita reduces income-poverty by 0.5 per cent:

$$\dot{Pov} = 1/2\left(\dot{GNP}pc\right)$$

This elasticity is consistent with those reported in Lipton and Ravallion (1995: 2603), although we have used a lower absolute value for the elasticity than the ones they report. The results under this conservative assumption still show important income-poverty reductions.

Life expectancy has been simulated using a logistic curve with an upper bound of 80. The level of per capita income affects the growth coefficient in the function:

$$\dot{Lifex} = \left(0.01 + 0.0001 GNPpc\right)/80\right)\left(80 - Lifex\right)$$

These equations are expanded by adding the synergetic terms. The coefficients used in these terms were estimated from a series of ordinary and two-stage least-squares regressions using average GNP per capita growth for the period 1960–94, the average level of income-poverty, life expectancy in 1960, 1994, and their difference, etc. However, the data set (twenty-nine countries) was relatively small due to the lack of consistent long series data on income-poverty. Thus, although in general the regressions were satisfactory, the estimated values for the coefficients of any individual regression should be not be taken as very definite. Consequently we relied on the average of different results. The equations used in the simulations were

$$GNPpc = 0.02 + 0.0002Lifex(100 - Pov)$$

where the last term means that the rate of growth is increased with higher levels of life expectancy and lower levels of income-poverty;

$$Pov = -1/2(GNPpc) - 0.00005GNPpc * Lifex$$

where both higher levels of per capita income and social development (captured through the higher life expectancy proxy) accelerates income-poverty reduction; and

$$Lifex = (0.01 + 0.0001GNPpc + 0.0001GNPpc(100 - Pov)/80)(80 - Lifex)$$

where the growth coefficient has been expanded to include the multiplicative term which incorporates the positive effect on social development of higher per capita income and lower income-poverty.

Notes

1. The phrase is Polanyi's (1944) and is often used to describe—in a positive way—the drastic changes towards the market in the last decade. However, it must be remembered that Polanyi equated the Great Transformation to a process which: (a) required strong state participation to create markets and marketable inputs, (b) had very negative consequences for most of the population, and (c) needed state action to limit those negative consequences. These elements would apply today to developing countries as they did to European ones in the nineteenth century.

2. The notions of poverty and economic growth are fraught with complexity. Poverty reduction refers to a decrease in the population considered poor. Although poverty is usually measured in terms of income or consumption levels, such measures ignore access to basic services, an important dimension of the problem, thus the term income-poverty will be used in the chapter. Also, the headcount measure of poverty fails to incorporate issues of distribution of income among the poor and of the depth of poverty. Thus, discussions of income-poverty cannot be wholly independent of income distribution. The concept of economic development is likewise complex. A simple way to measure it is by per capita GDP, perhaps 'corrected' for purchasing power parities. However, this is a very limited notion. A country could show a high rate of increase in per capita output (growth) but little if any change in its productive and employment structures, or the role of value-adding activities (development). Ignoring these complexities for the moment we attempt to draw some conclusions regarding the connections among social and economic development and income-poverty reduction as a means of improving well-being and human capabilities. While talking about economic growth and poverty in the rest of the chapter, the broader meaning we are implying in each case should be kept in mind.

3. Evans (1996) uses a similar concept of synergy while discussing the links between the State, citizens, and civil society in different settings. The virtuous circle he presents is different from (but not contradictory to) ours, because the elements involved are different. Nevertheless, in his argument the role of the State is crucial too.

4. See e.g. the criticism by Bhaduri and Nayyar (1996) of India's economic reforms in the early 1990s. In terms similar to ours, they characterize those policies as being dominated by a policy-making approach which is almost entirely oblivious of people.

5. Fishlow (1996) criticizes many of these studies for not considering the role played by land distribution, government policy, and the influence of Latin American countries in the sample. When these elements are taken into account the Kutznets hypothesis is partially revived and arguments for active redistribution (especially of land) policies are strengthened. We come back to these issues below.

6. Given that it was published by the World Bank at the time its President announced an all-out attack on poverty. Although the Bank did change its lending patterns (shifting its focus from infrastructure to agricultural investment) and at the same time the 'Green Revolution' started to have an impact, income distribution was not much affected.

7. Also Krueger (1974), Bhagwati (1982), and Lal (1983) could be mentioned.

8. Romer (1986), Lucas (1988), and Barro (1991) present original theoretical and empirical contributions, Verspagen (1992) is a review, and Pack (1992) stresses the weak empirical basis of these models.

9. Behrman (1990) presents serious questions about the theoretical and empirical validity of this approach from a neoclassical perspective. Darity (1994) and Kurz and Salvadori (1994) introduce more fundamental criticisms.

10. Such an approach is attempted in sect. 3.

11. e.g. Behrman (1995) argues that although increased education (especially of girls) has a strong effect on infant-mortality reduction, the effects of current spending on education will not be felt until ten or more years in the future. In this regard, he argues that direct health interventions (such as innoculations) must be carried out now (together with education).

12. Lucas (1993) adds free trade to the recommendation of universal basic education as the recipe for fast growth mainly based on a restricted view of the Korean experience. See section 4 below for a discussion of the role of integration to the world economy and foreign exchange in the growth process.

13. Datt and Ravallion (1992) and Ravallion and Datt (1995) are representative of an extensive field of research.

14. This does not mean that the State should be seen as a 'cure-all'. For different circumstances and state characteristics which allow them (or at least some state agencies) to play a 'developmentalist' role see Evans (1995). Although this issue is beyond the scope of this chapter it should always be kept in mind, in particular as implications for policies and state involvement are discussed below.

15. As a postcript, we found that UNDP (1996) presents a view very similar to ours. In particular, figure 3.7 (p. 82) is similar to our Tables 15.1 through 15.3. The difference is that instead of comparing only two variables (economic growth and changes in the Human Development Index) we present all the three possible combinations. Moreover, we attempt an explanation of the dynamics among the quadrants.

16. A similar view about the pace of growth is proposed by Rowthorn and Wells (1987) and Schor (1994) to solve the unemployment and environmental problems of industrialized countries.

17. While the incidence of poverty did decline in Brazil between 1970 and 1979 in both urban and rural areas (from 35 to 30 and 73 to 62% respectively) the absolute level remained very high. The rural households below the indigence line declined only from 42 to 35% and from 15 to 10% in urban areas. See ECLAC (1994). In India, per capita income grew faster in the 1980s

than in the preceding fifteen years leading to a decline in poverty incidence, but the percentage decline is disputed and in any case, the incidence of poverty remains very high, as does the absolute member of poor—the latter having shown little decline.

18. Neither of these phenomena requires we change our broad definition of growth, e.g. under conditions of wage repression more people can be employed in value-adding sectors without being able to share in the benefits of such activities.

19. In the case of India (and Pakistan), however, land redistribution would enhance both productivity as well as equity, for the well-known reason that labour input per unit of land is higher on smaller farms.

20. If there is no growth, there could not be any income-poverty reduction without redistribution. Redistribution, however, will not necessarily imply stagnant investment, as wage-led models have shown (Dutt, 1984; Taylor, 1991). The situation where a trade-off exists is considered in the text in order to analyse the 'most difficult' case.

21. Different growth strategies are discussed in the next section.

22. For a discussion of poverty in the ten high-achieving countries, see Ch. 2.

23. If the benefits of growth are not strongly biased in favour of those at the top of the income distribution.

24. The instability is not symmetric in the sense that universal provision of social services need not be directly hampered by the presence of income-poverty. The issue of sustainability of social development in the absence of growth is dealt with below.

25. These would normally be state led. However, circumstances when, in the presence of high social development, growth, and income-poverty reduction could start without state intervention are conceivable (e.g. exogenous changes in terms of trade) although unlikely given the historical evidence.

26. Notice that this would also result in higher aggregate growth rates.

27. For a discussion of economic growth in the ten high-achieving countries in this book, see Ch. 2.

28. Thus, *ceteris paribus*, if x% of output (at a given per capita income level) is sufficient to provide all the population with social services at time t, the same percentage (with the same per capita income) would also be sufficient at time $t + 1$. If anything, the percentage could decline if social development helps to hasten the demographic transition and stabilize the country's population.

29. However, if the economy stagnates sustainability of high social development could be impaired as the economy is more vulnerable to external shocks or other changes. Although this seems to have happened in the case of Zimbabwe in the 1990s quite quickly, in Sri Lanka, Kerala, and Cuba the social outcome indicators have been maintained, but the quality of services has been adversely affected (see Ch. 2).

30. These examples also show that a growth strategy requires an exogenous push (from the State), even if the other initial conditions are right.

31. 'Almost' is used because countries can grow in the absence of universal basic social services—an empirically rare event.

32. Although from a logical point of view any two of the three variables could be the focus of policy we could not find examples of successful combinations without either BSS or explicit pro-growth policies. This might mean that, although logically possible, they have not been implemented because their feasibility in practice is questionable.

33. The Korean example is particularly interesting because of its delayed health intervention. This does not contradict our hypothesis. It must be remembered that there are two circuits of

synergies: among the three variables and within social development. Consequently, although public health was relatively underfinanced, the strong education outcomes in conjunction with land redistribution and economic growth allowed good health outcomes to obtain too. Our contention is that this would not have been possible without the 'minimum' BSS intervention of providing universal education.

34. The simulation model has been based on a generalization of the symbiotic model introduced in Haken (1977, p. 296), for a two variable case. It applies to our case because its premiss is that the growth rate of a variable depends on its own level and a multiplicative term involving itself and the other variable in the system. This corresponds to the previous discussion where the effect of (say) investment on health and education is enhanced by the presence of higher economic growth and lower levels of income-poverty. The model is further explained in the appendix.

35. Although it is a very strong simplification, life expectancy is used to represent improvements in human capabilities because better health, education, and nutritional status would lead to longer lives.

36. See *inter alia* Lewis (1978), Pack (1988), and Singh (1994) for the theoretical argument and empirical evidence that dependence of growth on exports is not a viable alternative. Export-led growth is limited by international demands. Only learning by doing, producing locally, and technological change (both in agriculture and manufacturing) can be reliable sources of growth.

37. The weight given to each of these elements and how they are combined with other priorities and policies is country-specific. It should be noted we are not even assuming that industrialization is the only way ahead for developing countries as the above discussion on the role of agriculture attests.

38. Chen and Desai point out in Ch. 14 that the countries examined in the book were democracies, with the exception of Cuba and Korea. However, while Cuba may not be a liberal democracy, participation of civil society in the development process, especially women's groups, is well documented in the case-study and Korea is increasingly moving towards becoming a liberal democracy.

References

Adelman, Irma, and Morris C. T. (1973), *Economic Growth and Social Equity in Developing Countries*, Stanford, Calif.: Stanford University Press.

Alessina, A., and Perotti, R. (1994), 'The Political Economy of Growth: A Critical Survey of the Recent Literature', *World Bank Economic Review,* 8: 351–71.

—— and Rodrik, D. (1994), 'Distributive Politics and Economic Growth', *Quarterly Journal of Economics,* 109: 465–490.

Amsden, A. (1989), *Asia's Next Giant: South Korea and Late Industrialization*, New York: Oxford University Press.

Anand, Sudhir, and Kanbur, R. (1993), 'The Kuznets Process and the Inequality-Development Relationship', *Journal of Development Economics*, 40: 25–52.

Arrow, K. (1962), 'The Economic Implications of Learning by Doing', *Review of Economic Studies, 29*: 155–73.

Barro, R. (1991), 'Economic Growth in a Cross-Section of Countries', *Quarterly Journal of Economics, 106*: 407–44.

Becker, G. (1964), *Human Capital*, New York: Columbia University Press.

Behrman, J. (1990), *Human Resource Led Development?*, ILO-ARTEP.

—— (1995), 'The Contribution of Improved Human Resources to Productivity', mimeo.

—— and Deolalikar, A. (1988), 'Health and Nutrition', in H. B. Chenery and T. N. Srinivasan (eds.), *Handbook of Development Economics,* i, Amsterdam: North-Holland.

Bertola, G. (1992), 'Market Structure and Income Distribution in Endogenous Growth Models', *American Economic Review, 83.*

Bhaduri, A., and Nayyar, D. (1996), *An Intelligent Person's Guide to Liberalization*, New Dehli: Penguin.

Bhagwati, J. (1971), 'The Generalized Theory of Distortions and Welfare', in J. N. Bhagwati *et al.* (eds.), *Trade, Balance of Payments and Growth*, Amsterdam: North-Holland.

—— (1982), 'Directly Unproductive Profit-Seeking (DUP) Activities: A Welfare-Theoretic Synthesis and Generalization', *Journal of Political Economy, 90*: 988–1002.

Birdsall, N. (1988), 'Economic Approaches to Population Growth', in H. B. Chenery and T. N. Srinivasan (eds.), *Handbook of Development Economics*, i, Amsterdam: North-Holland.

—— and Griffin, C. (1993), 'Population Growth, Externalities, and Poverty', in M. Lipton and J. van der Gaag (eds.), *Including the Poor*, Washington DC: World Bank.

Chakravarty, S. (1987), *Development Planning: The Indian Experience*, Oxford: Clarendon Press.

Chenery, H, Ahluwalia, M. S., Bell, C. L. G., Duloy, J. H., and Jolly, R. (1974), *Redistribution with Growth*, Oxford: Oxford University Press.

—— (1986), 'Growth and Transformation', in H. B. Chenery, S. Robinson, and M. Syrquin (eds.), *Industrialization and Growth*, New York: Oxford University Press.

—— and Bruno, M. (1962), 'Development Alternatives in an Open Economy: The Case of Israel', *Economic Journal, 72*: 79–103.

Darity, W. (1994), 'What's so "new" about the "new" theories of technical change? Adam Smith, Robert Lucas Jr. and economic growth', in P. Davidson and J. Kregel (eds.), *Employment, Growth and Finance*, New York: Cambridge University Press.

Datt, G., and Ravallion, M. (1992), 'Growth and Redistribution Components of Changes in Poverty Measures: A Decomposition with Applications to Brazil and India in the 1980s', *Journal of Development Economics, 38*: 275–95.

De Janvry, A., and Sadoulet, E. (1995), 'Poverty, equity, and social welfare in Latin America: Determinants of change over growth spells', Geneva: ILO.

Dutt, A. (1984), 'Stagnation, Income Distribution, and Monopoly Power', *Cambridge Journal of Economics, 8*: 25–40.

ECLAC (1994), *Social Panorama*, Santiago, Chile.

Evans, P. (1995), *Embedded Autonomy*, Princeton: Princeton University Press.

—— (1996), 'Government Action, Social Capital and Development: Reviewing the Evidence on Synergy', *World Development, 4/6.*

Fanelli, J., Frenkel, R., and Rozenwurcel, G. (1990), 'Growth and Structural Reform in Latin America: Where We Stand', Buenos Aires: CEDES, mimeo.

—— —— and Taylor, L. (1992), 'The World Development Report 1991; A Critical Assessment', in *International Monetary and Financial Issues for the 1990s*, New York: United Nations.

Fishlow, A. (1996), 'Inequality, Poverty, and Growth: Where Do We Stand?' in M. Bruno and B. Pleskovic (eds.), *Annual World Bank Conference on Development Economics, 1995*, Washington, DC: World Bank.

Govt. of India (1994), *Economic Survey 1993–4*, New Delhi.

Haken, H. (1977), *Synergy*, Berlin and New York: Springer Verlag.

Hazell, P., and Haggblade, S. (1993), 'Farm-Non Farm Growth Linkages and the Welfare of the Poor', in M. Lipton and J. van der Gaag (eds.), *Including the Poor*, Washington, DC: World Bank

Hirschman, A. O. (1958), *The Strategy of Economic Development*, New Haven, Conn.: Yale University Press.

—— (1981), 'The rise and decline of development economics', in *Essays on Trespassing: Economics to Politics and Beyond*, New York: Cambridge University Press.

ILO (1976), *Employment, Growth and Basic Needs: A One-world Problem*, Geneva: ILO.

Kaldor, N (1957), 'A Model of Economic Growth', *Economic Journal, 82*: 591–624.

Kalecki, M. (1971), *Selected Essays On the Dynamics of the Capitalist Economy*, Cambridge: Cambridge University Press.

Katzenstein, P. (1985), *Small States in World Markets: Industrial Policy in Europe*, Ithaca, NY: Cornell University Press.

Keynes, J. M. (1936), *The General Theory of Employment, Interest, and Money*, Macmillan.

Krueger, A. (1974), 'The Political Economy of the Rent Seeking Society', *American Economic Review, 64*: 291–303.

Kurz, H., and Salvadori N. (1994) 'The "New" Growth, Theory: Old Wine in New Goatskins', mimeo.

Kuznets, S. (1955), 'Economic Growth and Income Inequality', *American Economic Review, 65*: 1–28.

Lal, D. (1983), *The Poverty of Development Economics*, London: Institute of Economic Affairs.

Lewis, W. A. (1978), *The Evolution of the International Economic Order*, Princeton: Princeton University Press.

Lipton, M. (1977), *Why Poor People Stay Poor: Urban Bias and World Development*, London: Temple Smith.

—— and Ravallion, M. (1994), 'Poverty and Policy', in J. Behrman and T. N. Srinivasan (eds.), *Handbook of Development Economics*, iii, Amsterdam: North-Holland.

—— and van der Gaag, J. (1993), 'Poverty: A Research and Policy Framework', in M. Lipton and J. van der Gaag (eds.), *Including the Poor*, Washington, DC: World Bank.

Little, I., Scitovsky, T., and Scott, M. (1970), *Industry and Trade in some Developing Countries: A Comparative Study*, Oxford: Oxford University Press.

Lucas, R. (1988), 'On the Mechanics of Economic Development', *Journal of Monetary Economics, 22*: 3–42.

—— (1993), 'Making a miracle', *Econometrica, 61*: 2.

Mahalanobis P. C. (1953), 'Some Observations on the Process of Growth of National Income', *Sankhya, 12*: 307–12.

Meade, J. (1964), *Efficiency, Equality and the Ownership of Property*, London: Allen & Unwin.

Mincer, J. (1962), 'On the job training,' *Journal of Political Economy, 70*: 50–79.

Nell, E. (1992), *Transformational Growth and Effective Demand: Economics after the Capital Critique*, New York: NYU Press.

Nurske, R. (1953), *Problems of Capital Formation in Underdeveloped Countries*, Oxford: Basil Blackwell.

Pack, H. (1988), 'Industrialization and trade', in H. B. Chenery and T. N. Srinivasan (eds.), *Handbook of Development Economics*, i, Amsterdam: North-Holland.

—— (1992), 'Endogenous Growth Theory: Intellectual Appeal and Empirical Shortcomings', *Journal of Economics Perspectives*, 8 (winter).

Perotti, R. (1993), 'Political Equilibrium, Income Distribution, and Growth', *Review of Economic Studies, 60*: 755–76.

Persson, T., and Tabellini, G. (1994), 'Is Inequity Harmful for Growth', *American Economic Review*, 84/3.

Polanyi, R. (1944), *The Great Transformation: The Political and Economic Origins of Our Times*, New York: Rinehart.

Porter, M. (1990), *The Competitive Advantage of Nations*, New York: Free Press.

Prebish, R. (1959), 'Commercial Policy in the Underdeveloped Countries', *American Economic Review, 49*: 257–69.

Psacharopoulos, G. (1985), 'Returns to Education: A Further International Update and Implications', *Journal of Human Resources, 20*: 583–604.

—— (1994), 'Returns to Investment in Education: A Global Update', *World Development*, 22: 9.

Ravallion, M., and Datt, G. (1995), 'How Important to India's Poor is the Sectoral Composition of Economic Growth?', Policy Research Department, World Bank, mimeo.

Romer, P. (1986), 'Increasing Returns and Long-Run Growth', *Journal of Political Economy, 94*: 1002–37.

Rosenstein-Rodan, P. (1943), 'Problems of Industrialization of Eastern and South-Eastern Europe', *Economic Journal, 53*: 202–11.

Rowthorn, R., and Wells, J. R. (1987), *De-industrialization and Foreign Trade*, New York: Cambridge University Press.

Saith, A. (1996), 'Reflections on South Asian Prospects in East Asian Perspective', Geneva: ILO.

Schor, J. (1991), 'Global Equity and Environmental Crisis: An Argument for Reducing Working Hours in the North', *World Development*, 19/1.

Schultz, T. W. (1961), 'Investment in Human Capital', *American Economic Review, 51*/1.

—— (1964), *Transforming Traditional Agriculture*, New Haven, Conn. Yale University Press.

Schumpeter, J. (1934), *The Theory of Economic Development*, Cambridge, Mass.: Harvard University Press.

Sen, A. (1985), *Commodities and Capabilities*, Amsterdam: North-Holland.

Shapiro, H., and Taylor, L. (1990), 'The State and Industrial Strategy', *World Development* 18/6.

Singh, A. (1990), *The Great Ascent*, Baltimore: Johns Hopkins University Press.

—— (1994), 'Openness and the Market Friendly Approach to Development: Learning the Right Lessons from Development Experience,' *World Development*, 22/12.

Streeten, P., *et al.* (1981), *First Things First: Meeting Basic Needs in Developing Countries*, New York: Oxford University Press.

Sundrum, R. M. (1991), *Income Distribution in Less Developed Countries*, London and New York: Routledge.

Syrquin, R. M. (1988), 'Patterns of Structural Change', in H. B. Chenery and T. N. Srinivasan (eds.), *Handbook of Development Economics*, i, Amsterdam: North-Holland.

Taylor, L. (1991), *Income Distribution, Inflation, and Growth*, Cambridge, Mass.: MIT Press.

—— and Pieper, U. (1996), 'Social Implications of Structural Adjustment: A Critical Survey', UNDP paper.

Timmer, P. (1988), 'The Agricultural Transformation', in H. B. Chenery and T. N. Srinivasan (eds.), *Handbook of Development Economics*, i, Amsterdam: North-Holland.

Todaro, M. (1982), *Economics for a Developing World*, 2nd edn., Longman.

UNCTAD (1993), *Handbook of International Trade and Development Statistics 1992*, New York: United Nations.

UNDP (1990), *Human Development Report*, New York: United Nations.

—— (1996), *Human Development Report*, New York: United Nations.

Verspagen, B. (1992), 'Endogenous Innovation in Neo-Classical Growth Models: A Survey', *Journal of Macroeconomics*, 4 / 14.

Wade, R. (1990), *Governing the Market: Economic Theory and the Role of the Government in East Asian Industrialization*, Princeton: Princeton University Press.

Williamson, J. (1989), 'What Washington Means by Policy Reform', in J. Williamson (ed.), *Latin American Adjustment: How much has happened?*, Washington, DC: Institute of International Economics.

World Bank (1990), *World Development Report: Poverty*, Oxford: Oxford University Press.

—— (1994), *World Development Report: Infrastructure for Development*, Oxford: Oxford University Press.

You, Jong-Il (1995), 'Income Distribution and Growth in East Asia', mimeo, paper presented for UNCTAD conference on income distribution and development, December 1995.

Index

Abdul Majid Ismail 309–10, 315
Abel-Smith, Brian, *see* Titmuss
abortion:
  Barbados 344
  Korea 275, 292
  Mauritius 154–5
  Sri Lanka 250
access:
  to education 94; Africa 68, 135, 165; Latin
    America 332, 360, 395; South Asia 215, 221,
    251
  to health services 34–5, 68, 100, 106; Africa 68,
    135, 165; Asia 68, 209, 221, 312; Latin
    America 68, 364
accommodation 423–4
accountability 16
Achio, M. 380
Adelman, Irma 267, 437
adjustment, *see* structural adjustment
Africa, sub-Saharan 5
  economic growth and poverty reduction 441–8,
    451–3, 455–6, 462–3
  education 19, 93, 396
  health policies 65–8, 105, 107
  population and demographic transition 6
  universal primary education policies 92–4, 108
  see also Botswana; Mauritius; Zimbabwe
Afro-pessimism 421
ageing populations 151, 168, 245, 274, 328
agriculture 28, 30–1, 38
  economic growth and poverty reduction 437,
    451, 453–4, 456
  see also drought; land tenure; nutrition; sugar *and*
    under individual case-studies
aid, *see* foreign aid; grant-aid; subsidies
AIDS/HIV:
  Barbados 344
  Botswana 119, 126, 142–3, 144
  Zimbabwe 184, 186, 188
Alailama, Patricia ix, 427
  on Sri Lanka 235–63
Albania 401
Alessina, A. 440
Alleyne, George 336
Alma Ata declaration (1978) 65, 71, 73, 101, 106,
  145, 248

Alvarez, E. 405
Ameringer, C. D. 358
AMP, *see* assistant medical practitioner
Amsden, Alice H. 268, 272, 273, 280, 441
anaemia 167–8, 411
Anand, Sudhia 23, 58, 415, 428, 432, 438
Andhra Pradesh:
  education 96, 206, 217, 226
  health 206, 225
Araya, *see* Hidalgo Araya
Argentina 369
  economic growth and poverty reduction 451
  GNP 385
  infant and child mortality 391–2
  literacy, adult 357
army, *see* defence
Arrow, K. 439
Asia 4, 6, 396
  see also East Asia; South Asia
Assam 206, 217, 225, 226
assistant medical practitioner (Sri Lanka) 248, 249
asthma 411
Ayurveda 70–1, 72, 249–50
Ayyankali 212

Baek, Hwa-Jong ix, 427
  on Korea 264–96
Bahamas 352
Bahrin, Shamsul 319
Balachander, J. 106
Bandaranaike-Chelvanayakam Pact 240
Bangladesh:
  economic growth 6, 443–4
  education 94
  health 70, 80, 107
  population and demographic transition 107,
    108
Bank of Korea 270
Barbados 323–54, 424
  agriculture 340; *see also under* sugar
  economic growth 30, 330, 426; crises 348–50;
    development plans 334, 344–5, 349; and
    poverty reduction 444, 445–6
  education 331–5, 352; decentralization 33–4;
    demand for 92; early development of
    primary 326–7; enrolment 26, 86–8, 324–5,

Index

Barbados (*cont.*):
    327, 330–1, 352; finances/expenditure 43,
    45–7, 89–91, 345–8, 349, 352; literacy 25–6,
    324–5, 335, 336; private 34, 331, 348;
    teachers 96, 332–3, 334; tertiary 332, 348;
    women 39–40, 96
  employment 31, 39–40
  facilitating factors 326–30
  finances/expenditure 49, 345–8, 352;
    crises 349–50; defence 48; non-public-sector
    346–8; *see also under* education *above and* health
    below
  health 25, 26–7, 335–45, 352; access 68; AIDS
    344; childbirth 68; finances/expenditure 29,
    42, 44, 47, 335, 338–9, 345–7, 349, 352;
    hospitals 337, 346; immunization 68, 69, 336,
    339–40; infant and child mortality 66, 325–6,
    335–6, 351, 352; life expectancy 66, 325–6;
    nutrition 77, 336, 340–1; primary care
    336–45; water and sanitation 82, 335, 336,
    341–3
  legislation 330, 331, 336, 344
  politics 33, 329
  population and demographic transition 58, 83–4,
    426; density 326, 327; emigration 245, 327–8,
    330; family planning 327, 328, 343–4
  poverty 53–5, 350, 444–6
  stability 329
  structural adjustment 349, 428
  tourism 330, 350, 426
  women 37–40, 328, 329–30, 332
Barbados Drug Service 338–9, 352
Barbados Family Planning Association 328, 343–4
Barnes Report 305
Barro, R. 461
basic needs approach 441
Batswana people 114, 132, 134, 424
BDP, *see* Botswana Democratic Party
BDS (Barbados Drug Service) 338–9, 352
Becker, G. 438
Behrman, J. R. 23, 439, 461
benefits, *see* social security
Berman, Peter 227
Berry, R. 268
Bertola, G. 440
BFPA, *see* Barbados Family Planning Association
BFV (Family Housing Voucher, Costa Rica) 369,
    371
Bhaduri, A. 461
Bhagwati, J. 438, 461
Bhalla, Surjit 320
Bharadwaj, Krishna 268

Bheenick, Rundheesing 161
Bhutan 107
BIDPA (Botswana) 122
Bihar:
  education 96, 97, 206, 217, 226, 227
  health 71, 206, 225
Birdsall, Nancy 22, 23, 266, 267, 268, 439
birth, *see* childbirth; family planning
Bishop, Myrtle D. ix
  on Barbados 323–54
BNF, *see* Botswana National Front
Board of Education (Barbados) 327
BOMAID (Botswana) 141
Bongaarts, John 84, 85
Bono Alimentario, Escolar and Familiar (vouchers in
    Costa Rica) 369, 371
Boo, Kum 319
Botswana 22, 113–48, 431, 433
  agriculture 113, 119, 124, 128, 129–31, 134
  drought 113, 124, 130–1, 134
  economic growth 17, 134–5, 142, 426; common
    elements and diversities 27, 28, 30, 32, 50–1;
    development plans 114–15, 120, 125, 134–5,
    139–40; and poverty reduction 443–4, 446, 456
  education 117, 120, 127–9, 135; demand for 92;
    enrolment 26, 28, 34, 38, 86–8, 117, 118,
    127–8, 142; finances/expenditure 43, 45–9,
    89–91, 94, 128, 133, 136–8, 140, 429–30;
    infrastructure 120–1; literacy, adult 117, 118;
    secondary 120, 127, 128, 129; teachers 96, 128,
    129; tertiary 129; and women 37–8, 96, 118,
    128, 129, 144
  employment 28, 31, 39–40
  equity 425
  finances/expenditure 29, 117–18, 135–41, 144,
    145–6; allocation 136–8, 145–6; defence 48,
    136, 138–9, 140; foreign aid 49, 117–18, 133,
    135, 139–41, 146; revenues from diamonds
    116, 118, 135–6, 139; *see also under* education
    above and health *below*
  health 66, 68, 124–7; access 68, 135; AIDS 119,
    126, 142–3, 144; common elements and
    diversities 25, 26–7; finances/expenditure 29,
    42, 44, 49, 76, 136, 137–8, 140, 429–30;
    immunization 68, 69, 118, 125, 141; infant and
    child mortality 66, 117, 118, 119, 125;
    infrastructure 120–1; life expectancy 32, 66,
    117, 118, 129; nutrition 77, 78, 118, 119, 124,
    125, 129–31; primary care 124–5, 135, 142, 145;
    private 122, 128, 141, 146; water and
    sanitation 82, 120, 126–7, 135
  infrastructure 114, 115, 120–1, 124, 138, 140

overall trends 113–24; social indicators 117–20;
see also diamonds
politics 131–5
population and demographic transition 82, 83–4,
102, 426; family planning 108; fertility and
growth 118
poverty 53–5, 56, 119, 122–4, 131, 143, 145;
reduction and economic growth 443–4, 446,
456
rural areas 119, 122–4, 128–30, 143
social security 120–2, 136, 144
urban areas/urbanization 118–19, 122–3, 138,
140, 143
women and education 37–8, 96, 118, 128, 129,
144
Botswana Democratic Party 131, 132–3
Botswana Development Corporation 133
Botswana National Front 132
Bowman, Larry W. 174
Brahmins (Kerala) 214
Bray, Mark 90
Brazil 369
economic growth 52, 53; and poverty
reduction 443–4, 446, 451–2, 456, 461
and Korea, comparison with 266–7
public action lacking 32
breastfeeding 77, 80
Barbados 352
GOBI–FFF programme 23, 40, 58, 73
Korea 283
Mauritius 170, 173
Bresser Pereira, L. C. 55
Bretton Woods 11, 455
Bridgetown 326
Britain:
and Barbados 326–7, 328, 329
and Botswana 113, 135, 146
and Cuba 414–15
health 33, 64, 70
and Kerala 207, 213
and Mauritius 149, 158, 174
pessimism in 7
poverty 5
and Zimbabwe 179
see also English language
Brundenius, Claes (on Cuba):
economic growth 385, 403, 415
health 393, 413, 414
women 400
Bruno, M. 437
Bruton, Henry J. 53, 319
Buddhism 33, 424

Bulawayo 186
Bulgaria 401, 402
Bumiputra (Malays) in Malaysia 297, 298, 302, 305,
319, 428
Burghers in Sri Lanka 247
Burkina Faso 94
Burn, Nalini 157, 173, 176
Business Rescue Plan (Costa Rica) 368

Cairo conference (1994) 15, 85
Caldwell, John C. 38, 64, 70, 208, 219
Canada 329
capabilities, enhancement of 21, 441
see also social development
Caribbean, *see* Latin America and Caribbean
CARICOM (Caribbean Community) 339, 352
Carnoy, Martin 395, 396, 399, 404
case-studies 8
Africa, *see* Botswana; Mauritius
East Asia, *see* Korea; Malaysia
Latin America, *see* Barbados; Costa Rica; Cuba
lessons from 421–34; *see also* governance;
integration; universality
South Asia, *see* Kerala; Sri Lanka
Cash, Richard 23
caste system in Kerala 208–10, 211–14
Castro, Fidel 395
Catholicism 211
CCSS (Costa Rican Social Security Fund) 366–7,
368, 373–4, 376
Central Bank:
of Barbados 345–7, 349
of Costa Rica 377
of Sri Lanka 238, 247, 250, 252, 256
Central Housing Authority (Mauritius) 160
Central Selling Organization 145
Central Statistical Office (Zimbabwe) 187, 195
Central Statistics Office (Botswana) 122
Centre for Women's Research (Sri Lanka) 255
CENWOR, *see* Centre for Women's Research
cerebrovascular disease 323, 325
Chad 107
Chakravarty, S. 456
Chasin, Barbara H. 204
Chatterji, Meera 69, 78, 106
Chee, Heng Leng 312, 314
Chen, Lincoln C. ix, 208, 219, 415, 463
on lessons from case-studies 421–34
Chenery, H. 437, 438, 440, 441
Chew, Tow Yow 308
Chief Medical Officer (Barbados) 337, 340, 344
Chikanza, I. 191

Child Day Care Act (Korea) 288
child supplementary feeding programme
   (Zimbabwe) 190
childbirth and pregnancy 67–8, 108, 277, 338, 388,
   390
   midwives 38, 70, 248, 249, 281, 312, 314
   prevention, *see* abortion; family planning
children:
   birth, *see* childbirth
   health, *see* immunization; infant and child
      mortality; nutrition
   labour by 86, 96, 104, 128, 327
   World Summit for 15, 16, 23, 172, 422
   see also child-care *under* women; education;
      UNICEF
Chile 100, 357, 365, 414
China:
   economic growth 4, 409; and poverty
      reduction 437, 444, 453
   education 88, 401
   health 70, 102, 401
   and Mauritius 149
   population and demographic transition 85, 107,
      108
Chinese people and language in Malaysia 97, 297,
   302, 305, 308, 428
Chisvo, Munhamo (on Zimbabwe) ix, 179–203
Cho, Nam-Hoon 275
cholera 219, 313
Chopak, Charles 190
Christianity:
   Barbados 327, 329, 331
   Kerala 209, 210, 211, 214, 218, 424
   Malaysia 305, 308
   Mauritius 424
   Sri Lanka 236
Chung, Fay 93, 94
CHWs, *see* community health workers
CIS, *see* Soviet Union, former
climate and weather 160
   see also drought
Cline, William 268
CMO, *see* Chief Medical Officer
Cochin, *see* Travancore-Cochin
cocoa 299
coconuts 244
coffee 426, 456
Colclough, Christopher 22, 92, 93
Colombia 451, 456
Colonial Development and Welfare Act (Britain,
   1945) 162
Colonial Office 162, 328

colonialism/imperialism 5
   see also Britain
Comecon (Council of Mutual Economic
   Assistance) 384, 386, 405–6, 408, 409–10
Committees for Defence of Revolution (Cuba) 388
commodity exports 49
   see also diamonds; rubber; sugar; tea; tin
common elements in high-achieving countries
   29–50, 63
   educational improvement preceding health 29,
      33–6
   state-supported social services 29, 32–3, 57
   see also education; finances/expenditure; health;
      nutrition; population; women
Commonwealth Sugar Agreement 158
communism 33
   Communist Party (Kerala) 33, 56
   see also Comecon; Cuba; Soviet Union, former
community health workers 72, 101
community involvement:
   Costa Rica 363, 366–7, 380
   educational expansion 93, 103
   Korea 286
   lacking 33
   Zimbabwe 180, 186, 195, 199
   see also NGOs
Comptroller General (Costa Rica) 372
conferences, global 15–16, 85, 422
   on children 15, 16, 23, 172, 422
Confucianism 268, 287, 424, 431
Congress Party (Kerala) 33, 56
consensus in Mauritius 174
Contingent of Militant Mothers for Education
   (Cuba) 402
contraception, *see* family planning
Convention on Elimination of All Forms of
   Discrimination against Women 330
Convention on Rights of Child 24, 172
Copenhagen Social Summit 15, 323, 422
Corbin, Rosalyn ix–x
   on Barbados 323–54
Cornia, Giovanni Andrea 19
Corporate Plan (Zimbabwe) 181
Costa Rica 355–83, 424, 433
   agriculture 360
   economic growth 359, 368–9, 371, 426; common
      elements and diversities 27, 30, 50–1; crisis
      428; and poverty reduction 443–4, 445–6
   education 100, 364–5, 369, 373; demand for 92;
      enrolment 26, 86–8; finances/expenditure 41,
      43, 45–7, 48, 89–91, 364, 372, 374, 375, 377,
      429–30; and health 105; literacy 25–6, 355–7,

364, 443–4, 445–6; private 374, 375;
    secondary 364, 367–8, 373, 375; teachers 96;
    tertiary 129; women 39–40, 96, 364
employment 31, 39–40, 358, 368, 369
equity 425
finances/expenditure 371–8, 427–8; defence 48;
    foreign aid 49, 377; revenues 368, 375–6; *see
    also under* education *above and* health *below*
foreign aid 377
health 362–3, 365; access 68; childbirth 68;
    common elements and diversities 25, 26–7;
    comparison with Cuba 414; finances/
    expenditure 29, 41, 42, 44, 46, 47, 73, 74, 107,
    363, 372, 374–7, 429–30; hospitals 363, 366;
    immunization 68, 69; infant and child
    mortality 66, 74, 355–7, 363, 367; life
    expectancy 66, 73, 74, 355–7, 363, 367;
    nutrition 73, 77, 80–81, 101, 104, 355–7, 363,
    366; personnel 363; primary care 73, 366–7,
    373, 380; private 373–4, 375, 432; water and
    sanitation 81–2, 357, 360, 363, 365, 373
history 358
housing 365, 369, 371, 373, 374, 377
lessons and future options 378–9
politics 33, 358–9, 370–1, 379–80
population and demographic transition 58, 83–4,
    426; density 362; family planning 73; fertility
    and growth 360–2, 380
poverty 53–5, 355–6, 360–1, 365–71, 374–5;
    reduction and economic growth 443–4, 445–6
rural areas 73, 106, 360–1, 366–8, 388
social security 366–7, 368, 373–4, 376, 377
stages in implementation of policy 359–71
structural adjustment 49, 368–70
tourism 426
urban areas/urbanization 355, 362, 368
women 37–40, 96, 364
Costa Rican Social Security Fund (Costa Rica), *see*
    CCSS
Côte d'Ivoire 105
Council of Mutual Economic Assistance, *see*
    Comecon
CPR (contraceptive prevalence rate) 83
    see also family planning
CSFP, *see* child supplementary feeding programme
CSO, *see* Central Statistical Office
Cuba 384–418, 424
    agriculture 397, 399, 403–4, 406, 410; sugar
        385–6, 397, 426
    economic growth 399, 403–7, 414–15, 426–7;
        common elements and diversities 29, 30, 32,
        50, 51; crisis 407–12, 413, 415; and poverty

reduction 443–4, 447, 450–1, 452, 462
    education 386–7, 395–400, 404, 414; demand
        for 92; enrolment 26, 86–8, 395, 396, 397–8,
        400; finances/expenditure 43, 46, 47, 89–91,
        396, 402–3; literacy 25–6, 97, 99, 104–5, 108,
        357, 395–7, 400–1, 414, 428, 429; secondary
        395, 396, 397–9, 400–1; teachers 395, 399, 401;
        tertiary 395, 396, 398–9; and women 39–40,
        395
    employment 31, 39–40
    finances/expenditure 402–3, 414, 427, 431;
        defence lacking 48; foreign aid 49, 386, 407;
        see also under education *above and* health *below*
    health 75, 387–95, 413; access 68; childbirth 68;
        common elements and diversities 25, 26–7,
        32–3; and education 104; finances/
        expenditure 29, 42, 44, 402–3; hospitals 388,
        389, 392; immunization 68, 69, 74, 389–91;
        infant and child mortality 32–3, 66, 74, 357,
        385, 387, 390–2, 400–1, 404, 411; life
        expectancy 33, 66, 392, 400–1; nutrition 77,
        102, 104, 107, 393–4, 410–11, 412; personnel
        388, 400–1, 413; primary care 387–8, 389;
        water and sanitation 82, 393, 415
    infrastructure 386, 411
    legislation 74, 388, 395, 409–10, 414
    politics 33, 402, 423
    population and demographic transition 58, 83–4,
        426; family planning 391, 395; fertility and
        growth 393–5
    poverty 53–5, 57, 385, 408–9; reduction and
        economic growth 443–4, 447, 450–1, 452, 462
    rural areas 74, 386, 387, 389, 393, 399, 402–4, 406,
        410
    social security 402–3
    structural adjustment 49, 404
    tourism 386, 426
    trade 393, 405–7, 410
    unemployment 385, 408
    urban areas/urbanization 388, 393, 399, 414
    women 37–40, 390, 395, 400–2, 404
Cuban Democracy Act 409–10
Cumpstone Report (Sri Lanka) 236
cyclones 160
Czechoslovakia, former 401, 402

Dahlgren, S. 139
Darity, W. 461
Datt, G. 461
DDT 248
De Beers diamond cartel 115–16, 145
Debswana (Botswana firm) 116

debt 183, 377, 454
  Botswana's lack of 115
Declaration of Rights of Child 16
defence and expenditure on 43, 45
  Africa 48, 136, 138–9, 140; lacking 175
  East Asia 48, 290, 307
  Latin America and Caribbean 48; abolished 358, 371, 380
  South Asia 48, 49, 245, 430
  see also wars
Delamonica, Enrique x
  on growth and poverty reduction 435–67
Dellimore, Jeffrey W. 350
democracy 33, 423, 463
  Botswana 114, 131–2
  Costa Rica 358–9
  Cuba 409–10
  Mauritius 149, 174
Demographic and Health Survey (Sri Lanka) 249
demographic transition, *see* population and demographic transition
Deolalikar, A. 23, 439
Department of Census and Statistics (Sri Lanka) 238, 241, 246–7, 250, 252
Department of Economics and Statistics (Kerala) 228
Department of Food Supply (Sri Lanka) 236
Department of Health Services (Sri Lanka) 239
Department of Medical Services (Barbados) 336
Desai, Meghnad x, 463
  on lessons from case-studies 421–34
development, *see* social development
Development Certificates (Mauritius) 158
Development Plans:
  Barbados 334, 344–5, 349
  Botswana 114–15, 120, 125, 134–5, 139–40
  India 71
  Korea (Five Year Plans) 265, 269, 274, 288
  Malaysia 309; First and Second 307, 312, 314; Fourth and Fifth 302, 312, 319; Sixth 301, 319
  Zimbabwe 181
diabetes 168, 323, 325
diamonds in Botswana, impact of 113, 114, 115–17, 145, 456
  revenues from 116, 118, 135–6, 139
diarrhoea 184, 221, 250, 304
  and malnutrition 23–4, 64, 77, 81
diphtheria 73, 105, 389, 390–1, 411
diseases and disorders, major:
  avoiding, *see* health; immunization
  see also in particular diarrhoea; malaria; measles; poliomyelitis; tetanus; tuberculosis; worms

diversities amongst high-achieving countries 50–6
  economic growth and rate of change of social indicators 50–3
  poverty alleviation 53–6
doctors, *see* personnel, health
Dominican Republic 369
Dommen, Edward and Bridget x, 426
  on Mauritius 149–78
Donoughmore Constitution (Sri Lanka) 235–6
Drèze, Jean:
  on health 95, 292, 366, 367
  on human capability 21
  on social services 33
  on women 38
drop-outs from school 96, 98, 99–100, 103, 104
  Africa 194
  East Asia 285
  Latin America and Caribbean 364
  South Asia 216, 217
  see also repetition rates
drought:
  Botswana 113, 124, 130–1, 134
  Sri Lanka 253
  Zimbabwe 182–3, 191
drugs:
  abuse 323
  therapeutic 338–9, 352
Duncan, Neville C. x, 431
  on Barbados 323–54
Duncan, Tyrrell x
  on Botswana 113–48
Dutt, A. 462

Earth Summit 15
East Asia:
  economic growth and poverty reduction 441, 443–4, 446, 447, 450, 452–4, 456
  health policies 72–3, 106, 107
  universal primary education policies 97–9
  see also China; Japan; Korea; Malaysia; NICs
Eastern Europe, *see* Soviet Union, former
ECLAC (Economic Commission for Latin America and Caribbean) 42, 53, 370, 414, 443, 461
economic growth 4, 6, 8, 11, 13, 15, 19
  common elements and diversities 22–3, 30, 57
  and poverty reduction 435–67; basic symbiotic model 459–60; patterns of growth 450–7, 463; and social indicators in development literature 436–42, 460–1; taxonomy of outcomes 442–50, 461–3
  see also GDP; industry; structural adjustment; trade *and under individual case-studies*

Economic Planning Board (Korea) 282, 284, 287, 290
Ecuador 52
Edirisinghe, N. 254
education 3, 10, 14, 438–9
  common elements and diversities 23–6, 28
  female, *see under* women
  finances/expenditure 258, 347, 348; common
    elements and diversities 41, 43, 45–9; and
    policies 88–92, 99, 103, 108; *see also under*
    individual case-studies
  improvement preceding health as common
    element 29, 33–6, 63–4, 100
  language of, *see* languages; mother-tongue
  legislation 96–7, 104
  and nutrition, *see* free meals
  policies, *see* universal primary education
  see also enrolment; literacy, adult; primary
    education; secondary education; teachers;
    tertiary education; training *and under individual*
    case-studies; UNESCO
Education Acts:
  Barbados 333, 352
  Malaysia 308
Education Ordinance (Sri Lanka) 252
Educational Consultants India Ltd 259
Egypt 105
emigration:
  from Barbados 245, 327–8, 330
  of doctors 74, 105, 187, 387; prevented or
    delayed 70, 72–3, 74, 101, 388
  from Kerala 52, 71, 98, 228, 229, 232
  of labourers, *see* labour *under* Middle East
  from Mauritius 155
  from Sri Lanka 98, 245
employment 28, 32, 37–40
  female, *see* working *under* women
  structure of 30–1
  see also agriculture; industry; personnel;
    unemployment *and under individual case-studies*
Employment of Disabled Persons Act (Mauritius)
  170
Encuesta Nacional de Ingresos y Gastos (Costa
  Rica) 374
English language in schools:
  Barbados 335
  Kerala 210, 211
  Malaysia 97, 306, 308
  Sri Lanka 251
enrolment in school, *see under* education *under*
  individual case-studies
enrolment in schools (mainly primary) 3, 19, 85–8,
  92, 93, 98, 108

common elements and diversities 24, 26, 28, 34,
  50
  see also secondary education *and under* education
    under individual case-studies
Environment and Development, Conference on
  15
EPB, *see* Economic Planning Board
EPI, *see* expanded programme on immunization
EPZ, *see* export processing zone
equity 423, 424–5
  gender, *see* women
  lacking, *see* inequality; poverty
Ernakulam 216
Ernst & Young 258
ESAP (economic structural-adjustment
  programme, Zimbabwe) 182–3, 199
ethnicity and ethnic conflict 424
  Malaysia 33, 297, 306, 318, 428
  Mauritius 149
  missing in Botswana 120, 424
  Sri Lanka 240, 243, 245, 424
  see also languages; multiculturalism; racism
Europe:
  and Botswana 139
  economic growth and poverty reduction 452,
    455–6
  European Union/Community/Common
    Market 158–9, 176
  population and demographic transition 85
  see also Britain
Evans, Peter 273, 460, 461
exchange rates 58
excreta disposal, *see* water and sanitation
expanded programme of immunization 67, 125,
  185–6, 339
expenditure, *see* finances/expenditure
export processing zones:
  Mauritius 156, 157–8, 159, 161, 173, 174, 175
  Sri Lanka 244
exports, *see* trade
Ezhavas (Kerala) 211–12, 213, 214

fair price shops (India) 102
family, *see* children; fertility; women
Family Housing Voucher, *see* BFV
Family Life and Peer Counselling Course
  (Barbados) 343–4
family planning 3, 72, 83–5, 102, 107–8
  GOBI–FFF programme 23, 40, 58, 73
  see also abortion; GOBI–FFF *and under* population
    under individual case-studies
Fanelli, J. 441, 454

Fawcus, S. 189
Feachem, R. G. 81, 107
Federal Land Consolidation and Rehabilitation
    Authority 300
Federal Land and Development Authority
    (Malaysia) 300–1, 315–17, 319
Federation of Cuban Women 390, 400, 402
FELCRA (Federal Land Consolidation and
    Rehabilitation Authority) 300
FELDA, *see* Federal Land and Development
    Authority
fertility rate 35, 83–4, 85
    see also family planning *and under* population
    under individual case-studies
fevers 221
Fiddler, Stephen 408
Fields, G. 360
Figueres, Jose 358, 360, 365, 380
finances/expenditure 12, 59, 75–6, 106, 429–30
    education, *see under* education
    family planning 84
    health, *see under* health
    international financial institutions, *see* IFIs
    as percentage of GDP 41–9, 58
    social development 427
    see also foreign aid; IMF; revenues; subsidies *and*
        also under individual case-studies
Finland 456
Fishlow, A. 461
focused programme 14–15
FODESAF (Social Development and Family
    Allowance Fund, Costa Rica) 365–6, 368
Fonseca, C. 369
food, *see* nutrition *and under* subsidies
Food Studies Group (Botswana) 131
foreign aid 11, 49, 437, 450
    Botswana 49, 117–18, 133, 135, 139–41, 146
    Costa Rica 49, 377
    Cuba 49, 386, 407
    Korea 49, 99, 266, 269, 286–7
    Malaysia 298
    Mauritius 159–60
    Sri Lanka 257
    Zimbabwe 49
    see also IMF
Fourth World Conference on Women (Beijing,
    1995) 15
France 103, 149
franchise 424
Franke, R. W. 204
free meals at school 78–81, 92, 95, 104, 107
    Kerala 215, 216

Sri Lanka 245, 251, 254, 259, 260
Zimbabwe 191–2
see also food *under* subsidies
Freeport Authority, Mauritius 175
future prospects 15–18, 175–6

Gaag, J. van der 441
Gabon 52, 53, 113, 117
Gaborone 119, 141
Gandhi, Mohandas Karamchand (Mahatma) 212
Garfield, R. 410, 411, 415
Garnier, Leonardo x–xi
    on Costa Rica 355–83
GDP and GNP (gross domestic and national
        products) 19, 30, 83
    Barbados 349, 352
    Botswana 113
    common elements and diversities 21, 27–30, 32,
        50–1, 54, 55
    Costa Rica 355–7, 359–60, 365, 368, 372, 379
    Cuba 385, 404
    Kerala 205, 206, 207, 224
    Korea 269–71
    Malaysia 297–8, 310–11
    Mauritius 155, 156
    social development expenditure as percentage of
        41–9, 58
    Sri Lanka 243, 244, 245–7
    tax ratio to 55
    see also economic growth
George, K. K. 204
GER (gross enrolment rate), *see* enrolment
Germany 139, 421
Ghana 102, 442
Gillespie, Stuart 40, 80
Gilmurray, J. 180
Global Conference on Human Settlements
        (Istanbul, 1996) 15
Global programme on AIDS 344
globalization 13
    see also conferences; trade
GMB, *see* Grain Marketing Board
GNP, *see* GDP and GNP
goals for future 15–18
GOBI–FFF programme 23, 40, 58, 73
Gómez, V. 380
Gonzalez Quiñones, Fernando 395
Gopinathan Nair, P. R. 210, 211, 213
governance 423–5
    accommodation 423–4
    equity 424–5
    responsive regime 423

see also politics; state
grain 189–90
  see also rice
Grain Marketing Board (Zimbabwe) 189, 190
grant-aid to schools 241, 332
  Kerala 211, 214, 215–16
'Green Revolution' 453, 461
Griffin, C. 367, 439
Grootaert, Christian 86
gross domestic and national products, *see* GDP and GNP
'Growth with Equity' strategy (Zimbabwe) 181
growth monitoring of children, *see* GOBI–FFF
Grynspan, Rebeca xi
  on Costa Rica 355–83
Guaranteed Price Scheme (Sri Lanka) 253
Güendel, L. 376
Guevara, Ernesto Che 413
Gujarat:
  education 96, 206, 217, 226
  health 206, 225
Gulf, *see* Middle East
Gunatilleke, G. 238, 248
Guyana 325, 346–8

Haggblade, S. 453
Haken, H. 463
Halstead, Scott B. 58
Haq, Mahbub 422
Harare 184, 188
Harvey, C. 113, 139
Haryana 51
  consumer expenditure 229
  education 206, 217, 226
  health 206, 225
Hazell, P. 453
HDI, *see* Human Development Index
head start in primary education, *see* enrolment
health 3
  common elements and diversities 23–7, 29
  finances/expenditure 29, 41, 42, 44, 45–8, 49, 75–6, 106
  policies 64–82, 105–8; Africa 65–8, 105, 107; demographic transition, *see* policies *under* population; East Asia 72–3, 106, 107; Latin America 73–5, 106, 107; mortality decline 100–2; nutritional interventions 76–81, 106–7; organization and funding 75–6, 106; South Asia 68–72, 105–6, 107; water and sanitation 81–2, 107
  workers, women as 38

see also access to health; hospitals; infant and child mortality; life expectancy; nutrition; population; primary health care; water and sanitation *and under individual case-studies*
Health Administration Reports (Sri Lanka) 238
Health Centre Law 278
Health Development Certificates (Mauritius) 168
Health Unit system (Sri Lanka) 248
heart disease 168, 250, 323, 325
Hein, Philippe 152, 154, 156, 157, 159, 161, 175
Heng, Leong Choon xi, 42
  on Malaysia 297–322
hepatitis 105, 315, 390, 414
herbalism 101, 278
Heyzer, Noeleen 288
Hidalgo, Roberto ix
  on Costa Rica 355–83
high-achieving countries 21–61
  choice of 24–9
  see also case-studies; common elements; diversities
higher education, *see* tertiary education
Hill, Terrel 106
Himachal Pradesh:
  consumer expenditure 229
  education 97, 206, 216–17, 226
  health 206, 225
Hinduism 210, 212–13
  see also caste system
Hirschman, A. O. 19, 379, 436
history 235–42, 264–5, 297–9, 358, 424
HIV, *see* AIDS/HIV
Hoey, Tan Siew xi
  on Malaysia 297–322
homoeopathy 71, 72, 101
Hong Kong 4
Hong, Sawon 292
hospitals:
  Barbados 337, 346
  Costa Rica 363, 366
  Cuba 388, 389, 392
  Kerala 220–1
  Korea 278, 279, 281
  Malaysia 311
  Mauritius 154
  Sri Lanka 238, 250
  Zimbabwe 184, 188
  see also health
Household Budget Survey (Barbados) 352
Household Income and Expenditure Surveys 122, 183, 241

housing:
  Africa 138, 140, 160–1
  East Asia 307
  Latin America and Caribbean 345, 365, 369, 371,
    373, 374, 377
Howard, Michael 349
Hoyos, F. A. 328, 329
human capital model 438–9
human development, *see* social development
Human Development Index (HDI) 422
  Barbados 323
  Botswana 117, 291
  Costa Rica 356, 379
  elements of, *see* education; enrolment; infant and
    child mortality; life expectancy; literacy
  Gabon 117
  Kerala 205, 206
  Malaysia 291
  Punjab 205
  Thailand 291
Human Development Reports 15, 18–19, 21
  and finances/expenditure 41, 46
  and Kerala 207
Human Rights, Conference on (Vienna, 1994) 15
Hungary 401, 402
hypertension 168, 250

ICA (Industrial Co-ordination Act, Malaysia)
    318–19
ideology 33;
  see also politics
IEC, *see* Information, Education and
    Communication
IFAD (International Fund for Agricultural
    Development) 53–4
IFIs (international financial institutions) 13, 438,
    440, 442, 453, 455, 458
ignorance, avoiding, *see* education
ILO (International Labour Organization):
  basic needs approach 441
  and Costa Rica 370
  and poverty 6–7
  and Zimbabwe 182, 191
IMAS, *see* Instituto Mixto de Ayuda Social
IMF (International Monetary Fund) 415
  and Barbados 349
  and defence 43, 45
  and economic growth 30
  and education 43, 45
  and health 42, 44
  and Mauritius 156–7
  and Sri Lanka 244

and structural adjustment 11
and Zimbabwe 182
immunization and vaccination 67–70, 73, 74, 100–1,
    105, 430
  Africa 68, 69, 74, 118, 125, 141, 165, 185–6, 336,
    339–40, 389–91
  expanded programme of 67, 125, 185–6, 339
  GOBI-FFF programme 23, 40, 58, 73
  Latin America and Caribbean 68, 69, 277, 312–13,
    315
  and mortality 34–5
  South Asia 68, 69, 219, 222
  see also under health *under individual case-studies*
imports, *see* trade
IMR (infant-mortality rate), *see* infant and child
    mortality
INA (National Vocational Training Institute, Costa
    Rica) 368
income distribution, *see* GDP; poverty; wages
India:
  economic growth 4, 6, 273; and poverty
    reduction 437, 443–4, 451–3, 456, 461–2
  education 94; drop-out rate 96; enrolment 97,
    217; finances/expenditure 88, 226; literacy 95,
    97
  finances/expenditure 225–6; defence 49
  health 71–2, 206, 225; access 221; and
    education 104; infant and child mortality 206;
    life expectancy 206, 219; nutrition 80, 102;
    personnel 67, 70; water and sanitation 81
  Indians in Malaysia 30, 97, 297, 302, 306, 308
  Indians in Sri Lanka 235, 243, 245, 246, 247
  and Mauritius 149
  oil 415
  population and demographic transition 85,
    223–4; fertility and family planning 107, 225,
    292
  poverty 18
  primary health care 71–2
  rent-seeking rampant 292
  see also Kerala
Indian Army 245
Indo-Sri Lanka Agreement 245
Indonesia:
  economic growth 4
  education 285
  health 102
  population and demographic transition 107, 108,
    304
  poverty 55
  public action lacking 32
Industrial Co-ordination Act (Malaysia) 318–19

industry:
  Barbados 350
  Costa Rica 360, 362
  Cuba 380, 389, 403–4, 408
  economic growth and poverty reduction 437, 441
  Korea 267–8, 269, 271–3, 288, 292
  Malaysia 297–8, 301
  Mauritius 159, 161
  sectors 27–31, 39
  Zimbabwe 179, 182
  see also economic growth; oil; trade
inequality 55
  low, growth stimulation and 266–8, 272
  see also equity
infant and child mortality 3, 8, 10, 12, 17, 19, 100,
    102
  common elements and diversities 24–7, 32
  and economic growth 50
  and education 34–5
  female 85
  and health policies 66, 68, 70
  see also under health *under individual case-studies*
infanticide, female 85
inflation 183, 272, 408
influenza 218
Information, Education and Communication
    programmes (Barbados) 328
infrastructure 64, 71
  Barbados 326
  Botswana 114, 115, 120–1, 124, 138, 140
  Costa Rica 359
  Cuba 386, 411
  Kerala 210–11
  Malaysia 299
  Mauritius 158, 159, 160–2
  Sri Lanka 244, 257, 259–60, 424
  see also housing; power supplies;
    telecommunications; transport; water and
    sanitation
Instituto Mixto de Ayuda Social (Costa Rica) 365
Instituto Nacional de Aprendizaje, *see* INA
insurance, health 73, 75, 76, 280, 291
integration of policies 423, 425–9
  external contact 426–7
  investment 427
  junctures, timing and sequencing 428–9
Inter-American Development Bank 415
International Conference on Population and
    Development (Cairo, 1994) 15, 85
international financial institutions, *see* IFIs
International Fund for Agricultural
    Development 53–4

International Labour Organization, *see* ILO
International Monetary Fund, *see* IMF
investment, *see* finances / expenditure
iodine deficiency 16, 17, 105, 106
Iran 58
iron deficiency 105, 106, 411
ISI strategy 438, 451, 452, 456
Islam:
  and family planning 107
  Kerala 209, 214
  Malaysia 83, 305
Italy 424
Ivanov, S. 152

Jamaica 330
  education 324, 325, 346–8, 352
  health 346–7, 348
Jammu and Kashmir 206, 217, 225, 226
Janasaviya programme 246, 255, 259
Janvry, A. De 452
Japan 421
  economic growth and poverty reduction 441,
    452, 456
  education and health 105
  and Korea 264, 266, 291, 292
  life expectancy 68
Jayantha, D. 243
Jayarajah, Carl 49
Jayasundera, P. B. 244, 256
Jayesuria, L. W. 310
Jayne, T. S. 190
Jefferis, Keith xi, 431
  on Botswana 113–48
Jeffrey, Robin 204, 213
Jennings Report (Sri Lanka) 236
Jolly, Richard viii, xii, 411, 421
  on success 3–20
Jose, A. V. 56
Joseph, Stephen 47
Joseph, Thomas A. 210
Joynathsing, M. 162

Kabir, M. 208, 209, 229
Kalahari, *see* Kgalagadi
Kaldor, N. 437, 440
Kanbur, Ravi 86, 438
Kannangara Report (Sri Lanka) 236, 251
Karnataka:
  education 96, 206, 217, 226
  health 206, 225
  women 38
Kaser, Michael 412, 415

Kashmir 206, 217, 225, 226

Katzenstein, P. 455

KEDI, *see* Korea Educational Development Institute

Kenya 93, 123

Kerala 204–34

accommodation 424

agriculture 51–2

creation 205, 207; *see also* Malabar; Travancore-Cochin

defence expenditure lacking 48

demand for services 431

economic growth 229–30, 425, 426; common elements and diversities 27, 29, 30, 32, 50, 51–2; constraints and sustainability 229–31; and poverty reduction 444, 445–6, 447, 462

education 206, 208–9, 210–18, 226; demand for 92; drop-out rates 103; enrolment 26, 34, 86–8, 97, 216–17; finances/expenditure 43, 45, 47, 89–91, 95–6, 226–7, 429, 430; and health 104; literacy 25–6, 51, 94, 95, 98, 205–6, 207, 213, 215–16; campaign 97, 99, 104–5, 108, 216, 397, 414; private 431–2; teachers 96, 215; and women 96, 213–15, 216, 218, 225

employment 31, 37–8, 39–40, 229–30

equity 425

finances/expenditure 49, 208, 225–8, 427; *see also under* education *above and* health *below*

health 75, 206, 208–9, 218–25, 228–9; access 68; childbirth 68; common elements and diversities 25, 26–7, 34; demand for 232; finances/expenditure 29, 42, 76, 221, 227–9, 429, 430; hospitals 220–1; immunization 68, 69, 219, 222; infant and child mortality 66, 70–1, 77–8, 205–6, 207, 218–20, 222, 232; life expectancy 66, 205–6, 207, 219, 224; nutrition 70, 76–9, 80, 102, 104, 107, 224; organization 71–2; primary care 101; private 71, 76, 211, 215, 222, 431–2; traditional 70–1, 101; utilization rates 106; water and sanitation 81, 82, 219, 224, 232

land tenure 51, 55

lessons from 424

as model of development 204–5

multicultural 424

politics 33

population and demographic transition 58, 83–4, 223–5, 426; emigration 52, 71, 98, 228, 229, 232; family planning 224–5; fertility and growth 206, 218, 221–4, 232

poverty 53–6, 57, 205–6; reduction and economic growth 444, 445–6, 447, 462

social intermediation, beginning of 207–10

women 37–40, 107, 429; and education 96, 213–15, 216, 218, 225

Keynes, John Maynard 7, 436

Kgalagadi desert (Botswana) 113, 132, 145

Khama, Sir Seretse 132

Kharas, Himi 320

KIFP, *see* Korea Institute of Family Planning

KIHASA, *see* Korea Institute of Health and Social Affairs

KIPH (Korea Institute of Population and Health) 277

Kleysen, D. 374

Klouda, Anthony 106

Korea 24, 264–96, 432–3

comparison with Cuba 387

economic growth 17, 267–8, 269–73, 290, 425; common elements and diversities 27, 30, 50–1, 52; development plans 265, 269, 274, 288; and poverty reduction 441, 443–4, 446, 447, 450, 453, 456

education 283–7, 427; demand for 92, 431; enrolment 26, 86–8, 264, 268, 283–4; finances/expenditure 41, 43, 45–7, 48, 89–91, 98, 267, 268, 271, 285–6, 290, 429, 430; and health 34; literacy 25–6, 34, 268, 283, 285; private 286, 424; secondary 264, 284, 286; teachers 96, 285; tertiary 267, 283; women 39–40, 96, 281, 291

employment 28, 31, 39–40, 271–2

equity 425

finances/expenditure 266–8, 272, 289–90, 427; defence 48, 290; foreign aid 49, 266, 269, 286–7; *see also under* education *above and* health *below*

health 276–83, 462; access 68; childbirth 68; common elements and diversities 25, 26–7, 34; crude death rate 428–9; finances/expenditure 29, 41, 44, 75, 106, 278, 430; hospitals 278, 279, 281; immunization 68, 69, 277; infant and child mortality 66, 276–7, 291; life expectancy 66, 276–7; nutrition 77, 281–3; personnel 277, 278, 279, 281; primary care 105; private 276–7, 278, 281; resources and policies 276–81; traditional 101; utilization 281; water and sanitation 82, 264, 277, 278

history of development 264–5

land tenure 264, 266, 272, 291, 427

legislation 266, 288, 289

politics 33, 265, 423

population and demographic transition 58, 82, 83–4, 273–6, 287, 426; family planning 108,

274–6, 292; fertility and growth 108, 273–4, 275
poverty 53–5, 56, 264, 267, 270, 275, 281, 288–9; reduction and economic growth 441, 443–4, 446, 447, 450, 453, 456
religion 268, 287, 424
roots of development 266–73
rural areas 264, 266, 269, 271–2, 291
social security 275, 288–9
structural adjustment 49, 272, 428
women 37–8, 287–8; education 39–40, 96, 281, 291; working 287–8, 299
Korea Educational Development Institute 270, 284
Korea Institute of Family Planning 275, 276–7, 282
Korea Institute of Health and Social Affairs 273, 275, 276–7
Korea Institute of Population and Health 277
Korean War 239, 264, 266, 268, 274, 286
Krishnan, T. N. xii
on Kerala 204–34
Krueger, A. 461
Kuntz, Diane 392, 410, 415
Kuravas (Kerala) 213
Kurz, H. 461
Kuznets, Simon 269, 292, 437, 438, 461

labour, *see* emigration; employment
Labour Party (Mauritius) 174
Lage, Carlos 391
Lagesse, Marcelle 175
Lal, D. 461
Lamusse, Roland 157, 159, 173, 175, 176
Land Reform Act (Korea) 266
land tenure and ownership (and reform):
Cuba 387
Kerala 51, 55
Korea 264, 266, 272, 291, 427
Malaysia 299, 300–1, 315–17, 319
Sri Lanka 56
see also agriculture
languages (mainly in schools)
Barbados 335
Botswana 132
Kerala 210–11, 214
Malaysia 97–8, 297, 302, 305, 306, 308, 318, 428
Sri Lanka 97, 240, 251
see also ethnicity; mother-tongue
Latin America and Caribbean 357
economic growth and poverty reduction 6, 441, 443–4, 445–6, 447, 450–5, 456, 461, 462

health 64, 73–5, 106, 107
military expenditure 380
social indicators 64, 357
universal primary education policies 99–100
see also Argentina; Barbados; Brazil; Costa Rica; Cuba
Lau, L. 105
law, *see* legislation
Laxmi Baya, Rani 210
Lee, Hung-Tak 275
legislation:
Barbados 330, 331, 336, 344
Britain 162
Cuba 74, 388, 395, 409–10, 414
education 96–7, 104
Korea 266, 288, 289
Malaysia 72, 314–15, 318–19
Mauritius 170, 171
León, M. 374, 375
Lesotho 53, 116–17
Lewis, S. R. 113, 123, 139
Lewis, W. A. 463
liberation struggle in Zimbabwe 33, 92
life expectancy 3, 14, 19
common elements and diversities 21, 24–5, 32, 33
and education 34–5
and health policies 66, 68, 72
and income 58
see also mortality *and under* health *under individual case-studies*
Lim, Ewe Seng 319
Lipton, Michael 7, 437, 440, 441, 459
literacy, adult 21, 24–6, 94
campaigns in Kerala and Cuba 97, 99, 104–5, 108, 397, 414, 428, 429
and economic growth 50
and health 34
and UNICEF 356, 357
see also under education *under individual case-studies*
Little, I. 438
Livelihood Protection Act (Korea) 289
Lloyd, C. B. 152
Lockheed, M. 94
Loewenson, Rene xii, 105
on Zimbabwe 179–203
Lucas, R. 450, 461
lunches, school, *see* free meals

Madhya Pradesh:
education 96, 206, 217, 226, 227
health 71, 206, 225

Mahabharata 214

Mahalanobis, P. C. 437, 450

Maharashtra:
education 96, 206, 216–17, 226
health 206, 225

Mahaweli River scheme (Sri Lanka) 244

maize 189–90

Maizels, Alfred 175

Malabar 205, 207, 232, 433
education 211, 213, 215–16, 218
health 218, 220–1, 222
population and demographic transition 223–4
see also Kerala

malaria 184, 389
Malaysia 304, 313, 315
Sri Lanka 248, 250, 430

Malayalam language (Kerala) 210–11, 214

Malays:
in Malaysia: language in schools 97–8, 305, 306,
308, 318; *see also* Bumiputra
in Sri Lanka 247

Malaysia 297–322, 433
accommodation 424
agriculture 297–8, 299–300, 307, 317
economic growth 297–300, 317, 426; common
elements and diversities 27, 30, 50–1, 52; and
poverty reduction 443–4, 446, 453–4, 456; *see
also under* Development Plans
education 303, 305–9, 316, 427; demand for 92,
97; drop-out rates 103; enrolment 26, 86–8,
303–4, 305–9; finances/expenditure 41, 43,
45–7, 48, 89–91, 98, 299, 304, 307, 311, 317, 430;
language of 97–8, 297, 302, 305, 306, 318, 428;
literacy 25–6; private 306, 308, 318; secondary
304, 308, 316, 318; teachers 96, 285, 306, 308,
316; and women 39–40, 96, 308–9
employment 28, 31, 39–40, 298
equity 425
finances/expenditure 49, 298–9, 307, 317–18,
427; defence 48, 307; foreign aid 298; revenues
317; *see also under* education *above and* health
below
health 75, 303–4, 309–15; access 68, 312;
childbirth 68; common elements and
diversities 25, 26–7; finances/expenditure 29,
41, 42, 44, 47, 106, 278, 299, 304, 307, 310–12,
430; hospitals 311; immunization 68, 69,
312–13, 315; infant and child mortality 66, 72,
81, 303, 312, 319; life expectancy 66, 72, 81,
277, 303, 309–10; nutrition 77, 312;
personnel 72–3, 311, 314–15; primary
care 101; private 318; water and

sanitation 81, 82, 315
history of development 297–9
land tenure 299, 300–1, 315–17, 319
legislation 72, 314–15, 318–19
multicultural 424
politics 33, 423
population and demographic transition 58, 82,
83–4, 102, 303–4, 426
poverty 53–5, 56, 72, 300–3, 315–17, 319;
reduction and economic growth 443–4, 446,
453–4, 456
religion 424
social cohesion 318–19
social security 304
structural adjustment 49, 298, 428
women 316; education 39–40, 96, 308–9
see also under rural areas

malnutrition, avoiding, *see* nutrition

Manipur 97

Mari Bhat, P. N. 223

Martorell, R. 107

Mason, Edward S. 98

Mason, E. R. 266, 269, 278, 286, 292

Mason, John 40, 80

Massiah, Joycelin 324, 327, 336

Mata, L. 73, 80, 106, 364, 366

maternal mortality rate 24–5, 67, 100
Botswana 119
Cuba 391–2
Korea 276–7
Malaysia 310
Sri Lanka 248
Zimbabwe 185, 189

matriliny in Kerala 214, 218

Mauritania 107

Mauritian Action for the Promotion of Breast-
Feeding and Nutrition 170

Mauritius 24, 149–78, 424, 433, 452
accommodation 424
economic growth 156–62, 426; common
elements and diversities 27, 28, 30, 32, 50–1,
52; infrastructure 160–2; phases of 156–7; and
population 155–6; and poverty reduction
443–4, 446, 447, 455–6; sugar 156, 157, 158–60,
426; wages and social justice 157–8; *see also*
sugar industry
education 162–4; demand for 92; enrolment 26,
86–8, 155, 162, 172; finances/expenditure 43,
45–7, 45–9, 89–91, 94, 150, 167, 169, 430;
literacy 25–6, 150; private 162, 164;
teachers 96; women 37–8, 96, 171–2
employment 31, 39–40

equity 425

finances/expenditure 49; defence 48; foreign
aid 159–60; revenues 158; *see also under*
education *above and* health *below*

future 175–6

health 164–8, 429, 430; access 68; childbirth 68;
common elements and diversities 25, 26–7;
finances/expenditure 29, 42, 44, 49, 150, 167,
169, 430; hospitals 154; immunization 68, 69,
165; infant and child mortality 66, 151–2, 153,
164–5; life expectancy 32, 66, 150, 171; new
problems 168; nutrition 77, 150, 167–8, 173;
personnel 150, 166–7; primary health care
163, 164–6; private 168; water and sanitation
82, 160–1

infrastructure 158, 159, 160–2

legislation 170, 171

multicultural 424

politics 33, 149

population and demographic transition 58, 83–4,
426; abortion 154–5; decline 150–6;
emigration 155; family planning 151–2,
153–4, 165, 170–1

poverty 53–5, 56; reduction and economic
growth 443–4, 446, 447, 455–6

social security 150, 167, 168–9

structural adjustment 49, 156–7, 428

sugar production 156, 157, 158–60, 426

tourism 156, 159, 174, 426, 456

women 37–40, 162, 170–3

Mauritius Freeport Authority 175

Maxwell Stamp 176

Mazur, R. 191

Meade, James E. 150, 156, 157, 158, 438, 441

meals at school, *see* free meals

measles 17, 23–4, 73, 77, 184, 185, 391

MEDIA (Mauritius) 175

medical personnel, *see* personnel, health

Medical Termination of Pregnancy Act (Barbados)
344

Meerman, Jocob 313

Mehrotra, Santosh viii, xii, 20, 422
on common elements and diversities 21–61
on Cuba 384–417
on growth and poverty reduction 435–67
on health and education policies 63–110
on Korea 264–96

meningitis 184, 391, 414

MEPD (Mauritius) 164

Mesa-Lago, Carmelo: (on Cuba) 30, 42, 43
economy 401, 407, 408, 412
expenditure 402, 403

health 388, 392, 413, 414

Mexico 100
economic growth and poverty reduction 55, 441,
443–4, 446, 451

MFDP, *see* Ministry of Finance and Development

MFPA (Mauritius Family Planning Association) 154,
165, 170

Middle East:
economic growth 6, 59
health 59, 67
infant and child mortality 58
labour migration to and remittances from 426;
Barbados 245; Kerala 52, 71, 98, 228, 229, 232;
Korea 272; Sri Lanka 98
trade with 292

Mideplan (UNDP) 360

midwives, *see under* childbirth

migration, *see* emigration

military state, *see* Korea

Mincer, J. 439

Mingat, Alain 88

mining 179, 271, 317, 319
Botswana, *see* diamonds
tin 317, 319, 426, 456

Ministry of Agriculture (Barbados) 340

Ministry of Education:
Barbados 331–5, 344, 349
Costa Rica 400
Cuba 414
Korea 285
Malaysia 305, 306, 308
Sri Lanka 251

Ministry of Education and Culture (Zimbabwe)
193, 194, 195

Ministry of Education and Science (Mauritius)
162–4

Ministry of Finance:
Costa Rica 373, 376
Malaysia 298, 302, 317
Zimbabwe 182

Ministry of Finance and Development (Botswana)
121, 137

Ministry of Health:
Barbados 340, 341, 344–5, 349
Malaysia 310, 311, 314
Mauritius 155, 173
Zimbabwe 181, 184, 189, 190

Ministry of Health and Social Affairs (Korea) 277,
279, 280–2

Ministry of Health and Welfare (Korea) 288

Ministry of Labour:
Costa Rica 369

Ministry of Labour (*cont.*):
   Korea 270
Ministry of Public Health (Cuba) 387, 388, 390–4, 402
Ministry of Public Service, Labour and Social Welfare (MPSLSW, Zimbabwe) 191
Minturn Leigh 215
Miranda, G. 356, 362, 363, 364, 366, 367
Misra 223
MLAWD/USAID 191
MMA (Malaysian Medical Association) 312, 314
MMM (Mouvement Militant Mauricien) 174
MMR, *see* maternal mortality rate
Mohs, Edgar 73
MOHSA, *see* Ministry of Health and Social Affairs
MOHW (Ministry of Health and Welfare) 288
Molutsi, Patrick xiii, 431
   on Botswana 113–48
Monge, Guillermo xi
   on Costa Rica 355–83
monitoring 16
Moors in Sri Lanka 246–7
moral incentives 386, 397
Morley 53
Morris, C. T. 437
mortality:
   decline and health policies 100–2
   see also abortion; infant and child mortality; life expectancy; maternal mortality
Mosley, Henry W. 219
mother and child, *see* childbirth; children; infant and child mortality; maternal mortality; women
mother-tongue education 92, 97–8, 103–4, 108
   Botswana 128
   Kerala 210–11
   Malaysia 305, 306, 308, 318
   Sri Lanka 251
Mother's Clubs, Family Planning (Korea) 275
Mouvement Militant Mauricien 174
Moyne Commission, *see* West India Royal Commission
Mozambique 198
multiculturalism 423–4
   countries with, *see* Kerala; Malaysia; Mauritius; Sri Lanka; Zimbabwe
   see also ethnicity
mumps 391
Murray, Christopher J. L. 208, 428
Muslims, *see* Islam
Myanmar 91

NACP, *see* national AIDS control programme
Nairs (Kerala) 212, 213, 214
Namboodiri Brahmins 214
Namibia 116–17
Napoleonic Code (Mauritius) 171
Narayana Guru 212
National Adoption Council (Mauritius) 172
national AIDS control programme (Botswana) 126
National Children's Council (Mauritius) 170, 172
National Commission for Education (Botswana) 128
National Council for Rehabilitation of Disabled Persons (Mauritius) 170
National Development Plans (Botswana) 114–15, 120, 125, 134–5, 139–40
National Housing Development Company (Mauritius) 161
National Liberation Party (Costa Rica), *see* PLN
National Literacy Mission (India) 97, 216
National Nutrition Centre and Survey (Barbados) 341, 352
National Nutrition Surveillance System (Botswana) 129
National Pension System (Korea) 289
National Population Censuses (Costa Rica) 356, 360, 362–4
National Programmes of Action 23
National Sample Survey (Kerala) 228
National Settlement Policy (Botswana) 127
National Statistical Office (Cuba) 398
National Statistical Office (Korea):
   economic growth 270, 271
   education 284
   finances/expenditure 290, 292
   health 277, 279
   population and demographic transition 274
   water and sanitation 287
National Survey of Income and Expenditure (Costa Rica) 374
National Vocational Training Institute (Costa Rica), *see* INA
National Water Master Plan (Botswana) 126
National Women's Council (Mauritius) 170
Navarro, V. 387
NCDs, *see* non-communicable diseases
NDPs, *see* National Development Plans
Nell, E. 440
NEP, *see* New Economic Policy
Netherlands 414–15
New Economic Policy (Malaysia) 298–9, 301, 303, 318, 319, 428

New Growth Theory 438–40
Newman, P. 248
NGOs (non-governmental organizations) 11, 97, 431
　Barbados 344
　Botswana 126, 143
　Kerala 216
　Korea 275
　limited 33
　Mauritius 170, 172
　Zimbabwe 67, 79, 186
　see also community involvement
NGT (New Growth Theory) 438–40
Nicaragua 377
NICs (newly industrialized countries) of East
　　Asia 4, 175, 357, 414, 441
　see also Korea; Taiwan
Nigeria 32, 64, 102
NNSS, *see* National Nutrition Surveillance System
non-communicable diseases 168, 171, 250, 304, 323, 325
non-governmental organizations, *see* NGOs
Norway 139
NSO, *see* National Statistical Office
nurses, *see under* personnel, health
Nurske, R. 436
nutrition 3, 10, 19, 64, 65, 102, 107
　health policies 76–81, 106–7
　and mortality 34–5, 36
　school feeding, *see* free meals
　supplements, *see* subsidies *under* food
　see also agriculture; breastfeeding *and under* health
　　under individual case-studies

OECD (Organization for Economic Co-operation
　　and Development), and Costa Rica 377
oil 52
　Cuba 410, 414–15
　Gabon 117
　Malaysia 317, 319, 426, 456
　prices 156, 267, 330, 438; windfall gains 32, 58, 59
oil palm, *see* palm oil
Oman 53, 58
One-Day Literacy Survey (Kerala) 216
oral rehydration, *see* GOBI-FFF
Organization for Economic Co-operation and
　　Development, *see* OECD
Orissa:
　education 96, 206, 217, 226
　health 206, 218, 225

Oshima, Harry 413
outcomes, taxonomy of 442–50, 461–3
output, *see* economic growth

Pack, H. 461, 463
Pakistan:
　economic growth and poverty reduction 443–4, 453, 462
　education 34, 94, 95, 268
　health 70, 80
palm oil 299, 300, 317, 319, 456
　Palm Oil Research Institute (Malaysia) 300
Pan-American Health Organization 341, 415
Panchamukhi, P. R. 213
Panikar, P. G. K. 107, 219
parasites 73, 167, 250, 389
Parayas (Kerala) 213
Parent Teachers' Associations:
　Barbados 333–4
　Korea 280
　Zimbabwe 103
Park, In-Hwa xiii, 427
　on Korea 264–96
Partido Liberación Nacional, *see* PLN
Patel, Sulekha 224–5, 232
Patel, Surendra 20
Patrinos, H. A. 86
Perera, P. D. A. 319
Pérez Izquierdo, Victoria 395
Perotti, R. 439, 440
personnel, education, *see* teachers
personnel, health:
　migration, *see under* emigration
　nurses 38, 67, 73, 105, 187, 279, 281, 314
　required to serve government 70, 72–3, 74, 101, 388
　training 67, 70, 73, 74, 101, 166, 249, 314–15, 389
　see also under health *under individual case-studies*
Persson, T. 440
pertussis 73, 390–1
pessimism 421–2
　and optimism 3–7
Pfeffermann, G. 367
PHC, *see* primary health care
PHI, *see* public health inspector
PHM, *see* primary health midwife
PIE (School Computer Programme, Costa Rica) 369
Pieper, U. 441
Pillai, Govinda P. 212

Pizarro, Cristostomo 55, 100, 267, 414
Plan de Compensacion Social (Costa Rica) 428
Planned Parenthood Federation of Korea 275
Planning Commission (India) 205
PLN (National Liberation Party, Costa Rica) 358, 368–9, 370, 379–80
pneumonia 184, 411
Poland 401, 402
poliomyelitis 16–17, 73, 315, 389, 390–1
politics:
  Barbados 33, 329
  Botswana 131–5
  Costa Rica 33, 358–9, 370–1, 379–80
  Cuba 33, 402, 423
  Kerala 33
  Korea 33, 265, 423
  Mauritius 33, 423
  Sri Lanka 33, 236
  Zimbabwe 33, 179
  see also democracy; governance
Polyani, R. 460
polyclinics 337–8
Population Council 84
population and demographic transition 3–4, 24, 64
  density 304, 326, 327, 362; sparse, see Botswana
  migration, see emigration
  total size 426
  see also family planning; fertility; fertility rate;
    mortality and under individual case-studies
Populist (Congress) Party (Kerala) 33, 56
PORIM (Palm Oil Research Institute, Malaysia) 300
Port Louis 161
Porter, M. 456
poverty and alleviation of 4–7, 13, 17, 18, 22, 53–6, 57, 72, 425
  see also under economic growth and individual case-studies
power supplies:
  Botswana 120–1
  Costa Rica 356, 360, 365
  Cuba 404
  Mauritius 160, 161
PPFK (Planned Parenthood Federation of Korea) 275
PREALC 370
Prebish, R. 436, 437
pregnancy, see childbirth and pregnancy
pre-primary education 164, 400
Presidential Task Force Report on Health (Sri Lanka) 258
press in Mauritius 175
Preston 428

primary education:
  finances/expenditure 46–7, 59;
  see also enrolment; universal primary education
primary health care 47, 65, 67, 101
  Barbados 336–45
  Botswana 124–5, 135, 142, 145
  Costa Rica 73, 366–7, 373, 380
  Cuba 387–8, 389
  India 71–2
  Mauritius 163, 164–6
  Sri Lanka 101, 248, 249
  Zimbabwe 101, 181, 184–5, 186–7
primary health midwife (Sri Lanka) 101, 248, 249
primary industry, see agriculture; mining
Pritchett, Lant 84, 107
private services 59, 431–2
  education 93, 94, 98; see also under individual case-studies
  health care 34, 75; see also under individual case-studies
profiles in success 3–20
  adjustment with human face 11–14
  goals for future 15–18
  lessons of 7–11, 14–15
  pessimism and optimism 3–7
  see also high-achieving countries
Programa de Informática Educativa, see PIE
Programme of Assistance to Approved Independent Schools (Barbados) 332, 352
promotion of children in schools, see repetition rates
Psacharapoulos, George 22, 350, 438
PTA, see Parent Teachers' Association
Public Health Act (Barbados) 336
public health inspector (Sri Lanka) 248
Public Health Institute (Malaysia) 314
public support, see state-supported
public-private mix 431–2
Pulayas (Kerala) 212–13
Punjab:
  consumer expenditure 229
  economic growth 51
  education 206, 217, 226, 227
  health 206, 225
purchasing power, see income
Purdah 214, 232
Pusan 278
Pushpangadan, K. 229
Putnam, Robert 423, 424

racism:
  South Africa 133–4, 184, 192

see also ethnicity and ethnic conflict
Raczynski, D. 365
RADs, *see* remote area dwellers
Rahman Talib Report (Malaysia) 308–9
Rajan, Irudaya 223
Rajasthan:
    education 96, 97, 206, 216, 217, 226
    health 71, 80, 206, 225
Rama, G. 359
Ramalingaswami, V. 79, 107
Ramayana 214
Ramsey, Frank C. 335, 336–7, 340
Rand Monetary Area 116, 117
Rao, M. S. A. 209
Ravallion, Martin 23, 58, 432, 440, 459, 460
Razak, Tun Abdul 305, 310
Razak report (Malaysia) 305–6, 308
recession, global 49
Red Cross, Botswana 126
religion, *see* Buddhism; Christianity; Confucianism
remittances 328, 330, 426
    see also labour *under* Middle East
remote area dwellers 145
Renfrew, A. 188–9
rent, *see* revenues; taxation
repetition rates and replacement by automatic
    promotion in schools 87–8, 98–9, 103, 192,
    285, 308, 333, 364
    see also drop-outs
resources, *see* finances/expenditure
respiratory diseases 185, 221
revenues 49, 51, 55
    see also foreign aid; remittances *and under*
    finances/expenditure *under individual case-*
    studies
Rhee, President Synghman 274
Rhodesia, *see* Zimbabwe
rice 107
    Malaysia 299, 300, 301
    Sri Lanka 236, 243, 244, 253
RISDA, *see* Rubber Industry Smallholders'
    Development Authority
roads 160, 326
Rodriguez, A. 375
Rodriguez, José Luis 414
Rodrik, D. 440
Rohrbach, D. D. 190
Romania 401
Romer, P. 461
Rosenstein-Rodan, P. 436
Rosero, L. (on Costa Rica):
    economic growth 360, 362

education 364, 365
    health 73, 80, 106, 363, 366, 367
Rovira, J. 358, 377
Rowthorn, R. 461
RRIM (Rubber Research Institute, Malaysia) 300
rubber 51, 426, 456
    Malaysia 299–300, 317, 319
    Sri Lanka 239, 244
Rubber Industry Smallholders' Development
    Authority (Malaysia) 299–300
Rubber Research Institute (Malaysia) 300
rubella 391
rural areas 452, 453–4, 456
    Botswana 119, 122–4, 128–30, 143
    Costa Rica 73, 106, 360–1, 366–8, 388
    Cuba 74, 386, 387, 389, 393, 399, 402–4, 406, 410
    health programmes and schemes: Costa Rica 73,
        105, 388; Cuba 74; health policies 65–7, 73;
        Malaysia 309–15; Zimbabwe 66–7
    Korea 264, 266, 269, 271–2, 291
    Malaysia: development and income generation
        298–300, 307; FELDA 300–1, 315–17, 319;
        health 309–15; poverty 300–2, 315–17
    Sri Lanka 244, 253
    Zimbabwe 66–7, 185–7, 189
    see also agriculture
Rural Medical Service Law:
    Costa Rica 388
    Cuba 74

SACU, *see* Southern African Customs Union
Sadhu Jana Paripalana Sabha (Kerala) 212
Sadoulet, E. 452
Saemaul Undong 275
Sáenz, L. 374, 375
Saith, A. 454
Salvadori, N. 461
samllpox 105
Samoff, Joel 395, 396, 399, 404
Sanderatne, Nimal xiii, 427, 430
    on Sri Lanka 235–63
Sanders, David 66, 105, 191
sanitation, *see* water and sanitation
Sarma 223
Saudi Arabia 58
Sauma, P. 370, 375
savings 55, 231, 269
schools, *see* education; free meals
Schor, J. 461
Schultz, T. Paul 22
Schultz, T. W. 437, 438
Schumpeter, J. 436

SDF, *see* social dimensions fund
Second World War 78, 167, 236, 266
secondary education 86, 88, 91, 93, 94, 98, 108
　Barbados 324, 331–2, 333, 334, 348
　Botswana 120, 127, 128, 129
　Costa Rica 364, 367–8, 373, 375
　Cuba 395, 396, 397–9, 400–1
　Korea 264, 284, 286
　Malaysia 304, 308, 316, 318
　Mauritius 162
　Sri Lanka 240, 241–2, 258
　Zimbabwe 194
secondary industry, *see* industry
security:
　food 129–30
　military, *see* defence
　see also social security
Seers, Dudley 413, 414
Seetohul, Brijlall D. 162
Selebi-Phikwe mine 145
Sen, Amartya:
　on health 85, 95, 292, 366, 367
　on human capability 21
　on social services 29, 33, 441
　on society 209
　on women 36, 38, 287, 402, 414
Sen, Gita 85
Sena, A. 191
Senanayake-Chelvanayakam Pact 240
Seoul 278
service industries 30–1
Setswana language and culture 128, 132, 145
Shapiro, H. 441
Sharma, R. 107
shift-working by teachers 103, 195, 285
shoes provided for children 167
Shop Corporation (Malaysia) 316
Siddiqui, F. 86
Silva, A. V. K. V. de 248
Simeonov, L. A. 249
Simmons, Adele Smith 174
Singapore 4, 357
Singh, A. 441, 463
Sinhala language 240, 251
Sinhalese people 243, 245, 247
Sivanandan, P. 209
SJP, *see* Sadhu Jana Paripalana
skills shortage 120, 133
　remedying, *see* education; training
SLFP, (Bandaranaike-Chelvanayakam Pact) 240
smallpox 219, 221, 315
Smith, Adam 436

SNDP, *see* Sree Narayana Dharma
Snodgrass, Donald R. 98, 239
Social Compensation Plan (Costa Rica) 368
social development:
　defined 422
　see also case-studies; common elements;
　　economic growth; education; health; high-
　　achieving countries; poverty; profiles in
　　success; women
Social Development and Family Allowance Fund
　(Costa Rica), *see* FODESAF
social dimensions fund (Zimbabwe) 191
social intermediation defined 208–9
　see also Kerala
social security:
　Botswana 120–2, 136, 144
　Costa Rica 366–7, 368, 373–4, 376, 377
　Cuba 402–3
　and health 73, 74, 75
　Korea 275, 288–9
　Malaysia 304
　Mauritius 150, 167, 168–9
　Sri Lanka 236, 238, 239, 240
South Africa:
　and Botswana 116–17, 139, 144
　poverty 123
　racism 133–4
　and Zimbabwe 48
South Asia:
　economic growth and poverty reduction 437,
　　443–4, 445–6, 447, 451–3, 456, 461–2
　health policies 68–72, 105–6, 107
　universal primary education policies 94–7, 108
　see also Bangladesh; India; Kerala; Pakistan; Sri
　　Lanka
South Korea, *see* Korea
Southern African Customs Union 116, 136
Soviet Union, former (and Eastern Europe) 26
　and Cuba 384, 386, 389, 400–1, 402, 404, 406–8,
　　412, 413, 415, 426–7
　economic decline 19
　economic growth and poverty reduction 437,
　　441, 452
　health and education expenditure 402
　pessimism 4
　population and demographic transition 85
　structural adjustment 49
Spain 385–6
Sree Narayana Dharma Paripalana Sanghom
　(Kerala) 212
Sri Lanka 235–63
　agriculture 253

demand for services 431

economic growth 17, 243–7, 425, 426; common elements and diversities 27, 29, 30, 32, 50–1; and poverty reduction 443–4, 445–6, 447, 462

education 251–3; demand for 92, 97; enrolment 26, 34, 86–8, 94, 235, 240–2, 252; finances/ expenditure 41, 43, 45–7, 89–91, 230, 239, 244, 256, 258–9, 430; and health 34; infrastructure 424; language of 97, 240, 251; literacy 25–6, 94–5, 98, 235, 241–2, 251; private 241; secondary 240, 241–2, 258; teachers 96; tertiary 162, 164, 240, 241, 243, 258–9; women 39–40, 96, 249, 251

employment 31, 39–40

equity 425

finances/expenditure 49, 255–9, 427; defence 48, 245, 430; foreign aid 257; revenues 239; sustainability problems 430, 431; *see also under* education *above and* health *below*

health 70, 248–51, 257, 430; access 68; childbirth 68, 70; common elements and diversities 25, 26–7; development 236–7; and education 103; finances/expenditure 29, 41, 42, 44, 76, 106, 236, 239, 244, 256–9, 430; hospitals 238, 250; immunization 68, 69; infant and child mortality 66, 68, 77–8, 235, 236, 248; infrastructure 424; life expectancy 66, 235; nutrition 76–9, 80, 102, 104, 107, 236, 239, 244–5, 251, 253–7, 260; personnel 238, 239, 248–9; primary care 101, 248, 249; private 105–6; technology 258; traditional 102; utilization rates 106; water and sanitation 82, 250, 260–1

history 235–42

infrastructure 244, 257, 259–60, 424

lessons of experience 259–61

multicultural 424

politics 33, 236

population and demographic transition 58, 83–4, 426; family planning 108, 239, 250; fertility and growth 108, 239, 245; migration 98, 245

poverty 53–6, 57, 244–5, 249–52, 254, 261; reduction and economic growth 443–4, 445–6, 447, 462

religion 33, 424

rural areas 244, 253

social security 236, 238, 239, 240

structural adjustment 244–7, 428

women 37–8, 107, 429; education 39–40, 96, 249, 251

stabilization, *see* structural adjustment

Stack, Jayne 190

stagnation, economic 51

State Committee on Statistics (Cuba) 394

State Planning Board (Kerala) 216–17

state-supported social services as common element 29, 32–3, 57, 459
not active in Korea health 276, 291
see also social development

Stevens, M. 139

Stewart, F. 19

stock-flow approach 428

Streeten, Paul 422, 441

structural adjustment 11–14, 19, 49, 57
Barbados 349, 428
Costa Rica 49, 368–70
Cuba 49, 404
IMF 11
Korea 49, 272, 428
Malaysia 49, 298, 428
Mauritius 49, 156–7, 428
Sri Lanka 244–7, 428
UNICEF 11, 12, 13, 19
World Bank 11, 156–7, 180, 182, 246, 368
Zimbabwe 49–50, 52, 180, 182–3, 195, 199, 428

subsidies 12–13, 273, 300, 301, 440
food 78–81, 106, 368; GOBI-FFF programme 23, 40, 58, 73; Sri Lanka 236, 239, 244–5, 251, 253–4, 256–7, 260; Zimbabwe 190, 191–2, 194; *see also* free meals
see also foreign aid; grant-aid

success, *see* profiles in success

sugar production:
Barbados 326, 330, 426
Cuba 385–6, 397, 426
Mauritius 156, 157, 158–60, 426

Suh, Sang Mok 288

Sunga, E. 190

supplementary feeding, *see* food *under* subsidies

supply and demand of social provision 420–1

sustainability 422, 429–30

Swaziland 116–17

Sweden 456

synergies, *see* economic growth and poverty reduction

syphilis 411

Syrquin, R. M. 440

Tabellini, G. 440

Taiwan 441, 456

Tamil Nadu:
education 96, 206, 216–17, 226
health 206, 225
nutrition 10

Tamils in Malaysia: language 97, 305, 306, 308
Tamils in Sri Lanka:
  Ceylon 245, 246, 247, 424
  Indian 235, 245, 246, 247
  language 240, 251
  Tamil United Liberation Front 243
Tan, Jee-Peng 88, 427
Tanzania 93, 123
targeting vs. universality 430–1
tax, *see* revenues
taxonomy of outcomes 442–50, 461–3
Taylor, Lance xiii
  on growth and poverty reduction 435–67
Taylor-Dormond, M. 374
TBAs (trained birth attendants) 105
tea 51, 244
teachers:
  shift-working 103, 195, 285
  training 93, 194–5, 196, 334, 399
  women 38, 95–6
  see also under education *under individual case-
    studies*
telecommunications:
  Botswana 120–1
  Costa Rica 356, 360
  Mauritius 161–2
Temple Entry Proclamation (Travancore) 213
tertiary education 88, 90–1
  Barbados 332, 348
  Botswana 129
  Costa Rica 373
  Cuba 395, 396, 398–9
  Korea 267, 283
  Sri Lanka 162, 164, 240, 241, 243, 258–9
tetanus 17, 73, 77, 184, 185, 222, 249, 315, 390–1
TFR (total fertility rate), *see* fertility
Thailand:
  economic growth 4
  HDI 291
  life expectancy 277
  population density 304
  poverty 55
  public action lacking 32
Thet, A. T. 47
Tilak, J. B. G. 22, 95, 97, 226–7
timing of policy integration 428–9
Timmer, P. 452
tin 317, 319, 426, 456
Titmuss, Richard M. (on Mauritius) 150, 151, 152,
    156, 158, 160, 164, 166, 167, 168, 173
Titmuss, Richard M. and Abel-Smith, Brian, Report
    on Mauritius 150

  economic growth 156, 158
  family planning 151, 152
  health 164, 166, 167
  housing 160
  social security 168
  women 173
Tobago, *see* Trinidad and Tobago
Todaro, M. 436
tourism 49
  Barbados 330, 350, 426
  Costa Rica 426
  Cuba 386, 426
  Mauritius 156, 159, 174, 426, 456
trade 426–7, 450–1, 454–6
  Costa Rica 360
  Cuba 393, 405–7, 410
  Korea 271, 292
  see also economic growth
trade unions 51, 70, 174, 215
traditional health care 101–2;
  see also Ayurveda; homoeopathy
trained birth attendants 105
training:
  medical personnel 67, 70, 73, 74, 101, 166, 249,
    314–15, 389
  settlers in Malaysia 316
  teachers 93, 194–5, 196, 334, 399
  see also education
Transitional National Development Plan
    (Zimbabwe) 181
transport systems 120–1, 160–1
Travancore-Cochin 205, 207, 232, 433
  education 210–11, 213–14, 215–16
  finances/expenditure 225–6
  health 218, 220–1
  population and demographic transition 223–4
  see also Kerala
Trejos, Juan Diego xiii
  on Costa Rica 355–83
tribalism 132
Trinidad and Tobago:
  education 324, 325, 346–8, 352, 357
  health 346–7, 348
Truslow 414
tuberculosis:
  Barbados 339–40
  Cuba 389, 391, 411
  Malaysia 304, 313, 315
  Zimbabwe 184, 185
Tulasidhar, V. B. 70
TULF (Tamil United Liberation Front) 243
Tunisia 291

Turkey 441
typhoid 313, 391

UAE (United Arab Emirates) 58
U5MR (under-5-mortality rate), *see* infant and child mortality
Uganda 94, 442
UNCTAD (United Nations Conference on Trade and Development) 453
UNDP (United Nations Development Programme) 19
  and capabilities 21
  and Costa Rica 357, 362, 363–4
  and Cuba 402
  and economic growth 30, 461
  and education 37, 357, 364
  and employment 39
  and finances/expenditure 41, 47
  and health 357, 363
  and Korea 264, 285
  and population and demographic transition 362
  and sustainable human development 422
  and women 37, 39, 402
  see also Human Development Index; Human Development Reports
unemployment 39, 421
  Africa 157, 182
  Latin America and Caribbean 323, 350, 385, 395, 408
  South Asia 243, 247
UNESCO (United Nations Educational, Scientific and Cultural Organization)
  and Cuba 396
  and education 396; efficiency 89; enrolment 88, 324; finances/expenditure 47, 90–1, 258, 347, 348; women teachers 96
  and finances/expenditure 396
UNICEF (United Nations Children's Fund) 16, 422
  and Barbados 336
  and Botswana 119
  and conceptual framework 23
  and Costa Rica 356, 357
  and Cuba 390, 399, 401, 415
  and debt 183
  and economic growth 30, 443
  and education 194, 401; common elements and diversities 25–6, 28, 35, 37, 194; enrolment 86–8, 357, 399; finances/expenditure 259; literacy, adult 356, 357
  and finances/expenditure 59
  and health 73, 119, 401; breakthrough 66; breastfeeding 80, 173; childbirth deaths 67;

common elements and diversities 25–6, 27, 35, 58; immunization 69, 101, 105, 176; input 68; life expectancy 357; mortality 184, 357; nutrition 167, 173, 357, 415; water 357
  and infant and child mortality 390
  and Mauritius 167, 173
  and poverty 53
  and social spending 145–6
  and Soviet Union, former 412
  and structural adjustment 11, 12, 13, 19
  and synergies 23
  and trends 3
  and universality 431
  and women 37
  and Zimbabwe 183, 184, 194
unions 51, 70, 174, 215
United Nations:
  System of National Accounts 38
  see also UNDP; UNESCO; UNICEF
United States 438
  and Barbados 329
  and Botswana 139
  and Costa Rica 377
  and Cuba 385–6, 414–15; embargo 384, 386, 407–8, 409–11, 427
  health 70, 392
  and Korea 33, 99, 264, 266, 268, 269, 286, 290, 291, 292
  poverty 5
universal primary education policies 85–100, 102–5, 108
  Africa 92–4, 108
  East Asia 97–9
  equity and cost-effectiveness in expenditure 88–92, 108
  Latin America 99–100
  South Asia 94–7, 108
  see also enrolment
universality of social provision 423, 429–32
  financing and sustainability 429–30
  public-private mix 431–2
  supply and demand 420–1
  targeting vs. 430–1
universities, *see* tertiary education
University of West Indies 348
UNP (Senanayake-Chelvanayakam Pact) 240
UPE, *see* universal primary education
urban areas/urbanization 452
  Botswana 118–19, 122–3, 138, 140, 143
  Costa Rica 355, 362, 368
  Cuba 388, 393, 399, 414
  health care 65, 67, 100

urban areas/urbanization (*cont.*):
  Korea 275
  Malaysia 301–2
  Zimbabwe 185–6, 189
Uruguay 385, 391–2
Uttar Pradesh:
  education 95, 96, 97, 206, 216–17, 226
  health 71, 206, 225
UWI (University of West Indies) 348

vaccination, *see* immunization
Vandemorrtele, Jan 20, 94, 108, 396
VCW (village community worker) 186
Venezuela 369, 385, 414
Verspagen, B. 461
Verspoor, A. M. 94
VHW (village health worker) 66, 186
Vidyasagara, N. W. 248
Vietnam 91, 409
village:
  community worker (Zimbabwe) 186
  health worker (Zimbabwe) 66, 186
  movement (Korea) 275
  see also rural areas
Villasuso, J. M. 368
vitamin deficiency 105, 106, 411

Wade, R. 441
wages 254
  Costa Rica 359–60, 368
  Cuba 386, 404
  Kerala 230–1
  Korea 267, 272, 285
  Mauritius 157–8
wars 6
  Costa Rica 358, 378, 379
  Cuban War of Independence 385–6
  Korean 239, 264, 266, 268, 274, 286
  Nicaragua 377
  Second World 78, 167, 236, 266
  see also defence
water and sanitation 3, 10, 16, 65, 102, 107
  common elements and diversities 24, 34–5
  health policies 73, 76, 77, 79, 81–2, 107
  see also under health *under individual case-studies*
Wee, V. 288
Weiner, Myron 96–7
Wells, J. R. 461
West Bengal:
  education 96, 206, 216–17, 226
  health 206, 225
West India Royal Commission 324–5, 327, 328, 329, 331, 335, 351

Western Europe, *see* Europe
WHO, *see* World Health Organization
Williamson, J. 440
Wilson, David 188
windfalls, *see* oil price
women 12, 29, 424
  child-care 36, 40, 77, 288; Mauritius 172–3
  convention against discrimination 330
  education 3, 22, 104, 107; and agency 36–41, 424; and economic growth 50–1; enrolment 36–7, 40; GOBI–FFF programme 23, 40, 58, 73; and health 34–5, 76–7, 102; literacy 36–7; teachers 38, 95–6
  health: nutrition 40, 76; workers 72, *see also* midwives; nurses
  matriliny 214, 218
  see also under individual case-studies
  structural adjustment 19
  working outside home (and freedom) 36, 38–40, 173, 328, 330, 400, 402, 404; *see also* health workers *above and under individual case-studies*
  see also maternal mortality *and under individual case-studies*
Woodhall, M. 22
World Bank 422
  and Barbados 352
  and Botswana 113, 145
  and capabilities 21
  and cost-efffectiveness 431
  and Costa Rica 368
  and Cuba 414, 415
  and drugs 352
  and economic growth 30–1; and poverty reduction 440, 443, 453, 455, 461
  and education 35, 37, 85, 108, 258, 285
  and health 35, 105; finances/expenditure 74, 187, 258, 280; input 185; life expectancy 303; nutrition 190, 281, 283, 408; outcome 185; personnel 67; private 106
  and industrial investment 298
  and Korea 280, 281–3, 285
  lessons from and for 141–5
  and Malaysia 298, 303
  and Mauritius 156–7
  and poverty 53–4; reduction and economic growth 440, 443, 453, 455, 461
  and private consumption 59
  and Sri Lanka 246, 258
  and structural adjustment 11, 156–7, 180, 182, 246, 368
  and women 37
  and Zimbabwe 180, 182, 183, 185, 187, 190, 193
World Food Programme 167, 340

World Health Organization:
  and access 165
  and AIDS 344
  and Barbados 336, 339, 341–2, 344, 352
  and breast-feeding 80
  and drugs 339, 352
  and immunization 69, 105
  and Malaysia 309
  and Mauritius 165
  and nutrition 81
  and organization of health services 75
  and poverty and subsidies 72
  water and sanitation 336, 341–2
World Summit for Children 15, 16, 23, 172, 422
World Summit for Social Development
    (Copenhagen) 15, 323, 422
worms and parasites 17, 73, 167, 250, 389
Worrell, DeLisle 349

yaws 315
yellow fever 105
Yeon, Hacheong 265
Yin, Pierre 173
You, Jong-Il 441
Youth Works Brigades 316
Yugoslavia, former 401
YWCA 126

Zachariah, K. C. 223, 224–5, 232
ZANU (Zimbabwe African National Union) 179
ZAPU (Zimbabwe African People's Union) 179
Zimbabwe 179–203, 433
  accommodation 424
  agriculture 179, 182–3
  and Botswana 134, 139
  drought 182–3, 191
  economic factors in sustainability of social
    investments 182–3
  economic growth 181–3; common elements and
    diversities 27, 28, 29, 30, 32, 50, 51, 52; and
    poverty reduction 443–7, 462, 463

education 92–4, 181, 192–6; buildings 103;
    demand for 92; drop-out rates 103;
    enrolment 26, 86–8, 192–4;
    finances/expenditure 43, 45–8, 49, 89–91, 98,
    193, 195, 430; literacy 25–6, 192; private 193;
    secondary 194; teachers 96, 194–5, 196, 285;
    women 37–8, 96
  employment 28, 31, 39–40, 182
  equity 425
  finances/expenditure 182–3, 427; debt 183;
    defence 48; foreign aid 49; revenues 181; *see
    also under* education *above and* health *below*
  health 65, 184–9; access 68; AIDS/HIV 184, 186,
    188; pre-independence 180–1, 184; childbirth
    67–8; common elements and diversities 25,
    26–7; and education 104; equity 105;
    finances/expenditure 29, 42, 44, 49, 75–6, 106,
    187–8, 430; hospitals 184, 188; immunization
    68, 69, 185–6; infant and child mortality 66,
    77–8, 184, 185; life expectancy 66, 185;
    nutrition 76–9, 80, 101, 102, 104, 189–92;
    personnel 67, 185–6, 187, 189; primary care
    101, 181, 184–5, 186–7; private 67, 184, 187;
    water and sanitation 82, 185
  multicultural 424
  policy support for social sector
    development 180–2
  politics 33, 179
  population and demographic transition 58, 82,
    83–4, 102, 196–7, 426; family planning 189;
    fertility and growth 181–2, 196
  poverty 53–5, 56, 57, 123, 183; reduction and
    economic growth 443–7, 462, 463
  rural areas 66–7, 185–7, 189
  structural adjustment 49–50, 52, 180, 182–3, 195,
    199, 428
  urban areas/urbanization 185–6, 189
  women 37–40, 96, 194
Zimbabwe Integrated National Teacher Education
    Course (ZINTEC) 93, 194